THE COMPLETE
HARLEY 2253 MANUSCRIPT

Volume 3

The Middle English Texts Series is designed for classroom use. Its goal is to make available to teachers, scholars, and students texts that occupy an important place in the literary and cultural canon but have not been readily available in student editions. The series does not include those authors, such as Chaucer, Langland, or Malory, whose English works are normally in print in good student editions. The focus is, instead, upon Middle English literature adjacent to those authors that teachers need in compiling the syllabuses they wish to teach. The editions maintain the linguistic integrity of the original work but within the parameters of modern reading conventions. The texts are printed in the modern alphabet and follow the practices of modern capitalization, word formation, and punctuation. Manuscript abbreviations are silently expanded, and *u/v* and *j/i* spellings are regularized according to modern orthography. Yogh (ʒ) is transcribed as *g, gh, y,* or *s,* according to the sound in Modern English spelling to which it corresponds; thorn (þ) and eth (ð) are transcribed as *th.* Distinction between the second person pronoun and the definite article is made by spelling the one *thee* and the other *the,* and final *-e* that receives full syllabic value is accented (e.g., *charité*). Hard words, difficult phrases, and unusual idioms are glossed either in the right margin or at the foot of the page. Explanatory and textual notes appear at the end of the text, often along with a glossary. The editions include short introductions on the history of the work, its merits and points of topical interest, and brief working bibliographies.

This series is published in association with the University of Rochester.

Medieval Institute Publications is a program of
The Medieval Institute, College of Arts and Sciences

 WESTERN MICHIGAN UNIVERSITY

THE COMPLETE
HARLEY 2253 MANUSCRIPT

Volume 3

Edited and Translated by

Susanna Fein

with

David Raybin and Jan Ziolkowski

TEAMS • Middle English Texts Series

MEDIEVAL INSTITUTE PUBLICATIONS
Western Michigan University
Kalamazoo

Library of Congress Cataloging-in-Publication Data

The Complete Harley 2253 Manuscript / edited and translated by Susanna Fein with David Raybin and Jan Ziolkowski.

    volumes cm. -- (Middle English texts series)

 Harley's contents are presented according to booklet structure; the grouping of seven booklets to make the Harley manuscript's full 140 leaves seems to have happened when the scribe was alive.

 For the Latin texts, Jan Ziolkowski provided translations of those obscure works; for translations of French, David Raybin has been a collaborator; initially, there was another collaborator for the French portions of Harley, Barbara Nolan, who before her death, had drafted English versions of some fabliaux, the translation of Gilote and Johane.

 Includes bibliographical references and indexes.

 ISBN 978-1-58044-205-3 (pbk. : alk. paper) -- ISBN 978-1-58044-198-8 (pbk. : alk. paper) -- ISBN 978-1-58044-199-5 (pbk. : alk. paper)

 1. English literature--Middle English, 1100-1500. 2. Anglo-Norman literature. 3. Latin literature, Medieval and modern--England. 4. Middle Ages--Literary collections. 5. Manuscripts, Medieval--England--London. 6. British Library. Manuscript. Harley 2253. I. Fein, Susanna Greer, editor, translator. II. Raybin, David B., 1951- translator. III. Ziolkowski, Jan M., 1956- translator. IV. Consortium for the Teaching of the Middle Ages. V. British Library. Manuscript. Harley 2253. VI. British Library. Manuscript. Harley 2253. English. VII. Title: Harley 2253.

 PR1120.M77 2014

 820.8'001--dc23

2014011645

ISBN 978-1-58044-199-5

P   5   4   3   2   1

 # CONTENTS

ACKNOWLEDGMENTS

This edition of MS Harley 2253 is indebted beyond words to many individuals. Most of all, Russell Peck's patient, unwavering support for the project and his own example as a great medieval scholar have motivated me in profound ways. Carter Revard has been ever-generous in sharing research and insights about the manuscript, and of course it is Carter's ground-breaking work that has allowed the main scribe to be precisely localized. When my Anglo-Norman transcriptions were still new and somewhat crude, Tony Hunt selflessly reviewed them all. As I have sought to emulate the stellar standards of the Anglo-Norman Text Society, his learned scholarship has been my model. For the Latin texts, Jan Ziolkowski was very good to provide, early on, faithful translations of those obscure works. For translations of French, David Raybin has been, as always, an incomparable collaborator; his work has enabled me to hear each Anglo-Norman author's distinctive style and voice. Initially, there was another collaborator for the French portions of MS Harley 2253: Barbara Nolan. Before her death, Barbara had drafted English versions of some fabliaux. The translation of *Gilote and Johane* published here bears witness to her splendid ear for lively comedy. For errors that remain in these volumes, in texts or translations, I bear responsibility.

Other debts accrued over the years have been either individual or institutional. I owe much to the wisdom of those who contributed essays to *Studies in the Harley Manuscript* in 2000 to advance research on a then still opaque textual artifact: besides Carter and Barbara, they include Marilyn Corrie, the late Mary Dove, David Jeffrey, Michael Kuczynski, Frances McSparran, Richard Newhauser, Helen Phillips, Karl Reichl, John Scattergood, Elizabeth Solopova, Theo Stemmler, and John Thompson. Ongoing conversations with each of them have been mainstays of my work, and Mary Dove is much missed. With others I have discussed the pioneering challenges of manuscript editing and scribal mapping. Here, particularly, I thank Julia Boffey, Martin Camargo, Martha Driver, Tony Edwards, Simon Horobin, Kathryn Kerby-Fulton, Linne Mooney, Derek Pearsall, Wendy Scase, Carl Schmidt, George Shuffelton, Eric Stanley, Thorlac Turville-Petre, and Míceál Vaughan. A new wave of Harley scholars has also emerged, and, for sharing their insights, I am grateful to Daniel Birkholz, Nancy Durling, John Hines, Seth Lerer, Ingrid Nelson, Justin O'Hearn, Jason O'Rourke, and Catherine Rock. I also reserve special thanks for my Kent State Latinist colleague Radd Ehrman and for the friendly counsels I depend on from Richard Firth Green, Kristen Figg, and John Block Friedman.

My first transcription of MS Harley 2253 was supported by an NEH Summer Stipend in 1997, a grant spurred by an invitation to create the *Harley Lyrics* chapter for *A Manual of Writings in Middle English*. For this impetus, I gratefully acknowledge the late Al Hartung and his editorial successor Peter Beidler. Unflagging institutional support has been granted by Kent State University through the Research Council, the Institute for Bibliography and Editing, the Department of English, and the Library staff. David Raybin's translations were supported by a grant from the Council on Faculty Research at Eastern Illinois University. The British Library has lent aid whenever I have had need to see Harley and related manuscripts; I thank especially Julian Harrison, Curator of Early Modern Manuscripts. The Medieval Song Network at University College London, organized by Ardis Butterfield and Helen Deeming, has created an innovative, supportive context for new work on lyrics. Finally, but not at all least, I thank the Harvard English Department, which is responsible not just for setting me on this path long ago when I was Larry Benson and Morton Bloomfield's student, but also for inviting me to return in Fall 2010 as a Bloomfield Fellow, lending momentum to this project. For this privilege, I must thank Daniel Donoghue, James Simpson, and Nicholas Watson, ever-gracious hosts.

At the University of Rochester, I sincerely thank METS Assistant Editor Martha M. Johnson-Olin and staff editors Katie VanWert, Kara L. McShane, Pamela M. Yee, and Alison Harper, whose sharp-eyed diligence improved the final product. At Western Michigan University's Medieval Institute Publications, I thank Editor Patricia Hollahan and her dedicated staff. At each location, Rochester and Kalamazoo, it is gratifying to experience great editorial care. The NEH has generously funded the METS Series in which this volume appears. Thanks are also due to David White, who provided early technical assistance, and to Rebecca Sargent, who worked meticulously on large swathes of the unedited Anglo-Norman poetry that will appear in Volume 1.

Above all, this edition of MS Harley 2253 owes its being to my family, and I therefore dedicate it with love to Elizabeth, Carolyn, and Jonathan.

⚜ INTRODUCTION

Manuscripts from medieval England are rarely presented to readers of today in the manner given here: each item edited beside a modern English translation.[1] No medieval book, however, warrants this exceptional treatment so much as does the famous Harley Lyrics manuscript.

London, British Library MS Harley 2253 is one of the most important literary books to survive from the English medieval era. In rarity, quality, and abundance, its secular love lyrics comprise an unrivaled collection. Intermingled with them are additional treasures for the student of Middle English: contemporary political songs as well as delicate lyrics designed to inspire religious devotion. And digging beyond these English gems, one readily discovers more prizes — less well-known ones — in French and Latin: four fabliaux (the largest set from medieval England), three lives of Anglo-Saxon saints, and a wealth of satires, comedies, debates, interludes, collected sayings, conduct literature, Bible stories, dream interpretations, and pilgrim guides. Rich in texts in three languages, the book's overall range is quite astounding. The Ludlow scribe, compiler and copyist of folios 49–140, shows himself to have been a man of unusual curiosity, acquisitiveness, and discerning connoisseurship.

THE HARLEY MANUSCRIPT: FOLIOS 1–48

Volume 1 of this three-volume edition prints what were originally two booklets, matched to each other in size and format and holding a rich assortment of religous narratives in Anglo-French verse and prose. These booklets are uniformly copied by an older scribe (not the Ludlow scribe) in a formal textura script. The texts themselves are complete, but Scribe A left open spaces at the heads of sections for the insertion of rubricated initials. The Ludlow scribe (Scribe B) clearly had these books in his possession, for he supplied in red ink titles for each work and four initials on folio 1r. Although not made by the main scribe of

---

[1] There are few precedents for this manner of presentation, but the approach seems to be gathering momentum. See, for example, recent editions of the Anglo-Saxon *Beowulf* manuscript (Fulk); the Latin *Cambridge Songs* manuscript, termed "the grandfather of the *Harley Lyrics*" (Ziolkowski 1998, p. xxx); and the Middle English *Pearl* manuscript, translated on CD-ROM (Andrew and Waldron). The English texts of the Kildare manuscript have been edited with translations (Lucas), and similar treatment has been given to the English saints' lives of Cambridge, St. John's College MSS N. 16 and N. 17 (Waters). Meanwhile, editions of entire codices, glossed but not translated, have started to appear in the METS Middle English Texts Series: MS Ashmole 61 (Shuffelton) and the Audelay manuscript (Fein 2009). Digital whole-manuscript transcriptions with facsimile images are also gradually emerging: the Auchinleck manuscript online (Burnley and Wiggins) and the Vernon manuscript on DVD-ROM (Scase and Kennedy).

interest, this portion of Harley 2253 represents what the Ludlow man had access to in his library. It contains lively works with imaginative appeal: moral sayings and exempla from the ancient desert fathers, absorbing accounts of Christ's trial and passion, and a well-crafted set of apostolic saints' legends.

THE HARLEY MANUSCRIPT: FOLIOS 49–140

The Ludlow scribe's robust achievement (printed in Volumes 2 and 3) appears on the codex's folios 49–140, leaves that are accessible in their original form by means of a high-quality facsimile (Ker). Excluded from that facsimile are the first forty-eight leaves because a different scribe — Scribe A — was responsible for their content. Working several decades earlier, this older scribe copied texts of religion exclusively in Anglo-Norman. At some point his products came into the possession of the Ludlow scribe (chronologically, Scribe B), whom we know owned and read these works because in around 1331 he wrote the titles in red found at the head of Scribe A's texts.[2] Thus what folios 49–140 represent is a long addendum produced by the Ludlow scribe from about 1331 to 1341 and then affixed by him to a preexisting older book, extending it to nearly three times its original length.

It is difficult to know how to classify a book so singular as the Harley manuscript. Is it a miscellany or an anthology? In reference to the Ludlow scribe's portion, one must categorize the book as something of a hybrid, that is, a miscellany that idiosyncratically and frequently veers toward the nature and purposes of an anthology.[3] That is to say, there is much evidence of meaningful layouts, linkages, and juxtapositions that work not only to join texts alike in language and genre, but also to create junctures that bridge the divides. This feature of the Harley manuscript has fascinated many modern readers, yet it also tends to make the book maddeningly hard to comprehend as a whole entity.

In this METS edition, the making available of the whole contents of MS Harley 2253 — edited texts set next to faithful translations of them — is designed to overcome what has been the major obstacle to study of the whole book, that is, simply put, the difficulty students and scholars encounter in *reading all of it*. The Ludlow scribe worked fluently in three languages. Sometimes, the mixing occurs within individual poems: different poets blended two or three languages in macaronic fashion, as in *Mary, Maiden Mild* and *Against the King's Taxes*. But at a most basic level it is the scribe's own work that is macaronic when he sets texts of different languages side by side in significant ways. Multilingual fluency is thus a constant, and with it one may detect a well-developed, ever-alert deployment of diverse linguistic registers, displayed by juxtaposition and textual selection. This fundamental

---

[2] Revard 2007, p. 98 n. 5. See also O'Rourke 2005, p. 55.

[3] The terms *miscellany* and *anthology* are often in flux as scholars work to categorize medieval manuscripts of mixed content (see, for example, the attempts at definition in Nichols and Wenzel). Codicological intentions frequently cannot be known, so organizing principles come to be detected internally and, hence, may seem overly ruled by subjective interpretation. The Harley manuscript is, as Scattergood observes, "organized to a degree" (2000a, p. 167). Wanley first described it as a trilingual miscellany: a book "upon several Subjects; partly in old French, partly in Latin, and partly in old English; partly in Verse, & partly in Prose" (2:585). More recently, Connolly has characterized it as "a complex compilation of secular and devotional material in verse and prose which has no discernible principle of organization" (p. 132). On categorizing the arrangement of contents in Harley, see especially Revard 1982, 2007; Stemmler 2000; Fein 2000b, 2007; and O'Rourke 2005.

feature suggests how the Ludlow scribe must have enjoyed interlingual wit unleashed for social play, piety, and pedagogy. Given how modern conventions of editing tend to downplay medieval contexts, this critically important aspect of the Harley reading experience has been largely unavailable to a modern audience.

My goal in making this edition is to give students the capacity to read and experience the whole book alongside viewing it in the facsimile, and also to enable scholars to better study and appraise the Ludlow scribe and the compilation he so creatively made. With texts printed continuously and translations at hand, the trilingualism of the Harley manuscript is here rendered transparent.[4] Readers may explore the scribe's accomplishment in its entirety rather than merely in its parts, as has typically characterized Harley studies. By printing everything in order, this edition exhibits the linguistic crossover points while simultaneously lessening temporal and verbal impediments: the flavor of the medieval texts can be experienced in original words *and* with modern English equivalencies. Students may thereby bridge linguistic boundaries with the fluency practiced by the scribe.[5]

Compartmented within linguistic spheres of study reinforced by traditional disciplines, many scholars of medieval texts work mainly inside single-language frameworks. In the case of MS Harley 2253, such a method is far less than ideal and will yield myopic results. Broadly speaking, it is Middle English scholars who have dealt with the English texts, especially the famous lyrics and political songs, while they have relegated to Anglo-Normanists the task of handling the French ones — the matter that comprises, in fact, the bulk of the collection. Consequently, the book's French has long lain in a state of neglect — often barely edited or not edited at all — because relatively few literary scholars in English *or* French departments work in the vast textual terrain of post-Norman-Conquest, French-speaking England. Lately, hopeful signs have emerged that, by means of valuable new tools and collaborative projects, this barren state is to be steadily remedied.[6] This METS edition contributes to the broader, sweeping impetus to bring the French of England — as well as much more early Middle English — to greater clarity and understanding.

Likewise has the book's "Latin of England" been largely ignored.[7] The versatile Ludlow scribe worked professionally in this *third* language, too, as legal scrivener and most probably

---

[4] One can, of course, see this diversity in the facsimile, but reading handwritten texts in three languages and medieval script is not easy for most, and the existence of the facsimile has not spurred scholarship of Harley 2253 much beyond examination of isolated textual clusters or themes. For notable exceptions, see Turville-Petre 1996 and Revard 2000b. That a comprehensive approach is ripe for adoption is indicated by two recent dissertations that embrace Harley's English and Anglo-Norman contents as a unified field (Maulsby, Nelson 2010), and another that does the same for the Ludlow scribe's three manuscripts (Rock).

[5] For translations, I am indebted to my collaborators David Raybin for Anglo-Norman and Jan Ziolkowski for Latin. For the final form each translation takes, I am responsible for errors.

[6] Some of these new tools and projects include the valuable comprehensive catalogue *Anglo-Norman Literature* (R. Dean and Boulton); the online *Anglo-Norman Dictionary*; the online *Production and Use of English Manuscripts 1060 to 1220* Project (Da Rold et al.); a ground-breaking collection of essays (Wogan-Browne et al.); and the French of England Translation Series (FRETS) of ACRMS Publications. All of these occurrences augment the already steady output of editorial scholarship from the Anglo-Norman Text Society (ANTS).

[7] MS Harley 2253 is never mentioned, for example, in the authoritative study of Anglo-Latin literature by Rigg 1992.

as chaplain. In the book's Latin one finds selections as intriguingly provocative as the vernacular ones. All of this Latin material appears, of course, in this edition in proper sequence with the French and English matter. Many bits of it — such as the prose lives of Ethelbert, Etfrid, and Wistan, each a foundational story of the region's Anglo-Saxon heritage — are here edited and printed for the first time.

The innovation of this full-manuscript edition-with-translation is, therefore, critical to its goal. The format is designed to treat Middle English, Anglo-Norman, and Latin evenly and to translate each in a manner that invites inspection of the originals.[8] In the past, individual Harley texts have been accessible only in scattered places and scattered ways. Many are in modern anthologies that typically reinforce divides of language or genre. Only a handful of editors have striven to include groups of Harley texts in one place, and anthologies of medieval verse typically print a number of English lyrics without the French ones.[9] Thomas Wright anthologized and translated the Harley political verse — English, French, and Latin — arranging them not together but rather in a broad selection of political songs from England (Wright 1839). Likewise, the Harley Anglo-Norman fabliaux appear in the definitive *Nouveau recueil complet des fabliaux*, but they must be sought there in separate volumes because they are treated within categories of Old French fabliaux.[10] Here, at last, is the Harley manuscript *in toto*.

BOOKLETS

The presentation of Harley's contents according to booklet structure introduces another significant breakthrough. Internal booklets were first delineated by N. R. Ker,[11] and they were given some attention in the 2000 collection *Studies in the Harley Manuscript*.[12] Reading the Harley manuscript according to its physical makeup — that is, by the individual quires or groups of quires that constitute independent blocks of texts — sheds light on what the

---

[8] As I initially planned the format (in discussions with METS General Editor Russell A. Peck), it was thought that Middle English texts would be glossed rather than translated, in accord with METS style. However, texts written in dialects of early Middle English bear a greater than normal need for the close analysis that modern translation brings, and they demand full utilization of the online *Middle English Dictionary*. Moreover, as my translation work proceeded, I was surprised to see how rarely the *Harley Lyrics* have been translated; how existing translations tend to be versified rather than close; how the very challenging vernacular satires (arts. 25a, 31, 40, 81, 88) have never been translated; and how some English items (i.e., arts. 32, 68, 85, 89) have seldom been printed, much less subjected to critical editing and translation.

[9] The major anthologies of select English contents are Böddeker, Brown 1932, Brown 1952, and Brook. The only anthology to mix English and French lyrics is Wright 1842. Editions of select Anglo-Norman are also found in Jeffrey and Levy, and in the unpublished dissertations of Dove and Kennedy.

[10] Noomen and van den Boogaard; see also Montaiglon and Raynaud; and Short and Pearcy. Revard has printed the fabliaux and some comic French items with verse translations (2004, 2005a, 2005b, 2005c).

[11] Ker, p. xvi. In listing the "independent blocks" of MS Harley 2253, Ker omitted the division that marks booklet 1 as separate from booklet 2.

[12] Fein 2000c (with a chart on pp. 371–76), Nolan, and Thompson 2000. See also O'Rourke 2005, Revard 2007, and Fein 2007. O'Rourke 2000 examines the booklets of London, British Library, Royal 12.C.12, another codex belonging to the Ludlow scribe.

first two scribes strove to accomplish within their portions of the book. We cannot assert that the Ludlow scribe's textual productions ever circulated in multiple booklets. Individual articles *did* get copied, however, into booklets in the manuscript's early making, even if only at the scribe's desk. Although now in a modern binding, the codex as we have it seems to date from the scribe's own time — an assumption based on the fact that the first two booklets (inscribed by Scribe A) were also the property of the Ludlow scribe. So the grouping of seven booklets to make the Harley manuscript — its full 140 leaves — seems to have happened when the scribe was alive.[13]

The booklet makeup yields tangible clues as to the two main scribes' local purposes. In particular, it begins to reveal rationales that underlie the Ludlow scribe's anthologizing impulses, showing how he arranged texts with an eye to clustering topics, themes, and/or antithetical arguments inside units smaller than the whole book. The following paragraphs provide an overview of the contents of each booklet in the manuscript.[14]

Booklet 1 (quires 1–2, fols. 1–22). This booklet holds the lengthy text of the *Vitas patrum* in Anglo-Norman verse with the story of Thais (drawn from the same work) appended at the end. The hand is that of the earlier Scribe A. The Ludlow scribe has written in red the title *Vitas patrum* on fol. 1. This booklet and the next one constitute the volume that the Ludlow scribe had in hand when he commenced his own copying endeavor.

Booklet 2 (quires 3–4, fols. 23–48). Scribe A's work continues in this booklet with more Anglo-Norman religious texts in both verse and prose. First there is a long verse paraphrase of the Gospels: Herman de Valenciennes's *La Passioun Nostre Seignour*. Coming next is the anonymous prose *Gospel of Nicodemus*, a work of biblical apocrypha enjoying broad dissemination in many languages throughout medieval Europe. Appended to *The Gospel of Nicodemus* are two of its traditional accretions, *The Letter of Pilate to Tiberius* and *The Letter of Pilate to Emperor Claudius*. Then Scribe A adds four prose saints' lives — those of John the Evangelist, John the Baptist, Bartholomew, and Peter — a textual cluster that has analogues in Old French manuscripts.[15] A history of the Passion and its aftermath (including saints from that historical era) is the spiritual knowledge conveyed by this booklet to a reader. Here again, the Ludlow scribe inserts titles in red. It is intriguing to think that he may have been acquainted with the elder Scribe A, for as the first scribe left lines blank for titles, it was the Ludlow scribe who filled them in when he acquired the book. The Ludlow's scribe's titles indicate, at the very least, that he knew the contents of the book in his possession.

---

[13] Alternatively, it may have happened soon after his death, when his library was still intact and an executor, relative, or associate sought to preserve it. Revard assumes that it was the Ludlow scribe who acted to join the fifteen quires (2007, pp. 98–99). Ker notes only that, because of the booklet makeup, "the quires need not be in their original order" (p. xvi). See also Fein 2013.

[14] In the presentation of texts in this edition, the divisions of booklet, quire, and folio are designated, and each item is keyed to its article number in the facsimile (Ker, pp. ix–xvi). Here I have occasionally refined Ker's numbering, that is, I have given separate numbers to arts. 1a, 3a, and 3b in Volume 1, and to art. 24a* in Volume 2 (see Appendix).

[15] This collection of lives has been edited by D. Russell 1989. Revard relates them to Ludlow-area churches having the same patron saints: "St John Evangelist is patron of the Palmers' Gild in Ludlow parish Church of St Lawrence; St John Baptist is patron saint of the Ludlow Hospital of St John Baptist; the parish Church of St Bartholomew is three miles south of Ludlow in Richard's Castle; and the Church of St Peter is at Leominster Priory, ten miles south of Ludlow" (2007, p. 100). Saint Peter also figures centrally in the Leominster-based life of Saint Etfrid found in booklet 6 (see art. 98).

Booklet 3 (quire 5, fols. 49–52). This booklet marks the start of the Ludlow scribe's portion of MS Harley 2253. Choosing a purposeful beginning and a radical shift in topic from booklets 1 and 2, the scribe starts off with an alphabet poem, the *ABC of Women*, followed by the *Debate between Winter and Summer*. Both of these entertainments are in Anglo–Norman verse. The booklet consists of just one quire of four leaves, and it originally ended with a column and a half of blank space (fol. 52v), on which a later person (hence, chronologically, Scribe C) added paint recipes. Such recipes pertain to the technical interests of a manuscript illuminator, and they may offer a clue as to the further ownership or use of MS Harley 2253 after its completion by the Ludlow scribe — perhaps, that is, after his death. The first evident user of the book (after the scribe or his patron) was someone who wished to retain instructions on how to make paint colors and apply silverfoil to parchment. This same person may have added the decorative initial *W* appearing on the last folio of MS Harley 2253 (fol. 140v). The break in topic from Scribe A's religious texts to the Ludlow scribe's courtly entertainments likely indicates that this booklet was initially separate from booklets 1–2 and was at first conceived to be so.

Booklet 4 (quire 6, fols. 53–62). Like booklet 3, this one consists of a single quire, yet, having ten leaves, it is more than twice the length. Distinctly moral in nature, it is filled with exempla of tragic men — wicked traitors and fallen heroes alike — who pass on to death and implicitly to the afterlives they deserve. The booklet starts off with the local, sanctified example of Saint Ethelbert, Anglo-Saxon patron martyr of Hereford Cathedral, delivered in Latin prose.[16] But the tone is most fully established by the presence of the English *Harrowing of Hell* and *Debate between Body and Soul* — humanity's cosmic fate beside that of the individual. Next there appear political poems on Richard of Cornwall ("Richard the trichard"), Simon de Montfort, William Wallace, and Simon Fraser, and tucked in between is a triad of moral proverbs in English, French, and Latin — the stark message universalized in every language. *The Three Foes of Man* closes this booklet with stern warning to watch one's own behavior and consider the eventual fate. Interlopers in this moralistic booklet introduce an edge of comedy or courtliness: *A Goliard's Feast*, *On the Follies of Fashion*, and *Lesson for True Lovers*. Read a certain way, these texts expose human foibles, but they veer more toward the light-heartedness of booklet 3.

Booklet 5 (quires 7–11, fols. 63–105). Numbering forty-three leaves, booklet 5 is the longest and most complex of the sections of MS Harley 2253. Its first half constitutes an extraordinary anthology of lyrics mostly in English, the finest such collection to survive from medieval Britain. In this sequence, secular love lyrics come first with religious poems following later, although such categories are not strictly maintained. In the secular section appears a comic monk's tale (a pseudo-saint's life), *The Life of Saint Marina*. Roughly dividing the secular from the religious sections are the rollicking French interlude *Gilote and Johane* and a pair of pilgrimage texts in French prose. This cluster seems to enact a meandering transition from sexual desires to Holy Land travels. It also marks an exit from quire 7 into quires 8–9, which hold delicate lyrics (still largely in English) that, for the most

---

[16] Revard suggests that *The Life of Saint Ethelbert* is the earliest of the texts appearing on fols. 49–140 (2007, p. 101), which might suggest that the Ludlow scribe initially designed booklet 4 to follow immediately on booklets 1 and 2. Like them (and unlike booklet 3), it is ruled in columns. The scribe evidently regarded the three Latin lives as texts of special reverence. He copied the others (Etfrid and Wistan) as the *concluding* items of their respective booklets.

part, honor Christ and Mary, with two historical poems paired and mixed in: *The Death of Edward I* and *The Flemish Insurrection*.

Anchoring the second half of booklet 5 are two long works: the English verse romance *King Horn* and the Ludlow scribe's never-before-edited Anglo-Norman prose translation of stories from Genesis, Exodus, and Numbers. These somewhat freely adapted stories stress the exploits of Joseph, Moses, and the priestly Levite tribe. *King Horn*, coming with a preface (a prayer-poem in French and English), occupies almost ten full folios on its own. The succeeding Bible stories occupy thirteen. In sheer length, then, these two texts constitute the core of the Ludlow scribe's continuous labor as represented on folios 49–140. Quires 10–11 were appended to the lyric anthology in order to provide room for *Horn* and the stories. On the last verso of booklet 5 — that is, its back cover if it once stood alone — the scribe has written in Latin a list of the books of the Bible. This list signals, perhaps, a pedagogical function residing behind this compilation of superb specimens in verse and dynamic models of virtuous male behavior.

Booklet 6 (quires 12–14, fols. 106–133). This booklet contains the largest collection of Anglo-Norman fabliaux to be found in England. In all, there are four here, each one told very cleverly, with two of them not recorded elsewhere. They seem grouped with many poems that argue the inherent flaws and merits of women (obviously a perennially favorite topic). Designed for social repartee, this theme is also evident in several booklet 5 items, although in booklet 6 it is more pronounced and more typically expressed in French. Displays of wit continue in the comic *Jongleur of Ely and the King of England*, which also participates in the booklet's deep interest in conveying wise advice and inculcating proper male conduct, especially as passed from father to son (Urbain to his son, Saint Louis to Philip), or from a named sage (Saint Bernard, Thomas of Erceldoune, Hending, and so on). Anglo-Norman prevails in this booklet, but there are still some interesting English items, such as the *Book of Dreaming*, the remarkable *Man in the Moon*, and the *contrefacta* on Jesus' love versus woman's love. The booklet also contains the second Latin saint's life, *The Legend of Saint Etfrid*, which commemorates another Anglo-Saxon saint with local resonance. Geographic lore with a crusading edge surfaces in texts on Saracen lands, international heraldic arms, and the relics housed in the cathedral of the Spanish city of Oviedo. In overall makeup, booklet 6 is an intriguing miscellany that suggests an audience of young men, perhaps pupils, as well as scripts for mixed-gender social settings at which comic entertainments could be read aloud, and perhaps enacted, for enjoyment and discussion.

Booklet 7 (quire 15, fols. 134–140). Consisting of one quire of seven leaves, booklet 7 is written entirely in French and Latin and mainly in prose. It is a handbook of practical religion that provides the reader with lists of occasions for prayers, masses, and psalms to be said in times of adversity, along with more lists of the reasons to fast on Friday, the propitious attributes of herbs, and Anselm's questions to be asked of the dying. A few longer texts stand out as somewhat detached from this purpose, and they give the booklet a more miscellaneous though still devout feel: the Latin moralization *All the World's a Chess Board*, which the scribe may have drawn from a copy of John of Wales's *Communeloquium*; the macaronic French/Latin political diatribe *Against the King's Taxes*; an intense, affective meditation focused on the hours of the Passion; and a commemoration of the life of Saint Wistan, Anglo-Saxon patron saint of the Ludlow scribe's neighboring Wistanstow. To judge by the script, this last text was added several years after the other texts were copied, in around 1347. As an end to the Harley manuscript, booklet 7 displays the piety of daily worship tied to the worldly concerns of a clergy opposed to oppressive taxation by the state. It is another booklet that might once have stood alone, although it should be noted that the last text of booklet 6, *Prayer for Protection*, offers a bridge to the practices and beliefs detailed here.

PROFILE OF THE LUDLOW SCRIBE

Much has been written about the Ludlow scribe, especially since Carter Revard's landmark research that dates his hand as it appears in three manuscripts and forty-one legal writs. Revard's report of these discoveries appeared just when the study of scribes exploded on the investigative scene of Middle English as an important technique by which to bring historical precision to the cultural mapping of manuscripts, their contents, and their readers. Such work has recently revolutionized the study of Chaucer, Langland, Gower, Trevisa, and Hoccleve, revealing previously unknown networks of metropolitan scribes — in particular, a pivotal group of men centered in the London Guildhall — who assiduously copied and promoted these authors.[17] Work on the Ludlow scribe runs parallel to this movement while illustrating a strand of the scribal networks operating outside of London. In this realm of Middle English literary-historical studies, the Ludlow scribe is someone of special interest, akin to the intriguing Rate (main scribe of MS Ashmole 61) and Robert Thornton of Yorkshire (compiler of two manuscripts in the fifteenth century). Many such scribes are like the Ludlow scribe in being entirely anonymous yet recognizable in their handiwork and proclivities. As the maker of a key manuscript, the Ludlow scribe is a leading figure among a growing company of copyists now recognized for the value of what they preserved. Increasingly, scholars are focusing on these figures so as to understand the historical purposes for which texts were made, and to learn how texts circulated, were used, and were selected to be copied. For a scribe as provocative and idiosyncratic in his choices as was the Ludlow scribe of MS Harley 2253, we also just want to know more about who he was, who he might have worked for, how he was educated, how he was trained as a scribe, and in what circles he moved in society.

Documents reveal that the scribe who copied folios 49–140 of the Harley manuscript flourished as a professional legal scribe in the vicinity of Ludlow from 1314 to 1349. The forty-one writs and charters in his hand recovered by Revard are dated from December 18, 1314, to April 13, 1349. If he was in his twenties when he inscribed the first of these documents, then he was born in the last decade of the thirteenth century. He may have died during the Black Death, which swept through England from 1348 to 1350, so his dates can roughly be set from about 1290 to about 1350.

The earliest writs hail from Ludlow, the scribe's apparent home base. There are sixteen documents from Ludlow itself, including one probably written for Sir Lawrence Ludlow of Stokesay Castle, which is located west of Ludlow in the direction of Wistanstow. In that village is the church built on the site of Saint Wistan's martyrdom as chronicled in the last text of MS Harley 2253. The most outlying document is from Edgton, a village west of Wistanstow. Another is from Stanton Lacy, which is to the north of Ludlow. All others are set south of Ludlow: in the town's neighboring outskirts, four from Ludford and one each from Sheet and Steventon; and from further south: fifteen from Overton, two from Ashford Carbonel, and one from Richard's Castle. With the exception of Edgton, all the writs and

---

[17] See Horobin; Mooney and Stubbs; and the important new online resource *Late Medieval English Scribes* (Mooney et al.).

charters are located within a three-mile radius of Ludlow. And Edgton is but two miles from Wistanstow, which is merely three miles from Stokesay Castle.

The other two Latin saints' lives affiliate the Harley manuscript with major centers directly on the road south from Ludlow. *The Life of Saint Ethelbert* commemorates the patron saint of Hereford and its cathedral.[18] *The Legend of Saint Etfrid* recounts the colorful story of a lion tamed by the saint's offer of bread, a dreamlike encounter that predicts an Anglo-Saxon king's conversion and the founding of a monastery in Leominster. The three saints' lives share a common thread of interest in regional saints from Anglo-Saxon times, that is, foundational stories for religious centers in the vicinity of the scribe's activity. In the case of *The Martyrdom of Saint Wistan*, it is conceivable that the scribe himself redacted the story and preached it to a congregation in Wistanstow to mark a feast day, or that it came from such a local source written for such a parochial purpose.

A considerable amount of further evidence about the Ludlow scribe's reading, collection habits, and tastes exists in two additional manuscripts, where his hand frequently appears in such a way as to suggest that he once owned them as well. These books are MS Harley 273 and MS Royal 12.C.12. Both are housed with the Harley manuscript in London at the British Library, and, to judge from the scribe's script, both predate it. Revard supplies good overviews of these books and dates the scribe's handwriting in each one.[19] Yet, except for attention paid to the Ludlow scribe's copies of some major works — such as the *Short Metrical Chronicle* (an abridgement of the Middle English *Brut*) and *Fouke le Fitz Waryn* (an outlaw tale in Anglo-Norman prose) — the intricate range of contents found in these two books and the various, sometimes stray insertions made by the scribe have not yet been systematically described.[20]

In characterizing who the Ludlow scribe was and exploring his probable occupations and training, one may borrow from an informed speculation as to the compiler-scribe of a comparable, older West Midland book, Oxford, Bodleian Library MS Digby 86. Here, it has been said, the scribe was likely "a cleric, perhaps the local parish-priest, more probably a private chaplain in a manorial household. . . . He had a dual function, to provide both spiritual guidance and also what one might call book-based entertainment."[21] This profile for the Digby scribe seems a good fit for the Ludlow scribe, too.[22] We may readily surmise

---

[18] The Ludlow scribe's seeming connections to Hereford and to Hereford Cathedral, a sophisticated center of learning with international ties, have long piqued scholarly curiosity. See especially Ker, pp. xxi–xxiii; Salter, pp. 32–33; Revard 2000b, pp. 23–30; Corrie 2003, pp. 78–79; Birkholz; and Fein 2013. McSparran notes that the scribe's orthography and dialect localize him to the vicinity of Leominster, which lies twelve miles north of Hereford and nine miles south of Ludlow, all lying on the same route (pp. 393–94, citing Samuels).

[19] Revard 2000b, pp. 65–73.

[20] The content of the writs and charters is presented in Revard 2000b, 30–64, 91–107. On MS Royal 12.C.12, see especially Ker, pp. xx–xxi; Hathaway et al., pp. xxxvii–liii; O'Farrell-Tate, pp. 46–50; and O'Rourke 2000. On all three books, see Walpole, pp. 29–40; and O'Rourke 2005, pp. 52–53.

[21] Frankis, p. 183. On the affiliations between the Harley and Digby manuscripts, see Corrie 2000; and Boffey, pp. 8–10.

[22] Scholars have, furthermore, detected a degree of cosmopolitan sophistication in the Ludlow scribe, whose selections "drew on material written abroad as well as works written more locally" (Corrie 2003, p. 79) and probably derived from "contact with high ecclesiastics, noble benefactors,

that his training was in Latin, religion, and law, subjects that all point to a clerical education. A distinct taste for secular performance pieces suggests his additional role as a master of entertainments, no doubt as a speaking reader, possibly even as a performer or director of others in performance. Marginal speech markers in *Harrowing of Hell* and *Gilote and Johane* preserve these articles' original theatricality, and many more of the Ludlow scribe's preserved debates, dialogues, and expressive monologues seem designed for dramatic show. Oral delivery is often announced from the start, and such openings surely indicate real occasions and are not just literate convention.[23] The scribe seems to have held some particular political leanings, which were probably common to his region: patriotic toward nation and king; sympathetic, however, to the barons' cause as formerly led by Simon de Montfort; and strongly opposed to petty, corrupt officialdom and unreasonable taxation. These attitudes show an empathy for the common populace, but they were also shared by many clergy, and a good degree of identification with the clerical authors expressing these views probably accounts for the scribe's inclusion of these outlooks.[24]

Of course, it may be that the scribe's social attitudes were also shaped to please a patron; various scholars have sought to identify who the scribe's patron might have been.[25] Because we cannot know the name of the patron any more than we can know the name of the scribe, it seems wisest to glean what we can of attitudes and social outlooks as they are suggested by the articles of MS Harley 2253 taken in aggregate and in combination. The meanings built by juxtaposition and selection would seem best explained as deriving from the intelligence of the scribe — someone with literary leanings and a freedom to pursue his own whims, choices, chance finds, and networks of texts. If an externally directed pattern is perceptible here, it runs toward edification and instruction. It would seem likely that the Ludlow scribe had some responsibility in the inculcation of manners and learning for a male heir or heirs in a well-bred, perhaps aristocratic setting. In this environment, he, his charges, and his patrons were accustomed to interact with one another in Anglo-Norman. Toward household members, his duties must also have included spiritual guidance, as from a professional chaplain.

The inclusion of the adventure stories of *King Horn* in the Harley manuscript and of *Fouke le Fitz Waryn* in MS Royal 12.C.12 seems well explained as directed toward an audience of boys whose morals were to be shaped by a clerical tutor or schoolmaster.[26] The Old Testament stories devote space to the God-ordained exploits of Joseph and Moses. The political and geographical works offer more instruction on history and knowledge of the world and local environs. And the debates on women's nature, the lyrics on secular love, and even the outrageously profane fabliaux provide provocative matter to be absorbed by inquisitive young men about the mysterious nature of the opposite gender. Most overtly, the literature

---

as well as with travelling scholars and minstrels" (Salter, p. 32). For other profiling insights, see especially O'Rourke 2000 (p. 222), 2005; and Revard 2007, pp. 99–102.

[23] Fein 2007, pp. 81, 88–91.

[24] See, for example, the explanatory notes to arts. 31, 109, and 114. On the collective political outlook of the Harley contents, see Scattergood 2000a; and also O'Rourke 2005, pp. 50–52.

[25] For recent proposals as to the unknown patron, patrons, or milieus, see Revard 2000b, esp. pp. 74–90; O'Rourke 2000; Hines, pp. 71–104; and Birkholz.

[26] For *Fouke le Fitz Waryn*, the chronicled history of a local family and namesake heir was surely a factor that compelled interest in the narrative, too. See Revard 2000b, pp. 87–90, 108–09; and Hanna.

of conduct and good manners clustered in booklet 6 seems designed for the schoolroom, whether directed at a single scion of a household or a group of pupils from aspirant Anglo-Norman homes.

Most interesting, perhaps, in considering the roles of the Ludlow scribe, is to observe how he sometimes assumed the task of author as well as a redactor and compiler. The Bible stories and *Fouke le Fitz Waryn* are now accepted as his own literate productions created by translating and adapting inherited material. For the former, extracts from the Vulgate Bible (and sometimes Peter Comestor) were converted from Latin to Anglo-Norman prose, with the scribe adding occasional lessons: a mnemonic couplet on the ten plagues, a multilingual explanation of the word *manna*, and a typological reading of the Synagogue as the "Church for Christians" ("eglise a chretiens"). For *Fouke*, an Anglo-Norman verse romance was remade as prose in the same language. Certain turns of phrase show the scribe to have been anglophone by birth, francophone by social standing and daily habit — as were, no doubt, his associates, his patrons, and their children.[27] To these French works now ascribed to him, works in other languages contend as more possibilities. One is *The Martyrdom of Saint Wistan*, a Latin redaction from a longer Latin prose life.[28] In English, too, he may have devised *A Bok of Swevenyng* by cobbling it from the Latin dreambook *Somniale Danielis* in his possession in MS Royal 12.C.12.

The lines that distinguish scribe from compiler and even from the higher offices of an author are sometimes blurred, therefore, as we reach for an accurate profile of this interesting man from medieval Ludlow. Regarding poetry of this period, Derek Pearsall has commented that "the scribe as much as the poet is the 'author' of what we have in extant copies."[29] Nowhere is this more true than in the command performance of the Ludlow scribe. He collected ephemeral songs, entertainments, and diatribes that survive nowhere else because they floated on broadsheets never intended for appearance among the records of a book. For some of the most vernacular items of local politics and social satire, the Ludlow scribe became, perhaps unconsciously, an innovator in preservation by new media when he inscribed *into booklets* comic complaints delivered in colorful alliterative idiom to ventriloquize the outlooks of monoglot, unlettered English people. Such scripts designed for performance and class-based mockery acquire a new, more politicized valence when — marked exclusively as *utterance* — they come eventually to dwell inside the boards of a bound document, thereby officially "recording" a marginal point of view.[30]

---

[27] Wilshere, and see explanatory notes to art. 71. The author of *Urbain the Courteous* (art. 79) advocates that French be taught to English children. In it, a father instructs his son: "I want, first of all, / For you to be wise and full of kindness, / Gracious and courteous, / And that you know how to speak French, / For highly is this language praised / By noblemen" (lines 15–20).

[28] This vita seems the most likely of the three to be the Ludlow scribe's own redaction, although the other two Latin lives — both adapted from longer vitae — may also have sprung from his efforts. See the explanatory notes to arts. 18, 98, and 114.

[29] Pearsall, p. 120.

[30] I have argued elsewhere that the scribe preserved these particular vernacular satires because he saw significant ways to pair and juxtapose them with other works (Fein 2007, pp. 91–94). When the English vernacular enters this textual/oral world as biting satire, there are subtle enactments of social class and register in play. So, too, when Latin enters, there are uplifted tones of clerical learning and moral teaching.

The Ludlow scribe's remarkable manuscript captures for us myriad snapshots of lived moments in the literate culture of the French-speaking English from the western Marches, giving us multiple perspectives on how that society sought entertainment and pursued mental enrichment a half-century before Chaucer. When we closely examine vernacular performance texts extant in other copies, like the *Harrowing of Hell* and *King Horn*, we readily discover how the scribe's distinct touch has perceptibly inflected his versions. At the same time, in the Ludlow scribe's selections and insertions, one may potentially trace his preferences and influences: Peter Comester, John of Wales, Albertus Magnus, Anselm of Canterbury, Hilary of Poitiers, Chrétien de Troyes, for example. The Hereford Franciscan poet and preacher William Herebert might have been one of his acquaintances.[31] In addition, the imaginatively rich, stylistically versatile narratives copied by Scribe A enhance our sense of the Anglo-French literary influences swirling within the scribe's easy reach. The Ludlow scribe's milieus, sources, range of training, professional activities, and goals as a copyist pose a challenging, fascinating domain for scholarly investigation. With this edition and translation, that domain is now fully open for reading and exploration.

FURTHER READING

Facsimile
Ker, N. R., intro. *Facsimile of British Museum MS. Harley 2253*. EETS o.s. 255. London, 1965.

Standard Edition of the English "Harley Lyrics"
Brook, G. L., ed. *The Harley Lyrics: The Middle English Lyrics of Ms. Harley 2253*. 4th ed. Manchester: Manchester University Press, 1968.

Descriptive Bibliography of the English "Harley Lyrics"
Fein, Susanna. "XXVII. The Lyrics of MS Harley 2253." In *A Manual of the Writings in Middle English, 1050–1500*. Ed. Peter G. Beidler. Vol. 11. New Haven, CT: Connecticut Academy of Arts and Sciences, 2005. Pp. 4168–4206, 4311–4361.

Other Editions of Multiple Harley Items
Böddeker, Karl, ed. *Altenglische Dichtungen des MS. Harl. 2253*. Berlin: Weidmannsche, 1878.
Brown, Carleton, ed. *English Lyrics of the XIIIth Century*. Oxford: Clarendon, 1932.
———, ed. *Religious Lyrics of the XIVth Century*. Oxford: Clarendon, 1924. Second edition. Rev. G. V. Smithers. Oxford: Clarendon, 1952.
Dove, Mary. *A Study of Some of the Lesser-Known Poems of British Museum Ms. Harley 2253*. D.Phil. dissertation. Cambridge: Girton College, Cambridge, 1969.
Jeffrey, David L., and Brian J. Levy, eds. *The Anglo-Norman Lyric: An Anthology*. Toronto: Pontifical Institute of Mediaeval Studies, 1990.
Kennedy, Thomas Corbin. *Anglo-Norman Poems about Love, Women, and Sex from British Museum MS. Harley 2253*. Ph.D. dissertation. New York: Columbia University, 1973.

---

[31] The Ludlow scribe includes one or two poems by the Franciscan Nicholas Bozon, whose writings appear in the Herebert manuscript (London, British Library, Addit. MS 46919). See explanatory notes to arts. 9 (often attributed to Bozon), 24a (also in the Herebert manuscript), and 78 (a Bozon text in the Herebert manuscript). The links are discussed by Jeffrey 2000, pp. 263, 269–70; and Revard 2007, pp. 104–05 n. 17.

Montaiglon, Anatole de, and Gaston Raynaud, eds. *Recueil général et complet des fabliaux des XIIIe et XIVe siècles*. 6 vols. 1872–90. Repr. New York, 1964.

Noomen, Willem, and Nico van den Boogaard, eds. *Nouveau recueil complet des fabliaux*. 10 vols. Assen: Van Gorcum, 1983–98.

Robbins, Rossell Hope, ed. *Historical Poems of the XIVth and XVth Centuries*. New York: Columbia University Press, 1959.

Turville-Petre, Thorlac, ed. *Alliterative Poetry of the Later Middle Ages: An Anthology*. Washington, DC: The Catholic University of America Press, 1989.

Wright, Thomas, ed. *Political Songs of England, from the Reign of John to That of Edward II*. 1839; repr. with an Intro. by Peter Coss. Cambridge: Cambridge University Press, 1996.

———, ed. *The Latin Poems Commonly Attributed to Walter Mapes*. 1841; repr. New York: AMS Press, 1968.

———, ed. *Specimens of Lyric Poetry, Composed in England in the Reign of Edward the First*. 1842; repr. New York: Johnson Reprint Corporation, 1965.

———, ed. "Early English Receipts for Painting, Gilding, &c." *Archaeological Journal* 1 (1844), 64–66.

Recent Editions of Select Harley Items

Hunt, Tony, ed., and Jane Bliss, trans. *"Cher alme": Texts of Anglo-Norman Piety*. French of England Translation Series. Tempe, AZ: Arizona Center for Medieval and Renaissance Studies, 2010.

Lerer, Seth. "'Dum ludis floribus': Language and Text in the Medieval English Lyric." *Philological Quarterly* 87 (2008), 237–55.

Millett, Bella. *Wessex Parallel WebTexts*. 2003. Online at http://www.soton.ac.uk/~wpwt/wpwt/contents.htm.

Pringle, Denys. *Pilgrimage to Jerusalem and the Holy Land, 1187–1291*. Burlington, VT: Ashgate, 2012. Pp. 229–36.

Revard, Carter. "*The Wife of Bath's Grandmother*: or How Gilote Showed Her Friend Johane that the Wages of Sin Is Worldly Pleasure, and How Both Then Preached This Gospel throughout England and Ireland." *Chaucer Review* 39 (2004), 117–36.

———. "Four Fabliaux from London, British Library MS Harley 2253, Translated into English Verse." *Chaucer Review* 40 (2005), 111–40.

———. "*A Goliard's Feast* and the Metanarrative of Harley 2253." *Revue Belge de Philologie et d'Histoire* 83 (2005), 841–67.

———. "The Outlaw's Song of Trailbaston." In *Medieval Outlaws: Twelve Tales in Modern English Translation*. Ed. Thomas H. Ohlgren. Second edition. West Lafayette, IN: Parlor Press, 2005. Pp. 151–64.

Short, Ian, and Roy Pearcy, eds. *Eighteen Anglo-Norman Fabliaux*. ANTS Plain Texts Series 14. London: Anglo-Norman Text Society, 2000.

Treharne, Elaine, ed. *Old and Middle English c.890–c.1450*. Third edition. Chichester: Wiley-Blackwell, 2010.

Woolgar, C. M., ed. *Household Accounts from Medieval England, Part 1: Introduction, Glossary, Diet Accounts (I)*. Records of Social and Economic History n.s. 17. Oxford: Oxford University Press for The British Academy, 1992. Pp. 174–77.

Essay Collection on MS Harley 2253

Fein, Susanna, ed. *Studies in the Harley Manuscript: The Scribes, Contents, and Social Contexts of British Library MS Harley 2253*. Kalamazoo, MI: Medieval Institute Publications, 2000. *Contents:*

- Susanna Fein. "British Library MS Harley 2253: The Lyrics, the Facsimile, and the Book." Pp. 1–20.
- Carter Revard. "Scribe and Provenance." Pp. 21–109.
- Theo Stemmler. "Miscellany or Anthology? The Structure of Medieval Manuscripts: MS Harley 2253, for Example." Pp. 111–21.
- Michael P. Kuczynski. "An 'Electric Stream': The Religious Contents." Pp. 123–61.
- John Scattergood. "Authority and Resistance: The Political Verse." Pp. 163–201.
- Richard Newhauser. "Historicity and Complaint in *Song of the Husbandman*." Pp. 203–17.
- Karl Reichl. "Debate Verse." Pp. 219–39.
- Helen Phillips. "Dreams and Dream Lore." Pp. 241–59.
- David L. Jeffrey. "Authors, Anthologists, and Franciscan Spirituality." Pp. 261–70.
- John J. Thompson. "'Frankis rimes here I redd, / Communlik in ilk[a] sted . . .': The French Bible Stories in Harley 2253." Pp. 271–88.
- Barbara Nolan. "Anthologizing Ribaldry: Five Anglo-Norman Fabliaux." Pp. 289–327.
- Mary Dove. "Evading Textual Intimacy: The French Secular Verse." Pp. 329–49.
- Susanna Fein. "A Saint 'Geynest under Gore': Marina and the Love Lyrics of the Seventh Quire." Pp. 351–76.
- Elizabeth Solopova. "Layout, Punctuation, and Stanza Patterns in the English Verse." Pp. 377–89.
- Frances McSparran. "The Language of the English Poems: The Harley Scribe and His Exemplars." Pp. 391–426.
- Marilyn Corrie. "Harley 2253, Digby 86, and the Circulation of Literature in Pre-Chaucerian England." Pp. 427–43.

Other Recent Criticism

Birkholz, Daniel. "Harley Lyrics and Hereford Clerics: The Implications of Mobility, c. 1300–1351." *Studies in the Age of Chaucer* 31 (2009), 175–230.

Boffey, Julia. "Middle English Lyrics and Manuscripts." In *A Companion to the Middle English Lyric*. Ed. Thomas G. Duncan. Cambridge: D. S. Brewer, 2005. Pp. 1–18.

Butterfield, Ardis. "English, French and Anglo-French: Language and Nation in the Fabliau." In *Mittelalterliche Novellistik im europäischen Kontext: Kulturwissenschaftliche Perspektiven*. Ed. Mark Chinca, Timo Reuvekamp-Felber, and Christopher Young. Berlin: Erich Schmidt, 2006. Pp. 238–59.

Cable, Thomas. "Foreign Influence, Native Continuation, and Metrical Typology in Alliterative Lyrics." In *Approaches to the Metres of Alliterative Verse*. Ed. Judith Jefferson and Ad Putter. Leeds Texts and Monographs, New Series 17. Leeds: University of Leeds, 2009. Pp. 219–34.

Choong, Kevin Teo Kia. "Bodies of Knowledge: Embodying Riotous Performance in the Harley Lyrics." In *"And Never Know the Joy": Sex and the Erotic in English Poetry*. Ed. C. C. Barfoot. Amsterdam: Rodopi, 2006. Pp. 13–32.

Corrie, Marilyn. "Kings and Kingship in British Library MS Harley 2253." *Yearbook of English Studies* 33 (2003), 64–79.

D'Arcy, Anne Marie. "The Middle English Lyrics." In *Readings in Medieval Texts: Interpreting Old and Middle English Literature*. Ed. David F. Johnson and Elaine Treharne. Oxford: Oxford University Press, 2005. Pp. 306–22.

Durling, Nancy Vine. "British Library MS Harley 2253: A New Reading of the Passion Lyrics in Their Manuscript Context." *Viator* 40 (2009), 271–307.

Fein, Susanna. "Harley Lyrics." In *The Oxford Encyclopedia of British Literature*. Ed. David Scott Kastan and Gail McMurray Gibson. 5 vols. Oxford: Oxford University Press, 2006. 2:519–22.

———. "Compilation and Purpose in MS Harley 2253." In *Essays in Manuscript Geography: Vernacular Manuscripts of the English West Midlands from the Conquest to the Sixteenth Century*. Ed. Wendy Scase. Turnhout: Brepols, 2007. Pp. 67–94.

———. "The Four Scribes of MS Harley 2253." *Journal of the Early Book Society* 16 (2013), 27–49.

———. "Literary Scribes: The Harley Scribe and Robert Thornton as Case Studies." In *Insular Books: Vernacular Miscellanies in Late Medieval Britain*. Ed. Margaret Connolly and Raluca Radulescu. Proceedings of the British Academy. London: The British Academy, forthcoming.

Fisher, Matthew. *Scribal Authorship and the Writing of History in Medieval England*. Columbus, OH: The Ohio State University Press, 2012. Pp. 100–45.

Hanna, Ralph. "The Matter of Fulk: Romance and the History of the Marches." *Journal of English and Germanic Philology* 110 (2011), 337–58.

Hines, John. *Voices in the Past: English Literature and Archaeology*. Cambridge: D. S. Brewer, 2004.

Kerby-Fulton, Kathryn, Maidie Hilmo, and Linda Olson. *Opening Up Middle English Manuscripts: Literary and Visual Approaches*. Ithaca, NY: Cornell University Press, 2012.

Kinch, Ashby. "Dying for Love: Dialogic Response in the Lyrics of BL MS Harley 2253." In *Courtly Literature and Clerical Culture*. Ed. Christopher Huber and Henrike Lähnemann. Tübingen: Attempto, 2002. Pp. 137–47.

Lerer, Seth. "Medieval English Literature and the Idea of the Anthology." *PMLA* 118 (2003), 1251–67.

Maulsby, Stephen C. *The Harley Lyrics Revisited: A Multilingual Textual Community*. Ph.D. dissertation. Washington, DC: Catholic University of America, 2008.

Nelson, Ingrid Lynn. *The Lyric in England, 1200–1400*. Ph.D. dissertation. Cambridge, MA: Harvard University, 2010.

———. "The Performance of Power in Medieval English Households: The Case of the *Harrowing of Hell*." *Journal of English and Germanic Philology* 112 (2013), 48–69.

O'Rourke, Jason. "British Library MS Royal 12 C. xii and the Problems of Patronage." *Journal of the Early Book Society* 3 (2000), 216–25.

———. "Imagining Book Production in Fourteenth-Century Herefordshire: The Scribe of British Library, Harley 2253 and His 'Organizing Principles.'" In *Imagining the Book*. Ed. Stephen Kelly and John J. Thompson. Turnhout: Brepols, 2005. Pp. 45–60.

Revard, Carter. "From French 'Fabliau Manuscripts' and MS Harley 2253 to the *Decameron* and the *Canterbury Tales*." *Medium Ævum* 69 (2000), 261–78.

———. "Oppositional Thematics and Metanarrative in MS Harley 2253, Quires 1–6." In *Essays in Manuscript Geography: Vernacular Manuscripts of the English West Midlands from the Conquest to the Sixteenth Century*. Ed. Wendy Scase. Turnhout: Brepols, 2007. Pp. 95–112.

Rock, Catherine A. *Romances Copied by the Ludlow Scribe*: Purgatoire Saint Patrice, Short Metrical Chronicle, Fouke le Fitz Waryn, *and* King Horn. Ph.D. dissertation. Kent, OH: Kent State University, 2008.

Scahill, John. "Trilingualism in Early Middle English Miscellanies: Languages and Literature." *Yearbook of English Studies* 33 (2003), 18–52.

Scase, Wendy. *Literature and Complaint in England 1272–1553*. Oxford: Oxford University Press, 2007.

Scattergood, John. *The Lost Tradition: Essays on Middle English Alliterative Poetry*. Dublin: Four Courts Press, 2000.

———. "The Love Lyric Before Chaucer." In *A Companion to the Middle English Lyric*. Ed. Thomas G. Duncan. Cambridge: D. S. Brewer, 2005. Pp. 39–67.

NOTE ON THE PRESENTATION OF TEXTS

The texts of MS Harley 2253 are printed in the modern alphabet and follow the conventions of the Middle English Texts Series. I list here several details of presentation that require special notice.

Transcriptions. Final *h* or final *k* with a medial horizontal line (often a looped flourish) is rendered as *he* or *ke*.

Final yogh is rendered as *s* in English texts, *z* in French texts.

The Ludlow scribe's form of *homme* ("man") consistently lacks a minim; previous editors have transcribed the word as either *houme* or *honme*. The form used in this edition is *honme*.

The distinction between the Ludlow scribe's *t* and *c* is frequently slight or nonexistent. Consequently, transcription of those letters may be governed by the language in question. For example, in French texts, *-cio(u)n* is the standard spelling of the suffix; in Latin texts, it is *-tion*.

In Latin texts, the letter *i* remains and does not become *j*.

Other editors' variations of the practices cited here are not recorded in the textual notes.

Abbreviations. The Ludlow scribe's ampersand is rendered *ant* in English texts, *e* in French texts, *et* in Latin texts, in accordance with his evident usage when the forms are spelled out. Scribe C's ampersand found in the English paint recipes (arts. 10–17) is also rendered *ant* (although he spells out both *ant* and *et*). The frequent transcription of ampersand in English texts as *and* by previous editors is not noted in the textual notes.

Scribe A's abbreviation *Jh'u* is rendered *Jhesu*. The Ludlow's scribe's abbreviation *ihc* is rendered *Jesu*, as supported by Ker (p. xix) and by the scribe's normal usage. There is only one occurrence of the spelling *ihesu* in the Ludlow scribe's work: *ABC of Women* (art. 8), line 63 (the first appearance of the word). Transcription as *Ihesu* or *Jhesu* by previous editors is not noted in the textual notes.

In French texts copied by the Ludlow scribe, *ns* with an expansion mark is rendered *nous*, as found at *ABC of Women* (art. 8), line 228; *vs* with an expansion mark is rendered *vous*, as found at *Debate between Winter and Summer* (art. 9), line 126. Expansions as *vus* and *nus* by previous editors are not recorded in the textual notes. In Scribe A's texts, these abbreviations are expanded to *nus* and *vus*, in accordance with the scribe's practice.

The abbreviation for *par* in French, English, and Latin texts (*p* with a medial line through the descender) is normally rendered *par*, but in some lexical contexts the form indicates *per* (i.e., *pernez, perdu, apertenant, spere*, etc.).

Likewise, the abbreviation *mlt* is rendered *molt* in French texts (the Ludlow scribe's attested spelling), *mult* in Latin texts. However, in some lexical contexts, the French abbreviation indicates *mult* (for example, *mlteplia* on fol. 95v near *multiplierent* spelled out).

In French texts, *q* with a macron is expanded to *que*, not *qe*. Expansion to *qe* by other editors (i.e., Kennedy) is not listed in the textual notes.

In French texts, the abbreviation *seign* with a flourish on the *n* is rendered *seignur*. The Ludlow scribe's spelling of this word fluctuates. For example, in *Debate between Winter and Summer* (art. 9), one finds the word abbreviated and spelled out as *seignur, seignor, seigneur,* and *seignour*.

Paragraphs and initials. Paraphs and large initials, typically in red ink, adorn the opening word of most texts and may also appear internally. All paraphs are recorded. Red initials are not indicated; wherever their placement may be meaningful, they are discussed in the explanatory notes. Boldface initials corresponding to scribal initials appear in two texts: first, in *ABC of Women* (art. 8) to highlight the ABC formula, and, second, in *The Life of Saint Ethelbert* (art. 18) to record how the scribe presents its divisions by initial letter and not by paraph.

Refrains and burdens. The Ludlow scribe's abbreviated indicators for lyric refrains and carol burdens are expanded and printed in full, in the manner in which they were intended to be recited or sung after each stanza. Refrains and burdens appear in italic font. The lines of the opening burden of carols (arts. 36 and 46) are not numbered.

Article numbers. The numbering of items in MS Harley 2253 is keyed to the Ker facsimile (pp. ix-xvi). It follows the enumeration first created by Wanley and then refined by Ker. Article 42 is vacant and therefore omitted (see Ker, p. ix). A Latin couplet (art. 24a*) is presented here as a separate article for the first time.

Foliation. Material from the manuscript is cited in the left margin by folio number, recto or verso ("r" or "v"), and column ("a," "b," or "c"). A vertical line appears in prose texts wherever a folio or column break occurs. Folio breaks rarely occur within lines of verse; where they do, the break is indicated by a vertical line.

Titles. The Middle English, Anglo-Norman, and Latin titles of original works found in MS Harley 2253 derive from first lines, incipits, or scholarly consensus. The titles of the translated texts reflect their standard modern English titles. Where no modern nomenclature exists, titles have been created by the editor.

Variant readings. Variant readings recorded by previous editors are compiled in the textual notes. Editions that modernize texts or regularize spellings are omitted. These notes are keyed to the editions listed for each work in the explanatory notes. Differences in word breaks and in the use of apostrophes in French words are not recorded. Words or letters clearly marked for deletion by the scribe are also not recorded. For a broader listing of the numerous editions of the famous *Harley Lyrics* (that is, the thirty-two poems selected by Brook), see Fein 2005.

BOOKLET 5 **QUIRES 7–11**

Ludlow Scribe, Estoyres de la Bible

[quire 10]
[art. 71]

92v]   ¶ Seigneurs, vous oy avetz molt sovent diverses estoyres de la Bible, que plusors
sunt de Adam, Seth, Noe, Habraham, Ysaac, e Jacob, e autres plusours de queux
ore leysyr me est de parler.

5   Jacob e Esau furent deus freres gemels de une porture engendrez. Esau par resoun
de nature dust primes aver issu de la ventre la mere que Jacob, e par resoun
ensement deveriot aver en la beneçoun que Jacob avoit. E pur ce que Dieu ne le
voleit mie, Jacob supplanta Esau de le un e de le autre. E pur ce est Jacob apelé
"supplaunteour." [*Compare Genesis 25:23–24, 27:36.*]

10   Ce fa Jacob avoit dosse fitz e une file de quatre femmes, dount la premere e la
dreyne furent fraunches, e les deus meenes femmes furent aunceles.

De Lya furent engendrez Ruben, Symeon, Levy, Judas, Yzacar, Zabulon, e une fyle
nomé Dyna.

De Bala auncele, il engendra Dan e Neptalym.

De Zelpha auncele, Gaad e Asser.

15   De [Rachel] fraunche, Josep e Benjamyn. [*Compare Genesis 34:1, 35:22–26.*]

Lya e Rachel furent sueres e les files Laban soun uncle, que Jacob esposa en
Aaram. [*Compare Genesis 29:16–30.*]

Jacob amoit Josep plus qe nul dos autres enfauntz. E Josep avoit, aprés la mort
Rachel sa mere, accosé ces freres que, quant lur plust, il avoeient dormy en lur
20   marastre. E pur ce les freres le hayent a la mort.

BOOKLET 5   **QUIRES 7–11**

Ludlow Scribe, Old Testament Stories   **[quire 10]**
                                                            [art. 71]

92v]   ¶ Lords, you have heard very often various stories from the Bible, of which many
       are of Adam, Seth, Noah, Abraham, Isaac, and Jacob, and many others of whom
       I now have leisure to speak.

       Jacob and Esau were two twin brothers begot of one pregnancy. Esau by natural law
5   ought to have had [the birthright] of having issued from his mother's womb before
       Jacob, and by the same law he ought to have had the blessing that Jacob had. And
       because God did not at all wish this, Jacob supplanted Esau of the one and the other.
       And for this is Jacob called "supplanter." [*Compare Genesis 25:23–24, 27:36.*]

       It happened that Jacob had twelve sons and one daughter by four women, of whom
10   the first and the next were free, and the two common women were handmaids.

       By Leah were conceived Reuben, Simeon, Levi, Judah, Issachar, Zabulun, and a
       daughter named Dinah.

       By handmaid Bilhah, he conceived Dan and Naphtali.

       By handmaid Zilpah, Gad and Asher.

15   By free [Rachel], Joseph and Benjamin. [*Compare Genesis 34:1, 35:22–26.*]

       Leah and Rachel were sisters and the daughters of Laban his uncle, whom Jacob
       married in Haran. [*Compare Genesis 29:16–30.*]

       Jacob loved Joseph more than any of the other children. And Joseph had, after the
       death of Rachel his mother, accused his brothers that, whenever it pleased them,
20   they had slept with their stepmothers. And for this his brothers hated him to the
       death.

Josep sounga que ces freres e ly lyerent garbes en les champs, e lur garbes se
aclynerent e aorerent le suen, e qe le solail e la lune e unze estoilles s'enclynerent
e ly aorerent. Josep counta son pere cet avisioun. E le pere ly dit, "Bel fitz, uncore
avendra que moi e mes unze fitz obeyermus a toi. E vous serrez seigneur de nous
25   tous, e nous vos serfs." E pur ce ces freres molt le plus le hayoyent. E diseyent qu'il
le ociereint.

Jacob comaunda Josep aler en les chaunps a ces freres e qu'il portast arere noveles
de eux e de lur bestes. Quar a icel temps la gent vesquirent a poi tot de lur bestes
e de lur arment, e les pastours furent hardis e vigerous a garder lur bestes de
30   lyouns e autres salvagines. Josep vint en un champ e ne trova mie ces freres. Atant
un vadlet ly demaunda quei quereit, e il ly dit ces freres. Fet il, "Je oy vos freres ore
93r]   eynz dire, 'Aloms en Dotaym,' e la | les troverez vous."

Quant ces freres le virent venyr de loynz, diseyent, "La vient le songeour. Ore
yparra quei ces sounges ly profiterount. Nous le ocieroms."

35   Ruben, le eynsne de tous, lur dit, "Ne espaundes mie son sang, mes soit mys en
cele viele cisterne la, e la morra." E ce disoit pur ce qu'il le voleit delyvrer de lur
maynz e le rendre vif al piere. E quant vint, le mistrent meyntenaunt en la
parfounde cisterne. E pus se assistrent a manger.

Aprés Ruben ala visiter les bestes. Ataunt vindrent marchauntz de Galaaht vers
40   Egipte. Donque lur dist Judas, "Aloms vendre Josep nostre frere a ces marchauntz,
que le amerront en estraunge terre ou plus jamés ne orroms de ly." Il le vendirens
as marchaunz pur xx deners.

Ne mie gueres aprés vint Ruben a le cisterne e vodera estrere Josep. E ne le trova
mie, e ne savoit rien de la vente. E se dementa fierement, entrenchaunt ces
45   vestures. E ne savoit que fere.

Les freres pristrent la gonele que son piere li avoit novele fet, e la teyndrent en
sang de une beste qu'il avoient ocis. E le aporterent a le piere. E demaunderent si
ce fust la gonele Josep son fitz. E quant Jacob le vit, si dit, "Mavoise beste salvagyne
ad devoré Josep mon fitz." E fist tiel duel que um ne poeit fere greynour. E dit
50   qu'il descendreit en enfern deploraunt son fitz. Nully ly poeit solacer, taunt avoit
dolour de son fitz qu'il tant ama. [*Compare Genesis 37.*]

Les marchauntz qe averent achaté Josep le vendirent a Putifar, le seneschal le roy
Pharaon de Egipte. E il dona, pur sa belté, a le roy pur ly servyr. E pur sa belté e
bounté, fust amez tous.

Joseph dreamed that his brothers and he bound sheaves in the fields, and their sheaves bowed down and worshiped him, and the sun and the moon and eleven stars bowed down and worshiped him. Joseph recounted this vision to his father. And the father said to him, "Dear son, it will yet happen that I and my eleven sons
25   shall obey you. And you shall be lord of us all, and we your slaves." And for this his brothers hated him all the more. And they said that they would kill him.

Jacob commanded Joseph to go into the fields to his brothers and bring back news of them and their animals. For at this time men lived close to their animals and their herds, and shepherds were hardy and strong so as to guard their animals
30   from lions and other wild beasts. Joseph came to a field and could not at all find his brothers. Thereupon a young man asked him what he was looking for, and he said to him his brothers. He said, "Just a bit earlier I heard your brothers say, 'Let
93r]   us go to Dothan,' and there | you shall find them."

When his brothers saw him coming from afar, they said, "Here comes the dreamer. Now it will be seen how these dreams will benefit him. We will kill him."

35   Reuben, the eldest of them all, said to them, "Do not in any way shed his blood, but let him be put in that old pit, and he will die there." And he said this because he wished to deliver him from their hands and return him living to the father. And when he came, they immediately put him in the deep pit. And then they sat down to eat.

Afterwards Reuben went to tend the animals. Thereupon merchants came from
40   Gilead toward Egypt. Then said Judah to them, "Let us sell Joseph our brother to these merchants, who will take him to a foreign land where we will never more hear anything of him." They sold him to the merchants for twenty deniers.

Not long afterwards Reuben came to the pit and wished to take Joseph out. But he did not find him at all, and knew nothing of the sale. And he lamented fiercely,
45   tearing his clothes. And he did not know what to do.

The brothers took the tunic that his father had newly made for him, and stained it with the blood of an animal that they had killed. And they carried it to the father. And they asked if this was the tunic of Joseph his son. And when Jacob saw it, he said, "A wicked wild beast has devoured Joseph my son." And he made such grief that no man could make greater. And he said that he would descend to hell
50   weeping for his son. No one was able to console him, so great was the sorrow for his son whom he loved so much. [*Compare Genesis 37.*]

The merchants who had bought Joseph sold him to Potiphar, the seneschal of King Pharaoh of Egypt. And he gave him, on account of his beauty, to the king in order to serve him. And for his beauty and goodness, he was loved by all.

55   Avint que la reygne privément ly pria dormyr ov ly. E il la dit, "Dame," fet il,
"nostre seigneur le roy me ayme taunt que quanqu'il ad est en ma garde, par soun
comandement. Estre vous, ma dame, la reyne, e te serroit grant tresoun si je
mespreise en cele manere a monseignur le roy."

     E s'enparti de la reyne, que a force detint son mauntel e comenca braier e crire. E dit
60   a tous que cely cerf Hebreu a force la vodra aver prise si ele ne out crié.

     Quant le rei le savoit, le comaunda enprisoner. E si fust longement en la prisone.
[*Compare Genesis 39.*]

     Josep ne manga rien des viandes des Egipcienz, que payenz furent, for soulement
de lur payn.

65   Les geolers taunt amerent Josep que tote avoit sa volenté de fere quanque ly plust
entre eux.

     ¶ Quynt que le mestre botiller e le mestre pestour de la court furent comandez a
meisme cele prisone pur trespas qu'il avoient fet al roy Pharaon.

     Le botyler sounga que un cep vist ester devant ly, de qui treis braunches issyrent,
70   floryrent, e taunt se enmeurerent que grapes evissirent: "De queux grapes je fesoi
vyn issyr, e enploy un hanap pur servyr le roy." Donque ly dit Josep, "Ce treis
braunches sunt treis jours, aprés queux vous serrez engitté de prisone e serverez
le roy en vostre office come avant feytes. E donque, pur Dieu, pensez de eyder
moy, qe si su a tort, Dieu le siet."

75   ¶ "Je songay," fet le pestour, "que je portoye sur mon chief treis corboillons
pleynes de payns e autres viaundes de mon office. E les oysels de le firmament
vindrent e mangerent de celes viaundes." Donqe li dit Josep, "Dedenz le tierz jour
serras estret de prisone, e pus pendu e decolé. E les oysels de le firmament
mangerount vostre char." En tot issi avynt come Josep avoit dit. [*Compare Genesis*
80   *40.*] |

93v]   Deus aunz aprés cel delyverement, sounga le roy Pharaon un songe qe nul savoit
interpreter. Donqe, primes, sovynt le botiler de Josep que longement avoit geu en
prisoun. E counta a le roy coment il e le pestour soungerent, e come Josep le
interpreta e dit a certes que lur avendreit.

85   Ly roi fist amener Josep devaunt ly, e dit, "Je songay l'autrer que, come je estois
pres de une eawe, je vi en une pasture molt plentyvouse. E seet vaches y pessoient
les plus grasses que je unque vi. E seet mesgres a demesure vindrent aprés, e
mangerent des herbes e devorerent les seet grasses vaches. E uncore remistrent
auxi mesgres ou plus que avant ne furent.

55   It happened that the queen privately asked him to sleep with her. And he said to her, "Lady," he said, "our lord the king loves me so much that whatever he has is in my keeping, by his command. You are, my lady, the queen, and it would do you great treason were I to wrong in this way my lord the king."

60   And he departed from the queen, who forcibly seized his cloak and began to cry out and shout. And she said to everyone that this Hebrew slave would have taken her by force had she not cried out.

When the king knew about this, he commanded him to be imprisoned. And he was in prison a long time. [*Compare Genesis 39.*]

Joseph did not eat any of the foods of the Egyptians, who were pagans, except for their bread.

65   The jailers loved Joseph so much that he was entirely free to do whatever he pleased among them.

¶ It happened that the master butler and master baker of the court were sentenced to that same prison for misdeeds that they had done to King Pharaoh.

70   The butler dreamed that a vine appeared before him, from which three branches issued, flowered, and ripened so much that grapes grew out: "From those grapes I made wine issue, and I used a goblet to serve the king." Then said Joseph to him, "The three branches are three days, after which you will be released from prison and will serve the king in your office as you did before. And then, for God's sake, think about helping me, who am here unjustly, as God knows."

75   ¶ "I dreamed," said the baker, "that I carried on my head three baskets full of breads and other foods of my office. And the birds of the sky came and ate those foods." Then said Joseph to him, "Upon the third day you will be released from prison, and then hung and beheaded. And the birds of the sky will eat your flesh."
80   And all this happened as Joseph said. [*Compare Genesis 40.*] |

93v] Two years after this deliverance, King Pharaoh dreamed a dream that no one knew how to interpret. Then, for the first time, the butler remembered Joseph who had for a long time remained in prison. And he recounted to the king how he and the baker dreamed, and how Joseph interpreted it and said exactly what would happen to them.

85   The king had Joseph brought before him, and said, "I dreamed the other night that, as I was near a river, I looked toward a very fertile pasture. And seven cows there weighed the fattest that I had ever seen. And seven exceedingly thin ones came afterwards, and ate the grass and devoured the seven fat cows. And they still remained as thin or more than they were before.

90   ¶ "E je songay aprés que me fust avis qe je vy seet espies molt bien engranees
      crestre, e set autres crestre de pres sauntz nul greyn aver. E si destruierent les seet
      espies engranés. Ces deus avisiouns esponez, si vous savez."

      "Sire," dit Josep, "ce deus avisiouns sunt une. Les seet grasse vaches e les espies bien
      engraneez signefient seet aunz que vendrount si plentivouses de herbes, greynz, e de
95   tote manere viande cressaunt que unque tieles vewes ne furent si habundauntz. Les
      seet mesgre vaches e les seet espies nient granez signefient seet aunz que
      vendrount meyntenaunt aprés e devorrount tote la plenté qe avaunt vint. E tiele
      famine serra que tot vostre pueple murra de faym si vous ne ovrez le plus sagement."

      ¶ Le roy Pharaon vist que Josep fust sages e averti. E parmi soun consail qu'il
100   adonque avoit, fist Josep mestre de tot le realme de Egipte. E comaunda que tous ces
      gentz fuissent entendamit a ly. E la garde de curres e de tous ces avers baylla a ly.

      E Pharaon prist de son dey soun anel e le mist a le dey Josep, e mist a son col un
      cercle oryn. E comaunda que tous se agenoillassent a ly, e ly fist estre apelé partot
      "Salveour du mounde." E tot le regne fust demené e governé par ly, e tot fust en
105   son bandon, salve que le roy soulement retint le noun de roy. Le roy ly maria a
      Assenethe, une pucele molt gente, la file Putyfares, un grant mestre e prestre de
      la ley Egipciene engendré a Helyopoleos, une riche cyté. Josep avoit passé xxx
      aunz quant il fust delyvrez de prisoun.

      Josep comaunda garder la quinte partie de chescun maner de greyn. E prist tot le
110   tresour le roi e achata blee partot le reigne. E fist gerners e le mist en bone garde.
      Quant les bons aunz furent passez, les cheres aunz vindrent. E dedenz les deus aunz
      premers fust tot le pays en famine. Josep vendi son blee e amassa tant de tresour que
      a merveille. Il achata a le cops le roy terres, rentes, e grant seignuries partot. Josep
      avoit de Deuz, les deus premers bons aunz, engendré de sa femme deus fitz:
115   Manassen fust le eynsnee e Effrahym le puisné. [*Compare Genesis 41, 47:13–21.*]

      En la terre de Canaan, que molt fust loynz, de le flum Jordan, la ou Jacob maneit,
      grant famyne y aveit. Jacob comanda ces dys fitz prendre or e argent, e aler en
      Egipte pur akatre forment. Benjamyn remist a meson ov son piere. Les dis freres
      vyndrent a Josep e s'engenulerent devant ly. E prierent qu'il lur vel fist | vendre
94r] de soun blee. Quant Josep les vist, meyntenaunt les conust, e saveit assez bien lur
121   langage. Mes rien ne voleit parler ov eux si par interpretour noun. Il lur
      demaunda dount erent.

90 ¶ "And I dreamed afterwards that it happened that I saw grow seven ears of corn full of kernels, and seven others grew nearby without having any kernels. And they destroyed the seven ears with kernels. Interpret these two visions, if you know how to."

"Sire," said Joseph, "these two visions are one. The seven fat cows and the ears with many kernels signify seven years that will arrive so abundant of grasses, grains, and
95 all kinds of growing food that never have such sights been so bountiful. The seven thin cows and the seven ears without kernels signify seven years that will arrive immediately afterwards and devour all the plenty that came before. And there will be such famine that all your people will die of hunger if you do not act very wisely."

¶ King Pharaoh saw that Joseph was wise and perceptive. And in accord with his
100 advisers that he then had, he made Joseph governor of all the realm of Egypt. And he commanded that all the people be under his direction. And custody of the chariots and all his possessions he entrusted to him.

And Pharaoh took from his finger his ring and placed it on Joseph's finger, and placed around his neck a gold chain. And he commanded that all kneel down before him, and had him called by everyone "Savior of the world." And all the
105 realm was led and governed by him, and all was under his jurisdiction, except that the king alone retained the name of king. The king married him to Asenath, a very noble girl, the daughter of Potiphera, a great teacher and priest of the Egyptian law born in Heliopolis, a rich city. Joseph had passed thirty years when he was delivered from prison.

Joseph commanded that the fifth part of every kind of grain be stored. And he
110 took all the king's treasure and bought grain throughout the realm. And he built granaries and placed them under strong guard. When the good years had passed, the scarce years came. And within the first two years all the country was in famine. Joseph sold his grain and amassed a wondrous amount of treasure. He bought at the king's expense fields, rents, and great estates everywhere. Joseph had begotten
115 by God, in the first two good years, two sons by his wife: Manasseh was the elder and Ephraim the younger. [*Compare Genesis 41, 47:13–21.*]

In the land of Canaan, which was very far away, by the river Jordan, where Jacob lived, there was great famine. Jacob commanded his ten sons to take gold and silver, and go to Egypt to buy wheat. Benjamin remained at home with his father. The ten brothers came to Joseph and kneeled before him. And they asked that he
94r] grant their wish | to sell from his grain. When Joseph saw them, he knew them at
121 once, and knew quite well their language. But he did not wish to speak with them without an interpreter. He asked them from whence they came.

Ruben le eysné ly dit que de terre Canaan, e la fust lur pere e Benjamyn lur menour frere, molt destreint pur defaute de blee, e si furent totis dis freres de un piere, e le unzyme a mesoun ov le pere, "e nostre dossyme frere fust perduz. Nous ne savoms ou il devynt."

125

"Je say bien," dit Josep, "qe vous estes fortz e vigerous, e que vous estes venuz pur espier nostre terre. E pur ce je vous retendrey en ma prisone. Mes si ce est voir que vous me avetz dit de vostre piere e de vostre menour frere, je voil qe un de vous aylle ov le forment qe je vous vendroy a vostre piere."

130

Il ly crierent merci, e diseient que lele gent furent. Il out pieté de ces freres, e lur dit, "Je voil que un de vous demeorge en ma prisone, e que ix allent a lur terre ov le blee. E quant vous revendrez arere, vous me amerrez vostre menour frere. E quant je voy que vous estes lele gent, dountz bien serra."

135 Ruben dit en son langage a ces freres, "E par resoun avom nous cest tribulacioun quar nous pecchames grantment en nostre frere. E je le vous disoy assez, e vous ne me vodriez oyr. E ensement en nostre piere, que ne cesse uncore soun dolour demener pur le pierte de ly."

Symeon remist en la prisone Josep. Lur sacz par le comaundement Josep furent
140 emplis de forment. E Josep comaunda a un son serjaunt que quanqu'il avoient doné pur le furment fust privément remis chescun en son sac. Il pristrent congié e s'en alerent. Symeon remist en garde. Quant vindrent a mesoun, conterent a Jacob tot lur affere. E il se tint tot engynez pur ce que Symeon remist en prison e pur Benjamyn que irreit en Egipte. Il overyrent lur sacz e troverent tot le aver que
145 il avoient doné, dount molt s'en merveillerent.

E Jacob ne savoit que fere. Mes queique avensist, ce dit, tendrount lur lealté.

Donque dit Ruben, "Sire, j'ay deus fitz lesqueux je vous delyveroy, si vous plest, tanque a la revenue Benjamyn." [*Compare Genesis 42.*]

"Ore vous appariletz e aletz o Dieu, bels fitz. Vous remeyne a joie arere."

150   ¶ Quant vindrent devant Josep, se mistrent a genoils devant ly. E ly rendyrent Benjamyn lur menour frere. Lors comaunda Josep que Symeon lur fust delyveré, e que lur sacz fuissent emplis de forment. E tot le aver qu'il il avoient aporté fust privément mis chescun en son sac. E en le sac Benjamyn fust mis un coupe que Josep avoit molt chere.

125 Reuben the eldest told him from the land of Canaan, and that their father and Benjamin their youngest brother were there, very distressed by lack of grain, and that they were all ten brothers of one father, and the eleventh at home with the father, "and our twelfth brother was lost. We do not know what became of him."

"I know well," said Joseph, "that you are strong and vigorous, and that you have come to spy upon our land. And for this I will hold you in my prison. But if it is true what you have told me about your father and your youngest brother, I want 130 one of you to go to your father with the wheat I will sell to you."

They cried out to him for mercy, and said that they were law-abiding people. He had compassion on his brothers, and said to them, "I want one of you to remain in my prison, and nine to go to their land with the grain. And when you return, you shall bring to me your youngest brother. And when I see that you are law-abiding people, then all will be well."

135 Reuben said in his language to his brothers, "It is right that we should have this trouble because we sinned deeply in respect to our brother. And I told you this often, and you did not want to listen to me. And likewise regarding our father, who still does not cease to show his sorrow for the loss of him."

Simeon remained in Joseph's prison. By the commandment of Joseph their sacks 140 were filled with wheat. And Joseph commanded his servant that whatever they had given for the wheat be returned secretly to each in his sack. They took leave and went away. Simeon remained under guard. When they returned home, they recounted to Jacob their whole business. And he considered himself wholly tricked because Simeon remained in prison and Benjamin had to go to Egypt. They 145 opened their sacks and found all the money that they had paid, at which they wondered greatly.

And Jacob did not know what to do. But whatever might happen, he said, they would tender their loyalty.

Then said Reuben, "Father, I have two sons whom I will give to you, if you please, until the return of Benjamin." [*Compare Genesis 42.*]

"Now prepare yourself and go with God, dear sons. May he lead you back in joy."

150 ¶ When they came before Joseph, they kneeled before him. And to him they rendered Benjamin their youngest brother. Then Joseph commanded that Simeon be restored to them, and that their sacks be filled with wheat. And all the money that they had brought was secretly given to each in his sack. And in Benjamin's sack was placed a cup that was very dear to Joseph.

155   Il demorerent la trois jours. E mangerent par eus meysmes pur ce que Hebreus
furent. E quanqu'il parleyent entre eux Josep le conust assez bien, e ce ne saveient
il poynt. E Josep meismes lur servi al manger. E de checun service Benjamyn avoit
plus qe autre deus, dont il s'en merveilerent e molt dotierent estre engynnez.

160   Ruben dit privément a le despencer. "Sire," fet il, "le forment qe nous
achatamus autre foiz ici, quant nous venimes a meson, nous trovamus en nos
sacz tot le aver qe nous vous paymes. E de ce avioms merveille. E pur ce, sire, ore
le avoms reporté a vous."

    "N'eiez garde de ce," fet il, "quar ce qe vous trovastes en vos sacz, vos dieus le vous
aveyent doné." [*Compare Genesis 43, 44:1–2.*]

165   ¶ Tous les freres, engonoylant, pristrent congié de Josep e s'en alerent. Ne avoient
gueres erré que deus serjantz e autres lur vindrent aprés. E les comaunderent

94v]   trestouz | arester e overyrent lur sacz. E troverent la coupe. Quant les freres ce
virent, molt s'enmayerent, e se tindrent enginez e al peryl de moryr.

170   Quant furent remenez devant Josep, il lur encheson a molt durement de la
coupe, e diseit que malement ly avoit rendu son bienfet que il lur fesoit.

    Il ne savoient qe fere. Ovés se rendirent trestous come ces serfs a sa volenté.

    Fet il, "Je vueil que vous tous an pez quitez, e vostre menour frere en qui sac ma
coupe fust trové, qu'il demeorge a ma volenté."

175   Dont dit Judas, "Sire, grantz mercis. Vueillez, sire, entendre que nostre piere est
molt auncien. E si cesti fitz ly fust toleit, il morreit pur duel quar pus qu'il perdi un
fitz qu'il avoit unque pus en sa confort, ne solas ne ly purreit valer. Pur Dieu, sire,
eiez merci de nostre piere e nous, que nous ne seioms enchesoun de sa mort."
[*Compare Genesis 44.*]

180   ¶ Josep en prist grant pieté, e les lermes ly cheyerent des oils. E comaunda tote
la meyne issir la sale. E il si fyrent. [*Not in the Bible.*]

    Dount dit Josep a haute vois, tendrement ploraunt, e parla Hebreu, "Je su Josep
vostre frere, que vous vendistes a les marchauntz que me amenerent
en Egipte. E pur vostre salu, Dieu me ordyna si. E si ay tote la seignurie
e la mestrie de tote Egipte, e tous sunt a mon comaundement. E si je avoy

185   fet le consail la reyne, Dieu ne me ust soffert avoir enjoyee cest honour. Ceste
chierté ad duree deus aunz e uncore durra synke. E pur ce vueil je qe nostre piere,
vos femmes, vos enfantz, e nostre perschem lignage vienge a moi. E je lur dorray
terre Gessem, ou il puissent habiter."

155 They stayed there three days. And they ate by themselves because they were Hebrews. And whatever they spoke among themselves Joseph understood quite well, and they did not know this at all. And Joseph himself served them food. And at each meal Benjamin received more than two others, about which they wondered and greatly feared that they were being tricked.

160 Reuben spoke privately to the server. "Sire," he said, "regarding the wheat that we bought here last time, when we came home, we found in our sacks all the money that we paid you. And we wondered at this. And for this, sire, now we have reported it to you."

"Do not be concerned about this," he said, "for what you found in your sacks, your gods have thus given to you." [*Compare Genesis 43, 44:1–2.*]

165 ¶ All the brothers, kneeling, took leave of Joseph and went away. They had barely proceeded before two servants and others came after them. And they commanded
94v] them all | to stop and open their sacks. And they found the cup. When the brothers saw this, they were quite dismayed, and held themselves tricked and in danger of death.

When they were brought before Joseph, he reproached them most harshly about the
170 cup, and said that they had repaid him badly for the kindness he had done them.

They did not know what to do. Therewith they all offered themselves as his slaves at his will.

He said, "I desire that you all depart in peace, and your youngest brother in whose sack my cup was found, that he remain at my will."

Then said Judah, "Sire, many thanks. Please, sire, understand that our father is
175 very old. And if this son is taken from him, he will die of grief because ever since he lost a son whom he never afterwards had for his comfort, no solace has been able to avail him. For God's sake, sire, have mercy on our father and on us, that we not be the cause of his death." [*Compare Genesis 44.*]

¶ Joseph felt great compassion at this, and tears fell from his eyes. And he com-
180 manded all his household to leave the room. And they went away. [*Not in the Bible.*]

Then said Joseph in a raised voice, weeping tenderly, and he spoke Hebrew, "I am Joseph your brother, whom you sold to the merchants that brought me to Egypt. And for your safety, God thus appointed me. And thus have I all lordship and governance over all Egypt, and all is at my command. And had I followed the
185 queen's counsel, God would not have permitted me to enjoy this honor. This scarcity has lasted two years and will continue five more. And for this I wish that our father, your wives, your children, and our close lineage come to me. And I will give to them the land of Goshen, where they will be able to live."

190   Le freres molt se merveillerent. Fet il, "Ne vous en merveillez mie. Je su vostre frere. E vous poez savoir qe je vous conois quar quant je vous assis al manger, je vous assis chescun en son degré, primes le eysné, pus le secunde, pus le tierce, e chescun de vous en son degré." E les acola e les beysa e les resçust a grant honour. Quant la meysné savoit qe ceux furent les freres Josep, molt les honorerent. E le roi meismes comaunda qe a grant fussent resçuz, e qu'il

195   envoyast honorablement pur tot son lygnage.

     ¶ Josep charga curres, someis, e dis asnes de viaundes, robes, e tresour pur fere lur apparayl, de amener son piere e ces proscheyziz a ly. E dona Benjamyn iij^c deners d'argent pur ly, e iij^c deners d'argent pur porter al piere, e synke vestures molt riches e cheos.

200   Quant vindrent a Jacob, lur ly counterent enterement coment vendirent Josep, e entierement la verité sauntz rien celer de nulle chose.

     Quant Jacob y ce oy, donque revesqui soun espyrit, e se releva come ce fust de dormyr. [*Compare Genesis 45.*]

     E tiele joie fesoit que ne poeit greynour fere, e dit, "Ore me sovynt de le songe
205   Josep moun fitz que je vous dysey, qu'il serroit mestre e seignour de nous tous. Ore
95r]   say je bien que ce que Dieu velt aver fet, nul ne le purra defere." | Jacob fist sacrifice a Dieu avaunt son aler en Egipte. E ly mostra Dieu qui il irreit en Egipte e il serreit ov ly.

210   ¶ Jacob e ces fitz e ces aliés furent resçu en Egipte a grant honour. E molt fu Josep lee qu'il avoit veu son piere. A molt grant joie demeuerent les Hebreus quant primes virent Josep. [*Not in the Bible.*]

     Le roi meismes les honora. E parla ov cynk de les freres Josep molt amiablement, e lur demaunda de quel mestier fuissent. E il dysent que pastours de lur arment furent e ces serfs, si ly plust a sa volenté. Le roy comaunda que la terre de Gessem
215   lur fust delyveré, e qu'il fuissent bien herbergé.

     ¶ Le roy demanda Jacob de quele age estoit. "Sire," fet il, "je su ore de la age de cent e trent aunz."

     Jacob e les suens a grant honour remistrent en la terre Gessem. Les gentz du pais e de les reignes entour a Josep e ly donerent or, argent, tot lur arment, terres,
220   rentes, e quanqu'il avoient, en eschaunche pur blee. E quant plus ne avoyent pur blee aquatre, il devyndrent serfs a le roy Pharaon pur lur stivaunce avoyr.

     ¶ Josep lur comaunda semer lur terres, e il lur trovereit semayl e quanque mestier lur fust si la qu'il avoient le premer croup engrangee.

190 The brothers wondered greatly. He said, "Do not at all wonder at this. I am your brother. And you may know that I knew you because when I seated you to eat, I seated you each according to his rank, first the eldest, then the second, then the third, and each of you according to his rank." And he hugged them and kissed them and received them with great honor. When his household knew that these were Joseph's brothers, they honored them greatly. And the king himself commanded that they

195 be received grandly, and that he should send honorably for his entire lineage.

¶ Joseph ordered chariots, pack horses, and ten asses to be equipped with food, robes, and treasure, in order that his father and kinsman be escorted back to him. And he gave Benjamin three hundred silver deniers for himself, and three hundred silver deniers to bring to his father, and five very costly and choice garments.

200 When they came to Jacob, they told him the whole story of how they had sold Joseph, and the whole truth without hiding anything.

When Jacob heard this, then his spirit came back to life, and he rose up as though from sleep. [*Compare Genesis 45.*]

And he made such joy that he could not make greater, and said, "Now I remember
205 the dream of Joseph my son about which I told you, that he would be governor and lord of us all. Now I understand well that whatever God wishes to have done, no one
95r] can undo." | Jacob made sacrifice to God before going to Egypt. And God showed [Jacob] that he would go to Egypt, and that he would be with him.

¶ Jacob and his sons and his kinsmen were received in Egypt with great honor. And
210 Joseph was very happy that he had seen his father. And the Hebrews experienced great joy when they first saw Joseph. [*Not in the Bible.*]

The king himself honored them. And he spoke with five of Joseph's brothers very amiably, and asked them what their trades were. And they said that they were shepherds of their herds and his slaves, if it were pleasing to his will. The king
215 commanded that the land of Goshen be given to them, and that they be lodged well.

¶ The king asked Jacob how old he was. "Sire," he said, "I am now of the age of one hundred and thirty years."

Jacob and his people settled with great honor in the land of Goshen. The people of the country and of the kingdoms surrounding Joseph gave him gold, silver, all
220 their herds, lands, rents, and whatever they had, in exchange for grain. And when they had no more to pay for grain, they became slaves to King Pharaoh in order to have their sustenance.

¶ Joseph commanded them to sow their lands, and he would find seed for them and also whatever necessity they had there until they had stored the first harvest.

225 E cel croup avereynt il quinte. E depus por tous jours, en reconoissance de homage, il rendrent al roy la quinte partie de lur forment cressant chescun an. E il le graunterent. E uncore dure cele rente en Egipte.

E pur ce que les proveyres de la terre ne devereynt vendre lur terres aportynauntes a lur temples (que furent ordynez a le service de lur temple), ne serfs devenyr pur lur sustinance avoir. E Josep lur ordina certeyn lyvereysoun des gerners le roy.

230 Jacob e son lygnage en la terre de Egipte furent des Egipciens apelé *Israel*. E *Israel* est taunt a entendre come "cely qe vist Dieu," quar is *id est "vir,"* ra *id est "videns,"* el *id est "Deum." Et sic* Israel *id est "vir videns Deum."*

¶ Jacob fust en Egipte dis e seet aunz. E quant approcha la mort, si fist apeler Josep. E ly comaunda e se fist affermer par serement que, quant il fust de vye, qu'il 235 le amerreit e freit ensevilyr son corps en la terre Canaan ov ces auncestres. [*Compare Genesis 47.*]

¶ Quant Josep vist qe son piere ne schapereit la mort, prist ces deus enfauntz, Effraym e Manasses, e les amena devant son piere, que donque fust de le age de cent synkaunte sept anz. E pria le piere doner benesoun a ly e a ces enfauntz. Jacob 240 benefia Josep son fitz quar tendrement le amad.

Josep prist Effrem son eysné fis e mist a la destre Jacob son pere, e Manassen le puysné a la senestre, e pria soun piere les benestre. Jacob transposa en manere de crois ces meyns, e mist la meyn destre sur le chief Manassen le puisné e la senestre sur le chief Effraym le eysné. "Sire," fet Josep, "metez vostre destre a le eysné, come 245 resoun velt, e la senestre al puisne." E vodra remuer les meyns son piere, e les meynz furent si peysauntz que Josep ne les poeit mover. "Donque," dit Jacob, "ambedeus serrount grantz, mes le puisné serra le greindre." [*Compare Genesis 48.*]

Quant Jacob fust mort, ces fitz, solum les costumes Egipcienes, demenerent lur duel quaraunte jours. Mes avant son moriant benedist tous ces fitz, chescun par son 250 noun. Ces fitz a grant honour le menerent vers Canaan, e quant avoient passé le 95v] flum Jordan, | la aresturent. E se reposerent tote une simaigne, e demenerent lur duel e lur pleynté. E pur cel duel que la fyrent, la gent du pays apelent cel lu le Egipciene Complegnement. Quant Jacob fust enterree en terre Canan delés Habraham e Ysaac, Josep e les autres tous retornerent en Egipte. Ces freres le 255 doterent grantment, e li prierent merci, qu'il ne les grevast pur le resoun qu'il ly aveynt trespassé e hay en sa juvente. Fet il, "Ne eyez ja gardé de ce je vous aym e ameroi tote ma vie comes mes freres doi?"

225 And of this crop he would have the fifth. And forever afterwards, as a sign of homage, they would render to the king the fifth part of their annual wheat harvest. And this they granted. And this rent still exists in Egypt.

And because the priests of the land were not obligated to sell the lands belonging to their temples (which were appointed to the service of their temple), they did not have to become slaves to have their sustenance. And Joseph appointed to them prescribed deliveries from the king's granaries.

230 Jacob and his lineage in the land of Egypt were called *Israel* by the Egyptians. And *Israel* is such as to say "he who sees God," because *is* means "man," *ra* means "seeing," *el* means "God." And thus *Israel* means "a man seeing God."

¶ Jacob was in Egypt seventeen years. And when he neared death, he called for Joseph. And he commanded him and had him swear by oath that, when he died, 235 he would carry him off and have his body buried in the land of Canaan with his ancestors. [*Compare Genesis 47.*]

¶ When Joseph saw that his father might not escape death, he took his two children, Ephraim and Manasseh, and led them before his father, who then was of the age of one hundred and fifty-seven years. And he asked his father to give his 240 blessing to him and his children. Jacob blessed Joseph his son because he loved him tenderly.

Joseph took Ephraim his elder son and placed him to the right of Jacob his father, and Manasseh the younger to the left, and asked his father to bless them. Jacob transposed his hands in the form of a cross, and placed his right hand on the head of Manasseh the younger and his left on the head of Ephraim the elder. "Father," 245 said Joseph, "place your right on the elder, as reason dictates, and the left on the younger." And he wished to move his father's hands, but the hands were so heavy that Joseph was not able to move them. "Therefore," said Jacob, "both will be great, but the younger will be the greater." [*Compare Genesis 48.*]

When Jacob was dead, his sons, according to the custom of the Egyptians, observed their mourning for forty days. But before his death he had blessed all his sons, each 250 by his name. His sons with great honor brought him toward Canaan, and when they 95v] had crossed the river Jordan, | they stopped there. And they rested for a whole week, and observed their mourning and their lamentation. And because of the mourning that they made, the people of the country call that place the Mourning of Egypt. When Jacob was buried in the land of Canaan alongside Abraham and Isaac, Joseph 255 and all the others returned to Egypt. His brothers feared him greatly, and they asked him for mercy, that he not harm them because they had trespassed against him and had hated him in his youth. He said, "Have you not seen that I love you and will love you all my life as I ought my brothers?"

Puis vesqui Josep longement en la pais ov ces freres e amys tant qu'il avoit acomply cent e dis aunz. E quant il en malady fist assembler ces amis, e lur pria que, quant

260 il serroit mort, qu'il ly feissent estre ensevely en Egipte, e, quant il departyrent de la terre de Egipte, qu'il amenasent ces os hors de la terre ovesque eux. Quant aveynt tote oy sa requeste, yl la graunterent. Josep morust en grant honour. Fust ensevely en Egipte. [*Compare Genesis 49–50.*]

E al temps que Jacob morust, remistrent en Egipte, de ces fitz e son lignage que

265 issist de ly, setaunce synke.

¶ Puis que Josep fust fyné, e le roy Pharaon son seignur fust mort, le pueple crust e multeplia si grantment qe a merveille. E tauntz furent des Hebreus que le roi de Egipte qe donque fust dota que eux ly e les Egipciens enchacerent de la terre. E dit qu'il les destrent dreit taunt par grevaunce e duresse de overeygnes que eux ne

270 avereint volenté de fere generacioun. E come plus furent destreint, plus multiplierent, le roi lur fesoit fere deus cités grantz.

E quant rien ne poeit esploiter par cele voie, ordyna deus dames, Suphia e Phua. E les comanda que eles fuissent a chescun enfauntement de les femmes Hebreus de Israel, e qu'il feissent ocire tous le madles e gardassent les femeles. Les dames

275 le graunterent, mes eles furent bones femes ne voleynt offendre Dieu. E ne velereit mie, ne oseyent pur pieté, nul ocyre.

Quant le roy savoit que nul fust ocis, demanda les dames pur quoy ne aveyent fet som comaundement. E eles ly diseyent, "Sire, les dames Hebreus de les fitz Israel sunt plus sages qe nous ne fumes, e sovent lur temps mieux qe nous ne savoms, e

280 aveyent enfaunté avant qe vous venimes a eux." Donqe ordyna le roy certeynes justices de aler partote la terre, e les madles qe erent nés serreient neiez, e les femmeles serreyent gardés. [*Compare Exodus 1.*]

¶ En icel temps une dame des Hebrus enfanta si avoit un fitz tres bel. E sa grant belté le mussa e garda a myeux que ele poeit. Issi qe ele le garda treis mois e grant

285 voit que plus ne le poeit garder qu'il ne serroit aparçu, si fist un vessel auqe bel e le fist bien peyer de dentz e dehors qe ewe ne poeit entre. E le mist suevement en une eawe. Marie le suere l'enfaunt aloit de loynz pur vere ce qe avendreit de cele chose. E grant duel fesoit. |

96r] Atant vint la fille Pharaon le roy, se deduiaunt pres de cele ewe. E vist cele vessele
290 flotant, e demanda quei ce fust. Le vessel fut tret hors de le ewe. E la damoisele vist qe ce fust un emfes. E dit que ele savoit bien qu'il fust Hebreu, e grant duel serreit ocyre si bel enfes. E dit que ele le freit noryr.

260 Then Joseph lived for a long time in the country with his brothers and kinsmen until he had reached one hundred and ten years. And when in sickness he had assembled his kinsmen, he asked them that, when he was dead, they bury him in Egypt, and that, when they departed from the land of Egypt, they bring his bones out of the country with them. When they had all heard his request, they granted it. Joseph died in great honor. He was buried in Egypt. [*Compare Genesis 49–50.*]

265 And at the time when Jacob died, there remained in Egypt, of his sons and his lineage that issued from him, seventy-five.

¶ When Joseph was dead, and King Pharaoh his lord was dead, the people increased and multiplied so greatly that it was wondrous. And there were so many Hebrews that he who then was the king of Egypt feared that they might drive him and the Egyptians from the land. And he said that he would oppress them at once with such great hardship and difficult labor that they would not wish to procreate.
270 And because the more they were oppressed, the more they multiplied, the king made them construct two great cities.

And when he was not able to accomplish anything by this method, he appointed two ladies, Shiphrah and Puah. And he commanded that they be at every birthing of the Hebrew women of Israel, and that they should have all the males killed and preserve the females. The ladies consented to this, but they were good women who
275 did not wish to offend God. And they did not wish at all, nor dare on account of piety, to kill any [of them].

When the king knew that none had been killed, he asked the ladies why they had not followed his command. And they said to him, "Sire, the Hebrew ladies of the sons of Israel are wiser than we are, and they know their times better than we know them,
280 and they have given birth before we come to them." Then the king appointed reliable justices to go throughout the land, and the males whom they found born were to be drowned, and the females were to be preserved. [*Compare Exodus 1.*]

¶ At this time a Hebrew lady gave birth and had a very handsome son. And she hid and protected his great beauty as best she could. When she had protected him for
285 three months and saw well that she could no longer hide him from detection, she made a sturdy vessel and had it well sealed inside and out so that water could not get in. And she placed it softly in a stream. Mary the baby's sister followed from a distance to see what would happen as a result of this. And she made great lamentation. |

96r]
290 Thereupon came the daughter of Pharaoh the king, amusing herself near this stream. And she saw this vessel floating, and asked what it was. The vessel was pulled from the water. And the young lady saw that it was a baby. And she said that she knew well that he was Hebrew, and it would be a deep sadness to kill so handsome a baby. And she said that she would have him nursed.

Atant vint Marie la suere l'enfant, e dit, "Ma damoysele, volez vous que je vous querge une feme Hebrewe pur norysser l'enfaunt?"

295   "Oil," fet ele, "je vous pri."

Marie vint corant a sa mere, e dit, "Mere, venez avant. La file le roi vous maund par moy qe vous viegnez a ly. E vous averez vostre enfaunt a noryr, e en nulle manere reconoissez qu'il est vostre."

La mere vint a la file le roy, e resçust l'enfaunt a noryr. E si avoit bels donus e
300   moltz pur la noreture. E la damoisele vint sovent a la noresse, e la noresse a ly, pur vere l'enfaunt. E pur ce qu'il fust trovez pres de l'ewe, fust apelé Moyses.

¶ E quant Moyses fust gueres de age, si fust molt bels. E la file le roy molt le ama, e le roi le ama molt tendrement pur la resoun sa fyle.

Un jour le roy prist sa coroune entaillé de un ydre e la mist sur le chief Moyses. E
305   il la prist e la gitta jus a terre. E le roy se corosa. Un proveyre de lur ley ce vist e corust sur l'enfaunt, e le vodra meyntenaunt aver ocis si sa dame ne ust esté. E dit que par cesti serra la coroune de Egipte abatue. E aprés issi fust.

¶ Quant Moyses fust bien parcru, vint la ou les Hebreus furent, par travals e opressiouns des overaignes, trop chargés e malmis. E vist un Egipcien feryr
310   ledement un Hebreu. Moyses out pieté de sa nacion. En eyde de le Hebreu, feri le Egipcien qu'il morust meyntenant. Moyses regarda entour ly e nully ne voit, e pur ce fust molt lié.

Un autre jour vynt Moises a les overours e vist un Egipcien ledement tenceron un Hebreu. Donqe dit Moyses en bone manere a le Egipcien que le tort aveit, "Vous
315   ne fetez mie issi de tencer cely qe coupe ne ad."

"Ha, ha," fet le Egipcien. "Vous ne me devez mie ocyre come feytes nyagueres mon compaignoun."

Quant Moyses saveit qe sum pecchié fust desconeit, molt fu dolent e ne savoit qe fere. Quant le fet fust mostré al roy, yl comaunda que, si il purreit estre pris, que
320   meyntenaunt fust ocis.

¶ Moyses ne savoit que fere mes s'en ala privément hors du pays. Vynt en la terre Madyan, bien loynz de Egipte, e se assist delees un puytz ou les pastours soleynt abeveryr lur bestes. Lors vindrent les seet

Thereupon came Mary the baby's sister, and said, "My young lady, would you like me to find for you a Hebrew woman to nurse the baby?"

295   "Yes," she said, "I beg of you."

Mary went running to her mother, and said, "Mother, come now. The king's daughter summons you through me that you come to her. And you will have your baby to nurse, but in no way make known that he is yours."

300   The mother went to the king's daughter, and received the baby to nurse. And then she had large and numerous gifts in return for the nursing. And the young lady came often to the nurse, and the nurse to her, to see the baby. And because he was found near the stream, he was called Moses.

¶ And when Moses was still young, he was very handsome. And the king's daughter loved him very much, and the king loved him very tenderly on account of his daughter.

305   One day the king took his crown adorned with an idol and placed it on Moses's head. And he took it and threw it to the ground. And the king grew angry. A priest of their faith saw this and was angry with the baby, and would have had him killed at once had his lady not been there. And he said that by this one would the crown of Egypt be brought down. And afterwards thus did it happen.

¶ When Moses was fully grown, he came to where the Hebrews were, by the toils and oppressions of their labors, overly burdened and poorly treated. And he saw
310   an Egyptian cruelly strike a Hebrew. Moses felt compassion for his people. In helping the Hebrew, he struck the Egyptian so that he died instantly. Moses looked about him and saw no one, and for this he felt very fortunate.

Another day Moses came to the workers and saw an Egyptian violently chide a Hebrew. Then in a kind manner Moses said to the Egyptian who had done the
315   wrongful act, "You are not sent here to chide one who is not at fault."

"Ha, ha," said the Egyptian. "You dare not kill me as you previously did my companion."

When Moses knew that his crime was discovered, he was very upset and did not know what to do. When the deed was revealed to the king, he commanded that, if
320   he could be seized, he should be killed at once.

¶ Moses did not know what to do other than depart the country secretly. He came to the land of Midian, very far from Egypt, and sat down beside a well where the shepherds were wont to water their flocks. Then there came the seven

325   filles Raguel, que fust de le lignage as Hebreus, e abevererent lur arment. Les
       pastours de la contresurvindrent pur abeveryr lur bestes devaunt eux.

       ¶ Moyses hardiement defendy les puceles, e fist, "Lur bestes come primes vindrent,
96v]   primes | estre enbeveris."

       Les puceles vindrent a mesone e counterent lur piere coment un home estraunge les
       delyvera des pastours. E il lur demaunda purquoi ne ly aveyent amené a mesone ov
330   eux. E il ly di, "Seynt sire, nous ne savyoms mie vostre volenté."

       "Alez tost," fet il, "pur ly."

       Une ala a cele fontaigne e le trova. E le mena ov ly a Raguel son piere, qe ly reçust,
       e retynt ov ly par serement. E pus ly dona Sephoran sa fille, de quele il engendra
       deus fitz, Eleazar e Gersan. E molt mercia Dieu que issi ly avoit delyvrés de la mayn
335   le roi Pharaon. Moises molt ama ces fitz, e les endocrina de amer Dieu e doter sa
       poesté sur totes choses. [Compare Exodus 2.]

       ¶ Pharaon le roi de Egipte morust. E un autre roy Pharaon vint aprés e regna en
       Egipte. E destreyneit le pueple Hebreu plus que son predecessour ne feseit a son
       poer. Mes Dieu par sa poesté les delyvera bien. [Compare Exodus 1:8–10.]

340   Un jour garda Moyses les onewayles Raguel son sogre en la pastoure vers le mount
       de Oreb. Si vist en le mount un busshon elluminé de cui merveillouse flaume
       evissist, e apparust fierement ardant e ne ardeit mie.

       Moyses voleit approchier le busshon. E une vois ly dist, "Moyses, esteez la, e ostez
       vos sondlers, quar le lu ou vous esterez est seint. Je su Dieu, que su venuz parler ov
345   tey. Je ay oy en ciel le clamour de mon pueple Hebreu, que le roi destreint si
       fierement en Egipte. E vous irrez a ly de par moy, e dirrez que je ly maund qu'il
       seofre mon pueple issir de son realme e aler la ou vous les amerrez. E je serroi en
       vostre bouche e vous aprendroi quanque vous dirrez."

       "Sire," fet il, "je ne su mie de bone eloquence. Maundez un autre, quel que vous
350   vodrez."

       E Dieu fist senblant de sei corocer, e dit, "Ore irrez, e vous encounterez Aaron
       vostre frere, qe quant joie averad de vous. E vous irrez ambedeus ensemble. E il est
       de bone eloquence e si sage qu'il siet bien fere mon message al roy. E je serroi en
       vos bouches a quanqe vous parlerez. E ceste verge porterez en vous, e en ceste
355   ferrez vous mes signes."

325 daughters of Reuel, who was of the Hebrew race, and they watered their herd. The shepherds drove them away from there to water their flocks before them.

¶ Moses bravely defended the maidens, and said, "As their flocks came first, | first
96v] shall they be watered."

The maidens went home and told their father how a foreign man had protected them from the shepherds. And he asked them why they had not brought him to
330 the house with them. And they told him, "Blessed father, we did not at all know your wish."

"Go quickly," he said, "after him."

One of them went to the well and found him. And she led him with her to Reuel her father, who received him, and retained his services with an oath. And then he gave him Zipporah his daughter, by whom he engendered two sons, Eliezer and
335 Gershom. And he thanked God greatly that he had freed him from the hand of King Pharaoh. Moses greatly loved his sons, and he taught them to love God and to fear his power above all things. [*Compare Exodus 2.*]

¶ Pharaoh the king of Egypt died. And another King Pharaoh came afterwards and reigned in Egypt. And with his power he suppressed the Hebrew people more than his predecessor had done. But God with his power freed them fully. [*Compare Exodus 1:8–10.*]

340 One day Moses watched the sheep of Reuel his father-in-law in the pasture near Mount Horeb. He saw on the hill a burning bush from which a wondrous flame emerged, and it appeared to burn fiercely and not to burn up at all.

Moses wished to approach the bush. And a voice said to him, "Moses, stay there, and remove your shoes, for the place where you are is holy. I am God, who am
345 come to speak with you. I have heard in heaven the cry of my Hebrew people, whom the king oppresses so cruelly in Egypt. And you shall go to him from me, and say that I command him to permit my people to leave his realm and go there where you shall lead them. And I shall be in your mouth and teach you whatever you are to say."

350 "Lord," said he, "I am not eloquent at all. Send another, whomever you wish."

And God pretended to be angered, and said, "Now go, and you shall meet Aaron your brother, who will have great joy of you. And the two of you shall go together. And he is very eloquent and so wise that he knows well how to convey my message to the king. And I shall be in your mouths whenever you speak. And this rod you
355 shall carry with you, and therewith shall you make my signs."

Moyses prist la verge, e Dieu ly dit, "Quei tenez vous?"

"Sire," fet il, "une verge."

"Oste la de vous."

Il la gitta a la terre, e meyntenant devynt une colnure. E Moyses comença fuyr.

360   E Dieu ly dist, "Pernez la par la cowe." E il la prist, e meyntenaunt devint verge.

Dist Dieu, "Metez vostre mayn en vostre seyn." E il si fist.

"Ore, retrahez la meyn." E il si fist. E donque fust la meyn feru de lepre si hidousement qe a merveille.

"Metez la meyn en ton seyn." E il si fist.

365   "Ore, la retrahez." E il si fist. E donque fust tote seyne.

"Par cestes signez," dist Dieu, "conoistra le pueple de Israel que vous avez parlé ov moy. E je lur dorray terre riche e plentyvouse decoraunte de let e mel, la terre Caney, Ethey, Amorey, Ferezey, Evey, Jebusey, Gergesey." |

97r]   ¶ Moyses ala prendre congié a Raguel soun sogre, e li counta le comaundement
370   Dieu. Prist Sephora sa femme e ces deus fis, e se mistrent en le chemyn vers Egipte. Atant vint un angel. E lur fust avis qu'il volent ocyre le eynsné fitz. E Sephora le aparçust, e prist tost un cayllon e circumsist son fitz. E le aungel donque s'en parti de eux. L'enfaunt seigna fierement, e Sephora dist a Moyses, "Pur vous ai je espandu le sang mon fitz, e vous estes espous de sang a mei. Si je usse pris espous
375   de le lignage dount je su nee, dont ne usse je meyn ensenglanté." E pur ce qe issi dit Moyses ne la vodra mener ov ly. E l'enfaunt fust molt fiebele. E pur ce les remaunda Moyses arere a sojorner ov Raguel soun piere.

¶ Lors s'en ala Moyses vers Egipte e encountra Aaron son frere, que molt fust leé de ly. Moyses ad counté coment Dieu ly avoit comaundé, e de la verge e de la meyn
380   e totes ces autres afferes. Vindrent al roy Pharaon e li counterent le maundement lur Dieu, e qu'il lessast le pueple Hebreu aler a trois jornés en le desert e fere sacrifice a ly.

Quant le roi le oy, molt despitousement lur dist, "Qui est cel Dieu? Je n'ay cure de vostre Dieu. Mes ore sai je bien par vous que le pueple
385   Hebreu est trop eesé en ma terre. E pur ce sunt il le plus orgoillous."

Moses took the rod, and God said to him, "What are you holding?"

"Lord," he said, "a rod."

"Throw it from you."

He threw it to the ground, and instantly it became a snake. And Moses began to flee.

360   And God said to him, "Take it by the tail." And he took it, and instantly it became a rod.

Said God, "Put your hand into your bosom." And he did so.

"Now, take out your hand." And he did so. And then the hand was stricken with leprosy so hideously that he was amazed.

"Put your hand into your bosom." And he did so.

365   "Now, take it out." And he did so. And then it was completely sound.

"By these signs," said God, "the people of Israel will know that you have spoken with me. And I shall give them a rich and bountiful land flowing with milk and honey, the land of the Canaanite, Hittite, Amorite, Perizzite, Hivite, Jebusite, Girgashite." |

97r]   ¶ Moses went to take leave of Reuel his father-in-law, and he told him the
370   commandment of God. He took Zipporah his wife and his two sons, and they proceeded on the road to Egypt. Thereupon came an angel. And it seemed to them that he wished to kill the older son. And Zipporah saw this, and she quickly took a stone and circumcised her son. And the angel then left them. The child bled fiercely, and Zipporah said to Moses, "For you I have shed the blood of my son, and you are married by blood to me. If I had taken a husband of the lineage to
375   which I was born, I would not have bloodied my hand like this." And for this Moses said he did not wish to take her with him. And the child was very weak. And for this Moses sent them back to stay with Reuel her father.

¶ Then Moses went toward Egypt and met Aaron his brother, who had much joy of him. Moses recounted what God had commanded of him, and about the rod and
380   the hand and all his other affairs. They came to King Pharaoh and informed him of the command of their God, and that he should let the Hebrew people go for three days into the wilderness and make a sacrifice to him.

When the king heard this, he spoke very contemptuously to them, "Who is this God? I do not care about your God. But now I know well from you that the Hebrew
385   people are too comfortable in my land. And for this they are excessively proud."

E comaunda que partot fuissent plus grevousement destreint qe avaunt ne furent. [*Compare Exodus 3–4, 5:1–9.*]

Moyses pria Dieu ayde. E Dieu repleny la terre Pharaon de mousches, quane grauntz anuys lur feseit partot. Mes en la terre de Gessem, la ou les Hebreus

390   demorerent, nulle moussche vynt.

Pharaon pria Moyses delyverer sa terre de mousches, e il lur grauntereit sacrefier en sa terre demeyne. E ce ne velt Moyses mes a trois jornés de sa terre. Le roy ly graunta. E quant fust delyvres de mouches, donque le roy desdit quaunque avoit eynz graunté.

395   Puis maundra Dieu partot le reigne Pharaon mortalité de bestes, e uncore ne vodra le roy granter Moyses sa requeste. Dieu comaunda Moyses e Aaron prendre le poudre de la terre e gittre sus. E il si fyrent. E tiel torment et malade de cors vint en Egipte que les enchateours le roi e tot le pueple furent si grevez que ne le poeint suffryr. E uncore ne vodra le roy granter.

400   Dieu maunda en la terre de Egipte grisil, vent, tonayres, sondres medlés de feu, que abati arbres, mesouns, foilles, herbes, arsist. Quant le roi vist qu'il ne le poeit endurer, donqe granta quaunqe Moyses velsist. E quant fust delyvres, donque tot le desdit.

405   Ces mesaventures e autres plusours manda Dieu sur la terre de Egipte, e la repleny de reynes e des verms. E al dreyn fist tiele mortalité de honmes qe de chescune mesone le eynsné fitz morust. E le fitz le roi meismes morust. E en tote Gessem unqe anuy ne damage vint de totes cestes mesaventures. E les mortz gyseyent desevelys.

Quant le roi ce vist, donque granta le pueple Hebreu aler. Mes, principalment, dis

97v]   plages maunda Dieu en Egipte avant que le pueple poeit | aver congié de passer

410   hors de la terre de Egipte a trois jornés pur lur sacrifice fere, les queux plages sunt notés par ces deus vers:

        ¶ *Sanguis, rana, culex, musce, pecus, ulcera, grando,*
        Brucus, caligo, mors optinuere necando.

¶ Donque fust le nounbre de Hebreus sis cent millers, estre les muliers, enfantz, e la

415   menue gent. Dieu lur comaunda appariller lur eyre, e apprompter de lur veysyns de Egipte les riche vestimentz, vessels, or e argent, e totes les richesses qu'il poeynt. E il lur a presteyent volenters quar il entendeyent que eux se retornassent hastivement. Quatre cent aunz e trent furent passé que les gentz de Israel primes vindrent a Josep en Egipte. [*Compare Exodus 7–12.*]

And he commanded that everywhere they should be more grievously oppressed than they were before. [*Compare Exodus 3–4, 5:1–9.*]

390 Moses asked God for help. And God filled Pharaoh's land with flies, which caused them great troubles everywhere. But in the land of Goshen, where the Hebrews lived, no fly came.

Pharaoh asked Moses to rid his land of flies, and he would permit them to sacrifice in his own land. And Moses did not wish this unless [it be] three days away from his land. The king granted this to him. And when they were rid of the flies, then the king revoked what he had previously granted.

395 Then God visited upon all of Pharaoh's realm the death of animals, and still the king did not want to grant Moses his request. God commanded Moses and Aaron to take the dust of the earth and throw it upward. And they did so. And such torment and bodily illness came to Egypt that the king's magicians and all the people were so distressed that they could not endure it. And still the king did not wish to comply.

400 God visited upon the land of Egypt hail, wind, thunders, lightning mixed with fire, which struck down trees, houses, arbors, grasses, in flames. When the king saw that he could not endure it, then he granted whatever Moses wished. And when they were delivered, then he quickly revoked it.

405 These misfortunes and many others God visited upon the land of Egypt, and filled it with frogs and with maggots. And in the end he made such mortality of men that in every house the eldest son died. And the son of the king himself died. And in all Goshen no trouble or damage came from all these misfortunes. And the dead lay unburied.

97v]
410 When the king saw this, then he permitted the Hebrew people to go. But, principally, God visited ten plagues upon Egypt before the people were able | to gain leave to go out of the land of Egypt for three days to make their sacrifice, the which plagues are indicated by these two verses:

¶ Blood, frog, gnat, flies, herd, ulcers, hail,
Locust, darkness, death seizes by killing.

415 ¶ Then was the number of the Hebrews six hundred thousand, not counting women, children, and servants. God commanded them to prepare for their journey and to borrow from their Egyptian neighbors their costly garments, vessels, gold and silver, and all the valuables that they might. And they lent them willingly to them because they understood that they would return quickly. Four hundred and thirty years had passed since the people of Israel first came to Joseph in Egypt. [*Compare Exodus 7–12.*]

420   Moyses prist les os Josep come eynz avoit pries a ces fitz, e s'en ala ov tot le pueple
       vers la Rouge Mer. E une mie en senblaunce de un pyler passa devant eux pur lur
       aprendre lur chemyn. E quant fust anuyeté, un clarté de su lur passa devant pur
       ce que eux ne devereint forneyer. E se herbergerent en Etham. [*Compare Exodus
       13:19–22.*]

425   E Dieu comaunda Moysen que le pueple alast avant e se herbergast entre
       Magdalom e la Rouge Mer. E le pueple si fist. E dit qe, si Pharaon donque venist,
       tous furent malballis quar il sunt enclos de mer e Magdalom, que fuir ne schaper
       porreint, "e par aventure nous sumes amenez ici de estre ici ocis, pur aver
       suffissaunce sepulcre que en Egipte aver ne purrons."

430   Donque dit Moyses, "Ne vous amaez de rien ne dotez le roi de rien quar Dieu
       combatera pur vous."

       Le roy assembla synt cent curres e grant host sauntz nounbre e tous les meillours
       de son reygne, e sywy les Hebreus. Moyses par le comaundement Dieu leva sa
       verge e ferist en la Rouge Mer. E la devynt une veie trobele, e la mer s'estut de une
435   part e d'autre come ce fust un mur. E le pueple Hebreu passa salvement cele mer
       par cel chemyn. Le roy e son host e ces curres entrerent meisme le chemyn. Mes
       quant Moyses ov son pueple fust aryvé, si fery de sa verge en la mer. E la mer
       encloist le roy e tous les suens qe unque un ne eschapa, que ne furent neiez
       trestous. [*Compare Exodus 14.*]

440   ¶ Moyses, Aaron, e Marie lur suere esturent e virent les curres le roy e ces gentz
       reversez en la mer. Molt furent leé. Marie prist son tympaigne e les autres dames,
       e chauntoient devant, e les autres aprés:

           ¶ "*Cantemus Domino gloriose*" etc.

       ¶ Treis jours alerent par le desert e ne troverent eawe. Pus vindrent en Marach e
445   troverent ewe a plenté, mes ele fust si amere qe nul la poeit goter, quar *mara* ert
       apelé, *id est*, "amara."

       Dieu mostra un fust a Moyses. E il le prist e mist en le ewe, e fust assez douce. E les
       Hebreus burent a plenté e enbeveryrent lur bestes. De ileque tornerent en Elym,
       e la troverent xii fountaignes e lxx palmers. [*Compare Exodus 15.*]

98r]   E demorerent en Syn, entre Synay e Elym, | en un molt delitable lu.

451   Le pueple fist grant grundilement a Moyses qu'il aveyent viaunde a plenté en
       Egipte, mes ore sunt estre lur gree mené en le desert e apoi viverent de faym.

420   Moses took the bones of Joseph, as that one had requested of his sons, and left with all the people toward the Red Sea. And a cloud in the form of a pillar passed before them to show them their path. And when night fell, a brightness from above passed before them so that they would not be led astray. And they encamped in Etham. [*Compare Exodus 13:19–22.*]

425   And God commanded Moses that the people move forward and encamp between Migdol and the Red Sea. And the people did this. And they said that, should Pharaoh then come, all would be ruined because they were enclosed by the sea and Migdol in such a way that they would not be able to flee or escape, "and perhaps we have been led here to be killed, so that we can have the number of graves that we were not able to have in Egypt."

430   Then said Moses, "Do not be dismayed by anything nor fear the king in anything because God will fight for you."

        The king assembled five hundred chariots and an innumerably large host and all the best men of his realm, and followed the Hebrews. Moses at the commandment of God raised his rod and struck upon the Red Sea. And a misty road appeared
435   there, and the sea stopped itself on one side and the other as though it were a wall. And the Hebrew people passed the sea safely by that path. The king and his host and his chariots entered the same path. But when Moses had arrived with his people, he then struck the sea with his rod. And the sea enclosed the king and all his people in such a way that not even one escaped, for they were all drowned. [*Compare Exodus 14.*]

440   ¶ Moses, Aaron, and Mary their sister stood and saw the king's chariots and his men overturned in the sea. They were very joyous. Mary took her tambourine with other women, and they sang first, and others sang after:

        ¶ "Let us sing to the Lord, for gloriously" etc.

        ¶ For three days they traveled through the wilderness and found no water.
445   Then they came to Marah and found plentiful water, but it was so bitter that none could consume it, for which reason it was called *marah*, that is, "bitterness."

        God showed a tree to Moses. And he took it and placed it in the water, and it was very sweet. And the Hebrews drank plentifully and watered their animals. From there they turned toward Elim, where they found twelve fountains and seventy palm trees. [*Compare Exodus 15.*]

98r]   And they rested in Sin, between Sinai and Elim, | in a very delightful place.

451   The people made a great grumbling to Moses that they had had abundant food in Egypt, but now they had been led against their will into the wilderness and scarcely survived on account of hunger.

Moises de ce parla a Dieu. E il ly dist qu'il pluereit payn de cel a eux. E comanda
qu'il le quilassent chescun jour ce que lur suffiereit, sauntz plus ou sauntz rien
455   estuer. E al syme jour, lur pluereit le double quar, al seme, rien ne pluereit. E a cel
sime jour quilassent pur deus jours.

Quant les Hebreus virent le payn de ciel chey entre eux, diseynt, "*Manhu, manhu,*"
en lur langage, en amerveillant, "quei est ce?" C'est a dire, "*Manna, manna, quid est
hoc?*" *Manna* est *interjectio admirantis,* e le payn est apelé manna. Puis dit fust qe le
460   pueple avent plus pris de cel payn que ne lur suffirreit, e qu'il l'aveit escué. Donque
Moyses se coroça grantement, e fist une mesure que fust apelé *gomor.* E ov cele
mesure departirent lur payn entre eux, e al sime jour le doublerent. E de tiel payn
vesquirent quaraunte aunz, tant come furent en le desert. [*Compare Exodus 16.*]

¶ E de Syn passa le pueple en Raphadyn. E quant ileque ewe ne troverent,
465   tencerent Dieu e Moyses. E Moyses se dota que il le velsist aver lapidé. E donque
comaunda Dieu a Moyses feryr sur la piere de Oreph ov sa verge. E il si fist. E
grant plenté de ewe issist de la dure piere, dount tous burent.

E Dieu prist de Hebreus vengaunce pur lur tensoun, quar Amalech le roy vint contre
eux en grant ost. E Moyses comaunda Josue ov les meillours des Hebreus issir a la
470   batayle contre Amalech. E les Hebreus furent bien armés. Moyses, Aaron, e Ur
monterent un terere pur vere les combataunz. Moyses ora a Dieu pur les Hebreus,
e leva ces mayns vers le ciel. E tant come ces mayns furent levez, son pueple aveit la
victorie. E quant furent abcesez, le pueple Amalech aveit la mestrie. E pur ce que
Moyses meismes ne poeynt sustenir ces mayns en levant, Aron e Ur les sustindrent
475   sus tanque a seyr, e son puple de Ebreus avoit la mestrie. [*Compare Exodus 17.*]

¶ De Raphadyn se tornerent e se herbergerent en un val desouz le mount de Synay.
Donque dit Dieu a Moysen, "Va seyntefiez ma gent, e comandez qu'il tienent mon
comandement. E dites que nul ces trois jours ne aproche al pié del Mont Synay ne
a sa mulier, mes que il facent laver lur dras. E je descendrey en une mie parler ov
480   eux e demostrer ma glorie. E si nul de eux autrement fra, de hydouse mort morra.

¶ Aprés le tierz jour passé, tonayre e sondre furent oys en le mound Synay, en
semblance de s'en descendi Jesu en le Mound e aprist oyauntz tous ces preceptz
tenir e la parole Dieu. La gent trembloit pur peur de la parole Dieu (taunt fust
98v]   espauntable!), e veient la fumé de le mount sus mon|ter, e la busyne oyent soner.
485   Moyses le dit que Dieu le fet pur eux esprover, e que eux li dussent le plus amer.
[*Compare Exodus 19.*]

Moses spoke to God about this. And he said to him that he would rain bread from the sky for them. And he commanded that they gather each day what was sufficient
455 for them, without [gathering] more and without storing any. And on the sixth day, double would rain for them because, on the seventh, nothing would rain. And on that sixth day they should gather for two days.

When the Hebrews saw the bread from the sky fall among them, they said, "*Manhu, manhu,*" in their language, wondering, "what is this?" That is to say, "*Manna, manna, quid est hoc?*" *Manna* is an interjection denoting wonder, and the bread is
460 called manna. Then it was said that the people had taken more of this bread than was sufficient for them, and that it had spoiled. Then Moses grew very angry, and he took a measure that was called a *gomor*. And with this measure they divided their bread among themselves, and on the sixth day they doubled it. And upon this bread they lived forty years, for as long as they were in the wilderness. [*Compare Exodus 16.*]

¶ And from Sin the people went to Rephidim. And when they found no water
465 there, they chided God and Moses. And Moses feared that they wished to stone him. And then God commanded Moses to strike upon the rock of Horeb with his rod. And he did so. And an abundance of water issued from the hard rock, from which all drank.

And God took vengeance on the Hebrews for their chiding, for King Amalek came against them with a large host. And Moses commanded Joshua with the best of the
470 Hebrews to issue forth in battle against Amalek. And the Hebrews were well armed. Moses, Aaron, and Hur climbed a hill to watch the combatants. Moses prayed to God for the Hebrews, and raised his hands toward the sky. And as long as his hands were raised, his people were victorious. And when they were lowered, Amalek's people had the advantage. And because Moses himself was not able to
475 keep his hands raised, Aaron and Hur held them up until evening, and his Hebrew people had the advantage. [*Compare Exodus 17.*]

¶ From Rephidim they journeyed and encamped in a valley beneath Mount Sinai. Then said God to Moses, "Go sanctify my people, and command that they keep my commandment. And say that for three days no one should approach either the foot of Mount Sinai or his wife, but that they should wash their clothes. And I will
480 descend in a cloud to speak with them and show my glory. And if any of them behaves otherwise, he will die a hideous death."

¶ The third day having passed, thunder and lightning were heard on Mount Sinai, in semblance of when Jesus descended from the Mount and taught all those listening to hold his precepts and the Word of God. The people trembled in fear of the Word of God (so fearful was it!), and saw the smoke from the mountain
98v] rise|up, and heard there the trumpet sound. Moses told them that God did it to
485 test them, and that they should love him the more. [*Compare Exodus 19.*]

Moyses mounta le mount de Synay e parla ov Dieu. E Dieu ly comaunda parler ov
son pueple qu'il preissent or e argent, pieres preciouses, vestimentz, e autres
grauntz richesses qu'il aveyent, e feissent fere une tabernacle solum le devys e
490   l'ordeynement Dieu. [*Compare Exodus 25–26.*]

Le fesure de le covre fust comaundé a Besselehel le fitz Ury e a Uolyab, que furent
sotils de chescun maner de overaigne. Le tabernacle fust fet solum l'ordeynement
Dieu meismes, e vous poez bien saver que richement, sotilement, e noblement fust
le tabernacle fet, que Dieu meismes ordyna. E as overours science dona de le
495   parfere a soun devis. Plus riche chose terriene ne poeit estre vewe de oyl quant tot
fut fet. Comaunda Dieu qe les riche vestimentz, le arche de le seintuayre, urcels,
chaundelabres, basyns, lavours, tables, auter, encensers, riches, dias de or corcynes
y furent myses. Dedenz le tabernacle la rychesse que la fust je ne vous say deviser.
[*Compare Exodus 31, 36–39.*]

500   ¶ En le secound an le premer meis, fust le tabernacle dressié. E Dies le covery de
une mie e de un feu de ciel. E tant come cele clarté y fust nul ni osa aprimer le
tabernacle.

Dieu comaunda Moyses fere deus busynes d'argent pur assembler la gent, e ordina
les fitz Aaron pur soner les busynes. E pur princes assembler, il les sonereynt un
505   petit a basse vois. "E pur ceus devers orient, les sonerez plus longement. E fetez
soner e resoner, si tous vels assembler. E pur ceus de mydy, aver fetez deus foyz le
soun partyr. Si vous volez trestous assembler, donque longement covent soner. Si
vous volez feste tener, doucement e peisiblement devez soner. E si pur guere soner
volez, bostoysement e durement les sonez." [*Compare Numbers 10:1–10.*]

510   Quant tous avoit Moises ensemblé, donque comanda tot le pueple en la garde
Aaron son frere e Ur. E disoit al pueple que si nul estrangerie lur survenist, qu'il
alast a Aron e Ur, e il lur dirreint quanque fere devereynt. E il meismes mountereit
le mount Synay pur parler ov Dieu. E en cel mount demora xl jours sauntz rien
manger ou beyvre. [*Compare Exodus 31:12–18.*]

515   Donque aprist Dieu a Moyses de bouche a bouche la ley qu'il aprendreit as
Hebreus. E prist deus tables, e escrit cele ley, e la bayla a Moyses. E les tables furent
de piere.

Dementiers que Moyses fust en le mount, le pueple vint a Aaron, e diseyent
que Moyses lur dustre fust passé de eux. E dyseyent que certeignement il
520   vueillent aver un dieu pur aorer. Aron dota lur malice, e ne lur osa
contredyre. E fust en doute qu'il le velsissent lapider. E lur graunta quanque
voleyent aver. E lur comaunda porter or, anels, firmayls, e autres gyeuls plusours.

490

Moses climbed Mount Sinai and spoke with God. And God commanded him to tell his people that they should take gold and silver, precious stones, vestments, and other costly valuables that they had, and that they should have a tabernacle built according to the plan and ordinance of God. [*Compare Exodus 25–26.*]

495

The building of the structure was assigned to Bezalel son of Uri and to Oholiab, who were skillful in every manner of work. The tabernacle was built according to the specifications of God himself, and you may well know that richly, skillfully, and nobly was the tabernacle built, as God himself ordained. And he gave the workers the knowledge to accomplish it according to his plan. A richer earthly thing could not be seen by eye when all was built. God commanded that the costly vestments, the ark of the sanctuary, cups, candelabras, basins, ewers, tables, altar, censers, valuables, and dias of twisted gold be placed there. I know not how to describe to you the richness that was there inside the tabernacle. [*Compare Exodus 31, 36–39.*]

500

¶ In the first month of the second year, the tabernacle was erected. And God covered it with a cloud and with a fire from the sky. And so great was this brightness there that no one dared to approach the tabernacle.

505

God commanded Moses to make two silver trumpets for assembling the people, and appointed the sons of Aaron to sound the trumpets. And to assemble the princes, they sounded them for a short time in low tones. "And for those in the east, you will sound them longer. And let them sound and resound if you wish everyone to assemble. And to have those of the south, let the sound go out twice. If you wish everyone to assemble, then it is appropriate to sound longer. If you wish to hold a feast, you ought to sound softly and peaceably. And if you wish to sound for war, sound them roughly and vigorously." [*Compare Numbers 10:1–10.*]

510

When Moses had everyone together, then he commanded all the people to be under the rule of Aaron his brother and Hur. And he said to the people that if anything strange should happen to them, they should go to Aaron and Hur, and they would tell them what they ought to do. And he himself would climb Mount Sinai in order to speak with God. And on that mountain he lived forty days without anything to eat or drink. [*Compare Exodus 31:12–18.*]

515

Then God taught Moses from mouth to mouth the law that he should teach to the Hebrews. And he took two tablets, and inscribed that law, and gave it to Moses. And the tablets were made of stone.

520

While Moses was on the mountain, the people came to Aaron, and said that Moses their leader had passed from them. And they said that they certainly wished to have a god to worship. Aaron feared their hostility, and dared not speak against them. And he was afraid that they wished to stone him. And he granted to them whatever they wanted to have. And he commanded them to bring gold, rings, brooches, and many other jewels.

99r]   E il les prist trestous, e les | gitta en un fornays. E quant de le fornais e de le fu
        issist un veel de or, tot le pueple le honora, e dit que ce fust lur dieu en qui il
525   creyent e que lur amena hors de Egipte. Aaron fust drescier un auter, e fist crier
        que lendemeyn serreit le solempnité de lur dieu, qu'il avoit fet d'or, celebré.

        Lendemeyn le pueple prist cores, tympaignes, e autres instrumentz. Chaunterent,
        carolerent, e melodie a demesure fyrent. E pur cel veel de or, oblierent Dieu, le
        Creatour de ciel e de terre.

530   Dieu dit a Moyses, "Le pueple de Israel m'ad tot gerpy, e tote vostre apryse ad
        lessé. E ad fet un veel d'or, e cel honourent, e lur dieu apelent. Soffrez que je me
        venge de eux e je les destrueray trestous, e je vous froy mestre de autre gentz."

        "Sire," fet il, "eyez merci de vostre pueple, e serez amentive de la promesse que
        vous, Sire, avez promis a cel pueple. E si vous preissez ciel vengement, donque
535   dirreynt les Egipciens que coyntement lur dieu lur avoit amené pur ocyre en le
        desert."

        Dieu dit, "S'il ne fust pur vous, ne serreit cel pueple esparnié."

        ¶ Moyses, descendi de le mount Synay, vint a Josue e as eynsnés que le atendoiens
        en un rescouns. E oyerent le cry e les busynes e la melodie que les gentz fyrent.
540   Josue dit, "Je crey que le pueple combat ov lur enymis."

        "Nanil," fet Moyses, "il n y a nul que lur asayle."

        Quant Moyses vint al pueple e vist ce qu'il avoient fet, e qu'il honorerent le veel
        d'or, gitta a un roche les tables de piere en qui Dieu de son dey avoit escrit la ley
        que le Hebreus devereynt tenyr. E les debrusa par corouse. E prist un bastoun e tot
545   de frussa le veel d'or e l'auter e quanque le pueple honoreit. E se coroça fierement,
        e dit que vengement enprendra. E demanda Aaron coment ce fut.

        E il ly pria merci, e ly counta de mot en autre coment il avoit fet a la requeste du
        pueple, e coment le veel d'or issist de le fornais e de le fu.

        E Moyses cria, e dit, "Tous ceux que sunt de Dieu, venent de cest part tot ycy." Se
550   treyent ly fitz Levy. "E armes vous tost, e ociez tot cel pueple la que aorerent le veel
        d'or. E nul n'esparnie — parent, frere, ami, conpaignoun, ne autre."

99r] And he took them all, and threw | them in a furnace. And when from the furnace and the fire there issued a golden calf, all the people worshiped it, and said that it

525 was their god in whom they believed and who had led them out of Egypt. Aaron had an altar raised, and had it proclaimed that on the next day the ceremony of their god, which he had made of gold, would be celebrated.

The next day the people took horns, tambourines, and other instruments. They sang, caroled, and unrestrainedly made music. And because of this golden calf, they forgot God, Creator of heaven and earth.

530 God said to Moses, "The people of Israel have entirely forsworn me, and have abandoned all your teaching. And they have made a golden calf, and worship it, and call it their god. Consent that I avenge myself upon them and destroy them all, and I shall make you the ruler of another people."

"Lord," he said, "have mercy on your people, and remember the promise that you, Lord, have vowed to this people. And if you take this vengeance, then the Egyptians

535 will say that their god has cleverly led them to be killed in the wilderness."

God said, "Were it not for you, this people would not be spared."

¶ Moses, having descended from Mount Sinai, came to Joshua and to the elders who awaited him in a hidden spot. And they heard the outcry and the trumpets

540 and the music that the people made. Joshua said, "I think the people fight with their enemies."

"Not at all," said Moses, "there is no one who assails them."

When Moses came to the people and saw what they had done, and that they worshiped the golden calf, he threw down on a rock the stone tablets upon which God with his finger had inscribed the law that the Hebrews ought to uphold. And he

545 shattered them in anger. And he took a stick and smashed completely the golden calf and the altar and whatever the people worshiped. And he grew fiercely angry, and said that he would exact vengeance. And he asked Aaron how this had happened.

And he begged him for mercy, and told him word for word how he had acted at the request of the people, and how the golden calf had issued from the furnace and the fire.

And Moses cried out, and said, "All those who are of God, come right here from

550 over there." And the sons of Levi drew near. "And arm yourselves quickly, and kill all those people who worshiped the golden calf. And spare no one — relative, brother, friend, companion, or other."

A cele occisioun, grant cri e noyse fust. E la furent ocis vynt treis milers del pueple que honora le veel d'or. E tiele vengaunce donqe fust prise pur cel pecchié.

555 Moyses seintefia le pueple que aveit cel occisioun fet, e molt reprist les autres de le assent que avoient assentuz le honorer le veel e lessir Dieu lur Creatour. "Ore irroi a Dieu e prieroi merci pur vous." Moyses molt pitousement pria Dieu merci pur son pueple. [*Compare Exodus 32.*]

"Moyses," dit Dieu, "le pueple est de sy dur cuer que il ne me creit, ne les myracles qu je faz ne veit. E tous que pecchent contre moi je les osteray de moun lyvre. E 560 envoieray un angel que destruerat Cananeum, Etheum, Amoreum, Ferezeum, Eveum, Jebuseum, e Gergeseum. E je dorray a ton lignage le terre que je promis a vos auncestres."

99v] Moyses fist descendre le tabernacle e le fist tendre en un autre lu. | Dieu descendy en un pyler de mie devant le us de le tabernacle. E tous, de lur herberges, 565 s'enclynoient a ly molt parfoundement.

Moises dit a Dieu, "Sire, que ferroi je de cest pueple? Je ne os remuer de yci le tabernacle, ne je ne pus cet pueple conduire ne amener de ycy si vous ne volez ov nous aler. Bel Sire Dieu, eyez merci pur vostre pieté de vostre pueple, e me grauntez, si vous plest, qe je pus vere vostre beneuré face."

570 Dieu ly dit, "Je vueil pur vostre amour aver merci de le pueple. Mes grace averez vous, e ma face ne poez vous vere. Venez demayn matyn a le mount, e je vous dirroi ce qe vous frez. E voiez que nully beste ne autre approchie al pié de le mount."

¶ Quant les autres furent endormy, Moyses mounta le mount ataunt vist le piler de la mie. E Moyses l'enclyna molt parfondement, e dit, "Bel Sire Reis e Dieu 575 onnipotent, eiez merci de vostre pueple e moi, e donez grace a nous qe nous vous puissoms amer, honorer, e servyr. E vyen ov nous, e nous gerpissez mie, quar bien savez qe de dur cuer est vostre pueple."

Dieu ly dit, "Je vous mosteray par signe que je su Dieu onnipotent e qe je vous aym. Tenez bien moun comaundement, e je destruerai tote gent que contre vous 580 sount. Je destrueray Amoreum, Cananeum, Ferezeum, Etheum, Gebuseum. E gardez qe ne eiez amisté ne compagnie a nul de lor vie. Destruez auters, temples, simulacres. E ne honorez nul dieu si mei noun, que parole a vous. E ce apernez al pueple. E portez ces deus tables ov vous, que je vous ay escrit. E lur apernez la ley."

Moyses prent ces tables e descent de le mount. E aprent le pueple 585 la parole Dieu. E le pueple que ly veit si ad grant merveille que il

Upon this killing, there was much outcry and noise. And killed there were twenty-three thousand people who worshiped the golden calf. And such vengeance thus was taken for this sin.

555 Moses sanctified the people who had done this killing, and highly reproved the others for the assent by which they had agreed to worship the calf and abandon God their Creator. "Now I will go to God and pray for mercy for you." Moses very devoutly prayed to God for mercy for his people. [*Compare Exodus 32.*]

560 "Moses," said God, "the people are so hard-hearted that they do not believe in me, nor do they see the miracles I perform. And all those who sin against me I will remove from my book. And I will send an angel who will destroy the Canaanite, Hittite, Amorite, Perizzite, Hivite, Jebusite, and Girgashite. And I will give to your lineage the land that I promised to your ancestors."

99v] Moses had the tabernacle taken down and had it pitched in another place. | God descended in a pillar of cloud before the entrance of the tabernacle. And all, from 565 their lodgings, bowed down to him very low.

Moses said to God, "Lord, what will I do with this people? I do not dare remove the tabernacle from here, nor may I conduct or lead this people from here if you do not wish to go with us. Dear Lord God, show mercy in your compassion for your people, and permit me, if it please you, that I may see your blessed face."

570 God said to him, "I wish for your love to have mercy on the people. But grace you shall have, though my face you cannot see. Come tomorrow morning to the mountain, and I shall tell you what to do. And see to it that no animal nor any other approach the foot of the mountain."

¶ When the others were asleep, Moses climbed the mountain until he saw the pillar of cloud. And Moses bowed very low before it, and said, "Dear Lord King and God 575 Omnipotent, have mercy on your people and me, and give grace to us so that we shall be able to love, worship, and serve you. And come with us, and never abandon us, for you well know that hard-hearted is your people."

God said to him, "I will show you by a sign that I am God Omnipotent and that I love you. Keep well my commandment, and I shall destroy all people who oppose 580 you. I shall destroy Amorite, Canaanite, Perizzite, Hivite, Jebusite. And take care that you have no friends or companions at all who are of their way of living. Destroy altars, temples, idols. And honor no god, other than me, who speaks to you. And teach this to the people. And carry these two tablets with you, which I have inscribed for you. And teach them the law."

585 Moses took the tablets and descended from the mountain. And he taught the people the word of God. And the people who saw him wondered greatly that he

ad deus cornes en sa teste, e targa aler a ly. E Moyses dit, "Purquoi ne venez vous a moy?" E le pueple ly dit, "Vous avez cornes que avant ne soliez aver." Quant Moyses le aparçust, covery sa face, e bien savoit qe ce fust de Dieu.

590   E tous jours la covery quant il fust hors de le tabernacle. E quant il fust leynz, donque la descovery. [*Compare Exodus 33–34.*]

¶ Moises conforta le pueple e le aprist ce que Dieu ly out comaundé. [*Not in the Bible.*]

¶ En le secound an pusqu'il enterent en le desert, vynt Dieu e comaunda Moyses qu'il enbrevast son pueple issi, qe ceux que furent de vynt aunz ou plus serreynt enbrevez a bataille (les menours e autres serreint escrit a altre diverse offis e
595   overaignes), e qe de chescun lygnage fust fet un prince pur a mestrer le pueple, estre de le lygnage Levy que ne serra escrit a bataille ne as overaignes. [*Compare Numbers 1:1–4.*]

Nota   ¶ De le lygnage Ruben le eysné, furent quaraunte sys millers, estre les femmes e les enfauntz, desqueux Elyzur la fitz Sedeur fust prince pur eux mener e lur bataille
600   ordyner. [*Compare Numbers 1:5, 1:20–21, 2:10–11.*]

¶ De lignage Symeon, synkaunte nuef myl e treis centz, estre les femmes e les enfauntz, de queux Salamyel fust prince. [*Compare Numbers 1:6, 1:22–23, 2:12–13.*] |

100r]   **[quire 11]** ¶ De le lignage Gaad, quaraunte synk mylers sis centz e synkaunte, de cui Elysab fust prince. [*Compare Numbers 1:14, 1:24–25, 2:14–15.*]

605   ¶ De le lignage Juda le bon guerreour, seissante quatosse mylers e sys centz, de cui Naason fitz Amynada fust prince. [*Compare Numbers 1:7, 1:26–27, 2:3–4.*]

¶ De le lygnage Ysacar, sinquaunte quatre myl quatre cent, de cui Nathanael le fitz Suhar fust prynce. [*Compare Numbers 1:8, 1:28–29, 2:5–6.*]

¶ De le lygnage Zabulon, synquante sept myl quatre centz, de cui Elyab le fitz Elon
610   fust prince. [*Compare Numbers 1:9, 1:30–31, 2:7–8.*]

¶ De Effraym e Manasse que furent les fitz Josepe, setaunte deus myl e sept centz, de le un lignage, Elysama, e de l'autre, Gamaliel. [*Compare Numbers 1:10, 1:32–35, 2:18–21.*]

¶ De le lignage Benjamyn, trent cynk myl e quatre cent, de cui Abidon fust prince.
615   [*Compare Numbers 1:11, 1:36–37, 2:22–23.*]

had two horns on his head, and hesitated to go to him. And Moses said, "Why do you not come to me?" And the people said to him, "You have horns that you did not have before." When Moses perceived this, he covered his face, and knew well that this was from God.

590   And he always covered it when he was outside the tabernacle. And when he was inside, then he uncovered it. [*Compare Exodus 33–34.*]

¶ Moses comforted the people and taught them as God had commanded him. [*Not in the Bible.*]

¶ In the second year after they had entered the wilderness, God came and commanded Moses that he should now record his people, that those who were twenty years old or more should be recorded in troops (the younger ones and
595   others were to be written down for various other offices and labors), and that from each lineage a prince would be made to govern the people, except that the lineage of Levi would not be written down for battle or for labor. [*Compare Numbers 1:1–4.*]

Note   ¶ Of the lineage of Reuben the eldest, were forty-six thousand, not counting women and children, of whom Elizur the son of Shedeur was prince to lead them
600   and organize their troop. [*Compare Numbers 1:5, 1:20–21, 2:10–11.*]

¶ Of the lineage of Simeon, fifty-nine thousand and three hundred, not counting women and children, of whom Shelumiel was prince. [*Compare Numbers 1:6, 1:22–23, 2:12–13.*] |

100r]   **[quire 11]** ¶ Of the lineage of Gad, forty-five thousand six hundred and fifty, of whom Eliasaph was prince. [*Compare Numbers 1:14, 1:24–25, 2:14–15.*]

605   ¶ Of the lineage of Judah the good warrior, seventy-four thousand and six hundred, of whom Nahshon son of Amminadab was prince. [*Compare Numbers 1:7, 1:26–27, 2:3–4.*]

¶ Of the lineage of Issachar, fifty-four thousand four hundred, of whom Nethanel the son of Zuar was prince. [*Compare Numbers 1:8, 1:28–29, 2:5–6.*]

¶ Of the lineage of Zabulun, fifty-seven thousand four hundred, of whom Eliab the
610   son of Helon was prince. [*Compare Numbers 1:9, 1:30–31, 2:7–8.*]

¶ Of Ephraim and Manasseh who were the sons of Joseph, seventy-two thousand and seven hundred, from the one lineage, Elishama, and from the other, Gamaliel. [*Compare Numbers 1:10, 1:32–35, 2:18–21.*]

¶ Of the lineage of Benjamin, thirty-five thousand and four hundred, of whom
615   Abidan was prince. [*Compare Numbers 1:11, 1:36–37, 2:22–23.*]

¶ De le lignage Daan, quaraunte deus myl e sept centz, de cui Ahiezel fust prince. [*Compare Numbers 1:12, 1:38–39, 2:25–26.*]

¶ De le lignage Asser, quaraunte un myl synk cent, de cui Phezyel fust prince. [*Compare Numbers 1:13, 1:40–41, 2:27–28.*]

620   ¶ De le lignage Neptalym, synkaunte treis myl quatre cent, de cui Ahyrac fust prince. [*Compare Numbers 1:15, 1:42–43, 2:29–30.*]

¶ Quant furent trestous nounbré, e ordiné, e escrit — soulement de ceux qe aveyent vynt aunz ou plus, que serreint entendaunt a bataille — donque fust la
Nota nounbre vj^c mil iij mil v c L de bone gent, estre les fenmes e les enfauntz e les
625   autres menu serjauntz, e estre le lyn Levy, de cui ne avetz uncore rien oy. [*Compare Numbers 1:44–47, 2:32–33.*]

Levy ¶ Dieu parla a Moysen e comaunda que le lignage Levy fust anounbree, de cui furent vynt deus myls, estre les femmes e les enfauntz. E de yceux, vynt myl synk centz e vintaunte furent de le age de xxx aunz ou plus. E a cel lignage, par le
630   comaundement Dieu, fust le tabernacle e le arche, e les riche vestimentz e aournementz que leynz furent baylés, a servyr e garder. E pur porter le tabernacle meismes, furent ordyné de les plus fortz de cel lyn, xliij myl. E a le arche e as autres choses — encensers, alters, lavours, basyns — furent ordynés, come mestrer fust. Les buefs, chamails, chyvals, e autres bestes que porterent les seintes choses
635   ou carierent rien apendant al tabernacle serount covertz molt estroytement de riche dras. E les seintes choses serrount envolupes molt richement en draps e instrumentz molt preciouses. [*Compare Numbers 1:48–54, 4:1–14.*]

Le premer mois de le secound an, must le pueple de le pie de le mount. E une mie en le desert covery le tabernacle, e une mie aloit, conduaunt le pueple devaunt.
640   [*Compare Numbers 9:1, 9:17.*]

¶ Lors dit Moyses a Abab le fitz Raguel de le lyn de Israel (frere le mulier Moyses), que vint a Moyses ov la femme e les deus fitz Moyses, Eliezel e Gersan, qu'il avoit engendré en la terre Madyan. E Raguel meismes y vynt quant Amalech fust vencu. E pria Moyses molt tendrement a Abab qu'il velsist aler ov eux. E il dit qu'il
100v]   retornereit a la terre Madian dont yl vynt. | Moyses ly dit que si il velsist aler ov
646   eux, il averoit grant mestrie sur tous quar bien savoit estre seygneur e dustre. Donque granta Abab aler ov eux.

Donque se must tot le pueple, e la mie lur passa devant. Quant avoient erré treis jornees, donque groundila le pueple veis Dieu e diseieit que
650   trop furent traveiles, e parlerent entre eux que malement avoient erree puis qu'il vyndrent de Egipte. Dount Dieu se corasa grantment,

¶ Of the lineage of Dan, forty-two thousand and seven hundred, of whom Ahiezer was prince. [*Compare Numbers 1:12, 1:38–39, 2:25–26.*]

¶ Of the lineage of Asher, forty-one thousand five hundred, of whom Pagiel was prince. [Compare *Numbers 1:13, 1:40–41, 2:27–28.*]

620   ¶ Of the lineage of Naphtali, fifty-three thousand four hundred, of whom Ahira was prince. [*Compare Numbers 1:15, 1:42–43, 2:29–30.*]

        ¶ When all were counted, appointed, and written down — only of those who were twenty years old or more, who would be engaging in battle — then the number was

Note   six hundred and three thousand five hundred fifty good men, not counting women
625   and children and also common servants, and not counting the line of Levi, of whom you have not heard anything yet. [*Compare Numbers 1:44–47, 2:32–33.*]

Levi   ¶ God spoke to Moses and commanded that the lineage of Levi be counted, of whom there were twenty-two thousand, not counting women and children. And of these, twenty thousand five hundred and fifty were thirty years old or more. And to
630   this lineage, by the commandment of God, was entrusted the tabernacle and the ark, and the precious vestments and ornaments that were inside, to serve and to protect. And to carry the tabernacle itself, it was ordained to the strongest of this line, fourteen thousand. And to the ark and other things — censers, altars, ewers, basins — they were ordained, as was their office. The cattle, camels, horses, and
635   other animals that bore the holy things or carried anything pertaining to the tabernacle were covered with well-fitted costly garments. And the holy things were enclosed very richly in most precious cloths and vessels. [*Compare Numbers 1:48–54, 4:1–14.*]

        In the first month of the second year, the people left the foot of the mountain. And a cloud in the wilderness covered the tabernacle, and a cloud moved, leading the
640   people forward. [*Compare Numbers 9:1, 9:17.*]

        ¶ Then Moses spoke to Hobab the son of Reuel of the line of Israel (the brother of Moses's wife), who came to Moses with the wife and two sons of Moses, Eliezer and Gershom, whom he had engendered in the land of Midian. And Reuel himself came there when Amalek was conquered. And Moses asked Hobab very tenderly if he might wish to go with them. And he said that he would return to the land of
100v]   Midian from which he came. | Moses said to him that if he wished to go with them,
646   he would have great authority over everyone because he knew well how to be a lord and leader. Then Hobab consented to go with them.

        Then all the people set out, and the cloud passed before them. When they had journeyed for three days, then the people grumbled against God and said that they
650   were tormented too much, and they spoke among themselves that they had journeyed with difficulty ever since they came from Egypt. Then God grew very angry,

e maunda un feu de ciel sur cel pueple, e destrueit plusours de eux. Lors pria
Moyses pur le pueple, e Dieu fist le feu cesser. E pur cel fu, fust le lu ou le fu fust
primes espris apelé Espernement.

655   ¶ Quant vindrent as Sepulcres de Coveytyse, ileque tendirent lur paveilons. E le
tabernacle fust tendu. Donque tensyrent le Hebreu Dieu pur ce qu'il n'avoient a
manger autre viande qe manna, e desirent aver char pur manger. Moyses oy le
groundilement de le pueple. E pria Dieu qu'il li grantast eyde de governer tant de
gent, e qu'il lur maundast de char quar forement le desirent.

660   Dieu descendy par la mie en le tabernacle, e comaunda Moyses qu'il amenast a le
tabernacle setaunte de les eysnes e plus sages Hebreus. E Moyses le fist. Dieu prist
de le espyrit Moyses e emply les setaunce Hebreus de cel espirit. E donque
devyndrent sages de prophecie e molt devoutz a le eyde Moyses. Dieu dist que le
pueple que desiroit aver char le avereit assez plenerement tot un mois entier.

665   Donqe dit Moyses, "Sire, ou averez vous taunt de bestes — buefs ou berbis — ou
char que suffysereit a taunt de pueple un meis enter?"

        Dieu savoit ce qu'il veleit fere. Un vent comença venter dont tant de quailles
        vindrent par les herberges e cheyrent partot si espessement que le pueple les
        quyleyt e grant mounceles fesoit. E tant avoit que le pueple ne savoit quey freit de
670   eux. Dieu prist vengement pur lur coveytise de le pueple: manda mortalité entre
        eux dount grant pueple morust. [*Compare Numbers 10–11.*]

        ¶ De ileque s'en alerent en Asserot. Donque dit Marie a Aaron, "Pur quey ne parle
        Dieu a nous come fet a Moyses nostre frere? E fet Dieu ce soulement pur ly, e ne
        mie pur nous e nostre desert?"

675   E Dieu, qe bien savoit que ele le disoit pur envye, descendi par la mie en le
        tabernacle, e parla a Marie devant Moyses e Aaron, e dit, "Coment fustes vu si osee
        de detrere mon serjaunt derere ly, a qui je meismes parle de bouche a bouche? E
101r]   je ly aym | e il moy, e je parle a ly e ne mie a vous ne a autre si noun par signe ou
        par sounge."

680   E pur cele detraccioun Dieu fery Marye de hydouse lepre. Aaron se esmaia
        grantment pur Marie sa suere, e pria Moises orer a Dieu pur ly. E Moyses si fist.

        Donqe ly dit Dieu, "Aprés seet jours serra tote seyne."

        Ele fust ostee e degitté de le pueple seet jours, aprés queux ele fust tote seyne e
        reprise a le pueple. [*Compare Numbers 12.*]

and visited a fire from the sky on this people, and destroyed many of them. Then Moses prayed for the people, and God had the fire end. And because of this fire, the place where the fire first burned is called the Burning.

655 ¶ When they came to the Graves of Covetousness, there they pitched their tents. And the tabernacle was raised. Then the Hebrews grumbled against God because they had no food to eat except manna, and they wanted to have meat to eat. Moses heard the grumbling of the people. And he prayed God that he grant him assistance in governing so many people, and that he send them meat because they desired it intensely.

660 God came down in the cloud into the tabernacle, and commanded Moses to bring to the tabernacle seventy of the oldest and wisest Hebrews. And Moses did it. God took of the spirit of Moses and filled the seventy Hebrews with this spirit. And then they became wise in prophecy and very devoted to assisting Moses. God said that the people who desired to have meat would have it plentifully enough for a whole month.

665 Then said Moses, "Lord, where might you have so many animals — cattle or sheep — or meat that would suffice for so many people a whole month?"

God knew what he wished to do. A wind began to blow in which many quail came through the pastures and fell down everywhere so thickly that the people gathered them and made large mounds. And there were so many that the people
670 did not know what to do with them. God took vengeance for the covetousness of the people: he sent plague among them by which many people died. [*Compare Numbers 10–11.*]

¶ From there they went to Hazeroth. Then said Mary to Aaron, "Why doesn't God speak to us as he does to Moses our brother? Does God do this only for him, and not at all for us and our merit?"

675 And God, who knew well that she said this through envy, came down in the cloud into the tabernacle, and spoke to Mary in front of Moses and Aaron, and said, "How are you so bold as to slander my servant behind his back, to whom I myself
101r] speak mouth to mouth? And I love him | and he me, and I speak to him and not at all to you nor to others except by sign or by dream."

680 And for this slander God struck Mary with hideous leprosy. Aaron was greatly dismayed on account of Mary his sister, and asked Moses to pray to God for her. And Moses did so.

Then said God to him, "After seven days she will be entirely healed."

She was removed and separated from the people seven days, after which she was entirely healed and returned to the people. [*Compare Numbers 12.*]

685 ¶ Donque tot le pueple se remua de Assarot en Pharan. Donque par le comaundement Dieu prist Moyses xij honmes de les xij lignages, c'est a savour Samuad, Saphat, Calef le fitz Zephone, Josue, Egal, Faltye, Gediel le fitz Zoty, Gaddy, Amyel, Stur le fitz Michael, Naaby, Guhel le fitz Machy. Ces xij furent maundez de Pharan pur espier la terre Canan que Dieu avoit promis as Hebreus.

690 Ceux xij alerent de Pharan par medy vers Canaan, e envyronerent la terre Canaan. E puis revyndrent, e diserent que la terre Canan fust molt riche e replenie de tous biens — bele tere e delitable de bois, ewes, prees, fontaignes assez beles, e plentivouse de totes frutz:

695 "Les cites sunt bien garnyes de murs. E les gentz sunt bien apris de guere. E la, sunt geauntz de lyn Enach, fortz e vaillauntz e grauntz. Vers medy meynt Amalech.

¶ "En le mountaignes sunt Ethey, Jebuzey, Amorey. Ly Cananen sunt joste la mer sur la ryvage de le flum Jordan. Trestous nous purront devorer, si il nous purreynt encountrer." [*Compare Numbers 13.*]

700 Lors Caleph e Josue vrent le Hebreus estre desconforté, diseynt, "Seignours, ne le creez pas! Aloms. Ov le eyde de Dieu, tous sunt les nos. Nous les prendroms tous a nostre volenté."

Les Hebreus furent molt esbahis, e diseynt que malement lur est avenu que issi sunt amenez de lur terre, ou il aveyent quanque mestier lur fut. E ore sunt en le desert, e apoy meorent de feym, e serrount ocis e destruit de lur enymis. E 705 murmurerent a Dieu e a Moyses. E Dieu se coroça fierement e descendy par la mie en le tabernacle, e dit qu'il destruerent tot le pueple pur lur dur cuer e maveise conscience e creaunce.

Moyses ly pria molt tendrement e molt pitousement merci. E Dieu ly dit, "Ceux que me ount tencé e detret e ne ount fet mon comandement ne verrount jamés 710 cele terre que je promis a lur auncestres. Mes a Josue e Caleph, qe me cryment, e a lur lignage, la dorroy. E tous ceux que furent enbrevee qe aveyent passé xx aunz taunt me ount mesfet qu'il morrount ici. E a lur enfauntz que ne furent enbrevez de xx aunz, dorroi cele terre. E ces enfauntz demorrount ici (taun qe les peres seient purris!), e quaraunte aunz les condueray par les desertz. E aprés lur dorray 715 cele terre."

685 ¶ Then all the people moved from Hazeroth to Paran. Then by the commandment of God Moses took twelve men from the twelve lineages, namely Shammua, Shaphat, Caleb the son of Jephunneh, Joshua, Igal, Palti, Gaddiel the son of Sodi, Gaddi, Ammiel, Sethur the son of Michael, Nahbi, Geuel the son of Machi. These twelve were sent from Paran to spy upon the land of Canaan that God had promised to the Hebrews.

690 These twelve went from Paran to the south toward Canaan, and they traversed the land of Canaan. And then they returned, and said that the land of Canaan was very rich and filled with all good things — a rich and delightful land with woods, waters, meadows, very beautiful springs, and abundant with all fruits:

"The cities are well furnished with walls. And the people are very ready for war.
695 And there, there are giants of the line of Anak, strong and brave and large. Toward the south dwells Amalek.

¶ "In the mountains are Hittites, Jebusites, Amorites. The Canaanites are next to the sea on the bank of the river Jordan. They would be capable of devouring us completely, were they to encounter us." [*Compare Numbers 13.*]

When Caleb and Joshua saw the Hebrews becoming disheartened, they said,
700 "Lords, do not believe it! Let us go on. With the aid of God, all is ours. We shall take all of them at our will."

The Hebrews were greatly dismayed, and said that it worked out badly for them that they were led here from their land, where they had had whatever they needed. And now they are in the wilderness, and are on the brink of dying from hunger,
705 and will be killed and destroyed by their enemies. And they grumbled to God and to Moses. And God grew fiercely angry, and came down in the cloud into the tabernacle, and said that he would destroy all the people on account of their hard hearts and bad conscience and faith.

Moses prayed him very tenderly and very reverently for mercy. And God said to him, "Those who have chided and slandered me and have not kept my com-
710 mandment shall never see that land that I promised to their ancestors. But to Joshua and Caleb, who feared me, and to their lineage, I shall give it. And all those who were written down who were over twenty years old have so wronged me that they shall die here. And to their children who were not written down as having twenty years, I shall give this land. And these children shall live here (so very wretched were their fathers!), and for forty years I shall lead them through the
715 wilderness. And afterwards I shall give them that land."

Moyses dist as Hebreus que Dieu prendroit greve vengaunce de lur mesfet. Il
plorerent e feseynt grant duel pur lur mesprise countre Dieu, e diseyent qu'il
irreyent a la terre Canaan e destruereynt tous lur enymis que purront trover.
Moyses dit, "Vous ne irrez mie sur vos enymis, quar Dieu n'est mie en vous. E pur |
101v]   ce vous ne poez espleyter de rien, mes serrez vileynement ledis par vos enymis."

721   Yl diseynt qe aler voleynt. Lendemeyn monterent un grant mont e virent lur
         enymis. Si descenderent e les corerent sur. Atant vynt Amalech de une part, e ly
         Cananen d'autre part, e feutre feryrent. E as Hebreus vint le pis, come Moyses lur
         avoit dit, quar Dieu ov eux ne fust. E plusours Hebreus furent ocis e plusours
725   malmis. E issi prist Dieu vengance de lur mesfet. [*Compare Numbers 14.*]

         ¶ En la Byble troverez vous ore en cet pas grant escripture de sacrifices que payens,
         judeux, e lur parenté soleyent fere de vels, aignels, e autre bestes. E ore le ount tot
         lessé pur ce qu'il sunt cheytyves entre nous. E en remenbraunce de lur Creatour,
         a ce qu'il dient, fount sculptures en pieres e peyntures chescun jour pur ce que il
730   ne ly vueillent oblier, quar peynture c'est lyvre a ceux qe ne ount conoissaunce de
         lettre. Mes ore de synagoge, que fust temple as gyus, ore est ordyné eglise a
         chretienz pur fere sacrifice chretiene. Al temps que cest escrit fut fet, mil aunz cent
         aunz e trente furent que Jesu Crist primes fust sacrifiez pur nostre pecchié, le quel
         sacrifice chescun jour entre chretienz est fet en remenbraunce de lur Creatour, e
735   serra tanque al fyn del mound. [*Not in the Bible.*]

         ¶ Lors deus centz e synkaunte compaignouns des Hebreus s'assemblerent.
         Vindrent a Moyses e Aaron. Desqueux compaignouns, mestre Chore, Datan, e
         Abyron furent principals. Donque dit Chore, "Moyses, rien n'avoms gayné parmi
         le seignorie e la mestrie qe vous avetz de nous. Vous ne serrez plus cheveynteyn ne
740   mestre sur cet pueple. Nous ne avoms cure de vostre prelacioun. Nous sumes tot
         seynt. Dieu est ov nous."

         Quant Moyses ce oy, molt fust dolent que le Deable les avoit issi desu par orgoyl
         e envye e par autre lede pecchié. E dit, "Chore, vous dites que vous estes seint.
         Demayn verroms nous votre seyntete. Portez demayn vostre encenser e vous —
745   ensement Datan e Abyron e tous vos compaignons — devant le tabernacle, e metez
         le encens as charbons. E donque serra veu qui de nous Dieu clyrra."

         Datan e Abyron, que malveis e orgoillous furent, diseyent que pur ly ne porterount
         encenser, e qe n'aveient afere de ly. Molt fust Moyses dolent que issi furent suppris
         de le Diable.

Moses said to the Hebrews that God would take great vengeance for their misdeeds. They wept and made great mourning for their crimes against God, and said that they would go to the land of Canaan and destroy all their enemies that they could find. Moses said, "You shall not go against your enemies at all, for God

101v] is not at all with you. And for | this you will not be able to accomplish anything, but you will be vilely abused by your enemies."

721 They said that they wished to go. The next day they climbed a large mountain and saw their enemies. Then they went down and ran against them. Thereupon Amalek came from one side, and the Canaanites from the other side, and struck upon them. And the Hebrews received the worst of it, as Moses had told them, for God

725 was not with them. And many Hebrews were killed and many hurt. And thus did God take vengeance for their misdeeds. [*Compare Numbers 14.*]

¶ In the Bible you will now find at this point much writing about the sacrifices that pagans, Jews, and their kin were wont to make of calves, lambs, and other animals. And now they have given up all that because they are captives among us. And in remembrance of their Creator, according to what they say, they make stone sculp-

730 tures and paintings every day because they do not want to forget him, for painting is a book for those who do not have understanding of letters. But now regarding the Synagogue, which was a temple for the Jews, now it is ordained a Church for Christians to make their Christian sacrifice. At the time that this writing was made, one thousand one hundred and thirty years had passed since Jesus Christ first was sacrificed for our sins, which sacrifice each day among Christians is made in remem-

735 brance of their Creator, and will be until the end of the world. [*Not in the Bible.*]

¶ Then two hundred and fifty companions of the Hebrews gathered together. They came to Moses and Aaron. Among these companions, Lord Korah, Dathan, and Abiram were the leaders. Then said Korah, "Moses, we have not gained anything during the lordship and governance that you have had over us. You shall no longer

740 be chief or governor over this people. We have no interest in your prelacy. We are all holy. God is with us."

When Moses heard this, he was very saddened that the Devil had so deceived them by pride and envy and by other ugly sins. And he said, "Korah, you say that you are holy. Tomorrow we shall see your holiness. Bear forth tomorrow your censer and

745 yourself — together with Dathan and Abiram and all your companions — before the tabernacle, and place the incense on the coals. And then it shall be seen which of us God calls."

Dathan and Abiram, who were wicked and proud, said that they would not carry a censer for him, and that they would have nothing to do with him. Moses was very saddened that they were taken by the Devil.

750   ¶ Lendemayn vindrent ov lur encensers les deus centz e sykaunte devant le
       tabernacle, mes Datan e Abyron ne vindrent mie. Donque dist Dieu a Moysen e
       Aaron, "Ostes vous de cele compaignie la que je me pus venger de eux *fortisme*."

       "Deus," fount il, "merci! Ne lessez taunt de gent peryr pur le mesfet de un honme
       ou de deus."

755   Moyses par le comaundement Dieu prist gent assez des Hebreus. Vint as herberges
       Datan e Abyron, e les fist hors trayre. E dit al pueple, "Seigneurs, Dieu prendra
       vengement de Datan e Abyron. E si il ne prenge autre vengaunce de eux que
       unque ne fist des autres, ne ly creez jamés qu'il soit verroi Dieu. E ce verrez vous |
102r] apertement, quar a trop demesure par lor orgoil, haltesse, elacion, e inobedience
760   qu'il ount pecchié contre Dieu lur Creatour, qe grant honour entre vous lur fist."

       Quant Moyses avoit ce dit devaunt tot le pueple que fust assemblé pur vere ce que
       Moyses freit, la terre se departy e overy, e devora e tranglota Datan e Abyron tot
       vifs. E issi cheyrent cri, "Le profound put de enfern!" E rien remist de quanque lur
       fust que la terre ignel pas ne devora.

765   Tot le pueple que ce veiet coreit sus e jus partot, e ne saveient qe fere. E tous se
       tindrent peris. E crierent merci a Dieu, e prierent Moyses orer pur els. E molt se
       tindrent desconforté.

       Atant vint un feu molt horyble de ciel. E, veaunt tot le pueple, la ou les deus cent
       e synkante compaignouns offryrent lur encenz, e les esprist e les mist tous en
770   flaume. E tiele vengance prist Dieu de ces deus cent e synkaunte compaignouns
       des Hebreus pur lur trespas.

       ¶ Donqe comaunda Moyses par le precept Dieu qe Eleazar le fitz Aaron presist les
       encencers de ceus que furent peris, e esparpilast le fu, e fesist des encensers pieces,
       e les fichist as auters, quar il sunt seintefiez en les mortz des peccheours. Issi que
775   ce pust estre signe a les fitz de Israel que nul de eux approchie a le auter de offryr
       encens si il ne soit de lygnage Aaron, si il ne veillent peryr come Chore, Datan,
       Abyron, e les autres fyrent.

       ¶ Le secounde jour le pueple de Hebreus grundila e fyrent grant noyse a Moyses e
       Aaron. E diseit le pueple que Moyses e Aaron aveient occis le pueple Dieu. E pur
780   doute de le pueple, Moyses e Aaron fuyrent al tabernacle. E entrent eynz, e la glorie

750   ¶ The next day the two hundred and fifty came with their censers before the tabernacle, but Dathan and Abiram did not come at all. Then God said to Moses and Aaron, "Remove yourselves from that company so that I may avenge myself upon them most mightily."

"God," they said, "have mercy! Do not permit so many people to perish for the misdeeds of one or two men."

755   Moses by the commandment of God took a good many Hebrews. He came to the lodgings of Dathan and Abiram, and had them dragged outside. And he said to the people, "Sirs, God will take vengeance upon Dathan and Abiram. And should he not take a vengeance upon them different from what he has ever taken upon

102r]   others, do not ever believe that he is the true God. And you will see this | openly, for too excessively in their pride, haughtiness, arrogance, and disobedience have

760   they sinned against God their Creator, who has granted to them great honor among us."

When Moses had said this before all the people who were assembled to see what Moses would do, the earth drew apart and opened, and devoured and swallowed up Dathan and Abiram entirely alive. And they let out a cry, "The deep pit of hell!" And nothing remained of whatever was theirs which the earth did not devour quickly.

765   All the people who saw this ran up and down everywhere, and did not know what to do. And they all thought they would perish. And they cried to God for mercy, and asked Moses to pray for them. And they thought they would be utterly destroyed.

Thereupon came a most horrible fire from the sky. And, in the sight of all the people, there where the two hundred and fifty companions offered their incense,

770   it seized them and entirely engulfed them in flames. And such vengeance did God take upon these two hundred and fifty companions of the Hebrews for their misdeeds.

¶ Then commanded Moses by the precept of God that Eleazar the son of Aaron take the censers of those who had perished, and scatter the fire, and fashion pieces from the censers, and fasten them to the altars, for they are sanctified by the death

775   of the sinners. Thus may this be a sign to the sons of Israel that none of them should approach the altar to offer incense if he not be of the lineage of Aaron, should he not wish to perish as Korah, Dathan, Abiram, and the others did.

¶ The following day the Hebrew people complained and made great noise to Moses and Aaron. And the people said that Moses and Aaron had killed the

780   people of God. And for fear of the people, Moses and Aaron fled to the tabernacle. And they entered inside, and the glory of God appeared to them.

Dieu lur apparust. E Dieu mist arsoun desus cel pueple. E Moyses comaunda Aaron
prendre un encenser, e ester enmy le pueple, e orer pur le pueple. E il si fist. E le
arsoun cessa, mes avant la cessacioun, furent xiiij^m e vij^c des Hebreus peris.
[*Compare Numbers 16.*]

785   ¶ Dieu comanda Moysen prendre de chescun lygnage une verge, e en celes xij
verges escrivre le noun de le prince en chascune verge, e une verge contendra les
nounz de touz lur meisgnes, e les mettre en le tabernacle "en signe qe je ay ov vous
parlé. E la verge de qy je choyseray floryra." E Moyses fist le comaundement Dieu,
e mist les verges en le tabernacle.

790   Lendemeyn trova Moyses en la mesone Levy la verge Aaron burgoynant e portaunt
flours, e les foilles de cele verge ostes devyndrent alemauntz. Donque porta Moyses
a les fitz de Israel e dona a chescun sa verge, mes la verge Aaron demora en le
tabernacle en signe des rebels fitz de Israel, e que eux cessassent lur
102v]   grondylementz e pleyntes, | que eux ne muergent. [*Compare Numbers 17.*]

795   Lors dit Dieu a Aaron, "Vous e vos fitz e la mesone toun piere sustendrez les
pecchiés de les sacerdocies e porterez la iniquité de seyntuarie. E pernez vos freres
de le lyn Levy e le septre toun piere ovesque vous. E vous e vos freres garderez le
sacerdocie e quanqe a le auter apent. E si nul autre le approche, serra ocis. E je
vous doynz la garde des primices e offrendres e sacrefices, e quei que est doné ou
800   offert a moy pur pecchié ou trespas le vostre ert. Primices de bles, terres, vynz,
oylles seient les vos, e de ce vyverez.

"Ce que primes vient hors de la ventre de chescune — femme ou autre beste — ert
le vostre. Issi, qe pur issue de femme, receverez pris. E de chescune beste nyent
net, receverez rauçoun, le quel raunçon serra fet aprés un meys. E le raunçon
805   serra un cycle d'argent, c'est, xx maylles.   .

"Des buefs, oeilles, chevres, e tieles — bestes netz — nul rauçoun serra, mes lur
sang serra espandu desuz le auter, e vous mangerez les chars. E la greese serra
ardenz, e dorra odour a Seignour. De la terre des Hebreus rien ne averez, quar je
meismes serroi vostre terre e vostre heritage. E a les fitz Levy ay je doné tous les
810   dismes des fitz Israel en possession pur lur service qe eux me fount en le
tabernacle." [*Compare Numbers 18.*]

¶ Moyses par le precept Dieu comaunda les fitz Israel amener une vache rouge de
entiere age qe unqe ne porta jug e que nulle tecche ne ad, e soit baylé a Eleazar le
prestre, e il fia le sacrifice de cele vache hors des chastels, veauntz tous, e mettra
815   son dey en le sang, e le esparpillera set foiz devant les portes de le tabernacle,
e si fra tote la char mettre en fume e flaume. E les cendres de la vache serrount

And God placed a fire above the people. And Moses commanded Aaron to take a censer, and stand in the midst of the people, and pray for the people. And he did so. And the fire ceased, but before the cessation, fourteen thousand and seven hundred of the Hebrews perished. [*Compare Numbers 16.*]

785 ¶ God commanded Moses to take from each lineage a rod, and upon these twelve rods to write the name of the prince on each rod, and one rod shall contain the names of all their households, and to put them in the tabernacle "as a sign that I have spoken with you. And the rod of the one I choose shall flower." And Moses did the commandment of God, and placed the rods in the tabernacle.

790 The next day Moses found in the house of Levi the rod of Aaron budding and bearing flowers, and the leaves extracted from this rod became almonds. Then Moses carried [the rods] to the sons of Israel and gave to each his rod, but Aaron's rod remained in the tabernacle as a sign to the rebellious sons of Israel, and that they
102v] should cease their grumbling and complaints, | so that they not die. [*Compare Numbers 17.*]

795 Then said God to Aaron, "You and your sons and the house of your father shall bear the sins of the priesthood and shall carry the iniquity of the sanctuary. And take with you your brothers of the line of Levi and the scepter of your father. And you and your brothers will be in charge of the priesthood and all that relates to the altar. If any other approach it, he will be killed. And I give you custody of the first fruits of offerings and sacrifices, and whatever is given or offered to me for sins or
800 violations is yours. The first fruits of corn, lands, wines, and oils are yours, and you shall live upon this.

"Whatever comes first out of the womb of each one — woman or else beast — is yours. Thus, for the issue of a woman, you shall be given a fee. And for each unclean beast, you shall receive a payment, which payment shall be made after a month. And
805 the payment shall be a silver shekel, that is, twenty halfpennies.

"For cattle, sheep, goats, and such — clean beasts — there shall be no payment, but their blood shall be spread upon the altar, and you shall eat their flesh. And the fat shall be burned, and the aroma shall be given to the Lord. Of the land of the Hebrews you shall have nothing, for I myself shall be your land and your inheritance. And to the sons of Levi I have given possession of all the tithes of the
810 children of Israel for the service that they perform for me in the tabernacle." [*Compare Numbers 18.*]

¶ Moses by the precept of God commanded that the children of Israel bring a red cow of full age that had never worn a yoke and had no blemish, and that it be given to Eleazar the priest, and that he make the sacrifice of this cow
815 outside the enclosure, in the sight of all, and put his finger in the blood, and sprinkle it seven times before the doors of the tabernacle, and then have all the flesh placed in smoke and fire. And the ashes of the cow shall be placed

mys en un lyw bel e net en la garde de la pueple de Israel, pur ce que ele fust arsé
pur pecché. E celes cendres serrount melles de ewe pure, e esparpilé sur les fitz de
Israel en signe de purgacioun / de pecchiés. [*Compare Numbers 19.*]

820   ¶ Le pueple de Israel vint en le desert Syn le premer meys. E demora en Cades. E
        la morust Marie la suere Moises e Aaron. E la fust ensevely.

        E le pueple avoit graunt defaute de ewe, e grondillerent vers Moysen e Aaron. E
        eux vindrent a le tabernacle, e prierent Dieu qu'il donast al pueple eawe vyve. E
        Dieu comanda Moysen e Arron, veiantz tous, feryr de lor verge deus foiz sur le
825   caylowe, e eawe issereit a plente. E yl si fyrent. Donque lur dist Moyses, "Vous de
        dure creaunce entendez qe nous par la vertu de Dieu ne vous puissoms doner eawe
        vyve de la dure piere. Ore veiez apertement qe si pooms. Lessez vostre
        groundylement, ou Dieu prendra greve vengaunce de vos tous." |

103r]   ¶ Lors dit Dieu a Moyses e Aaron, "Pur ce qe vous creistes poynt qe vous me
830   seyntefiastes devant les fitz Israel, vous ne amerrez poynt cest pueple a la terre qe
        je lur ay promys."

        ¶ Moyses maunda messagers de Cades a le roy Edom, e ly pria que le pueple de
        Israel poeit passer parmy sa terre sauntz nulle part torner hors de le chemyn, ou
        rien de le suen ou de soun pueple aver ou prendre. E le roy Edom ne le velt en
835   nulle manere graunter. E le pueple de Israel desturna de ly. E se must de Cades,
        e vint en le mount de Hor, qu'est en les synz de la terre de Edom.

        Donque dist Dieu a Moysen, "Pernez Aaron e Eleazar son fitz, e les menez en le
        somet de cest mount. E ostez les dras Aaron, e de celes dras vestez Eleazar son fitz.
        E la morra Aaron, quar je ne vueil mie qu'il entre la Terre de Promissioun pur ce
840   qu'il ne me crust poynt de mey seyntefier a le Eawe de Contradiccion devant les fitz
        de Israel."

        E Moyses fist le comandement Dieu. E quant le pueple vist qe Aaron fust mort, fist
        grant duel, e plora sur le cors xxx jours. [*Compare Numbers 20.*]

        ¶ Quant le roy Cananens savoit par ces espies le venue de la pueple Hebreu,
845   assembla grant pueple de son realme de Arad e se combaty as Hebreus. E illeque fust
        le roy vencu. E les Hebreus appelerent le lyw de la bataille Horma, e c'est a dyre,
        taunt come Anathema, c'est a savoyr "eschumegé." Les Hebreus s'en partyrent dehor
        par la dreyte veye vers le Rouge Mer. E voleynt envyroner le terre de Edom,

in a beautiful and clean place in the keeping of the people of Israel, because it was burned for sin. And the ashes shall be mixed with pure water, and sprinkled on all the sons of Israel as a sign of purgation of sin. [*Compare Numbers 19.*]

820 ¶ The people of Israel came into the wilderness of Sin in the first month. And they lived in Kadesh. And there died Mary the sister of Moses and Aaron. And she was buried there.

And the people had a great dearth of water, and complained against Moses and Aaron. And they came to the tabernacle, and asked God that he give living water to the people. And God commanded Moses and Aaron, in the sight of all, to strike
825 with their rods twice on the stone, and water would issue abundantly. And they did so. Then Moses said to them, "You of hard-hearted belief think that we by the power of God are not able to give you living water from the hard rock. Now you may see openly that we can. Cease your complaining, or God will take heavy vengeance upon you all." |

103r] ¶ Then said God to Moses and Aaron, "Because you did not believe entirely that
830 you should honor me before the sons of Israel, you will never lead this people to the land that I have promised them."

¶ Moses sent messengers from Kadesh to the king of Edom, and asked him that the people of Israel might pass through his land without turning anywhere from the path, or [without] having or taking anything belonging to him or his people. And
835 the king of Edom did not wish in any way to grant this. And the people of Israel turned away from him. And they set out from Kadesh, and came to Mount Hor, which is on the boundary of the land of Edom.

Then said God to Moses, "Take Aaron and Eleazar his son, and lead them to the top of this mountain. And remove Aaron's garments, and with these garments clothe Eleazar his son. And Aaron will die there, for I do not wish at all that he
840 enter the Promised Land because he did not believe in me so entirely as to honor me at the Waters of Contradiction before the sons of Israel."

And Moses did the commandment of God. And when the people saw that Aaron was dead, they made great mourning, and wept over the corpse for thirty days. [*Compare Numbers 20.*]

¶ When the king of Canaan learned through his spies of the coming of the Hebrew
845 people, he gathered a large people from his realm of Arad and fought with the Hebrews. And there was the king vanquished. And the Hebrews called the place of the battle Hormah, that is to say, something like Anathema, which means "excommunicated." The Hebrews left from there by the direct road toward the Red Sea. And they wished to go around the perimeter of the land of Edom, and

850 e devyndrent molt las pur lur travayl. E se corocerent vers Dieu e vers Moysen, e dyseynt que payn lur faylleit e eawe ne aveynt, e lur alme nausea desur si legere viaunde.

Dount Dieu se corouça grantment, e maunda partot le desert serpentz esprises de feu pur ocyre e malmener le pueple que en ly ne creyt poynt ne en ces vertuz. Les Hebreus de Israel ne poeynt mye endurer la persecucioun des serpentz, e crierent
855 a Moysen qu'il lur fesyst remedie.

Moyses pria a Dieu pur le pueple. E Dieu ly comaunda fere une serpente de erraym, e mettre al somet de une launce, issi qe la gent ferue des serpentz puissent vere cele serpente de erraym e serreynt sanez de lur entouchementz.

¶ De yleque ala le pueple en Oboch. E de yleque en Iebarym en le desert vers
860 Moab countre le est. E de yleque alerent a le torrent Zareht. E de yleque se herbigerent deprés Arnon, qu'est en le desert devers les fyns d'Amoreye.

Arnon c'est le fyn de Moab, departaunt les Moabites des Amorienz.

Moyses par le comaundement Dieu assembla le pueple des Hebreus, e Dieu lur
103v] dona une puce de eawe. E yleque chaunta Israel dyte, "*Ascendat puteus*" etc. | De
865 ileque s'en a la Israel en Mathana, e pus a Naalyel, pus en Bamoth. Bamoth est une valeye en la region de Moab en le somet de Phasga, devers le desert.

¶ Israel maunda messagers a Seon roy de Amorienz, e pria qu'il porreit passer parmy sa terre, e de nulle part torner ne rien de le suen aver. E le roi ne le vodera graunter. Mes fist assembler grant ost e encountra Israel en Jasa. E la fust le roy e
870 son pueple vencu. E debatu fust sa terre de Arnon tanque a Jeboc. Israel prist les cités le roy Seon, e habita en Amorei, Essebon e autres vylees. La cité de Essebon fust al roy Seon de Amorienz, qui combaty countre le roy Moab e prist totes ces terres desque Arnon.

Israel prist Jazer e tous ces habitatours, e se torna par la veie de Basan. E Og le roy
875 de Basan vint ou grant pueple countre Israel en Edray e vodera ocyre Israele. E Nostre Sire dit a Moysen, "Ne dotez ja le roy Og ne soun grant pueple. Je les dorroi tous en vostre meyn come je fesoy Seon roy de Amorienz." E quant le roy Og vint a la bataille, meintenaunt fust desconfist. [*Compare Numbers 21.*]

E Israel, en les champs de Moab vers la Jordan, ou Jerico est assis, prist son
880 herbergement.

850 they grew very weary from their labor. And they grew angry against God and Moses, and said that they lacked bread and did not have water, and their spirits were made sick by such meager food.

God grew very angry at this, and sent fiery serpents throughout the wilderness to kill and mislead the people who did not believe at all in him or in his power. The Hebrews of Israel could not endure at all the persecution of the serpents, and cried

855 out to Moses that he devise a cure for them.

Moses prayed to God for the people. And God commanded him to make a serpent of brass, and place it at the tip of a spear, so that the people struck by the serpents might behold this serpent of brass and be cured of their poisoning.

¶ From there the people went to Oboth. And from there to Iye-abarim in the

860 wilderness near Moab toward the east. And from there they went to the torrent Zered. And from there they lodged near Arnon, which is in the wilderness near the border of the Amorites.

Arnon is the border of Moab, separating the Moabites from the Amorites.

Moses by the commandment of God gathered the people of the Hebrews, and God gave them a well of water. And then Israel sang this song, "Let the well spring up"

103v] etc. | From there Israel went to Mattanah, and then to Nahaliel, then to Bamoth.

866 Bamoth is a valley in the region of Moab by the summit of Pisgah, facing the wilderness.

¶ Israel sent messengers to Sihon king of the Amorites, and asked that it might pass through his land, and neither turn aside anywhere nor take anything of his. And the king did not wish to permit this. But he gathered a large host, and met

870 Israel in Jahaz. And there the king and his people were conquered. And his land was fought over from Arnon to Jabbok. Israel took the towns of King Sihon, and lived among Amorites, [in] Heshbon and other cities. The town of Heshbon belonged to King Sihon of the Amorites, who had fought against the king of Moab and taken all his lands up to Arnon.

Israel took Jazer and all its inhabitants, and turned by the way of Bashan. And Og

875 the king of Bashan came with many people against Israel in Edrei and wished to kill Israel. And Our Lord said to Moses, "Do not ever fear King Og nor his many people. I will deliver them all into your hand as I did Sihon king of the Amorites." And when King Og came to battle, immediately he was defeated. [*Compare Numbers 21.*]

And Israel, in the fields of Moab by the Jordan, where Jericho is situated, made its

880 encampment.

¶ Lors dit Balaach le fitz Sephor a les greindres de Madyan, "Cest pueple Israel nous devorra tous come fet le buef la herbe." Cesti Balaach fust en icel temps roy en Moab. E maunda par messagers a Balaham fitz Beor, le dyvynour que habitout la flume de la terre le fitz Amon, qu'il venist a ly e veist la multitude de le pueple
885　Hebreu que vint de Egipte.

Issi qu'il les poeit vere e doner malessoun a cel pueple, parount cel pueple serroit le plustost vencu, quar ce, dit il, savoit bien qe cely qe Balaham voleit maldyre serreint maldit, e cely qu'il voleit benedyre serreit beneyt.

Les messagers vindrent a Balaham, e porterent le pris de la divinacioun. E
890　counterent a ly ce dont furent chargé. E il lur dit qu'il attendreint desque lendemeyn, e il parleroit a son mestre e pus lur respoundreit. La nuit vint Dieu a Balaham e ly demaunda quei cele gent la fyrent. Balaham ly trestut counta, de mot en autre. E Dieu ly comanda qu'il ne alast ovesque eux, e qu'il ne maldiseit son pueple.

895　Lendemeyn leva Balaham, e dit as messagers qu'il alassent arere a lur seygneur, e deissent que Dieu ly avoit defendu de aler a ly. Quant ceste responce vynt al roy Balac le fitz Sephor, prist autre messagers que furent de greyndre valour que les premers ne furent, e maunda a Balaham en meysme la manere qu'il
104r]　avoit avant fet. E Balaham lur pria | cele nuit demorer. E il sy fyrent.

900　La nuit vynt Dieu a Balaham, e dit, "Si cele gentz sunt purvous sa venuz, alez ou eux, e rien ne facez si ce noun que je vous comaund."

Balaham leva matyn, e prist ces deus fitz, e mounta sa asne. E chevaucha ov les messagers vers le roy Balac. E come Balaham chyvalcha sa asne, le aungel Dieu estut enmy la voye ov une espere trete e deneya la asne le voie. E la asne le veit
905　bien, e Balaham ne le poeit vere. La asne se destourna de la voye, e Balaham, que ne savoit l'enchesoun, la batyst e defola a demesure. E s'en prist a aler par autre voye, e le aungel vynt encontre ov l'espee trete. E la asne ne poeit avaunt. E Balaham la defola e batist a merveille durement. Balaham assaya le tierce voie, e le aungel vynt si pres de la asne que ele cheye a terre. E Balaham sayly sus e
910　comensa batre sa asne.

Donque par le ordeygnement Dieu parla cele asne a Balaham son mestre, e dit, "Purquoi me bates tu ore la tierz foiz? Quei vous ai je mesfet? Je ne vous fesey unqe taunt de mesprisioun, come ore ay fet, e ce n'est mie soulement par moy."

Adonque overy Dieu les oyls Balaham, e yl vist le aungel ov le espee. E
915　s'enmerveilla durement de cele vewe. E chey a terre e honora le aungel.

¶ Then said Balak the son of Zippor to the elders of Midian, "This people of Israel will devour us all as the ox does the grass." This Balak was at that time king in Moab. And he summoned by means of envoys Balaam the son of Beor, the soothsayer who dwelt by the river of the land of the children of Ammon, that he come to him and see the multitude of the Hebrew people who came from Egypt.

885

Thus might he see and curse this people, whereby this people would be conquered the more quickly, because, he said, he knew well that those whom Balaam wished to curse would be cursed, and those whom he wished to bless would be blessed.

The envoys came to Balaam, and carried the fee of divination. And they explained to him that with which they were charged. And he said to them that they should wait until the next day, and he would speak to his master and then answer them. That night God came to Balaam and asked him who those men were. Balaam recounted everything to him, word for word. And God commanded that he not go with them, and that he not curse his people.

890

The next day Balaam arose, and said to the envoys that they should go back to their lord, and say that God had forbidden him to go with them. When this response came to King Balak the son of Zippor, he took other envoys who were of higher rank than were the first, and summoned Balaam in the same way that he had done before. And Balaam asked them | to remain for the night. And they did so.

895

104r]

That night God came to Balaam, and said, "If these people have provided for your coming, go with them, and do not do anything other than what I command you."

900

Balaam arose in the morning, and took his two sons, and mounted his ass. And he rode with the envoys toward King Balak. And as Balaam rode his ass, the angel of God stood in the middle of the path with a drawn sword and denied the ass the path. And the ass saw him well, but Balaam could not see him. The ass turned from the path, and Balaam, who did not know the reason, beat and smote her immoderately. And he began to go by another path, and the angel came against [him] with his sword raised. And the ass could not go forward. And Balaam smote and beat her exceedingly hard. Balaam tried the third path, and the angel came so close to the ass that she fell down to the ground. And Balaam jumped off and began to beat his ass.

905

910

Then by the ordinance of God this ass spoke to Balaam her master, and said, "Why do you beat me now for the third time? What have I done to you? I have never at any time done any insults against you, as I now have done, and this is not at all by my own doing."

Then God opened Balaam's eyes, and he saw the angel with the sword. And he wondered greatly at this sight. And he fell to the ground and did honor to the angel.

915

Donque ly dist le aungel, "Je vienke sa pur ce qe je vous voderay encounterer e ocyre, e lesser la asne vyvre."

Donque ly dist Balaham, "Je ay pecchié, e je ne savoy qe vous y fustes. E si vous plest qe je retourne, je le froy volenters."

920 Donqe dit le aungel, "Alez ov ces princes, e rien ne parlez si noun ce qe je vous comandroy."

Quant le roy Balac savoit sa venue, sy vint countre ly, e a grant honour le reçust.

¶ Lendemeyn le roy amena Balaham a un mount apelé Balal, la ou yl poeit vere le dreyne partie de le pueple Hebreu. [*Compare Numbers 22.*]

925 Lors dit Balaham, "Apparillez issi set auters, set veans, e set owailles." Donqe prist Balaham e mist desuz chescun auter un veel e un owaille. E dist al roy, "Atendez si une piece pres de le auter. Je irroi ver si je pus parler a Dieu, e donqe vous dirroi je quanqe vous demaundrez."

Balaham parla ou Dieu. E tost revynt al roy, e dit oyauntz tous, "De Aram me
930 amena Balac le roy de Moabytes, de les mountz de orient, pur maldyre Jacob e escumeger Israel. Coment purroi je maldire le pueple qe unqe Dieu ne maldist?
104v] Come purroi je escumeger qe unqe | Dieu ne eschumega? Qui purra nounbrer la poudre purra nounbrer la progenie Jacob, e conustre le nounbre de Israel qui purra? Meorge ma alme en la mort de dreiturels, seient mes dreynetes fetz
935 semblale a eux."

Issi prophetiza Balaham plusours choses de Israel.

Le roy Balac se coroça, e dist, "Je vous fis quere pur ce qe vous me dussez plere e maldyre mes enymis, e vous fetes tot le contrarie."

Donque dit Balaham, "Je disoi a vos messagers e pri a vous que ne poy rien fere
940 ne dyre si noun a la volenté Dieu."

¶ Lors amena le roy Balaham en un halt mount qe um apele Phasga, la ou il poeit vere plus de le pueple Hebreu que avant ne fist. Donque fist Balaham set auters, e mist set veals e set owailles, e s'enloigna de le roy pur orrer. E pus revynt quant out parlé ov Dieu. E dist al roy, oyauntz tous ces princes, "Dieu ne est pas sicome
945 autre gent, a quei vous menteroy je, ne sicome le fitz de honme pur estre tousjours chaungé. Pur benesoun doner su je ament, e je ne pus benesoun deneyer. Yl n'y ad poynt ydle en Jacob, ne simulacre en Israel. Dieu Nostre Seigneur est ov eux, que tousjours est benet. E pur ce autre chose ne pus je doner a eux qe benesoun."

Then the angel said to him, "I came here because I wished to meet and kill you, and to permit the ass to live."

Then said Balaam to him, "I have sinned, and I did not know you were there. And if it pleases you that I should turn back, I will do it willingly."

920 Then said the angel, "Go with these princes, and do not say anything except as I shall command you."

When King Balak knew of his coming, he went to meet him, and received him with great honor.

¶ The next day the king led Balaam to a mountain called Baal, where he could see the larger part of the Hebrew people. [*Compare Numbers 22.*]

925 Then said Balaam, "Make ready here seven altars, seven calves, and seven sheep." Then Balaam took and placed on each altar a calf and a sheep. And he said to the king, "Wait here awhile near the altar. I will go to see if I may speak to God, and then I will tell you whatever you ask."

Balaam spoke with God. And he quickly returned to the king, and said for all to 930 hear, "Balak king of the Moabites brought me from Aram, from the mountains of the east, to curse Jacob and anathematize Israel. How can I curse the people that 104v] God has never cursed? How can I anathematize what | God has never anathematized? He who can count the dust will be able to count the progeny of Jacob, and who can know the number of Israel? May my soul die in the death of 935 the righteous, and may my final fate be similar to theirs."

Thus prophesied Balaam many things concerning Israel.

King Balak grew angry, and said, "I sent for you so that you would please me and curse my enemies, and you do exactly the opposite."

Then said Balaam, "I said to your envoys and affirmed to you that I cannot do or 940 say anything except at the will of God."

¶ Then the king brought Balaam to a high mountain that is called Pisgah, where he could see more of the Hebrew people than he had before been able to. Then Balaam made seven altars, and placed [on them] seven calves and seven sheep, and went away from the king to pray. And then he returned when he had spoken with God. And he said to the king, for all the princes to hear, "God is not as other 945 people, about whom I would lie to you, nor as the son of man who is constantly changing. I was led here to give a blessing, and I cannot withhold the blessing. There is no idol at all in Jacob, nor any effigies in Israel. God Our Lord is with them, who always is blessed. And for this I cannot give to them anything but a blessing."

Prophecies plusours dit Balaham de Israel.

950   Donque Balac le roy se coroça, e amena Balaham en le mont de Phegor pur vere si yl poeit maldyre Israel. E fist yleque set auters, set veals, e set owailes, come avant aveit fet, e lessa le roy e ces privés demorer ileque. E Balaham s'enloigna de eux e vist le pueple de Israel. E savoit bien sauntz dyvynaille fere, qe la volenté de Dieu fust benedyre Israel.

955   Revynt e dit al roy prophecies, e dit, "Quy benediera le pueple de Israel, yl serra benet. E quy le maldirra serra maldit."

Donque se corosa le roy fierement, e dit, "Je vous fis quere pur ce qe vous dussez maldire mes enymis, e vous avetz fet ore le revers treis foiz.

¶ "Retornez a vostre mesone dount vous venistes. Je vous avoi en pensé de aver
960   honoré devant tous de cest realme, e vous ne le avetz deservy."

Balaham ly dist, "Je dysoi qe je ne vous poey rien fere pur tous les bienz de mounde si noun a la volenté Dieu Nostre Seigneur. E sa volenté est que Israel seit beneit sur totes gentz."

E parla Balaham plusours profecies desqueux mester n'est ore de parler. Donque
965   se retorna Balaham a sa mesone dont il vynt. [*Compare Numbers 23–24.*]

¶ En ycel temps Israel demora en Sythem, e le pueple fist fornicacioun ov les filles
105r]   Moab. E les apelerent a sacrifices e aorerent malveis dieus. Dount | se coroça Dieu, e dit a Moysen, "Pernez tous les princes de cest pueple, e les fetes pendre countre le solail en patibles si la que ma corouce seit torné de eux."

970   Lors dit Moyses a les juges de Israel, "Chescun de vous ocie ces preomes."

E come yl entreparlerent de cel comaundement Dieu, un des fitz Israel veauntz Moyses e tot le pueple entra le bordel de Madyanytes. E plusours de le pueple Israel esturent devant la porte de le tabernacle e plorerent. E quant Phynees le fitz Eleazar (le fitz Aaron le chapeleyn) veist cely entrer le bordel, prist un dart e
975   tresperça parmy le honme e ensement la femme. E adonque cessa cele vengaunce entre les fils de Israel, mes avaunt furent ocis par la vengaunce de Dieu xxiiij^m des honmes pur lur fornicaciouns.

¶ Lors dit Dieu a Phynees, "Vous avez torné ma yre de les fitz de Israel, e je say qe vous me avez pur ce qe vous preistes vengaunce de mes enymis." E cely qe Fynees
980   ocist fust apelé Zambry le fitz Salu *myht*. E la femme Madianyte fust apelé Cozby la file Sur, le noble prince des Madianytes. Uncore dit Dieu a Moysen, "Ferez les Madianytes pur ce que eux se porterent enymiablement encountre nous."

Many prophecies did Balaam speak regarding Israel.

950 Then Balak the king grew angry, and led Balaam to the mountain of Peor to see if he would curse Israel. And there he made seven altars, seven calves, and seven sheep, as he had done before, and left the king and his ministers to stay there. And Balaam went away from them and saw the people of Israel. And he knew well without divination what to do, that the will of God was to bless Israel.

955 He returned and spoke prophecies to the king, and said, "Whoever blesses the people of Israel, he shall be blessed. And whoever curses them shall be cursed."

Then the king grew extremely angry, and said, "I deliberately sought you that you should curse my enemies, and you have now done the opposite three times.

960 ¶ "Return to your house from which you came. I had intended to honor you above all in this realm, and you have not earned it."

Balaam said to him, "I said that I could do nothing for you for all the wealth of the world except at the will of God Our Lord. And his will is that Israel be blessed over all people."

965 And Balaam spoke many prophecies of which there is now no need to speak. Then Balaam returned to his house from whence he came. [*Compare Numbers 23–24.*]

105r] ¶ At that time Israel dwelt in Shittim, and the people committed fornication with the daughters of Moab. And they summoned them to sacrifices and worshiped wicked gods. At this | God grew angry, and said to Moses, "Take all the princes of this people, and have them hung against the sun on gibbets until my anger is turned from them."

970 Then said Moses to the judges of Israel, "Let every one of you kill his neighbors."

And as they spoke together about this commandment of God, one of the sons of Israel in the sight of Moses and all the people entered the brothel of the Midianites. And many people of Israel stood before the door of the tabernacle and wept. And when Phinehas the son of Eleazar (the son of Aaron the priest) saw this one enter the

975 brothel, he took a javelin and pierced through the middle the man and woman together. And thus ended that vengeance among the sons of Israel, but first were killed by the vengeance of God twenty-four thousand men for their fornications.

¶ Then said God to Phinehas, "You have turned my anger from the sons of Israel, and I know that you belong to me because you took vengeance upon my enemies."

980 And the one that Phinehas killed was called Zimri the son of mighty Salu. And the Midianite woman was called Cozbi the daughter of Zur, the noble prince of the Midianites. Again God said to Moses, "Kill the Midianites because they carry themselves in enmity against you."

¶ E de cel temps en avaunt fust Fynees grant mestre e seigneur entre les Hebreus, e de Dieu privé e amé. [*Compare Numbers 25.*]

985   E de cet histoyre qui plus oyer vodra en la Byble en le lyvre de Nounbre le trovera, e ce apoy al fyn de meysme le lyvre. E qe bon fyn avera la joie de ciel ne perdra.

¶ Nomina librorum bibliotece   [art. 72]

105va]   ¶ Genesis
              Exodus
              Leviticus   libri legales
              Numerus
5   Deutronomius
           ¶ Josue
           ¶ Judicum
           ¶ Ruth
           ¶ Regum   iiii libri
10   ¶ Paralipominum   ii libri
           ¶ Esdras   iii libri
           ¶ Thobias
           ¶ Judith
           ¶ Ester
15   ¶ Job
           ¶ Parabole Salamonis
           ¶ Ecclesiastes
           ¶ Cantica
           ¶ Sapiencia
20   ¶ Ecclesiasticus
           ¶ Ysayas
           ¶ Jeremias
           ¶ Trene
           ¶ Baruch
25   ¶ Ezechiel
           ¶ Daniel
           ¶ Ozeas
           ¶ Joel
           ¶ Amos
30   ¶ Abdyas
           ¶ Jonas
           ¶ Mycheas
           ¶ Naum
           ¶ Abacuc
35   ¶ Sophonias

¶ And from this time forward Phinehas was a great leader and lord among the Hebrews, and an intimate and friend of God. [*Compare Numbers 25.*]

985   And of this history he who wishes to hear more will find it in the Bible in the book of Numbers, and this is almost at the end of the same book. And he who has a good end will not lose the joy of heaven.

¶ Names of the Books of the Bible   **[art. 72]**

105va]	¶ Genesis	
	Exodus	
	Leviticus	books of laws
	Numbers	
5	Deuteronomy	
	¶ Joshua	
	¶ Judges	
	¶ Ruth	
	¶ Kings	four books
10	¶ Paralipomenon	two books
	¶ Ezra	three books
	¶ Tobit	
	¶ Judith	
	¶ Esther	
15	¶ Job	
	¶ Parables of Solomon	
	¶ Ecclesiastes	
	¶ Canticle of Canticles	
	¶ Wisdom	
20	¶ Ecclesiasticus	
	¶ Isaiah	
	¶ Jeremiah	
	¶ Lamentations	
	¶ Baruch	
25	¶ Ezekiel	
	¶ Daniel	
	¶ Hosea	
	¶ Joel	
	¶ Amos	
30	¶ Obadiah	
	¶ Jonah	
	¶ Micah	
	¶ Nahum	
	¶ Habakkuk	
35	¶ Zephaniah	

¶ Aggeus
¶ Zacharias
¶ Malachias
¶ Machabeus
40   ¶ Marcus
¶ Matheus
¶ Lucas
¶ Johannes
¶ Ad Romanos
105vb]   ¶ Ad Corinthios   ii epistolas
46   ¶ Ad Galathas
¶ Ad Ephesios
¶ Ad Philipenses
¶ Ad Colosenses
50   ¶ Ad Thesalonicenses
¶ Ad Thimotheum   ii epistolas
¶ Ad Titum
¶ Ad Philomonem
¶ Ad Hebreos
55   ¶ Actus Apostolorum
¶ Epistola Jacobi
¶ Epistola Petri
¶ Epistola Johannis   iii
¶ Epistola Jude
60   ¶ Apocalipsis
¶ Psalterium
¶ Interpretationes Hebreorum nominatum, incipiencium secundem ordinem
  alphabeti

                    / Usualis: continet pedem et dimidium.
¶ Cubitorum:
65   / Major continet nonos pedes, et de illis archa Noe
                                   fiebat.
                    \ Geometricus:
                               \ Minor continet sex pedes.

¶ Haggai
¶ Zechariah
¶ Malachi
¶ Maccabees
40   ¶ Mark
¶ Matthew
¶ Luke
¶ John
¶ Romans
105vb] ¶ Corinthians   two epistles
46   ¶ Galatians
¶ Ephesians
¶ Philippians
¶ Colossians
50   ¶ Thessalonians
¶ Timothy   two epistles
¶ Titus
¶ Philemon
¶ Hebrews
55   ¶ Acts of the Apostles
¶ Epistle of James
¶ Epistle of Peter
¶ Epistles of John   three
¶ Epistle of Jude
60   ¶ Apocalypse
¶ Psalter
¶ Interpretations of Hebrew names, beginning according to the order of the
alphabet

/ Usual: contains one and a half feet.
¶ Of Cubits:
65   / The greater contains nine feet, and Noah's ark was
made according to them.
\ Geometric:
\ The lesser contains six feet.

BOOKLET 6   **QUIRES 12–14**

God that al this myhtes may   **[quire 12]**
                                                  [art. 73]

106r]   ¶ God that al this myhtes may,
        In hevene ant erthe thy wille ys oo.
        Ichabbe be losed mony a day —
        Er ant late Y be thy foo.
5   Ich wes to wyte, ant wiste my lay;
        Longe habbe holde me therfro.
        Vol of merci thou art ay;
        Al ungreythe Ich am to the to go.

        To go to him that hath ous boht,
10   My gode deden bueth fol smalle.
        Of the werkes that Ich ha wroht,
        The beste is bittrore then the galle.
        My god Ich wiste. Y nolde hit noht;
        In folie me wes luef to falle.
15   When Y myself have thourhsoht,
        Y knowe me for the worst of alle.

        God that deyedest on the rod,
        Al this world to forthren ant fylle,
        For ous thou sheddest thi suete blod.
20   That Y ha don, me lyketh ylle,
        Bote er ageyn the stith Y stod,
        Er ant late, loude ant stille.
        Of myne deden fynde Y non god.
        Lord, of me, thou do thy wille.

25   In herte ne myhte Y never bowe,
        Ne to my kunde Louerd drawe;
        My meste vo ys my loves trowe;
        Crist ne stod me never hawe.
        Ich holde me vilore then a Gyw,
30   Ant Y myself wolde bue knowe.
        Lord, merci! Rewe me now!
        Reyse up that ys falle lowe.

        God that al this world shal hede,
        Thy gode myht thou hast in wolde;
35   On erthe thou come for oure nede,
        For ous sunful, were boht ant solde.
        When we bueth dempned after ur dede
        A Domesday, when ryhtes bueth tolde,

BOOKLET 6   **QUIRES 12-14**

God Who Wields All This Might   [quire 12]
                                                                      [art. 73]

106r] ¶ God who wields all this might,
    In heaven and earth your will endures.
    I've gone astray many a day —
    Early and late I am your foe.
5   I was to blame, and knew my faith;
    I've long withheld myself from it.
    Full of mercy you always are;
    I'm all unready to go to you.

    To go to him who's bought us,
10   My good deeds are too meager.
    Of the works that I've performed,
    The best is more bitter than gall.
    My good I knew. I wanted it not.
    In foolishness I was happy to fall.
15   When I have fully examined myself,
    I perceive myself the worst of all.

    God who died on the cross,
    All this world to benefit and perfect,
    You shed for us your sweet blood.
20   What I have done, I little like,
    For ever against you I firmly stood,
    Early and late, at every turn.
    Among my deeds I find none good.
    Lord, with me, do your will.

25   I never bow down in heart or might,
    Nor draw toward my kind Lord;
    My greatest foe is my trust in praise;
    I never stood in awe of Christ.
    I consider myself baser than a Jew,
30   And I want myself to be known.
    Lord, mercy! Pity me now!
    Raise up that one who's fallen low.

    God whom all this world must heed,
    You have control of your good might;
35   To earth you came for our need,
    For sinful us, were bought and sold.
    When we shall be judged by our works
    On Doomsday, when justice shall be reckoned,

When we shule suen thy wounde blede,
40   To speke thenne we bueth unbolde.

Unbold Ich am to bidde the bote;
Swythe unreken ys my rees;
Thy wille ne welk Y ner afote;
To wickede werkes Y me chees.
45   Fals Y wes in crop ant rote
When Y seyde thy lore was lees;
Jesu Crist, thou be mi bote —
So boun Ich am to make my pees.

Al unreken ys my ro.
50   Louerd Crist, whet shal Y say?
Of myne deden fynde Y non fro,
Ne nothyng that Y thenke may.
Unworth Ich am to come the to!
Y serve the nouther nyht ne day.
55   In thy merci Y me do,
God that al this myhtes may.

Lustneth, alle, a lutel throwe [art. 74]

106ra] ¶ Lustneth, alle, a lutel throwe,
Ye that wolleth ouselve yknowe.
    Unwys thah Y be,
Ichulle telle ou, ase Y con,
5   Hou Holy Wryt speketh of mon:
    Herkneth nou to me!

The holy man sayth in is bok
That mon is worm ant wormes kok,
    Ant wormes he shal vede;
106rb] When is lif is hym byreved,
11   In is rug ant in ys heued
    He shal foule wormes brede.

The fleyhs shal rotie from the bon,
The senewes untuen everuchon,
15   The body shal tofye.
Ye that wolleth that sothe ysuen —
Under grases, ther hue buen,
    Byholdeth wet ther lye!

106va] Mon is mad of feble fom,
20   Ne hath he no syker hom,

When we shall see your wounds bleed,
40   To speak then we shall lack courage.

I lack the courage to call you savior;
Very unpleasant is my rashness;
I never walked afoot by your will;
I chose for myself wicked works.
45   False I was in every way
When I said your lore was lies;
Jesus Christ, be my remedy —
So ready I am to make my peace.

All uneasy is my rest.
50   Lord Christ, what shall I say?
In my deeds I find no relief,
Nor in anything else I can think of.
Unworthy I am to come to you!
I serve you neither night nor day.
55   Into your mercy I commit myself,
God who wields all this might.

The Sayings of Saint Bernard   [art. 74]

106ra]   ¶ Listen, everyone, for a moment,
You who want to know yourselves.
    Though I be unwise,
I'll tell you, as I know,
5   How Holy Writ speaks of man:
    Hearken now to me!

The holy man says in his book
That man is worm and food for worms,
    And worms he shall feed;
106rb]   When his life is stolen from him,
11   In his rib and in his head
    He shall breed foul worms.

The flesh shall rot from the bone,
All the sinews come unbound,
15   The body shall decay.
You who want to see the truth —
Under grass, there they are,
    Behold what lies there!

106va]   Man is made of feeble froth,
20   He doesn't have a stable home,

To stunte allewey stille;
Ys ryhte stude is elleswher —
Jesu, bring us alle ther
   Yef hit be thy wille.

25   The fleysh stont ageyn the gost.
When thou shalt deye ner thou nost,
   Nouther day ne nyht.
On stede ne sitte thou ner so heye,
Yet, alast, thou shalt deye.
30   Greyth the whil thou myht!

In false wonyng is monnes lyf.
When Deth draweth is sharpe knyf,
   Do the sone to shryve.
For yef thou const loke ariht,
35   Nast thou nothyng bote fyht
   Whil thou art alyve.

Nou thou hast wrong, ant nou ryht;
Nou thou art hevy, ant nou lyht;
   Thou lepest ase a roo.
40   Nou thou art sekest, ant nou holest;
Nou thou art rychest, ant nou porest —
   Nis this muche woo?

Thy fleysh ne swyketh nyht ne day;
Hit wol han eyse whil hit may,
45   Ant the soule sayth, "Nay,
Yef Ich the buere to muche meth,
Thou wolt me bringe to helle-deth,
   Ant wo that lesteth ay."

Thus hit geth bituene hem tuo —
50   That on saith, "Let!" That other seyth, "Do!"
   Ne conne hue nout lynne.
Wel we mowe alle yse:
The soule shulde maister be,
   The pris forte wynne.

55   Ne be thou nout thi fleysh uncouth;
Loke wet cometh out of thy mouth
   Ant elleswher wythoute.
106vb] Yef thou nymest wel god keep,
Ne fyndest thou non so fyl dung heep
60   Ant thou loke aboute.

To pause ever still;
His proper place is elsewhere —
Jesus, bring us all there
    If it be your will.

25   The flesh stands against the soul.
You'll never know when you shall die,
    Neither day nor night.
In seat no matter how high you sit,
Still, in the end, you shall die.
30   Prepare while you can!

In false housing is man's life.
When Death draws his sharp knife,
    Go soon to confession.
For if you might see truthfully,
35   You are nothing but a battle
    While you are alive.

Now you've done wrong, and now right;
Now you're heavy, and now light;
    You're restless as a roe.
40   Now you're sickest, and now healthiest;
Now you're richest, and now poorest —
    Isn't this quite woeful?

Your flesh won't toil night or day;
It wants comfort whenever it may,
45   And the soul says, "No,
If I allow you too much leisure,
You'll want to bring me to hell-death,
    And woe that lasts forever."

Thus it goes between them two —
50   That one says, "Stop!" That other says, "Do!"
    They're not able to quit.
Truly we must all perceive:
The soul should be the master,
    So as to win the prize.

55   Be not unseemly in your flesh;
Watch what comes out of your mouth
    And out from other places.
106vb] If you pay very good attention,
You'll never find so foul a dung heap
60   If you look about.

Nou thou hast in that foul hous
A thyng that is ful precious;
   Ful duere hit ys aboht.
Icholde the ful wilde ant wod
65   Yef thou lesest so muche god,
   Ant yevest hit for noht.

Mon, be war ant eke wis:
Yef thou fallest, sone arys;
   Ne ly thou none stounde.
70   With al thi myhte thou do this,
Thy soule sit — ant soth hit ys —
   Blysse, Ichave yfounde.

Mon, thou havest wicked fon
(The alreworst is that on),
75   Here nomes Y shal telle:
Thyn oune Fleysh, thy worldes fend
That best shulde be thy frend,
   That most doth the to quelle.

Thou clothest him in feir shroud,
80   Ant makest thy fomon fat ant proud,
   Yef Y durste seyn.
Thou dest thyselve muche wrong;
Thou makest him bo fat ant strong
   To fyhte the ageyn.

85   Do my counsail ant my reed:
Withdrah hym ofte of is breed,
   Ant yef him water drynke;
Ne let hym nothing ydel go,
Bote pyne do hym ant wo,
90   Ant ofte let hym swynke.

Coveytise of mony thyng
The World the bringeth, in fleish lykyng,
   Ant yeveth the more ant more.
Fals he is ant feyr he semeth:
95   Arlebest, when he the quemeth,
   He byndeth the fol sore.

107ra] Thenne shal he go to notht:
Nast thou nothing hyder ybroht,
   Ne nout shalt buere wyth the.
100   Thou shalt alone go thy wey,

Now you have in that foul house
A thing that's very precious;
 Quite dearly is it purchased.
I think you extremely wayward and mad
65 If you lose so much good,
 And give it away for nothing.

Man, be wary and also wise:
If you fall, quickly get up;
 Don't lie down for an instant.
70 If you do this with all your power,
Your soul shall sit — and true it is —
 In bliss, I have discovered.

Man, you have wicked foes
(The worst of all is that one),
75 Their names I shall reveal:
Your own Flesh, your worldly foe
Who best should be your friend,
 He does the most to kill you.

You clothe him in a fair garment,
80 And make your enemy fat and proud,
 If I may dare say.
You do yourself great wrong;
You make him both fat and strong
 In order to fight against you.

85 Follow my counsel and my advice:
Often withhold from him his food,
 And give him water to drink;
Don't allow him to be idle at all,
But cause him pain and suffering,
90 And often make him toil.

Greediness for many things
The World brings you, in fleshly desire,
 And gives you more and more.
False he is and fair he seems:
95 Most of all, when he pleases you,
 He binds you very sorely.

107ra] Then shall he change to nothingness:
You've brought nothing hither,
 And shall bear nothing with you.
100 You'll go your way alone,

Withoute stede ant palefrey,
   Withoute gold ant fee.

Lucifer, that foule wyht,
That wes himselve so feyr ant bryht,
105   Thurh prude fel to helle.
With foule wille ant foul thoht,
He fondeth bringe the to noht,
   Ant the forte quelle.

Thench that he the nes nout god,
110 He wolde have thyn huerte blod —
   War the for his hoke!
Do nou ase Ichave the seyd,
Ant alle thre shule ben aleyd
   With huere foule croke.

115 Yef thou seist my spel ys hard,
That thou ne mist this foreward
   Holde ne dreye.
A lutel thyng Y aske the:
Sey me soth, par charite,
120   Therof that thou ne lye.

Wher beth hue byforen us were?
Lordes, ledyes, that hauekes bere,
   Haden feld ant wode?
The ryche ledies in huere bour,
125 That wereden gold on huere tressour,
   With huere bryhte rode?

Hue eten ant dronken ant maden huem glad;
Huere lyf al with joie ylad;
   Me knelede huem byfore.
130 Hue beren huem so swythe heye,
Ant in a twynglyng of an eye,
   So hue buen forlore!

Wher bueth hue, thy wedes longe?
This muchele murthe, joie ant songe?
135   This hauekes ant this houndes?
Al that weole is wend away,
Ant al is turnd to "weylaway,"
   To monye harde stoundes.

107rb] Huere parais hue maden here,
140   Ant nou hue liggeth in helle yfere —

Without steed or horse,
    Without gold or money.

Lucifer, that evil creature,
Who was himself so fair and bright,
105   Through pride fell to hell.
With evil will and evil intent,
He plots to bring you to nought,
    And to make you die.

Should he think you're not good,
110   He'll plan to have your life-blood —
    Beware of his hook!
Do now as I've advised you,
And all three shall be allayed
    With their wicked tricks.

115   If you say my teaching is hard,
That this contract you're unable
    To hold or perform,
A little thing I ask of you:
Tell me truly, for charity,
120   That you won't lie about it.

Where are they who before us went?
Lords, ladies, who bore hawks,
    Ruled field and wood?
The rich ladies in their bowers,
125   Who wore gold on their hairnets,
    With their bright complexions?

They ate and drank and pleased themselves;
They led their lives entirely in joy;
    Men kneeled before them.
130   They bore themselves so very proudly,
And in a twinkling of an eye,
    Thus are they gone!

Where are they, your sumptuous robes?
This plentiful mirth, joy and song?
135   These hawks and these hounds?
All that wealth is gone away,
And all is turned to "wailaway,"
    To many difficult times.

107rb] They made their paradise here,
140   And now they lie in hell together —

That fur huem berneth ever!
Stronge y pyne, ant stronge in wo,
Longe is ay, ant longe ys o —
    Out ne cometh hue never!

145   Yef the Feond, the foule thyng,
Thourh wycked werk other eggyng,
    Adoun hath the ycast,
Up ant be god champioun!
Stond ant fal no more adoun
150   For a lutel blast.

Tac the rode to thy staf,
Ant thenke on him that for the gaf
    His lyf that wes so luef.
He hit gef, thou thonke hym;
155   Ageyn thy fo, such staf thou nym,
    Ant wreke the on that thuef!

Le jongleur d'Ely e le roi d'Angleterre   [art. 75]

107va]   ¶ Seygnours, escotez un petit,
Si orrez un tres bon desduit
De un menestral que passa la terre
Pur merveille e aventure quere.
5   Si vint de sa Loundres, en un pree
Encountra le Roy e sa meisnee.
Entour son col porta soun tabour,
Depeynt de or e riche atour.
    Le Roi demaund, "Par amour,
10   Ov qy este vous, sire Joglour?"
    E il respount sauntz pour,
"Sire, je su ov mon seignour."
    "Quy est toun seignur?" fet le Roy.
    "Le baroun ma dame, par ma foy."
15   "Quy est ta dame, par amour?"
    "Sire, la femme mon seignour."
    "Coment estes vous apellee?"
    "Sire, come cely qe m'ad levee."
    "Cesti qe te leva, quel noun aveit?"
20   "Itel come je, sire, tot dreit."
    "Ou va tu?" "Je vois dela."
    "Dont vien tu?" "Je vienke desa."
    "Dont estez vous? Ditez saunz gyle!"
    "Sire, je su de nostre vile."
25   "Ou est vostre vile, daunz Jogler?"

That fire burns them forever!
Fiercely in pain, and fiercely in woe,
Long is ever, and long is always —
    Escape may they never!

145 If the Fiend, the evil thing,
Through wicked deed or urging,
    Has cast you down,
Get up and be a good champion!
Stand and fall down no more
150   For a little setback.

Take the cross as your staff,
And remember him who for you gave
    His life that was so precious.
He gave it, you must thank him;
155 Against your foe, grab such a staff,
    And avenge yourself on that thief!

The Jongleur of Ely and the King of England   [art. 75]

107va]   ¶ Lords, listen a little while,
And you'll hear a good diversion
About a minstrel who traversed the land
Seeking marvels and wonders.
5   When he came to London, in a meadow
He met the King and his retinue.
Around his neck he wore his drum,
Painted with gold and rich ornament.
    The King asks, "If you please,
10   Whose man are you, Lord Jongleur?"
    And he answers fearlessly,
"Lord, I am my lord's."
    "Who's your lord?" says the King.
    "The husband of my lady, by my faith."
15   "Who's your lady, if you please?"
    "Lord, the wife of my lord."
    "How are you called?"
    "Lord, like he who raised me."
    "He who raised you, what name did he have?"
20   "Such as I, lord, quite properly."
    "Where are you going?" "I go over there."
    "Where do you come from?" "I come from here."
    "From where are you? Speak without guile!"
    "Lord, I'm from our town."
25   "Where's your town, Master Jongleur?"

　　　　"Sire, entour le moster."
　　　　"Ou est le moster, bel amy?"
　　　　"Sire, en la vile de Ely."
　　　　"Ou est Ely qy siet?"
30　　"Sire, sur l'ewe estiet."
　　　　"Quei est le ewe apelé, par amours?"
　　　　"L'em ne l'apele pas, eynz vient tous jours
　　Volenters par son eyndegré,
　　Que ja n'estovera estre apelee."
35　　"Tot ce savoi je bien avaunt."
　　　　"Donqe demandez com enfaunt.
　　A quei fere me demaundez
　　Chose qe vous meismes bien savez?"
　　　　"Si m'aid Dieus," fet le Roy,
40　　"Uncore plus vous demaundroy.
　　Vendras tu ton roncyn a moy?"
　　　　"Sire, plus volenters qe ne le dorroy."
107vb]　　"Pur combien le vendras tu?"
　　　　"Pur taunt com il serra vendu."
45　　"E pur combien le vendras?"
　　　　"Pur taunt come tu me dorras."
　　　　"E pur combien le averoi?"
　　　　"Pur taunt come je receveroy."
　　　　"Est il jevene?" "Oil, assez
50　　Yl n'avoit unqe la barbe reez."
　　　　"Vet il bien, par amours?"
　　　　"Oil, pis de nuit qe de jours."
　　　　"Mange il bien? Ce savez dire!"
　　　　"Oil, certes, bel douz sire.
55　　Yl mangereit plus un jour d'aveyne
　　Que vous ne frez partote la symeyne."
　　　　"Beit il bien, si Dieu vous gard?"
　　　　"Oil, sire, par seint Leonard,
　　De ewe a une foiz plus bevera
60　　Que vous ne frez taunt come la symeyne durra."
　　　　"Court il bien e isnelement?"
　　　　"Ce demaundez tot pur nient.
　　Je ne sai taunt poindre en la rywe
　　Qe la teste n'est devaunt la cowe!"
65　　"Amy, ne siet il point trere?"
　　　　"Je ne vous menterei — a quei fere?
　　D'arke ne d'arblastre, ne siet il rien.
　　Je ne le vi unqe trere pus qu'il fust mien."
　　　　"Passe il bien le pas?"
70　　"Oil, ce n'est mie gas.
　　Vous ne troverez en nulle route
　　Buef ne vache que il doute."

"Lord, near the church."
"Where's the church, good friend?"
"Lord, in the town of Ely."
"Where is Ely situated?"
30   "Lord, upon the water it stands."
"What's the water called, if you please?"
"One doesn't call it, but it always comes
Gladly of its own free will,
So that it need never be called."
35   "I knew all this well before."
"Then you ask like a child.
To what purpose do you ask me
Things you already understand?"
"God help me," says the King,
40   "Still more will I ask you.
Will you sell your horse to me?"
"Lord, more gladly than I'd give it."
107vb]   "For how much will you sell it?"
"For as much as it'll be sold."
45   "And for how much will you sell it?"
"For as much as you'll give me."
"And for how much will I have it?"
"For as much as I'll receive."
"Is it young?" "Yes, young enough
50   He's never had his beard shaved."
"Does he do well, if you please?"
"Yes, worse by night than by day."
"Does he eat well? Say what you know!"
"Yes, certainly, fair sweet lord.
55   He'd eat more oats in a day
Than you'll have in a whole week."
"Does he drink well also, God protect you?"
"Yes, lord, by Saint Leonard,
He'll drink more water at one time
60   Than you'll do as long as a week lasts."
"Does he run well and quickly?"
"You ask all this for nothing.
I can't spur so vigorously on the road
That his head not be in front of his tail!"
65   "Friend, is he able to draw at all?"
"I'll not lie to you — for what purpose?
Of bows and of crossbows, he knows nothing.
I've never seen him draw since he's been mine."
"Does he step his pace well?"
70   "Yes, he's not at all foolish.
You won't find along any route
Bull or cow that he fears."

"Emble il bien, com vous est avis?"
"Yl ne fust unqe de larcyn pris.
75   Tant come ov moi ad esté,
Ne fust mes de larcyn prové."
"Amis, si Dieu vous espleit,
Je demaund si il porte dreit."
Fet le Jogler, "Si Deu me eyt,
80   Qy en son lit coché serreit
Plus suef avereit repos
Qe si yl ne fust mounté soun dors!"
108ra]   "Ces paroles," dit le Roi, "sunt veynz!
Ore me dirrez si il est seinz."
85   "Seintz n'est il mie, ce sachez bien,
Car, si il fust seintz, ne fust pas mien.
Les noirs moynes le m'eussent toleyt
Pur mettre en fertre, come s'en serreit,
Auxi come autres seintz cors sunt
90   Partot le universe mount,
Pur pardoun receyvre e penance fere
A tote gent de la terre."
"Seinte Marie!" fet le Roy,
"Comment parles tu a moy!"
95   "Je dy sauntz de gales e sorenz
E d'autre mals e tormentz,"
Fet le Jogler al Roy.
"Yl ne se pleynt unque a moy
De maladie qu'il out en sey
100   Ne a autre myr, par ma fey."
"Bels amis, ad il bons piés?"
"Je ne mangay unqe, ce sachez,"
Ensi le Joglour respount,
"Pur ce, ne say je si bons sunt."
105   "Qe vous est, daun Rybaut?
Sunt il durs, si Dieu vous saut!"
"Durs sunt il, verroiement,
Come je quide a mon escient:
Yl usereit plus fers un meis
110   Qe je ne feisse mettre en treis."
"Est il hardy e fort?"
"Oil, il ne doute point la mort.
S'il fust en une grange soulement,
Yl ne dotereit, verroiement,
115   Ne ja n'avereit il poour
Ne de nuit ne de jour."
"Ditez moi s'il ad lange bone."
"Entre si e Leons-sur-Rone,
N'ad nulle meilour, come je quyt,

"Does he amble well, in your opinion?"
"He's never been seized for theft —
75   For as long as he's been with me,
He's never been convicted of theft."
"Friend, God care for you,
I ask if he carries comfortably."
Says the Jongleur, "God help me,
80   He who'd lie asleep in his bed
Would have a softer rest
Than were he mounted on his back!"
108ra]   "These words," says the King, "are empty!
Now tell me if he be healthy."
85   "He's not at all saintly, as you well know,
For, were he a saint, he'd not be mine.
The Black Monks would've taken him from me
To put him in a shrine, as would be sensible,
Just as other saints' bodies are
90   Throughout the entire world,
So that all the people of earth
May receive pardon and do penance."
"Saint Mary!" says the King,
"How you speak to me!"
95   "I speak without jests or games
Or other malice or evils,"
Says the Jongleur to the King.
"He has never complained to me
Of sickness that he had in him
100   Nor to any doctor, by my faith."
"Dear friend, has he good feet?"
"I've never eaten them, you know,"
Thus the Jongleur answers,
"As a result, I don't know if they're good."
105   "What's the matter with you, Master Scoundrel?
Are they hard, God save you?"
"Hard they are, truly,
As I know by my experience:
He uses up more iron in a month
110   Than I could put on in three."
"Is he hardy and strong?"
"Yes, he's not at all afraid of death.
If he were in a barn alone,
He wouldn't be afraid, truly,
115   Nor would he ever have fear
By night or day."
"Tell me if he has a good tongue."
"Between here and Lyons-sur-Rhone
There's none better, as I believe,

120   Car unqe mensonge ne dit,
       Ne, si bien, noun de son veysyn
       Ne dirreit, pur cent marcz d'or fyn,
       Mes qu'il ly voleit apertement fere
       Mavesté de chescune matere,
108rb] Ou larcyn par le pays,
126   Ou homicide, qe valt pys.
       Sire Roy, ce sachez:
       Par ly ne serrez acusez."
           Fet le Roi, "Je ne prise pas vos dys!"
130   "Ne je les vos, que vaillent pys.
       Je di bourde pur fere gent ryre,
       E je vous en countray, bel douz syre."
           "Responez a droit, daunz Joglours.
       De quele terre estez vous?"
135   "Sire, estez vous tywlers ou potters
       Qe si folement demaundez?
       Purquoi demandez 'de quele tere'?
       Volez vous de moi potz fere?"
           "E qe diables avez vous
140   Que si responez a rebours?
       Tiel ribaud ne oy je unqe mes!
       Diez de quel manere tu es."
           "Je vous dirroi, par seint Pere,
       Volenters, de ma manere.
145   Nous sumes compaignouns plusours,
       E de tiele manere sumes nous
       Qe nous mangeroms plus volenters
       La ou nous sumez priez,
       E plus volenters e plus tost,
150   Qe la ou nous payoms nostre escot.
       E bevoms plus volenters en seaunt
       Qe nous ne fesoms en esteaunt,
       E aprés manger qe devant,
       Pleyn hanap, gros e grant,
155   E si vodroms assez aver,
       Mes nous ne avoms cure de travyler.
       E purroms molt bien deporter
       D'aler matyn a mostier;
       E ce est le nostre us
160   De gysyr longement en nos lys,
       E a nonne sus lever,
       E pus aler a manger.
       Si, n'avoms cure de pleder,
       Car il n'apent a nostre mester;
165   E nous vodroms estre totdis,
       Si nous pussoms, en gyw e rys.

120   Since he never tells a lie,
Nor would he speak of any of his neighbors,
Either, for a hundred marks of fine gold,
Unless he wished openly to do
Wickedness of some kind,
108rb]   Or theft in the countryside,
126   Or murder, which is worse.
Lord King, know this:
By him you'll never be accused."
    Says the King, "I don't value your words!"
130   "Nor I yours, which are worth less.
I tell jokes to make people laugh,
And I'll tell you some, dear sweet lord."
    "Answer properly, Master Jongleur.
Of what land are you?"
135   "Lord, are you a tiler or a potter
That you ask so foolishly?
Why do you ask 'of what earth'?
Do you want to make a pot out of me?"
    "And what devils possess you
140   That you answer backwards?
I've never heard such a scoundrel!
Explain in what way you live."
    "I'll tell you, by Saint Peter,
About my manner of life, freely.
145   We're many companions,
And of such ways we are
That we'll eat more freely
There where we're invited,
And more gladly and more quickly,
150   Than where we pay our share.
And we drink more freely sitting
Than we do standing,
And [more] after eating than before,
A full goblet, thick and large.
155   And also we want to have enough,
Although we don't care for working.
And we can very well abstain from
Going in the morning to church;
And it's our custom
160   To lie a long time in our beds,
And to get up at noon,
And then go to eat.
Also, we don't care for begging,
Because it doesn't befit our office;
165   And we want to be always,
If we can, in play and laughter.

108va] E si vodroms aprompter e prendre,
        E, a nostre poer, malement rendre.
        Nous n'avoms cure de avre
170   For qe nous eyoms assez a manger.
        Plus despendroms a un digner
        Q'en un mois purroms gayner,
        E uncore volum plus
        Quar orgoil est nostre us.
175   E a bele dames acoynter,
        Ce apent a nostre mester.
        Ore savez une partie
        Coment amenoms nostre vie.
        Plus ne pus, pur vileynye,
180   Counter de nostre rybaudie.
        Sire Roi, ore me diez
        Si vostre vie est bone assez?"
            Le Roy respoygnant ly dit,
        "Certes, je preise molt petit
185   Vostre vie ou vostre manere,
        Quar ele ne valt mie une piere!
        Pur ce qe vous vivez en folie,
        Datheheit qe preyse vostre vie!"
            "Sire Roi," fet le Jogler,
190   "Quei valt sen ou saver?
        Ataunt valt vivre en folye
        Come en sen ou corteysie.
        E tot vous mostroi par ensample
        Qu'est si large e si aunple
195   E si pleyn de resoun
        Qe um ne dirra si bien noun.
            Si vous estez simple e sage honm,
        Vous estez tenuz pur feloun.
            Si vous parlez sovent e volenters,
200   Vous estes tenuz un janglers.
            Si vous eiez riant semblaunt,
        Vous estez tenuz pur enfaunt.
            Si vous riez en veyn,
        Vous estez tenuz pur vileyn.
205   Si vous estes riche chivaler
        E ne volez point torneyer,
108vb] Donqe dirra ascun honme,
        'Vous ne valez pas un purry poume!'
            Si vous estes hardy e pruytz
210   E hauntez places de desduytz:
        'Cesti cheitif ne siet nul bien —
        Taunt despent qu'il n'a rien!'
            Si vous estes honme puissaunt

108va] And we also want to borrow and take,
   And, as we're able, give bad return.
   We don't care for working
170 So long as we have enough to eat.
   We spend more on a meal
   Than we're able to earn in a month,
   And we want still more
   Because pride is our practice.
175 And to know lovely ladies,
   That befits our office.
   Now you know a portion
   Of how we lead our lives.
   I cannot, for rudeness,
180 Explain more of our ribaldry.
   Lord King, now tell me
   Whether your life is as good?"
    The King in response says to him,
   "Indeed, I value very little
185 Your life and your manner,
   For it's not worth even a stone!
   Because you live in folly,
   Cursed be he who values your life!"
    "Lord King," says the Jongleur,
190 "What's knowledge or wisdom worth?
   It's as valuable to live in folly
   As in good sense or courtliness.
   And I'll show you everything by example
   So broad and so wide
195 And so full of reason
   That no one shall speak against it.
    If you're a man humble and wise,
   You're considered a felon.
    If you speak often and gladly,
200 You're considered a chatterer.
    If you have a smiling face,
   You're considered a child.
    If you laugh at everything,
   You're considered a yokel.
205   If you're a powerful knight
   And you don't at all wish to joust,
108vb] Then some man will say,
   'You aren't worth a rotten apple!'
    If you're brave and bold
210 And frequent places of pleasure:
   'This wretch knows nothing good —
   He spends so much, he's got nothing!'
    If you're a powerful man

E seiez riche e manaunt,
215   Dount, dirra hom meyntenaunt,
'De par le Deable ou ad il taunt!'
   S'il est povre e n'ad dount vyvre:
'Cest cheitif tot ditz est yvre!'
   Si il vent sa tere pur ly ayder:
220   'Quel diable ly vodera terre doner?
Yl siet despendre e nient gaigner!'
Chescun ly velt cheytyf clamer.
   S'il achate terres par la vyle,
Si lur estoit autrement dire:
225   'Avez veu de cel mesel,
Come il resemble le bocerel
Qe unqe de terre ne fust pleyn?
Ensi est il de cel vileyn!'
   Si vous estes jeovene bachiler
230   E n'avez terre a gaygner,
E en compagnie volez aler
E la taverne haunter,
Vous troverez meint qe dirrat,
'Ou trovera il ce qu'il ad?
235   Unqe ne fust gayné a dreit
Ce qu'il mangue e ce qu'il beit!'
   Si vous alez poi en compagnie
E taverne ne hauntez mye:
'Cesti est escars, avers, e cheytif.
240   C'est damage qu'il est vyf!
Yl ne despendi unqe dener
S'il ne fust dolent al departer —
De son gayn Dieu li doint pert!
Yl n'out unqe la bourse overt!'
245   Si vous estes vesti quoyntement,
Donqe dirrount la gent,
'Avez veu de cel pautener,
Com il est orguillous e fier?
109ra] Ataunt usse je de or real,
250   Com il se tient valer fient de chyval!
Yl n'i averoit si riche honme, par Dé,
En Londres la riche cité!'
   Si vostre cote seit large e lee,
Si dirra ascun de soun gree,
255   'Ce n'est mie cote de esté!'
Donqe dirra le premer,
'Assez est bone — lessez ester! —
Yl resemble un mavois bover!'
   Si vostre teste soit despyné,
260   E soit haut estauncé:

And are rich and influential,
215   Of this, a man will readily say,
     'It's from the Devil that he's got so much!'
        If he's poor and doesn't have means to live:
     'This wretch is always drunk!'
        If he sells his land to help himself:
220   'What devil wanted to give land to him?
     He knows how to spend and earns nothing!'
     Everyone wants to call him a wretch.
        If he buys lands by the town,
     Then it's their custom to say the opposite:
225   'Have you seen this leper,
     How he looks like a little goat
     Who's never had his fill of land?
     That's how it is with this peasant!'
        If you're a young man
230   And don't have lands to cultivate,
     And want to go out with friends
     And frequent the tavern,
     You'll find many who'll say,
     'Where did he find what he has?
235   He never earned honestly
     What he eats and what he drinks!'
        If you seldom go out with friends
     And don't at all frequent the tavern:
     'This one's stingy, miserly, and wretched.
240   It's a pity that he's alive!
     He's never spent a penny
     That he wasn't sad to part with —
     God give him loss of his profit!
     He never has an open purse!'
245   If you're dressed elegantly,
     Then people will say,
     'Have you seen this rascal,
     How he's haughty and proud?
109ra]   For as much royal gold as I spend,
250   He holds it worth horse dung!
     There isn't so wealthy a man, by God,
     In the wealthy city of London!'
        If your tunic is broad and wide,
     Then someone will say of his own accord,
255   'It's not at all a summer coat!'
     Then the first one will say,
     'It's good enough — let him be! —
     He looks like a wicked herdsman!'
        If your head is spiked,
260   And its hair be cut high:

'C'est un moygne eschapé!'
    Si vostre teste seit plané,
E vos cheveus crestre lessé,
Yl serra meintenaunt dit,
265   'C'est la manere de ypocrit!'
    Si vostre coyfe seit blanche e bele:
'S'amie est une damoysele
Qe ly vodra plus coyfes trover
Qe ly rybaud pust decyrer!'
270   Si ele est neyre a desresoun:
Yl est un fevre, par seint Symoun —
Veiez come est teint de charboun!'
    Si vous estes cointement chaucé,
E avez bons soudlers al pié,
275   Si serra ascun par delee
Que vous avera al dey mostree,
E a soun compaignoun est torné:
'Ce n'est mie tot, pur Dé,
De estre si estroit chaucé.'
280   Dirra l'autre, 'A noun Dé,
C'est pur orgoil e fierté
Qe li est el cuer entree.'
    Si vous estes largement chaucé,
E avez botes feutré
285   E de une pane envolupé,
Donqe dirra ascun de gree,
'Beneit soit le moigne de Dee
Qe ces veyle botes, par charité,
Ad a cesti cheytyf doné!'
290   E si vous les femmes amez
E ov eux sovent parlez,
109rb]   E lowés ou honorez
Ou sovent revysitez,
Ou si vous mostrez par semblaunt
295   Qe a eux estes bien vueyllaunt,
Donqe dirra ascun pautener,
'Veiez cesti mavois holer —
Come il siet son mester! —
De son affere bien mostrer!'
300   Si vous ne les volez regarder
Ne volenters ov eux parler,
Si averount mensounge trové
Qe vous estes descoillé.
    Auxi, di je, par dela,
305   Come l'ensaunple gist par desa:
Si ascune dame bele,
Ou bien norrie damoysele,

'It's an escaped monk!'
  If your head is flat,
And your hair stops growing,
It will immediately be said,
265   'It's the look of a hypocrite!'
  If your hood is white and handsome:
'His friend is a young lady
Who wants him to find more hoods
Than the scoundrel can imagine!'
270   If it's extremely black:
'He's a blacksmith, by Saint Simon —
See how he's stained with coal!'
  If you're elegantly shod,
And have good shoes on your feet,
275   Then there'll be somebody nearby
Who'll have pointed at you,
And turned to his companion:
'It's not everything, by God,
To be so tightly shod.'
280   The other will say, 'In God's name,
It's on account of haughtiness and pride
That's entered his heart.'
  If you're generously shod,
And have boots felted
285   And covered in a fur lining,
Then someone will say of his own accord,
'Blessed be the monk of God
Who these old boots, out of charity,
Gave to this wretch!'
290   And if you love women
And often speak with them,
109rb] And praise or honor [them]
Or often exchange visits,
Or if you show by your countenance
295   That you desire them greatly,
Then some rascal will say,
'Look at this wicked dissolute —
How he knows his trade! —
Displaying openly his business!'
300   If you don't want to look at them
Or speak freely with them,
Then they'll have invented the lie
That you're castrated.
  Next, I say, in contrast,
305   As the example lies the other way:
If a certain lovely lady,
Or well-bred maiden,

      Pur sa nateresse e bounté,
      De nulli seit privee,
310   Ou si ele taunt ne quant
      Face a nully bel semblaunt,
      Ou si ele vueille juer:
      'Cele est femme de mester
      E de pute manere,
315   E a gayner trop legere!'
        Si ele soit auqe hountouse
      E de juer daungerouse:
      'Veiez come ele se tient souche —
      Bure ne descorreit en sa bouche!'
320   Coment qe ele ameyne sa vie,
      Rybaudz en dirrount vileynye.
        Si volenters alez a mostier
      E a Dieu volez prier
      De vos pecchiés remissioun,
325   E de fere satisfaccioun,
      Si dirra ascun qe vous regart:
      'Ja de vos prieres n'ey je part —
      Quar vous n'estes qe un papelart
      Vos prieres serrount oys tart.'
330   E si vous alez par le mostrer,
      E ne volez point entrer,
      Donqe dirra vostre veysyn,
      'Cesti ne vaut plus qe un mastyn!
      Si Dieu me doint de son bien —
335   Cesti ne valt plus qe un chien!'
109va]   Si vous volenters volez juner
      Pur vos pecchiés amender,
      Dount dirra ly maloré,
      'Ov a deables ad il esté —
340   Yl ad soun pere ou mere tué
      Ou ascun de soun parentee,
      Ou femme, file, ou enfaunt!
      Pur ce qu'il june taunt!'
        Si vous sovent ne junez,
345   Donqe dirrount malorez,
      'Cesti maveis chien recreaunt
      Ne puet juner taunt ne quant
      Le bon vendredy ahorree!
      Prendreit il bien charité,
350   Trestot par soun eyndegré —
      Ja de prestre ne querreit congé.'
        Si je su mesgre, bels douz cher:
      'Mort est de faym! Il n'a qe manger!'
        E si je su gros e gras,

On account of her upbringing or goodness,
Should be private with anyone,
310 Or if she in any way at all
Casts a fair glance at someone,
Or should she wish to play:
'That one's a prostitute
And a kind of whore,
315 And too easy to win!'
    If she's at all bashful
And reluctant to play:
'Look how she holds aloof —
Butter wouldn't melt in her mouth!'
320 No matter how she leads her life,
Scoundrels will say filth about her.
    If you go gladly to church,
And you wish to pray to God
For remission of your sins,
325 And do satisfaction,
Then someone will say of you:
'I'll have no part of your prayers —
Because you're just a hypocrite,
Your prayers will be heard late.'
330 And if you go by the church
And don't at all wish to go in,
Then your neighbor will say,
'This one's not worth a hound!
God grant me his goodness,
335 This one's not worth a dog!'
109va]   If you gladly wish to fast
To make amends for your sins,
Then the wicked will say,
'He's been with a devil —
340 He's killed his father or mother
Or one of his relatives,
Or his wife, daughter, or child!
It's for this that he fasts so much!'
    If you don't fast often,
345 Then the wicked ones will say,
'This evil, cowardly dog
Can't fast in any way at all
On the blessed Good Friday!
He'd certainly accept charity,
350 Fully of his own free will —
He'd never seek a priest's permission.'
    If I'm thin, fair sweet dear:
'He's dead of hunger! He needs to eat!'
    And if I am large and fat,

355   Si me dirra ascun en cas:
        'Dieu, come cesti dorreit graunt flaut
        En une longayne s'il cheit de haut!'
            Si j'ay long nees, asque croku,
        Tost dirrount, 'C'est un bescu.'
360   Si j'ay court nees tot en desus,
        Um dirrat, 'C'est un camus.'
            Si j'ay la barbe long pendaunt:
        'Est cesti chevre ou pelrynaunt?'
            E si je n'ay barbe, 'Par seint Michel,
365   Cesti n'est mie madle, mes femmel!'
            E si je su long e graunt,
        Je serroi apelé geaunt.
            E si petitz sei de estat,
        Serroi apelé naym e mat.
370   Dieu, come le siecle est maloré —
        Qe nul puet vivre sanz estre blamé!
        Plus y avereit a counter,
        E assez plus a demaunder,
        Mes je ne vueil estudier
375   Si vous ne me volez del vostre doner.
109vb] Car ensi va de tote rienz —
        E des mals e des bienz —
        Quar nulle rien ne purroi fere
        Qe um ne trovera la countrere."
380   Donqe dit le Roi, "Verroiement,
        Vous dites voir, a mien asscient.
        Quei me saverez vous counsiler
        Coment me pus countener
        E sauntz blame me garder,
385   Que um ne me vueille mesparler?"
            Respound le Joglour al Roy,
        "Sire, moun counsail vous dirroy:
        Si vous vostre estat vueillez bien garder,
        Ne devez trop encrueler
390   Ne trop simple vers ta gent,
        Mes vous portez meenement.
        Quar vos meymes savez bien
        Qe nul trop valt rien.
        Qy par mesure tote ryen fra
395   Ja prudhome ne ly blamera.
        Par mesure, meenement,
        Come est escrit apertement,
        E le latyn est ensi:
        'Medium tenuere beati.'"
400   Qy ceste trufle velt entendre
        Auke de sen purra aprendre,

355   Then someone will say to me in that case:
'God, how this one would spew a great flood
In a privy if he should shit from above!'
    If I have a long nose, rather crooked,
All will say, 'It's a beak.'
360   If I have a nose all short on top,
They'll say, 'It's a pug nose.'
    If I have a long hanging beard:
'Is this one a goat or a pilgrim?'
    And if I don't have a beard, 'By Saint Michael,
365   This one isn't male at all, but female!'
    And if I'm tall and big,
I'll be called a giant.
    And if I'm short of stature,
I'll be called a dwarf and low.
370   God, how the world is accursed —
That none may live without being blamed!
There would be more to tell,
And plenty more to ask,
But I don't want to belabor the matter
375   Lest you decide not to give me of your means.
109vb] For thus go all things —
Both the bad and the good —
For I can't do anything
Without someone finding the opposite."
380   Then says the King, "In truth,
You tell the truth, by my experience.
Can you advise me
How I ought to conduct myself
And govern myself without blame,
385   Such that none will speak ill of me?"
    Answers the Jongleur to the King,
"Lord, I'll give you my advice:
If you want to protect well your estate,
You ought to be neither too cruel
390   Nor too familiar toward the people,
But bear yourself with moderation.
For you yourself know well
That excess is worth nothing.
He who does all in accordance with measure
395   Shall never be blamed by a worthy man.
[Act] in accordance with measure, moderately,
As it is clearly written,
And the Latin is thus:
'Blessed be he who holds the middle way.'"
400   He who wants to heed this trifle
Could learn some sense,

Car um puet oyr sovent
Un fol parler sagement.
Sage est qe parle sagement;
405   Fol, come parle folement.

Les trois dames qui troverent un vit   [art. 75a]

110ra]   ¶ Puis que de fabler ay comencé,
Ja n'y ert, pur moun travail, lessé.
De *Trois Dames* comenceroy —
Assez brievement le counteroy.
5   Que al Mount-Seint-Michel aloient
En pelrynage come vowé avoyent.
Ne voderount plus demorer
De lur promesse aquiter,
E de ce, fesoient qe senees.
10   Ja avoient alé deus jornees
E l'endemein fust le tierce,
Quant vint a l'houre de tierce
La une garda en un senter
Si trova un vit, gros e plener,
15   Envolupé en un drapel.
N'i out descovert qe le musel.
La dame le prist meyntenaunt
E de la trovure fust joyaunt,
Quar ele savoit quei ce estoit.
20   E cele que aprés aloit
Dit que ele avereit part.
    "Certes," fet ele, "vous le averez tart.
Ja part de ce ne averez!"
    "Coment deble estes! Vous devez!
25   Je dis al trovour, demy myen!
E si je ne le ey, ce n'est mie bien!
Dreit est qe je part eye,
Quar je su vostre compaigne verreie.
Vous savez bien, si Dieu m'enjoie,
30   Qe nous sumes en ceste voie
Compaignes e bones amyes."
    "Yl ne me chaut voir qe tu dies —
Ja n'averez part ne prow!"
    L'autre ne le tient pas a gyw,
35   Mes jure soun chief qe si avera
Quaunqe juggé ly serra.
    "Par foi," fet l'autre, "Il me plest.
Dite moi donqe qy ce est
Qy dorra le jugement,

For one may often hear
A fool speak wisely.
Wise is he who speaks wisely;
405   Foolish, when he speaks foolishly.

The Three Ladies Who Found a Prick   [art. 75a]

110ra]   ¶ Since I've begun telling idle tales,
Surely, on account of my effort, I won't quit.
I'll begin with *Three Ladies* —
I'll recount it quite briefly.
5   They were going to Mont-Saint-Michel
On a pilgrimage as they had vowed.
They didn't want to delay any longer
In keeping their promise,
And concerning this, they were acting sensibly.
10   They had already traveled two days
And the next day was the third,
When it happened at the hour of terce
That one looked down on a path
And found a prick, thick and swollen,
15   Wrapped in a piece of cloth.
Only the tip was uncovered.
The lady picked it up at once
And was delighted by her find,
For she knew what it was.
20   And the one who walked behind her
Said that she would have a part.
"Indeed," she says, "you'll have it later.
You'll never have part of this one!"
"You're such a devil! You have to!
25   I say to the finder, it's half mine!
And if I don't have it, that's not fair at all!
It's only fair that I have a part,
For I'm your true companion.
You well know, God bring me joy,
30   That we're on this journey
As companions and good friends."
"I really don't care what you say —
You'll never have any part at all!"
The other doesn't think it a game,
35   But swears on her head that she'll have
Whatever will be judged hers.
"By my faith," says the other, "that pleases me.
Tell me then who it is
Who ought to give judgment,

40 E je le grant bonement."
110rb]   "Devant nous est une mesone de noneynz,
      Mout seinte dames e chapeleynz
      Que Dieu servent nuit e jour.
      La abbesse, pur nul amour,
45   Ne lerra juger verité."
         "E je le grant, de par Dé."
         Tant ount erree qe eles sunt venues —
      Ce m'est avis — al chief des rywes,
      La ou l'abbesse manoit.
50   Tant ount alé, tort e droit,
      Qe en l'abbeye sunt entreez,
      E meyntenant ount demaundez
      Noveles de la abbesse.
         E um lur dit, "Ele oyt sa messe.
55   Si vous volez a ly parler,
      Yl vous covient demorer."
         Eles dient que si frount.
      Atant assises se sount
      En le parlour sur un desgree.
60   Mes il ne urent qe poi estee
      Quant venir virent la abbesse —
      Ensemble ov ly, la prioresse,
      D'autre part, la celerere.
         E cele qe estoit premere
65   Se leve e dit meyntenaunt:
      "Dame, bien seiez vous viegnaunt!
      Veiez si une moie compaigne
      Qe doner ma part ne me deygne
      De une chose qe ele ad trové.
70   Pur ce, qe ele ne m'en a donee
      Ma part, come fere deveroit."
      E si counte tot le droit
      Come la chose fust trovee.
         E sur ly est le jugement tornee,
75   E dit la abbesse meyntenaunt:
      "Seit la chose mys avaunt,
      E nous le droit jugeroms
      E vos dreytures a vous rendroms."
         "Par foi," fet l'autre, "je le graunt.
80   Compaygne, metez le vyt avaunt.
110va] L'abbesse dirra verité."
         E cele qe le vit out trovee
      Le treyst erroument de son seyn
      E le mist devant un noneyn,
85   Qe mout le garda de bon oyl.
         De l'abbesse, counter voil

40   And I grant it graciously."
110rb]   "In front of us is a house of nuns,
        Very holy ladies and chaplains
        Who serve God night and day.
        The abbess, having no bias,
45   Will never fail to judge truth."
            "I agree to it, on God's part."
            They've traveled so far that they've arrived —
        It's my opinion — at the end of the road,
        There where the abbess lived.
50   They've gone so far, wrong and right,
        That they've entered the abbey,
        And now they've asked for
        Tidings of the abbess.
            And one tells them, "She's hearing Mass.
55   If you wish to speak with her,
        It's necessary that you wait."
            They say that they'll do so,
        And so they're seated
        On a bench in the parlor.
60   But they've been there only a little while
        When they saw the abbess coming —
        Together with her, the prioress,
        And beside her, the cellaress.
            And the one who was in front
65   Gets up and says at once:
        "Lady, how welcome is your arrival!
        See here one of my companions
        Who doesn't deign to give me my part
        Of a thing she's found.
70   As a result, she hasn't given to me
        My part, as she should do."
        And here she tells exactly
        How the thing was found.
            Thus the judgment is turned over to her,
75   And the abbess says at once:
        "Let the thing be displayed,
        And we'll judge the rightful owner
        And render to you your rights."
            "By my faith," says the other, "I agree to it.
80   Companion, display the prick.
110va] The abbess will speak the truth."
            And the one who had found the prick
        Drew it promptly from her breast
        And put it in front of a nun,
85   Who gazed at it with much favor.
            Regarding the abbess, I wish to report

Qe molt le regarda volenters.
Granz suspirs fist, longz e enters,
Pus dit aprés, "Oiez bel plet:
90   Quei vueillent il, qe ore seit fet.
Le jugement se prent pur nous.
C'est, de nostre porte, le verrous
Qe l'autre jour fust adyrrez.
Je comaund qu'il soit bien gardez
95   Come ce qu'est nostre chose demeyne.
Alez," fet ele, "dame Eleyne,
Qe estes pruz e bien legere,
Je comaund qu'il soit mis arere
La dount il fust ostez e pris."
100   E ma dame Eleyne ad pris
Le vit, qe fust long e grant,
E sachez qe ele meyntenaunt
Le prist e gitta en sa maunche,
Que molt estoit delgé e blaunche.
105   Les dames qe la chose troverent,
Quant le jugement entenderent,
Molt sunt dolent e irassuz
Qe la chose est issi perduz.
            E molt marris s'en partoient
110   E l'abbesse molt maldisoient,
E distrent qe jamés n'assenteround
Ne jugement demaunderound
De tiele chose aprester,
Ne en autre manere juger.
115   Mes cele qe la trovera
A tous jours la tendra
Come relyke molt desirree
E de totes dames honoree.

Le dit des femmes   [art. 76]

110vb]   ¶ Seignours e dames, ore escotez —
Ce qe vous dirroi l'entendez!
Quy le vodre entendre
Grant bien il purra aprendre.
5   A comencement de ma resoun,
De femmes froy mon sermoun.
Si, vous dirra en escripture
De lor bounté e de lur nature.
            Molt lur avyent bel aventure.
10   Quar Dieu les fist par grant cure —
Le noun de *femme* lur dona

That she looked at it very gladly.
She heaves great sighs, long and full,
Then says next, "Hear a just decision,
90   What they demand, it shall now be done.
The judgment falls to us.
It is, of our door, the bolt
Which was lost the other day.
I order that it be well guarded
95   As that which is our property.
Go," she says, "Lady Helen,
You who are prudent and gentle,
I command that it be put back
There where it was lifted off and taken."
100   And my Lady Helen has taken
The prick, which was long and huge,
And know that she quickly
Took it and thrust it into her sleeve,
Which was slender and white.
105   The ladies who found the thing,
When they heard the judgment,
Are very upset and angry
That the thing is here lost.
Thus they departed very unhappy
110   And bitterly cursed the abbess,
And said that they'd never again
Consent to or demand a judgment
To share such a thing,
Or in any way express an opinion.
115   But whoever shall find it
Shall always hold onto it
As a relic much desired
And honored by all women.

The Song on Women   [art. 76]

110vb]   ¶ Lords and ladies, now listen —
Hearken to what I'll tell you!
He who wishes to comprehend it
Can learn something very fine.
5   To begin my argument,
I'll make my sermon about women.
Indeed, it will inform you in writing
About their goodness and their nature.
Greatly does good fortune befall them,
10   For God made them with much care —
The name of *femme* [*fame*] he gave them

Pur sa mere, qe taunt ama.
E pus les fist bones e pleynes de bounté,
E beles sauntz iniquité.
15   Avenauntes sunt, e de bele porture,
Bien afeytés e de grant mesure.
D'amer gent est lur nature,
De fere eux joie e enveysure.
Femme est la plus douce rien
20   Qe unqe fist Dieu — ce di je bien!
Tous les espieces de cest mount
Ne sunt si douces come femmes sunt —
Gyngyvre, sucre, ne lycorys,
Ne tous les espieces de Paris,
25   Certes, galingal ne mas
N'est vaillaunt a femme un pygas!
De femme plus savoure un beiser
Qe plein poyn de lorer.
Eles sunt gentiles a demesure —
30   Greeles, bien fetes par la seinture —
E tous jours sunt de bele chere
Devaunt la gent e derere.
En eux ne trovera um taunt ne quant
Fors grant joie e bel semblaunt,
35   E reheitent gent ov bele enveysure.
De folie fere n'en ount cure:
Ja ne verrez femme foleier
Ne fust de honme le bel parler.
Ja ne freit ele folement
40   Ne fust de honme l'enchauntement,
Mes tous jours remeindreint virgines.
De netteté fuissent totes pleynes,
111ra] Mes um les bosoigne tous jours,
Pur aver de eux lur amours.
45   E ensi, par grant priere,
Receyvent sovent encombrere.
Qui a eux mesfet ou mesdit,
Ja ne serrount ov Die eslit.
Ja Dieu ne eyme qe femme het,
50   Quar nulle enchesoun trover set.
N'est clerc taunt aparceyvaunt,
Ne nul autre taunt vaillaunt,
Qe femmes vueillent blamer
Ne rien countre eux desputer,
55   S'il ne soit de vileyne nacioun;
Pur ce, ne dient si bien noun.
Grant amour a ly attret
Cely qe honour a femme fet.

For his mother's sake, whom he greatly loved.
And then he made them virtuous and full of goodness,
And beautiful without wickedness.
15   Welcoming they are, and of pleasing deportment,
Well formed and of excellent figure.
To love men is their nature,
So as to give them joy and gladness.
    Woman is the sweetest thing
20   That God ever made — this I affirm!
All the spices of this world
Aren't as sweet as women are —
Not ginger, sugar, nor licorice,
Nor all the spices of Paris,
25   Indeed, not galingale nor mace
Is worth a thing compared to woman!
One kiss from a woman is more delicious
Than a hand filled with laurel.
    They are elegant beyond measure —
30   Slender, well-made around the waist —
And always they're amiable
Toward people and behind their backs.
In them one won't find anything at all
Except profound joy and lovely appearance,
35   And they refresh men with pleasant mirth.
    They take care not to be foolish:
You'll never see a woman be a fool
Were it not for the sweet speech of men.
She'd never act foolish
40   Were it not for men's enchantment,
But always they'd remain virgins.
Of purity they'd be filled entirely,
111ra] Were it not that men always woo them,
To have from them their love.
45   And thus, because of grand pleading,
They often receive encumbrance.
    Whoever harms or slanders them,
He'll never be chosen by God.
God never loves the man who hates woman,
50   No matter what reason he can produce.
There's no clerk so shrewd,
Nor any other so worthy,
Who would want to blame women
Nor argue anything against them,
55   Unless he be of base lineage.
Because of this, they say nothing but good.
    By profound love she's attracted to
He who gives honor to woman.

Ly gentil ne les despyt
60   Ne vileynie de femme dit.
Dieu ayme femmes bonement
Ataunt com il fet la gent
Pur sa douce mere Marie,
Par qy recovri est la vie.
65   Dount chescun doit honorer
E femmes sur tous preyser.
Dieu les fist par grant leysir
Pur servyr gentz a pleysyr.
    Pur ce, les doit um loer
70   E en nul point despiser,
Car de femmes sunt gent estret
E suef nory de lur let.
Roys, countz, e barouns,
Evesques, freres que fount sermounz,
75   Prestres, moygnes, e abbés,
De femmes sunt engendrez.
Par femme est le siecle sustenu,
Molt avauncé e molt cru.
    Si femmes nu fuissent, verroiment,
80   Cest siecle ne vaudra nyent.
Ja ne fust il lee en cuer
Que ne savoit femme amer.
Qy a femme fet vyleynie,
Dieu ly doynt male vie!
85   Femme est la plus preciouse chose
Que le mound ad enclose.
111rb] Je aym femme sour tote rien,
Car yl me ount fet grant bien.
Je ay femme ov le cors gent!
90   De mon cuer lur faz present.
De femmes vienent les pruesses,
Les honeurs e le hautesses,
Tote bounté e drywerye!
    Dount, m'est avis, qu'il fet folye
95   Qe de eux se fet hayer —
Ja ne ly verrez bien chever.
Ceux qe a femmes mesdirrount
Ja bon fyn ne averount.
Nul honme deit de eux mentyr
100 S'il ne duissent mort soffryr.
Certes pur rien qe femme fra
Peyne d'enfern ne verra,
Quar Dieu lur ad doné le doun
Qe eles ne verront si bien noun.
105   N'est honme qe soit de femme neez

The noble man doesn't despise them

60   Or say base things about woman.

God loves women as graciously

As he does men

For the sake of his sweet mother Mary,

By whom life is recovered.

65   Therefore each man ought to honor

And value women above all.

God made them in a leisurely fashion

In order to serve men's pleasure.

    For this reason, one ought to praise them

70   And in no way despise them,

For from women are men birthed

And gently nourished with their milk.

Kings, counts, and barons,

Bishops, friars who make sermons,

75   Priests, monks, and abbots,

By women are conceived.

By woman is the world sustained,

Greatly advanced and greatly increased.

    If woman didn't exist, truly,

80   This world would be worth nothing.

Never would he be happy of heart

Unless he knew how to love a woman.

He who acts basely toward a woman,

May God give him a difficult life!

85   Woman is the most precious thing

That the world has within it.

111rb]   I love women above all things,

For they've done me great good.

I have a woman with an elegant body!

90   I make them a gift of my heart.

From women come noble deeds,

Honors and glories,

All goodness and affection!

    Thus, in my opinion, he commits folly

95   Who makes himself hated by them —

Never shall you see him finish well.

Those who slander women

Shall never have a good end.

No man should lie about them

100   Lest he be made to suffer death.

Indeed, for nothing that a woman does

Shall she ever see the pain of hell,

For God has given them the gift

Of perceiving only what is good.

105   There's no man born of woman

Qe tous siet dire lur bountez.
Je n'ai mie dit le centisme part,
Mes molt les lowe matin e tart.
Ne say dyre ne penser
110 La grant bounté de lur cuer,
Mes a Dieu les comaund, femmes beles!
Ensement, totes puceles
E totes femmes qe sunt nees
A Dieu soient comaundeez!

Le blasme des femmes [art. 77]

111rb]   ¶ Quy femme prent a compagnie,
Veiez si il fet sen ou folye —
Qy en femme despent sa cure,
Oiez sa mort e sa dreiture!
5 Qy femme eyme e femme creit
Sa mort brace, sa mort beyt.
Qy coveyte ou femme preyse
Sa mort quert e nulle eyse.
Sauntz pris e sauntz loer, se vend
10 E fet la lace dount yl se pend.
111va] Cui ces vers ad en remenbraunce,
Yl doute femme plus qe launce.
    Femme est racyne de tous maus.
Femme engendre ires mortaus.
15 Femme deceit bons amys.
De deus freres, fet enymys.
Femme departe le fitz del pere,
A force le toud de sa mere.
Femme par sa fauce parole
20 Blaundist le honme e pus le afole.
Femme afole les plus sachauntz;
Les plus riches, fet paynquerauntz.
Femme fet bataille e guere,
Occyre gentz, destrure terre.
25 Ard chastiels, prent cités.
Femme refuse fermetés.
Femme fet prendre les tornois,
E fet fere les desrois.
Femme fet fere les mesleez,
30 Trere cotels e espeez.
Femme fet chastiels graventer,
Chevalers e serjauntz anuyer.
Femme fet ume de ordre issir
E le service Dieu guerpyr.

Who can tell all their goodness.
I've not said even the hundredth part,
Though I highly praise them morn and eve.
I know not how to say or conceive
110   The deep goodness of their hearts,
But to God I commend them, lovely women!
Likewise, may all maidens
And all women alive
Be commended to God!

The Blame of Women   [art. 77]

111rb]   ¶ He who takes woman for a companion,
Consider whether he acts wisely or foolishly.
He who expends his care upon a woman,
Hear regarding his death and just desert!
5   He who woman loves and woman believes
Contrives his death, drinks his death.
He who desires or prizes a woman
Seeks his own death and no comfort.
Without honor or praise, he sells himself
10   And makes the noose to hang himself.
111va]   He who memorizes these verses
Shall fear woman more than the spear.
  Woman is the root of all evils.
Woman begets mortal angers.
15   Woman deceives good friends.
Between two brothers, she makes enemies.
Woman divides son from father,
Forcibly refts him from his mother.
Woman by her false speech
20   Flatters man and then deceives him.
Woman deceives the wisest;
Of the richest, makes beggars.
Woman causes battle and wars,
To kill people, to destroy lands.
25   She burns castles, captures cities.
Woman demolishes fortresses.
Woman causes tournaments to be taken up,
And causes devastation to occur.
Woman causes fights to commence,
30   Knives and swords to be drawn.
Woman causes castles to be overthrown,
Knights and men-at-arms to be injured.
Woman causes men to forsake holy orders
And abandon God's service.

35   Femme engendre en poi de houre
        Dount tote la countré emploure.
            Femme est jolyf pur ly demostrer:
        Femme est lyoun pur devorer.
        Femme est gopil pur gent deceyvre.
40   Femme est ourse pur cours receyvre.
        Femme est fotere pur tous prendre.
        Femme est ostour pur preie atteindre.
        Femme est esperver pur haut voler.
        Femme est houel pur haut mounter.
45   Femme est heyroun de suef payl.
        Femme est plus aspre que chamail.
        Femme est chyval de grant luxure.
        Femme est dragoun de grant arsure.
            Unqe languor ne conoit
50   Qe femme a compaigne ne avoit.
        Femme est fontaigne desouz vaye,
        Que tot recet e tot abaye.
        Femme est taverne que ne faut,
        Qui qe vine e qy qe vaut.
55   Femme est enfern que tot receit;
        Touz jours ad seif e tous jours beit.
111vb] De femme ce est la nature —
        Meynz la creez come plus jure!
        Femme n'ert ja pris privee
60   Si desouz loer ne soit trovee.
        Femme est leger come le vent —
        Cent foiz le jour chaunge talent.
            Mes quy vodera femme joyr,
        Je ly dirroi, sauntz mentyr,
65   Qu'il ly donast poy a manger,
        E mal a vestir e a chaucer,
        E la batist menu e sovent —
        Donqe freit il de femme son talent!
        N'est mie sage que femme creit,
70   Mere ne suere qui qe seit.
            Car ly sage Salamoun —
        Que de sen out graunt renoun
        Qe plus sage de ly ne fu —
        Par sa femme fust desçu.
75   Auxi fust Sampson forcyn,
        Car femme par son engyn:
        Tot en dormant, il perdy
        Ce dount fust si enforci.
        En femme est molt malveysyn
80   Car l'emperour Constantyn
        Out par sa femme tiele hountage,

35   Woman begets in a little while
That for which the whole country weeps.
   Woman is happy in demonstrating this:
Woman is a lion in devouring.
Woman is a fox in deceiving men.
40   Woman is a bear in maiming bodies.
Woman is a vulture in taking all.
Woman is a goshawk in capturing prey.
Woman is a sparrow hawk in flying high.
Woman is an owl in high climbing.
45   Woman is a heron of soft coat.
Woman is more rough than a camel.
Woman is a horse of great debauchery.
Woman is a dragon of burning heat.
   One doesn't know debilitating fatigue
50   Unless he has a woman for companion.
Woman is a fountain beneath the way,
Who receives and engulfs all.
Woman is a tavern that doesn't run out,
Whoever comes and whoever goes.
55   Woman is a hell that receives all;
She's always thirsty and always drinks.
111vb] This is woman's nature —
Believe her the less as she swears the more!
Woman is never taken privately
60   Who hasn't been found to be beneath praise.
Woman is light as the wind —
One hundred times a day she changes her will.
   But one who would wish to enjoy a woman,
I shall say to him, without lying,
65   That he should give her little to eat,
And dress and shoe her badly,
And he should beat her fast and thick —
Thus will he have his will with a woman!
He's not at all wise who believes a woman,
70   Though she be mother or sister.
   For the wise Solomon —
Who for wit was so very famous
That there was none wiser than he —
Was deceived by his wife.
75   And so was strong Samson,
By a woman with her tricks:
Fast asleep, he lost
What made him so strong.
In woman is such wickedness
80   That even Emperor Constantine
Had shame on account of his wife,

Car ele cocha par folage
Ov le naym de lede figure,
Sicome honme treove en escripture.
85 E ly bon myr Ypocras,
Qe tant savoit de medicyne artz,
Fust par sa femme desçu —
Ceste chose est bien aparsu.
Pur ce, vous dy, tart e matyn,
90 Gardez vous de femel engyn!
Nul honme puet a chief trere —
Taunt ad en femme mal affere!
    Plus ne vueil de femmes parler —
Chescun se gard de eux a son poer!
95 E je vous dy tot sauntz fable:
Femme siet un art plus que le Deable!

Nicholas Bozon, Femmes a la pye   [art. 78]

112ra] ¶ Femmes a la pye
Portent compagnye
    En maners e en mours.
Escotez que vous dye
5 E quele assocye
    Yl tienent en amours.

La pie de costume
Porte penne e plume
    De divers colours,
10 E femme se delite
En estraunge habite
    De divers atours.

La pie ad longe cowe
Que pend en la bowe
15   Pur la pesauncie,
E femme fet la sowe
Plus long que nule cowe
    De poun ou de pye.

La pie est jangleresse
20 E reelement cesse
    De mostrer ou ele est,
E la femme par son us
D'assez jangle plus.
    Issi nature crest.

For she slept in wantonness
With the ugly-faced dwarf,
As one may find in writing.
85   And the good doctor Hippocrates,
Who knew so well the arts of medicine,
Was deceived by his wife —
This thing is well known.
For this, I tell you, all day long,
90   Watch out for feminine trickery!
No man can reach a good end,
So terrible is the evil of woman!
    I don't wish to speak further about women —
Let each protect himself from them as best he can!
95   And I tell you this entirely without lying:
Woman is one trick ahead of the Devil!

Nicholas Bozon, Women and Magpies   [art. 78]

112ra]   ¶ Women with magpies
Keep close company
    In manners and in morals.
Listen to what I tell you
5   And what likenesses
    They maintain in love.

Magpie by custom
Wears feather and plumage
    Of various colors,
10   And woman delights
In outlandish clothes
    Of various ornament.

Magpie has a long tail
That hangs in the mud
15   For heaviness,
And woman makes her own
Longer than any tail
    Of peacock or magpie.

Magpie is a chatterbox
20   And she rarely ceases
    Revealing where she is,
And it's woman's habit
To chatter even more.
    Thus she expands nature.

25　　Par jangle de la pie,
　　　Um vient a troverye
　　　　　De gopyl e de chat;
　　　Femme par parole
　　　Meynt honme afole
30　　　　E ly rend tot mat.

　　　Vous troverez la pye
　　　Si pleyne de boydie
　　　　　Que ele se garde bien,
　　　Mes la femme pase
35　　La pie en cele grace,
　　　　　Quar ele ne doute rien.

　　　La pie en arbre haut
　　　En freit e en chaut
　　　　　Prent soun repos,
40　　E femme velt reposer
　　　En hautesse de cuer
　　　　　E desyre los.

　　　La pie quant ele greve
　　　Countre son mary leve
45　　　　E l'enchace de ly,
　　　E femme de grant cuer
　　　Son baroun par tencer
　　　　　Fet autresy.
112rb]　Pour icele gyse,
50　　Je lou que un se avyse
　　　　　Avaunt qu'l soit mary.

　　　E, nequedent, la pye
　　　Soun compaignoun espye
　　　　　De quel part s'en va,
55　　E la femme auxi
　　　Espie son mary
　　　　　Par gelosie que ele a.

　　　La pie par yre
　　　Les gardyns empire
60　　　　Par braunche debruser,
　　　E en femme corocee
　　　Rien serra celee
　　　　　Quant ele se puet venger.

　　　Hom dit que la pie
65　　En sa nature crye,

25   By magpie's chatter,
        One comes to the discovery
            Of fox and cat;
        Woman by speech
        Drives man crazy
30   And entirely breaks him.

        You'll find magpie
        So full of trickery
            That she keeps herself safe,
        Yet woman surpasses
35   Magpie in this talent,
            For she's afraid of nothing.

        Magpie in lofty tree
        In cold and in heat
            Takes its rest,
40   And woman wants to rest
        In loftiness of spirit
            And wishes for praise.

        Magpie when she's upset
        Rises up against her mate
45   And drives him from her,
        And proud-hearted woman
        When scolding her husband
            Does likewise.
112rb] Given this behavior,
50   I advise that one reflect
            Before he gets married.

        And, nonetheless, magpie
        Spies on her companion
            Regarding where he goes,
55   And likewise woman
        Spies on her husband
            For the jealousy she feels.

        Magpie in anger
        Harms gardens
60   By breaking branches,
        And from enraged woman
        Nothing may be hidden
            When she's bent on revenge.

        They say that magpie
65   By her nature announces,

    "Il nous viegnent gestes."
E la femme puet dire
A soun mary, "Syre,
    Par moi averez blestes."

70   La pie siet musser
    Quanqe ele puet gayner
      En un privé lu,
    E la femme se purveit
    Avant qe ele vidve seit
75   Dount ert sustenu.

    Bien dust la pie,
    Queiqe um en die,
     A femme estre chere,
    Puis qe lur vie
80   Par tiele compagnie
      Acordent en manere.

Un sage honme de grant valour   [art. 79]

112rc]   ¶ Un sage honme de grant valour,
    Qe longement vesqui en honour,
    Urban estoit apelee.
    En son temps molt fust amee.
5   De son enfant molt se purpensa
    E son bon sen ly mostra.
     E dit, "Ben fiz, ore escotez.
    Ce qe je dy sy l'entendez.
    Noreture vous vueil aprendre
10   Tant come vous estes d'age tendre,
    Quar, pur verité, le vous dy,
    Celi est hony que n'est nory.
    Ore escotez, mon chere fitz,
    Coment je vueil que seiez noris.
15   "Je vueil, tot al premour,
    Que sages seiez e plein de douçour,
    Seiez debonere e corteis,
    E qeu vous sachez parler fraunceis,
    Quar molt est langage alosee
20   De gentil honme, e molt amee.
     "Vous devez amer Dieu puissant,
    Tenyr sa ley e son comaunt,
    Volenters alez a mostier,
    Si escotez le Dieu mestier,
25   Quar de le service Dieu oyr

      "Glorious events come to us."
      And woman can say
      To her husband, "Lord,
        By me you'll have setbacks."

70   Magpie knows how to hide
      Whatever she can acquire
        In a secret place,
      And woman provides for herself
      Before she becomes a widow
75   What will be her sustenance.

      Well ought the magpie,
      Whatever one may say,
        Be dear to woman,
      Since their lives
80   By such comparison
        Accord in behavior.

Urbain the Courteous   [art. 79]

112rc]   ¶ A wise man of great refinement,
      Who lived a long time in honor,
      Was named Urbain.
      In his day he was dearly beloved.
5   He gave much thought to his child
      And wished to share with him his wisdom.
        And he said, "Good son, now listen.
      Be attentive to what I say.
      I want to teach you about good breeding
10   While you're still of tender age,
      For, in truth, I tell you,
      Shamed is he who's not well bred.
      Now listen, my dear son,
      To how I want you to be raised.
15   "I want, first of all,
      For you to be wise and full of kindness,
      Gracious and courteous,
      And that you know how to speak French,
      For highly is this language praised
20   By noblemen, and much loved.
        "You ought to love almighty God,
      Follow his law and his command,
      Gladly go to church,
      And listen to the Lord's office,
25   For by hearing the Lord's service

Ne puet nul mal avenyr.
Seiez de grant debonereté
E touz jours gardez verité,
Mes jamés a vostre voil
30 Ne seiez vencu d'orgoil.
Quar celi qu'est orguillous
Yl del tot est a rebours.
Que unqe ly noble Rodlaund
Ne valsist le demy tant,
35 Come il fet, a son quider,
E si ne valt il mye Olyver.
E plus quide estre beals
Qe Absolon ly juvenceals,
Ou Ypomedes estoit,
40 Qe tote beautés avoit,
E plus estre corteis e seyn
Que ne fust sire Gaweyn
112va] Ou que nul autre ne fu,
E si est ledement desçu.
45   "Apré, vueil que seiez sage
E qe ne facez nul outrage,
Ne procurez nulli de malfere,
Ne losenge ne mensonge crere.
De tote rien que fere devez,
50 A comencement vous purpensez
A quel chief vous le poez trere:
Si il est bon, bien fet a fere;
S'il est mavois, le lessez,
E de mieu fere vous penez.
55 De yveresse vous gardez auxi,
Quar ly yvres sachez de fy,
S'il eit mal vice al cors,
Meintenant le mettreit hors.
Ce ne creyint mie plusours.
60   "Si vous volez aver mes amours,
Seiez totdis bon cristien
E amez Dieu sur tote rien.
Dotez Dieu e seinte Eglise,
Si vous delitez en son service.
65 A tote gentz fetes honours —
Le mieux vous avendra touz jours —
E a femmes, nomément.
Ce est droit afeytement,
Quar, ce, prent um molt agree,
70 E ce vous serra molt alowee.
De femmes vienent hautesses,
Honours, e moltz proesses —

No evil can come about.
Be very gracious
And always maintain truth,
But never willingly
30   Be conquered by pride.
For he who's proud
Is backward in everything.
Thus the noble Roland
Was never worth half as much,
35   For all that he did, as he thought,
And he isn't at all as worthy as Oliver.
And he who imagines himself more handsome
Than was Absolon the young,
Or Hippomedes,
40   Who had surpassing beauty,
Or more courteous and hale
Than Sir Gawain
112va]   Or anyone else was,
Is thus evilly deceived.
45   "Next, I want you to be wise
And commit no excesses,
Nor cause anyone to do wrong,
Nor believe flattery or lies.
In all that you have to do,
50   From the start reflect on
The end to which you can bring it:
If it's good, it's good to do it;
If it's bad, give it up,
And apply yourself to do better.
55   Refrain from drunkenness as well,
For know indeed that the drunkard,
If he has wicked vice in his body,
Soon he'll show it outwardly.
Many don't believe this at all.
60   "If you want to have my love,
Always be a good Christian
And love God above everything.
Fear God and Holy Church,
And take delight in his service.
65   Toward all people be respectful —
It will turn out ever the better for you —
And toward women, in particular.
This is correct behavior,
For, in this, people take great pleasure,
70   And it will be highly praised in you.
From women come lofty status,
Honors, and many noble deeds —

Les bienz joies, a un mot.
Dont me semble il est sot
75   Qe de eux se fet hayer —
Ja ly ne verrez bien chever.
        "Mes de une chose vous gardez,
E si frez que senez:
Prendre femme tost ne hastez,
80   Ne ja femme ne pernez
Pur sa valour ou son pris
Santz consail de vos amys.
Si par tei meismes prise l'averez,
De lur aie bien faudrez.
85   Ne pernez nulle pur sa beautee,
Ne qe soit en lyvre lettree
112vb] (Quar sovent sunt decevables,
E relement sunt estables),
Mes pernez une que soit sage,
90   Sauntz malice ou outrage.
E si fis engendrez,
Touz mester les apernez.
Ceux que a mester mis sunt
Relement a hounte vount.
95   Ta femme espousé ben amez,
En nul autre ne delitez,
Quar de Dieu hay serrez,
E de ton prome poi amez.
        "Amez sen e leaulté;
100   Lessez folie e pecchié;
E si ne parlez une trop,
Quar ganglour en tenu sot.
Quant vous devez parler
E vostre resoun mostrer,
105   Veiez que vous eiez resoun,
Santz mesdire e tençoun.
Ensi serrez plus preysez
Qe si touz jours ganglez.
Acointez vous a bone gent,
110   E parlez debonerement.
Servez petitz e grauntz.
Apernez les noun sachanz.
Entre les bonz partot alez,
E corteysement vous portez,
115   Quar jamés, ce vous affy,
Ne serrez de un court bien norry.
        "Amez armes e chivals
Si les eiez bons e beals,
E les donez sivilement

In a word, virtuous joys.
Thus it seems to me that one is stupid
75 If he makes himself hated by them —
You'll never see him finish well.
 "But take heed of something,
And thus behave as a wise man:
Don't rush to take a wife immediately,
80 Nor ever to take a wife
For her refinement or reputation
Without your friends' advice.
If you've chosen her on your own,
You'll surely miss their help.
85 Don't take someone for her beauty,
Or because she's learned in books
112vb] (For often they're deceitful
And rarely steadfast),
But take one who's wise,
90 Without malice or insolence.
And if you beget sons,
Teach them all a trade.
Those who are put to a trade
Rarely come to shame.
95 Love well your wedded wife,
And don't delight in any other,
For you'll be hated by God,
And little loved by your relatives.
 "Love wisdom and loyalty;
100 Give up folly and sin;
And also don't speak too much,
For a chatterer is held a fool.
When you must speak
And show your reasoning,
105 Be sure that you're correct,
Without slander or animosity.
Then you'll be esteemed more
Than if you chatter constantly.
Acquaint yourself with good people,
110 And speak graciously.
Give service to small and great.
Teach the ignorant.
Go everywhere among the virtuous,
And courteously conduct yourself,
115 For, as I affirm to you, you'll never
Be well cared for at court.
 "Love arms and horses
If you have good and fair ones,
And give them away nonchalantly

120   Cum s'il valsissent nyent.
       Mes si terre devez doner,
       Pensez de le bien emploier.
       Metez cet un vostre cuer:
       Apernez richement a doner.
125   Vous dorrez a comencement
       Manger e beyvre leement
       A touz ceux de le pais.
       Issi crestra vostre pris.
112vc] Ce que um vous doine ne le obliez,
130   Mes de le rendre purpensez.
       E, pur Dieu, vous gardez bien
       Que vous ne promettez rien
       Que vous ne volez fere ou doner,
       Quar ce fet le fol conforter
135   E si est ce grant vileynye,
       Grant pecchié, e grant folie.
       E hounte de molt promettre
       E la promesse en obli mettre.
       Qy tiele chose ad en us
140   Serra faus sovent tenus.
          "Gardez qe ne seiez losengour
       Vers amy ne seignour,
       E s'il desirent lur deshonour
       Ou lur mal com font plusour,
145   E vous savez lur penser
       E les devez counsiler,
       Ne pensez mie de eux payer
       Pur lur gree donqe aver,
       Ne pur nully pleyser.
150   Ne lur devez losenger,
       Mes, a mieux que vous savez,
       Lel counsail lur donez.
       E si, a cele foiz, corocer
       Se vueillent ou tempester,
155   Autre foiz vous saverount gree
       Pur vostre fei e lealtee,
       Ou Dieu, qe ne oblye rien,
       Le vous guerdonera bien.
          "Pur Dieu, ne vous acostumez
160   D'escharnyr nul que vous veiez,
       Tot seit il povre ou bosoynus,
       Ou il ne seit si bel com vous,
       Si riche ne si avenaunt,
       Si corteis ne si sachant.
165   Pur ce ne ly escharnyes,
       Mes molt bel le salvez,

120   As if they're worth nothing.
      But if you must give away land,
      Think to put it to good use.
      Put this in your heart:
      Learn to give richly.
125   Give from the start
      Food and drink cheerfully
      To all those of the countryside.
      Thus will your reputation grow.
112vc] Don't forget what one gives you,
130   But plan on repaying it.
      And, for God's sake, take good care
      That you not promise anything
      That you don't want to do or give,
      For this encourages the fool
135   And is thus great rudeness,
      Great sin, and great foolishness.
      And [it's] shameful to promise much
      And forget the promise.
      He who makes a practice of such things
140   Will often be thought false.
          "Take care not to be a flatterer
      Of friend or lord,
      And if they desire their own dishonor
      Or what's bad for them, as many do,
145   And you know their thinking
      And must advise them,
      Don't think at all of pleasing them
      To have their favor later,
      Nor of satisfying anyone.
150   Nor should you flatter them,
      But, as best as you know how,
      Give them trustworthy advice.
      And if, at that time, they grow angry
      Or want to fly into a rage,
155   Later they'll feel grateful
      For your faith and loyalty,
      Or else God, who forgets nothing,
      Will thereafter reward you well for it.
          "For God's sake, don't make it a habit
160   To mock someone you see,
      However poor or needy he may be,
      Or if he isn't as handsome as you,
      As rich or as pleasing,
      As courteous or as knowledgeable.
165   Don't mock him for this,
      But greet him quite graciously,

   Quar pur escharn, ce sachez,
   Ne serrez ja bien alosez,
   Mes serra al chief de tour,
170 Escharny ly escharnisour.
113ra] "Si ascun honme vous velt mesdire,
   Ne sailez mie, pur ce, en yre.
   Lessez ly dire ces volenteez,
   Quar mieux vencre ne ly poez.
175 E quant il avera tot tencee,
   Yl serra pur fol clamee
   E vous sage tenuz,
   Le mieux amé e cremuz.
    "Quant vous passez par le pais,
180 Le vel chemyn tenez totdis.
   Amez vostre viel compagnoun.
   E ce tieng je greyndre resoun
   De un amy tener
   Qe de dis gayner.
185 "De nulle rien vous avauntez,
   Mes tot coy vous tenez,
   Que tous ceux del pays
   Parlent bien de vos dys.
   Vos meynz, vos piés, en parlant,
190 Ne les movez tant ne quant,
   Mes la lange soulement.
   Respoigne molt cortoisement,
   Que nully ne eyt poer
   De vous en nul point blamer
195 Ne vous dire vyleynye,
   Mes tote corteysie.
    "Entre les bonz sovent alez,
   E mavois fuer devez,
   Quar des bons bienz vendrount,
200 E de mavois mals serrount.
   De ta viaunde ne seiez escars,
   Mes cortois seiez de tote partz.
   Donez a ceux que bien vous fount
   E que ton doun bien rendrount.
205 Je ne di mie que dorrez a tous,
   Mes a ceux que fount pur vous.
   E si le vostre ferm tenez,
   D'autrui doun rien averez.
    "A autry table, ne janglez trop,
210 Que tu ne seiez tenu pur sot:
   Quant ton congié avez pris,
   Escharny serrez pur vos dys;
113rb] Pur fol serrez ileque tenu,

For, know this, because of that mockery
You'll never be well praised,
But in the end,
170   The mocker will be mocked.
113ra]   "If anyone wants to slander you,
Don't at all, because of this, start in anger.
Let him say what he wants,
For you cannot defeat him in a better way.
175   And when he's finished complaining,
He'll be proclaimed a fool
And you considered wise,
The better loved and feared.
    "When you pass through the countryside,
180   Hold always to the old path.
Love your old companion.
And I hold it more sensible
To keep one friend
Than to gain ten.
185   "Don't boast about anything,
But keep yourself wholly silent,
So that all those of the countryside
Speak well of your remarks.
Your hands, your feet, when speaking,
190   Don't move them at all,
But only your tongue.
Answer very courteously,
So that none will be able
To blame you in any way
195   Or speak evil about you,
But only courtesy.
    "Associate often with the good,
And you must avoid the bad,
For from good things will come good,
200   And from bad things there'll be bad.
Be not stingy with your food,
But be courteous on all sides.
Give to those who treat you well
And who'll return your kindness.
205   I'm not saying that you ought to give to all,
But only to those who act on your behalf.
And if you cling firmly to what's your own,
You'll have nothing from others.
    "At another's table, don't chatter too much,
210   Lest you be taken for an idiot:
When you've taken your leave,
You'll be mocked for your words;
113rb]   You'll be considered there a fool,

E dirront vous estes en bu.
215   "Si tu soiez enchiminaunt
E encontrez petit ou grant,
Volenters li salvez:
Le mieux serras de li amez.
S'il vous salve a premour,
220   Responce donez en douçour.
Si vous ne fetez en cele manere,
Donqe dirra le fitz al piere,
'Le Deable ly dust salver —
Yl ne velt respounz doner!'
225   "S'il avient a chef de tour
Que vous seiez grant seignour,
Ne seiez trop simple a tes gentz,
Ne soffrez trop lur talentz.
Si trop ount lur volentee,
230   A vous ne tornera a bountee.
Ne seiez trop simple ne trop haut,
Ne trop nice ne trop baud.
        "Si entre gestes servyr devez,
Gardez qe soiez avisez.
235   Ore vous dirroi de servise:
Quant le nap serra mise,
Metez salers, esquilers,
Pus trenchours e payns enters,
E pus vin ou cervoise,
240   E priez qe se facent a eysé.
Queiqu'il eient a manger,
Sovent lur devez conforter.
Par gruschure ne servez
Que tu ne seiez mauloseez.
245   Confortez petitz e grantz,
E apernez les noun sachantz.
C'est le Dieu comandement
D'aprendre non sachaunte gent.
Si nul mesfet, petit ou grant,
250   Ne li tencez tant ne quant,
Mes diez ly privément,
'Ce su malfet devant gent.
Autrefoiz seiez garny,
Qe tu ne seiez de gent hony.'
113rc] Cely diez entre vous deus;
256   Ne ly facez autre maus
Pur estranges que ileque sunt,
Que mal los ne vous porterunt
Quant ton congié devez prendre.
260   "Je vous faz bien entendre,

And they'll say you were drunk.
215   "If you're traveling
And meet someone small or great,
Gladly greet him:
You'll be better loved by him.
If he greets you first,
220   Give a response with kindness.
If you don't act in this manner,
Then son will say to father,
'The Devil ought to greet him —
He doesn't care to answer!'
225   "If it should happen in the end
That you become a great lord,
Don't be too familiar with your people,
Nor grant too much their desires.
If they have their will too much,
230   It won't turn to your profit.
Don't be too familiar or too aloof,
Nor too silly or too merry.
    "If among guests you're obliged to serve,
Take care that you're well informed.
235   Now I'll tell you about the service:
When the tablecloth's been spread,
Put out saltcellars, spoons,
Then carving knives and whole loaves,
And then wine or beer,
240   And ask that they make themselves comfortable.
Whatever they've had to eat,
You ought to encourage them often.
Do not serve while grumbling
Lest you be little praised.
245   Encourage the small and the great,
And teach the ignorant.
It's God's commandment
To teach ignorant people.
If anyone acts badly, small or great,
250   Don't scold him at all,
But say to him privately,
'This was done poorly in front of people.
Next time, be advised,
Lest you be shamed by people.'
113rc]   Say this between the two of you;
256   Don't cause him other troubles
Because of the strangers present there,
So that they not bear ill report of you
When you must take your leave.
260   "I'd have you know well,

Si robe vous doint ou cointise
Cel jour pur vostre service,
Volenters le recevez
E molt al seigneur merciez;
265   Pus la donez ov bel semblant
A ascun tuen serjant.
Son doun ne refusez mie
E ne le metez en oblie,
Qu'il ne pust aillours dire,
270   'C'est un estout syre.
De noreture siet il rien
Ne corteysie plus que un chien.'
E, pur Dieu, vous purpensez
Que yvres ne seiez.
275   "Bon enfant a manger
Devant son seignur deit ester
Bone aprise escoter,
Sa vewe bien garder.
Al pareie ne deit muser.
280   A post ne se doit puer.
Sa nue char ne deit grater.
Ne doit ryre n'eschyner.
Ne a nully mosker.
Meurement se doit porter.
285   Issi porra seignours payer.
     "Si clerc seiez, com bien puet estre,
Totdis amez vostre mestre.
Lessez puteynz e hasardrie.
La taverne ne hauntez mie.
290   Si l'em vous doint petit ou grant,
Le recevez en merciant.
     "Quant vous estes avauncé,
Pensez de humilité,
Honorez ceux que fyrent vous,
295   E lur fetes tous honours.
Honorez piere e mere,
Vostre suere e vostre frere,
113va] E les autres de vostre lyn.
Si en averez bon fyn.
300   "Si um vous mesdit de nule part,
Gardez bien cet art:
Respounce a ly ne donez,
Mes la place voidez.
Si vous responez al janglour,
305   Le pis averez, saunz retour.
     "Pur vostre pais combatez
En tous lyws ou vous serrez.

If one gives you a cloak or elegant thing
That day for your service,
Gladly receive it
And thank the lord very much;
265   Then give it with a smile
To one of your servants.
Do not at all refuse his gift
And do not forget it,
So that he can't say elsewhere,
270   'That's an arrogant lord.
He knows no more of manners
Or courtesy than a dog.'
And, for God's sake, take care
That you not get drunk.
275   "A good child eating
Before his lord ought to be
Well taught to listen,
To control well his sight.
He ought not stare at the wall.
280   He ought not lean on the post.
He ought not scratch his bare skin.
He ought not laugh or grimace,
Or mock anyone.
He ought to carry himself maturely.
285   Thus can he please lords.
    "If you're to be a cleric, as well may be,
Always love your master.
Avoid prostitutes and gambling.
Don't frequent the tavern at all.
290   If one gives you something small or great,
Receive it with thanks.
    "When you're promoted,
Give thought to humility,
Honor those who made you,
295   And do them all honors.
Honor father and mother,
Your sister and your brother,
113va] And the others of your line.
Thus shall you have a good end.
300   "If someone slanders you in any place,
Keep well this practice:
Do not give him a response,
But leave the place.
If you answer a slanderer,
305   You'll be worse off, without fail.
    "Fight for your country
In every place you may be.

N'oiez de ly si bien noun,
Que tu ne le defendez par resoun.
310   Si counter devez a nully,
Quant il sa resoun ad fyny,
Responez amiablement
Sanz mesdire e serement.
Piés ne meynz ne movez
315   Quant resoun parler devez.
Tot eiez vous la victorie.
   "Eiez ce en memorie:
A nully devez manacer,
Ne malfere ne mauparler.
320   Mon ami, je vous defent.
Ne diez rien derere gent
Si vous ne le poez avower
E a bon fyn torner.
N'encusez nully par derere.
325   N'est pas tot leals que lange lere.
Desouz cel, n'a tresoun sy fere
Com faus lang ov bele chere.
   "Pernez femme de honours
E que soit de bons mours,
330   E veiez qe ele seit sage,
Que tei ne peyse la mariage.
Seiez de bele porture
E cortois saunz ordure.
Queique vostre femme vous die,
335   Trop ne la creyez mye
Si ele ne seit profitable
Saunz mensonge ou fable.
   "Je vous defend, sur tote rien:
Jamés ne serez autrui chien,
340   Quar le chien, a qy qu'il soit,
Poez feryr mal en froit.
   "Amenez ensi vostre vie
Qe vous ayme le fitz Marie,
113vb] E priez Dieu omnipotent,
345   Qe soffry peyne e torment,
Qe vous eiez l'amour de ly
E de sa douce mere ansi.
113vc] E nous doint la sue grace
E vewe de sa douce face."
   Amen.

Hear only what's good of it,
Lest you fail to defend it justly.
310   If you must argue with someone,
When he's ended his argument,
Answer in an amiable way
Without slander or swearing.
Move neither feet nor hands
315   When you must present your argument.
You'll quickly have the victory.
    "Hold this in memory:
You ought not threaten anyone,
Nor do or speak evil.
320   My friend, I forbid you.
Say nothing behind people's backs
If you cannot swear to it
And convert it to good purpose.
Don't accuse anyone behind his back.
325   What the tongue lets slip isn't always loyal.
Under heaven, there's no treason so fierce
As a false tongue with a kind face.
    "Take an honorable wife
Who has good morals,
330   And see that she's wise,
So that marriage doesn't weigh on you.
Be of gracious bearing
And courteous without impurity.
Whatever your wife tells you,
335   Don't believe her too much
Unless she's prudent
Without falsity or lying.
    "I forbid you, above all:
Never be another's dog,
340   For a dog, whoever he belongs to,
You can kick into the cold.
    "Lead thus your life
So that Mary's son may love you,
113vb]   And pray to omnipotent God,
345   Who suffered pain and torment,
That you may have love from him
And from his sweet mother too.
113vc]   And may he give us his grace
And the sight of his sweet face."
    Amen.

Talent me prent de rymer e de geste fere   [art. 80]

113vb] ¶ Talent me prent de rymer e de geste fere
        D'une purveaunce qe purveu est en la terre.
        Mieux valsit uncore que la chose fust a fere.
        Si Dieu ne prenge garde, je quy que sourdra guere.

5   Ce sunt les articles de Trayllebastoun.
        Salve le roi meismes, de Dieu eit maleysoun
        Qe a de primes graunta tiel commissioun,
        Quar en ascuns des pointz n'est mie resoun.

        Sire, si je voderoi mon garsoun chastier
10   De une buffe ou de deus, pur ly amender,
        Sur moi betera bille e me frad atachier,
        E avant qe isse de prisone raunsoun grant doner.

        Quaraunte souz pernent pur ma raunsoun,
        E la viscounte vint a son guerdoun
15   Qu'il ne me mette en parfounde prisoun.
        Ore agardez, seigneurs, est ce resoun?

        Pur ce me tendroi antre bois sur le jolyf umbray,
        La n'y a fauceté ne nulle male lay,
        En le bois de Belregard, ou vole le jay,
20   E chaunte russinole touz jours santz delay.

        Mes le male deseynes — dount Dieu n'eit ja pieté! —
        Parmi lur fauce bouches me ount enditee
        De male robberies e autre mavestee,
        Que je n'os entre mes amis estre receptee.

25   J'ai servi my sire le roy en pees e en guere,
        En Flaundres, Escoce, en Gascoyne sa terre,
        Mes ore ne me sai je point chevisaunce fere.
        Tot mon temps ay mis en veyn pur tiel honme plere!

        Si ces maveis jurours ne se vueillent amender
30   Que je pus a mon pais chevalcher e aler,
        Si je les pus ateindre, la teste lur froi voler!
        De touz lur manaces ne dorroi un dener.

        Ly Martyn e ly Knoville sunt gent de pieté,
        E prient pur les povres qu'il eyent sauveté.
35   Spigurnel e Belflour sunt gent de cruelté:
        Si il fuissent e ma baylie, ne serreynt retornee.

Trailbaston   [art. 80]

113vb]   ¶ Survival compels me to rhyme and compose a story
          About an ordinance that's ordained in the land.
          It'd be much better were the thing still undone.
          If God doesn't prevent it, I think war will arise.

5   It concerns the articles of Trailbaston.
          Except for the King himself, may God's curse fall
          Upon he who first granted such a commission,
          For there's no justice at all in any of its points.

          Sir, should I wish to punish my knave
10   With a blow or two, in order to correct him,
          He'll seek a bill against me and have me arrested,
          And before leaving prison I must pay a big ransom.

          Forty shillings they take for my ransom,
          And the sheriff comes for his reward
15   For not consigning me to a deep dungeon.
          Now consider, lords, is this just?

          That's why I shall stay in the woods under lovely shade,
          Where there's neither treachery nor any bad law,
          In the forest of Belregard, where the jay flies,
20   And the nightingale always sings without ceasing.

          But the false accusers — may God never pity them! —
          Have indicted me with their lying mouths
          For wicked robberies and other crimes,
          So that I dare not be received by my friends.

25   I've served my lord the King in peace and in war,
          In Flanders, Scotland, in his own land of Gascony,
          But now I don't have any idea how to make a deal.
          I've spent all my time in vain to please such a man!

          If these wicked jurors won't set things right
30   So that I'm able to ride and go about in my country,
          Should I catch up with them, I'll make their heads fly!
          I wouldn't give a penny for all their threats.

          Judge Martin and Judge Knoville are men of piety,
          And they pray for the poor that they may be safe;
35   Spigurnel and Belflour are men of cruelty:
          Were they in my power, they wouldn't be returned.

114r]   Je lur aprendroy le giw de Traylebastoun: **[quire 13]**
           E lur bruseroy l'eschyne e le cropoun,
           Les bras e les jaunbes — ce serreit resoun! —
40   La lange lur tondroy, e la bouche ensoun!

           Qy cestes choses primes comença,
           Ja jour de sa vie, amendé ne serra.
           Je vous di, pur veyr, trop graunt pecché en a,
           Quar pur doute de prisone meint laroun serra.

45   Ycel devendra leres que ne fust unque mes,
           Que, pur doute de prisone, ne ose venir a pes:
           Vivre, covient avoir chescum jour adés.
           Qy ceste chose comença yl emprist grant fes.

           Bien devoient marchaunz e moygnes doner maliçoun
50   A tous iceux que ordinerent le Traillebastoun.
           Ne lur vaudra un ayle le roial proteccioun
           Que il ne rendrount les deners sauntz regerdoun.

           Vous qy estes endité, je lou venez a moy,
           Al vert bois de Belregard la n'y a nul ploy,
55   Forque beste savage e jolyf umbroy,
           Car trop est dotouse la commune loy!

           Si tu sachez de lettrure e estes coronee,
           Devaunt les justices serrez appellee.
           Uncore, poez estre a prisone retornee,
60   En garde de le evesque, jesque seiez purgee.

           . . . .
           . . . .
           E soffryr messayse e trop dure penaunce,
           E par cas n'averez jamés delyveraunce.

65   Pur ce valt plus ov moi a bois demorer
           Q'en prisone le evesque fyergé gyser.
           Trop est la penaunce e dure a soffrer!
           Quy le mieux puet eslyre fol est qe ne velt choyser.

           Avant savoy poy de bien; ore su je meins sage.
70   Ce me fount les male leis par mout grant outrage
           Qe n'os a la pes venyr entre mon lignage.
           Les riches sunt a raunsoun, povres a escolage.

           Fort serroit engager ce qe ne puet estre aquytee —
           C'est la vie de honme, que taunt est cher amee.

114r]   I'd teach them the game of Trailbaston:
         I'd break their spines and rumps,
         Their arms and legs — that would be justice! —
40   Their tongues I'd cut out, and their mouths as well!

         He who first started these affairs,
         In all the days of his life, will never be reformed.
         I tell you, truly, he sins too greatly in it,
         For many a man will be a thief for fear of prison.

45   He'll become a thief who was never one before,
         Who, for fear of prison, dares not come to peace:
         To live, it's essential to have nourishment each day.
         Whoever began this business undertook a huge task.

         Well ought merchants and monks heap curses
50   On all those who ordained the Trailbaston.
         Royal protection won't be worth a straw to them
         Unless they pay back their money without recompense.

         You who are indicted, I advise you to come to me,
         To the greenwood of Belregard where there's no worry,
55   Only wild animals and beautiful shade,
         For the common law is too frightening!

         If you know how to read and are tonsured,
         You shall be summoned before the judges.
         Still, you may be returned to prison,
60   Under guard of the bishop, until you're cleared.

         . . . .
         . . . .
         And suffer hardship and extremely harsh punishment,
         And perhaps you shall never be freed.

65   That's why it's better to live with me in the forest
         Than to lie fettered in the bishop's prison.
         The punishment is too great and hard to endure!
         Whoever knows what's better is a fool if he doesn't choose it.

         I used to know a little about virtue; now I'm less wise.
70   Bad laws inflict this on me by such great abuse
         That I don't dare return peacefully to my relatives.
         The rich are fined, the poor dwindle away.

         It'd be bitter to pledge what can't be discharged —
         A man's life, which is so dearly loved.

114v]   E je n'ay mye le chatel de estre rechatee.
76   Mes si je fusse en lur baundoun, a mort serroi lyveree.

         Uncore, attendroy grace e orroi gent parler.
         Tiels me dient le mal, que me ne osent aprochier,
         E volenters verroient mon corps ledenger.
80   Mes entre myl debles Dieu puet un honme sauver.

         Cely me pust salver que est le fitz Marie,
         Car je ne su coupable — endité su par envye!
         Qy en cesti lu me mist Dieu lur maldie.
         Le siecle est si variant fous est qe s'affye.

85   Si je sei compagnoun e sache de archerye,
         Mon veisyn irra disaunt, "Cesti est de compagnie
         De aler bercer a bois e fere autre folie.
         Que ore vueille vivre, come pork merra sa vye."

         Si je sache plus de ley qe ne sevent eux,
90   Yl dirrount, "Cesti conspyratour comence de estre faus,"
         E le heyre n'aprocheroy de x lywes ou deus.
         De tous veysinages, hony seient ceux!

         Je pri tote bone gent qe pur moi vueillent prier
         Qe je pus a mon pais aler e chyvaucher.
95   Unqe ne fu homicide, certes a moun voler,
         Ne mal robberes pur gent damager.

         Cest rym fust fet al bois desouz un lorer,
         La chaunte merle, russinole, e eyre l'esperver.
         Escrit estoit en parchemyn pur mout remenbrer,
100   E gitté en haut chemyn qe um le dust trover.

Mon in the mone stond ant strit   [art. 81]

114v]   ¶ Mon in the mone stond ant strit;
         On is bot-forke is burthen he bereth.
         Hit is muche wonder that he nadoun slyt —
         For doute leste he valle, he shoddreth ant shereth.
5   When the forst freseth, muche chele he byd.
         The thornes beth kene, is hattren totereth.
         Nis no wytht in the world that wot wen he syt,
         Ne, bote hit bue the hegge, whet wedes he wereth.

115r]   Whider trowe this mon ha the wey take?
10   He hath set is o fot is other toforen;

114v]   And I don't have any property by which to be redeemed.
76   Were I ever in their power, I'd be handed over to death.

          Even now, I'll wait for a pardon and hear people talk.
          Some, who don't dare to approach me, speak of me badly,
          And would happily see my body injured.
80   But amid a thousand devils God can save a man.

          The one who can save me is the son of Mary,
          For I'm not guilty — I'm indicted out of envy!
          May God curse whoever put me in this place.
          The world's so fickle that he's a fool who trusts it.

85   If I'm one of a company and know about archery,
          My neighbor will go about saying, "This one's from the gang
          That goes hunting in the forest and commits other sin.
          Should he want to live now, let him live like a pig."

          If I should know more about the law than they know,
90   They'll say, "This conspirator starts to be treacherous,"
          And I won't approach home within ten leagues or twenty.
          Among all neighbors, shame on them!

          I ask that all good men should pray for me
          So that I may go to my country and ride about.
95   I was never a murderer, surely not by my will,
          Nor a wicked robber for the intent of harming people.

          This rhyme was made in the forest under a laurel,
          Where sing blackbird and nightingale, and sparrow hawk flies.
          It was written on parchment to be better remembered,
100   And thrown on the highway so that someone might find it.

The Man in the Moon   [art. 81]

114v]   ¶ The man in the moon stands and strides;
          On his forked stick he bears his bundle.
          It's a great wonder that he doesn't fall down —
          For fear lest he fall, he trembles and veers.
5   When the frost freezes, he endures much cold.
          The thorns are sharp, [they] tatter his clothes.
          There's no one in the world who knows when he sits,
          Nor, unless it be the hedge, what clothes he wears.

115r]   Which way do you think this man's taken his path?
10   He's set his one foot in front of the other;

For non hithte that he hath, ne sytht me hym ner shake.
He is the sloweste mon that ever wes yboren!
Wher he were o the feld pycchynde stake,
For hope of ys thornes to dutten is doren,
15   He mot myd is twybyl other trous make,
Other al is dayes werk ther were yloren.

This ilke mon upon heh, when-er he were,
Wher he were y the mone boren ant yfed,
He leneth on is forke ase a grey frere —
20   This crokede caynard, sore he is adred!
Hit is mony day go that he was here;
Ichot of is ernde he nath nout ysped.
He hath hewe sumwher a burthen of brere;
Tharefore sum hayward hath taken ys wed.

25   Yef thy wed ys ytake, bring hom the trous!
Sete forth thyn other fot! Stryd over sty!
We shule preye the haywart hom to ur hous,
Ant maken hym at heyse, for the maystry,
Drynke to hym deorly of fol god bous,
30   Ant oure dame douse shal sitten hym by.
When that he is dronke ase a dreynt mous,
Thenne we schule borewe the wed ate bayly.

This mon hereth me nout, thah Ich to hym crye!
Ichot the cherl is def! The Del hym todrawe!
35   Thah Ich yeye upon heth, nulle nout hye;
The lostlase ladde con nout o lawe.
Hupe forth, Hubert, hosede pye!
Ichot thart amarscled into the mawe!
Thah me teone with hym that myn teh mye,
40   The cherld nul nout adoun er the day dawe!

Le chevaler e la corbaylle   [art. 82]

115va]   ¶ Pur ce que plusours ount mervaille
De *Le chevaler e la corbaylle*,
Ore le vous vueil je counter,
Si vous plest a escoter.
5   Un chevaler de grant valour
E une dame de honour
S'entreamerent jadis d'amour,
Leaument ov grant douçour.
Mes il ne se poeint assembler,
10   Ne pur geiter ne pur embler,

Despite any effort taken, one never sees him move.
He's the slowest man that ever was born!
Where he's in the field fastening stakes,
In the hope of closing his doors with his thorns,
15   He must make a bundle with his two-edged axe,
Or else all his day's work there is lost.

This very man upon high, whenever he appears,
There in the moon where he was born and reared,
He leans on his forked stick like a gray friar —
20   This hunched idler, he's terribly frightened!
It's many days ago that he was here;
I know he's not succeeded in his errand.
He's hewn somewhere a burden of briars;
Therefore some hayward has taken his pledge.

25   If your pledge is taken, bring home the hedge-cuttings!
Set forth your other foot! Stride over the path!
We shall ask the hayward home to our house,
And put him at ease, in a comfortable manner,
Drink to him affectionately with very stiff drink,
30   And our gentle wife shall sit near him.
When he is as drunk as a drowned mouse,
Then we shall obtain the pledge from the bailiff.

This man hears me not, though I call out to him!
I think the churl is deaf! May the Devil pull him to bits!
35   Though I cry out on high, he won't at all hurry;
The lazy lad knows nothing of the law.
Hop forth, Hubert, magpie in stockings!
I think you're stuffed full in the stomach!
Though I'm so angry with him that my teeth grate,
40   The churl won't come down before the day dawns!

The Knight and the Basket   [art. 82]

115va]   ¶ Because many people marvel
About *The Knight and the Basket*,
Now I wish to tell it to you,
If it should please you to listen.
5   A very courageous knight
And an honorable lady
Once loved each other dearly,
Loyally with great tenderness.
But they could never be together,
10   Either by watching out or by stealth,

Fors a parler taun soulement,
Quar molt estoit estreitement
La dame closé e enmuree.
Mesone ne clos ne ount duree
15   Vers femme, quar son engyn pase
Tot ce q'autre engyn compasse.
   Le chevaler l'out d'amour pryé,
E la dame s'ert otryé
A ly, quant vendreint en eyse.
20   Mes mester est qe um se teyse
Vers pucele e chaunbrere,
E qe ele se tienge en sa barrere
En pes, quar soun mary l'ageyte
E fet geiter, a grant deceyte.
25   E mes qu'il geytee ne l'aust,
Si ne say come l'em pust
Approcher a tiele chasteleyne,
Si ce ne fust a tro grant peyne,
Quar trop y a murs e fosseez.
30   Cil qe tous les avereit passeez
E feist taunt qu'il poeit estre
Dedenz cele chambre le plus mestre,
Ou la dame dort e repose,
Uncore, ne serreit legere chose
35   D'aver tote sa volenté,
Quar en yver e en esté
La gueyte une veele talevace.
E si la dame remuer se face
Une houre, qe ele ne la veist,
40   Meintenaunt ele deist
115vb] A le seigneur (qu'estoit soun fis),
E il crerroit bien tost ces dys.
   Le chevaler mout sovent
Soleyt aler a tornoyement,
45   Sicome ryche baroun deit fere.
Le chevaler de basse affere,
Que longement se avoit mussee,
E en mussaunt soun temps usee,
Un jour se purpensa
50   Qe la dame vere irra
Quaunt erré fust le chasteleyn.
   Le porter ne fust mie vileyn.
Eynz, son message a la dame fist.
E meintenant a le porter dist,
55   "Amis, lessez saeynz venyr,
Quar a counsail le vueil tenyr
De un affere qe je pens."

Except only to speak,
For very strictly
Was the lady enclosed and walled in.
Neither house nor enclosure may hold back
15   A woman, for her ingeniousness exceeds
All that any other ingenuity devises.
    The knight had asked for her love,
And the lady had assented
To him, whenever opportunity should arise.
20   But it's necessary that they keep quiet
Around maidservant and chambermaid,
And that she keep herself within her bounds
Docilely, for her husband watches her
And has her watched, most deceitfully.
25   And even were he not to keep watch,
I don't know how anyone could
Approach such a lady of the castle,
Unless it were with very great difficulty,
For there are too many walls and moats.
30   If one were to pass through all of them
And do as much as he could to enter
Into that room of most importance,
Where the lady sleeps and rests,
Even so, it would be no easy matter
35   To have all his desire,
For in winter and in summer
An old hag-shield watches her.
And if the lady should absent herself
For an hour, and she [the old woman] not see her,
40   At once she'd inform
115vb]   The lord (who was her son),
And he'd quite readily believe her report.
    The knight quite often
Would go to tournaments,
45   As a wealthy baron should.
The knight of modest circumstances,
Who had languished for a long time,
And passed his time in languishing,
One day decided
50   That he'd go see the lady
While the castellan was out traveling.
    The porter wasn't rude at all.
Instead, he took his message to the lady.
And at once she said to the porter,
55   "Friend, let him enter here,
For I wish to seek his advice
Concerning an affair I'm pondering."

          Ataunt entra saunz defens,
          E les chevalers qe leynz furent
60   Ly fyrent joie qe ly conurent.
          La dame molt bel le reçust,
          Mes la veeille ne ly pust
          Salver si a grant peyne noun,
          Quar ele le avoit en suspecioun.
65   Desus un tapit se assistrent;
          D'amours un parlement y mistrent.
          Trop fust pres la veeille frouncie —
          Que male passioun la ocie,
          Quar de parler ont poi d'espace!
70   "Dame," fet il, "ja Dieu ne place
          Qe ceste veille vyvre puisse:
          Que ele n'eit brusé ou bras ou quisse,
          Que ele soit clope ou contrayte,
          Quar si ele ust la lange trayte,
75   Certes ce serroit charité,
          Qe mensounge ne verité
          Ne issent jamés de ces denz!"
              "Sire, mout ad en le cuer dedenz,"
116ra] Fet la dame, "feloun corage!
80   Mort la prenge e male rage!
          Trop ad en ly male racyne!
          Mes, qui m'enseignast la medicine
          Par quei ele fust asourdee,
          Je l'en donasse grant soudee,
85   Quar petit dort e longes veyle,
          Si a tro clere l'oreyle,
          Auxi de nuytz come de jours.
          Um dit qe veeille gent sunt sourdz,
          Mes ceste ad trop clere l'oye."
90   "La male goute, bele amye,"
          Fet il, "nous em pusse venger —
          Je ne vous say autre enseigner.
          Mes, pur Dieu, que frez vous de moi,
          Qe taunt vous aym, en bone foy?
95   Grant pieté a, e bien le savez,
          Grant pecchié de moy avez!"
              "Pecché?" fet ele. "Bels amis chers,
          Ja estes vous ly chevalers
          Que je plus aym; si je pusse,
100   E je le loyser usse.
          Veiez tauntz barrez e tanz murs!
          Je vodroi estre ov vous aillours,
          En Espaigne ou en Lumbardye."
              "Dame," fet il, "par coardye,

Then he entered without hindrance,
And the knights who were inside
60   Joyfully welcomed him for they knew him.
The lady received him very graciously,
But the old woman could not
Greet him without great distress,
For she was suspicious of him.
65   On a tapestry they sat down together;
There they engaged in love talk.
Too near was the wrinkled old woman —
May a terrible disease kill her,
For they had little space to talk!
70   "Lady," he says, "may it never please God
That this old woman should live:
Were she to break an arm or thigh,
Were she lame or crippled,
Or if she were to have her tongue pulled out,
75   Certainly it would be a charitable thing,
For neither lies nor truth
Would ever again issue from her teeth!"
        "Lord, certainly she has in her heart,"
116ra] The lady says, "a wicked spirit!
80   May death and evil madness take her!
There's a malicious core in her!
Indeed, if someone could show me the drug
Whereby she'd be made deaf,
I'd give him a large reward,
85   For she sleeps little and watches long,
And she has ears that are too sharp,
As much by night as by day.
They say that old people are deaf,
But this one has hearing that's too keen."
90   "A bad malady, dear friend,"
He says, "might be able to avenge us —
I know no other way to advise you.
But, for God's sake, what will you do for me,
Who loves you so much, in good faith?
95   Have mercy, and well you know how to.
You've grievously sinned on my account!"
        "Sinned?" she says. "Dear sweet friend,
Truly you are the knight
Whom I most love, if only I could,
100   And if I had the opportunity.
Look how many barriers and walls there are!
I'd like to be with you somewhere else,
In Spain or in Lombardy."
        "Lady," he says, "by no cowardice,

105   Si Dieu pust mon cors salver,
        Ne lerroi je pas a entrer
        En cet hostel, e tant feroi
        Qe uncore anuit seynz serroi.
        Si, de vous, quidroi esploiter."
110   "Venez dounc saunz respiter,"
        Fet ele, "anuit, bels douz amis,
        Quar si saeynz vous estoiez mis
        Qe de nul aparsu fussez,
        Mon cors gayné averez;
115   Quar pus ne faudrez vous ja
        De venir desque cel us la,
        Ou je serroye countre vous."
            "Ensi," fet il, "le ferrom nous,
116rb] Je y vendroi anuit sauntz faile."
120   "Bien," fet ele, "vous y vaile."
            Ataunt, lessent le conciler.
        De le oriller e d'escoter,
        Molt fust la veeille entremise,
        Mes n'out pas la chose aprise.
125   La dame demanda le vyn.
        Le chevaler — ce fust la fyn —
        En bust, e ne mie grantment.
        Eynz, regarde ententivement.
        La sale, qe ad murs feytis
130   Estoit assise a pentis,
        Devers le mur fust descoverte.
        Si ja ne fust fenestre overte,
        Si pout um vere de lover
        Quar um porroit un bover
135   Launcer parmi ov tous ces buefs!
        E pensa qe ce serroit a soun oefs.
            Un soun esquier apela,
        Privément le councila
        Qu'il s'en isse e s'en aut muscer
140   Joste la sale en un ligner.
        Q'estoit apuez al mur,
        E soit la desqu'il soit obscur
        E que la gent se soit cochie,
        Pus mounte le mur tot a celee
145   Si le atende a un kernel.
        Cely, qe ne fust gueres bel
        De remeyndre en si grant doute,
        Graunta sa volenté toute,
        Quar ne le osa fere autrement.
150   Vers le ligner va belement,
        Enbuchez est dedenz la buche,

105 So God save my body,
   Would I hold off from entering
   This house, and I'll do whatever it takes
   To be inside it again tonight.
   Thus, with you, I plan to make it happen."
110   "Then come without delay,"
   She says, "tonight, dear sweet friend,
   For were you to be placed here within
   In such a way that you're seen by no one,
   You shall have won my body;
115 For then you won't neglect
   To come as far as that door,
   Where I'll be expecting you."
    "Just so," he says, "shall we do it,
116rb] I'll come there tonight without fail."
120   "Good," she says, "that's brave of you."
    With that, they ended the meeting.
   In hearing and listening to them,
   The old woman was very much concerned,
   But she hadn't understood what they said.
125   The lady asked for wine.
   The knight — this was the plot —
   Drank some, but not at all heavily.
   Instead, he looks around carefully.
   The hall, which with well-made walls
130 Was constructed and fitted,
   Was open-roofed near the wall.
   Even though no window was open,
   One could see by means of the open turret
   Such that one might allow a cowherd
135 To pass through with all his oxen!
   And he decided this would be his means of action.
    He called one of his squires,
   Privately advising him
   That he should go out and hide himself
140 Next to the hall in a woodshed
   That was up against the wall,
   And stay there till it's dark
   And the people have gone to bed,
   Then climb up the wall very secretly
145 And wait for him on the battlements.
   This one, who was not so pleased
   To stay there at such great risk,
   Granted his whole desire,
   For he didn't dare do otherwise.
150 He goes quietly toward the woodshed,
   Is concealed within the logs,

E tint en sa meyn une rusche.
　　E quant la gueyte avoit cornee,
Le chevaler se ert atornee.
155　Quant quida qe fust endormie,
La gent lors ne se oblia mie:
Le chevaler ad fet taunt
Que grant piece aprés l'anuytant
116va]　Sy vint dehors les murs ester,
160　E um ly fet aporter
Une corbaille bièn tornee
De cordes bien avyronee.
Ov la aye cely desus,
Le chevaler (qe remist jus)
165　S'est dedenz la corbaille cochee,
E cil l'ount sus le mur saké,
E molt tost l'ount mis avale
De le mur desqe en la sale.
Bien ad deservy son deduit!
170　　E la dame unqe cele nuit
Ne dormi. Einz, fust en entente
Tant q'ele oie ou qu'ele sente
De son amy le aviegnement.
Vers la chaunbre va belement
175　Ou la dame l'entendoit.
Bon guerdoun rendre l'en doit,
La dame qe grant joie en a!
Dedenz la chaunbre le mena,
E firent quanque fere durent:
180　A molt grant joie ensemble furent.
　　Mes la veille gysoit molt pres,
Qe molt avoit le cuer engrés,
E n'ert pas uncore endormie.
Entre lur deus litz n'i avoit mie
185　Une teyse, ce m'est avys.
Un soul covertour coveroit lur lis —
Qe bon e bel e graunt estoit
Le covertour qe les deus litz coveroit!
Come le chevaler fist son mester,
190　Le covertour comença crouler.
　　La maveise veille demaunda,
"File, ton covertour quey a,
Qe tant le oie aler e venir?"
　　"Dame, je ne pus tenir,"
195　Fet ele, "de grater une houre.
Seigne, ce quid, me demoure."
Cele quide qe voir ly dye.
　　Mes longes ne demorra mie

And holds some rushes in his hand.
    And when the watch had blown the horn,
The knight had made himself ready.
155   When he thought that he [the watch] was asleep,
Then he didn't forget his people at all:
The knight had done so much
That a good while after nightfall
116va] He arrives there outside the walls,
160   And there's delivered to him
A well-made basket
Entirely wrapped in ropes.
With the help of the one above,
The knight (who remained below)
165   Has lain down inside the basket,
And these have pulled him up the wall,
And very quickly lowered him down
From the wall into the hall.
He's well earned his delight!
170   And that night the lady never
Slept. Instead, she was listening
Until she hears or until she senses
The arrival of her friend.
He goes quietly toward the room
175   Where the lady waits for him.
She ought to render him a good reward,
The lady, who has great joy in it!
She led him into her room,
And they did whatever they ought to do:
180   They had very great joy together.
    But close by lay the old woman,
Who had a vicious heart,
And she was not yet asleep.
Between their two beds there was not
185   Even a space, in my opinion.
A single blanket covered their beds —
How good and beautiful and large
Was the blanket that covered the two beds!
As the knight did his work,
190   The blanket began to shake.
    The wicked old woman asked,
"Daughter, what's with your blanket,
That I hear it go and come so much?"
    "Lady, I cannot keep,"
195   She says, "from scratching constantly.
My itch, believe this, remains unrelieved."
That one thinks she tells the truth.
    But he did not slow down at all

116vb] Que il ne fist le covertour crouler.
200   Bien, sout les coupes le roy doner,
         Le chevaler, mien esscient,
         Quar il ne se repose nent.
         Molt ert vaillaunt en cel estour;
         Sovent fesoit le covertour
205   Crouler e torner de une part.
         E la veille qe mout soud de art
         E d'engyn e de trycherye,
         Pensa qe unqe pur graterye
         Ne ala le covertour ensi.
210   De son lit la veille issi,
         Une chaundele prist desteinte,
         E de aler suef ne se est feynte.
         Vers la cusyne tint sa voie,
         Mes parmi la sale forvoie
215   Taunt q'en la corbaille chay!
          Cil quiderent estre trahy,
         Qe les cordes braunler sentirent.
         Vistement la corbaille tyrent.
         Sus trehent la veille chanue.
220   Le ciel fust estoillé, saunt nue,
         Quant ele vint pres de le lover.
         Donqe conurent l'esquier
         Qe ce n'ert mie lur seignour.
          Donqe la demeynent a dolour,
225   Quar la corbaille balauncerent.
         De tref en autre la launcerent.
         Unqe la veille ne ala a tiele hounte!
         Primes aval, e pus amounte,
         En tele peyne e torment
230   La ont demenee longement
         Pur poi ne la ount toly la vie.
         Bien quide qu'il la eyent ravye —
         Deables ou autre malfees!
          Quant il furent eschaufeez
235   De crouler, les cordes guerpissent.
         La corbaille a terre flatissent,
         E la veille a une part vole.
117ra] Qaunt ele leva, se fist que fole.
         A quoi ferroi je long sermoun?
240   Taunt hordly par la mesoun
         Qu'a son lit est venue,
         Tremblaunt come fueille menue
         Que le vent de byse demeyne,
         Sicome poeit parler a peyne.
245   Dit a la dame, a grant tristour:

116vb] In making the blanket shake.
200   Indeed, he knew how to give the royal strokes,
        The knight, as best I know,
        For he doesn't rest at all.
        He was very brave in this combat;
        He often made the blanket
205   Shake and turn on one side.
        And the old woman, who understood craft
        And ingenuity and trickery,
        Thought that never on account of scratching
        Would a blanket move in this way.
210   The old woman rose up from her bed,
        Took an unlit candle,
        And didn't hesitate to go softly.
        Toward the kitchen she made her way,
        But within the hall she went awry
215   So much that she fell into the basket!
          They thought themselves betrayed,
        Those who felt the ropes tighten.
        Quickly they pulled in the basket.
        Up they draw the old gray-haired woman.
220   The sky was starry, without a cloud,
        When she came close to the louvred turret.
        Then the squires knew
        This was not at all their lord.
          Then they made it grievous for her,
225   For they swung the basket.
        From one beam to another they threw it.
        Never had the old woman felt such abuse!
        First down, and then up,
        In such pain and torment
230   Have they tossed her for so long
        That they've nearly taken her life.
        She really thinks they've ravished her —
        Devils or other demons!
          When they were made all hot
235   From the shaking, they let go of the ropes.
        The basket they let fall to the ground,
        And the old woman flies out to the side.
117ra] When she got up, she acted senseless.
        Why should I make a long tale?
240   She hurtled so much about the house
        Till she came to her bed,
        Trembling like a fragile leaf
        That the north wind shakes,
        Like one who could hardly talk.
245   She says to the lady, with extreme grief:

"Mal feu arde ton covertour!
Tele noise ad anuit demenee!
Malement me ad atornee.
Les dames que errerent par nuit!"
250   Mout en urent grant desduit —
Les deus amantz, quant le oevre surent,
E ceux qe balauncé le urent.
Ensi le chevaler ala e vynt.
Unque plus a la veille ne avynt
255   Que ele levast puis qe fu cochee —
Quant ly sovynt de sa haschee,
N'avoit talent de hors issyr!
Unqe puis — taunt ne oy crouler
Le covertour — qe se remust
260   Pur nulle bosoigne qe ele ust.
Pur ce est droit qe mal purchace
Qe a la foiz mal ly face.
     Ataunt finist, sauntz fayle,
De la veille e de la corbayle.

De mal mariage   [art. 83]

117ra]   ¶ Bené soit Dieu omnipotent,
Qe delivre d'enconbrement
Ceux qu'en li ont affiaunce
Par bone foi e dreite creaunce.
5   Par moi, le di qe, l'ay provee.
Gawein par noun su nomee.
Dieu me salva par sa puissaunce
De grant anuy e d'enconbraunce,
Si vous dirroi bien coment.
10   Ore escotez bonement.
117rb]   Jadis voloi femme prendre
Une pucele bele e tendre
Qe mout estoit de grant belté.
Devant totes l'avoi amee.
15   De lui esposer fust trop somounz
E conseillee des compaignoms
Que femmes prises avoient
E en sposailles viveient.
Mout preyserent cele vie
20   Pur moi trere a lur compagnie,
Qu'il se puissent de moi gabber
Quaunt yl me verrount repenter,
Sicome eux meismes feseient.
De lur affere se repenteient!

"May an evil fire burn your blanket!
Such an uproar's been stirred up tonight!
I've been given a wicked turn.
[Cursed are] ladies out traveling by night!"
250   They took great entertainment in it —
The two lovers when they knew the deed,
And those who had tossed her.
Thus did the knight come and go.
Never more would the old woman
255   Get up after she'd gone to bed —
When she remembered her suffering,
She had no desire to go out!
Never afterwards — no matter how much she heard
The blanket shake — did she get up
260   For any need that she might have.
For it's right that one who strives for wrong
Should in turn have wrong done to him.
    Thus ends, without fail,
The Old Woman and the Basket.

Against Marriage   [art. 83]

117ra]   ¶ Blessed be God omnipotent,
Who delivers from hardship
Those who trust in him
With good faith and right belief.
5   For myself, I affirm, I've experienced it.
Gawain am I called by name.
God saved me by his power
From great trouble and hardship,
And I'll tell you exactly how.
10   Now listen kindly.
117rb]   Once I wanted to take a wife
A fair and tender maiden
Who was extremely beautiful.
I had loved her above all others.
15   To marry her I was pressured
And advised by friends
Who had taken wives
And lived in wedlock.
They highly praised that life
20   In order to draw me into their company,
So that they could mock me
When they'd see me repent,
Just as they themselves had done.
They repented of their deed!

25 Tant me mistrent en le oraille,
  E taunt preyserent esposaille,
  Qe je fu tot consillee
  M'amie aver esposee —
  E me aver mis en aconbraunce
30 E tote ma vie en peysaunce!
   Mes Dieu par sa merci
  Me salva, come eynz vous di.
  Par sa merci me salva,
  Par treis aungles qu'il m'envoia
35 En une valoie come aloy
  Tot soul juer, come dirroi.
   Coment les aungles furent nomez
  Q'a moi furent maundez:
  Pieres de Corbloi fust le premer
40 Qe vint a moi come messager.
  Le secounde out noun Laurence,
  Honme de grant sapience.
  E le tierz compaignoun
  Johan ov la bouche d'or appelom.
45 Treis aungles les nomay,
  Si vous dirroi bien pur quay:
  En seinte Escripture um puet lyre
  Qe *aungel* valt taunt a dyre,
  "Come cely qu'est bon messager,
50 Que bone chose vint nouncier."
117va] E bone chose ount nouncié,
  Ces trois aungles, pur verité,
  Quar par eux su eschapé
  Longe peyne la, merci Dé!
55 Pieres dit qe femme est frele,
  Ja ne soit ele si bele.
  Laurence dit que ele est chaungable,
  Fauce, fole, e movable.
  Johan dit qe ele est corousouse,
60 Decevable, e orguillouse.
  Veiez ci povre comencement
  A doner honme bon talent!
  De femme prendre en esposaille
  N'est mie bon, je dy sauntz faille!
65 Pieres dit, "Qe femme prent,
  Yl se charge grevement,
  De tiel fees s'en est chargee
  Dount ja ne serra deschargee.
  Entre femme e soun marry —
70 Par cel affere, ce vous dy —
  Qe c'est charnele compagnie.

25   So much did they make me listen,
       And so highly praised wedlock,
       That I was wholly determined
       To marry my love —
       To place myself in servitude
30   And all my life in heaviness!
           But God in his mercy
       Saved me, as I've just told you.
       He saved me by his mercy,
       By means of three angels he sent to me
35   In a valley as I traveled
       All by myself to play, as I shall recount.
           [Here's] how were named the angels
       Who were sent to me:
       Peter of Corbeil was the first
40   Who came to me as a messenger.
       The second had the name Lawrence,
       A man of great wisdom.
       And the third companion
       We call John of the golden mouth.
45   I've called them three angels,
       And I'll tell you exactly why:
       In Holy Scripture one can read
       That *angel* is as much as to say,
       "He who's a good messenger,
50   Who's come to announce a good thing."
117va] And a good thing they've announced,
       These three angels, in truth,
       For by them I've escaped
       Long suffering there, thank God!
55   Peter says that woman is frail,
       However beautiful she may be.
       Lawrence says that she's fickle,
       False, foolish, and unsteady.
       John says that she's wrathful,
60   Deceptive, and proud.
       Here's a poor beginning
       To give a man courage!
       Taking a woman in marriage
       Is not at all good, I affirm without doubt!
65   Peter says, "Whoever takes a wife,
       He burdens himself grievously,
       He's charged with a load
       Of which he'll never be unburdened.
       Between a wife and her husband —
70   Of this business, I tell you this —
       It's fleshly companionship.

Quant le baroun ne puet mie
Fere le si sovent
Come la femme avereit talent,
75   Donqe prent, a grant honeysoun,
Un ou deus desouz soun baroun
(Ou assez plus, par aventure)
Pur estauncher cel ordure.
E uncore, sachez vous,
80   Ja ne soit il si prous,
Ne la puet assez trover
A soun talent de cel mester.
Nota   Bien puet estre lasse devendra,
Mes jamés saulee ne serra.
85   Pur ce, Gaweyn, fetez que sage,
Gardez vous de tiel outrage!"
Pieres sa resone ad fyny,
Qe bien est digne d'estre oy,
E pri qe um ly vueill entendre
90   E sa resoun de rien mesprendre.
        Ore vint avaunt Laurence,
117vb] E sa resone issi comence:
"Femme est fole e trop legere,
De fol semblant e fole chere,
95   Trop variable e trop coveitaunt,
Meinte chose desirraunt.
Quar si le baroun ne puet
Trover la quanqe ele veut,
Meintenaunt se dorra
100   A un que trover la porra.
Riche atyr, noble vesture,
Bele robe ov riche pelure —
Coment qu'il aile, force ne fet
For que ele eit son pleisir tret.
105   Dieu, quel dolour e damage
Avient sovent de mal mariage!
Pur ce, Gaweyn, bel douz amy,
Seiez avysé e garni:
De femme prendre ne le fetes mye!
110   Dont, serrez sages, quei qe um en dye."
        E Johan, le tierz compaignoun,
Ore comence sa resoun:
"Certes," fet il, "mariage
Est la plus haute servage
115   Qe soit pur honme qe vit;
Car il n'avera jamés respit,
Nient plus qe le buef joynt
En la charue, qu'est point

When the husband cannot
Do it as often
As the wife desires,
75 Then she takes, very shamefully,
One or two lower than her husband
(Or many more, perhaps)
To staunch this filth.
Moreover, as you know,
80 Be he ever so worthy,
He can't for her muster enough
For her desire in this office.
Note It may well be she'll grow tired,
But never will she be sated.
85 Therefore, Gawain, act wisely,
Guard yourself against such excess!"
Peter has finished his argument,
Which is worthy of being heard,
And I pray people will want to heed him
90 And not mistake his argument at all.
    Now Lawrence comes forward,
117vb] And thus begins his argument:
"Woman is silly and too shallow,
Of silly looks and silly bearing,
95 Too variable and too greedy,
Desiring many things.
For if the husband cannot
Provide whatever she wants,
Quickly she'll give herself
100 To one who can get it for her.
Rich attire, noble clothing,
A beautiful robe with rich fur —
However it goes, she makes no fuss
So long as she gets her pleasure.
105 God, what suffering and harm
Often comes of a bad marriage!
Therefore, Gawain, dear sweet friend,
Be advised and warned:
Don't take a wife at all!
110 In this, you'll be wise, whatever people say."
    And John, the third companion,
Now begins his argument:
"Certainly," he says, "marriage
Is the greatest servitude
115 That exists for living man;
For he'll never have rest,
No more than the ox yoked
To the plow, which is poked

Sovent d'aguilloun agu,
120   Sovent maldit e feru.
Tot ensi ce veiomz nous
Avient del cheytif um espous:
Si tous jours ne soit traveillant,
Eynz e hors purchassaunt,
125   Sa femme sovent ly poindra
De le aguilloun qe ele a —
C'est la lange trop legere
De mesdire, e trop amere!
Meintefoiz serra tencé,
130   Mesdit, hounie, e ledengee.
Tant l'orra mesdire e tencer
118ra] Qu'il ne savera quel part torner!
'Allas' fet il, 'qe unqe fu mary!'
'Allas' fet ele, 'qe unque vous vy!'
135   'Allas' fet yl, 'que su vyfs!'
'Allas' fet ele, 'qe unqe vous pris!'
'Allas' de sa, 'allas' de la —
Ou qu'il tourne, 'allas' y a!
Mes coment qu'il 'allas' en die,
140   Yl ne puet eschaper mye.
Soffryr ly covient cele peyne
Tous les jours de la symeygne.
Bien, dust estre, par resoun,
Sire e seigneur de la mesoun,
145   Mes ele velt la seignurye
Tot aver e la mestrye.
E, ov ce, le hounte sourt,
Car ele tence sovent e plourt,
E le prodhonme leve sus,
150   Si s'en va hors a le hus,
E soule la lesse covenyr,
Fere e dire soun pleysyr.
Nota   Femme, plue, fumé, e tensoun
Enchacent honme de sa mesoun.
155   De tote peynes, la plus amere
Est mort en sa manere,
Mes male femme a soun tort
Est pluz cruele qe la mort.
Car mort passe en poi de ure,
160   E femme est languor qe trop dure!
Mieux valsist par temps morir
Qe longement al col languyr.
Languir covent, verroiment,
Qe male femme a compaigne prent!
165   Pur ce, Gaweyn, fetes qe sage.

Often by the sharp goad,
120   Often cursed and beaten.
Exactly thus do we see it
Happen to the wretched married man:
If he's not always exerting himself,
Running after things inside and out,
125   His wife frequently prods him
With the goad that she's got —
It's the tongue ever ready
With curses, and too bitter!
Often he'll be contradicted,
130   Cursed, shamed, and slandered.
He'll hear her curse and argue so much
118ra]   That he won't know which way to turn!
'Alas,' says he, 'that ever I was married!'
'Alas,' says she, 'that ever I saw you!'
135   'Alas,' says he, 'that I'm alive!'
'Alas,' says she, 'that ever I took you!'
'Alas' here, 'alas' there —
Wherever he turns, there's an 'alas'!
But however much he says 'alas,'
140   He's not able at all to escape.
He must suffer that torment
Every day of the week.
Certainly, he ought to be, by rights,
Lord and master of the house,
145   But she wants entirely to have
The lordship and the mastery.
And, with this, the shame begins,
For she argues often and weeps,
And the good man gets up,
150   Then goes out by the door,
And leaves the decision to her alone,
To do and speak as she wishes.
Note   Woman, rain, smoke, and argument
Drive a man out of his house.
155   Of all torments, the most bitter
Is death in its way,
But a bad wife by her wrongdoing
Is more cruel than death.
For death passes in a little while,
160   And a wife is disease that lasts too long!
It would be better to die quickly
Than hang by the neck a long time.
He must suffer, truly,
Who takes a bad woman for a mate!
165   Therefore, Gawain, act wisely.

Gardez vous de mal mariage!"
    Quant ces trois ount parlé
E moi ensi councylé,
Je respoundy brevement,
170   "Bels seigneurs, e je consent."
Tot ensi su eschapé
Longe peyne, merci Dé!
118rb]   En le noun de le Piere e de le Fis
E de le seintz Espyritz,
175   A cui honour e gloire apent,
Sauntz fyn e sauntz comencement,
Sicome est, fust, e serra,
En le siecle qe tous jours durra.

La gagure, ou L'esquier e la chaunbrere   [art. 84]

118rb]   ¶ Une fable vueil comencer
Qe je oy l'autrer counter
De *Un esquier e une chaunbrere*,
Que comence en ytiele manere.
5   Un chevaler jadis estoit
Que une tres bele femme avoit,
Mes ele n'amoit pas soun lygnage.
De ce, ne fist ele que sage.
Son frere estoit son esquier,
10   Si ly servy de tiel mestier
Come a esquier apent.
E la dame ensement
Avoit une sue cosyne,
Qe molt estoit gente meschyne.
15   E l'esquyer la daunea,
E de molt fyn cuer la ama.
    Avynt issi par un jour,
Que l'esquier la requist d'amour,
E cele a sa dame counte
20   Coment l'esquier requist sa hounte.
    E dit la dame, "Savez bien
Qu'il vous ayme sur tote rien?"
    "Oil, certes, ma dame.
Ce me jure il par s'alme."
25   "Ore arere tost va
E ditez vostre amour ne avera
Quar vous ne poez saver
Qu'il vous ayme de cuer enter
Si il ne vous feist une rien,
30   E de ce vous asseurist bien:

Watch out for a bad marriage!"
When these three had spoken
And advised me in this manner,
I answered briefly,
170 "Good lords, I consent."
In this way I completely escaped
Long-lasting pain, thank God!
118rb] In the name of the Father and the Son
And the Holy Ghost,
175 To whom honor and glory belong,
Without end and without beginning,
Just as it is, was, and ever shall be,
In the world that will last forever.

The Wager, or The Squire and the Chambermaid [art. 84]

118rb] ¶ I want to begin an idle tale
That I heard told the other day
About *A Squire and a Chambermaid*,
Which begins in this way.
5 There was once a knight
Who had a very fair wife,
But she didn't love his lineage.
In this, she wasn't being at all wise.
His brother was his squire,
10 And he served him in such office
As is expected of a squire.
And the lady likewise
Had [in service] one of her cousins,
Who was a very refined girl.
15 And the squire courted her,
And loved her sincerely.
It happened thus one day,
That the squire asked for her love,
And she tells her lady
20 How the squire asked for her disgrace.
And the lady says, "Know you well
That he loves you above all things?"
"Yes, indeed, my lady.
He swears this to me upon his soul."
25 "Now go back quickly
And tell him he won't have your love
Because you're not able to know
Whether he loves you with his whole heart
Till he does a trivial thing for you,
30 And by this gives you proof:

Vostre cul beiser, premerement,
Si que ne sache pas la gent.
118va]   E quant avera toun cul beisé,
De toi fra sa volenté.
35   E, pus, me dirrez la verité
Quant il vous avera ce graunté."
La pucele ne s'est oblié.
A l'esquier est repeyré,
Que li dit tot son talent.
40   La pucele dit erralment
Que ele ne puet crere ne quider
Qu'il l'ayme de cuer entier.
Pur ce, si il velt s'amour aver,
S'il li covent son cul beyser,
45   E ce si privément
Qu'il ne soit aparsu de la gent,
"Quar de ce n'averez ja blame."
"Volenters," fet il, "par m'alme!
Ore tost terme me metez."
50   "Tauntost," fet ele, "si vous volez,
La sus en cel jardyn
Desouz le perer jahenyn.
Alez e ileque m'atendez.
Je y vendroi, ce sachez."
55   L'esquier avant ala,
E la pucele retorna
A sa dame si l'a countee,
Que molt ad joie demenee.
A l'esquier la envoia.
60   E a soun seigneur meismes ala
Ov bele chere, ov bel semblant.
"Sire," fet ele, "venez avaunt
Si verrez vostre frere
Beyser le cul ma chaunbrere."
65   "Certes," dit il, "je ne quid mie
Qu'il freit tiele vyleynie.
Si frez, par seint Martyn,
Ce mettroi un tonel de vyn."
La gagure ount affermee
70   E as fenestres sunt alee.
La damoisele se est venue
A l'esquier, que la salue.
118vb]   Yl leve sus les dras derer.
Pus pensout, "Si a bon mester!"
75   L'esquier, a soun voler,
De son affere ne vodra failler.
Yl sake avaunt bon bordoun,

To kiss your ass, first,
In such a way that people won't know,

118va]   And when he's kissed your ass,
He'll have from you what he wants.

35   And, then, tell me truly
When he's granted you this."
       The girl doesn't waste time.
She's gone back to the squire,
Who tells her all his will.

40   Forthwith the girl says
That she can't believe or think
That he loves her with his whole heart.
For this reason, if he wants to have her love,
It's necessary that he kiss her ass,

45   And this so secretly
That he not be seen by people,
"So you won't ever be blamed for this."
       "Gladly," he says, "upon my soul!
Now quickly give me a time."

50   "Right away," she says, "if you want,
Up there in that garden
Under the pear-jonette tree.
Go there and wait for me.
I'll come there, I promise."

55   The squire went forth,
And the girl returned
To her lady and told her about this,
Which has made the lady quite merry.
To the squire she sent her.

60   And to her lord she herself went
With glad look, with glad expression.
"Lord," she says, "come out
And you'll see your brother
Kiss my chambermaid's ass."

65   "Certainly," he says, "I don't believe
That he'd do something so crude.
If you're willing, by Saint Martin,
I'll wager a cask of wine."
       They've agreed on the wager

70   And have gone to the windows.
The young lady has come
To the squire, who greets her.

118vb]   He lifts up her gown in the back.
Then he thought, "Here's a good office!"

75   The squire, following his will,
Didn't want to fail in his business.
He draws out the sturdy staff,

      Si l'a donné enmy le coun.
      Un gros vit, long e quarré,
80   Si ly a enmy le coun doné.
      Si la ensi a ly de ces bras afferma
      Qu'ele ne poeit gwenchir, sa ne la.
         E la dame ly escria
      E hastivement a li parla
85   Ov grosse voiz e longe aleyne:
      "Gwenchez, trestresse! Gwenchez, puteyne!
      Gwenchez! Dieu te doint mal fyn!
      J'ay perdu le tonel de vyn!"
         E ly sire ly dist, en riaunt:
90   "Tien tei, leres, je te comaunt!
      Frapez la bien e vistement,
      Je te comaund, hardiement!
      De lower averez, par seint Thomas,
      Un cheval qe vaudra dis mars!
95   Ore, dame, me diez, par amour,
      Ay je gayné le wagour?
      E, dame, vous ne fetez mie qe sage
      De haier ceux qe sunt de mon lynage,
      De pus qe je tendrement
100 Aym les vos entierement."
         Le prodhome fist son frere
      Esposer cele chaunbrere,
      E pus aprés ycel jour
      La dame ama par tendrour
105 Ceux qe soun seygneur ama,
      E molt de cuer les honora.
      De *La chaunbrere e l'esquier*,
      N'est ore plus a treter.

A bok of swevenyng [art. 85]

119ra]   ¶ Her comenses a bok of swevenyng:
      That men meteth in slepyng.
      Thurth David hit yfounden ys,
      That wes prophete of gret pris
5   Tho he was in a cyte
      Of Babyloyne of gret pouste.
      The princes him bysohten alle,
      Bothe in toun ant in halle,
      That he huere swevenes aredde,
10   That huem thothte anyht in bedde;
      Ant undude huere swevenes ariht
      Thurh the Holi Gostes myht.

And gives it to her in the center of the cunt.
A big prick, long and thick,
80   He's given her in the center of the cunt.
And he's so bound her to him with his arms
That she can't turn away, this way or that.
   And the lady cried out to her
And hastily spoke to her
85   With a big voice and a long breath:
"Turn away, traitress! Turn away, whore!
Turn away! God give you a bad end!
I've lost the cask of wine!"
   And, laughing, the lord said to him:
90   "Hold on tight, rascal, I command you!
Strike her well and quickly,
I command you, heartily!
As a reward you'll have, by Saint Thomas,
A horse that'll be worth ten marks!
95   Now, lady, tell me, for love's sake,
Have I won the wager?
And, lady, you're not acting at all wisely
To hate those who are of my lineage,
Since I tenderly
100   Love yours thoroughly."
   The good man had his brother
Marry the chambermaid,
And ever since that day
The lady loved with tenderness
105   Those whom her lord loved,
And honored them sincerely.
Of *The Chambermaid and the Squire*,
There's now no more to discuss.

A Book of Dreaming   [art. 85]

119ra]   ¶ Here commences a book of dreaming:
What people encounter in sleep.
It is composed by Da[niel],
Who was a prophet of high renown
5   While he dwelled in Babylon,
A city of great dominion.
All the princes sought him out,
Both in town and in hall,
So that he might interpret their dreams,
10   What they thought at night in bed;
And he correctly unraveled their dreams
Through power of the Holy Ghost.

Mon that bryddes syth, slepynde:
 Him is toward gret wynnynge.

15 Mon that meteth of lomb ant got:
 That tokneth confort, God yt wot.

Mon that thuncheth he breketh armes:
 That ywis bytokneth harmes.

Mon that syth tren blowe ant bere:
20 *Bitokneth wynnyng ant no lere.*

Mon that styth on tre an heh:
 Gode tidynge him is neh.

Mon that syth the sky wes clere:
 Of somthing he worth yboden here.

25 Mon that syth briddes cokkynde:
 Of wraththe that is toknynge.

Mon that thuncheth him bestes dryven:
 His enimy wol with him striven.

Mon that of cartes met:
30 *Of dede mon tidyng he het.*

Mon that shet ant bowe bent:
 Of somthing he worth ysend.

Mon that met of broche ant ryng:
 That bitokneth syker thyng.

35 Mon that broche other ryng forlest:
 He bith bitreyed alre nest.

Selver seon ant gold bryht:
 That is weder cler ant lyht.

Eysil drynke ant bittre thyng:
40 *Som serewe him is comyng.*

119rb] Mon that to God doth offryng:
 Of gladnesse hit is tydyng.

Mon in albe other cloth whit:
 Of joie that is gret delit.

One who, sleeping, sees birds:
> *He will receive great reward.*

15   One who dreams of lamb and goat:
> *That betokens comfort, as God knows.*

One who thinks he breaks his arms:
> *That assuredly betokens injuries.*

One who sees trees blown and bare:
20   *That betokens gain and no loss.*

One who climbs a tree on high:
> *His good tidings are nearby.*

One who sees the sky was clear:
> *He can expect something to happen here.*

25   One who sees birds fighting:
> *That is a sign of anger.*

One who thinks himself chased by animals:
> *His enemy will fight with him.*

One who encounters carts:
30   *He summons news of someone dead.*

One who shoots and bends a bow:
> *He can expect something to be sent.*

One who encounters brooch or ring:
> *That signifies a sure thing.*

35   One who loses a brooch or ring:
> *Next of all he'll be betrayed.*

To see silver and bright gold:
> *That means clear and sunny weather.*

To drink vinegar and something bitter:
40   *Some sorrow is coming to him.*

119rb] One who gives offering to God:
> *It is a sign of gladness.*

One clothed in an alb or other white cloth:
> *That signifies great delight of joy.*

45   Armes ysen ant eke bataille:
            Hit is strif ant wrake, withoute faille.

        Thilke that hath berd gret ant long:
            He worth of power gret ant strong.

        Mon that thuncheth is berd ys shave:
50   *That bitokneth harm to have.*

        Armes habbe grete ant longe:
            That is power, Ich onderstonde.

        Armes habbe sherte ant lene:
            That is feblesse ase at ene.

55   Gerlaund whose hath ant croune:
            Forsoth him worth honour in toune.

        Mon that sith the hevene undon:
            To al the world hit is wycked won.

        Buen yshrud in gode clothe:
60   *That is sykernesse ant counfort bothe.*

        Mon that wolde erne ah he ne may:
            That is seknesse, par fay.

        Tapres make ant condle lyhte:
            That is joie, day ant nyhte.

65   Bokes rede other here reden:
            That is tidyng of god deden.

        Mon that is in lokyng:
            Deceyte him is comyng.

        With kyng speke other emperour:
70   *That is dignete ant honour.*

        Heren symphayne other harpe:
            That bitokneth wordes sharpe.

        Ye that falleth toht other tweyn:
            Thi nexte frendes shule deyn.

75   Yef thou makest houses newe:
            Joie ant blisse the shal siwe.

45   To see arms and also battle:
            It means strife and enmity, without doubt.

        He who has a beard thick and long:
            He'll gain power great and strong.

        One who thinks his beard is shaved:
50   *That signifies a harm he'll have.*

        Having arms large and long:
            That means power, I understand.

        Having arms short and lean:
            That means weakness once and for all.

55   Whoever has a garland and crown:
            Truly he'll experience public honor.

        One who sees heaven undone:
            It means cruel disaster for all the world.

        To be dressed in fine cloth:
60   *That means both security and comfort.*

        One who desires what he may not have:
            That signifies sickness, in faith.

        Making tapers and lighting candle:
            That means joy, day and night.

65   Reading books or hearing them read:
            That means hearing of good deeds.

        One who is peering in:
            Deceit is coming to him.

        Speaking with king or emperor:
70   *That means dignity and honor.*

        To hear an instrument or harp:
            That betokens sharp words.

        You who lose a tooth or two:
            Your nearest friends will die.

75   If you build new houses:
            Joy and bliss will follow you.

Yef thin hous falleth mid the wowe:
The worth harm ant eken howe.

119va] Yef thou ridest on hors whyt:
80   *That is joie ant delyt.*

Reed hors seon other ryden:
Gode tidinge that wol tiden.

On blac hors ryden other seon:
That wol luere ant tuene buen.

85   Mon that meteth himself sek ys:
Of wommon accusynge that is.

That sith himself gomeninge ant wod:
Bitokneth serewe ant no god.

With suerd other knif whose is smyte:
90   *Of tuene he shal eft ywyte.*

Mon that thuncheth he hath feir face:
Bitokneth god ant feir grace.

Mon that sith him in water cler:
Of longe lyve he worth her.

95   Blac whose sith is oune face:
Him worth blame in uche place.

Water passen cler ant stille:
Bitokneth sikernesse ant wille.

In water thikke ant trouble buen:
100   *Bytokneth bo deceyte ant tuen.*

In diches falle grete ant deope:
From blame ne shal he him kepe.

In grete water ase Temese is throwe:
Evel toward he may trowe.

105   Mon that syth gret snow ant hayl:
Hit bitokneth gret travail.

With swerd other knyf fyhte:
That is deceyte al aryhte.

If your house falls amid the flood:
> *You'll receive harm and also distress.*

119va] If you ride on a white horse:
80 .   *That means joy and delight.*

To see or ride a red horse:
> *Good news that will come about.*

To ride or see a black horse:
> *That will mean peril and destruction.*

85   One who dreams that he is sick:
> *That is about blaming women.*

He who sees himself silly and mad:
> *That signifies sorrow and no good.*

Whoever is struck with sword or knife:
90   *He will know repeated trouble.*

One who thinks he has a fair face:
> *It signifies good and fair grace.*

One who sees himself in clear water:
> *He'll have here a long life.*

95   Whoever sees his own face black:
> *He'll experience blame everywhere.*

To cross water clear and still:
> *Signifies safety and purpose.*

To be in water dark and turbulent:
100   *Signifies both deceit and harm.*

Falling into ditches large and deep:
> *He'll not keep himself from blame.*

To be thrown into water vast as the Thames:
> *He may believe that evil approaches.*

105   One who sees great snow and hail:
> *It signifies arduous effort.*

Fighting with sword or knife:
> *That means deceit very certainly.*

Lombren suen other calf:
110   *Bytokneth plente on uch half.*

Mon that sith gestes come:
         Ywayted he is to buen ynome.

Whose sith is fomon in bataille:
         Anguisse him tid withoute faille.

115   Lahtoun make ant todelve:
         Bytokneth joie of himselve.

Man yturnd into beste:
         That is wraththe ant eke cheste.

Mon that sith is hous bernynde:
119vb]   *Ful gret peryl him is comynde.*

121   Whose hym wossheth of cler water other welle:
         Of joie ant wynnyng he shal telle.

That is hed is wyt whose meteth:
         Gret byyete hit bytokneth.

125   Whose thuncheth is hed is shave:
         Strong hit is from luere him save.

Whose meteth is her is long:
         He worth of poer gret ant strong.

On whan houndes berketh fele:
130   *Is fomon him foundeth tele.*

Yef thou hast on newe shon:
         Thou shalt joie underfon.

Yef the meteth thin shon beth olde:
         In anguisse the worth yholde.

135   Yef the meteth me wossheth thin heued:
         Sunne ant peril the worth byreved.

Yef thou etest of thystles yurne:
         Thy fomon the freteth on uche hurne.

Yyf thou sist two mone:
140   *In pouste thou shalt waxe sone.*

To follow lambs or a calf:
110   *Betokens plenty on every side.*

One who sees guests arrive:
         He may expect to be captured.

Whoever sees his enemies in battle:
         Anguish will come to him without fail.

115   To make and to dig up a garden:
         Signifies joy in oneself.

One turned into beast:
         That means anger and also strife.

One who sees his house burning:
119vb]   *Extreme peril is coming to him.*

121   Whoever washes himself in clear water or well:
         He will accrue joy and reward.

Whoever dreams his head is white:
         It signifies great profit.

125   Whoever thinks his head is shaved:
         It clearly indicates he'll be saved from harm.

Whoever dreams his hair is long:
         He'll have strength great and strong.

He at whom hounds often bark:
130   *His enemies will slander him.*

If you have new shoes on:
         You will obtain joy.

If you dream your shoes are old:
         Anguish will take hold of you.

135   If you dream that someone washes your head:
         Harm and peril will be taken from you.

If you eat thistles eagerly:
         Your enemies threaten you everywhere.

If you see two moons:
140   *In power you will wax soon.*

Yef the thuncheth thou sist the mone:
Shapen of hard the worth to done.

Yef the thuncheth thou ybounden art:
Lattynge the worth strong ant smart.

145   Yef thou hast a bed of pris:
The worth a trewe wyf, ywis.

Yef thou sist the see ful cler:
The is god toward ner ant ner.

Yef the see is yn tempeste:
150   *The tid anguisse ant eke cheste.*

Whose foule sith is honde:
He is fol of sunne ant shonde.

Whose meteth him lasse ymaked:
Of is power he byth aslaked.

155   Yef thou more ant more wext:
Of god poer thou shalt buen hext.

Yef mon thuncheth that he is wedded:
120ra]   *Longe he worth seek in bedde.*

Mon that thuncheth he ded ys:
160   *Newe hous ant confort shal buen his.*

Yef thou with dede mon spext:
Muche joie the is next.

Whose thuncheth himself adreint:
Of desturbaunce he bith ateint.

165   Whose briddes nest hath yfounde:
Good shal to him abounde.

Yef thou sist thyn hauek flen:
In joie thou shalt weole ysen.

Brudale oper songes heren:
170   *Bytokneth plente to alle feren.*

Yef the thuncheth thou gest barefot:
Bytokneth serewe ant no god.

If you think you see the moon:
Your actions will be full of hardship.

If you think you are restrained:
You'll experience hindrance sharp and painful.

145   If you have an expensive bed:
You'll have a true wife, indeed.

If you see the sea be quite clear:
Good is approaching you nearer and nearer.

If the sea is in tempest:
150   *To you will come anguish and also suffering.*

Whoever sees his hand look foul:
He is full of sin and disgrace.

Whoever dreams himself made shorter:
He is decreased in his strength.

155   If you grow more and more:
You will be promised good power.

If one thinks that he is married:
120ra]   *He will be long time sick in bed.*

One who thinks he is dead:
160   *A new house and comfort shall be his.*

If you speak with a dead man:
Much joy is near you.

Whoever thinks himself drowned:
Of a disturbance he'll be convicted.

165   Whoever has found a bird's nest:
Good will abound to him.

If you see your hawk fly:
In joy you'll see good fortune.

To hear a wedding feast or songs:
170   *It betokens plenty for all mates.*

If you think you go barefoot:
It betokens sorrow and no good.

Yef the thuncheth thou takest veil:
Bitokneth joie, god, ant eyl.

175   Tren with frut whose sith:
Biyete, forsothe, that byth.

Eyr mysty whose syth:
Desturbaunce that bith.

Of bestes him hated whose sith:
180   *Luere of frend that byth.*

Cartes urne whose sith:
Wraththe of frend that byth.

Drynke eysil whose syth:
To sothe, seknesse that bith.

185   Eryen lond whose him syth:
Travail, forsothe, that bith.

Berd shave whose sith:
Muche joie that bith.

Armes other legges misturnd wose syth:
190   *Langour ant mournyng that bith.*

Croune underfonge whose syth:
Heththe ant menske that byth.

Whit heued whose syth:
Gret byyete that byth.

195   Heued shave whose syth:
Wyte him wel, deceyte that bith.

120rb]   Houndes berkynde whose syth:
Proude von the speketh with.

With houndes biset whose him syth:
200   *Tuene of enymis that bith.*

Wosshen is heued wose syth:
Of sunne ant peril tolyvred he byth.

Thistles eten whose him syth:
Evel speche of fon that byth.

If you think you take veil [become a nun]:
It betokens joy, virtue, and health.

175   Whoever sees a tree with fruit:
That means, truly, procreation.

Whoever sees foggy air:
That means disturbance.

Whoever sees beasts he hates:
180   *That means the loss of a friend.*

Whoever sees carts run:
That means a friend's wrath.

Whoever sees bitter drink:
Truly, that means sickness.

185   Whoever sees himself till land:
That means, truly, suffering.

Whoever sees a shaved beard:
That means great joy.

Whoever sees crooked arms or legs:
190   *That means illness and mourning.*

Whoever sees a seized crown:
That means health and honor.

Whoever sees a white head:
That means great profit.

195   Whoever sees a shaved head:
Take good heed, that means deceit.

120rb] Whoever sees dogs barking:
You will speak with haughty foes.

Whoever sees himself surrounded by dogs:
200   *That means adversity from enemies.*

Whoever sees his head washed:
He'll be delivered from harm and peril.

Whoever sees thistles eaten:
That signifies the evil speech of foes.

205   Hevene yleyed wose syth:
           Harm in huerte, sothliche, hit byth.

       Urne feintliche whose him sith:
           Seknesse that tokneth ant byth.

       Caroles make ant condles lyhte:
210   *That is joie ant murthe bryhte.*

       With maide wedded whose him syth:
           Anguisse on soule mon saith that byth.

       Mantel werie whose him sytht:
           Confort ant joie that byth.

215   Whose the dede speketh wyth,
       Fader other moder whose hit bith:
           Ase the Latyn seith, ywis,
           That is muche joie ant blis.

       Casten drynke other mete:
220   *That a mon hath er y-ete.*

       Other with soster have to donne,
       Other soster taken him to monne:
           That is a bytokenyng
           Of sunne ant of mournyng.

225   His teth falle whose syth:
           Luere of frend Ychot that byth.

       Wong-teth blede ant tharewith falle:
           Deth of cun we mowe calle.

       Hous falle other berne whose syth:
230   *Sclaundre ne may he wyten him wyth.*

       White hors ant rede habbe:
           God tydynge, withoute gabbe.

       Wondrynde whose hym syth:
           Mournyng that bytokneth ant byth.

235   Blake hors other falewe habbe:
           Apeyrement, Y nul nout gabbe.

205 Whoever sees heaven set on fire:
     It means, truly, heartache.

   Whoever sees himself run feebly:
     That betokens and means sickness.

   To make carols and light candles:
210   *That means joy and sparkling mirth.*

   Whoever sees himself wedded to a maiden:
     Anguish of soul they say that means.

   Whoever sees himself wear a cloak:
     That means comfort and joy.

215 Whoever speaks with the dead,
   Whether it be father or mother:
     As the Latin says, indeed,
     That means much joy and happiness.

   Throwing away drink or food:
220   *That [means] one has previously eaten.*

   One who has to do with his sister,
   Or his sister takes him physically:
     That is a sign
     Of sin and of grief.

225 Whoever sees his teeth fall out:
     I know that means loss of a friend.

   Molars bleed and then fall out:
     We must receive the death of kin.

   Whoever sees a house or barn fall down:
230   *He may not protect himself from slander.*

   Having a white and red horse:
     [Means] good tiding, without lie.

   One who sees himself traveling:
     That betokens and means mourning.

235 Having a black or bay horse:
     [Means] injury, I will not lie.

120va] Hymselve dronke whose syth,
Led drawen other swyn, therwyth:
Feblesse of body that ilke byth.

240 Galded other seek whose hym syth,
Robbed other outlawed, therwyth:
Wreynge ant gret blame that byth.

With yrne ysmite whose hym syth:
Mournyng that illke byth.

245 His face in water whose syth:
Long lyf that ilke byth.

Ys face feyr whose syth:
Joie ant menske that ilke byth.

Ys face lodlych whose syth:
250 *Bytoknyng of sunne that byth.*

Water cler whose syth:
Bytoknyng of sykernesse that byth.

Water trouble whose syth:
Wreynge, forsothe, that ylke bith.

255 Wallen suen ant of hem drynke,
Other in house walle sprynge:
Joie ant biyete that is toknynge.

Water into hous ybore whose sith:
Tocknynge of peril that byth.

260 Children bueren other habbe:
That is harm, withoute gabbe.

Joie in swevenyng whose syth:
Mournyng that tokneth ant byth.

Mon yturnd into beste:
265 *He wraththed God, atte leste.*

Uncomely to bataille gon:
That is shome of is fon.

Whose thuncheth him in prisoun:
That is chalenge ant raunsoun.

120va] Whoever sees himself drunk,
A tortured man or churl, as well:
That means feebleness of body.

240   Whoever sees himself gelded or sick,
Robbed or banished, as well:
That means denunciation and great blame.

Whoever sees himself struck by iron:
Grief will that one have.

245   Whoever sees his face in water:
Long life will that one have.

Whoever sees his face as fair:
Joy and honor will that one have.

Whoever sees his face as ugly:
250   *That is a sign of sin.*

Whoever sees clear water:
That is a token of safety.

Whoever sees troubled water:
Denunciation, truly, that one will have.

255   To see fountains and drink from them,
Or a fountain flow in a house:
That is a sign of joy and profit.

Whoever sees water seeping into a house:
That is a sign of peril.

260   To bear or have children:
That means harm, without lie.

Whoever sees joy in dreaming:
That signifies and means mourning.

One turned into a beast:
265   *He has angered God, at the least.*

To go unprepared into battle:
That means shame at the hands of his foes.

Whoever thinks he is in prison:
That means accusation and ransom.

270   Whose him thuncheth ben peint on bord:
              That is long lif, at lut word.

         The mone blody other doun falle:
              Travail ant peril me may calle.

         Himself ybounde whose may sen,
275   Other in swymmynge ben,
120vb]   Other wycchen, other weddyng:
              That is travail other gret lattyng.

         Sheren shep whose syth:
              Sothliche, harm that byth.

280   Whose wepeth in swevenyng,
         Other meteth of cussyng,
         Other palmen may ysen:
              Joie ant blisse that wol ben.

         The sonne cler whose syth:
285   *That bitokneth pes ant gryth.*

         The sonne derk whose may se:
              Peril of kynges that wol be.

         The sonne reed whose syth:
              Shedyng of blod that tokne byth.

290   Sterren of the hevene falle:
              Gret bataille that is withalle.

         Tueyn monen at eve ysen:
              Chaunge of kyng other prince that mai ben.

         Thourne whose thuncheth he syth:
295   *That beth grete wordes ant styth.*

         The erthequaque whose may sen:
              Harm to thilke stude wol ben.

         Whose geth on hontyng:
              That bytokneth purchasyng.

300   Whose thuncheth that he flyth:
              Chaunge of stude that ilke bith.

270   Whoever believes himself painted on a board:
         That means long life, to speak briefly.

     The moon bloody or else fallen down:
         One may receive effort and peril.

     Whoever may see himself restrained,
275   Or in the act of swimming,
120vb] Or bewitching, or marrying:
         That means effort or other hard hindrance.

     Whoever sees sheep being sheared:
         Truly, that means harm.

280   Whoever weeps in dreaming,
     Or dreams of kissing,
     Or may see palm leaves:
         That will mean joy and happiness.

     Whoever sees the clear sun:
285   *That signifies peace and lawful order.*

     Whoever may see the dark sun:
         That will mean danger to kings.

     Whoever sees the red sun:
         That means shedding of blood.

290   Stars falling from the heaven:
         That means great battle overall.

     To see two moons in the evening:
         That may mean a change of king or prince.

     Whoever thinks he sees a thorn:
295   *That means proud and harsh words.*

     Whoever may see an earthquake:
         That will mean injury to this place.

     Whoever goes hunting:
         That signifies acquisition.

300   Whoever thinks that he flies:
         That very dream means change of place.

Whose sith clothes bernynde:
Deceite is the bytoknynge.

Folle vesseles in house ysen:
305 *Plente that tokneth to ben.*

Whose thuncheth he God sith,
Other out that to him biliht:
That, ase suggeth this clerkes,
Bytokneth gode werkes.
310 *Somme seggeth hit is ylle,*
Ant that be at Godes wille.

Gurdel wosshen whose syth:
Choste, Ychot, that ylke byth.

121ra] Of alle swevenes that men metetht
315 Day other nytht, when hue slepetht,
No mon ne con that sothe thyng
Telle bote the hevene kyng.
He us wyte ant warde bo,
Ant ever shilde us from ur fo.

Ordre de bel ayse [art. 86]

121ra] ¶ Qui vodra a moi entendre
Oyr purra e aprendre
L'estoyre de un ordre novel
Qe mout est delitous e bel.
5 Je le vous dirroi come l'ay apris
Des freres de mon pays.
L'ordre est si foundé a droit
Qe de tous ordres un point estroit;
N'i ad ordre en cest mound
10 Dont si n'i ad ascun point.
Le noun de l'ordre vous vueil dyre
Qe um ne me pust blamer de lire —
Qy oyr velt, si se teyse! —
C'est le Ordre de Bel Eyse.
15 De l'ordre vous dirroi la sonme,
Quar en l'ordre est meint prodhonme
E meinte bele e bone dame.
En cel ordre sunt, sanz blame,
Esquiers, vadletz, e serjauntz,
20 Mes a ribaldz e a pesauntz
Est l'ordre del tot defendu.

Whoever sees burning clothes:
  Deceit is the betokening.

To see full vessels in a house:
305   *That betokens plenty.*

Whoever thinks he sees God,
Or something that brings him illumination:
  That, as these clerks say,
  Betokens good works.
310   *Some say it is an ill omen,*
  And that it is by God's will.

Whoever sees a girdle washed:
  Chaste, I believe, that same one is.

121ra] Of all the dreams that men encounter
315   Day or night, when they sleep,
No one can tell the ultimate truth
Except for heaven's king.
May he both guide and protect us,
And always shield us from our foe.

The Order of Fair Ease   [art. 86]

121ra]   ¶ He who wishes to listen to me
Will be able to hear and learn
The history of a new order
That's most delightful and fair.
5   I'll tell you about it as I learned it
From the brothers of my country.
The order is founded so properly
That from every order it draws a rule;
Nor is there an order in this world
10   From which it doesn't take some rule.
I wish to tell you the name of the order
Lest anyone blame me for speaking —
Whoever wishes to hear, now be still! —
It's the Order of Fair Ease.
15   I'll tell you the substance of the order,
For in the order are many good men
And many fair and good ladies.
In this order are, without reproach,
Squires, pages, and men-at-arms,
20   But to scoundrels and peasants
The order is strictly forbidden.

Qe ja nul ne soit resçu,
Quar il frount a l'ordre hounte.
121rb] Quant rybaud ou vyleyn mounte
25   En hautesse ou baylie,
La ou il puet aver mestrie,
N'i ad plus de mesure en eux
Qe al le luop qe devoure aigneux.
De cele gent lerroi ataunt,
30   E de le ordre dirroi avaunt.
En cel ordre dount je vous dy,
Est primes issi estably
Que ceux qe a l'ordre serrount.
De Sympringham averount
35   Un point qe bien pleysant serra.
Come l'abbeie de Sympringham a
Freres e sueres ensemble,
C'est bon ordre, come me semble.
Mes de tant ert changié, pur veyr,
40   Q'a Sympringham doit aver
Entre les freres e les sorours
(Qe desplest a plusours)
Fossés e murs de haute teyse.
Mes en cet Ordre de Bel Eyse
45   Ne doit fossé ne mur aver,
Ne nul autre destourber
Qe les freres, a lur pleysyr,
Ne pussent a lor sueres venyr,
E qu'il n'eit point de chalaunge.
50   Ja n'i avera ne lyn ne launge
Entre eux, e si le peil y a,
Ja pur ce ne remeindra.
De yleoque, est ensi purveu
Qe cil q'a l'ordre serrount rendu
55   De l'abbé deyvent bien estre,
E ce comaund nostre mestre:
Pur bien manger e a talent
Treis foiz le jour e plus sovent.
E s'il le fount pur compagnye,
121va] Le ordre pur ce ne remeindra mie.
61   De Beverleye ont un point treit
Qe serra tenu bien e dreit:
Pur beyvre bien a mangier,
E pus aprés desqu'a soper;
65   E aprés, al collacioun,
Deit chescun aver un copoun
De chandelle long desqu'al coute,
E tant come remeindra goute

May none ever be received in it,
For they'd bring shame to the order.
121rb] When a scoundrel or a peasant rises
25 To high rank or authority,
To where he can have mastery,
There's no more moderation in them
Than in the wolf who devours lambs.
Of such people I've said enough.
30 And I'll now speak further of the order.
    In this order of which I tell you,
It was first established
That those who shall be in the order
Will have from Sempringham
35 One rule that's most pleasing.
Since Sempringham Abbey allows
Brothers and sisters to be together,
It's a good order, it seems to me.
But so shall it be changed, in truth,
40 Since at Sempringham there must be
Between the brothers and sisters
(Which displeases many of them)
Ditches and walls standing high.
But in this Order of Fair Ease
45 There shall be no ditch or wall,
Nor anything else to prevent
The brothers, as they like,
From coming to the sisters,
Nor shall there be any rule against it.
50 Never shall there be linen or wool
Between them, and if there's skin,
Never shall one be hindered by that.
From there, it's also provided
That those given to the order
55 Shall be well received by the abbot,
And this our master commands:
To eat well and freely
Three times a day and more often.
And if they do it for good company,
121va] The order shall never be the less for that.
61   From Beverley they've drawn one rule
That shall be held strictly and precisely:
To drink heartily at dinner,
And then afterwards till supper;
65 And afterwards, at the collation,
Each shall have a piece
Of candle the length of a forearm,
And as long as there remains a drop

De la chandeille a arder,
70   Deivent les freres a beyvre ser!
        Un point unt tret de Hospitlers,
        Qe sunt molt corteis chevalers
        E ount robes bien avenauntz
        Longes desqu'al pié traynantz,
75   Soudlers e chausés bien seantz,
        E gros palefrois, bien amblantz.
        Si deyvent, en nostre ordre, aver
        Les freres e sueres, pur veyr.
        De chanoynes ont un point pris
80   Qu'en l'ordre ert bien assis:
        Quar chanoygnes pur grant peyne
        Mangent, en la symeygne,
        Char en le refreitour treis jours.
        Auxi, deyvent nos sorours
85   E nos freres chescun jour
        Char mangier en refreitour,
        Fors le vendredi soulement
        E le samadi ensement.
        E si issint avenist
90   Q'al samadi hoste fust
        E l'em ne ust plenté de pesshon,
        L'estor qe fust en la mesoun
        Purreint il par congié prendre.
        Ja l'ordre ne serra le meindre.
95   Un point ont tret de moyne neirs,
        Que volenters beyvent, pur veyrs,
121vb] E sount cheschun jour yvre,
        Quar ne sevent autre vivre,
        Mes il le fount pur compagnie
100   E ne mie pur glotonie.
        Auxi, est il purveu
        Que chescun frere soit enbu
        De jour en jour, tot adés,
        Devant manger e aprés.
105   E si il avenist ensi
        Qe a frere venist amy
        (Dount se deyvent ensorter
        Pur les freres solacer)
        Qui savera bien juer le seyr —
110   Ce vous di je, de veir:
        Yl dormira grant matinee,
        Desque la male fumee
        Seit de la teste issue,
        Pur grant peril de la vewe.
115   Des chanoynes seculers,

Of the candle to burn,
70   The brothers shall be set to drink!
           One rule they've drawn from the Hospitallers,
Who are most courteous knights
And have very comely robes
Trailing down to their feet,
75   Stylish shoes and boots,
And large palfreys, nicely ambling.
In our order, so also shall receive
The brothers and sisters, in truth.
           From the Canons they've taken one rule
80   That shall be well established in the order:
For the Canons in strict penance
Eat, during the week,
Meat in the refectory three days.
Likewise, shall our sisters
85   And our brothers every day
Eat meat in the refectory,
Except only Friday
And also Saturday.
And if it should happen
90   That there's a guest on Saturday
And sufficient fish is not available,
The provisions in the house
Shall with permission be used.
The order won't be any the less for it.
95   One rule they've drawn from the Black Monks,
Who gladly drink, in truth,
121vb] And are drunk every day,
For they don't know any other life,
But they do it for good company
100   And not at all for gluttony.
Likewise, it's planned
That every brother shall be inebriated
Day to day, continuously,
Before eating and afterwards.
105   And if it should so happen
(As will occur
For the brothers' pleasure)
That a brother should be visited by a friend
Who well knows how to spend the evening —
110   I say this to you, in truth:
He [the brother] shall sleep late in the morning,
Until the bad stupor
Is gone from his head,
Endangering his eyesight.
115   From the secular canons,

Qe dames servent volenters,
Ont nos mestres un point treit,
E vueillent qe cel point seit
Bien tenuz e bien useez,
120   Quar c'est le point — bien sachez —
Que pluz ad en l'ordre mester.
Pur les sueres solacer,
Si est sur eschumygement,
Comaundé molt estroitement,
125   Que chescun frere a sa sorour
Deit fere le giw d'amour
Devant matines adescement,
E aprés matines ensement.
E s'il le fet, avant son departyr,
130   Troiz foiz a soun pleysyr,
Ja le frere blame ne avera,
Ne le ordre enpeyré serra.
　　　Gris moignes sunt dure gent,
E de lur ordre, nequedent,
122ra]   Vueillent nos mestres, pur grever   [quire 14]
136   L'ordre, un des lur poyntz aver,
E si n'est geres corteis,
Quar a matines vont sanz breys!
Auxi deyvent nos freres fere,
140   Pur estre prest a lur affere.
E quant il fount nul oreysoun,
Si deyvent estre a genulloun,
Pur aver greindre devocioun
A fere lur execucioun,
145   E ov un seyn sonnent, santz plus:
C'est lur ordre e lur us.
Mes nos freres, pur doubler,
Ov deus seynz deyvent soner.
De taunt est nostre ordre dyvers
150   Qe nos sueres deyvent envers
Gysyr, e orer countre mount;
Par grant devocioun le fount.
Issi pernent en pacience
Cest point de l'ordre de cilence.
155   Charthous est bon ordre, sanz faile;
N'est nul des autres qe taunt vayle.
Pur ce, vueillent ascun point trere
De cel ordre a nostre affere.
Chescun est en sa celle enclos
160   Pur estre soul en repos.
Auxi deyvent nos freres estre:
Si doit chescun, a sa fenestre,

> Who gladly serve ladies,
> Our masters have drawn one rule,
> And wish that this rule be
> Well maintained and well employed,
120 For it's the rule — know it well —
> That has most authority in the order.
> So as to entertain the sisters,
> Thus is it ordered very strictly,
> On pain of excommunication,
125 That each brother with his sister
> Shall play the game of love
> Before matins continuously,
> And after matins as well.
> And if, before leaving, he does it
130 Three times for her pleasure,
> The brother shall never be reproached,
> Nor will the order be impaired.
>   The Gray Monks are strict men,
> And from their order, nonetheless,

122ra] Our masters wish, in order to add weight   **[quire 14]**
136 To the order, to take one of their rules,
> And it's hardly a courtly one,
> For at matins they go without breeches!
> Our brothers shall do likewise,
140 To be ready for their office.
> And when they say any prayer,
> Then they must be on their knees,
> In order to have greater devotion
> To perform their work,
145 And they ring with one bell, no more:
> That's their rule and their custom.
> But our brothers, to give double measure,
> With two bells shall ring.
> Thus is our order so distinctive
150 That our sisters shall on their backs
> Lie down, and pray facing upwards;
> Out of great devotion they do it.
> Thus they take in patience
> This rule of the silent order.
155   The Carthusians are a good order, without doubt;
> Among the others there's none so worthy.
> Because of this, they wish to draw some rule
> From this order for our office.
> Each one is shut in his cell
160 So as to be alone at rest.
> Our brothers shall be likewise:
> Thus each one shall, at his window,

De l'herber aver pur solas,
E la suere entre ces bras,
165   E estre enclos privément
Pur survenue de la gent.
    Ne devomz pas entreoblier,
Si nostre ordre deit durer,
Les frere menours, a nul fuer,
170   Qe Dieu servent de bon cuer.
Si devomz ascun point aver
De lur ordre pur mieux valer.
Lur ordre est fondé en poverté,
122rb]   Pur quei yl vont la voie apierté
175   En ciel, tot plenerement.
Si vous dirroi bien coment
Yl querent poverté totdis:
Quaunt il vont par le pays,
Al chief baroun ou chivaler,
180   Se lerrount il herberger
Ou a chief persone ou prestre,
La ou il purrount a eese estre,
Mes, par seint Piere de Roume,
Ne se herbigerount ov povre honme!
185   Taunt come plus riches serrount,
Ostiel plustost demanderount.
Ne ne deyvent nos freres fere
Ostiel en autre lyu quere
Fors la ou il sevent plenté.
190   E la deyvent en charité,
Char mangier e ce qu'il ount,
Auxi come les menours fount.
    Pus qe avomz des menours,
Auxi averomz des prechours.
195   Ne vont come les autres nuyz peez;
Eynz, vont precher tot chauceez,
E s'il avient ascune feez
Qu'il seient malades as piés,
Yl purrount, s'il ount talent,
200   Chevalcher tot plenerement
Tote la jornee entiere.
Mes tot en autre manere
Deyvent nos freres fere
Quant il prechent par la terre,
205   Car il deyvent, tot, adés,
Totdis, chevalcher loinz e pres,
E quant il fount nul sermoun,
Si deyvent estre dedenz mesoun.
E tote foiz aprés manger

Have some plants for comfort,
And his sister in his arms,
165   And be shut up privately
Lest people interrupt them.
    We must not forget,
If our order is to continue,
The Friars Minor, at any rate,
170   Who serve God with good will.
Thus we shall have some rule
From their order so as to be the more worthy.
Their order is founded on poverty,
122rb]   By which they take the open path
175   To heaven, full plainly.
And I'll tell you how
They seek after poverty every day:
When they go through the country,
They allow themselves to lodge
180   With a powerful baron or knight,
Or with a prominent parson or priest,
Where they can be made comfortable,
But, by Saint Peter of Rome,
They'll not lodge with a poor man!
185   So long as there are richer men,
The more readily will they ask for lodging.
Likewise our brothers shall not try
To seek out lodging in any place other
Than where they know there's affluence.
190   And there they shall, in charity,
Eat meat and whatever they have,
Just as the Minors do.
    Since we've borrowed from the Minors,
Likewise we'll borrow from the Preachers.
195   They don't go barefoot like the others;
Instead, they go properly shod,
And if it should happen at any time
That they have sore feet,
They may, if they desire,
200   Ride freely on horseback
All the long day.
But in an entirely different way
Shall our brothers act
When they preach across the land,
205   For they shall, absolutely, all the time,
Every day, ride far and near on horseback,
And when they deliver any sermon,
They shall be in a house.
And always after dinner

210   Deyvent il de dreit precher,
        Quar meint honme est de tiele manere
        Qu'il ad le cuer pluz dur qe piere,
        Mes quant il avera aukes bu
122va] Tost avera le ordre entendu,
215   E les cuers serront enmoistez,
        De plus leger serrount oyez,
        Qe a l'ordre se rendrount
        Quant le sermon oy averont.
            Ensi est nostre ordre foundé.
220   E si ount nos freres en pensee
        Qe chescun counté doit aver
        Un abbé qe eit poer
        A receyvre sueres e freres
        E fere e tenyr ordres pleneres.
225   E qe les pointz seient tenuz
        Qe nos mestres ount purveuz,
        Un provyncial en la terre
        Doit aler e enquere
        Pur saver qy l'ordre tendra.
230   E cely qe le enfreindra
        Serra privément chastié
        E de son mesfet reprové.
        E ceux qe serront trovez
        Qe l'ordre averount bien usez,
235   Si deyvent, pur lur humilité,
        Estre mis en digneté,
        E serrount abbés ou priours
        A tenyr l'ordre en honeurs.
        (Issi fount les Augustyns
240   Qe tant sevent de devyns.)
        Par tot enquergent pleynement
        Qy tienent l'ordre lealment.
        E ceux qe l'ordre tendrount
        Par tot loé serrount!
245   Atant fine nostre ordre,
        Q'a touz bonz ordres se acorde,
        E c'est l'Ordre de Bel Eyse.
        Qe a plusours tro bien pleyse!

Le chevaler qui fist les cons parler   [art. 87]

122vb]   ¶ Aventures e enseignement
        Fount solas molt sovent,
        E solas fet releggement —
        Ce dit Gwaryn, que ne ment.

210   They shall preach of goodness,
    For many a man is of such character
    That he's got a heart harder than stone,
    But once he's drunk a little

122va] He'll readily listen to the order,

215   And their hearts will be moist,
    However inattentively they've listened,
    So that they'll confess to the order
    When they've heard the sermon.
      Thus is our order founded.

220   And so our brothers have in mind
    That each shire shall have
    An abbot who holds the power
    To receive sisters and brothers
    And make and keep sumptuous orders.

225   And so that the rules may be kept
    As our masters have planned,
    An officer throughout the land
    Must go and inquire
    To find out who's adhered to the order.

230   And the one who violates it
    Shall be chastised privately
    And chided for his misconduct.
    And those who shall be found
    To have well observed the order,

235   Thus shall, for their humility,
    Be placed in positions of authority,
    And they shall be abbots and priors
    To maintain the order in its honors.
    (Just so behave the Augustinians,

240   Who know so much of divine things.)
    They [shall] make full inquiry everywhere
    About who holds faithfully to the order,
    And those who adhere to the order
    Shall be praised by everyone!

245   Now ends our order,
    Which accords with all good orders,
    And it is the Order of Fair Ease.
    May it be very pleasing to many!

The Knight Who Made Vaginas Talk [art. 87]

122vb]   ¶ Adventures and a lesson
    Very often bring solace,
    And solace brings refreshment —
    So says Guerin, who doesn't lie.

5　　　　E pur solas demostrer,
　　　　　Une trufle vueil comencer.
　　　　　Quant um parle de trufle e rage,
　　　　　Ne pense de autre fere damage.
　　　　　E pur ce a cet comensement,
10　　　Counteroi assez brievement
　　　　　Le counte de *Le chyvaler*
　　　　　Qe sout fere le coun parler.
　　　　　　Un chevaler estoit jadis,
　　　　　Mout vaillaunt e de grant pris,
15　　　Hardi, pruz, bel bachiler.
　　　　　De touz, se fesoit molt amer,
　　　　　Mes il ne avoit rente ne terre.
　　　　　E pur sa tres noble affere,
　　　　　Fust il fet chivaler,
20　　　E touz jours remist seuder.
　　　　　E, si, out un esquier
　　　　　Qe Huet se fesoit nomer.
　　　　　Qei, par doner e largesse,
　　　　　Anientist mout sa richesse.
25　　　Pur ce, dit um molt sovent:
　　　　　"Qe petit ad e petit prent,
　　　　　E velt despendre largement,
　　　　　Ne purra durer longement;
　　　　　E, pur ce, il fet qe sage
30　　　Qe se prent a le avauntage."
　　　　　　Issi remist un an entier
　　　　　Qu'il n'out rien qe de aprompter.
　　　　　Puis avynt, neqedent,
　　　　　Qu'il oy parler de un tornoiement.
35　　　E apela son esquier,
　　　　　E tot ice ly fet counter,
　　　　　E ly demaund consail e aye
　　　　　Si nul y sache qu'il ly die.
　　　　　　"Certes, sire, ileque aloms.
123ra]　C'est le mieux que fere purroms,
41　　　Quar ileque gaygnerez
　　　　　Par ount vos gages aquiterez."
　　　　　　Lur herneis fount appariller.
　　　　　Al tornoiement vodrount aler
45　　　Par priories e abbeyes;
　　　　　Lur covenist aler, tote veies,
　　　　　Pur ce qe petit avoient
　　　　　Qe despendre purroient,
　　　　　E ce n'est mye greindre folie
50　　　De aler ov la nees sire Elye —
　　　　　Yl n'est point tenuz tous jours pur sot

5   And in order to provide solace,
            I want to begin a trifling jest.
            When one speaks of trifles and foolery,
            He doesn't think of injuring anyone.
            And therefore with this opening,
10   I'll tell somewhat briefly
            The story of *The Knight*
            Who Knew How To Make Cunts Talk.
               There was once a knight,
            Very brave and high-ranking,
15   A bold, worthy, handsome young man.
            Among all, he made himself much loved,
            But he had neither income nor land.
            Yet because of his very noble conduct,
            He was made a knight,
20   And he lived always as a mercenary.
            And, also, he had a squire
            Who was named Huet.
            He, by gifts and generosity,
            Squandered most of his wealth.
25   Thus, it's very often said:
            "He who has little and receives little,
            And wishes to spend freely,
            Won't be able to last for long;
            And, therefore, he acts wisely
30   Who takes for his own advantage."
               Thus it lasted an entire year
            That he had nothing except by borrowing.
            Then it happened, nonetheless,
            That he heard word of a tournament.
35   And he called his squire,
            And tells him all this,
            And asks for his advice and help
            So that none there would know he'd advised him.
               "Certainly, lord, let's go there.
123ra] It's the best we can do,
41   For there you may earn
            What you need to pay your debts."
               They've had their gear made ready.
            They want to go to the tournament
45   By way of priories and abbeys;
            They needed to go [that way], in any case,
            Because they had little
            That they could spend,
            And it's not at all the greater folly
50   To go in Lord Elijah's boat —
            He's never at all taken for a fool

      Qe siet aler ov le nees Elyot!
        Ce fust en esté, quant la flour
      Verdist e doint bon odour,
55   E les oylsels sunt chauntanz
      E demenent solas graunz.
      Come il errerent en une pleyne
      Qe ert delees une fonteyne,
      Si virent un petit russhel,
60   Auke petit mes molt bel.
      Yleque virent treis damoiseles,
      Sages, cortoises, e tres beles,
      Qu'en la russhele se baynerent,
      Se desdurent e solacerent.
65   Huet les vit meintenaunt,
      E dit, "Sire, chevalchez avaunt,
      E je vous atteindroi
      A plus tost qe je purroi."
      Huet vers les damoiseles ala
70   E lur despoille enporta.
      Yl ly prierent qu'il lur rendeit
      Lur despoille, e pus parteit.
      Yl lur dit qe ce ne freit,
      Mes la despoille gardereit.
75   Yl crierent a le chevaler
      E ly prierent retorner,
      E la despoille deliverer
      Que Huet out son esquier,
123rb] E il li dorreint tiel guerdoun
80   Qe rien lur savereit si gree noun.
       La eyné dit, "Sire chivaler,
      Un doun vous vueil je doner:
      En tous lyus ou vous vendrez,
      De tous honoré serrez,
85   E molt chery e molt amez
      Taunt come ileque demorrez,
      E ceux qe vous encounterount
      De vous grant joie demerrount."
       La puisné dit erraument,
90   "Un doun te doynz je, ensement:
      Ne est dame ne damoisele —
      Ne seit ele ja si bele —
      Si sa amour desirrez
      E de vous amer la prierez,
95   Qe s'amour ne vous grantera
      E tous vos pleysirs en fra."
       Donc dit la tierce damoysele,
      Qe s'estuit en la russhele,

Who's able to go in Elijah's boat!
   This was in the summer, when flowers
Grow green and give a sweet odor,
55   And the birds are singing
And provide deep solace.
As they were traveling upon a plain
That was near a spring,
They saw a small stream,
60   Rather small yet quite pleasant.
There they saw three young ladies,
Wise, courteous, and very fair,
Who were bathing in the stream,
Enjoying and refreshing themselves.
65   Huet sees them immediately,
And says, "Lord, ride ahead,
And I'll catch up with you
As soon as I can."
Huet went toward the young ladies
70   And carried away their clothes.
They asked him to return to them
Their clothes, and then go away.
He told them that he wouldn't do this,
But would keep the clothes.
75   They cried out to the knight
And asked him to turn back,
And to bring back the clothes
That Huet his squire had taken,
123rb] And they'd give him such a reward
80   That he'd be ever thankful to them.
   The eldest says, "Sir Knight,
I wish to give you a gift:
Everywhere you go,
You'll be honored by all,
85   And deeply cherished and loved
As long as you stay there,
And those who meet you
Will be very pleased to stay with you."
   The youngest says at once,
90   "A gift I give you, likewise:
There's no woman or girl —
No matter how lovely she is —
Who, if you wish for her love
And ask her to love you,
95   Will not grant you her love
And do all your pleasure."
   Then says the third young lady,
Standing in the stream,

        "Bel sire chevaler,
100   Qe estes si cortois e si fer,
        Un doun te vueil je doner
        Dont meint se doit enmerviller:
        Je vous dorroi le poer
        De fere cul e coun parler
105   A vostre requeste, communement
        Derere e devant la gent —
        De quanque vous lur demaunderez,
        Certeyn respounz averez."
            "Damoisele, grant mercis."
110   A ceste parole, sunt partis.
        La despoille yleqe lessa,
        Congié prist, e s'en ala.
           Ne demora gueres, come errerent,
        Qe un chapeleyn ne acountrerent
115   Une jumente chevalchant,
        Qe molt suef va, portaunt.
123va] Quant yl vist le chevaler,
        Grant joie comença demener,
        Ov bel semblant le honora,
120   E a ly del tot se abaundona.
           Dit Huet, "Bon est de assaier
        De fere le coun al jumente parler."
           "Vous ditez bien! Par seint Richer,
        Je le vueil assayer!
125   Ou va tu, daun Coun? Ne le celez mie!"
           "Sire, je porte a mesoun le prestre a s'amie."
           "Ad yl amie verroiement?"
           "Oil, sire, certeignement,
        E dis marcz en s'almonere
130   Qu'il dorra a sa amie chere."
           Le prestre dit a le chevaler,
        "Merci, vous cri! Sire cher,
        Quanque j'ai vous vueil doner
        Ne me fetes si vergounder!"
135   Les dis mars ileque lessa,
        E a sa amie avant ala,
        Que molt li sout mal gré
        Pur ce qu'il out si erré.
           Le chevaler s'en ala
140   Que grant joie demena.
        Si est lee a demesure
        De si merveillouse aventure,
        E a Dieu graces rent
        Qu'il ad esploité si richement.
145   Tant ont par le pais erree

"Good Sir Knight,
100   So courteous and so brave,
       I wish to give you a gift
       That will astonish many:
       I'll give you the power
       To make asshole and cunt talk
105   At your request, both
       The person's back and front —
       Whatever you ask them about,
       You'll have a trustworthy answer."
          "Ladies, many thanks."
110   With this word, they departed.
       He left the clothes there,
       Took his leave, and went away.
          Hardly had they gone, as they traveled,
       Before they met a chaplain
115   Riding on a mare,
       Which, bearing him, ambled very softly.
123va] When he saw the knight,
       He started to greet him with joy,
       Politely honored him,
120   And gladly offered to stay with him.
          Huet says, "It's good to try
       To make the mare's cunt speak."
          "You're right! By Saint Richer,
       I wish to try it!
125   Where are you going, Master Cunt? Don't hide anything!"
          "Lord, I'm carrying the priest home to his mistress."
          "Does he truly have a mistress?"
          "Yes, lord, certainly,
       And ten marks in his alms-sack
130   That he'll give to his dear mistress."
          The priest says to the knight,
       "Mercy, I pray you! Dear lord,
       I wish to give you whatever I have
       So that you'll not bring me to disgrace!"
135   He left the ten marks there,
       And went on ahead to his mistress,
       Who was quite irritated with him
       Because he had strayed so far.
          The knight went forth
140   Showing much delight.
       He's happy beyond measure
       About so wondrous an adventure,
       And gives thanks to God
       That he's achieved so rich an exploit.
145   They've traveled through the country

Qu'il fust a poi avespree.
Si virent un chastiel bien assis,
Halt, bel, e de grant pris.
Un counte ileqe maneit —
150   Tot le pais suen esteit.
Yleque vodreint herbiger;
Pur nuit, ne poeint avant aler.
Al chastiel sunt descenduz,
Yleqe sunt molt bien reçuz.
155   Le counte quant yl les veit,
123vb]   Mout durement les honoreit,
E la countesse ensement.
Grant joie ly fyrent communement —
Esquiers, vadletz, e serjauntz,
160   Trestous petitz e grauntz.
    Quant al soper furent assis,
Richement furent servis.
Une damoisele e le chevaler
Ensemble sistrent al soper.
165   Le chevaler primes parla,
E la damoisele enresona
E la pria e requist
Qe ele amer ly velsist.
A quoi dirroi je longement?
170   Ele ly graunta soun talent,
E qe la nuit a ly vendreit
Ensemble ov li la nuit cochereit.
La damoisele ne se oblia.
A le chevaler s'en ala,
175   E come en le lit se cocherent,
Estroitement s'entreacolerent.
    Donqe dit le chivaler,
"Daun Coun, ne pus tu nient parler?"
    "Oil, mi syre, verroiement,
180   Tot a vostre comaundement."
    "Me diez si vostre dammoisele
Seit uncore pucele."
    "Nanyl, syre, certeignement!
Ele ad eu plus que cent
185   Coillouns a soun derere
Qe ount purfendu sa banere!"
    La dammoysele se tynt abay.
"Allas!" fet ele, "Qe vienke ycy!
Trop su honyé ledement
190   E engyné vylement!"
A plus tost qe ele pout,
De le chevaler eschapout.

Till it was nearly nightfall.
Then they saw a well-situated castle,
Tall, attractive, and impressive.
A count lived there —
150   All the countryside was his.
There they wished to lodge;
As it was night, they couldn't go further.
At the castle they've dismounted,
Where they are very well received.
155   When the count sees them,
123vb]   He honors them most heartily,
And the countess likewise.
Everyone together welcomed them —
Squires, valets, and servants,
160   All the small and the great.
     When they were seated at supper,
They were richly served.
A young lady and the knight
Sat together at supper.
165   The knight spoke first,
And he addressed the young lady
And asked her and requested
That she consent to love him.
What's the point of saying more?
170   She granted him his desire,
That by night she'd come to him
And lie together with him all night.
The lady didn't forget.
She went to the knight,
175   And as they lay together in bed,
They tightly embraced each other.
     Then the knight says,
"Master Cunt, can't you say anything?"
   "Yes, my lord, truly,
180   Entirely at your command."
     "Tell me if your lady
Is still a virgin."
     "Not at all, lord, certainly!
She's had more than a hundred
185   Balls at her rear
That have split her banner!"
     The young woman was abashed.
"Alas," she says, "that I've come here!
I'm wickedly disgraced
190   And vilely tricked!"
And as quickly as she could,
She escaped from the knight.

        Quant sa dame fust levee

124ra]   Lendemeyn, ly chay al pié

195   E la cria sovent mercie,

        E dit, "Dame, je su honie!

        Si vous le volez celer,

        La verité vous vueil counter."

          "Oil, certes, a mon poer,

200   Vostre priveté vueil celer."

          "Le chevaler qe vint er sa

        De ly amer me pria,

        E je ly grauntay son desduit

        E a son lit venyr la nuit.

205   Quant a son lit venuz estoie,

        Yl me acola e fist grant joie.

        E meyntenaunt — nel vueil celer —

        Fist moun coun a ly parler,

        E tiele parole mist avant

210   Dount je avoi honte grant!

        E a plus tost qe je poeyé,

        De soun lyt eschapeyé."

         "Tes!" fet la dame. "C'est folye!"

         "Certes, dame, je ne mente mye."

215   La dame jure Dampnedee

        Qe ele savera la veritee.

        Meisme le jour, aprés manger,

        La dame comença a parler,

        E dit al counte, "Sire, saunz faille,

220   Vous orrez de une grant merveille —

        Yl y ad seynz un chevaler

        Qe siet fere le coun parler."

         Ly sire dist, "Lessez ester!

        Ne le pus crere ne quider!"

225   "Certes, le chevaler qe siet la,

        Um le dit qu'il le fra."

         "Sire chevaler, dit ele verité?"

         "Oil, sire, a noun Dee.

        Parlera ele sovent,

230   Sire, a mon comaundement."

         La dame dit meyntenant,

        "Sire chevaler, venez avaunt.

124rb]   Je mettroi de moneie cent lyvres

        Qe vous ne frez mon coun sy yvres

235   Que de ly respounce ne averez

        A chose qe vous demaundrez."

         "E je mettroi mon chyval

        Qe ele respoundra, de bien e mal,

        E parlera apertement

	When her lady had risen
124ra]	On the morrow, she fell at her feet
195	And asked repeatedly for mercy,
	And says, "Lady, I'm disgraced!
	If you're willing to keep it secret,
	I want to tell you the truth."
	"Yes, certainly, as I'm able,
200	I'm willing to hide your secret."
	"The knight who came here yesterday
	Asked me to love him,
	And I granted him his delight
	And to come to his bed at night.
205	When I came to his bed,
	He embraced me and made great joy.
	And immediately — to hide nothing —
	He made my cunt talk to him,
	And such speech it put forth
210	That I had great shame!
	And as soon as I could,
	I escaped from his bed."
	"Be still!" says the lady. "That's absurd!"
	"Indeed, lady, I'm not at all lying."
215	The lady swears by the Lord God
	That she'll know the truth.
	That very day, after dinner,
	The lady began to speak,
	And says to the count, "Lord, without fail,
220	You'll hear of a great marvel —
	In this house there's a knight
	Who knows how to make cunts talk."
	The lord said, "That's impossible!
	I can't believe or think it!"
225	"Indeed, the knight who's sitting there,
	It is said that he can do it."
	"Sir Knight, is she speaking the truth?"
	"Yes, lord, in God's name.
	It will often talk,
230	Lord, at my command."
	The lady says immediately,
	"Sir Knight, come forward.
124rb]	I'll bet a hundred pounds in money
	That you won't make my cunt so drunk
235	That you'll get an answer from it
	About anything that you ask."
	"And I'll bet my horse
	That it will respond, for good or ill,
	And that it will talk openly

240 Oyauntz tous communement."
    La dame un petit suzryst.
"En ma chaunbre entroy," ce dist,
"E bien tost revendroy,
E vostre coyntise assayeroi."
245   La dame prist de cotoun
Si parempli bien le coun,
E la fist si empler
Qu'il n'y purra plus entrer.
Bien quatre lyvres de cotoun
250 La dame mist en soun coun.
Pus la sale entra
E le chyvaler demaunda
Qu'yl dust assayer
De fere soun coun parler.
255 E quaunt le chevaler fere ne le pust,
Certeignement mult ly desplust,
E se tynt engynez.
    "Syre," dit Huet, "quei pensez?
Sovyegnez vous de le cul
260 Que respoundra a vostre vueil!"
    "Cul, cul, qe fet le coun?"
    "Sire, est empli de cotoun
Que me destreint si ferement
Que je ne pus apertement
265 Une soule parole parler —
Taunt me fet encombrer!"
    Tous diseyent a un acord,
"Dame, vous ly fetez tort!"
Ov un long croke, le cotoun
270 Fyrent trere hors del coun.
    Le chevaler al coun demaunda
124va] Purquoy respounce ne ly dona.
    "Sire, je ne purroi verroiement,
Taunt fu estranglé vylement."
275   Le counte dit meintenant,
"Dame, dame, je vous comaunt:
Fetes pees al chevaler,
E pus le lessez aler."
    E la dame ensi fist.
280 E le chevaler congié prist.
Vers son pais s'en velt aler.
Assez emporte de aver.
Ore ad assez dont out mester
Pur ces gages acquiter.
285   E quaunt cest aventure fust sue,
E entre gent oye e vewe,

240   In everyone's common hearing."
           The lady smiled a little.
       "I'll go to my chamber," she said,
       "And be back very soon,
       And I shall test your cunning."
245   The lady took cotton
       And thoroughly filled up her cunt,
       And made it so full
       That no more could go in.
       A full four pounds of cotton
250   The lady put into her cunt.
       Then she entered the hall
       And ordered the knight
       That he had to try
       To make her cunt talk.
255   And when the knight couldn't do it,
       Indeed, it much displeased him,
       And he thought himself defeated.
           "Lord," says Huet, "what're you thinking?
       Remember the asshole
260   That will answer at your will!"
           "Asshole, asshole, what's the cunt doing?"
           "Lord, it's filled with cotton
       That crowds me so forcibly
       That I can't clearly
265   Say a single word —
       So much does it encumber me!"
           Everyone said with one accord,
       "Lady, you do him wrong!"
       With a long hook, they had
270   The cotton drawn out of her cunt.
           The knight asked the cunt
124va] Why it hadn't given him an answer.
           "Lord, I couldn't, truly,
       So wickedly was I choked up."
275   The count says immediately,
       "Lady, lady, I command you:
       Make peace with the knight,
       And then permit him to go."
           And so the lady did.
280   And the knight took his leave.
       Toward his country he wished to go.
       He carries a good sum of money.
       Now he's got enough of what he needs
       To pay off his debts.
285   And when this adventure was known,
       And among the people heard and seen,

Sy ly mistrent un surnoun,
E le apelerent "Chevaler de Coun,"
E son esquier Huet,
290   Le sournoun "de Culet."
Chyvaler de Coun, Huet de Culet.
Fous y est que plus y met!

Of rybauds Y ryme ant red o my rolle   [art. 88]

124va] ¶ Of rybauds Y ryme ant red o my rolle,
Of gedelynges, gromes, of Colyn ant of Colle,
Harlotes, hors-knaves, bi pate ant by polle —
To Devel Ich hem tolyvre, ant take to tolle!

124vb] The gedelynges were gedered of gonnylde gnoste,
6   Palefreiours ant pages ant boyes with boste —
Alle weren yhaht of an horse thoste!
The Devel huem afretye, rau other aroste!

The Shuppare that huem shupte, to shome he huem shadde
10   To fles ant to fleye, to tyke ant to tadde;
So seyth romauns, whose ryht radde:
"Fleh com of flore, ant lous com of ladde."

The harlotes bueth horlynges ant haunteth the plawe,
The gedelynges bueth glotouns ant drynketh er hit dawe,
15   Sathanas, huere syre, seyde on is sawe:
"Gobelyn made is gerner of gromene mawe."

The knave crommeth is crop er the cok crawe;
He momeleth ant moccheth ant marreth is mawe;
When he is al forlaped ant lad over lawe,
20   A doseyn of doggen ne myhte hyre drawe!

The rybauds aryseth er the day rewe;
He shrapeth on is shabbes ant draweth huem to dewe;
Sene is on is browe ant on is eyebrewe
125r] That he louseth a losynger ant shoyeth a shrewe!

25   Nou beth capel-claweres with shome toshrude;
Hue bosketh huem wyth botouns ase hit were a brude,
With lowe-lacede shon of an hayfre hude —
Hue pyketh of here provendre al huere prude.

Whose rykeneth with knaves huere coustage —
30   The luthernesse of the ladde, the prude of the page —

Then they gave him a surname,
Calling him "Knight of the Cunt,"
And [for] his squire Huet,
290   The surname "Little Asshole."
           Knight of the Cunt, Huet of Little Asshole.
           Foolish is he who would add more here!

Satire on the Retinues of the Great   [art. 88]

124va]   ¶ Of rascals I rhyme and recount in my roll,
           Of low rogues, grooms, of Colin and of Colle,
           Scoundrels, horse-knaves, by pate and by head —
           I deliver them to the Devil, and offer tribute!

124vb]   The bastards were assembled from cannon's spark,
6   Stable-hands and pages and boasting boys —
           All were hatched from a horse's turd!
           May the Devil devour them, raw or roasted!

           The Shaper who shaped them, shamefully he spawned them
10   From fleas and flies, mongrels and toads;
           As stories tell, whoever reads rightly:
           "Flea comes of flour, and louse comes of churl."

           The scoundrels are lechers and chase after pleasure,
           The bastards are gluttons and drink till it dawns,
15   Satan, their sire, said in his proverb:
           "Goblin set his storehouse in a groom's belly."

           The knave crams his paunch before the cock crows;
           He mumbles and munches and ruins his guts;
           When he's fully drunk and fallen over low,
20   Dogs by the dozen couldn't drag him away!

           The rascal arises before the day dawns;
           He picks at his scabs and makes them ooze;
           It's seen on his forehead and his eyebrow
125r]   That he delouses a wastrel and shoes a villain!

25   Now are horse-clawers shamefully clothed;
           They dress up with buttons as if they're bridegrooms,
           With low-laced shoes made of a heifer's hide —
           They filch all their finery from their fodder.

           Whoever settles wages with scurrilous fellows —
30   The insolence of the churl, the pride of the page —

Thah he yeve hem cattes dryt to huere companage,
Yet hym shulde arewen of the arrerage!

Whil God wes on erthe ant wondrede wyde,
Whet wes the resoun why he nolde ryde?
35   For he nolde no grom to go by ys syde,
Ne grucchyng of no gedelyng, to chaule ne to chyde!

Spedeth ou to spewen ase me doth to spelle!
The Fend ou afretie with fleis ant with felle!
Herkneth hideward, horsmen, a tidyng Ich ou telle —
40   That ye shulen hongen ant herbarewen in helle!

Mon that wol of wysdam heren   [art. 89]

125ra] ¶ Mon that wol of wysdam heren
At wyse Hendyng he may leren,
      That wes Marcolves sone,
Gode thonkes ant monie thewes
5   Forte teche fele shrewes,
      For that wes ever is wone.

Jesu Crist al folkes red,
That for us alle tholede ded
      Upon the rode-tre;
10   Lene us alle to ben wys
Ant to ende in his servys.
      Amen, par charite.
      "God biginning
      Maketh god endyng,"
15   Quoth Hendyng.

125rb] Wyt ant wysdom lurneth yerne,
Ant loke that non other werne
      To be wys ant hende,
For betere were to bue wis
20   Then forte where feh ant grys,
      Wherso mon shal ende.
      "Wyt ant wysdom
      Is god warysoun,"
            Quoth Hendyng.

25   Ne may no mon that is in londe,
For nothyng that he con fonde,
      Wonen at home ant spede
So fele thewes forte leorne

Though he give them cat droppings for their earned board,
They'd still complain about the balance due!

When God was on earth and traveled far and wide,
What was the reason he preferred not to ride?
35   Because he wanted no groom to go by his side,
Nor any knave's grumbling, to chatter and chide!

You spew as speedily as I speak insult!
May the Fiend devour you in both flesh and skin!
Listen here, stablemen, I tell you a tiding —
40   You'll surely hang and find lodgings in hell!

Hending   [art. 89]

125ra] ¶ He who wants to hear wisdom
May learn from wise Hending,
     Who was Marcolf's son,
Good principles and many morals
5   To teach many unruly children,
     For that was always his manner.

May Jesus Christ counsel all people,
Who for us all suffered death
     Upon the cross-tree;
10   Permit us all to be wise
And to die in his service.
     Amen, for charity.
"Good beginning
     Makes good ending,"
15   Says Hending.

125rb] Eagerly learn wit and wisdom,
And see that no one else be hindered
     From being wise and courteous,
For better it is to be wise
20   Than to wear fur-lined clothes,
     However one may fare.
"Wit and wisdom
     Is good treasure,"
        Says Hending.

25   Nor may anyone on earth,
No matter how hard he tries,
     Stay at home and prosper
In learning many morals

Ase he that hath ysotht yeorne

125va]   In wel fele theode.

31   *"Ase fele thede,*
            Ase fele thewes,"
                Quoth Hendyng.

        Ne bue thi child never so duere,

35   Ant hit wolle unthewes lere,
            Bet hit other whyle,
        Mote hit al habben is wille,
        Woltou nultou, hit wol spille
            Ant bicome a fule.

40   *"Luef child*
            Lore byhoveth,"
                Quoth Hendyng.

        Such lores ase thou lerest
        After that thou sist ant herest,

45   Mon in thyne youthe,
        Shule the on elde folewe,
        Bothe an eve ant amorewe,
            Ant bue the fol couthe.
        "Whose yong lerneth,

50   *Olt he ne leseth,"*
                Quoth Hendyng.

        Yef the biste a sunne don
        Ant thy thoht bue al theron,
            Yet is god to blynne,

55   For when the hete is overcome
        Ant thou have thy wyt ynome,
            Hit shal the lyke wynne.
        "Let lust overgon;
            Eft hit shal the lyke,"

60   Quoth Hendyng.

        Yef thou art of thohtes lyht,
        Ant thou falle for unmytht
            In a wycked synne,
        Loke that thou do hit so selde

65   In that sunne that thou ne elde
            That thou ne deye therinne.
        "Betere is eye sor
            Then al blynd,"
                Quoth Hendyng.

So well as he who's diligently looked

125va]   In very many places.

31   *"So many countries,*
       So many customs,"
         Says Hending.

However precious your child is,

35   Should it learn evil habits,
       Or otherwise,
If it must have all its will,
Despite your wishes, it will fail
     And become a fool.

40   *"Precious child*
       Needs instruction,"
         Says Hending.

Such wisdoms as you learn
From what you see and hear,

45   Man in your youth,
Shall follow you into old age,
Both morning and night,
     And be very well known to you.
"What one learns in youth,
     He does not lose in old age,"

50   Says Hending.

If you are about to commit a sin
And your intent is entirely set on it,
     Still it is good to refrain,

55   For when the passion is overcome
And you have recovered your wits,
     It shall win you pleasure.
"Let desire be conquered;
     In return you shall be pleased,"

60   Says Hending.

If you are weak of conviction,
And you fall on account of frailty
     Into a wicked sin,
See that you commit it so seldom

65   That you do not grow old in that sin
     Nor die therein.
"Better is eye sore
     Than all blind,"
         Says Hending.

70   Me may lere a sely fode,
        That is ever toward gode,
                With a lutel lore;
        Yef me nul him forther teche,
        Thenne is herte wol areche
75   Forte lerne more.
        "*Sely chyld*
                Is sone ylered,"
                        Quoth Hendyng.

        Yef thou wolt fleyshe-lust overcome,
80   Thou most fiht ant fle ylome
                With eye ant with huerte.
125vb] Of fleysh-lust cometh shame.
        Thath hit thunche the body game,
                Hit doth the soule smerte.
85   "*Wel fytht*
                That wel flyth,"
                        Quoth Hendyng.

        Wis mon halt is wordes ynne, ·
        For he nul no gle bygynne
90   Er he have tempred is pype.
        Sot is sot, ant that is sene,
        For he wol speke wordes grene
                Er then hue buen rype.
        "*Sottes bolt*
95   *Is sone shote*,"
                        Quoth Hendyng.

        Tel thou never thy fomon
        Shome ne teone that the is on,
                Thi care ne thy wo,
100   For he wol fonde, yef he may,
        Bothe by nyhtes ant by day,
                Of on to make two.
        "*Tel thou never thy fo*
                That thy fot aketh,"
105   Quoth Hendyng.

        Yef thou havest bred ant ale,
        Ne put thou nout al in thy male;
                Thou del it sum aboute.
        Be thou fre of thy meeles;
110   Wherso me eny mete deles,
                Gest thou nout withoute.
        "*Betere is appel y-yeve*

70   One may teach an innocent child,
        Who is ever inclined to good,
            With a bit of lore;
        If one doesn't teach him further,
        Then his heart will reach out
75   To learn more.
        "Innocent child
            Is quickly taught,"
                Says Hending.

        If you will conquer fleshly lust,
80   You must fight and flee often
            With eye and with heart.
125vb] From fleshly lust comes shame.
        Though the body thinks it a sport,
            It does afflict the soul.
85   *"Well fights*
            That well flees,"
                Says Hending.

        The wise man holds his words in,
        For he will begin no minstrelsy
90   Before he has tuned his pipe.
        A fool is a fool, and that is clear,
        For he will speak immature words
            Before they are ripe.
        "A fool's bolt
95   *Is soon shot,"*
                Says Hending.

        Never tell your enemy
        A shame or injury that you're in,
            Your care nor your distress,
100   For he will discover, if he may,
        Both by night and by day,
            How to make two from one.
        "Never tell your foe
            That your foot aches,"
105   Says Hending.

        If you have bread and ale,
        Don't put all in your pouch;
            Serve some of it about.
        Be generous with your meals;
110   Wherever one serves any food,
            You'll not go without.
        "Better is apple given

Then y-ete,"
  Quoth Hendyng.

115 Alle whyle Ich wes on erthe,
  Never lykede me my werthe
   For none wynes fylle,
  Bote myn ant myn owen won—
  Wyn ant water, stoke ant ston —
120   Al goth to my wille.
  "Este bueth
   Oune brondes,"
    Quoth Hendyng.

  Yef the lacketh mete other clotht,
125 Ne make the nout forthy to wrotht,
   Thath thou byde ant borewe,
  For he that haveth is god ploth
  Ant of worldes wele ynoh,
   Ne wot he of no sorewe.
126ra] *"Gredy is*
131   *The godles,"*
    Quoth Hendyng.

  Yef thou art riche ant wel ytold,
  Ne be thou notht tharefore to bold,
135   Ne wax thou nout to wilde,
  Ah ber the feyre in al thyng,
  Ant thou miht habbe blessyng,
   Ant be meke ant mylde.
  "When the coppe is follest,
140   *Thenne ber hire feyrest,"*
    Quoth Hendyng.

  Yef thou art an old mon,
  Tac thou the no yong wommon
   Forte be thi spouse;
145 For love thou hire ner so muche,
  Hue wol telle to the lute
   In thin oune house.
  "Moni mon syngeth
  When he hom bringeth
150   *Is yonge wyf.*
  Wyste wot he brohte
  Wepen he mohte
   Er syth his lyf,"
    Quoth Hendyng.

Than eaten,"
Says Hending.

115   All the time I was on earth,
My possessions never pleased me
    For none satisfied me,
But my things and my own ways —
Wine and water, stick and stone —
120   All goes as I wish.
"Pleasant is
   One's own hearth fire,"
    Says Hending.

If you lack food or clothing,
125   Don't be therefore too upset,
    Though you beg and borrow,
For he who has his good plow
And enough of worldly fortune,
    He knows no sorrow.
126ra] *"Greedy is*
131   *The one without goods,"*
    Says Hending.

If you are rich and highly regarded,
Don't be too proud because of that,
135   Nor become too unrestrained,
But bear yourself properly in all affairs,
And you might obtain blessing,
    And be meek and humble.
"When the cup is fullest,
140   *Then bear it most carefully,"*
    Says Hending.

If you are an old man,
Take no young woman
   To be your spouse;
145   For no matter how much you love her,
She will tell you too little truth
   In your own house.
"Many man sings
When he home brings
150   *His young wife.*
If he knew what he brought,
Weep he must
   For the rest of his life,"
    Says Hending.

155   Thah thou muche thenche, ne spek thou nout al;
       Bynd thine tonge with bonene wal.
       Let hit don synke ther hit up swal;
       Thenne mytht thou fynde frend overal.
       "Tonge breketh bon
160   *Ant nad hireselve non,"*
           Quoth Hendyng.

       Hit is mony gedelyng,
       When me him yeveth a lutel thyng,
         Waxen wol unsatht;
165   Hy telle he deth wel by me
       That me yeveth a lutel fe,
         Ant oweth me riht naht.
       "That me lutel yeveth,
         He my lyf ys on,"
170   Quoth Hendyng.

       Mon that is luef don ylle
       When the world goth after is wille,
         Sore may him drede,
       For yef hit tyde so that he falle,
175   Men shal, of is owen galle,
126rb]   Shenchen him at nede.
       "The bet the be,
         The bet the byse,"
         Quoth Hendyng.

180   Thah the wolde wel bycome
       Forte make houses roume,
         Thou most nede abyde
       Ant in a lutel house wone,
       Forte thou fele that thou mone
185   Withouten evel pryde.
       "Under boske
         Shal men weder abide,"
         Quoth Hendyng.

       Holde Ich no mon for unsele
190   Otherwhyle thah he fele
         Sumthyng that him smerte;
       For when mon is in treye ant tene,
       Thenne hereth God ys bene,
         That he byd myd herte.
195   *"When the bale is hest,*
         Thenne is the bote nest,"
         Quoth Hendyng.

155   Though you think much, don't say all;
        Bind your tongue with bony wall.
        Let it sink down where up it swelled;
        Then might you find friends overall.
        "Tongue breaks bone
160   *Though itself has none,"*
                Says Hending.

        There is many a fellow who,
        When one gives him a small amount,
                Becomes all dissatisfied;
165   They say he does well by me
        Who gives me a little fee,
                And owes me nothing at all.
        "He who gives me little
            Benefits my life,"
170   Says Hending.

        One who is prone to do evil
        When the world follows his will,
                Should be sorely afraid,
        For should it happen that he fall,
175   Men will, with his own gall,
126rb]   Serve him in his need.
        "The better off you are,
            The more you should take care,"
                Says Hending.

180   Although you would fully wish
        To make houses roomy,
                You must be patient
        And dwell in a little house,
        As you know that you must
185   Without evil pride.
        "Under bush
            One must wait out weather,"
                Says Hending.

        I maintain that no one is wretched
190   Even though he feels
                Something that pains him;
        For when one is in trouble and grief,
        Then God hears his request,
                Which he earnestly prays.
195   *"When the pain is highest,*
            Then is the remedy nighest,"
                Says Hending.

Drath thyn hond sone ageyn
Yef men the doth a wycke theyn
200   Ther thyn ahte ys lend,
So that child withdraweth is hond
From the fur ant the brond,
       That hath byfore bue brend.
"Brend child
205   *Fur dredeth,"*
           Quoth Hendyng.

Such mon have Ich land my cloth
That hath maked me fol wroth
       Er hit come ageyn;
210   Ah he that me ene serveth so,
Ant he eft bidde mo,
       He shal me fynde unfeyn.
"Selde cometh lone
       Lahynde hom,"
215   Quoth Hendyng.

Yef thou trost to borewyng,
The shal fayle mony thyng
       Loth when the ware;
Yef thou have thin oune won,
220   Thenne is thy treye overgon,
       Al wythoute care.
126va] *"Owen ys owen*
       Ant other mennes edueth,"
           Quoth Hendyng.

225   This worldes love ys a wrecche —
Whose hit here, me ne recche,
       Thah Y speke heye —
For Y se that on brother
Lutel recche of that other,
230   Be he out of ys eye.
"Fer from eye,
       Fer from herte,"
           Quoth Hendyng.

Thah, uch mon byswyke me
235   That of my god maketh him fre
       Forte gete word,
Ant himself is the meste qued
That may breke eny bred
       At ys oune bord.
240   *"Of unboht hude*

Withdraw your hand immediately
If one does to you a wicked turn
200   Where your favor is lent,
Just as a child withdraws his hand
From the fire and the brand,
    Who's been burnt before.
"Burnt child
205   *Fire dreads,"*
      Says Hending.

To such men have I lent my garb
That it made me quite angry
    Before it was returned;
210 But he who serves me so once,
If he were to ask again,
    Will find me unwilling.
"Seldom does a loan come
    Laughing home,"
215   Says Hending.

If you rely on borrowing,
Many things shall fail you
    When you least wish;
If you have your own possession,
220 Then your vexation is overcome,
    All without care.
126va] *"Own is one's own*
    And another man's shame,"
      Says Hending.

225 This world's love is a wretched thing —
Whoever hears it, I don't care,
    Though I speak sternly —
For I see that one brother
Little cares about the other,
230   When he's out of sight.
"Far from eye,
    Far from heart,"
      Says Hending.

However, each one defrauds me
235 Who helps himself to my goods
    To gain a good reputation,
While he himself is the most miserly
Ever to break bread
    At his own table.
240 *"From unbought leather*

Men kerveth brod thong,"
        Quoth Hendyng.

            Moni men seith, were he ryche,
            "Ne shulde non be me ylyche
245   To be god ant fre,"
            For when he hath oht bygeten,
            Al the fredome is foryeten
                Ant leyd under kne.
            "He is fre of hors
250   *That ner nade non,"*
                        Quoth Hendyng.

            Moni mon mid a lutel ahte
            Yeveth is dohter an unmahte,
                Ant lutel is the bette,
255   Ant myhte withoute fere,
            Wis mon yef he were,
                Wel hire have bysette.
            "Lytht chep
                Luthere yeldes,"
260   Quoth Hendyng.

            Strong ys ahte forte gete,
            Ant wicke when me hit shal lete;
                Wys mon, take thou yeme!
            Al to dere is botht that ware
126vb] That ne may, wythoute care,
266   Monnes herte queme.
            "Dere is botht the hony
                That is licked of the thorne,"
                        Quoth Hendyng.

270   Mon that munteth over flod
            Whiles that the wynd ys wod
                Abyde fayre ant stille;
            Abyd stille, yef that thou may,
            Ant thou shalt have another day
275   Weder after wille.
            "Wel abit,
                That wel may tholye,"
                        Quoth Hendyng.

            That Y telle an evel lype:
280   Mon that doth him into shype
                Whil the weder is wod —
            For be he come to the depe,

One cuts a broad thong,"
      Says Hending.

Many say that, were they rich,
"There'd be none like me
      In goodness or generosity,"
245
But when he has obtained anything,
All the generosity is forgotten
      And hidden under knee.
"*He is generous of horse*
250
      Who never had one,"
      Says Hending.

Many a man of little property
Gives his daughter a poor match,
      And little is the better,
255
Yet he might without fear,
If he were a wise man,
      Have bestowed her well.
"*Cheap bargain*
      Yields poorly,"
260
      Says Hending.

Property is arduous to acquire,
And evil when one loses it;
      Wise man, take heed!
All too dearly is bought that ware
126vb] That may not, without care,
266
      Satisfy man's heart.
"*Dearly bought is the honey*
      Licked off the thorn,"
      Says Hending.

270
One who intends to go over the sea
While the wind is turbulent
      Should wait patiently and calmly;
Wait calmly, if you can,
And you shall have another day
275
      Weather to your liking.
"*Well abides*,
      He who well may suffer,"
      Says Hending.

Thus I describe an evil leap:
280
One who boards a ship
      When the weather is wild —
Should he come into the deep,

He mai wrynge hond ant wepe,
    Ant be of drery mod.
285   *"Ofte rap*
       Reweth,"
          Quoth Hendyng.

Mihte the luther mon
Don al the wonder that he con,
290   Al the world forferde;
He fareth so doth the luther grom
That men ever beteth on
      With one smerte yerde.
"Of alle mester men,
295   *Mest me hongeth theves,"*
         Quoth Hendyng.

Wicke mon ant wicke wyf,
When hue ledeth wicke lyf,
    Ant buen in wicked synne,
300   Hue ne shule hit so wende
That hit ne shal, atte ende,
      Showe himself wythynne.
"Ever out cometh
      Evel sponne web,"
305   Quoth Hendyng.

Betere were a riche mon
Forte spouse a god womon,
    Thath hue be sumdel pore,
127ra] Then to brynge into his hous
310   A proud quene ant daungerous,
      That is sumdel hore.
"Moni mon for londe
      Wyveth to shonde,"
         Quoth Hendyng.

315   Ne leve no mon, child, ne wyf,
When he shal wende of this lyf
    Ant drawe to the dethe,
For mowe he the bones bydelve,
Ant the ahte welde hemselve,
320   Of thi soule huem ys ethe.
"Frendles
      Ys the dede,"
         Quoth Hendyng.

He may wring his hands and weep,
 And be of sorry spirit.
285 *"Often haste*
  Regrets,"
   Says Hending.

The treacherous man might
Commit all the crimes that he can,
290   Ravaging all the world;
He fares just like the worthless servant
Continually beaten up by men
  With a painful rod.
"Of all tradesmen,
295   *Thieves they hang most,"*
   Says Hending.

Wicked man and wicked woman,
When they lead wicked lives,
  And remain in wicked sin,
300 They shall fare in such a way
That it'll happen, in the end,
  They'll expose their inner selves.
"Always unravels
  The evilly spun web,"
305   Says Hending.

Better it were for a rich man
To marry a good woman,
  Though she be somewhat poor,
127ra] Than to bring into his house
310 A proud and haughty noblewoman,
  Who's something of a whore.
"Many a man for land
  Marries to his disgrace,"
   Says Hending.

315 Do not trust man, child, or woman,
When [you] shall depart from this life
  And draw toward death,
For though they may bury the bones,
And the property govern themselves,
320   Of your soul they are indifferent.
"Friendless
  Is the dead,"
   Says Hending.

The glotoun ther he fynt god ale,
325   He put so muche in ys male,
    Ne leteth he for non eye,
So longe he doth uch mon ryht,
That he wendeth hom by nyht
    Ant lyth ded by the weye.
330   *"Drynke eft lasse*
    Ant go by lyhte hom,"
      Quoth Hendyng.

Riche ant pore, yonge ant olde,
Whil ye habbeth wyt at wolde,
335   Secheth ore soule bote.
For when ye weneth alrebest
Forte have ro ant rest,
    The ax is at the rote.
"Hope of long lyf
340   *Gyleth mony god wyf,"*
      Quoth Hendyng.

Hendyng seith soth of mony thyng.
Jesu Crist, hevene kyng,
    Us to blisse brynge,
345   For his swete moder love,
That sit in hevene us above,
    Yeve us god endynge. Amen.

When man as mad a kyng of a capped man   [art. 90]

127rb]   ¶ La countesse de Donbar demanda a Thomas de Essedoune quant la guere
d'Escoce prendreit fyn, e yl la respoundy e dyt:

When man as mad a kyng of a capped man.

When mon is levere other mones thyng then is owen.

5   When Londyon ys forest, ant forest ys felde.

When hares kendles o the herston.

When Wyt ant Wille werres togedere.

When mon makes stables of kyrkes ant steles castles wyth styes.

When Rokesbourh nys no burgh, ant market is at Forwyleye.

Where the glutton finds good ale,
325   He puts so much in his belly,
     He stops for nothing.
He regales each man so long
That he travels home by night
     And lies dead by the road.
330   *"Drink again less*
     And go home by daylight,"
     Says Hending.

Rich and poor, young and old,
While you have control of your wit,
335   Seek your soul's remedy,
For when you think it's best of all
To have peace and rest,
     The ax is at the root.
"Hope of long life
340   *Beguiles many a good wife,"*
     Says Hending.

Hending speaks truth about many things.
Jesus Christ, heaven's king,
     Bring us to bliss,
345   For his sweet mother's love,
Who sits in heaven us above,
     Give us good ending. Amen.

The Prophecy of Thomas of Erceldoune [art. 90]

127rb] ¶ The Countess of Dunbar asked Thomas of Erceldoune when the Scottish war should come to an end, and he responded to her and said:

When one has made a fool's cap a king.

When one would have another's thing more than his own.

5   When London is forest, and forest is field.

When hares kindle on the hearthstone.

When Wit and Will battle each other.

When one makes stables from churches and steals castles with ladders.

When Roxburgh is no borough, and market is at Forwyleye.

10   When the alde is gan ant the newe is come, that don notht.

          When Bambourne is donged wyth dede men.

          When men ledes men in ropes to buyen ant to sellen.

          When a quarter of whaty whete is chaunged for a colt of ten markes.

          When Prude prikes, ant Pees is leyd in prisoun.

15   When a Scot ne may hym hude ase hare in forme that the Englysshe ne shal hym
          fynde. |

127va]   When Rytht ant Wrong ascenteth togedere.

          When laddes weddeth levedis.

          When Scottes flen so faste that for faute of ship hy drouneth hemselve.

20   Whenne shal this be? Nouther in thine tyme ne in myne, ah comen ant gon
          withinne twenty wynter ant on.

La destinccioun de la estature Jesu Crist Nostre Seigneur   [art. 91]

127va]   ¶ C'est la destinccioun de la estature Jesu Crist Nostre Seigneur.

          ¶ Trouvee est en auncien estoire de Rome de Jesu Crist que dit fust de la gent
          prophetes veritables, qu'il estoit menement de haut estature e voutable a regarder.
          Le volt avoit honorable, si que ceux que ly vyrent amer le poeyent e doter. Cheveus
5   avoit de la colour de menue noys, c'est a dyre, de auke rouses, desque as oreilles
          vers val crespé, auke jaunes e lusauntz, e as espaudles pendauntz. Grye né avoit a
          la gyse de Nazarenz, frount pleyn e cler, la face sauntz frounte e tecche, e colour
          auke vermail, que molt bien le enbelist. De nees ne de bouche ne avoit que
127vb]   reprendre. Barbe | avoit yl, jeovene mes a plenté, de la colour de ces chevels, ne
10   pas longe mes al mentoun fourché; simple e de meure regardure; lé oyls neyres e
          clers. En repernaunt, estoit espauntable; en amonestaunt, douz e amiable. Heyté
          estoit menement. Ascune foiz plora, unqe ne rist. La estature du cors fust dreit a
          lygne, bras e meynz deliciouz a regarder. Sa paroule estoit meure, reulé e sueve,
          e plein de resoun. A bon droit dit le prophete David: "Speciosus forma pre filiis
15   hominum" [*Psalm 44:3*]. |

10   When the old is gone and the new is come, which does nothing.

When Bannockburn is dunged with dead men.

When men lead men in ropes to buy and to sell.

When a quarter of foul wheat is exchanged for a colt worth ten marks.

When Pride gallops, and Peace is held in prison.

15   When a Scotsman can't hide himself like a hare in a burrow so that the English won't find him. |

127va]   When Right and Wrong agree with each other.

When churls wed ladies.

When Scotsmen flee so fast that for lack of ship they drown themselves.

20   When shall this be? Neither in your time nor in mine, but it shall come and go within twenty winters plus one.

Distinguishing Features of the Bodily Form of Jesus Christ Our Lord [art. 91]

127va]   ¶ These are the distinguishing features of the bodily form of Jesus Christ Our Lord.

¶ It is recorded in the ancient history of Rome regarding Jesus Christ that he was of the race of true prophets, that he was moderately tall in stature and fair in appearance. He had an honorable face, so that those who saw him were able to love

5   and revere him. He had hair the color of a walnut, that is to say, somewhat red, curling downward from the ears, somewhat yellow and gleaming, and hanging to the shoulders. He had a Greek nose in the Nazarene manner, a forehead smooth and fine, a face without wrinkle or blemish, reddish in color, which endowed him with great beauty. Neither his nose nor his mouth had anything that might be

127vb]   criticized. A beard | he had, youthful yet full, the color of his hair, not long but

10   forked at the chin; a look innocent and mature; eyes black and sparkling. When reproaching, he was fearsome; when admonishing, sweet and amiable. He was moderately happy. He cried sometimes, laughed never. His bodily stature was truly straight, arms and hands delightful to behold. His voice was mature, temperate and pleasant, and wise. Truly spoke the prophet David: "Thou art beautiful

15   beyond the sons of men" [*Psalm 44:3*]. |

Lutel wot hit any mon hou love hym haveth ybounde   [art. 92]

128r] ¶ Lutel wot hit any mon
       Hou love hym haveth ybounde,
       That for us o the rode ron
       Ant bohte us with is wounde.
5   The love of him us haveth ymaked sounde,
           Ant ycast the grimly Gost to grounde.
               Ever ant oo, nyht ant day, he haveth us in is thohte,
               He nul nout leose that he so deore bohte.

       He bohte us with is holy blod —
10   What shulde he don us more?
       He is so meoke, milde, ant good —
       He na gulte nout therfore.
           That we han ydon, Y rede, we reowen sore,
           Ant crien ever to Jesu, "Crist, thyn ore!"
15   *Ever ant oo, niht ant day, he haveth us in is thohte,*
               He nul nout leose that he so deore bohte.

       He seh his Fader so wonder wroht
       With mon, that wes yfalle;
       With herte sor he seide is oht:
20   Whe shulde abuggen alle!
           His suete Sone to hym gon clepe ant calle,
           Ant preiede he moste deye for us alle.
               Ever ant oo, nyht ant day, he haveth us in is thohte,
               He nul nout leose that he so deore bohte.

25   He brohte us alle from the deth,
       Ant dude us frendes dede.
       Suete Jesu of Nazareth,
       Thou do us hevene mede
           Upon the rode. Why nulle we taken hede?
30   His greve wounde so grimly conne blede.
               Ever ant oo, nyht ant day, he haveth us in is thohte,
               He nul nout leose that he so deore bohte.

       His deope wounden bledeth fast;
       Of hem we ohte munne.
35   He hath ous out of helle ycast,
       Ybroht us out of sunne.
           For love of us he wonges waxeth thunne;
           His hert blod he yef for al monkunne.
               Ever ant oo, nyht ant day, he haveth us in is thohte,
40   *He nul nout leose that he so deore bohte.*

The Way of Christ's Love   **[art. 92]**

128r]   ¶ Little does anyone know
         How love has bound him,
         Who bled for us on the cross
         And redeemed us with his wounds.
5   His love has made us whole,
             And cast the cruel Demon to ground.
                 Ever and always, night and day, he has us in his thought,
                 He doesn't want to lose what he so dearly bought.

         He bought us with his holy blood —
10   What more might he do for us?
         He is so meek, gentle, and good —
         He did not sin in any way.
             I advise that what we've done, we earnestly repent,
             And cry always to Jesus, "Christ, your grace!"
15   *Ever and always, night and day, he has us in his thought,*
                 He doesn't want to lose what he so dearly bought.

         He saw his Father so very angry
         At mankind, who had fallen;
         With grieved heart he made his vow:
20   We all should pay the penalty!
             His sweet Son to him did speak and make appeal,
             And pleaded that he might die for us all.
                 Ever and always, night and day, he has us in his thought,
                 He doesn't want to lose what he so dearly bought.

25   He brought us all out of death,
         And did us a friend's deed.
         Sweet Jesus of Nazareth,
         You gave us heaven's reward
             Upon the cross. Why won't we take heed?
30   His fresh wounds did bleed so terribly.
                 Ever and always, night and day, he has us in his thought,
                 He doesn't want to lose what he so dearly bought.

         His deep wounds bleed plentifully;
         Of them we ought be mindful.
35   He's delivered us out of hell,
         Brought us out of sin.
             For love of us his cheeks grow thin;
             He gave his heart's blood for all mankind.
                 Ever and always, night and day, he has us in his thought,
40   *He doesn't want to lose what he so dearly bought.*

Lutel wot hit any mon hou derne love may stonde   [art. 93]

128r]   ¶ Lutel wot hit any mon
         Hou derne love may stonde,
         Bote hit were a fre wymmon
         That muche of love had fonde.
5   The love of hire ne lesteth no wyht longe;
             Heo haveth me plyht, ant wyteth me wyth wronge.
                 Ever ant oo, for my leof, Ich am in grete thohte,
                 Y thenche on hire that Y ne seo nout ofte.

         Y wolde nemne hyre today
10   Ant Y dorste hire munne;
         Heo is that feireste may
         Of uch ende of hire kunne;
             Bote heo me love, of me heo haves sunne.
             Who is him that loveth the love that he ne may ner ywynne!
15   *Ever ant oo, for my leof, Ich am in grete thohte,*
                 Y thenche on hire that Y ne seo nout ofte.

         Adoun Y fel to hire anon
         Ant crie, "Ledy, thyn ore!
         Ledy, ha mercy of thy mon.
20   Lef thou no false lore.
             Yef thou dost, hit wol me reowe sore.
             Love dreccheth me that Y ne may lyve namore."
                 Ever ant oo, for my leof, Ich am in grete thohte,
                 Y thenche on hire that Y ne seo nout ofte.

25   Mury hit ys in hyre tour
         Wyth hatheles ant wyth heowes.
         So hit is in hyre bour,
         With gomenes ant with gleowes.
128v]   Bote heo me lovye, sore hit wol me rewe.
30   Wo is him that loveth the love that ner nul be trewe!
                 Ever ant oo, for my leof, Ich am in grete thohte,
                 Y thenche on hire that Y ne seo nout ofte.

         Fayrest fode upo loft,
         My gode luef, Y the greete
35   Ase fele sythe ant oft
         As dewes dropes beth weete,
             Ase sterres beth in welkne, ant grases sour ant suete.
             Whose loveth untrewe, his herte is selde seete.
                 Ever ant oo, for my leof, Ich am in grete thohte,
40   *Y thenche on hire that Y ne seo nout ofte.*

The Way of Woman's Love [art. 93]

128r] ¶ Little does anyone know
How secret love may last,
Unless she be a noble woman
Who's had much practice in love.
5   Her love lasts not at all long;
She's promised me, yet blames me unjustly.
    Ever and always, for my love, I am lost in thought,
    I muse on her in my mind, the one I seldom see.

I would name her today
10   If I dared mention her;
She is the fairest maiden
Of all members of her kin.
    Unless she loves me, she'll commit sin on my account.
    Woeful is he who loves the love that he may never win!
15   *Ever and always, for my love, I am lost in thought,*
    I muse on her in my mind, the one I seldom see.

Down I fell before her soon
And cried, "Lady, your grace!
Lady, have mercy on your man.
20   Believe no false tales.
    If you do, it will grieve me sorely.
    Love afflicts me such that I may live no more."
    Ever and always, for my love, I am lost in thought,
    I muse on her in my mind, the one I seldom see.

25   It is pleasing in her tower
With knights and with servants.
So too is it in her chamber,
With games and with love songs.
128v]   Unless she loves me, will it grieve me terribly.
30   Woe is he who loves the love that never will be true!
    Ever and always, for my love, I am lost in thought,
    I muse on her in my mind, the one I seldom see.

Fairest creature alive,
My good beloved, I greet you
35   As many times and as often
As dewdrops be wet,
    As stars be in the sky, and herbs be bitter and sweet.
    He who loves one untrue, his heart is seldom content.
    Ever and always, for my love, I am lost in thought,
40   *I muse on her in my mind, the one I seldom see.*

Enseignements de saint Lewis a Philip soun fitz   **[art. 94]**

128v]   ¶ Ce est le aprise que le roy Lewis de Fraunce aprist a Philip soun fitz quant il
estoit en lit mortiel a Tunes.

¶ Tres cher fiz, je te aprenk a comencement que tu aymez Dieu de tot toun cuer e
de tote ta vertue, quar saunz ce n'est salut a nully. Gardez toi de totes choses que
5   despleisent a Dieu, e de tot mortiel pecchié te garde en tiele manere que vueilletz
mieux soffryr martire que fere nul. Si Dieu te envoie ascun adverseté, pren la
debonerement, en rendant graces a Nostre Seigneur, e pensez que ele te est avenu
pur toun bien, e que tu le as bien deservi pur toun mesfet.

E si Dieu te envoie prosperité, le regraciez sovent a ly, quar ce est pur sa
10   deboneré noun pas pur vostre desert, quar tu ne dois pas Dieu corocer ne
guerrer de ces bienfetz.

Soiez confés sovent, e elisez sage confessour que, solum ton quider, te sache
aprendre ce que tu dois fere, e te sache garnyr ce que tu dois lesser. E te contien
en tiele manere que ton confessour e tes amys te osent seurement reprendre quant
15   vous meserrez. Devoutement e volentiers oiez le service Dieu e de seinte Eglise, e
gardez que ta regardure ne soit volage taunt come vous estez en la eglise. E ileque
ne parlez vileynie ne chose veyne, mes priez Dieu devoutement de bouche e de
cuer, e enforcez ta pensee a devocioun, e nomément a le houre que le cors Dieu
est sacree, c'est a dire, a le sacrement de la messe.

20   Eyez pitous cuer as cheytyfs e as povres e a tormentez, e solum ton poer eidez les
e confortez. Si tu as nul dolour au cuer, di la a toun confessour ou autre leaus e
prodhome, e quant il te avera conforté, tu le aporteras plus legerement.

Amez compagnie des bonez gentz, lequel qu'il seient religious ou seculers, e fuez
compagnie des malveis.

25   Oyez volenters prechementz en segreez e en apert, e te purchacez pardouns.

E tes preomes amez e le bien, e haiez le mal.

Ne soffrez qe um die devant toy nulle parole atrayaunt a pecchié, ne que um parle
129r]   mal | de autruy par derere.

E gardez que tu ne oyez parole ou Dieu soit moské, ne nul de sez seyntz.

The Teachings of Saint Louis to His Son Philip   [art. 94]

128v]   ¶ This is the teaching that King Louis of France taught his son Philip when he was on his deathbed in Tunis.

¶ Dearest son, I instruct you first that you ought to love God with all your heart and all your strength, for without this no one can be saved. Keep yourself from all

5   things that are displeasing to God, and keep yourself from every mortal sin in such a way that you would prefer to endure martyrdom rather than commit any. Should God send you any adversity, accept it graciously, giving thanks to Our Lord, and think that it has happened to you for your good, and that you have fully deserved it on account of your misdeeds.

And should God send you prosperity, thank him often, because it is on account of

10   his goodness and not for your merit, for you should neither anger God nor war against his kindnesses.

Confess often, and choose a wise confessor who, to the best of your knowledge, knows how to teach you what you ought to do, and knows how to warn you of what you ought to refrain from doing. And behave in such a way that your confessor and your friends will venture without fear to retrieve you when you go astray. Listen

15   devoutly and gladly to the service of God and Holy Church, and take care that your manner not be frivolous so long as you are in church. And do not speak evil or vain things there, but pray devoutly to God with mouth and heart, and direct your thought to devotion, especially at the hour when God's body is consecrated, that is to say, at the sacrament of the Mass.

20   Have a compassionate heart for the wretched and the poor and the tormented, and aid and comfort them as best you can. If you have any sorrow of heart, tell it to your confessor or to another loyal and worthy man, and when he has comforted you, you will bear it the more lightly.

Enjoy the company of good men, whether they be religious or secular, and shun the company of the wicked.

25   Listen gladly to admonitions in private and in public, and obtain pardons.

And love your worthy men and what is good, and hate what is bad.

Do not permit anyone to say in your presence any word leading to sin, nor anyone

129r]   to speak ill | of another behind his back.

And take care that you do not hear a word where God is mocked, nor any of his saints.

30   E si tu le as oy, je te comant que tu ly vengez en cely que le avera dit, e issi ren graces a Dieu des biens qu'il te ad fet que tu soiez dignes a recevoir greynures.

Vers tes sogetz te porte si dreiturelement que tu tiengez tous jours la lygne de dreiture ne enclinez a destre ne a senestre, e nepurquant tien toi auques plus vers la partie du povre que du ryche, si la que tu sachez la verité.

35   Si ascun ad querele contre toy, seiez de la sue part si la que tu sachez la verité de la querele. E par ce, avendra que vos concilers meintendrount volenters dreiture pus qu'il veient que tu le meyntegnez countre toi meymes.

Si tu vois que tu tienez ascune chose de autrui a tort, ou de tempz de tes auncestres ou de tuen, ren la acely a qy ele dust estre. E si la chose soit oscure, fetes enquere
40   la verité e pus en facez dreiture.

Soiez ententifs que tous tes sogetz soient meintenuz en dreiture e en misericorde quant tu veiez que tu la pussez fere sauntz fere tort, e nomément eiez en amour les persones de seinte Eglise e de religioun.

Je oy counter que un des consilers le roy Philip dist au roy que les clers ly fesoient
45   grantz damages en purpenant ces dreitures, e molt se merveillot qu'il le voleit soffryr. E le roy respoundy, "Bien croy, mes quant je regard les grauntz bontez que Dieu me ad fait, e le poy de bien que je ay deservy, je vueil mieux endurer damage de siecle en bienz temporals que mover esclaundre entre seinte Eglise e moy." Amez donqe les clerkes pur le amour e la reverence de Nostre Seigneur, e eiez pes
50   a seinte Eglise e a eux. Amez especialment gentz de religion e les eydez en lur bosoignes, e nomément ceux par qy Dieux est plus honoré en cest mound.

Honorez tes parentz e tien lur comaundementz en tote reverence. Benefices de seinte Eglise donez as bones gentz e as digne persones, par le counsail de prodeshonmes, e nomément a ceux que ne ount gareisoun de nul benefis.

55   Gardez que guerre ne movez sauntz grant counsail, e nomément countre cristien. E si ce comenge guerrer, gardez que ceux que coupe ne ount seient damagez en nulle manere a toun poer, e que seinte Eglise seit sauvé en tous ces dreitures. E fetez pees a plustost qe tu porras de tes guerres e de tes contenks, sicome fesoit seint Martyn.

129v]   Seiez ententifs que tu eiez leals bailifs, provotz, e ministres, | e que soient gentz de
61   bone conscience, e fetes enquere sovent coment eux si portent en lur offices. E ce cointement que vous poez fere les redresses ou mestier est de amendement. E ensi fetes de ceux de vostre hostiel.

30   And if you have heard it, I command you to avenge it against the one who has said it, and so give thanks to God for the good things that he has done for you so that you may be worthy to receive greater things.

Bear yourself toward your subjects so justly that you hold always to the rule of justice without inclining to right or left, and nonetheless always stand more toward the interest of the poor than the rich, insofar as you know the truth.

35   If anyone has a complaint against you, take his side until you know the truth of the complaint. And as a result of this, your counselors will uphold justice willingly since they see that you support it even against yourself.

If you see that you possess wrongly anything that belongs to someone else, whether from the time of your ancestors or your own, return it to him to whom it belongs.
40   And if the question is unclear, search out the truth and then do what is right.

Be attentive that all your subjects are maintained in justice and mercy when you see that you are able to do so without doing wrong, and especially hold in love the people of Holy Church and in religious orders.

I have heard tell that one of King Philip's counselors said to the king that the
45   clergy did great harm to him with regard to his rights, and that he greatly marveled that he would willingly allow this. And the king answered, "That is right, but when I look at the great favors that the Lord has done for me, and the little good that I have deserved, I prefer to endure worldly harm in temporal goods rather than provoke slander between Holy Church and myself." Love therefore the
50   clergy for the love and reverence of Our Lord, and be at peace with Holy Church and with them. Love especially men in religious orders and help them with their needs, and particularly those by whom God is most honored in this world.

Honor your parents and hold their commands in full reverence. Give the benefices of Holy Church to good men and worthy persons, following the counsel of prudent men, and especially to those who do not have the provision of any benefice.

55   Take care not to initiate war without great deliberation, particularly against Christians. And if war should begin, take care that those not at fault are not hurt in any way by your power, and that Holy Church is secure in all its rights. And make peace as soon as you can from your wars and your quarrels, as did Saint Martin.

129v]   Be mindful that you have loyal bailiffs, provosts, and ministers, | and that they be
61   men of good conscience, and make inquiry often about how they comport themselves in their duties. And do this so prudently that you are able to make redress where there is a matter to be amended. And do the same with those of your household.

65 Seiez obedient e devout a la eglise de Rome e a le apostoille come a vostre piere
espirital e come a cely que puet fere e desfere, lyer e deslyer, en cel e en terre.

Laborez a ce que pecchié e moskerie de Dieu e heresie seient hostez de vostre
roialme. Voiez que les despences de vostre hostiel seient mesurables, issi que vous
pussez vivre de vostre sauntz aprompt ou ravyne fere entre vos southmys.

70 Je vous pri que, si je muerge eynz de toy, eidez ma alme en messes e en oreisounz,
e envoiez a mesouns de religiouns e priez lur que ma alme eit part de lur bienfetz.

Je te doyn ma benesoun, e pri que tote la Trinité e touz seintz te gardent en tiele
manere que Dieu soit honoré par toy, e que tu facez ensi sa volenté, que aprés ceste
cheytive vie venoms ambedeus a ly veoir, amer, e loer sauntz fyn. Amen.

L'enqueste que le patriarche de Jerusalem fist   [art. 95]

129v] ¶ C'est l'enqueste que le patriarche de Jerusalem fist de la terre a sarazyns par le
comaundement le apostoille pur ensenser les chretiens.

¶ Saladyn e Saphadyn furent freres en la Terre Seinte e morirent.

5 Saladyn avoit un fitz apelee Foradyn. Yl tint par heritage tote la terre de Halape,
plus qe cent cités e chastels fortz.

Saphadyn out xv fitz.

Melalyn, le premer, tint aprés son piere tote la terre de Alisaundre, Kayre,
Babiloyne, Damyote, Egipte vers Ynde, e sire fut de ces freres.

10 Coradyn, le secunde fitz, tint la terre de Jerusalem e la Terre de Promission qe
chretienz ount perdu, plus que trois cent cytés e chastels.

Melchifas, le tierce fitz, tint la terre de Caine, plus qe quatre cent cités e chastels
fortz.

Melamadaim, le quart fitz, tient le reygne d'Asye e tot qe afert, qe chastels que cités
ccc e plus estre les viles.

Nota Melchifatan, le quinte fitz, tint la terre de Sarce, ou Abel fust ocis, bien a vii^c cités.

65 Be obedient and devoted to the Church of Rome and the Apostles in the same way as to your spiritual Father and the one who can make and unmake, bind and unbind, in heaven and on earth.

Work to ensure that sin and mockery of God and heresy are eliminated from your realm. See that the expenses of your household be moderate, so that you are able to live by your own means without borrowing or causing plunder among your subjects.

70 I ask you that, should I die before you, you assist my soul in masses and in prayers, and send word to the religious houses asking them that my soul share in their good works.

I give you my blessing, and pray that all the Trinity and all the saints look after you in such a way that God is honored by you, and that you act according to his will, so that after this wretched life we may both come to see, love, and praise him without end. Amen.

The Land of the Saracens [art. 95]

129v] ¶ This is the inquest that the patriarch of Jerusalem made of the land of the Saracens in accord with the Apostles' order to instruct the Christians.

¶ Saladin and Saphadin were brothers in the Holy Land and died.

5 Saladin had a son named Foradin. He holds in inheritance all the land of Aleppo, more than one hundred cities and fortified castles.

Saphadin had fifteen sons.

Melalin, the first, holds from his father all the land of Alexandria, Cairo, Babylon, Damietta, Egypt toward India, and is lord of his brothers.

10 Coradin, the second son, holds the land of Jerusalem and the Promised Land that Christians had lost, more than three hundred cities and castles.

Melchifas, the third son, holds the land of Canaan, more than four hundred cities and fortified castles.

Melamadaim, the fourth son, holds the kingdom of Asia and all that belongs to it, both castles and more than three hundred cities in addition to the towns.

Note Melchifatan, the fifth son, holds the land of Syria, where Abel was killed, fully seven hundred cities.

16 Makemet, le sisme fitz, tint tote la terre de Baldac, ou le apostoille dé sarazyns meint en la cité de Kalife. Cesti apostoille ne doit estre veu for deuz foith par an quant il va aorer Mahomet soun dieu. Yl est dé sarazyns come le apostoille de Rome des chretienz.

20 Saraphas, le septime frere, est ov soun frere eynsné e porte sa banere.

Le utisme fitz e le nefyme gardent le Sepulcre Nostre Seignour Jesu Crist, e lur office valt par an quatre myl besauntz d'or.

130r] Le disme frere e le unzyme, duzyme, e tressyme — ceux quatre ont le rente de la eawe qu'est | apelé Nyl, que aruse cheschun aust la terre de Egipte, e lur office valt 25 par an x^m besauntz.

Les deus puisné fitz gardent lur Mahomet en fertre.

Jerusalem est enmy le mounde. Vers orient est la terre de Arabye. Vers le south est la terre de Egipte. Vers le occident est la grant Mier Gregeis. Vers le north est la terre de Surie e la Mier de Cypre.

30 De Jerusalem a Acres sunt trois jornés.

A Dames, v jornés.

Dames est une bone cité e forte. La est une ymage de Nostre Dame qe fust depeint en Constantinople e est en le mount de Sardayné, e de sa mamele yst oille qe fet medicine a chescun maner enfermeté.

35 Pres de Antioche ad une gentz hautasyns qe vyvent saunz ley, quar il gisent ov lur mieres e ov lur sueres e files. Ly sire de cele terre ad un tres bel palois en un montaigne qu'est apelé Parays. La fet il norir les fitz de ces vileyns, qe jamés ne verrount honme si lur mester noun, que les fet entendre que tiele vie averount perdurable pur fere le comaundement lur seigneur. Quant chretiens entrent la 40 terre, le seigneur lur baille totels en veniment, e les premettent parays pur les ocyre.

Fenice est un grant regioun en la quele est Surs, Acres, Cete, Baruch, Sarepte, Sydoygne, Sache, Gibelete, Triple, e le mount Lyban.

Surs est le chief citee de Fenice.

45 En Baruch est une ymage de Jesu Crist crucifié, qe un Giw feri de une launce, e le sang en issist, par quele miracle tote la terre convertist a Dieu.

De le mont Lyban issint deus fluvies, Abban e Phar. Abban court a la mier ou Placidas perdi ces fitz. Phar court par Surie vers Antioche.

16   Makemet, the sixth son, holds all the land of Baghdad, where the apostle of the Saracens dwelled in the city of the Caliph. This apostle may not be seen except twice each year when he goes to worship Mahomet his god. He is to Saracens as the Apostle of Rome is to Christians.

20   Saraphas, the seventh brother, is with his eldest brother and carries his banner.

The eighth son and the ninth guard the Sepulcher of Our Lord Jesus Christ, and their office is worth 4,000 gold bezants a year.

The tenth son and the eleventh, twelfth, and thirteenth — these four have the income from the river that is | called the Nile, which each August waters the land of Egypt, and their office is worth 10,000 bezants a year.

130r]
25

The two youngest sons guard their idol Mahomet in his tomb.

Jerusalem is in the middle of the world. Toward the east is the land of Arabia. Toward the south is the land of Egypt. Toward the west is the great Greek Sea [the Mediterranean]. Toward the north is the land of Syria and the [Isle] of Cyprus.

30   From Jerusalem to Acre is three days' journey.

To Damascus, five days.

Damascus is an important and strong city. In that place is an image of Our Lady that was painted in Constantinople and is on Mount Sardenay, and from her breast flows an oil that produces medicine for every kind of infirmity.

35   Near Antioch is a very haughty people who live without law, for they lie with their mothers and with their sisters and daughters. The lord of this land has a very fine palace on a mountain that is called Paradise. In that place he raises the sons of his peasants, who will never see any man other than their master, who has them understand that they will gain that everlasting life for performing the commands

40   of their lord. When Christians enter the land, the lord hands them all over to them on arrival, and promises them paradise for killing them.

Phoenicia is a large region in which are found Tyre, Acre, Safita, Beirut, Sarepta, Sidon, Nablus, Yibna, Tripoli, and Mount Lebanon.

Tyre is the capital city of Phoenicia.

45   In Beirut is an image of Jesus Christ crucified, which a Jew struck with a lance, and blood flows from it, by which miracle all the land converted to God.

From Mount Lebanon flow two rivers, the Abban and the Phar. The Abban flows to the sea where Placidas lost his sons. The Phar flows through Syria toward Antioch.

50   En cele terre sunt deus fluvies, Jor e Dan, qe se assemblent juste le mont Sibboe e est donqe apelé Jordan. La le roy Saul fust ocys e Jesu baptizé. Trois lues de Jerico ceste fluvie devise la terre de Jerusalem e de Galylé e de Ydumee.

De Antioche a Acres sunt xij jornés par terre, e iiij par myer.

De Acres a Nazareth ad vj lues.

55   A mont Tabor, vynt lues; al mont Cayphas, iiij lius; a le chastel peregrin, vij lyus; a Japhet, xij lyus.

A Ascaloyne, vij lyus.

De Jerusalem a le flum, ix lyus.

A Bedlehem, iij lyus.

A Damas, v jornés.

60   Gadres est une cité sur la mer pres de Ascaloyne, ou Sampson le fort enporta les portes.

De Jerusalem al mont Synay, ou gist seinte Katerine, sunt xij jornees. La terre parent est deserte e poy de eawe.

130v]   De une part est la Rouge Mer, | la ou Moises passa ov lé Hebreus e le roy Pharaon
65   fust neyé. Aprés est Arabie e pus Egipte.

Egipte est une terre molt chaude quar poy y pluet. La court le avantdite eawe de Nyl, que norist molt des peisshouns, mes poi sunt bons. La sont cocatris e autres verms.

70   Nyl comence a crestre enmy joyn desqe enmy septembre. E quant ele est destrue, si seme un tote maneres blees, e les sient en mars.

La ou Nil chet en la mer est Damiote, la cité que chief est de paynyme e de pors vers chretiens.

Cele cité est enclos de xxx grantz tours e xl toreles. Enmy le eawe est un grant tour qe garde les entrees e les issues par trois grosse cheynes.

75   De Damiote a le mont Synay ad xij jornés.

50   In this land are two rivers, the Jor and the Dan, which join together near Mount Gelboe and are therefore called the Jordan. In that place King Saul was killed and Jesus baptized. Three leagues from Jericho this river separates the land of Jerusalem from both Galilee and Idumea.

From Antioch to Acre is twelve days' journey by land and four by sea.

From Acre to Nazareth is six leagues.

55   To Mount Tabor, twenty leagues; to Mount Haifa, four leagues; to the Pilgrims' Castle, seven leagues; to Jaffa, twelve leagues.

To Ascalon, seven leagues.

From Jerusalem to the river, nine leagues.

To Bethlehem, three leagues.

To Damascus, five days' journey.

60   Gaza is a city on the sea near Ascalon, where Samson the strong brought down the gates.

From Jerusalem to Mount Sinai, where Saint Catherine lies buried, is twelve days' journey. The land in between is uninhabited and lacking in water.

130v]
65   On one side is the Red Sea, | where Moses crossed with the Hebrews and King Pharaoh was drowned. Beyond is Arabia and then Egypt.

Egypt is a very hot land where it rains little. The aforesaid water of the Nile flows there, which nourishes many fish, but few are good. In that place are crocodiles and other reptiles.

70   The Nile begins to rise from mid-June to mid-September. And when it has receded, all kinds of grains are sowed, and they are harvested in March.

In that place where the Nile flows into the sea is Damietta, the city that is the capital of the pagan lands and the port for Christians.

This city is enclosed by thirty large towers and forty turrets. In the middle of the bay is a large tower that guards the entries and the exits by means of three thick chains.

75   From Damietta to Mount Sinai is twelve days' journey.

De Damiote a Attanise, un autre port, ad un jorné, e ces deus portz plus desturbent chretiens qe tot le remenaunt de paynyme.

De Damiote a la novele Babiloyne ad iiij journés, e pus a Kayre une lue. E la hauntent tote manere des gentz, e chescun tient sa ley.

80   La est un arbre que porte la baume q'est resçu en vessels de veer e pus est purgé demi an en fient de collonbes. Verroi balme n'est pas en cele terre si cele noun.

Pres de Kayre ad une fonteyne ou Nostre Dame soleit laver les draps son fitz quant ele fust demoraunt en Egipte. La est un palmer que porte dates, qe se abeissa e dona fruit a le petit enfaunt Jesu. Puis un sarazyn le coupa, e lendemeyn fust trovee
85   redressé. E uncore honurent cel lu.

Trois Babiloynes sunt: le grant Babiloyne sur le flum de Cobar ou regna Nabugodonosor; un autre en Egipte ou fust le roy Pharaon. E ces deus sunt destrutes. En la novele Babiloyne en Egipte reygne le Soudan dé sarazyns.

De yleqe a Alysaundre sunt trois jornés par terre e vj par mier.

90   Alisaundre est une riche cité, mes yl n'y a point de eawe fresshe si par condut noun. La habitent plusours chretienz que rendent truage par an al Soudan.

La fust seint Matheu le Ewangeliste martirize pur la parole Dieu, e gist en fertre.

Les berbitz e chievres de cele terre founissent deu foyth par an. |

Les armes des roys   [art. 96]

131r]   ¶ C'est la conisaunce de les armes des roys.

¶ Le Roy de Jerusalem porte l'escu d'asure ov crois e crucifix d'or.

¶ Roy d'Espaygne porte escu quartroné de goules e d'argent ov deus chastiels d'or e deus lyouns de sable.

5   ¶ Roy de Fraunce porte l'escu d'asure poudré ov flur de lyls d'or.

¶ Roy d'Alemaigne porte escu d'or ov un egle de sable.

¶ Roy d'Engleterre porte escu de goules ov trois leopardz d'or.

From Damietta to Tennis, another port, is a day's journey, and these two ports distress Christians more than all other pagan lands.

From Damietta to the new Babylon is four days' journey, and then to Cairo one league. And all manner of people dwell there, and each follows its own law.

80   In that place is a tree that bears the balm that is gathered in vessels of glass and then is refined for half a year in the dung of doves. There is no true balm in this land if not this one.

Near Cairo is a fountain where Our Lady used to wash her son's clothes when she was living in Egypt. In that place is a palm tree that bears dates, which lowered
85   itself and gave fruit to the little baby Jesus. Then a Saracen cut it down, and the next day it was found standing again. And they still honor this place.

There are three Babylons: the great Babylon on the Khabur River where Nabuchodnosor reigned; another in Egypt where King Pharaoh was. And these two are destroyed. In the new Babylon in Egypt reigns the Sultan of the Saracens.

From there to Alexandria is three days' journey by land and six by sea.

90   Alexandria is a rich city, but there is fresh water only by means of aqueduct. In that place live many Christians who pay tribute each year to the Sultan.

In that place Saint Matthew the Evangelist was martyred for the sake of God's word, and he lies in a tomb.

The sheep and goats of this land produce twice a year. |

Heraldic Arms of Kings   [art. 96]

131r]   ¶ Here are the emblems on the kings' arms.

¶ The King of Jerusalem carries the blue shield with a cross and gold crucifix.

¶ King of Spain carries a shield quartered in red and silver with two gold castles and two sable lions.

5   ¶ King of France carries the blue shield decorated with gold fleur-de-lys.

¶ King of Germany carries a gold shield with a sable eagle.

¶ King of England carries a red shield with three gold leopards.

¶ Roy de Navarre porte escu de goules ov deus cercles d'or e translaté de corner a autre d'or, un saphyr en my lyw.

10 ¶ Roy de Cicile: come le Roy de Fraunce ov vns espece de goules e d'argent.

¶ Roy de Ermenye: l'escu d'asure ov trois corounes d'or.

¶ Roy de Denemarche: escu de goules ov un leon raunpant d'or portant une hasche d'or.

¶ Roy de Erminak: escu quartroné de goules e d'asure ov vj oysels e ij egles de or.

15 ¶ Roy d'Escoce: escu d'or ov deus cercles poudrés ov flur de lyls e ov un leoun de goules.

¶ Roy d'Aragoun: escu palee de goules e d'or .s. vj.

¶ Roy de Tharse: escu de goules ov treis testes de leouns d'or.

¶ Roy de Cypre: escu de goules ov un crois d'or, le pé grece.

20 ¶ Roy de Hungrie: escu de goules ov treis leverers d'argent.

¶ Roy de Portigal: escu d'or ov treis papejays de vert, les pés de goules.

¶ Roy de Constantyn: escu d'or ov treis foils de vigne de vert, ov un cheveroun de goules poudré ov roses d'argent.

¶ Roy de Norweye: escu de goules ov un nef d'or.

25 ¶ Roy de Gres: escu d'asure ov treis dees d'argent, les poyntz vi, v, iiij.

¶ Roy de Mailogris: escu de goules ov treis testes de cerf d'or.

¶ Roy d'Orkeneye: escu d'or ov un cabal de goules.

¶ Roy de Man: escu d'asure ov iij jaunbes armez e jointz ensemble en my lyw d'argent esperonez a or.

30 ¶ Roy de Gryfonye: escu de goules ov un griffoun d'or.

¶ Roy de Hasteney: escu de goules ov un chastiel d'or.

¶ Roy de Ostrice: escu d'asure ov un leverer d'or. |

¶ King of Navarre carries a red shield with two gold rings and traversed from one corner to the other with gold, a sapphire in the middle.

10   ¶ King of Sicily: like the king of France with a design in red and silver.

¶ King of Armenia: the blue shield with three gold crowns.

¶ King of Denmark: red shield with a gold lion rampant carrying a gold battleaxe.

¶ King of Armagnac: shield quartered in red and blue with six birds and two gold eagles.

15   ¶ King of Scotland: gold shield with two rings decorated with fleur-de-lys and a red lion.

¶ King of Aragon: shield striped in red and gold .s. six.

¶ King of Tars: red shield with three gold lion heads.

¶ King of Cyprus: red shield with a gold cross, Greek-footed.

20   ¶ King of Hungary: red shield with three silver hounds.

¶ King of Portugal: gold shield with three green parrots, red-footed.

¶ King of Constantinople: gold shield with three green vine leaves, with a red chevron decorated with silver roses.

¶ King of Norway: red shield with a gold ship.

25   ¶ King of Greece: blue shield with three silver dice, the points six, five, four.

¶ King of Mallorca: red shield with three gold deer heads.

¶ King of Orkeney: gold shield with a red horse.

¶ King of [the Isle of] Man: blue shield with three silver legs armored and joined together in the middle by a gold spur.

30   ¶ King of Griffony: red shield with a gold griffon.

¶ King of Estonia: red shield with a gold castle.

¶ King of Austria: blue shield with a gold hound. |

Scriptum quod peregrini deferunt   [art. 97]

131v]   ¶ Scriptum quod peregrini deferunt ab Ecclesia Sancti Salvatoris in Asturiis.

¶ Dilectissimi fratres in Christo, qui Deum in celis atque in terra omnia quecunque vult posse non dubitatis, manifesta vobis relatione et firma veritate intimamus que, vos audientes, ortamur ut fide vera et plena credatis: quod Deus omnipotens,
5   mirabili potencia et secreto suo consilio, archam de lignis inputribilibus ab apostolorum dicipulis factam sive fabricatam, innumeris Dei magnalibus plenam. Ab urbe Ierosolimitana transtulit in Affricam, ab Affrica in Cartaginem, a Cartagine in Yspalym, ab Yspali in Tholetum, a Tholeto in Asturias ad Ecclesiam Sancti Salvatoris, loco qui dicitur Ovetum. Que archa ibidem aperta exstuit. In qua,
10   aperientes plures invenerunt arcellas aureas, argenteas, et eboreas. Quas aperire cum Dei timore ac reverencia presumentes viderunt oculis in eisdem subscripta Dei, magnalia contineri appositis scriptis, per se quie predicta manifestissime declarabant.

Invenerunt siquidem cristallinam ampullam cum cruore Domini fuso, videlicet,
15   de latere illius ymaginis quam quidem fideles ad similitudinem Christi fecerunt quam perfidi Iudei, antiqua perfidia obstinati, ligno affixerunt, et lancea ut veri vivi Christi latus percusserunt. Ex qua ad fidem passionis Christi astruendam exiuit sanguis et aqua. De vera cruce Domini maximam partem; de sepulcro Domini; partem spinee corone; de sindone Domini; de sudario Domini; de tunica
20   Domini; de pannis in quibus Dominus iacuit in presepio involutus; de pane quo saciavit Dominus quinque milia hominum; de pane cene Domini; de manna qua pluit Dominus filiis Israel; de terra montis Oliveti ubi Dominus ascensurus in celum pedes tenuit; de terra ubi pedes tenuit quando Lazarum suscitavit; de sepulcro ipsius Lazari; de lacte matris Domini; de capillis et vestimentis eius;
25   pallium quod dedit ipsa regina celi Yldefonti tunc archiepiscopo Tholotane sedis; de pallio Elye; manus sancti Stephani prothomartiris; sandale dextrum beati Petri apostoli; frons beati Iohannis Baptiste et de capillis eius; de ossibus Innocencium et de articulis digitorum; de ossibus trium puerorum Ananye, Azarie, et Mysaelis; de capillis cum quibus Maria Magdalena tersit pedes Domini;
30   de lapide cum quo signatum est sepulcrum Domini; de oliva quam Dominus tenuit in festo ramis palmarum; de petra montis Synay supra quam Moyses ieiunavit; de virga cum qua divisit Moyses Mare Rubrum filiis Israel; partem piscis assi et favum mellis; multa preterea corpora sanctorum; ossa prophetarum; multa etiam aliorum sanctorum, martirum, confessorum, et virginum. Diversa ibi
35   pignora in capsis aureis, argenteis, et eboreis, tenentur recondita, quorum numerum sola Dei sciencia colligit. Extra ipsam archam habentur corpora sanctorum martirum Eulogii et Lucricie et beate Eulalie; emeritensis sancti Pelagii,

Letter for Pilgrims on the Relics at Oviedo [art. 97]

131v] ¶ A text that pilgrims bring from the Church of the Holy Savior in Asturias.

¶ Most beloved brothers in Christ, who do not doubt that God can accomplish everything whatsoever he wishes in heaven and on earth, we confide in you with a clear report and firm truth things with which we encourage you, as you listen, that you believe with full and true faith: that all-powerful God, according to his marvel-

5 ous power and secret resolution, moved an ark made or crafted of incorruptible wood by the disciples of the Apostles, filled with countless wondrous objects of God. He moved it from the city of Jerusalem to Africa, from Africa to Carthage, from Carthage to Seville, from Seville to Toledo, from Toledo to Asturias to the Church of the Holy Savior, in a place that is called Oviedo. There the ark was opened. In

10 it, the people opening it found many little gold, silver, and ivory arks. Those who with fear and reverence of God presumed to open these little arks saw with their own eyes that in them were contained the wondrous objects of God, signed with writings attached to them, which declared very clearly the aforementioned things.

Indeed, they found an ampule of crystal with the gore that poured forth from the

15 Lord, which is to say, from the side of that image which, in fact, the faithful made in the likeness of Christ and which treacherous Jews, persevering in their ancient treachery, affixed to wood, the side of which they struck with a lance as if it had been that of the true living Christ. From this image came forth blood and water to add to the faithful recreation of the Passion of Christ. They found a very great part of the Lord's true cross; [part] of the Lord's tomb; part of the crown of thorns; of

20 the Lord's muslin; of the Lord's shroud; of the Lord's tunic; of the swaddling clothes in which the Lord lay wrapped in the manger; of the bread with which the Lord satisfied five thousand people; of the bread of the Lord's last supper; of the manna that the Lord rained down for the sons of Israel; of earth from Mount Olive where the Lord set his feet as he was about to ascend to heaven; of earth where he set his feet when he brought back Lazarus; of the tomb of Lazarus himself; of the

25 milk of the Lord's mother; of his hair and clothing; the mantle that the queen of heaven herself gave to Ildephonsus then when he was archbishop of the see of Toledo; of the mantle of Elijah; the hand of the first martyr Saint Stephen; the right sandal of the blessed apostle Peter; the forehead of the blessed John the Baptist and some of his hair; some of the bones and finger joints of the Innocents; some of the bones of the three boys Ananias, Azarias, and Misael; some of the hair

30 with which Mary Magdalen washed the Lord's feet; some of the stone with which the Lord's tomb was sealed; some of the olive that the Lord held on the festival with palm branches; some of the rock of Mount Sinai upon which Moses fasted; some of the rod with which Moses parted the Red Sea for the sons of Israel; part of the roast fish and honeycomb; plus many bodies of saints; bones of prophets; many too of other saints, martyrs, confessors, and virgins. Various tokens are hidden away there

35 in gold, silver, and ivory casks, the number of which only the wisdom of God grasps. In addition to the ark itself, there are held there the bodies of the sainted martyrs Eulogius and Lucretia and blessed Eulalia; of the early Saint Pelagius,

132r]   martiris; sancti Vincencii, martiris, atque | Alberis; et sancti Serani, episcopi, et
          sancti Iuliani, pontificis, qui predicam archam a Domino benedicam a Tholeto
40   Ovetum transtulit; et corpus regis Costi, qui Ecclesiam Sancti Salvatoris fundavit;
          et corpus sancte Florentine, virginis. Crux etiam ibi monstratur opere angelico
          fabricata spectabili modo; sporte apostolorum Petri et Andree; lignum cuiusdam
          trabis deficientis ad edificium eiusdem ecclesie quod Deus mirabiliter augmentavit.
          In ipsa autem, principali ecclesia habetur una de sex ydriis in quibus Dominus in
45   nupciis aquam convertit in vinum. Quisquis autem, divina inspiratione vocatus tam
          preciosa ac gloriosa sanctorum insignia visitare meruerit, auctoritate Dei et
          beatorum apostulorum Petri et Pauli et a Romana ecclesia. Ipsi ecclesie vel eidem
          Ecclesie Sancti Salvatoris auctoritate Dei vel hac auctoritate concessa, sciat sibi ab
          episcopo eiusdem sedis et a ministris eiusdem terciam partem iuncte sibi
50   penitencie condonari sive dimitti, et se in confraternitatem eiusdem ecclesie recipi,
          ita ut vir et femina faciat singulas missas celebrare singulis annis vite sue pro
          defunctis confraribus Ovetenensis ecclesie. Et, in obitu suo, mittat pro se oblationem
          quam voluerit. Et tunc sui confratres debita pro eo persolvent officia, etc.

Legenda de sancto Etfrido, presbitero de Leoministria   [art. 98]

132r]   Incipit legenda de sancto Etfrido, presbitero de Leoministria.

          I. Erat Merwaldus rex Merciorum, paganismo deditus, quando sanctus presbiter
          Etfridus, vir doctrina clarus et vita magnificus, ad eum convertendum venit a
          Norhthimbrorum partibus. Celesti oraculo premonitus — ut, autem, fertur
5   divinum ipse susceperat oraculum — ut in terra Mercio loco Reodesmouht vocato
          pergeret, ibique, verbum Dei predicans, regem et eius gentem paganos ad
          christianismum converteret. Segregatus, itaque sacerdos Etfridus, tanquam alter
          apostolus, in opus predicationis viam arripuit, ignorans regem et locum quo
          pergere iussus fuit. Celitus ei via precipitur, et celitus ad locum usque perducitur.
10   Demum ergo locum attigit, et sol occasum adiit, nocte dies obducitur. Tecto
          carens, novus hospes clyno nocte tegitur, ubi, vero, ne desolaretur ambiguo
          proventu sue peregrinationis, divinitus visitatur presagio regie conversionis.

132r]   martyr; of saint Vincent, martyr, and | Alvaro; and of Saint Seranus, bishop, and
         of Saint Julian, pontiff, who moved the aforesaid ark that had been blessed by the
40   Lord from Toledo to Oviedo; and the body of King Costus, who founded the
         Church of the Holy Savior; and the body of Saint Florentina, virgin. Also on
         display there is a cross handcrafted by the work of angels in remarkable fashion;
         the baskets of the apostles Peter and Andrew; the wood of a certain beam that was
         insufficient for the construction of the same church, which God miraculously
45   enlarged. What's more, in the main church is kept one of the six jugs in which the
         Lord converted water into wine at the wedding. Moreover, whoever is summoned by
         divine inspiration to visit such precious and glorious trophies of the saints will gain
         merit by the authority of God and of the blessed apostles Peter and Paul and by the
         Roman Church. By the authority of God, or by this authority granted to the Church
         itself or to the Church of the Holy Savior, let him know that a third part of the
50   penance imposed on him is pardoned or remitted by the bishop of the same see and
         by its ministers, and that he is received into the confraternity of the same church
         in such a way that a man and a woman may have celebrated every single mass for
         every single year of their life for the dead confreres of the church of Oviedo. And,
         upon his decease, may the person have sent on his behalf an offering as he willed.
         And then his confreres will perform offices for him as contracted, and so forth.

The Legend of Saint Etfrid, Priest of Leominster   [art. 98]

132r]   Here begins the legend of Saint Etfrid, priest of Leominster.

         I. Merewald was king of the Mercians, devoted to paganism, when the saintly priest
         Etfrid, a man renowned for his learning and splendid in his life, came from the
         regions of the Northumbrians to convert him. He had been forewarned by a heavenly
5   oracle — as it is reported, moreover, he himself received the divine oracle — that he
         should go into the land of the Mercians to the place called Redesmouth, and that
         there, preaching the word of God, he should convert the pagan king and his people
         to Christianity. And so the priest Etfrid, having separated himself, undertook his
         route toward the work of preaching, like another apostle, not knowing the king and
         the place where he had been bidden to go. The route is commanded to him by hea-
10   ven, and by heaven he is conducted to the place. Therefore at last he reached the
         place, and the sun approached setting, day is swallowed by night. Lacking shelter, the
         new guest is sheltered by descending night, in which, truly, so that he should not be
         forsaken in the uncertain progress of his pilgrimage, he is visited by a heaven-sent
         omen of the king's conversion.

II. ¶ Cum enim assedisset cenulam sub vesperta noctis — prius Deo debitis solutis laudibus et noctis — adest leo inmanissimus, iubis per collum crispantibus. Cui visio, vir sanctus ut deifer intrepidus nullatinus cessit, set tanquam celesti misso fractum de pane suo porrexit. | Porrectum autem ipse, iam non leo set mansuetior agno, ritu blando suscepit, susceptum ante pedes porrigentis se provoluens, ut mansuetus commedit. Quid multa? Leo pastus disparuit, vir autem sanctus in loco pernoctavit. Sol redit ad superos, dies fulsit aurea. De loco surgit vir, predicus advena, cernit queque loci confinia, devenit ubi rex quesitus manebat et eius familia ad hospitandum. Sibi domus eligitur, et a quodam regis milite suscipitur.

III. ¶ Subsequenti autem nocte rex vidit sompnium. Quod mane facto suis prolatum solvere sibi, poterat nemo suorum. Regi tandem suggerit memoratus miles de suscepto eius hospite, velut suus pincerna Pharaoni de Iosep sompniorum coniectore. "Domine mi rex," inquit, "iubeat excellentia tua tibi virum quemdam presentari, quem meum nocte transacta pro hospite sub tecto recepi. Cuius mores a nostris videntur alieni. Qui nisi fallor, cultor est fidei christiane. Diis, nanque, nostris detrahit et calumpniatur, nobis eorum ob cultum mortis eterne supplicium promittit et minatur. Qui fortassis si domini mei regis sompnium audierit, non falsus ut arbitror interpres eius erit." Rex ad militem, "Accersiatur huc," inquit, "ocius talis hospes tuus."

IIII. ¶ Accersito Christi legato coram rege, rex sompnium ita cepit edicere: "Nox preterita dum me sompno datum in stratu tenebat, videbar michi videre duos canes teterrimos et inmanes me per iugulum arripere. E regione, vero, personam quamdam venerabili facie, tonsa per aures in coronam cesarie. Michi presidio adesse et de canum dentibus aurea cum clave quam in manu ferebat me potenter eruere. Quo set mihi, hinc terreat me tanta canum inmanitas et eorum in me grassabunda rapacitas, inde foveat tam festina ab eis ereptio et iocunda ereptoris mei visio. Set quia nescio quid portenti habeat tam tetra bestia tam insolens et effera, quid auspicii tam grata persona, ereptrix mea, tam decens et clavigera. Utrobique, mens mea redditur soli ritu."

V. ¶ Rex desierat loqui. Subinfert assecla Christi: "Rex, gratulare tue visioni, famulatur enim tue perpetue saluti. Quid, ergo, portentat sic canum in te grassantium et te iugulare violentium tam horrenda species, quid auspicetur clavigere persone, liberatricis tue, tam iocunda facies, rex, accipe et intellige. Teterrimi canes et inmanes sunt fulliginosi Plutonis satellites, vite et salutis tue mortiferi hostes, quorum tu faucibus in predam et devorationem daberis.

II. ¶ For when he had sat down to a little meal at the evening time of the night — beforehand he had rendered the praises due to God at night — a most monstrous

15   lion is near, its mane standing on end along its neck. When he had seen it, the saintly man as a fearless missionary yielded not a bit, but held out a piece of his

132v]   bread as if to a heavenly emissary. | The lion, not now a lion but gentler than a lamb, took meekly what was held out, and stretching itself out at the feet of the man offering the bread, it ate the bread offered as if it were tame. What need is there to elaborate? After being fed, the lion vanished, but the saintly man spent the night in the place. The sun returned to the heavens, and the day shone bright gold. The

20   aforesaid man, the new arrival, arose from his place, saw all the boundaries of the place, and arrived where the king he was seeking and his retinue were staying. A house is selected for his lodging, and he is taken in by a certain knight of the king.

III. ¶ Moreover, on the next night the king saw a dream. When it had been made known to his men after morning came, none of them was able to analyze it for him. Finally the knight, reminded of the guest he has taken in, makes a suggestion to the king, just as his butler did to Pharoah about Joseph the dream interpreter.

25   "Lord my king," he says, "may your excellency command that a certain man be presented to you, whom I took in as my guest last night under my roof. His customs seem different from ours. Unless I am mistaken, he is a devotee of the Christian faith. In fact, he utters detractions and slanders against our gods, and promises and threatens the torment of eternal death upon us for worshiping them. Perhaps if he

30   hears of the dream of my lord king, he will not be a mistaken interpreter." The king says to the knight, "Let this guest of yours be summoned here quickly."

IV. ¶ When Christ's emissary had been summoned into the king's presence, the king began in this way to make known his dream: "As last night held me given over to sleep on my bed, I seemed to myself to see two most hideous and monstrous dogs grab me by the throat. Face to face I seemed to see present as a protector to me a certain person with a venerable face, his hair cut in a crown over the ears. And I seemed to see him rip me powerfully out of the dogs' teeth with a golden key that he carried in his hand. In this way it happens to me that on the one side such monstrous dogs and their violent rapacity against me frighten me, on the other so rapid a deliverance from them and so pleasant a sight of my deliverer encourage me. But I do not know what significance so hideous, insolent, and savage a beast

40   holds, what promise so welcome a person, my deliverer, and so decent a key-bearer. And either way, my mind is restored in the usual way."

V. ¶ The king ceased speaking. Christ's follower replies: "King, give thanks for your vision, for it serves your everlasting salvation. King, learn and understand, therefore, what meaning there is in the so very frightful appearance of the dogs threatening violence against you and wanting to tear your throat, what omen the

45   very pleasant face of the key-bearing person, your liberator, holds. The most hideous and monstrous dogs are the soot-black henchmen of Pluto, the deadly enemies of your life and well-being, into whose jaws you will be given as prey to be devoured.

Ubi devoratur semper devorandus eris, ut sic usque moriens et nunquam morte
finiens, perpetuis terroribus, sulphureis fetoribus, dentium stridoribus, ignium
50   ardoribus, penis inmanibus et intollorabilibus, cum ipsis in tartari medio crucieris,
nisi funditus abnegaveris paganismum, et ex toto te corde converteris ad Christum,
Dei vivi Filium. |

133r]   VI. ¶ "Reverendus ille claviger, cuius potencia liberaris, sicut tibi videtur, de beluis
tam efferis et voracibus, ianitor est principis regni celestis et in terra Christi
55   Salvatoris mundi vicarius. Clavis enim aurea celestis est potentia qua quicquid ipse
ligat ligatur, quicquid liberat liberatur. Cui, tu domum edificabis in regno tuo ad
agendas laudes et gratias die noctuque Regi superno. In quem in corde credens,
quem ore confitens, cuius quoque baptismi vestem induens, vite gentilis
demoniacos abdicaveris ritus, et idolatrie prophanos abiuraveris cultus, ut superni
60   regni sedibus merearis fieri ydoneus. Cuius regni frequens et beata leticia,
delectatus que mortis est nescia. Cuius, tu felix et perhennis heres eris, cum
liberatus de canum dentibus fueris per susceptionem sancte fidei, beati Petri,
liberatoris tui, qui confessione Christi, Filii Dei vivi, claves meruit et principatum
paradisi."

65   VII. ¶ Viis et multimodis rudimentis fidei, sacer heros regi Christum preconatur,
Christo regem conformari preconando conatur. Quibus diligenter auditis, rex ait
ad interpretem sue salutis, "Quicquid tua me christiana docuerit eruditio, mea
paratur suscipere devota subiectio quatinus evadere queam tam horribilis bellue
rictus." Preventus itaque rex superna clemencia sua queque destruit, et pessumdat
70   ydola, deponit regni insignia, septrum, purpuram, et diadema. Cinere conspersus,
cilicio induitur, dolet, ingemit, et totus in penitentia compungitur. Sancti pedibus
advoluitur, paganismum abiurat, cultum Dei profitetur, sacro fonte renascitur,
Christicola sanctus efficitur prompte devocionis ad omnia quibus eum cathezizat
suus ewangelista.

Anno   VIII. ¶ Iam, vero, lustra bis sena (lx) sexies (vi^c) vicena peregerat cursus Dominice
Domine incarnationis quando Merwaldus rex Merciorum a sancto presbitero Etfrido
vi^{c}lx   baptizatur. Ecce, rex, hactenus ut leo prefiguratus leone superius memorato,
iam non ferox ut leo set mitior agno, erroris sui de luco se reum fatendo prodiit,
et veritatis fidem vite panem ab eius conviva fidei, scilicet, et vite dogmatista,
80   percepit. Ubi, vero, regis conversio per leonem, ut dictum est (viro Dei divinitus
presagitur locus), fundationi domus regio liberatori regni, celestis ianitori,
eligitur. Unde, locus ipse postea vertitur in Leonis monasterium. Domus autem
fundata faleratur, rebus et opibus regiis opulenter ditatur. Cui beatus Edfridus,
cuius doctrina vere lucis gratia primo refulsit in plaga Merciorum hesperia.

50 You will be devoured where devouring is forever, so that thus even dying and never finishing with death, you will be tormented in the middle of hell by everlasting terrors, sulfurous stenches, gnashing of teeth, heats of fires, monstrous and unbearable tortures, unless you renounce paganism entirely and convert whole-heartedly to Christ, Son of the living God. |

133r] VI. ¶ "That venerable key-bearer, by whose power you are freed, as it seems to you, from such wild and voracious beasts, is the doorkeeper of the prince of the heaven-ly realm and the representative on earth of Christ Savior of the world.

55 The golden key is, in fact, the heavenly power by which whatever he binds is bound, whatever he frees is freed. For him, you will construct a house in your kingdom to give praise and thanks day and night to the celestial king. Believing in him in your heart, acknowledging him in your mouth, and donning also the garment of his baptism, you will renounce the demonic customs of pagan life, and you will forswear the profane practices of idolatry, so that you may deserve to become

60 suitable for the seats of the heavenly realm. The joy of his realm is continuous and blessed, a delight that knows no death. Of this, you will be a blessed and perpetual heir, when you have been freed from the dogs' teeth by taking the saintly faith of your liberator, blessed Peter, who merited the keys and chieftainship of paradise through his profession of Christ, Son of the living God."

65 VII. ¶ Through the ways and manifold elements of the faith, the sacred hero makes Christ known to the king, and in making him known he tries to have the king conform to Christ. After hearing these matters, the king says to the mediator of his salvation, "Whatever your Christian learning will teach me, with my pious submission I am ready to receive so that I may be able to escape the open maw of so frightful a beast." And so the king, won over by heavenly mercy, destroys all his

70 possessions, brings to ruin idols, sets aside the trappings of his rule, the scepter, royal purple, and diadem. Strewn with ashes, he dons sackcloth, grieves, moans, and entirely penitent shows remorse. He throws himself at the feet of the saint, forswears paganism, professes the worship of God, is reborn in the sacred font, is rendered a Christ-worshiping saint of ready devotion to all things in which his evangelist catechizes him.

Year of the Lord 660 VIII. ¶ Now, indeed, 660 years had passed since the Lord's incarnation when King Merewald of the Mercians is baptized by the saintly priest Etfrid. Behold, the king, up to now prefigured as a lion on account of the lion recalled above, now not ferocious as a lion but meeker than a lamb, confessed himself guilty of his sin and came forth from the slime, and received the faith of truth and bread of life from

80 his guest, which is to say, his instructor in faith and life. In fact, where the conver-sion of the king through a lion is foreshown divinely to the man of God, a place is chosen for the foundation of a house for the royal liberator, doorkeeper of heaven. For that reason, the place is afterward turned into the Monastery of the Lion. The house that is founded is adorned, made opulently rich with royal things and wealth. To it belongs blessed Etfrid, whose teaching shone first with the grace of the true

85 Cuius ibi digne pro meritis est recolenda celebris et felix memoria. Cui honor et
gloria in seculorum secula. Amen. |

Quy chescun jour de bon cuer cest oreisoun dirra   [art. 99]

133v] ¶ Quy chescun jour de bon cuer cest oreisoun dirra remissioun de ces pecchiés
avera, ne de mal mort morra, mes bon fyn avera.

Sy ascun bon chemyn aler volez, cest oreysoun le jour dirrez, e ja en voye desturbé
ne serrez mes pees en chemyn averez. E devaunt chescun ou vous vendrez. Honour,
5 amour, e grace troverez.

Si vous estes en mer travylé de tempeste, pernez un hanap pleyn de ewe de la mer
e dites cest oreysoun outre le ewe. E pus la gittez en la mer, e la tempeste cessera.

E quy en bataille vodra aler die cest oreysoun outre la ceynture de son espé, e pus
se ceynte de ce, e le myeux ly avendra. Ne ocys ne playe mortel avera.

10 Ditez ces oreysoun outre ewe coraunte, e donez a boire a ceux que sount
enfantesmé, e eux devendront seynz.

E a chescune foiz e en chescun lu, al comencement diez la Pater Nostre e Ave
Maria.

E qy cest oreysoun dirra sages devendra e l'eritage Dieu a dreyn recevera. Nul siet
15 la grant vertu que cet oreysoun ad as creauntz for Dieu soul.

In nomine Patris et Filii et Spiritus Sancti. Amen.

Ditez ces trois salmes devant le oreysoun: "Deus misereatur nostri" [*Psalm 66*], "De
profundis" [*Psalm 129*], "Voce mea ad Dominum clamavi" [*Psalm 141*].

Domine Deus, omnipotens Pater, Filius, et Spiritus Sanctus, da mihi, n[omine],
20 famulo tuo, per virtutem sancte crucis victoriam contra omnes et super omnes
inimicos meos ut non possint mihi resistere nec contradicere; set dirigatur
virtus, potestas, et consilium eorum in bonum. Set tu, Deus, sis fortitudo mea,
clipeus defensorius, et turris inexpungnabilis quatinus dispergentur et
confundantur omnes adversarii mei. Deus Habraham, Deus Ysaac, et Deus
25 Iacob, Deus omnium bene vivencium, libera me, n[omine], famulum tuum, de
omnibus peccatis et angustiis meis, de necessitatibus et angustiis sine periculis. Et
da mihi sermonem rectum et bene sonantem in os meum, ut placita sint verba mea

85   light in the western zone of the Mercians. His renowned and joyous memory is there cherished on account of his merits. To him may there be honor and glory forever and ever. Amen. |

Prayer for Protection [art. 99]

133v]   ¶ One who says this prayer with good heart each day will have remission for his sins, will not die a bad death, but will have a good end.

If you wish to have a good journey, say this prayer on that day, and you will not be disturbed in your passage but will have peace in your journey. And in the presence
5   of each person wherever you arrive, you will find honor, love, and grace.

If you are troubled by a storm at sea, take a goblet full of seawater and say this prayer over the water. And then throw it in the sea, and the storm will end.

And one who wishes to go into battle should say this prayer over the belt of his sword, and then gird it about himself, and the best will come to him. He'll have neither death nor a mortal wound.

10   Say this prayer over running water, and give a drink to those who are bewitched, and they will become healthy.

And at each time and in each place, in the beginning say the Paternoster and Ave Maria.

And one who says this prayer will become wise and will receive God's inheritance
15   in the end. No one knows the great power this prayer has for believers except God alone.

In the name of the Father and Son and Holy Spirit. Amen.

Say these three psalms before the prayer: "May God have mercy on us" [*Psalm 66*], "Out of the depths" [*Psalm 129*], and "I cried to the Lord with my voice" [*Psalm 141*].

20   Lord God, all-powerful Father, Son, and Holy Spirit, grant me, n[ame], your servant, by the power of the holy cross victory against all and over all my foes so that they be unable to resist me or to speak against me; but may their strength, power, and counsel be guided to a good end. But you, God, be my bravery, shield of protection, and unassailable tower so that all my opponents may be scattered and routed.
25   God of Abraham, God of Isaac, and God of Jacob, God of all good living men, free me, n[ame], your servant, from all my sins and anguishes, from needs and anxieties without dangers. And grant me speech sounding right and good in my mouth,

vultus et opera omnibus hominibus me videntibus. Propheta clamat, apostulus dicat, "Christus in se confidentes salvat." Christus vincit, Christus regnat. Christus
30   imperare dignetur me esse triumphatorem omnium adversariorum meorum ut sicut non timebo quid faciat mihi homo. Deus, in nomine tuo salvum me fac, et ab hoste visibili et invisibili libera me. Amen.

Domine Iesu Christe Nazarene, Fili Dei vivi, qui in cruce suspensus fuisti et lancea latus tuum perforari permisisti, etiam de tuo sanguine nos redemisti; et Susannam
35   de falso crimine liberasti [*Daniel 13*]; et tres pueros de camino ignis ardentis eruisti [*Daniel 3*]; et Danielem de lacu leonum et eorum impetu salvasti [*Daniel 6:16–27*]. Ita salva et libera me, famulum tuum, ab omni opere malo, et conserva in omni opere bono, et perduc ad vitam eternam. "Voce mea ad Dominum clamavi" etc. usque "donec retribuas michi" [*Psalm 141*]. |

BOOKLET 7   QUIRE 15

Quant vous levez le matyn   [art. 100]

134r]   ¶ Quant vous levez le matyn, pensez de seint Michael, e vous averez honour le jour.

¶ Qaunt vous oyez toneyre, pensez de seint Gabriel, e ren serrez grevez.

¶ Quant vous mangerez ou beverez, pensez de seint Raphael, e totes choses vous habounderount.

5   ¶ Quant vous irrez nul chemyn, pensez de seint Raguel, e rien doterez.

¶ Quant vous vendrez al jugement, pensez de seint Rachel, e vous averez vostre volenté en bien.

¶ Quant vous vendrez a feste, pensez de seint Pantesseron, e vous serrez honorez.

¶ Pensez de seint Abyel e de seint Brachiel quant vous vendrez devant prince ou
10   seigneur, e vous avendra bien.

¶ Pensez de seint Uryel e de seint Tobye quant vous entrez en nef, e vous passerez sauntz peryl.

30 that the words of my countenance and my deeds be pleasing to all people who see me. The prophet cries out, the apostle says, "Christ saves those who trust in him." Christ triumphs. Christ rules. May Christ deign to command that I be victor over all my opponents in such a way that I will not fear what a man may do to me. God, make me safe in your name, and free me from the enemy seen and unseen. Amen.

35 Lord Jesus Christ the Nazarene, Son of the living God, you who were hanged on the cross and permitted your side to be pierced by a lance, even as by your blood you redeemed us; and you freed Susanna from false accusation [*Daniel 13*]; and you wrested away the three boys from the furnace of glowing fire [*Daniel 3*]; and you saved Daniel from the den of lions and from their attack [*Daniel 6:16–27*]. So too save me and free me, your servant, from every bad deed, and maintain me in every good deed, and guide me through to eternal life. "I cried to the Lord with my voice" etc. up to "until thou reward me" [*Psalm 141*]. |

BOOKLET 7 **QUIRE 15**

Occasions for Angels [art. 100]

134r] ¶ When you rise in the morning, think on Saint Michael, and you will have honor that day.

¶ When you hear thunder, think on Saint Gabriel, and nothing will harm you.

¶ When you eat or drink, think on Saint Raphael, and all things will be abundant for you.

5 ¶ When you go on any road, think on Saint Raguel, and you need not fear anything.

¶ When you face a judgment, think on Saint Rachel, and you will gain just what you wish.

¶ When you come to a feast, think on Saint Pantesseron, and you will be honored.

10 ¶ Think on Saint Abiel and Saint Brachiel when you come before a prince or lord, and it will go well for you.

¶ Think on Saint Uriel and Saint Tobias when you get on a boat, and you will cross without danger.

Quy velt que Dieu sovyegne de ly   [art. 101]

134r]   ¶ Quy velt que Dieu sovyegne de ly, die troi foiz cest salme: "Usquequo Domine"
          [*Psalm 12*].

          ¶ Qui de rien se doute, die troiz foiz cest salme: "In te Domine speravi" [*Psalm 30*].

          ¶ Si vous volez estre deliveré del poer del Deable, ditez le jour trey foiz cest salme:
5   "In te Domine speravi" [*Psalm 30*].

          ¶ Quant vous devez aler la ou vous avez pour ou doute, dites ceste salme: "Iudica
          Domine nocentes me expungna [expungnantes me]" etc. [*Psalm 34*].

          ¶ Quant temptacion de vostre char vous prent, ditez, "Iudica me Deus et discerne"
          [*Psalm 42*].

10   ¶ Quant vous levetz de vostre lit, dites, "Deus in nomine tuo" [*Psalm 53*].

          ¶ Si vous estes en ascun adversité, dites sept foiz, "Exaudi Deus orationem meam
          cum deprecor" [*Psalm 63*].

          ¶ Si vous devez pleder ov vostre enymy, dites, "Miserere mei Deus [miserere mei]
          quoniam in te confidit [anima mea]" [*Psalm 56*].

15   ¶ Si vous devez combatre, ditez cest salme: "Eripe me de inimicis" [*Psalm 58*].

          ¶ Si vous seiez en pecchié, dites, "Deus misereatur nostri" [*Psalm 66*].

          ¶ Si vous estes environé de vos enimys, dites, "Exurgat Deus" [*Psalm 67*].

          ¶ Quant vous estes en tribulacioun, dites, "Salvum me fac Deus quoniam
          intraverunt [aquae]" [*Psalm 68*].

20   ¶ Quant vous volez rien comencer, dites, "Deus in adiutorium [meum intende]"
          [*Psalm 69*].

          ¶ Si vous volez qe Dieu receyve ta priere, ditez, "Deus venerunt gentes" [*Psalm 78*].

          ¶ Si vous estes en tribulacioun e volez estre delyvrez, "Domine refugium [tu factus
          es nobis]" [*Psalm 89*].

Occasions for Psalms in French [art. 101]

134r] ¶ One who wishes that God remember him, say this psalm three times: "How long, O Lord" [*Psalm 12*].

¶ One who is fearful of anything, say this psalm three times: "In thee, O Lord, have I hoped" [*Psalm 30*].

5 ¶ If you wish to be freed from the power of the Devil, say this psalm three times in the day: "In thee, O Lord, have I hoped" [*Psalm 30*].

¶ When you must go where you are afraid or in fear, say this psalm: "Judge thou, O Lord, them that wrong me: overthrow them that fight against me" etc. [*Psalm 34*].

¶ When the temptation of your flesh takes hold of you, say, "Judge me, O God, and distinguish" [*Psalm 42*].

10 ¶ When you rise from your bed, say, "O God, by thy name" [*Psalm 53*].

¶ If you are in any adversity, say seven times, "Hear, O God, my prayer when I make supplication to thee" [*Psalm 63*].

¶ If you must plead against your enemy, say, "Have mercy on me, O God, have mercy on me: for my soul trusteth in thee" [*Psalm 56*].

15 ¶ If you must fight, say this psalm: "Deliver me from my enemies" [*Psalm 58*].

¶ If you should be in sin, say, "May God have mercy on us" [*Psalm 66*].

¶ If you are surrounded by your enemies, say, "Let God arise" [*Psalm 67*].

¶ When you are in tribulation, say, "Save me, O God, for the waters are come in" [*Psalm 68*].

20 ¶ When you wish to begin something, say, "O God, come to my assistance" [*Psalm 69*].

¶ If you wish that God accept your prayer, say, "O God, the heathens are come" [*Psalm 78*].

¶ If you are in tribulation and wish to be delivered, "Lord, thou hast been our refuge" [*Psalm 89*].

25   ¶ Si vous estes pris e mys en destresse, dites, "Domine probasti" [*Psalm 138*].

        ¶ Cestes salmes avant nomez serrount ditez en genoillant ov grant devocioun e
        chescun a meynz troi foiz ou plus. |

Gloria in excelsis Deo en fraunceis   [art. 102]

134v]   ¶ Gloria in excelsis Deo en fraunceis

        Joyous honour lasus en haut seit a Dampnedé,
        E pees en terre soit a gent de bone volenté;
        Loé soit Sire Dieu, beneit e aoré;
        A joie vous rendrum graces pur vostre grant bonté,
5   Sire Deu, roy de ciel, Piere de poesté.
        E vous, Sire Jesu Crist, le Fitz Dieu benuré,
        Fitz e Piere tut puissant, Aignel Dieu apelé,
        Nos pecchiez nous pardonez e recevez a gré
        Les preeyeres que nous fesoms pur nostre necessité.
10   Vous q'a destre seez la Piere en magesté,
        Eyez merci de nous, Jesu Crist, e pieté,
        Que soul estes Sires, seint e trehauncé,
        Ov Dieu le Piere e Seint Espirit en joye en deyté,
        Quar ensi est, sauntz fyn, en herité.
            Amen.

Confiteor tibi, Deus, omnia peccata mea   [art. 103]

134v]   ¶ Confiteor tibi, Deus, omnia peccata mea, quia tu Deus es sine peccato, et obsecro
        te, Deus meus, Domine Iesu Christe Nazarene, Fili Dei vivi, per passionem tuam,
        et per lignum salutiffere crucis tue, et per effusionem sancti sanguinis tui, mihi
        concedere remissionem omnium peccatorum meorum. Peto, Domine, ut iudicas
5   me secundum iudicium indulgencie tue, et per misericordiam tuam exoro ut
        digneris inserere in me amorem tuum. Suscita in me veram penitenciam, et adiuva
        me. Dele iniquitatem meam a conspectu tuo, et ne avertas faciem tuam ab oratione
        mea ne derelinquas me, Deus meus, set confirma me in tua voluntate. Doce me
        quod agere debeam. Defende me, Domine Deus meus, contra omnes inimicos meos
10   visibiles et invisibiles. Defende me, Domine Iesu Christe, contra iacula Diabolica
        et contra angelos tartareos, suadentes et docentes me mala facere. Domine, ne
        discedas a me, et ne derelinquas me, Domine Deus meus, et ne proicias me,
        miserum famulum tuum, sed adiuva me, Domine Deus meus, et perfice in me
        doctrinam tuam et veram confessionem, quia tu es Deus, Creator meus et Dominus
15   meus, qui cum Patre, Filio, et Spiritu Sancto vivis et regnas in secula seculorum.
        Amen.

25 ¶ If you are captured and placed in confinement, say, "Lord, thou hast proved [me]" [*Psalm 138*].

¶ These psalms named above should be said while kneeling with great devotion and each at least three times or more. |

Glory to God in the Highest in French [art. 102]

134v] ¶ Glory to God in the highest in French

Joyful honor be to Lord God in the highest,
And peace on earth be among men of goodwill;
Praised be Lord God, blessed and adored;
Joyfully we thank thee for thy great goodness,
5 Lord God, king of heaven, Father of might.
And you, Lord Jesus Christ, blessed Son of God,
Son and almighty Father, called the Lamb of God,
Pardon us our sins and receive willingly
The prayers that we make in our need.
10 You who sit at the Father's right hand in majesty,
Have mercy on us, Jesus Christ, and compassion,
Who alone are Lord, holy and most high,
With God the Father and Holy Spirit in joy in godhead,
For such is, without end, your heritage.
    Amen.

Prayer of Confession [art. 103]

134v] ¶ I confess to you, God, all my sins, because you are God without sin, and I beseech you, my God, Lord Jesus Christ of Nazareth, Son of living God, by your passion, and by the wood of your salvational cross, and by the spilling of your sainted blood, to grant me remission of all my sins. I ask, Lord, that you judge me according to
5 the judgment of your indulgence, and I entreat by your mercy that you deign to implant in me your love. Awaken in me true penance, and aid me. Wipe away my iniquity from your sight, and do not turn away your face from my prayer or abandon me, my God, but strengthen me in your will. Teach me what I ought to
10 do. Protect me, Lord my God, against all my enemies seen and unseen. Protect me, Lord Jesus Christ, against the Devil's darts and against hell's angels, persuading and teaching me to commit wrongs. Lord, do not leave me, do not abandon me, Lord my God, and do not cast me out, your wretched servant, but aid me, Lord my God, and perfect in me your teaching and true confession, because you are God,
15 my Creator and my Lord, who as the Father, Son, and Holy Ghost lives and reigns forever. Amen.

Gloriouse Dame   [art. 104]

134v]   ¶ Icest oreysoun enveia Nostre Dame seinte Marie a seint Moris evesque de Parys
e ly comanda qu'il le aprist al pueple, e qui chescun jour ov bon devocion le dirra
hounte en le siecle ne avera, ne de l'Enymy engyné serra, ne passioun en terre
soffrera, ne femme d'enfant periera, ne mesaventure ne avendra, ne desconfés
5   murra:

¶ Gloriouse Dame, que le Fitz Dieu portastes,
E a ta benuré porture, sanz conysaunce de honme, conçustes,
Sauntz dolour, e sauve ta virgineté, le Fitz Dieu enfauntastes,
E de virginal let virginalment le letastes,
10   Dame, si veroiement come c'est voirs, e je fermement le croy,
Eyez en garde l'alme e le cors de moy.

E pur celes noundisables joyes que le Fitz Dieu e le vostre vous fist quant il releva
de mort e vewablement a vous apparust, e que avyez quant il mounta en ciel veaunt
vos eux, e que avyez quant vynt tot festinauntz countre vous ov la court tote
15   celestre, si vous assist al destre de ly, e vous corona reigne de cel e de terre, pur |
135r]   iceles seintisme joyes, je vous cry merci, e requer qu'en totes mes bosoignes me
vueillez counsiller e ayder, moy e tous iceux pur queux prier vous doy, ma
tresdouce Dame Virge Marie. Amen.

Rex seculorum et Domine dominator   [art. 105]

135r]   ¶ Rex seculorum et Domine dominator qui me, creasti dona mihi veram
memoriam, veram penitenciam, et veram confessionem quam me oporteat et que
tibi placeat. Da mihi, Domine Iesu Nazerene, veram cordis compunctionem et
fontem lacrimarum quibus peccatorum meorum dissolvere vinculam; et
5   misericordiam, tuam que mihi ad perseveranciam boni operis perducat nunc et in
evum. Amen.

Um doit plus volentiers juner le vendredy   [art. 106]

135r]   ¶ Um doit plus volentiers juner le vendredy qe nul autre jour de la simaigne pur
ce qe a vendredi entrerent les fitz Israel le Terre de Promission. Vendredi morust
Moises le prophete al mount de Alban.

Vendredy ocist David le prophete Golyas.

5   Vendredy fust decollez Helyas le prophete.

Vendredi fust decollés seint Johan le Baptiste.

Prayer on the Five Joys of Our Lady [art. 104]

134v] ¶ This prayer Our Lady Saint Mary sent to Saint Maurice Bishop of Paris and commanded him that he teach it to the people, and he who says it each day with good devotion will never know shame in this world, nor encounter snares of the Enemy, nor feel suffering on earth, nor woman perish in childbirth, nor come
5 upon misfortune, nor die unshriven:

¶ Glorious Lady, who bore the Son of God,
And in your blessed pregnancy, without knowing man, conceived,
Without pain, and your virginity intact, the Son of God birthed,
And with virginal milk as a virgin him suckled,
10 Lady, thus truly as it is true, and I steadfastly believe it,
Take me body and soul into your care.

And for those ineffable joys that God's Son and yours made for you when he rose from the dead and appeared visibly to you, and that you had when he ascended to heaven before your eyes, and that you had when he came all festively before you with
15 the entire celestial court, and seated you at his right side, and crowned you queen of
135r] heaven and earth, for | those most holy joys, I beg your mercy, and ask that you advise and help me in all my needs, for myself and all those for whom it is my duty to pray to you, my most sweet Lady Virgin Mary. Amen.

Prayer for Contrition [art. 105]

135r] ¶ King of the ages and Lord overlord who created me, grant me true memory, true penance, and true confession as behooves me and which pleases you. Grant me, Lord Jesus of Nazareth, true remorse of the heart and a fountain of tears with
5 which to undo the bonds of my sins; and grant me your mercy, to lead me through to persistence in good work now and forever. Amen.

Reasons for Fasting on Friday [art. 106]

135r] ¶ One should fast more willingly on Friday than on any other day of the week because on Friday the sons of Israel entered the Promised Land. Friday the prophet Moses died on Mount Nebo.

Friday the prophet David killed Goliath.

5 Friday the prophet Elijah was beheaded.

Friday Saint John the Baptist was beheaded.

Vendredy ocist Herodes cent millers e quaraunte quatre millers des Innocens, e cele occisioun comença par vendredi.

Gabriel anuncia par vendredi a Nostre Dame que Jesu serreit nee de ly.

10   A vendredi fust seint Piere crucifié.

Vendredy fust Dieu crucifiez.

Vendredi trespassa Nostre Dame a cyel.

Vendredi fust seint Estevene lapidé e seint Paul decollé.

Vendredy Enoc e Elyas combaterount ov Antecrist.

Quy est en tristour [art. 107]

135r]   ¶ Quy est en tristour, prisone, poverté, ou chiet en maladie, face dire messes come desouz est escrit, e yl serra aydé.

Face dire une messe de la Trinité par digmange: e illumer treis chaundeles e doner treis almoignes as povres e offryr a la messe e ester.

5   Lundy, une messe de seint Michel e de tous angeles e archangles: e illumer sept chaundeilles e doner sept almoignes, offryr, e ester.

Mardy, de Seint Espirit: e illumer sept chandeilles e doner sept almoignes, offryr, e ester.

Mesgredy, de seint Johan le Baptiste e des patriarches: illumer iiij chandeilles,
10   doner iiij almoynes, offrer, ester.

Jeovedy, de seint Piere e des apostles: illumer xij chandeilles e doner xij almoignes, offryr, e ester.

Vendredi, de la croys: illumer v chaundeilles, doner v almoignes, offryr, e ester.

Samady, de Nostre Dame e de totes virgines: illumer une chaundeille e doner une
15   almoigne e offryr e ester. |

Friday Herod killed one hundred forty-four thousand Innocents, and this slaughter began on Friday.

Gabriel proclaimed to Our Lady on Friday that Jesus would be born to her.

10   On Friday Saint Peter was crucified.

Friday God was crucified.

Friday Our Lady passed on to heaven.

Friday Saint Stephen was stoned and Saint Paul beheaded.

Friday Enoch and Elijah will battle with Antichrist.

Seven Masses To Be Said in Misfortune   [art. 107]

135r]   ¶ One who is in sadness, prison, poverty, or falls in sickness, should say masses as is written below, and he will be helped.

He should say a Mass of the Trinity on Sunday: and light three candles and give three alms to the poor and make an offering at the Mass and stand.

5   Monday, a Mass of Saint Michael and all angels and archangels: and light seven candles and give seven alms, make an offering, and stand.

Tuesday, of the Holy Spirit: and light seven candles and give seven alms, make an offering, and stand.

Wednesday, of Saint John the Baptist and the patriarchs: light four candles, give
10   four alms, make an offering, stand.

Thursday, of Saint Peter and the Apostles: light twelve candles and give twelve alms, make an offering, and stand.

Friday, of the Cross: light five candles, give five alms, make an offering, and stand.

Saturday, of Our Lady and all virgins: light one candle and give one alms and
15   make an offering and stand. |

Cely que fra ces messes chaunter   [art. 108]

135v]   ¶ Cely que fra ces messes chaunter en le honour de Dieu e de seint Gyle yl avera ce
         qu'il ov dreite fey demaundera:

         La premere serra de l'Annunciacion Nostre Dame: "Rorate cely."

         La secounde de Noel: "Puer natus."

5   La tierce: "Nos autem gloriari [oportet]."

         La quarte de Pasche: "Resurexi."

         La quinte de l'Ascencion: "Viri Galiley."

         La sisme de Pentecoste: "Spiritus Domini."

         La septisme de le Assumpcion de Nostre Dame: "Gaudeamus" etc.

Je vous requer, Jaspar, Melchior, e Baltazar   [art. 108a]

135v]   ¶ Je vous requer, Jaspar, Melchior, e Baltazar, rois coronez, que Jesum alastes
         quere quant il fust né de la virge Marie, par icel douçour que vous vers ly ustes
         quant vous quere ly alastes, e pur cele joye que vous ustes quant ly trovastes e vos
         douns ly offristes, que vous me consilez de ce dont je vous requer sicome Dieu vous
5   oy e vos offrendres resçust. Verroi Dieu, auxi come lur offrendres reçustes, recevez
         huy ma oreisoun pur lur amour; e auxi come l'estoille lur apparust en orient, que
         lur mena a vous al lu qu'il urent grantment desire, auxi, Sire Dieu, aemplez mon
         desir a leesse e joie. Otreiez moi que je puisse avoir e vere ce que mon cuer desyre,
         a la loenge Dieu e ma Dame seinte Marie. Amen.

Mundus iste totus quoddam scaccarium est   [art. 109]

135v]   ¶ Mundus iste totus quoddam scaccarium est, cuius unus punctus albus est alius
         vero niger propter duplicem statum vite et mortis, gratie et culpe. Familia autem
         huius scaccarii sunt homines huius mundi, qui de uno sacculo materno
         extrahuntur, et collocantur in diversis locis huius mundi, et singuli habent diversa
5   nomina. Primus enim rex est, alter regina, tertius rocus, quartus miles, quintus
         alphinus, sextus pedinus.

Seven Masses in Honor of God and Saint Giles [art. 108]

135v] ¶ One who has these masses sung in honor of God and Saint Giles will have what he asks for with true faith:

The first will be of the Annunciation to Our Lady: "Drop down ye heavens."

The second of Christmas: "A child is born."

5 The third: "But it behooves us to glory."

The fourth of Easter: "I am risen."

The fifth of the Ascension: "Men of Galilee."

The sixth of Pentecost: "Spirit of the Lord."

The seventh of the Assumption of Our Lady: "Let us rejoice" etc.

Prayer to the Three Kings [art. 108a]

135v] ¶ I entreat you, Jaspar, Melchior, and Balthazar, crowned kings, who went to seek Jesus when he was born of the Virgin Mary, for that sweetness you felt toward him when you went to seek him, and for that joy you felt when you found him and offered him your gifts, that you advise me regarding that which I ask you inasmuch 5 as God hears you and accepted your gifts. True God, as you accepted their gifts, may you accept today my prayer on account of their love; and as the star appeared to them in the east, which led them to you in the place they had so greatly desired, so too, Lord God, you filled my desire for gladness and joy. Grant me that I may have and behold what my heart desires, for the praise of God and my Lady Saint Mary. Amen.

All the World's a Chess Board [art. 109]

135v] ¶ This whole world is a kind of chessboard, of which one square is white but another black on account of the twofold state of life and death, of grace and sin. Moreover, the pieces of this chessboard are the people of this world, who are drawn out of one bag — a mother's womb — and are positioned in various places of this 5 world, and every single one has a different name. For the first is the king, the second the queen, the third the rook, the fourth the knight, the fifth the bishop, the sixth the pawn.

Istius autem ioci condicio talis est ut unus alterum capiat, et cum ludum compleverint, sicut de uno sacculo exierunt, ita iterum reponuntur, nec est differencia inter regem et peditem pauperem quia simul in unum dives et pauper;
10 et sepe contingit quod quando familia scaccarii reponitur in sacculum, rex inferius collocatur et reponitur. Sic fere quique maiores in transitu huius seculi inferius collocantur, scilicet, in inferno sepeliuntur, pauperes in sinum Habrahe deportantur.

In isto autem ludo REX vadit ubique et capit undique directe, in signum quod rex
15 omnia iuste corrigat et in nullo omissa iusticia obliquari debet. Set quicquid agit rex iusticia reputatur, quia quicquid principi placet legis habet vigorem.

REGINA, que dicitur *ferce*, vadit oblique et capit undique indirecte, quia cum avarissimum sit genus mulierum, nichil capit — nisi mere detur ex gratia — nisi rapina et iniusticia.

20 ROCUS est iusticiarius, perambulans totam terram directe in linia, in signum quod omnia iuste corrigat et in nullo omissa iusticia muneribus coruptus, obliquari debet.
136r] Set modo est quod pervertit iudicium, ut scribitur: "Pervertisti iu|dicium in amaritudinem, et fructum iusticie in absinthium" [*Amos 6:13*].

MILES tres punctos pertransit, duos directos, in signum quod milites et terreni
25 domini possunt iuste capere redditus sibi debitos et iustas emendas secundum exigenciam delicti, set tertium punctum obliquant cum tallagia et exactiones iniustas extorquent a subditis.

ALPHINI vero sunt episcopi non ut Moyses, ex colloquio divino, set potius regio imperio prece vel pretio sublimati. Et sic promoti, isti alphini oblique currunt, et
30 tres punctos, currendo pertranseunt indirecte quia fere omnes prelati odio, amore, munere, seu favore pervertuntur ne delinquentes corrigant. Et contra vicia latrant, set potius annuo censu peccata ad firmam tradant. Sic Diabolum ditant. Unde qui debuerunt esse viciorum extirpatores iam per cupiditatem facti sunt viciorum promotores et Diaboli procuratores.

35 PEDINI pauperculi sunt qui, incedendo, duos punctos pertranseunt directos quia dum pauper manet, in sua simplicitate et paupertate semper directe vivit. Set cum capere vult, obliquat quia cum cupit aliquid temporale vel honores, consequi, semper capiendo cum falsis iuramentis, vel adulationibus, seu mendaciis obliquat, donec ad summum gradum scaccarii perveniat. Et tunc de *poun* fit *fierce*, et tunc
40 incontinenti capit cum maximo dominio, et tres punctos pertransit, quia, ut dicitur in Alexandro, "asperius nichil est humili cum surgit in altum."

The conduct of this game is such that one captures another, and when they have finished the game, they are put back again in one bag, just as they came out of one, and there is not a difference between a king and a poor pawn because the rich and poor are together at the same time; and it often happens that when the pieces of this chessboard are put back in the sack, the king is positioned and put back lower. In this way almost all those who are greater during the passage through this world are placed lower, which is to say, they are buried in hell, whereas the poor are carried off into the lap of Abraham.

Furthermore, in this game the KING moves everywhere and takes from all directions directly, to indicate that a king corrects everything justly and that in no case ought justice be omitted and shunted aside. But whatever the king does is regarded as justice, because whatever suits the prince has the rigor of law.

The QUEEN, who is called *fers*, moves obliquely and takes from all directions indirectly, because since womankind is most greedy, it takes nothing — unless it be given purely as a favor — if not by seizure and injustice.

The ROOK is a judge, traversing the entire board in a straight line, as an indication that he corrects everything and that in no case ought justice be omitted and shunted aside, corrupted by bribes. But now it happens that it perverts judgment, as it is written: "You have perverted judg|ment into bitterness, and the fruit of justice into wormwood" [*Amos 6:13*].

The KNIGHT moves three squares, two of them in a straight line, as an indication that knights and earthly lords can justly take the incomes owed them and justly impose correction in keeping with the requirement of the crime, but they move aside a third square when they extort unjust taxes and exactions from their subjects.

The ALFINS are bishops elevated not like Moses, because of a discussion with God, but rather because of royal power and thanks to entreaty or payment. And having been promoted in this way, these bishops glide at an angle, and gliding three squares, they pass indirectly because almost all prelates are perverted by hate, love, bribery, or bias not to correct sinners. And they bark out against vices, but they hand over sins for rent by a yearly payment. In this way they enrich the Devil. They who ought to be the exterminators of vices have become through their avidity promoters of vices and agents of the Devil.

The PAWNS are the poor and humble who, in advancing, traverse two squares in a straight line because so long as a person remains poor, he always lives in a direct fashion in his simplicity and poverty. But when he wishes to take, he moves at an angle because when he desires to obtain something worldly or honors, he moves at an angle, always taking with false oaths, flattery, or lies, until he arrives at the final move of the chess game. And then from a *poun* he becomes a *fers*, and then immediately he takes with greatest power and traverses three squares because, as is said in Alexander, "nothing is harsher than a humble man when he rises."

In isto autem ludo Diabolus dicit "eschek," insultando vel percuciendo aliquem peccati iaculo. Qui percussus, nisi cicius dicat "lyveret," ad penitenciam et cordis compunctionem transeundo, Diabolus dicit ei "mat," animam secum ad tartara

45   deducendo, ubi non liberabitur, nec prece nec pretio quia in inferno nulla est redempcio.

Quy chescun jour denz seissaunte jours   [art. 109a]

136r]   ¶ Quy chescun jour denz seissaunte jours trente foiz "Veni Creator Spiritus" etc. "Qui [diceris] Paraclitus" etc., trente foiz "Gloria in excelsis [Deo]," e trente foiz "De profundis" [*Psalm 129*] dirra, de la preiere qu'il fra dreitement a Dieu, ja ne faudra.

Contra inimicos si quos habes   [art. 110]

136r]   ¶ Contra inimicos si quos habes, lege hunc psalmum lxiii, "Exaudi Deus orationem meam cum deprecor." Super has philatirias, et ligas eas in brachio tuo et vinces eos.

        ¶ Si quis factus fuerit egenus et pauper, dicat hunc psalmum cotidie, sepcies in die
5   et sepcies in sero, et convertetur eius inopia in diviciis: "In te Domine speravi" i^{m} [*Psalm 30*], "Deus venerunt [gentes]" [*Psalm 78*].

        ¶ Si quis timuerit temptationem, leget hunc psalmum, "Salvum me fac Deus" [*Psalm 68*], et fiet tranquillitas magna in terra et in mari, et saneberis in quo volueris.

136v]   ¶ Scribe hunc psalmum in carta (et nomine infirmantis), | et suffumiga incenso in
10   trivio, et quadrivio, et cotidie lege hunc psalmum, "Deus in adiutorium meum intende" [*Psalm 69*], et sanabitur.

        ¶ Si placitare debeas cum maiore vel potenciore, antequam exeas ad placitum, dic hunc psalmum: "In te Domine speravi" [*Psalm 70*].

        ¶ Et contra adversarios et maliciosos, dic, "Deus laudem [meam ne tacueris]" [*Psalm
15   108*].

        ¶ Scribe hunc psalmum in nomine cuius vis et nomine martiris eius, et liga in brachio tuo — "Deus iudicium tuum regi da" [*Psalm 71*] — et habebis dilectionem ab eo maximam.

45 Moreover, in this game the Devil says "check," insulting or destroying someone with the dart of sin. When someone is stricken, unless he quickly says "delivered," passing over to penitence and remorse of the heart, the Devil says to him "mate," leading off his soul with him to hell, where he will not be freed by entreaty or payment because in hell there is no redemption.

Three Prayers That Never Fail [art. 109a]

136r] ¶ Whoever each day during sixty days will say thirty times "Come, Creator Spirit" etc. [and] "Comforter, to thee we cry" etc., thirty times "Glory be to God on high," and thirty times "Out of the depths" [*Psalm 129*], the prayer that he makes directly to God will never fail.

Occasions for Psalms in Latin [art. 110]

136r] ¶ Against enemies if you have them, read this Psalm 63, "Hear, O God, my prayer, when I make supplication to thee." Concerning these phylacteries, you both tie them on your arm and bind them.

5 ¶ If anyone becomes destitute and a pauper, let him say this psalm daily, seven times during the day and seven times in the evening, and his need will be turned into wealth: "In thee, O Lord, have I hoped" the first [*Psalm 30*], "O God, the heathens are come" [*Psalm 78*].

¶ If anyone bears temptation, he will read this psalm, "Save me, O God" [*Psalm 68*], and a great calm will be made upon earth and sea, and you will be restored as you wish.

136v]
11 ¶ Write this psalm on paper (and with the name of the person suffering debility), | and fumigate with incense at the meeting of three roads, and of four, and daily read this psalm, "O God, come to my assistance" [*Psalm 69*], and he will be restored.

¶ If you must make a plea with a greater or more powerful person, before you go forth to plea, say this psalm: "In thee, O Lord, I have hoped" [*Psalm 70*].

15 ¶ And against opponents and evildoers, say, "O God, be thou not silent in my praise" [*Psalm 108*].

¶ Write this psalm in the name of whomever you will and in the name of his martyr saint, and bind it on your arm — "Give to the king thy judgment, O God" [*Psalm 71*] — and you will have the greatest delight from him.

20   ¶ Scribe hunc psalmum, "Quam bonus Israel [Deus]" [*Psalm 72*], et suspende in brachio tuo, et dabitur tibi quod postularis a principe vel potestate.

¶ Scribe hunc salmum, "Ut quid Deus rep[p]ulisti" [*Psalm 73*], in nomine inimici tui simul, et nomen tuum, et has philatirias et mitte in ignem, et dispergentur statim.

25   ¶ Quod non planget puer, scribe hunc psalmum totum et liga in brachio pueri, et non planget: "Nonne Deo subiecta [erit anima mea]" [*Psalm 61*].

¶ Ad elevationem corporis Christi, dic hunc psalmum, "Te Deum laudamus."

Seint Hillere archevesque de Peyters ordina ces salmes   [art. 111]

136v]   ¶ Seint Hillere archevesque de Peyters ordina ces salmes pur prier a Dieu.

¶ Qui velt rien prier a soy, die ov devocion devaunt la croys, "Ad te Domine levavi animam meam Deus meus in te confido" etc. [*Psalm 24*], e "Inclina Domine aurem tuam et exaudi me quoniam inops" etc. [*Psalm 85*].

5   ¶ Quy est environee de ses enimis, die ov devocion cestes psaumes, e il serra delyverez: "Exurgat Deus" [*Psalm 67*], e "Deus laudem meam [ne tacueris]" [*Psalm 108*].

¶ Si vous estes chey en bosoigne, eiez bone esperaunce en Dieu. Dites, "In te Domine speravi" le premer [*Psalm 30*].

10   ¶ Si ascun vueille aler la ou il se doute, die treis foiz ov devocion, "Iudica me Deus et discerne" etc. [*Psalm 42*], e ayle seurement.

¶ Si vous estes molt en meseisse de cuer e volez que Dieus vous delyvre, diez a genoils ov lermes vij foiz, "Exaudi Deus orationem meam et ne despexeris" etc. [*Psalm 54*], "Miserere mei Deus quoniam conculcavit [me homo]" etc. [*Psalm 55*].

15   ¶ Si vous devez pleder ov vostre sovereine, priez Dieu humblement qu'il vous doint force e poer de acontrester vostre adversarie, e ditez, "Miserere mei Deus [miserere mei] quoniam in te confidit [anima mea]" [*Psalm 56*].

¶ Quy deyve aler a bataille, die un ascun die pur ly, "Eripe me de inimicis meis Deus et ab insurgentibus [in me libera me]" [*Psalm 58*], "Exaudi Deus
20   deprecationem meam intende orationi mee" [*Psalm 60*], "Exaudi Deus orationem meam cum deprecor" etc. [*Psalm 63*].

20   ¶ Write this psalm, "How good is God to Israel" [*Psalm 72*], and hang it on your arm, and what you demand of a prince or an authority will be granted to you.

¶ Write this psalm, "O God, why hast thou cast us off" [*Psalm 73*], in the name of your enemy, and [write] your name, and put these phylacteries into the fire, and they will be scattered immediately.

25   ¶ So that a child will not whine, write this whole psalm and bind it on the child's arm, and he will not whine: "Shall not my soul be subject to God" [*Psalm 61*].

¶ At the Levation of Christ's body, say this hymn, "We praise you, God."

Occasions for Psalms Ordained by Saint Hilary of Poitiers   [art. 111]

136v]   ¶ Saint Hilary the Archbishop of Poitiers ordained these psalms for praying to God.

¶ He who wishes to pray for something for himself, say with devotion before the cross, "To thee, O Lord, have I lifted up my soul. In thee, O my God, I put my trust" etc. [*Psalm 24*], and "Incline thy ear, O Lord, and hear me: for I am needy" etc. [*Psalm 85*].

5   ¶ He who is surrounded by his enemies, say with devotion these psalms, and he will be delivered: "Let God arise" [*Psalm 67*], and "O God, be thou not silent in my praise" [*Psalm 108*].

¶ If you have fallen in need, have good hope in God. Say, "In thee, O Lord, have I hoped" the first [*Psalm 30*].

10   ¶ If anyone wishes to go where he is fearful, say three times with devotion, "Judge me, O God, and distinguish" etc. [*Psalm 42*], and go safely.

¶ If you are in great affliction of heart and wish for God to deliver you, say on your knees with tears seven times, "Hear, O God, my prayer, and despise not" etc. [*Psalm 54*], "Have mercy on me, O God, for man hath trodden me underfoot" etc. [*Psalm 55*].

15   ¶ If you must plead before your sovereign, pray to God humbly that he give you strength and power to oppose your adversary, and say, "Have mercy on me, O God, have mercy on me: for my soul trusteth in thee" [*Psalm 56*].

¶ He who must go into battle, say or let someone say for him, "Deliver me from my enemies, O my God, and defend me from them that rise up against me" [*Psalm 58*], "Hear, O God, my supplication: be attentive to my prayer" [*Psalm 60*], "Hear, O God, my prayer, when I make supplication to thee" etc. [*Psalm 63*].

20

¶ Quant vous levez le matyn, dites, "Deus in nomine tuo salvum me fac" [*Psalm 53*], "Deus repulisti [nos]" [*Psalm 59*], treis Paternoster, treis Ave Maria, e passerez cel jour sauntz encombraunce.

25   ¶ Qui ad volenté de peccher, prie Dieu devoutement qu'il ly doint repentaunce, e veroyment il serra delyvrez s'il die, "Deus misereatur" [*Psalm 66*].

¶ Quant vous alez vers vostre enymy ou ad vostre adversarie, dites ov devocioun, "Iudica Domine nocentes me" [*Psalm 34*], e il ne avera poer de vous nuyre.

¶ Quant vous avez de rien songié, alez lendemain devant le crucifix en la eglise, e
30   dites, "Ad Dominum cum tribularer [clamavi]" [*Psalm 119*], Paternoster, Ave Maria, e Credo.

¶ Si ascun soit enprisonee, si se conffesse bien e nettement, e puis die ces psalmes.
137r]   E si yl ne les puet dire, die ascun autre pur ly mes, | qu'il soit bien e nettement
          confés, e pus les die quaraunte foiz, "Domine probasti me" [*Psalm 138*], "Eripe me
35   Domine ab homine malo a viro iniquo [eripe me]" etc. [*Psalm 139*].

¶ Si ascun vueille comencer ascune graunde chose, si prie l'eyde de Dieu, e s'estende devant l'auter, e die synk foiz, "Deus in adiutorium [meum intende]" [*Psalm 69*].

¶ Si ascun se doute que le Deble eit poer de ly, die trei foiz cest salme, "In te
40   Domine speravi" le secounde [*Psalm 70*].   .

¶ Si ascun chese en defaute de siecle, die nuef foiz a genoils devant le croys ov bon devocioun, e Dieu ly aydera: "Deus venerunt gentes" [*Psalm 78*].

¶ Si ascun vuelle requere la merci de Dieu, e qu'il otreye sa preeyere e paremplisse soun desir en bien, die x foiz, "Ad te levavi oculos meos" [*Psalm 122*], "Ad te
45   Domine clamabo" [*Psalm 27*], "Usquequo Domine" [*Psalm 12*].

¶ Si ascun soit en anguisse ou tribulacion, die par un digmange devant le cors Nostre Seigneur, "Domine quid multiplicati" [*Psalm 3*], "Salvum me fac Deus" [*Psalm 68*], "Domine refugium [tu factus es nobis]" [*Psalm 89*].

¶ Si ascun soit grevement en malady, die, "Domine refugium [tu factus es nobis]"
50   [*Psalm 89*], e il sentira aleggaunce.

¶ En memoire de la passioun Jesu Christ, deit um dire ov bon devocioun, "Deus Deus meus respice [me]" [*Psalm 21*], e a la elevacion, "Te Deum laudemus."

¶ When you rise in the morning, say, "Save me, O God, by thy name" [*Psalm 53*], "O God, thou hast cast us off" [*Psalm 59*], three Paternosters, three Ave Marias, and you will go through the day without encumbrance.

25 ¶ He who has a desire to sin, pray to God devoutly that he give him repentance, and he will truly be delivered if he says, "May God have mercy" [*Psalm 66*].

¶ When you go toward your enemy or against your adversary, say with devotion, "Judge thou, O Lord, them that wrong me" [*Psalm 34*], and he will not have power to harm you.

30 ¶ When you have dreamed of something, go on the morrow before the crucifix in church, and say, "In my trouble I cried to the Lord" [*Psalm 119*], Paternoster, Ave Maria, and Creed.

¶ If anyone should be imprisoned, let him confess himself well and cleanly, and then say these psalms. And if he is not able to say them, let someone else speak for
137r] him instead, | so long as he is well and cleanly confessed, and then say these forty times, "Lord, thou hast proved me" [*Psalm 138*], "Deliver me, O Lord, from the evil
35 man; rescue me from the unjust man" etc. [*Psalm 139*].

¶ If anyone should wish to begin a great matter, pray thus for God's help, and lie prostrate before the altar, and say five times, "O God, come to my assistance" [*Psalm 69*].

¶ If anyone fears that the Devil may have power over him, say this psalm three
40 times, "In thee, O Lord, I have hoped" the second [*Psalm 70*].

¶ If anyone should fall on account of the world, say nine times on his knees before the cross with good devotion, and God will help him: "O God, the heathens are come" [*Psalm 78*].

¶ If anyone should wish to ask for God's mercy, and that he might grant his prayer and well fulfill his desire, say ten times, "To thee I have lifted up my eyes" [*Psalm*
45 *122*], "Unto thee I will cry, O Lord" [*Psalm 27*], "How long, O Lord" [*Psalm 12*].

¶ If anyone should be in anguish or tribulation, say on Sunday before the body of Our Lord, "Why, O Lord, are they multiplied" [*Psalm 3*], "Save me, O God" [*Psalm 68*], "Lord, thou hast been our refuge" [*Psalm 89*].

¶ If anyone should be gravely ill, say, "Lord, you have been our refuge" [*Psalm 89*],
50 and he will feel relief.

¶ In memory of the Passion of Jesus Christ, one ought to say with good devotion, "O God my God, look upon me" [*Psalm 21*], and at the Levation, "Te Deum laudemus."

Eulotropia et celidonia [art. 112]

137r]   ¶ Est autem herba que vocatur apud Caldeos *yryos*, apud Grecos *mauchiel*, apud Latinos *eulotropia*, id est, solsequium. Que si colligatur in estate sole existente in Virgine (sicut dicitur in Augusto sol in Virgine) et voluatur in folio lauri, et addatur dens lupi, sciatis quod nullus contra ipsum poterit habere colloquium nisi verba

5   pacifica. Et si quid furatur in nocte, subtus capud tuum ponatur, videbis furem et omnes eius conditiones. Et si ponatur in templo ubi sunt mulieres, quarum connubium per sui defectum frangatur nunquam poterit exire de templo antequam deponatur.

    ¶ Est enim herba que vocatur a Caldeis *aquibare*, a Latinis *celidonia*. Hanc herbam

10   si quis cum corde talpe habuerit simuli, devinceret omnes hostes et omnes causas et lites removebit. Et si ponatur sub capite infirmi, si debeat in illa infirmitate mori, statim cantabit alta voce; si non, mox incipiet lacrimari.

De interrogandi moribundis beati Anselmi [art. 113]

137r]   ¶ Hec est doctrina beati Anselmi, Cantuariensis archiepiscopi.

    Sic debet frater vel soror proximus vel proxima morti interrogari:

    "Frater vel soror, letaris quod in fide christiana morieris?" Respondeat: "Etiam."

    "Gaudes quod morieris in habitu clericali vel statu viduali, seu virginali, coniugali,

5   vel monachico?" "Etiam." |

137v]   "Fateris te non tam bene vixisse quam debuisses?" "Etiam."

    "Penitet te?" "Etiam."

    "Habes voluntatem emendandi si spacium haberes vivendi?" "Etiam."

    "Credis quod pro te mortuus est Dominus Iesu Christus, Filius Dei vivi?" "Etiam."

10   "Agis ei gratias?" "Etiam."

    "Credis te ne posse nisi per mortem eius saluari?" "Etiam."

Heliotrope and Celandine   [art. 112]

137r]   ¶ There is an herb which is called *yryos* among the Chaldeans, *mauchiel* among the
          Greeks, *heliotrope* among Latin speakers, which is to say, marigold. If collected in
          summer when the sun is in Virgo (as in August the sun is said to be in Virgo) and
          wrapped in a laurel leaf, and if the tooth of a wolf is added, know that no one will
5   be able to have speech against it except calm words. And if anything is stolen in the
          night, let it be placed under your head, and you will see the thief and all his
          circumstances. And if it is put in a church when there are women, those whose
          marriage vows are being broken through a failing of theirs will never be able to
          leave the church before it is put away.

          ¶ There is an herb that is called *aquibare* by the Chaldeans, *celandine* by Latin
10   speakers. If anyone should have this herb together with the heart of a mole, he
          would overcome all enemies and remove all quarrels and contentions. And if it
          should be put under the head of a sick man, if he is bound to die of that sickness,
          he will at once sing in a loud voice; if not, he will begin to weep.

Saint Anselm's Questions to the Dying   [art. 113]

137r]   ¶ This is the teaching of Saint Anselm, Archbishop of Canterbury.

          So ought a brother or sister who is near death be asked:

          "Brother or sister, are you happy that you are dying in the Christian faith?" May
          he or she respond: "Yes indeed."

5   "You rejoice that you are dying as a cleric or in a state of widowhood, virginity,
          marriage, or monasticism?" "Yes." |

137v]   "You confess that you have not lived as well as you ought to have?" "Yes."

          "Do you repent?" "Yes."

          "Do you have the desire to do correction if you should still have a span of life?"
          "Yes."

          "Do you believe that the Lord Jesus Christ, Son of the living God, died for you?"
          "Yes."

10   "Do you give thanks to him?" "Yes."

          "Do you believe that you cannot be saved except through his death?" "Yes."

"Age ergo, dum superest in te anima; in hac sola morte totam fiduciam tuam constitue, et in nulla alia re fiduciam habeas. Huic morti te totum vel totam inmitte, hac morte te totum vel totam contege, hac morte te totum vel totam involue.

15   "Et si Dominus Deus te voluerit iudicare, dic,

"'Domine, mortem Domini nostri Iesu Christi obicio inter me et iudicium tuum. Aliter tecum non contendo.'

"Si dixerit quod merueris dampnationem, dic,

"'Domine, mortem Domini nostri Iesu Christi obicio inter me et mala merita mea,
20   ipsiusque meritum offero pro merito quod ego debuissem habere non habeo.' Et dic iterum,

"'Domine, mortem Domini nostri Iesu Christi pono inter me et te et iram tuam.'"

Deinde dicat ter,

"In manus tuas, Domine, comendo spiritum meum. Redemisti me, Domine Deus
25   veritatis. Amen."

Cui hec premissa ante mortem dicantur, mortem non gustabit in eternum.

Dieu, roy de magesté   [art. 114]

137v]   ¶ Dieu, roy de magesté,
            Ob Personas Trinas,
        Nostre roy e sa meyné
            Ne perire sinas!
5   Grantz mals ly fist aver
            Gravesque ruinas —
        Celi qe ly fist passer
            Partes transmarinas.
                Rex ut salvetur,
10   Falsis maledictio detur!

        Roy ne doit, a feore de gere,
            Extra regnum ire,
        For si la commune de sa terre
            Velint consentire.
15   Par tresoun, voit honme sovent

"Come then, while the soul remains in you; in this lonely death assemble all your faith, and may you have faith in no other thing. Throw yourself entirely into this death, cover yourself over entirely with this death, enclose yourself entirely in this death.

15   "And if the Lord God should wish to judge you, say,

"'Lord, I interpose the death of our Lord Jesus Christ between your judgment and me. Otherwise I offer you no resistance.'

"If he should say that you deserve damnation, say,

20   "'Lord, I interpose the death of our Lord Jesus Christ between my wicked deserts and myself, and I offer his merit in place of the merit that I ought to have but do not.' And say again,

"'Lord, I interpose the death of our Lord Jesus Christ between me and you and your anger.'"

Then let him say three times,

25   "Into your hands, Lord, I commend my spirit. You have redeemed me, Lord God of truth. Amen."

To whom the preceding words are pronounced before death, he will not taste everlasting death.

Against the King's Taxes   **[art. 114]**

137v]   ¶ God, king of majesty,
       For the sake of the Triune Persons,
   May our king and his household
       Not perish!
5   He caused him to suffer great harm
       And grievous ruin —
   That one who made him travel
       Over the sea.
       That the king prosper,
10   May false ones be accursed!

   A king should not, in a warlike way,
       Depart from his realm,
   Unless the commons of his land
       Wish to consent.
15   On account of treason, one often sees

Quam plures perire.
A quy en fier seurement
   Nemo potest scire.
      Non est ex regno
20   Rex sine consilio.

Ore court en Engletere
   De anno in annum
Le quinzyme dener pur fere,
   Sic commune dampnum.
25 E fet avaler que soleyent
   Sedere super scannum,
E vendre fet commune gent
   Vaccas, vas, et pannum.
      Non placet ad summum,
30   Quindenum, sic, dare nummum.

Une chose est countre foy
   Unde gens gravatur:
Que la meyté ne vient al roy
   In regno quod levatur!
35 Pur ce qu'il n'ad tot l'enter
   Prout sibi datur,
La pueple doit le plus doner,
   Et sic sincopatur.
      Nam que taxantur
40   Regi non omnia dantur.

Unquore plus greve a simple gent
   Collectio lanarum.
Que vendre fet, communement,
   Divicias earum.
138r] Ne puet estre que tiel consail
46   Constat Deo carum,
Issi destrure le poverail
   Pondus per amarum!
      Non est lex sana
50   Quod regi sit mea lana!

Uncore est plus outre peis,
   Ut testantur gentes,
En le sac deus per ou treis
   Per vim retinentes.
55 A quy remeindra cele leyne?
      Quidam respondentes
Que ja n'avera roy ne reygne,
   Set tantum colligentes.

Many perish.
He in whom one can trust securely
  No one can know.
    May the king not leave his realm
20   Without good counsel.

Now proceeds in England
  From year to year
The tax of the fifteenth penny,
  Thus inflicting a common harm.
25 And it brings down those wont
  To sit upon the bench,
And it forces common folk to sell
  Cows, utensils, and clothing.
    Most unpleasant is it,
30   Therefore, to pay the entire fifteenth.

There is a thing contrary to faith
  By which people are oppressed:
To the king comes not half
  Of what's raised in the realm!
35 Since he doesn't receive the whole
  As it's granted to him,
The people must pay more,
  And thus they're cut short.
    For the taxes that are raised
40   Are not all given to the king.

Still more oppressive for simple folk
  Is the wool collection.
Commonly, it forces them to sell
  Their valuables.
138r] It cannot be that such a policy
46   Is pleasing to God,
Thus to crush the poor
  Under a bitter burden!
    It is no just law
50   That gives my wool to the king!

It is of still greater weight,
  As people bear witness,
That from the sack two or three measures
  Are retained by force.
55 By whom will this wool be taken?
  Some respond
That neither king nor realm will have it,
  But only the wool collectors.

           Pondus lanarum
60   Tam falsum constat amarum!

       Depus que le roy vodera
          Tam multum cepisse,
       Entre les riches si purra
          Satis invenisse.
65   E plus, a ce que m'est avys,
          Et melius fecisse
       Des grantz partie aver pris,
          Et parvis pepercisse.
             Qui capit argentum,
70   Sine causa, peccat egentum.

       Honme ne doit a roy retter
          Talem pravitatem,
       Mes al maveis consiler
          Per ferocitatem.
75   Le roy est jeovene bachiler,
          Nec habet etatem
       Nulle malice compasser,
          Set omnem probitatem.
             Consilium tale
80   Dampnum confert generale.

       Rien greve les grantz graunter
          Regi sic tributum;
       Les simples deyvent tot doner,
          Contra Dei nutum.
85   Cest consail n'est mye bien,
          Sed viciis pollutum.
       Ceux que grauntent ne paient rien
          Est male constitutum.
             Nam concedentes
90   Nil dant regi, set egentes.

       Coment fra honme bon espleit
          Ex pauperum sudore,
       Que les riches esparnyer deit
          Dono vel favore?
95   Des grantz um le dust lever,
          Dei pro timore,
       Le pueple plus esparnyer
          Que vivit in dolore.
             Qui satis es dives,
100   Non sic ex paupere vives!

             Such a false weight of wool
60   Constitutes a bitter thing!

         Since the king wants
             To take so much,
         Among the rich he may thus
             Find enough.
65   And besides, in my opinion,
             He would do better
         To have taken a portion from the great,
             And have spared the lowly.
                 He who, without cause, takes money
70   From the needy commits sin.

         One ought not to the king
             Assign such depravity,
         But to an evil counselor
             In his savagery.
75   The king is a young man,
             And is not of an age
         To devise any malice,
             But possesses all honesty.
                 Such a policy
80   Confers general harm.

         It doesn't oppress the great at all
             To thus yield tribute to the king;
         The simple have to give all,
             Contrary to God's will.
85   This policy is not good at all,
             But is sullied with vice.
         For those tax-makers to pay nothing
             Is wrongly ordained.
                 For the policy-makers
90   Give nothing to the king, only the needy.

         How may one bring forth good
             From the sweat of the poor,
         One who's obliged to spare the rich
             On account of gift or favor?
95   One ought to levy the tax upon the great,
             In fear of God,
         To spare more the people
             Who live in affliction.
                 You who are rich enough,
100   Live not thus upon the poor!

Je voy en siecle qu'ore court
   Gentes superbire,
D'autre biens tenir grant court,
   Quod cito vult transire.

105   Quant vendra le haut juggement,
   Magna dies ire,
S'il ne facent amendement,
   Tunc debent perire.
     Rex dicit reprobis,
110   "Ite." "Venite," probis.

Dieu, que fustes coronee
   Cum acuta spina,
De vostre pueple eiez pitee,
   Gratia divina.

115   Que le siecle soit aleggee
   De tali ruina.
A dire grosse veritee,
   Est quasi rapina.
     Res inopum capita
120   Nisi gratis est quasi rapta.

Tel tribut a nul feor
   Diu nequit durare.
De voyde qy puet doner,
   Vel manibus tractare?

125   Gentz sunt a tiel meschief
   Quod nequeunt plus dare;
Je me doute, s'ils ussent chief,
   Quod vellent levare.
     Sepe facit stultas
130   Gentes vacuata facultas.

Yl y a tant escarceté
   Monete inter gentes
Qe honme puet en marché,
   Quam parci sunt ementes

135   (Tot eyt honme drap ou blee,
   Porcos vel bidentes),
Rien lever, en verité,
   Tam multi sunt engentes.
     Gens non est leta
140   Cum sit tam parca moneta.

138v]   Si le roy freyt moun consail,
   Tunc vellem laudare:

I see at the present time
　　How people grow prideful,
Holding great pomp with others' goods,
　　Which will briefly pass away.
105　When comes the Last Judgment,
　　That great day of wrath,
Unless they mend their ways,
　　They must then perish.
　　　　The king says to the unrighteous,
110　　"Go." "Come," to the righteous.

God, who was crowned
　　With sharp thorns,
Have mercy on your people,
　　With heavenly grace.
115　May the world be spared
　　From such calamity.
To tell the plain truth,
　　It is just like stealing.
　　　　Taking goods from the poor against their will
120　　Is the same as if it were stolen.

Such tribute can by no means
　　Last for long.
Who can give from emptiness,
　　Or touch it with his hands?
125　People are in such bad straits
　　That they cannot give more;
I fear that, had they a leader,
　　They would rise in rebellion.
　　　　Often people turn foolish
130　　From loss of possessions.

There is so much scarcity
　　Of money among people
That at market one is able,
　　Because buyers are so few
135　(For all the cloth or corn one might have,
　　Pigs or sheep),
To gain nothing, in truth,
　　For so many are needy.
　　　　The people are not happy
140　　When money is so scarce.

138v]　Were the king to heed my advice,
　　Then I would praise him:

D'argent prendre le vessel,
   Monetamque parare.
145 Mieu valdreit de fust manger
   Pro victu nummos dare,
Qe d'argent le cors servyr
   Et lignum pacare.
    Est vicii signum
150   Pro victu solvere lignum!

Lur commissiouns sunt tro chiers
   Qui sunt ultra mare;
Ore lur terres n'ount povers
   Eosdem sustentare.
155 Je ne say coment purrount
   Animas salvare,
Que d'autrui vivre voderount
   Et propria servare.
    Non dubitant penas
160   Cupientes res alienas.

Dieu, pur soun seintime noun,
   Confundat errores,
E ceux que pensent fere tresoun,
   Et pacis turbatores!
165 E vengaunce en facez
   Ad tales vexatores,
E confermez e grantez
   Inter reges amores!
    Perdat solamen
170   Qui pacem destruit!
    Amen.

Contemplacioun de la passioun Jesu Crist   [art. 115]

138v] ¶ Ici comence contemplacioun de la passioun Jesu Crist. E comence a comply pur
ce que a cel oure Judas Scarioth ly vendy.

  ¶ Quant vous dites comply, pensir devez mout ententivement coment Judas vendy
Nostre Seigneur pur xxx deners, e pur ce, a ciel oure, vous rendez coupable a Dieu
5 priveement en vostre cuer — e a prestre de bouche, si vous le poez avoir — de
quanque vous avez le jour mesfait encountre les comaundementz Dieu, e de ce qe
vous avetz en delit en vanités, e si vous eiez malement ou deshonestement parlé,
ou de vos yeux folement regardé, e de quanqe vous quidez le jour par nul de vos
synk sentz encountre la volenté de vostre Creatour avoir pecchié. Si en requerez
10 devoutement merci e pardoun, e certeyne esperaunce eyez que vous averez ce que

Take the vessels of silver,
    And make money with them.
145   Better would it be to eat off wood
    And pay in coin for food,
Than to serve the body with silver
    And pay with wood.
      It is a sign of vice
150   To pay for food with wood!

The maintenance is too costly
    For those who are across the sea;
Now their lands haven't the power
    To sustain them.
155   I don't know how they'll be able
    To save their souls,
Those who would live on others
    And preserve what's their own.
      They fear no penalties
160   In coveting others' things.

May God, for his most holy name,
    Confound errant ones,
And those who plan to do treason,
    And disturbers of the peace!
165   And may you take vengeance
    On such oppressors,
And confirm and grant
    Love between kings!
      May he lose consolation
170   Who destroys the peace!
      Amen.

Seven Hours of the Passion of Jesus Christ   [art. 115]

138v]   ¶ Here begins the contemplation of the Passion of Jesus Christ. And it begins at compline because at that hour Judas Iscariot sold him.

¶ When you say compline, you must meditate attentively on how Judas sold Our Lord for thirty deniers, and for this, at that hour, you confess guilt to God privately in your heart — and to a priest by mouth, if you are able to do this — for whatever misdeeds you have done that day against the commandments of God, and for what you have done for the delight of vain things, and if you might have spoken wickedly or dishonestly, or with your eyes looked foolishly, and for whatever you consider yourself to have sinned on that day by any of your five senses against the will of your Creator. Thus you should ask devoutly for mercy and pardon, and have

vous dreitement requerez en bounté, eynssi qe vous soiez verroiement repentant e bien confés, quar ce dit Nostre Seigneur en le Ewangelye, "Requerez e vous receverez."

Dites donque, a cest COMPLY, einsi:

15   ¶ "Douz Sire Jesu Crist, je te renk graces, qe a oure de comply estoiez trahy de Judas Scarioth e vendy pur xxx deners. E aprés cest comply, tu dys a trois de tes deciples, 'Veilles e horez que vous ne entrez en temptacioun,' e pus t'en alas tu un poy de tes deciples a la mountaunce de tant come um porreit rochier une piere, e te cochas a la terre, e prias troiz foiz ton Piere que cele passioun, qu'adonque te fust
139r] en venant, passast outre de toy, si ce | pust estre. E donque apparust un aungle a
21   toi e te counforta, e tant come tu fus en t'oreysoun, tu suas d'angoyse goutes de sang. E dementiers dormirent tes desciples, mes tu soul ne dormys pointe jesque ataunt qe tu moruz en la croys. E pus dormys el sepulcre jesqe au jour de ta resurexioun. E adonqe eveillas."

25   ¶ A MATINES, devez mout ententivement penser, eynsi e dire:

      ¶ "Je te renk graces, douz Seignur Jesu Crist, qe fus a matin, par la tresoun Judas ton desciple, pur nous pris. Aprés fus lyé, despoillé, batu, buffeté, escharny, fausement acusé, de la orde salyve as Gyus soillé, de lur despitouse paroles ledengé, de tous tes desciples gerpi, tot soul lessé, de toun apostre refusé pur Seigneur, e
30   toute cele nuyt vilement e crueument treité e defolé, dount je te mercy, tresdouz Seigneur, de tout moun cuer."

      ¶ A houre de PRIME, dites:

      "Je te renk graces, douz Sire Jesu Crist, de ce qe a houre de prime fuz come lere lyé e mené a la court devant Pylat, e a ly baillé pur estre a tort jugié. E a ciel houre,
35   reporta Judas arere les xxx deners qu'il avoit resçu pur sa tresoun faire, e tantost se pendy meismes de deol par deseperaunce.

      "A ycel houre, tresdouz Seignur, te acuserent les Gyus a Pylat de trois choses. Primes te surmistrent eux fausement que tu avoyez deffendu que l'em ne donast point truage au roy Cesar, en qui subjeccioun eux estoient. Puis te surmistrent
40   fausement que tu te fes roy pur tolyr a Cesar son regne terrien. Aprés ce, te accuserent de ce qe tu dys e voirs fu, que tu fuz le Fitz Dieu.

      "A icel houre, fus tu envoyé e presenté de par Pylat a Herodes. Si ne voleyes yleqe mot soner, dont l'em te tynt a fol, e en escharnissement e moskerye te fist um vestir de une vesture blaunche come fol. E tout ensi fus tu reenvoyé a Pylat."

firm hope that you will have what you rightly ask for in good will, as long as you be truly repentant and well confessed, because this is what Our Lord says in the Gospel, "Ask and you will receive."

Speak then, at this COMPLINE, in this manner:

15 ¶ "Sweet Lord Jesus Christ, I render thanks to you, who at the hour of compline were betrayed by Judas Iscariot and sold for thirty deniers. And after this compline, you said to three of your disciples, 'Watch and pray lest you enter into temptation,' and then you went a little way from your disciples as far as a man is able to throw a stone, and laid yourself on the ground, and prayed three times to your Father that this passion, whatever might happen to you, might pass from you, if this |

139r] might be. And then appeared an angel to you and comforted you, and as long as
21 you were in prayer, you sweated in anguish drops of blood. And meanwhile your disciples slept, but you alone did not sleep at all until the time that you died on the cross. And then you slept in the sepulcher until the day of your resurrection. And at that time you woke up."

25 ¶ At MATINS, you ought to meditate very attentively, and speak in this manner:

¶ "I render thanks to you, sweet Lord Jesus Christ, who in the morning, by the treason of your disciple Judas, for us were taken. Afterwards you were bound, stripped, beaten, buffeted, mocked, falsely accused, dirtied with filthy saliva by the Jews, insulted by their contemptuous words, abandoned by all your disciples, left all alone, by your apostle denied as Lord, and all that night vilely and cruelly drawn
30 and defiled, for which I thank you, most sweet Lord, with all my heart."

¶ At the hour of PRIME, say:

"I render thanks to you, sweet Lord Jesus Christ, because at the hour of prime you were like a thief bound and led to the court before Pilate, and handed over to him
35 to be unjustly judged. And at that hour, Judas returned the thirty deniers that he had received to commit his treason, and immediately hanged himself in grief through despair.

"At that hour, most sweet Lord, the Jews accused you before Pilate of three things. First they falsely accused you that you had forbidden anyone to give any tribute to
40 King Caesar, under whose authority they lived. Next they falsely accused you that you made yourself king to take from Caesar his earthly realm. After this, they accused you for what you said and what you were, that you were the Son of God.

"At that hour, you were sent and presented on Pilate's behalf to Herod. Then you did not wish to speak a word there, on account of which men held you to be a fool, and with taunts and mockery made you dress in white clothes like a fool. And thus were you sent back to Pilate."

45   ¶ A houre de Tierce, dites:

"Je te renk graces, douz Seigneur Jesu Crist, de ce qe tu soffris si debonayrement qe, a houre de tierce, les felouns Gyus crierent encountre toy si hydousement, 'Crucifiez le! Crucifiez le!' Adonque, fus tu mené hors taunt come eus treterent de ta mort e countroverent la sentence de ta perdicioun.

139v]   "A icele | houre, maunda la femme Pilat a soun seigneur qu'il ne s'entremeist mes
51   de toy, e ce par l'entisement de Diable que voleit desturber nostre redempcioun, pur laquiele tu deignas soffryr si dure passioun.

"A icel houre, lava Pilat ses mayns e ne se voloit plus entremettre de toy. E par ice se quida il fere net e quites qu'il ne fust coupable de ta mort. A icele houre, fus tu
55   lyé al pyler tot nu, e tant batu de escourges qu'il n'y avoit lu en ton cors que ne fust dolerousement sanglante.

"A cele houre, te vestirent d'un mauntel purpre, e plyerent une coroune d'espynes e la mistrent sur ta teste, e en moskaunt te saluerent, e distrent, 'Dieu te salve, Roy des Gyus,' e te ferirent en la teste, e escrachierent en ta face, e, en genullaunt, te
60   'ahorerent.' E pus te ousterent le mauntel de pourpre, e te vestirent tes autres dras, e te chacerent vers le mount de Calvarye pur pendre e crucifier.

"A cele houre, te sywy ta douce mere ensemblement ové autres femes anguissousement plorauntz pur toy, a quieles tu te tournas e prias qe eles ne plorassent pas pur toi.

65   "Cestes peynes e mout plus souffris tu pur nous entre tierce e mydy."

¶ A houre de Mydy, dites:

"Je te renk graces, douz Seigneur Jesu Crist, qe, a houre de midy, estendis ton benet cors en la croys, e soffris tes mayns e tes piés de grosse clous si penousement trespersier e atachier en cele croys, en laquele furent quatre manere de fuist: quar
70   le fuist qu'estoit dressié countremount fu de cedre, le traversein fu de palmer, e le soverein de tous (en lequel fust escrit en Hebreu, Gryu, e Latyn, 'Iesu Nazarenus, Rex Iudeorum') estoit d'olyve, e le fuist desouth (que porta e soustint tous les autres) estoit de cyprés.

"A icel houre, requis tu nostre tres merciable Dieu ton Piere qu'il pardonast as
75   felouns Gyus ta mort tant cruele.

"A icel houre, departirent ils tes dras, mes la cote demora entiere, pur laquele eux mistrent sort pur savoir a qui ele dust escheyer. A icel houre, te escrierent e blasfemerent, te escharnisoient e te despisoient, les trespassauntz par le chemyn.

45 ¶ At the hour of TIERCE, say:

"I render thanks to you, sweet Lord Jesus Christ, for what you suffered so graciously when, at the hour of tierce, the wicked Jews cried out against you so hideously, 'Crucify him! Crucify him!' And at that time, you were led outside even as they discussed your death and devised the sentence of your destruction.

139v]
51
"At that | hour, Pilate's wife sent word to her lord that he should no longer concern himself with you, and this at the instigation of the Devil who wished to interfere with our redemption, for which you deigned to suffer so hard a passion.

55
"At that hour, Pilate washed his hands and no longer wished to concern himself with you. And by this he thought to make himself clean and free such that he would not be guilty of your death. At that hour, you were tied to the pillar entirely naked, and so beaten with whips that there was no place on your body that was not grievously bleeding.

60
"At that hour, they dressed you with a purple cloak, and wove a crown of thorns and placed it on your head, and mockingly saluted you, and said, 'God save you, King of the Jews,' and struck you on the head, and spit in your face, and, kneeling, 'worshiped' you. And then they removed the purple cloak, and clothed you [in] your other garments, and drove you toward Mount Calvary to be hanged and crucified.

"At that hour, your sweet mother followed you together with other women crying in anguish for you, to whom you turned and asked that they not cry for you.

65 "These pains and many more you suffered for us between tierce and sext."

¶ At the hour of SEXT, say:

70
"I render thanks to you, sweet Lord Jesus Christ, who, at the hour of sext, stretched your blessed body on the cross, and permitted your hands and your feet to be pierced so painfully with large nails and to be attached to that cross, in which there were four kinds of wood: for the wood that was raised upwards was of cedar, the traverse was of palm, and the highest part of all (on which was written in Hebrew, Greek, and Latin, 'Jesus of Nazareth, King of the Jews') was of olive, and the wood underneath (which carried and held up all the others) was of cyprus.

75
"At that hour, you asked our very merciful God your Father that he pardon the wicked Jews for your death so cruel.

"At that hour, they divided up your garments, but the tunic remained whole, for which they cast lots to know to whom it should fall. At that hour, the passersby on the road defamed and blasphemed you, and mocked you and insulted you.

"A icel houre, promis tu al laroun paradys.

80 "A cele houre, baillas tu ta tres seintisme mere a seint Johan l'Ewangeliste a garder. A cele houre, devynt le solail obscur e tenebrous, e jeske a haute nonne perdi sa clareté."

¶ A houre de NONNE, dites:

"Je te renk graces, douz Seignur Jesu Crist, qe, a houre de nonne, levas un grant
85 cry en la croys, la ou tu pendys, e dys en Hebreu, 'Dieux, Dieux, purquoi m'as tu
140r] guerpy?' Ce ne dis tu pas | pur ce que tu fussez de Dieu ton Piere gerpy — quar ce ne fet une a crere — mes pur ce que vis si poi des bien creauntz en toi, de tous ceux pur qui redempcion e salu tu avoies souffert. E uncore, adonque, soffris taunt de tormyntz e peynes, quar de tout le mound ne poeit um trover que en toi fermement
90 crust, a cel houre, for qe vostre beneitte mere e un soul laroun qe pendy pres de toi. Par quoi, tu (qui es Fontaigne de Vie!), tu pleinsies adonque que tu ustes seif, e les enfruntz Giws te tendirent eysyl medlé ov fyel, de quoi tu ne voleies beyvre. A quel houre, tu dis, 'Tout est acomply,' quar donque fust fet e chevy quant que fust affere devant ta preciouse mort. Adonqe, crias tu a haute vois, 'In manus tuas,
95 Domine, comendo spiritum meum.' Ensi rendis tu le espirit.

"A icel houre, fendirent les peres, e avynt grant terremeot. Monumentz desclostrent, e en issirent plousours cors des seintz, la coverture del temple fendy parmy. Pur queles merveilles e plousours autres, que adonqe avindrent, dit Centurio e les justes que ov ly erent, 'Verroiement le Fitz Dieu estoit cesti.' Adonqe, vindrent
100 les Gews e rompirent les jaunbes dé deus larouns que pendirent pres de toi, d'une part e d'autre. E lé vostres ne briserent il point car ils te troverent mort. A cel houre, mes, un chivaler qe avoit a noun Longieus te vint ferir de une lance parmi le costie, e tantost en issi sang e eawe pur nous rechater hors del poer del Deable e laver nos almes de le ordure de pecchié."

105 ¶ A houre de VESPERS, dites:

"Je te renke graces, douz Sire Jesu Crist, qe soffris qe Josep de Arymathie e Nichodemus (lesqueux ne consentirent pas a ta mort) venissent, a houre de vespers, en le honour de toi pur oustier ton seintisme cors de la crois, lesqueux par le congié de Pilat le pristrent jus de cele crois, e le cochierent a terre, e le oyndrent
110 de myrre, e le envoluperent en un drap delyé, e le mistrent en sepulcre veant ta benette mere, que estoit mout dolente pur toy." |

"At that hour, you promised paradise to the thief.

80   "At that hour, you entrusted your very holy mother to Saint John the Evangelist to
protect. At that hour, the sun became dark and clouded, and until high noon it lost
its brightness."

¶ At the hour of None, say:

"I render thanks to you, sweet Lord Jesus Christ, who, at the hour of none, raised
85   a great cry on the cross, where you were hanging, and said in Hebrew, 'God, God,
140r]   why have you forsaken me?' You did not say this | because you had been forsaken
by God your Father — since this would not be something to believe — but because
you saw so few who believed truly in you, among all those for whose redemption
and health you had suffered. And still, at that time, you suffered so many torments
and pains, because in all the world no one could be found who believed strongly
90   in you, at that hour, except your blessed mother and a single thief who hung near
you. For which reason, you (who are the Fountain of Life!), you complained still
that you were thirsty, and the ravenous Jews offered you vinegar mixed with gall,
of which you did not wish to drink. At that hour, you said, 'All is fulfilled,' because
then was done and achieved whatever was to be done before your precious death.
95   At that time, you cried out in a raised voice, 'Into your hands, Lord, I entrust my
spirit.' Thus you gave up your soul.

"At that hour, the tombstones split, and a great earthquake occurred. Tombs were
unsealed, and out from them came many bodies of saints, the roof of the temple
bursting among them. For these marvels and many others, which occurred at that
time, said the centurion and the righteous ones with him, 'Truly this one is the Son
100   of God.' At that time, the Jews came and broke the legs of the two thieves who
hung near you, on one side and the other. And yours they did not break at all
because they found you dead. At that hour, however, a knight who had the name
Longinus happened to strike you with a lance in the side, and immediately issued
from it blood and water to redeem us from the power of the Devil and to cleanse
our souls of the filth of sin."

105   ¶ At the hour of Vespers, say:

"I render thanks to you, sweet Lord Jesus Christ, who permitted that Joseph of
Arimathea and Nicodemus (those who did not consent to your death) came, at the
hour of vespers, in your honor to remove your holy body from the cross, who with
Pilate's permission took it down from that cross, and placed it in the earth, and
110   anointed it with myrrh, and wrapped it in a fine cloth, and placed it in the
sepulcher in the sight of your blessed mother, who was very mournful for you." |

De martirio sancti Wistani   [art. 116]

140v]   De martirio sancti Wistani.

Wiglafus rex Merciorum, vir illustris, genuit de Kyneswytha regina uxore sua filium
nomine Wygmundum. Defuncto Wiglafo rege Merciorum anno regni sui
terciodecimo sepultrique apud Repedone, Wigmundus filius eius successit in
5   regnum Merciorum et duxit in uxorem Ealfledam filiam Cheolwolfi regis, de qua
generavit Wystanum. Qui sese tota animi diligencia divino mancipavit obsequio.
Deinde, defuncto Wigmundo patre suo, comprovinciales Wistanum pecierunt ut
regni que iure hereditario sibi competere debebant gubernacula reciperet. Puer
vero Wistanus, malens celestis regni quam temporalis fieri coheres, singula
10   mundana neglexit imperia.

Quod audiens, quidam consul nomine Brithfardus, cognatus et compater Wistani,
misit nuncios, scilicet, Wibaldum, Man, et Ethulfum, ad Ealfledam reginam,
matrem Wistani, ut eam duceret in uxorem et sic regnum Merciorum sibi
adquireret. Quod audiens, Wistanus dixit matri sue, "Mater mea dulcissima,
15   habuisti patrem meum regem Wigmundum in maritum, qui iam mortuus est. Pro
cuius morte dolores infinitos sustinuisti et adhuc sustines in presenti. Operare de
meo concilio, et maritum habebis immortalem pro quo nunquam dolere set
eternaliter gaudere videberis." Cuius concilio regina se promisit adquiescere.

Tunc Wistanus, filiolus et cognatus Brithfardi consulis, per legatos suos predictos
20   sibi notificavit commatrem uxoremque cognati ducere non posse. Quod cum
audivisset Brithfardus consul, misit amicabiliter ad Wistanum ut specialiter ad
certum locum assignatum cum tribus sociis de necessariis diversis secum
colloquiturum adveniret. Quem cum vidisset Brithfardus in loco assignato, accessit
et osculatus est. Cum quo facto, extraxit gladium quem latenter habuit, et Wistani
25   capitis summitatem in cono amputavit, et socios eius qui secum venerant perforavit.
Et statim amens effectus est.

Corpus vero Wistani apud Reopedune monasterium, tunc temporis famosum,
delatum est, et in mausoleo Wiglafi regis avi sui tumulatum est. De loco nempe ubi
innocenter occisus est, columpna lucis — usque ad oculum porrecta — omnibus
30   eiusdem loci incolis per triginta dies conspicua stabat. Passus est puer sanctus sub
die kalendas Iunii prima feria anno incarnationis Dominice octingentesimo
quinquagesimo. Pro quo Deus diversa et infinita operatur miracula.

The Martyrdom of Saint Wistan [art. 116]

140v]   On the martyrdom of Saint Wistan.

King Wiglaf of the Mercians, a noble man, fathered by his wife Queen Cyneswitha
a son named Wigmund. When King Wiglaf of the Mercians died in the thirteenth
year of his reign and was buried at Repton, his son Wigmund succeeded him in the
5   realm of the Mercians and took as wife Elfleda, daughter of King Ceolwulf, by
whom he fathered Wistan. Wistan dedicated himself with the entire steadfastness
of his soul to the worship of God. Then, when his father Wigmund died, his fellow
Mercians asked Wistan to accept the direction of the realm which by right of
inheritance was owed to him. But the boy Wistan, preferring to become coheir of
10   a heavenly rather than temporal realm, neglected every earthly rule.

Hearing this, a certain consul named Brithfard, a relation and godfather of Wistan,
sent messengers, that is, Wibald, Man, and Ethulf, to Queen Elfleda, Wistan's
mother, that he intended to take her as his wife and thus acquire the realm of the
Mercians for himself. Hearing this, Wistan said to his mother, "My sweet, sweet
15   mother, you had as husband my father King Wigmund, who has now died. For his
death you endured countless sorrows and you still endure them even now. Act in
accord with my counsel, and you will have an undying husband for whom you will
be seen never to grieve but rather to rejoice everlastingly." The queen promised to
accept his counsel.

Then Wistan, her young son and the relative of the consul Brithfard, made known
20   to him through his legates that he could not marry the mother and wife of his
relation. When consul Brithfard had heard this, he send word in friendly fashion
to Wistan that he should come to a certain designated place with three companions
to confer with him about various important matters. When Brithfard had seen him
in the designated place, he approached and kissed him. With that done, he drew
a sword that he had hidden, and he cut off the peak of Wistan's head at the apex
25   of his helmet, and he pierced through the companions who had come with him.
And at once he was made insane.

But the body of Wistan was conveyed to the monastery of Repton, which was at that
time famous, and was entombed in the mausoleum of his grandfather King Wiglaf.
From the place where he was innocently slain, a column of light — stretched out
as far as the eye could see — was visible thirty days to all the inhabitants of the
30   place. The saintly boy suffered his death on the calends of June in the 850th year
of the Lord's incarnation. On his account God performs countless miracles of
different types.

EXPLANATORY NOTES

ABBREVIATIONS: *AND*: *Anglo-Norman Dictionary*; *ANL*: *Anglo-Norman Literature: A Guide to Texts and Manuscripts* (R. Dean and Boulton); **BL**: British Library (London); **Bodl.**: Bodleian Library (Oxford); **CUL**: Cambridge University Library (Cambridge); **DOML**: Dumbarton Oaks Medieval Library; *FDT*: *French Devotional Texts of the Middle Ages* (Sinclair 1979); *FDT-1*: *French Devotional Texts of the Middle Ages, . . . First Supplement* (Sinclair 1982); *IMEV*: *The Index of Middle English Verse* (Brown and Robbins); *MED*: *Middle English Dictionary*; *MWME*: *A Manual of the Writings in Middle English, 1050–1500* (Severs et al.); *NIMEV*: *A New Index of Middle English Verse* (Boffey and Edwards); **NLS**: National Library of Scotland (Edinburgh).

BOOKLET 5

LUDLOW SCRIBE, ESTOYRES DE LA BIBLE / OLD TESTAMENT STORIES   [ART. 71]

A lively assemblage of Old Testament stories in Anglo-Norman prose constitutes the longest and most central text in MS Harley 2253. This work has not been previously edited or translated. By careful analysis of its dialect and idiom, scholars ascribe authorship to the Ludlow scribe (Wilshere 1988, pp. 87–88; *ANL* 463). Comparative study of linguistic features points, in addition, to the same person as the translator of the Anglo-Norman outlaw tale *Fouke le Fitz Warin*, which the scribe copied into London, BL MS Royal 12.C.12. *Fouke* is apparently a prose redaction of a lost verse romance. Both *Fouke* and this item provide opportunity, therefore, for observing the preoccupations and compositional talents of this otherwise elusive scribe. The cumulative evidence points to a "substratum influence of English," that is, to an anglophone writer of French prose (Thompson 2000, p. 280). The scribe may also be the composer of a translation from Latin to English, *A Book of Dreaming* (art. 85), and an adapted Latin saint's life, *Martyrdom of Saint Wistan* (art. 116).

In *Old Testament Stories* we observe the Ludlow scribe engaging in the pious literary practice of translating, paraphrasing, and summarizing biblical matter. His method is to combine story elements from the Vulgate Bible with exegesis from Peter Comestor's *Historia scholastica* and other sources, and also to add a few comments of his own. His selections suggest the pedagogical foci of a schoolmaster who wants to pass along knowledge of the history of the Hebrew tribes, details of Holy Land geography, and precepts of the priestly profession. He especially wants his readers to hear about the responsibilities and privileges of the tribe of Levi and to understand that their role is prescribed by God. As Kuczynski remarks, "The attention drawn to the Levites, the priestly class, in these biblical paraphrases and glosses might, then, point to a clerical hand in the copying of Harley" (2000, p. 130).

In stories extracted from Genesis, Exodus, and Numbers, the central figures are Joseph and Moses, divinely appointed leaders of the Hebrew race who overcame substantial adversities in childhood (rather like the romance hero Horn). With what might seem to be an appeal aimed at boy pupils, the Ludlow scribe offers many episodes of godly divination and magic: Joseph's ability to decipher dreams, Moses's spectacular tricks with his rod, Moses's capacity to converse with God, Balaam's soothsaying aided by a she-ass with miraculous speech and a private angel. He provides his audience, in the manner of a teacher, with a mnemonic in Latin verse by which to recall the ten plagues of Egypt (lines 412–13). Here and there the Ludlow scribe includes christological allusions found in Old Testament events: how Joseph is named "Savior of the World" (line 104), how an aged Jacob crosses his arms to bless his grandsons (lines 242–43), how God's presence on Sinai is like Christ's on the Mount (lines 481–83), and how Church has replaced Synagogue (lines 731–32). The stories embed implicit moralizing upon the dangers of false idols, covetousness, and arrogant pride, as opposed to true signs, righteous piety, and humble obedience. They teach lessons of filial duty and narrate moments of righteous victory. When the author pauses to dissect words etymologically, or to explain how Joseph switched from one language to another, his storytelling showcases his own fascination with cross-lingual understanding.

Essays by Wilshere, Kuczynski, and Thompson constitute the only commentaries on this work to date. Kuczynski outlines the contents by biblical book and chapter (2000, pp. 128–30). Thompson examines the codicological context whereby MS Harley 2253 preserves other French Bible translations, namely, those copied by Scribe A in the older portion of MS Harley 2253, fols. 1–48 (2000, pp. 280–87). Wilshere analyzes the nature of the retold tales, and he pinpoints several of the Ludlow scribe's linguistic and spelling habits, which show his mother tongue to be English (1988). On the handful of orthographical errors provoked by thorns or yoghs, see the textual notes to this edition.

In preparing this text, I have inserted modern paragraphing to indicate speech changes and natural breaks. I have also used the rubrication and paraph signs of the Ludlow scribe as guideposts. Wherever he has marked the first letter of a sentence in red, I have begun a new paragraph. Proper names for biblical persons, places, and books are translated as their standard modern forms in accord with those found in the DOML edition of the Vulgate Bible with Douay-Rheims translation, edited by Edgar. For example, "Noe," "Josue," and "Pharao," are rendered "Noah," "Joshua," and "Pharaoh," respectively. I have exempted one name from this practice: the scribe's "Marie" for the sister of Moses and Aaron is here retained as "Mary" per the original Douay-Rheims, not as modern "Miriam." The following explanatory notes sometimes cite additional exegesis as found in the Douay-Rheims Catholic Bible (accessible online at http://www.dbro.org), but omitted from the DOML edition.

[Fols. 92v–105r. *ANL* 463. **Scribe:** B (Ludlow scribe). **Quires:** 10–11. **Layout:** No columns, as prose. **Editions:** None. **Other MSS:** None. **Translations:** None.]

15   *Rachel*. The manuscript reading *Lia* is a clear error by the scribe.

28–30   The gloss on how shepherds guarded their flocks is added by the author. See
            Wilshere 1988, p. 84.

43   *vodera estrere*. The author's habits in regard to his usage of the verb *voloir* become a marker that identifies him as the same person who created the Anglo-Norman prose *Fouke le Fitz Waryn*. See Wilshere 1988, p. 85.

46   *gonele*. The manuscript reading *gonenele* is a scribal error for *gonele*, in Old French "a long loose coat or robe" (*MED*). The word recurs in line 48.

55–60   The would-be seducer in the Bible is Potiphar's wife, not the Egyptian queen (Genesis 39:7–20). The confusion existed in non-Vulgate/Comestor sources that the author may have known. See Thompson 2000, p. 282; and Wilshere 1988, pp. 79.

63–64   Wilshere points to this passage about Joseph's eating restrictions as an example of how the author sometimes adds an individualized understanding to the stories (1988, p. 83). The scribe sets off this sentence by marking its capital with red ink.

105–07   The author adds this sentence on Asenath and her father, which appears in neither the Vulgate Bible nor Comestor, although her story is prominent in Vincent of Beauvais' *Speculum Tristoreale*, VI. cap.cxviii–cxxiiii (Latin c. 1260; French 1325). The passage is discussed by Thompson 2000, p. 283 n. 29. See also "The Storie of Asneth" where such interpolation is expanded from Hebrew commentaries into a full-fledged romance first in Greek, Syriac (6th century), Armenian, Ethiopic, Slavic, and Latin (12th century) and, ultimately, a 933-line Middle English romance. See Peck 1991, pp. 1–67.

119   *s'engenulerent*. Wilshere points out that the frequent bowing to Joseph by the brothers, which the author adds, is a fourteenth-century anachronism (1988, p. 84). See also Thompson 2000, p. 283.

131   *lele gent*. "Law-abiding people," a little-attested late Anglo-Norman phrase. This phrase also appears in line 134 and in *Fouke le Fitz Warin*. See Wilshere 1988, p. 85.

172   *pez*. The scribal form *gez* (MS *geʒ*) does not make sense. The Vulgate word here is *liberi*, "free" (Genesis 44:17); Joseph tells his brothers they are free to go away, but they must leave Benjamin behind.

179–80   The author adds this sentence of household action as a way to transition from Judah's speech to Joseph's revelation of his identity. Joseph clears the room of Egyptians before he speaks to his brothers in Hebrew. The switch in language is another detail added by the author.

184–85   The idea that Joseph's virtuous resistance of the queen's advances has helped him to maintain his chosen status with God is an original insertion by the author.

223   *si la qu'il*. "Until." On this distinctive construction, which occurs in *Fouke le Fitz Warin* as well, see Wilshere 1988, p. 85.

227–29   The scribe adds this sentence (drawn from Genesis 47:22) by writing it at the base of fol. 95r and indicating its place with a caret. It underscores the appropriate relationship between the state and the priesthood. See Thompson 2000, p. 284.

230–32   The Latin gloss on the name *Israel* derives not from the Bible but from Comestor's *Historia scholastica*. See Wilshere 1988, pp. 81–82.

241–42   The author here contradicts the Bible, and himself earlier, regarding which son is the elder and which the younger. Compare line 115.

252–53   *le Egipciene Complegnement*. "The Mourning of Egypt," a site called "Planctus Aegypti" in the Vulgate Bible (Genesis 50:11).

253   On the burial site of Jacob, see Genesis 49:29–31, 50:13. Elsewhere in MS Harley 2253, see *Pilgrimages in the Holy Land* (art. 38), lines 113–14.

286   *suevement*. See explanatory note to lines 545–46.

287   *Marie le suere l'enfaunt*. The naming of Moses's sister does not occur here in the Bible. The author may derive the information from Peter Comester. See Wilshere 1988, p. 82.

304–07   The story of the crown is found in Comestor, not the Bible. See Wilshere 1988, p. 82.

309–11   In the Bible (Exodus 2:11–15), both workers are Hebrew; here, the one who chides a Hebrew is Egyptian.

312   *lié*. "Felt fortunate, rejoiced." See Hindley, Langley, and Levy, eds., *Old French Dictionary, Leese*$_2$.

324   In the Bible Reuel is not a Hebrew, but rather a priest of Midian. See Exodus 3:1, Numbers 10:29.

368   *Gergesey*. "Girgashites," one of the biblical tribes of Canaan. In Douay-Rheims, see Genesis 10:16, Genesis 15:19–21, Joshua 3:10, 1 Paralipomenon [1 Chronicles] 1:14. The author's frequent, extrascriptural insertion of this tribe probably derives from Peter Comester. See Wilshere 1988, p. 82.

383   *despitousement*. See explanatory note to lines 545–46.

412–13   This mnemonic couplet on the ten plagues is set off and made prominent by the scribe's use of a crude textura script. Its presence in many medieval manuscripts — English and Continental — indicates that it was widely known and taught. It appears, for example, among the works of William de Montibus (ca. 1140–1213) (ed. Goering, p. 176), where *pignora prima* is found in place of *optinuere*. Another common variant for *optinuere* is *obtinuere*. See comments by Wilshere 1988, p. 80, and Kuczynski 2000, p. 130. The scribe's summarized account of the plagues does not set them in the right order, but the Latin couplet conveys the biblical sequence accurately.

443   *Cantemus, Domino gloriose*. The Canticle of Miriam from the Vulgate Bible, Exodus 15:21.

458–59   *Manna, manna, quid est hoc?* Paraphrased from the Vulgate Bible, Exodus 16:15.

481–83   *Jesu.* The author deploys a typological reading of God on Mount Sinai as a precursor for Christ on the Mount. Wilshere mistakenly reads this christological reference as authorial error, and suggests that the scribe accidently substituted *Jesu* for *Dieu* (1988, p. 80).

545–46   It is typical of the author's style to intensify and dramatize actions with adverbs not found in the Bible. Here Moses acts in anger, and his fury advances with a declaration that he is fiercely (*fierement*) angry and in search of vengeance. These phrases amplify the account of Exodus 32:19–20. Other examples of authorial modifiers are *suevement* (line 286) and *despitousement* (line 383).

547   *de mot en autre.* "Word for word." This idiom appears also in lines 892–93, and in *Fouke le Fitz Warin.* See Wilshere 1988, p. 86.

585–88   On the author's treatment of Moses's horns, a notorious biblical crux, see Wilshere 1988, p. 83. Here the poet does not mention Peter Comestor's gloss of the horn as light radiating from Moses's face.

598   The word *Nota* appears here in red ink in the margin to point out the listing of the twelve tribes of Israel, after the author has noted that the Levites are not included in the list. See Kuczynski 2000, p. 130; and Thompson 2000, p. 283.

624   The word *Nota* appears in red ink in the margin, pointing to the census of Israelites ready to go to war. The author notes again that the tally has omitted the Levites. See Kuczynski 2000, p. 130; and Thompson 2000, p. 283.

627   The word *Levy* appears in red ink in the margin, signaling the scribe's interest in the privileges and responsibilities granted to the priestly class. See Kuczynski 2000, p. 130; and Thompson 2000, pp. 283–84.

654   *Espernement.* The "Burning," or in the Vulgate "Incensio." See Numbers 11:3.

655   *Sepulcres de Coveytyse.* "Graves of Covetousness." In the Vulgate, these are the "Sepulchra Concupiscentiae," and in Douay-Rheims, the "Graves of Lust" (Numbers 11:34). The vice of *covetyse* is inserted into the story of how the people are fed. Compare line 670.

670   *coveytise.* See explanatory note to line 656.

726–35   Wilshere characterizes this passage as the author's "brief homily on the superiority of Christianity" in which he "describes the Israelites as *payens Judeaux*" (1988, p. 80). On this digression, the longest in the text, see also Thompson 2000, pp. 284–85.

732–33   The date of composition is given as 1163. Wilshere plausibly accepts this date as a relic from one of the author's sources, Comestor's *Historia scholastica* (1988, p. 83). See also Thompson 2000, p. 284.

736–77   The author expands the story of the rebellion of Korah, Dathan, and Abiram, adding the Devil and a lesson on pride. See Wilshere 1988, p. 84. The Douay-Rheims gloss on the tale indicates that it warns against "pretending to the priesthood without being lawfully called or sent."

752 *fortisme*. From the Vulgate Bible, Numbers 16:22.

765 *sus e jus*. "Up and down." This idiom appears also in *Fouke le Fitz Warin*. See Wilshere 1988, p. 86.

773 *fesist des encensers pieces*. "Fashion pieces from the censers." The word *pieces* is an error for the similar-in-appearance word *plates*. Compare Numbers 16:38, "beat them into plates."

805 *maylles*. That is, halfpennies, or in the Vulgate Latin, "obolos" (obols). See Numbers 18:16.

840 *le Eawe de Contradiccion*. "The Waters of Contradiction," or in the Vulgate, "Aquas Contradictionis." See Numbers 20:24.

847 *Anathema*. Glossed as "a thing devoted to utter destruction" in the Douay-Rheims Bible (Numbers 21:3).

850 *nausea*. The author coins a French verb from the Latin original: "anima nostra iam nauseat super cibo isto levissimo" (Numbers 21:5) (Wilshere 1988, p. 81).

864 *Ascendat puteus*. From the Vulgate Bible, Numbers 21:17.

865–66 In the Bible Bamoth is a place of high elevation (Numbers 21:19–20). The author's mistake in calling it a valley may derive from Comestor. See Wilshere 1988, p. 83.

902–17 *sa asne*. The author maintains the feminine gender of Balaam's ass, as in the Vulgate Bible. This feature is discussed by Wilshere 1988, p. 81.

939 From this point on, the scribe alters his manner of rubrication. He now marks off the first letters of select speeches as well as the opening of select sentences. He has marked *J* in *Je* (line 939), *J* in *Je* (line 957), and *C* in *Chescun* (line 970).

941 *Phasga*. The scribe writes *Plasga*, an error for *Phasga* (Pisgah), which he spelled appropriately at line 866.

964 *E parla Balaham plusours profecies*. For a later Middle English rendering of Balaam and his prophecies, see the Chester play *The Ten Commandments, Balaam and Balak, and the Prophets* (Bevington, pp. 337–54). The play sets Balaam in a line of prophets that begins with Moses receiving the tablet, then Balaam (as here), and then seven more prophets: Isaiah, Ezekiel, Jeremiah, Jonah, David, Joel, and Micah.

980 *Salu myht*. "Mighty Salu." The phrase appears to be a coinage from English of the Vulgate's "Salu dux" (Salu prince). The Bible identifies Salu as a prince of the kindred and tribe of Simeon (Numbers 25:14).

NOMINA LIBRORUM BIBLIOTECE / NAMES OF THE BOOKS OF THE BIBLE **[ART. 72]**

  This Latin list of the biblical books appears immediately after the Anglo-Norman Bible stories on the last verso of quire 11. As a conclusion to the Bible stories, which begin in

Genesis, it should be regarded as not simply a filler of blank space. It provides "a comprehensive sense of the great book from which the foregoing narratives were excerpted" (Kuczynski 2000, p. 130). With several apocryphal books included, the list reflects the typical contents of thirteenth-century Bibles (Ker, p. xiii). Two notes are appended to it, one on interpretation of Hebrew names (a normal item at the end of medieval Bibles), and another on the types and lengths of a cubit. Paraphs adorn each book name except for the single grouping of the five books of the Pentateuch ("libri legales"). Some anomalies occur in the order of books. For example, Mark is listed before Matthew, and Psalms appears in final position.

Proper names for biblical books are here translated into modern spellings in accord with the DOML edition of the Vulgate Bible with Douay-Rheims translation, edited by Edgar (pp. xxxi–xxxiii).

[Fol. 105va–b. **Scribe:** B (Ludlow scribe). **Quire:** 11. **Layout:** Double columns. The title is written by the scribe and underlined in red. **Editions:** None. **Translations:** None.]

16	*Parabole Salamonis.* "Parables of Solomon," that is, Proverbs.
16–20	The scribe brackets these lines. The bracketed books are those traditionally associated with Solomon: Parables (Proverbs, the book of Solomon's middle age) Ecclesiastes (the book of the king's old age), Canticle of Canticles (the songs of his youth), and Wisdom and Ecclesiasticus (apocryphal books of his wisdom).
61	*Psalterium.* The Psalter comes last rather than in its canonical position before Proverbs. See the discussion by Kuczynski 2000, p. 131.

BOOKLET 6

GOD THAT AL THIS MYHTES MAY / GOD WHO WIELDS ALL THIS MIGHT   [ART. 73]

God Who Wields All This Might is an English penitential lyric fashioned as a prayer. The speaker voices contrition over how his innately errant nature has caused him to withhold what he owes to God, who has sacrificed all for his eternal welfare. The speaker expresses his abject unworthiness, his personal lack of sufficient humility, virtue, courage, or stamina. He stands before God's almighty power, a power that frames the lyric in the first and last lines: "God that al this myhtes may." Frequent end-stopped verses give the lyric a staccato movement, an effect that may be meant to dramatize the speaker's state of penitential anguish: speech, the necessary instrument for confessing personal weaknesses, comes haltingly.

As the text that opens booklet 6, *God Who Wields All This Might* summons a mood of piety and submission, in address to God and on God's name. Despite the fact that booklet 6 holds quite a lot of secular and ribald material, it will eventually end in the pious *Prayer for Protection* (art. 99). The first two stanzas of *God Who Wields All This Might* appear in a manuscript that predates Harley: Cambridge, CUL Addit. MS 2585(b). The other manuscripts are later. For commentary on this poem, see the bibliography in *MWME* 11:4356–58.

[Fol. 106r. *IMEV, NIMEV* 968. *MWME* 11:4201 [29]. **Quire:** 12. **Scribe:** B (Ludlow scribe). **Meter:** Seven 8-line stanzas, abababab$_4$. **Layout:** No columns, two verses per manuscript line. **Editions:** Wright 1842, pp. 99–101 (no. 36); Böddeker, pp. 222–24; Patterson, pp. 64–66; Brown 1932, pp. 156–58 (no. 88); Brook, pp. 68–69 (no. 29). **Other MSS:** New York, Columbia University, Plimpton Addenda 3, fol. 238v (ed. Brown 1932, p. 158); London, BL Addit. MS 5901, fol. 325v (a modern transcription of the New York MS); Cambridge, CUL Addit. MS 2585(b), fol. 2v (2 stanzas).]

2   *thy wille ys oo.* Literally God's will is "one," i.e., "constant"; I have translated *ys oo* as "endure," the sense being that God's will is perpetual and the same both on earth and in heaven.

27   *my loves trowe.* "My trust in praise"; see Brook, p. 87. *Loves* is the genitive of OE *lof*, "praise."

41   *the bote.* "You savior" (redeemer, and remedy). See *MED, bote* (n.(1)), sense 2.(e). Compare *bote* in line 47.

45   *in crop ant rote.* "In every way," literally, "in plant and root."

LUSTNETH, ALLE, A LUTEL THROWE / THE SAYINGS OF SAINT BERNARD   [ART. 74]

To judge by its preservation in five books and a roll, this homily in English verse enjoyed good readership and circulation in the fourteenth century. The group of important manuscripts that hold it is fascinating: besides MS Harley 2253, they are MS Laud Misc. 108 (containing *The South English Legendary, King Horn,* and *Havelok the Dane*), MS Digby 86, the Auchinleck manuscript, and the Vernon manuscript, with the number of stanzas varying from copy to copy. The lesson of the poet falls into three parts: (1) moral sayings on mortal existence attributed to Saint Bernard, which starkly inform a person that he shall be food for worms; (2) a warning about mankind's three foes: the Flesh, the World, and the Devil; and (3) a classic *ubi sunt* lament on the passing of former generations who had looked splendid and seemed invincible. The third section is pared down in Harley and given its own heading in Digby. It occupies all of the fragment that remains in Auchinleck (Cross).

In the context of booklet 6, the attribution of sayings to Saint Bernard may be compared to the proverb collection *Hending* (art. 89) and to other authoritative precepts for proper conduct offered in many French texts, some serious and some less so (e.g., arts. 75, 79, 83, 94). Bernard's moral warnings complement, too, several texts in booklet 4: *Debate between Body and Soul, Earth upon Earth,* and *The Three Foes of Man* (arts. 22, 24b, 27).

[Fols. 106ra–107rb. *IMEV, NIMEV* 3310. *MWME* 9:3008 [205]. **Scribe:** B (Ludlow scribe). **Quire:** 12. **Meter:** Twenty-six 6-line stanzas, aa$_4$b$_3$cc$_4$b$_3$. **Layout:** Double columns. **Editions:** Wright 1842, pp. 101–06 (no. 37); Böddeker, pp. 225–30; Furnivall, pp. 511–21. **Other MSS:** Oxford, Bodl. MS Laud Misc. 108, fols. 198r–199r (ed. Furnivall, pp. 511–22); Oxford, Bodl. MS Digby 86, fols. 125v–127v (Tschann and Parkes, p. xxv [nos. 43–44]; ed. Furnivall, pp. 757–63); Vernon MS (Oxford, Bodl. MS Eng. Poet. A.1), fols. 303 (ed. Furnivall, pp. 511–22); Oxford, Bodl. Addit. MS E.6 (a roll; ed. Monda, pp. 299–307);

Auchinleck MS (Edinburgh, NLS MS Advocates 19.2.1), fols. 324ra–325vb (ed. Burnley and Wiggins, online facsimile).]

7	*holy man.* That is, Saint Bernard, as the author of *Meditationes piisimae de cognitione humanae conditionis.*
31	*false wonyng.* "False housing, false dwelling" i.e., the body. See *MED*, *woning(e* (ger. (1)), sense 3.
143	Compare the refrain of *The Way of Love* poems (arts. 92, 93).

LE JONGLEUR D'ELY ET LE ROI D'ANGLETERRE / THE JONGLEUR . . . ENGLAND   [ART. 75]

The Jongleur of Ely and the King of England is a performance text that starts off as joking banter, that is, as quick repartee between a clown and a straight man. It is full of delightfully agile puns and wordplay. It then devolves into a satiric monologue on backbiting, and it closes with a light moral lesson on following moderation in all things. The cogent message delivered to the king is that one must know how to govern oneself. The piece is set up as a dialogue between a jongleur and a king, placing it in the tradition of the Marcolf and Solomon dialogues — rustic wisdom delivered bluntly to powerful authority (Ziolkowski 2008; Bradbury 2008; Bradbury and Bradbury). Often, because of its persistent comic air, scholars categorize it as a fabliau, though it lacks the developed plot and extremely bawdy humor one expects from that genre. In MS Harley 2253 its closest cousin is the interlude-dialogue *Gilote and Johane* (art. 37). Nolan discusses it in the context of the Harley fabliaux (arts. 75a, 82, 84, 87), and Reichl 2000 positions it as a Harley debate poem beside arts. 9, 22, 35, 64. In the context of booklet 6, it comes amid several works that ascribe authority to a wise individual: Saint Bernard, Urbain the Courteous, Daniel (or David), Hending (named as Marcolf's son), Thomas of Erceldoune, and Saint Louis (arts. 74, 79, 85, 89, 90, 94). The jongleur who speaks words that seem cryptic and silly, yet turn out be truthful and pure, belongs with these types of truth-tellers. He speaks to an open-minded king who can glean wisdom from what he hears, to the benefit of all society.

The king and the jongleur in this Anglo-Norman poem are both English. R. Dean dates the item's composition in the thirteenth century (*ANL* 195). It exists in Continental versions, where it is known as *La riote du monde.* An Anglo-Norman analogue, a longer work in prose, survives in a manuscript and a fragment. For further discussion of the work, see Bloch, pp. 1–21; Reichl 2000, pp. 231–33; Nolan, pp. 292–94, 296–307, 310–11; Corrie 2003, pp. 72–76; and Butterfield, pp. 242, 254–59. Interestingly, a French fabliau names *La riote du monde* in the performance repertoire of minstrels (Bloch, pp. 47–48).

[Fols. 107va–109vb. *ANL* 195. Nykrog, no. 126. Långfors, p. 368. Vising §268. **Scribe:** B (Ludlow scribe). **Quire:** 12. **Meter:** Octosyllabic couplets. **Layout:** Double columns. **Edition:** Ulrich, pp. 275–79. **Altered Edition:** Montaiglon and Raynaud 2:242–56 (see Holbrook). **Other MSS:** None. **Anglo–Norman Analogue:** *La riote du monde* in prose: Cambridge, Trinity College MS O.2.45, pp. 331–36 (ed. Ulrich, pp. 279–89); Stratford-upon-Avon, Gild Records, Div. XII, No. 206 (ed. Brereton, pp. 95–99). **Old French Version:** *La riote du monde* in prose (ed. Ulrich, pp. 279–89). **Translations:** None.]

9   *Par amour*. Idiomatically, this phrase in this text means "if you please."

17–18   The wordplay is on the double meaning of *coment*, "how?" and "like what?"

29–30   The wordplay is on similar words for where a place is situated: it "sits" (*seer*) or it "stands" (*ester*).

51   The word *vet* can mean either "go" or "do."

58   *seint Leonard*. Saint Leonard of Noblac (d. ca. 559), the patron saint of horses.

69–72   The jongleur converts the word for "step" (*pas*) to a second meaning, "pass."

73   *Emble*. The jongleur quibbles on how this word can mean "steal."

84   *seinz*. The wordplay is on the meanings "sound, healthy" and "saintly, holy."

87   *Les noirs moynes*. The Black Monks, that is, the Benedictines, who are satirized in *The Order of Fair Ease* (art. 86), lines 95–100.

163   *pleder*. This word means "begging" while it also carries the legal sense of pleading a formal case. See *MED*, *pleden* (v.).

370–85   On this concern for avoiding the blame of others, compare *Urbain the Courteous* (art. 79), lines 185–96.

375   The jongleur requests a contribution. The prose analogues include a section on how the king should respond to beggars.

389–90   Compare this advice with that found in *Urbain the Courteous* (art. 79), lines 227–32.

LES TROIS DAMES QUI TROVERENT UN VIT / THE THREE . . . FOUND A PRICK   [ART. 75A]

The sophisticated sense of humor found in this fabliau has been aptly characterized as "surreally obscene" (Pearcy 2007, p. 50). Three ladies travel together on pilgrimage when one of them happens to find a *vit* (penis) lying on the ground. It is wrapped in a cloth with only its tip showing. Feeling lucky in her discovery, the finder intends to keep her prize, but one companion claims she must share it equally. The rest of the fabliau is about who holds rightful claim to this precious relic. Its acquisition and promised rewards form the core of the tale's religious parody, as the once harmonious ladies now dispute who shall have a "part" of this body part — which is what actual saints' relics often were. The *vit* implicitly becomes "the desired goal of the female quest for saving bliss" (Nolan, p. 309). Eventually, the ladies decide to set the matter before an abbess as arbiter, a move that allows the author to add a twist of satire on judicial corruption. To the ladies' dismay, the abbess invents a third answer. She names the convent as the *vit*'s rightful owner and immediately confiscates the relic: it is, she claims, the bolt to the convent door, recently lost but now happily recovered. Upon the abbess's orders, a nun with the secular name Helen appropriates the *vit*, slipping it into her slender white sleeve. The original ladies leave the convent in disappointment, but now they are wiser when it comes to matters of finders and keepers.

For various discussions of this fabliau, see Bloch, pp. 91–92; Lacy, pp. 131–49; Nolan, pp. 305–11, 316–17; Revard 2000a, p. 262, and 2005a, p. 114; and Pearcy 2007, p. 50.

[Fol. 110ra–va. *ANL* 185. Nykrog, no. 55. Långfors, p. 294. Vising §218. **Scribe:** B (Ludlow scribe). **Quire:** 12. **Meter:** Octosyllabic couplets. **Layout:** Double columns. **Editions:** Kennedy, pp. 220–29 (no. 12); Noomen and van den Boogaard 8:269–82, 384–86 (no. 96); Short and Pearcy, pp. 28–29 (no. 15); Revard 2005a, pp. 114–17. **Altered Edition:** Montaiglon and Raynaud, 4:128–32 (see Holbrook). **Other MSS:** None. **French Analogue:** Paris, Bibl. Nat. fr. 1593, fols. 149v–150v. **Translations:** Kennedy, pp. 220–29; Revard 2005a, pp. 114–17.]

1–2   Nolan, p. 306, notes that these two lines are borrowed from Marie de France's lai *Yonec*, lines 1–2.

44   *amour*. Means both "bias" and "love-longing." The ladies assume that the abbess, vowed to celibacy, will be wholly impartial.

85   *garda*. "Looked upon, gazed." Compare the word's recurrence in line 94.

89   *bel plet*. The term, "just decision," reinforces the situation with legal language.

LE DIT DES FEMMES / THE SONG ON WOMEN [ART. 76]

Called a sermon in writing, this poem showers praise on womankind because, according to its author, God favors all women for the sake of the blessed Virgin Mary. Moreover, women are so innately virtuous that they will never see the torments of hell (lines 101–04). They are attractive, elegant, and pleasing to men. Anyone who would slander or harm women acts ignobly and foolishly. This discourse generalizing on the virtues of one gender is openly paired in the manuscript with its rhetorical opposite, *The Blame of Women* (art. 77). Both belong to a dense cluster of playful verse, mostly in booklet 6, on the question of women's natural goodness or malevolence. The Ludlow scribe chose the subject of praising and defending women as the opener for his portion of the manuscript: *ABC of Women* (art. 8). He thus sees to it that both sides of the argument are expounded, perhaps as a way to spur fun and stimulate conversation among a mixed group of men and women. Such literature contributes to a complementary debate raised in other texts, that is, the marriage question: whether to marry, the dangers for men in doing so, and the qualities sought in a wife.

The Anglo-Norman text in MS Harley 2253 is unique, but some verses from the French *Bien des femmes* crop up in it and in *Urbain the Courteous* (art. 79) (*ANL* 197; Nolan, p. 296 n. 15). For discussions of the debate on women in the Harley manuscript, as well as on this poem in particular, see Dove 2000, pp. 343–44; and Nolan, pp. 310, 319.

[Fols. 110vb–111rb. *ANL* 197. Långfors, p. 369. Vising §277. **Scribe:** B (Ludlow scribe). **Quire:** 12. **Meter:** Octosyllabic couplets. **Layout:** Double columns. **Editions:** Wright and Halliwell, 2:218–21; Kennedy, pp. 95–102 (no. 6). Dove 1969, pp. 89–91. **Altered Edition:** Jubinal, pp. 334–38. **Other MSS:** None. **Old French Analogue**: *Bien des femmes* (ed. and trans. Fiero et al., pp. 105–18). **Translation:** Kennedy, pp. 95–102.]

11   *femme*. The idea seems to be that God named women *femme* because the word
            also means "fame, renown, good repute" (a pun on AN *fame*).

26   *N'est vaillaunt a femme un pygas*. "Not worth a thing compared to a woman." The
            word *pigace* appears idiomatically in expressions of comparison, defined as
            "slipper" in the *AND*, and as "horse's foot" in the *MED*.

94–96   These lines echo *Urbain the Courteous* (art. 79), lines 74–76.

LE BLASME DES FEMMES / THE BLAME OF WOMEN   [ART. 77]

A companion to *The Song on Women* (art. 76), this poem presents women in an
unflattering and pejorative light. It is so hyperbolically misogynist in its claim that women
start wars, burn castles, and so on that it seems to deflate its own bombast. The dominant
motive for arguments against women in MS Harley 2253 would seem to be humor, for they
counter the pro-women poems that insist that men who slander women must be
condemned. Another motive may be pedagogical and even nurturing: presenting the debate
not just for entertainment, but also to introduce the young and inexperienced (mainly boys,
perhaps) to some pros and cons of gender relations. Moreover, both sides of the argument
exist in other works that offer more balanced comments on human nature, occasionally even
inclusive of women.

This relatively popular poem survives in various forms in two Anglo-Norman and
numerous Old French versions. One of the Anglo-Norman manuscripts is MS Digby 86, a
book with many similarities to MS Harley 2253 (Corrie 2000, p. 439). Another book of near-
total religious content, MS Douce 210, possesses *The Blame of Women* and *Against Marriage*
(art. 83) as its only secular items. In such a one-sided context, the misogyny of both poems
would seem to be taken seriously (Dove 2000, p. 345). However, it is more usual to find texts
such as this one in secular settings and sometimes, as here, beside fabliaux. *The Blame of
Women* then becomes sexist background noise for bawdy narratives that show women
behaving largely in the ways stated (Nolan, pp. 319). MS Harley 2253 is notable for how
densely clustered in booklet 6 are pieces that speak of women's nature and issues of
marriage. Harley texts on "what women are like" include: in French, arts. 8, 37, 76, 77, 78,
83; in English, arts. 25a, 33, 35, 44, 89, 93; and in Latin, art. 109. For further discussion,
see Dove 2000, pp. 335–49; and Nolan, pp. 310, 319.

[Fol. 111rb–vb. *ANL* 202. Långfors, p. 325. Vising §60. **Scribe:** B (Ludlow scribe). **Quire:**
12. **Meter:** Octosyllabic couplets. **Layout:** Double columns. **Editions:** Wright and Halliwell,
2:221–23; Kennedy, pp. 103–18 (no. 7); Dove 1969, pp. 68–70. **Altered Edition:** Jubinal,
pp. 330–33. **Other MSS:** Oxford, Bodl. MS Digby 86, fols. 113v–114r (Tschann and Parkes,
p. xxiii–xxiv [nos. 35–37]); Cambridge, CUL MS Gg.1.1, fols. 627r–628r (ed. and trans.
Fiero et al., pp. 119–47). **Old French Analogues:** Six MSS (see *ANL* 202, to which Dove
adds Oxford, Bodl. MS Douce 210 [2000, p. 345]; and Fiero et al., pp. 12–16.) **Translation:**
Kennedy, pp. 103–18.]

41   *fotere*. "Vulture," with a possible play on French *futre*, "fuck." See *MED*, *vulture*
            (n.), which lists the Anglo-French form *voutre*.

45   *payl.* "Hair, coat"; see *AND, peil.*

46   *aspre.* "rough, violent, harsh"; see *AND, aspre*; *MED, aspre* (adj.).

96   On the rhetorical dichotomy of woman as either an angel or a devil, see Dove's discussion (2000, pp. 344–45).

NICHOLAS BOZON, FEMMES A LA PYE / WOMEN AND MAGPIES   [ART. 78]

Another copy of this poem appears in the Herebert manuscript (BL Addit. MS 46919), a book dated a bit earlier than the Harley manuscript (Reimer, pp. 8–9). It contains sermons and poems by the Franciscan friar William Herebert of Hereford and later of Oxford (ca. 1270–1333). It also includes many Anglo-Norman poems by another Franciscan, Nicholas Bozon (fl. 1300–1320), a prolific writer about whom little is known (Jeffrey and Levy, pp. 14–15). In Addit. MS 46919, the antifeminist *Women and Magpies* carries an ascription to Bozon: "Cest tretys fist frere Nich. Boioun del ordre de freres menours." Bozon's poetic oeuvre, however, plays both sides of the debate on women: he also composed the pro-feminine *De bounté des femmes.* A major variant between the Additional and Harley versions of *Women and Magpies* is the insertion of lines 49–51 in Harley. Extending the length of the stanza, these lines warn against marriage: "Given this behavior [of women], / I advise that one reflect / Before he gets married." The Ludlow scribe may be the one who adds this advice. Regarding other Harley contents, Bozon has been hypothesized to be the author of *Debate between Winter and Summer* (art. 9) (Reichl 2000, p. 230). In addition, Bozon's *Pleynte d'amour* appears elsewhere in the Ludlow scribe's library (London, BL MS Harley 273, fols. 199r–203v).

Women and Magpies continues the blame of women heard in art. 77. Here, women's deplorable traits make them like the magpie bird, in "pride in clothes, their chatter, laziness, quarrelling, jealousy, and hoarding" (Turville-Petre 1996, p. 202). In satirizing the vanity of proud attire, the poem holds a likeness to the English *On the Follies of Fashion* (art. 25a), where an extreme hairstyle makes girls look like baited pigs. In its scathing comparison of women to animals, however, *Femmes a la pye* is most like the catalogue of similes in the adjacent *Blame of Women* (art. 77), lines 38–48. It is also like Richard de Fournival's *Bestiaire d'amour* (see Beer), found in the Ludlow scribe's MS Harley 273, fols. 70v–81r. For discussion of this work, see Jeffrey and Levy, pp. 227–29; Jeffrey 2000, pp. 263, 270 (on identifying Bozon as "Bohun"); and Dove 2000, pp. 339–40, 345.

[Fol. 112ra–b. *ANL* 205. Långfors, p. 142. Vising §282. **Scribe:** B (Ludlow scribe). **Quire:** 12. **Meter:** Twelve 6-line stanzas (aabaab or aabccb) and one 9-line stanza (aabccbddb), in lines of five or six syllables. **Layout:** Triple columns. **Editions:** Wright 1842, pp. 107–09 (no. 38); Kennedy, pp. 119–26 (no. 8); Dove 1969, pp. 86–88. **Altered Edition:** Jubinal, pp. 326–29. **Other MS:** London, BL Addit. MS 46919, fol. 75r–v. (ed. and trans. Jeffrey and Levy, pp. 223–29 [no. 43]). **Translation:** Kennedy, pp. 119–26.]

13   Compare the long robes of the proud in *The Sayings of St. Bernard* (art. 74), line 133.

49–51   This warning about marriage, which Jeffrey and Levy call "gratuitious and slightly clumsy" (p. 228), expands the stanza and is not found in BL Addit. MS 46919.

69   *blestes*. "Setbacks." Compare *The Sayings of Saint Bernard* (art. 74), line 150. According to the poet, a magpie predicts future glory, while a woman's presence promises the opposite.

UN SAGE HONME DE GRANT VALOUR / URBAIN THE COURTEOUS   [ART. 79]

Composed in the second half of the thirteenth century, *Urbain the Courteous* was a popular treatise on morals, manners, and conduct for boys and young men. Read and disseminated among noble families in Anglo-Norman England, the work is a medley of proverbial and practical precepts. Redactions of varying length and arrangement survive in eleven manuscripts. In 1929, not knowing the Harley text, Parsons (pp. 386–90) identified two distinct versions, which she called the Earlier Version (244 lines) and the Later Version (321 lines). The Harley text's 349 lines is a mixture of passages from both versions. The longest of all, it is published here for the first time. Kennedy's valuable edition appears in an unpublished dissertation.

Regarding the Harley compiler's interest in courtesy literature, this treatise may be compared to *The Teachings of Saint Louis to His Son Philip* and *Hending* (arts. 94, 89), both of which also appear in booklet 6. *Urbain the Courteous* is, like *Teachings*, directed at nobility and written in French. In contrast, the English *Hending* seems targeted at a wider audience, rich and poor alike. It is noteworthy that *Urbain the Courteous* includes a passage on how important it is that a child learn to speak French because that language is much prized among nobles (lines 18–20). Such advice stresses how French was a cultivated, learned language among English families seeking to attain or maintain a social status marked not just by wealth, manners, and affiliations, but also by language. In a treatise framed as advice from a father to his son, such counsel, delivered in French, tells a boy what is expected: he must augment his mother tongue with the superior "father" tongue that befits his birthright.

Parsons's edition provides an important analysis of *Urbain the Courteous* but unfortunately does so without the Harley version. For other commentary, see Kennedy, pp. 1–9, 24–53; Nicholls, pp. 69, 154–55, 187; Nolan, pp. 310, 325; and Dove 2000, pp. 341–42.

[Fols. 112rc–113vc. *ANL* 231. Långfors, p. 432. Vising §247, §248. **Scribe:** B (Ludlow scribe). **Quire:** 12. **Meter:** Octosyllabic couplets. **Layout:** Triple columns. **Edition:** Kennedy, pp. 24–53 (no. 4). **Other MSS:** Eleven MSS: see *ANL* 231. Parsons produced a critical edition of eight MSS, not including MS Harley 2253. **Translation:** Kennedy, pp. 24–53.]

33–44   A parallel to this passage is found in just one other manuscript, Oxford, Bodl. MS Selden supra 74 (dated second half of the thirteenth century). The passage there cites Roland and Oliver for valor, Gawain for courtesy, Horn and Ipomadon for beauty. Here, Gawain is similarly exemplary in courtesy, prideful Roland is worth less than Oliver, and the handsome ones are Absolon and Hippomedes (i.e., Ipomadon). See Parsons, pp. 394, 411; Nicholls, pp. 54–55;

and Kennedy, pp. 27–28. *Ipomadon* (ca. 1180) is an Anglo-Norman romance that was adapted several times in Middle English. Its author was Hue de Rotelande, who possibly wrote it in Herefordshire.

74–76   These lines echo *The Song on Women* (art. 76), lines 94–96.

119   *sivilement.* "Nonchalantly, easily." Kennedy reads *si vilement*, which he translates "cheaply."

185–96   On this concern for avoiding the blame of others, compare *The Jongleur of Ely and the King of England* (art. 75), lines 370–85.

227–32   Compare this advice with that found in *The Jongleur of Ely and the King of England* (art. 75), lines 389–90.

TALENT ME PRENT DE RYMER E DE GESTE FERE / TRAILBASTON   [ART. 80]

This Anglo-Norman poem is a song of political complaint voiced by a man exiled from society. He claims that he has been falsely accused and made an outlaw as a result of the articles of Trailbaston, a series of fourteenth-century statutes enacted and strenuously enforced to raise funds needed for the crown's military campaigns. The speaker names four men — Martin, Knoville, Spigurnel, and Belflour (lines 33–36) — who were four of the five justices assigned to the southwestern counties of England from April 1305 to February 1307. Consequently, the poem can be dated with precision and placed in the same region as the Harley manuscript. The author, if we may understand him to be writing autobiographically, must have lived under the jurisdiction of these justices. The two named as pious (Martin and Knoville) were local men, and they are accorded a degree of respect. The two named as cruel (Spigurnel and Belflour) were from outside the area (Aspin, pp. 67–68). Revard (2005c, pp. 152–53) hypothesizes that the author was William of Billebury, chamberlain to Maud Mortimer, the ancestor of a possible patron of the Ludlow scribe.

The speaker has fled to the greenwood — that is, the forest of Belregard — to escape prison, and there he finds protective shelter and solace. Passing references to archery and a band of outlaws establish the song in the larger body of outlaw lore that precedes the popular Robin Hood ballads of succeeding centuries. Elsewhere, the Ludlow scribe is responsible for the sole copy of an important outlaw romance, *Fouke le Fitz Waryn*, in London, BL MS Royal 12.C.12 (ed. Hathaway et al.). The stated means of publication for *Trailbaston* is as a bill thrown into the highway (lines 97–100), a desperate way to issue a plea of innocence and lodge a political complaint. Scase sees in *Trailbaston* an instance of literature framed as legal plaint (2007, p. 173), a category in which other Harley poems might be set, for example, *Song of the Husbandman* and *Satire on the Retinues of the Great* (arts. 31, 88).

For discussions of *Trailbaston*, see Aspin, pp. 67–68; Dobson and Taylor, pp. 250–51; Green 1999, pp. 171–73; Scattergood 2000a, pp. 185–88; Revard 2000b, pp. 75–76 (on the contemporary relevance of the poem in the year 1341), and 2005c, pp. 151–55; and Scase 2007, pp. 42–48, 173.

[Fols. 113vb–114v. *ANL* 93. Långfors, p. 400. **Scribe:** B (Ludlow scribe). **Quires:** 12–13 (fol. 114 opens quire 13). **Meter:** Twenty-five monorhymed quatrains. Each line has ten to fifteen syllables. Two lines are lost from stanza 16. **Layout:** Begins in a wide right column and finishes with no columns. **Editions:** Wright 1839, pp. 231–36; Ritson 1877, pp. 19–24; Aspin, pp. 67–78 (no. 7). **Other MSS:** None. **Translations:** Wright 1839, pp. 231–36; Aspin, pp. 73–76; Dobson and Taylor, pp. 250–54; Revard 2005c, pp. 151–64.]

1   *Talent.* "Survival instinct, need, desperation." See *MED, talent* (n.), sense 3.

91   *x lywes ou deus.* "Ten leagues or twenty." The phrase *ou deus* literally means "or two," but it seems to mean in this context "ten leagues or twice that."

MON IN THE MONE STOND ANT STRIT / THE MAN IN THE MOON [ART. 81]

The Man in the Moon provides a glimpse of what performed comedy in English was like in the early fourteenth century. It is a funny dramatic monologue that would have required theatrical talent for mimicry and an exquisite sense of timing. In the Harley manuscript it belongs with *On the Follies of Fashion, Song of the Husbandman, Satire on the Consistory Courts, An Old Man's Prayer,* and *Satire on the Retinues of the Great* (arts. 25a, 31, 40, 45, 88) — each one a miniature masterpiece of controlled tone, dramatic effect, and alliterative idiom. Such pieces tend to draw their psychological power from how they mix political comment with personal aggrievement. The language is learned in its verbal acrobatics, yet the speaker is ostensibly a member of the illiterate underclass who is suffering a lamentable crisis. In some poems (e.g., arts. 31, 45), the pathos of the situation feels authentic and moving. But in others, an element of mockery creeps in as the speaker shows himself unaware of how his pose invites ridicule. Such works draw class-based laughter upon an English-speaking clown who complains over something a French-speaking audience — regarding itself as more sophisticated — will think absurd.

This lyric bases its colloquial dramatics on a folkloric fiction, the man in the moon, imagined as a poor peasant engaged in hedge-robbing. The speaker greets him colloquially by first name (Hubert) and graciously offers him a means to avoid paying the stiff penalty imposed by a local officer (the hayward). By the speaker's elaborate plan, the hayward shall be invited to his own home, where the speaker's attractive wife will distract him and see that he gets as drunk as a drowned mouse. They then will filch the pledge and release the man in the moon. But Hubert, frozen in a stationary pose, offers no response to these kind and generous overtures. The piece ends with the speaker's angry frustration that a churl should be so ungrateful.

For further comment on this lyric, see Menner, pp. 1–14; Fein 2007, pp. 91–92; and Scase 2007, pp. 38 n. 130, 143 n. 24.

[Fols. 114v–115r. *IMEV, NIMEV* 2066. *MWME* 11:4202 [30]. **Scribe:** B (Ludlow scribe). **Quire:** 13. **Meter:** Five 8-line stanzas, ababab ab$_4$, with alliterative ornament. **Layout:** No columns, written as prose. **Editions:** Wright 1842, pp. 110–11 (no. 39); Ritson 1877, pp. 58–60; Böddeker, pp. 176–77; Brown 1932, pp. 160–61 (no. 89); Brook, pp. 69–70 (no. 30); Bennett and Smithers, pp. 127–28; Turville-Petre 1989, pp. 32–33. **Other MSS:** None.]

19   *grey frere*. "Gray friar," that is, a friar of the Franciscan order.

30   *dame douse*. Turville-Petre 1989 and Ritson 1877 read *douce* as the wife's proper name, "Sweetheart."

LE CHEVALER E LA CORBAYLLE / THE KNIGHT AND THE BASKET   [ART. 82]

The author of this fabliau gives it two internal titles. To start with, it is *The Knight and the Basket*; by the end, it is *The Old Woman and the Basket*. Hanging in balance, the titles respond to the tale's content and to the contrastive rides in the basket, its main prop. First, the basket swings the aspirant lover into the castle; then it tosses and disorients the old woman. Each character finds a deserved fate — his reward or her punishment — by riding in the basket.

Known only in the Harley manuscript, this fabliau follows a plot of adultery enabled by an elaborate, ingenious scheme, such as is found in *Dame Sirith* or Chaucer's *Miller's Tale*. Its fun lies in its spatial and architectural precision enhanced by a mechanical gadgetry that achieves the technology needed for the wife and knight to consummate their passion. The castle walls are thick rock and the castellan's wife is well guarded, but, with a good scheme and the wife's compliance, the castle can be scaled via a few ropes, a flimsy, porous vehicle of conveyance (the basket), and a few accomplices with strong arms. A hallway with a louvred roof, open at one end, is key to the operation. Meanwhile, there are the human impediments: the husband and his meddlesome mother, depicted (through the eyes of the lovers) as wicked and malevolent. She is given the derogatory term *talevace* (antiquated, wooden shield) to show how she is a worthless barrier to love. While the aspirant knight is seen as brave in his single-minded exploit, a positive hero in his quest, the castellan-husband is depicted as an errant knight who roams away to tourney while his rival zeroes in on his vulnerable domestic space. The mother-in-law, too, becomes an ill-fated wanderer when she makes the mistake of getting out of bed and falling into the basket. She takes the tossing she receives as a form of bewitchment and vows never again to roam at night, no matter how the blanket she shares with the wife tosses and turns. In its movements, the blanket becomes a prop that complements the basket. The old woman has to endure these unusual doings in the night, accepting the blanket so as not to suffer the basket. The tale thus plays out the classic fabliau theme: youth's lustful vitality and ingenuity prevailing over age's confusion and weakness.

For further discussion of this fabliau, see Nolan, pp. 311–17.

[Fols. 115va–117ra. *ANL* 186. Långfors, p. 284. Vising §43, §217. Nykrog, no. 24. **Scribe:** B (Ludlow scribe). **Quire:** 13. **Meter:** Octosyllabic couplets. **Layout:** Double columns. **Editions:** Kennedy, pp. 199–219 (no. 11); Noomen and van den Boogaard 9:263–78, 314 (no. 113); Revard 2005a, pp. 117–23. **Altered Editions:** Montaiglon and Raynaud, 2:183–92, 333 (see Holbrook); Short and Pearcy, pp. 15–18 (no. 12). **Other MSS:** None. **Translations:** Kennedy, pp. 199–219; Revard 2005a, pp. 117–23.]

37   *talevace*. In Anglo-Norman, "wooden shield used for protection against arrows." In *Gilote and Johan* (art. 37), line 337, the term seems to be a euphemism for the

pudendum (see explanatory note). A similar, more derogatory slur may be intended here. See Revard 2005a, p. 137 n. 15.

90   *goute*. The word means either "malady" or "drop," i.e., as of poison; see *MED*, *goute* (n.(1)) and (n.(2)). The first meaning seems more probable. By the end, the old woman suffers an unsettling disorientation that makes her feel ill.

136   *oefs*. "Means of action, operation, affair"; see *AND*, *ovre*. The knight has detected in the louvred roof his means of entry into the castle via the basket.

152   *rusche*. "Rushes, reeds," apparently held by the squire as camouflage. The word has an Old English derivation (*rysc*) and hence is unusual in this French work; see *MED*, *rishe* (n.), sense 1. The prop exists perhaps to associate this maneuver with the basket.

248   *atornee*. A literal "turn" (i.e., being tossed) and also "turn of events, circuitous course, or spell." The old woman fears she's been afflicted by demons, and associates this affliction with her night-wandering. Compare the tossing of Mak in a blanket to drive out evil spirits in the Wakefield *Second Shepherds' Pageant* (Bevington, p. 404).

260   *bosoigne*. "Need." The word resonates with the lady's earlier "itch" (line 196). While the lady can continue to assuage her need, the old woman will never again arise from bed to satisfy her curiosity.

DE MAL MARIAGE / AGAINST MARRIAGE   [ART. 83]

This Anglo-Norman anti-matrimonial satire is freely adapted from a well-known Latin poem, *De conjuge non ducenda*, composed in the second quarter of the thirteenth century. As in the source, whose structure is followed quite closely, the narrator Gawain explains how he had planned to marry and was keenly encouraged to do so by his married friends, but actually they just want him to join them in misery. He was saved from this fate by God's benevolence. Three angels visit him as heavenly emissaries — Peter of Corbeil, Lawrence of Durham, and Saint John Chrysostom — and they explain, each in turn, various aspects of woman's flawed nature. Every speech closes in direct warning to Gawain, the last one admonishing, "Therefore, Gawain, act wisely. / Watch out for a bad marriage! [*Gardez vous de mal mariage!*]" (lines 165–66). Gawain agrees to avoid marriage, and he thanks God for rescuing him by divine intervention.

The item belongs with other pieces in the Harley manuscript that grossly defame women (arts. 77, 78). It is flanked by two fabliaux (arts. 82, 84) that might be thought to illustrate its truth in their portrayals of wives who scheme, cheat, and work to gain advantage over their husbands. It also contributes vigorous satire to a broader conversation in booklet 6 on marriage and its potential pitfalls (arts. 79, 89). Elsewhere in MS Harley 2253, the perspective offered in *Against Marriage* is countered by a different set of misogamist arguments in the satiric *Gilote and Johane* (art. 37). The Ludlow scribe twice flags passages by inserting the word "Nota" in the margin (perhaps following a source). At line 83, the meaning concerns the impossibility of ever satisfying a woman. At line 153, the highlighted passage is a proverb similarly used by Chaucer's Wife of Bath: that woman, rain, smoke, and argument are the torments that drive a man from his own house.

In Latin analogues, the protagonist is variously called Gawain, Golias, Galterus, and so on. The name may be meant to give the author's real name, but it seems more probably to be a fictional construct. As "Gawain," the name may evoke the womanizing reputation of the Arthurian knight. For further discussion of this poem, see Rigg 1986, p. 102; Dove 2000, pp. 340–41, 345, 347; and Nolan, p. 316.

[Fols. 117ra–118rb. *ANL* 206. Långfors, p. 45. **Scribe:** B (Ludlow scribe). **Quire:** 13. **Meter:** Octosyllabic couplets. **Layout:** Double columns. **Editions:** Wright 1841, pp. 292–94; Kennedy, pp. 127–45 (no. 9); Dove 1969, pp. 77–85. **Other MS:** Oxford, Bodl. MS Douce 210, fols. 48r–49v. **Latin Source:** *De coniuge non ducenda* (ed. Wright 1841, pp. 77–85; ed. and trans. Rigg 1992, pp. 66–99; selection trans. Blamires, pp. 125–29). **Translation:** Kennedy, pp. 127–45.]

5   *provee*. "Experienced." The manuscript reading is *prorree* or *proriee*, an error for *provee*, the reading found in MS Douce 210 (Kennedy, p. 127). This reading makes better sense than *priee*, "prayed," the word read by Wright 1841, Dove 1969, and Kennedy.

39   *Pieres de Corbloi*. Peter of Corbeil (d. 1222) was a scholastic philosopher at the University of Paris who was appointed Archbishop of Sens in 1200.

41   *Laurence*. Lawrence of Durham (d. 1154), an English prelate, poet, and hagiographer.

44   *Johan ov la bouche d'or*. Saint John Chrysostom (ca. 349–407), a Greek saint known for eloquence as a preacher. By legend, he committed one act of fornication and for this sin and others, he suffered excruciating penance for years, crawling on his hands and knees and grazing like an animal, until he earned forgiveness. He was also known for his censure of women (Blamires, pp. 58–59).

83–84   This warning to unmarried men about women's sexual insatiability is signaled by the scribe with a marginal *Nota*. Compare the second *Nota* on nagging women at lines 153–54.

153–54   These lines, marked *Nota*, express a folksy/academic commonplace on evil women (Whiting, T267), occasionally repeated in Chaucer's *Canterbury Tales*. See, in the prose Tale of Melibee: "that is to seyn, smoke, droppyng of reyn, and wikked wyves" (line 1086); and the Wife of Bath's variant on the idea: "Thow seyst that dropping houses, and eek smoke, / And chiding wyves maken men to flee / Out of hir owene houses; a, benedicitee!" (Wife of Bath's Prologue, lines 278–280). See also the Parson's Tale, line 631, and compare Proverbs 27:15: "Roofs dropping through in a cold day, and a contentious woman are alike." For further background, see *The Riverside Chaucer*, p. 925 (note to line 1086).

LA GAGURE, OU L'ESQUIER E LA CHAUNBRERE / THE WAGER . . . CHAMBERMAID   [ART. 84]

Like an earlier Harley fabliau, *The Knight and the Basket* (art. 82), this one has a dual internal title — *The Squire and the Chambermaid* or *The Chambermaid and the Squire* — which reflects how power shifts as the plot progresses. Among scholars, this fabliau (known only in the Harley manuscript) is called *The Wager*. There are four protagonists: a knight, his wife, and their two young relatives. The knight's brother serves him as squire, and the lady's female cousin serves her as chambermaid or lady-in-waiting. An unseemly rivalry exists between the married pair, for the wife thinks her family is loftier than her husband's. Her conviction of social superiority, expressed as disdain for the family to which she is married, motivates the wager and the fabliau plot that ensues.

The lady has passed her proud attitude to her young cousin, for when the squire professes love, the chambermaid runs to her lady and tells her about this insult. Coaching the girl, the lady tells her to set up a test: the squire should willingly kiss her *cul* before she grants him her love. The word *cul*, "ass, asshole, buttocks," is, like *coun* and *vit*, a vulgar name for a nether body part, and thereby a staple of fabliau vocabulary and plotting (compare arts. 75a, 87). The test itself is a parody of the acts of self-abasement that a lady in romance can reasonably require of a knight who truly loves her, like Guenivere telling Lancelot to "do his worst" in a tournament. This particular gesture, in its display of vulgarity and debasement, is also meant to symbolize "the superiority of an upper-class lady's family over that of her lower-class husband" (Muscatine, p. 45). The anticipated encounter then becomes a wager between the knight and his wife, who will observe their relatives from a window. The husband is convinced that his brother will never perform such a low, peasant deed.

Thus the encounter is set up as a bet between the contentious and voyeuristic older couple, and also as an initiation in "love" between the youngsters. From the window the elder pair shout and encourage their protegés as if at a sports event. The win goes to the knight: his squire proves his social worth by reconfiguring the asked-for gesture. Rather than kiss the maiden's behind, he connects more natural body parts of his own and hers, showing everyone his true lineage and breeding. The blunt action quells the lady's disdain for her husband's family, and the knight has the squire honorably marry the chambermaid — thus expanding the family alliance and solidifying his own domestic peace with his now more compliant wife.

For further discussion of this fabliau, see Cooke, p. 151; Pearcy 1978, pp. 76–83; Muscatine, pp. 30, 120; Nolan, pp. 316–19; and Revard 2000a, p. 263, and 2005a, p. 124.

[Fol. 118rb–vb. *ANL* 187. Nykrog, no. 73. Långfors, p. 419. Vising §221. **Scribe:** B (Ludlow scribe). **Quire:** 13. **Meter:** Octosyllabic couplets. **Layout:** Double columns. **Editions:** Kennedy, pp. 230–37 (no. 13); Noomen and van den Boogaard 10:1–10, 339 (no. 114); Revard 2005a, pp. 124–27. **Altered Editions:** Montaiglon and Raynaud, 2:193–96, 336 (see Holbrook); Short and Pearcy, pp. 30–31 (no. 16). **Other MSS:** None. **Translations:** Kennedy, pp. 230–37; Revard 2005a, pp. 124–27.]

52   *le perer jahenyn.* "An early-ripening pear (tree)." See *MED*, *pere-jonette* (n.); and
          Kennedy, p. 234.

67   *seint Martyn*. Saint Martin of Tours, whose autumnal festival was associated throughout western Europe with the maturation of wine and the harvest. A period of fasting began after St. Martin's Day, November 11, so the festival was associated with hearty eating and drinking.

93   *seint Thomas*. The reference could be to Thomas of Canterbury, martyr (d. 1170), or it may point to another English saint with local resonance in the West Midlands: Thomas of Cantilupe (ca. 1218–1282), Bishop of Hereford (1275–82) and, briefly, Chancellor of England (1264). He favored Simon de Montfort's cause during the Barons' War (compare arts. 23, 24).

A BOK OF SWEVENYNG / A BOOK OF DREAMING   [ART. 85]

A Book of Dreaming is composed in couplets with a twelve-line introduction, a six-line conclusion, and, in its body, 144 dream prognostications. The poet's usual method of presentation is to provide in a single couplet the dream image matched to its meaning. Occasionally he alters the pattern so that a dream interpretation spans three monorhyming lines or a pair of couplets. This dream-with-meaning structure is highlighted in this edition by italics and layout.

    The source text for *A Book of Dreaming* is the Latin *Somniale Danielis*. The Ludlow scribe had access to this work in his book London, BL MS Royal 12.C.12, fols. 81vb–86ra, a version that remains unedited. The Royal copy may be the direct source for this version, and the scribe himself may be the English poet. In the *Somniale Danielis*, each type of dream is listed in alphabetical order for ease of reference. Ironically, when translated to English, this indexing method is utterly invisible; the resultant order, based on Latin words by letter, comes to seem entirely random, even bewildering. Moreover, the attribution of the book to the prophet Daniel, an expert in dreams, is muddled by the Ludlow scribe when he copies *Dauid* instead of *Daniel* in line 3 (the translation is emended to *Daniel* in this edition). A few other dreambooks were made in English, all of them in prose and with fewer interpretations.

    The scribe betrays an interest in dream prognostication elsewhere in his telling of the story of Joseph in the Anglo-Norman *Old Testament Stories* (art. 71) and by allusion to Joseph in the Latin *Legend of Saint Etfrid, Priest of Leominster* (art. 98) — an allusion he may have inserted. In addition, the plot of the romance *King Horn* (art. 70) depends on several important dreams, and the *Debate between Body and Soul* (art. 22) possesses the atmospherics of a dream vision. For further discussion of dream lore in MS Harley 2253, see Phillips.

[Fols. 119ra–121ra. *IMEV, NIMEV* 1196. *MWME* 10:3625 [125]. **Scribe:** B (Ludlow scribe). **Quire:** 13. **Meter:** Octosyllabic couplets. **Layout:** Double columns. **Editions:** Förster, pp. 36–47; Wright and Halliwell, 1:261–68. **Other MSS:** None. **Latin Source:** *Somniale Danielis* (ed. L. Martin). **Middle English Prose Analogues:** See *MWME* 10:3621, 3625 [86, 126–27].]

3   *David*. The scribe writes *Dauid* for *Daniel*, a simple error caused by the likeness of *d* to *el*.

77   *wowe*. This word could mean "wall" instead of "wave." Compare *MED*, *wough* (n.(1)) and *waue* (n.). The dreamed house is either destroyed by flood or suffers its walls falling down.

111   *gestes*. "Guests." Alternatively, this word could mean "adventures." Compare *MED, gest* (n.) and *geste* (n.(1)).

144   *Lattynge*. "Injury, harm, trouble." See *MED, letting(e* (ger.), sense 3.

174   *eyl*. "Health." See *MED, heil* (n.).

238   This line is difficult to translate. See *MED, led(e* (n.(2)), sense 1.(a), "a person, a man" and 1.(c), "a prince, lord"; and *swin(e* (n.), sense 2.(a), "a lazy, dirty, lustful person" or 1(a), "a domestic pig."

ORDRE DE BEL AYSE / THE ORDER OF FAIR EASE [ART. 86]

The Anglo-Norman *Order of Fair Ease* follows a vogue for religious satire known in the twelfth century in the Latin works of Walter Map, Gerald of Wales, and Wirecker. Dated roughly around 1300 and known only in the Harley manuscript, this parody makes fun of the religious orders of England. Its speaker's premise is that a new order, one better than all the others, has just been created and will be accepting initiates. It is the finest of all orders in the land because it judiciously borrows a single ordinance from the rule of each well-known order of monks, nuns, canons, and friars — that is, it takes the most appealing rule of each — to form the "Ordre de Bel Ayse." The name is thus appropriate because the new order is pleasing in all respects. A characteristic of each English order is thus targeted for keen satire: it is adopted not as a stringent ascetic practice, but as an excuse for sanctioning an opulent, licentious way of life such as, by implication, the religious orders now enjoy. The new order shall be open only to noble persons — a way of saying "that the powerful rich have appropriated the religious orders and remade them for their own advantage and in their own images" (Scattergood 2000a, p. 197). Near the beginning, the speaker asserts that rogues and peasants will be strictly forbidden from joining the order, for when one of their class rises in authority, "There's no more moderation in them / Than in the wolf who devours lambs" (lines 27–28). This attitude, somewhat hard to gauge in its irony, can be compared to notions on class presented in the Latin *All the World's a Chess Board* (art. 109). For further discussion of this work, see Aspin, pp. 130–42; Tucker, p. 58; Turville-Petre 1996, pp. 200–01; and Scattergood 2000a, pp. 195–97.

[Fols. 121ra–122va. *ANL* 96. Långfors, p. 342. **Scribe:** B (Ludlow scribe). **Quires:** 13–14 (fol. 122 opens quire 14). **Meter:** Octosyllabic couplets. **Layout:** Double columns. **Editions:** Wright 1839, pp. 137–48; Aspin, pp. 130–42 (no. 12). **Other MSS:** None. **Translations:** Wright 1839, pp. 137–48; Aspin, pp. 138–41.]

34   *Sympringham*. Sempringham, Lincolnshire, the home of the Gilbertine Order of canons regular, founded around 1130. It was mixed order of monks and nuns.

61   *Beverleye*. A local monastery was founded at Beverley Minster around the year 700.

71   *Hospitlers*. The order of the Knights Hospitallers of Saint John of Jerusalem, which is dedicated to hospitality, religion, and militancy. Hospitallers were present in England from at least the mid-twelfth century onwards.

| 79 | *chanoynes*. According to Aspin, these are "presumably the Augustinian or regular canons. They lived a quasi-monastic life" (p. 141). |

79   *chanoynes*. According to Aspin, these are "presumably the Augustinian or regular canons. They lived a quasi-monastic life" (p. 141).

95   *moyne neirs*. The Black Monks are the Benedictines.

115   *chanoynes seculers*. The secular canons are the clergy who served in cathedrals and important churches. They lived outside of a monastery by rules of discipline.

133   *Gris moignes*. The Gray Monks are the Cistercians.

148   *seynz*. "Bells," which becomes a euphemism for "testicles."

155   *Charthous*. The Carthusians, who lived isolated within individual cells (miniature dwellings), which would include space to grow vegetables and herbs in a walled garden.

169   *frere menours*. The Friars Minor, that is, the Franciscans.

177–92   One is reminded of Chaucer's Friar, committed to *poverté*, who preaches the easy way to heaven and prefers the company of women and franklins, where he can have good food and board and be made comfortable, rather than lodge with a *povre honme*. Compare the General Prologue to the *Canterbury Tales*, lines 215–17.

194   *prechours*. The Order of Preachers, that is, the Dominican friars.

215   The satiric point, regarding how an understanding friar will accept penance from one who is too hard-hearted to weep, resembles a detail in Chaucer's Friar's portrait in the General Prologue to the *Canterbury Tales*, lines 228–32.

239   *Augustyns*. The Augustinian Order of friars.

LE CHEVALER QUI FIST LES CONS PARLER / THE KNIGHT . . . MADE VAGINAS TALK [ART. 87]

Booklet 6 contains all four of the fabliaux found in the Harley manuscript. This one occurs fourth, after *The Three Ladies Who Found a Prick*, *The Knight and the Basket*, and *The Wager* (arts. 75a, 82, 84). Muscatine labels it an "hilarious parody of the romance motif of the magical gift" (p. 91). It tells of an adventuring knight who is handsome and worthy, but also a mercenary down on his luck. Accompanying him is his clever squire Huet, without whom it seems none of his adventures would pan out. Low on resources, the knight decides to try to increase his fortune by going to tournaments. In this, he has Huet's encouragement, but they are so poor that they must lodge along the way in religious houses ("Lord Elijah's boat," lines 43–52).

On a pleasant summer day they come upon three nymphs bathing. Exercising his valuable ingenuity and foresight, Huet steals their clothes. To get them back, the maidens, who are fairies, appeal to the young knight and promise him three gifts in return for this contrived favor. The first gift conforms to romance: he will be welcomed and cherished wherever he is a guest. The second adds an element of sexual fantasy: all women and girls will gladly grant him their love. The third advances into the bawdy, surreal world of fabliau with something considered truly noteworthy: he will have the power to make *culs* and *couns* talk and always tell the truth. He is now on his way to becoming the Knight Who Made Vaginas Talk.

The fabliau proceeds to narrate the knight's adventures. The first involves an encounter with a chaplain riding a mare. After Huet reminds the knight to try out his gift, the mare's *coun* exposes the chaplain's shameful destination: the house of his mistress. Then the knight arrives at a castle where he is enthusiastically welcomed in accord with the first gift. By the second gift, he is graciously rewarded when a young lady visits him in his bed. But, now operating without Huet's aid, the knight ungallantly questions the girl's *coun*: it reveals an unflattering truth about the girl, and she leaves him in horror and shame. The final adventure occurs when the girl divulges the knight's unusual talent to the lady of the castle. The countess's test of the knight — in which she tries to cheat him — nearly overcomes his capacity to make *couns* talk, but trusty Huet reminds him just in time that his gift governs *culs* too. In the end, the two adventurers earn their honors — *Knight of the Cunt, Huet of Little Asshole* — in a line that could double as the title for the fabliau. The talking body parts and the story (the *conte*) seem to merge on a metaphorical level. The tale comes to exemplify Bloch's observation on how there is often, in fabliaux, "no difference between the desire so often expressed in sexual terms on the level of theme and the desire for the story itself" (p. 109).

The Harley manuscript preserves the only copy of this fabliau in Anglo-Norman, but its popularity on the Continent is indicated by survival of its Old French analogues in six manuscripts. For additional commentary, see Honeycutt, pp. 76–80; Cooke, p. 152; Muscatine, pp. 89–91; Bloch, pp. 107–09; Nolan, pp. 320–25; and Revard 2000a, pp. 262–63, and 2005a, pp. 127–28.

[Fols. 122vb–124va. *ANL* 188. Nykrog, no. 28. Långfors, p. 35. Vising §219. **Scribe:** B (Ludlow scribe). **Quire:** 14. **Meter:** Octosyllabic couplets. **Layout:** Double columns. **Editions:** Kennedy, pp. 238–53 (no. 14); Noomen and van den Boogaard 3:47–50, 57–155 (no. 15); Short and Pearcy, pp. 25–28 (no. 14); Revard 2005a, pp. 127–35. **Altered Edition:** Montaiglon and Raynaud, 6:198–205. **Other MSS:** None. **Old French Version:** Six MSS (ed. Noomen and van den Boogaard 3:47–173; trans. Hellman and O'Gorman, pp. 105–21; trans. Dubin, pp. 142–77). **Translations:** Kennedy, pp. 238–53; Revard 2005a, pp. 127–35.]

2   *solas*. The fabliau author uses here the same term that Chaucer draws upon to describe the entertainment value of the *Canterbury Tales*. Nolan observes how the prologue of this Harley fabliau (lines 1–6) differs in this way from each of the Old French analogues (pp. 320–21).

4   *Gwaryn*. On the name Guerin, perhaps the author, see Hellman and O'Gorman, p. 121; and Nykrog, p. 313.

12   *coun*. This impolite word for a female body part requires translation into its even less polite English cognate. Fabliaux often expose private body parts and relish the crude words applied to them. All of the Harley fabliaux share this feature to some degree. See, too, the explanatory notes for the English love lyric *Annot and John* (art. 28), line 15, and the English *Life of Saint Marina* (art. 32), line 217.

50–52   *la nees sire Elye*. "Lord Elijah's boat," a phrase that suggests they lodged at religious houses along the way. On this puzzling expression, see the lengthy discussion by Revard (2005a, pp. 138–40 n. 21).

120   *a ly del tot se abaundona*. Literally, "completely gave himself over to him." The
        magical first and second gifts are having an effect on the chaplain!

123   *seint Richer*. Perhaps this is a reference to Richer(us) of Reims (ca. 940–998), a
        monk of St.-Remigius, who wrote a Latin chronicle of West-Frankish political
        events of the tenth century. The reason for the reference is unclear. It may evoke
        Richer's association with eloquence and embellished style, or perhaps his
        knowledge of medical science. He was not canonized.

244   *coyntise*. "Cunning," with a wordplay on *coun*, the knight's specialized kind of
        cunning.

OF RYBAUDS Y RYME ANT RED O MY ROLLE / SATIRE ON . . . THE GREAT   [ART. 88]

This monologue against the pretensions of low-born horse grooms is a riotous jumble
of alliterative invective and coarse insult. Such crude horse-handlers, it seems to say, are the
polar opposite of what is chivalric (a word related to French *cheval*, "horse"). The insults
carry a good dose of moral condemnation, with the speaker sending the *rybauds* to the Devil
as tribute. The poem is framed as a roll — a presentation of an unpaid bill — with the
scoundrels being itemized in their disgusting habits and vices. The eighth stanza highlights
the lyric's raucous vernacularity by inserting Anglo-Norman business language (in rhyme-
words) to sharpen the crudity of the churls' greedy transactions. The last stanza equates
hurling insult with spewing vomit. As the speaker draws the lineaments of the groomsmen's
repulsive vulgarity, his dip into the genre of insult seems to taint himself as well.

Comparable comic poems in English in the Harley manuscript include *On the Follies of
Fashion*, *Satire on the Consistory Courts*, and *The Man in the Moon* (arts. 25a, 40, 81). All employ
dazzling alliteration and masterful pacing for strong dramatic effect. They seem to be
entertainments designed for oral performance. In the arrangement of items in the Harley
manuscript, this poem is paired with *Hending* (art. 89), which showcases the innate wisdom
of English proverb in stark contrast to the degenerate stupidity depicted here. On how this
lyric participates in a contemporary political and legal debate on the practice of purveyance,
and on how it pursues the themes of taxation and peasant poverty often embedded in
Harley texts, see Scase 2005. Like *Song of the Husbandman* and *Trailbaston* (arts. 31, 80), this
poem draws on the documentary form of legal plaint. For other recent commentary, see
Turville-Petre 1996, pp. 200–01; Scattergood 2000a, pp. 193–94; Fein 2007, pp. 91–92; and
Scase 2007, pp. 33–41, 84.

[Fols. 124va–125r. *IMEV*, *NIMEV* 2649. *MWME* 5:1407 [31]. **Scribe:** B (Ludlow scribe).
Quire: 14. **Meter:** Ten monorhyming alliterative long-line quatrains, aaaa. **Layout:** Begins
in double columns and ends with no columns. Lines 1–24 are written in half-lines. **Editions:**
Wright 1839, pp. 237–40; Böddeker, pp. 135–38; Robbins 1959, pp. 27–29 (no. 7); Turville-
Petre 1989, pp. 34–35. **Other MSS:** None.]

12   *"Fleh com of flore, ant lous com of ladde."* Apparently invented by the poet, this
        comic proverb bears a cynical wit worthy of *Hending* (art. 89).

16   *"Gobelyn made is gerner of gromene mawe."* This proverb on the evil of gluttony is
            said to come straight from the Devil. The mock-proverbial quality of this poem
            matches it to *Hending* (art. 89).

35–36   Christ's rationale for avoiding horse grooms is delivered more as punch line
            than proverb. It fits, however, with the two insults already delivered by the poet
            as proverbs. The Devil and Christ agree in denigrating horse grooms, and both
            act as truthful authorities in the poem juxtaposed with *Hending* (art. 89).

MON THAT WOL OF WYSDAM HEREN / HENDING   [ART. 89]

In this long poem, the sage Hending ("skilled one") is said to be Marcolf's son, an
affiliation that sets the poem in the tradition of the rustic fool who speaks wisdom to power,
a tradition well reflected in *The Jongleur of Ely and the King of England* (art. 75). Such
literature depicts Marcolf in earthy, comic dialogue with Solomon as a way to showcase how
his clever native wit matches or exceeds a king's authoritative learnedness (Ziolkowski 2008;
Bradbury 2008; Bradbury and Bradbury). In the layout of the Harley manuscript, *Hending*
is paired with *Satire on the Retinues of the Great* (art. 88), the two set up as a vernacular diptych
on folly and wisdom (Fein 2007, p. 91).

Hending survives in three versions of different length and varying content. These
Hending poems belong to a larger class of Middle English lyric and debate based in
proverbial lore, sometimes attributed to a single philosopher (Aristotle, Cato, Alfred, etc.).
Harley's pithy *Earth upon Earth* (art. 24b) speaks, too, in the gnomic tone of English proverb.
As a form of advice literature, *Hending* is related to the French *Urbain the Courteous* and *The
Teachings of Saint Louis to His Son Philip* (arts. 79, 94), both framed as solicitous counsel from
a father to a son. Lacking the overt paternal element, the composer of *Hending* is still quite
careful to include proverbs on wise child-rearing, and especially on how to inculcate good
morals, discipline, and learning. Many proverbs discuss the etiquette of lending and
borrowing, as does Urbain. Other advice on the choosing of a wife puts this text in dialogue
with many in French that discuss women and marriage (arts. 76, 77, 78, 83). According to
Louis, "many of the proverbs deal with human relations in a very cynical way" (*MWME*
9:2975), but it should also be noted that they frequently convey an outlook of wry humor
along with compassion for the precariousness of human existence.

Hending bears the air of a schoolroom, wherein proverbs would be taught and
explained. For older boys, a heavier emphasis would be placed on Latin proverbs. An
important audience for Hending may be, then, the very young schoolboy, for whom an early
education in native precept would be thought suitable study. Aside from their being indexed
in catalogues such as Whiting's, the body of Middle English proverbial lore in poems like
this one is understudied by modern literary scholars. In *Hending,* each stanza elaborates a
native proverb by prefacing it with a hypothetical explanation of its use in the world. Then
the proverb is pronounced and the sage named: "Quoth Hendyng." To highlight this
standard stanzaic structure, this edition sets the prose-like proverb in italics, usually as two
lines divided at a natural caesura. The method resembles somewhat the style of the more
openly learned *Against the King's Taxes* (art. 114), wherein each stanza closes with a Latin
couplet that makes an authoritative moral statement, much like a vernacular proverb.

Like the English *Book of Dreaming* (art. 85), *Hending* boasts an expandable internal structure ready to contain as many interpretations or proverbs as the author wants to pack in. It has, nonetheless, a real beginning and end based cleverly in proverb: "*God biginning / Maketh god endyng*" (lines 13–14), and "*Hope of long lyf / Gyleth mony a god wyf*" (lines 339–40). The final proverb prepares for the concluding stanza: the line "Hendyng seith soth of mony thyng" is joined to a prayer, "Yeve us god endynge" (lines 342, 347). Thus does the poet find through *Hendyng* an "ending" rhyme.

[Fols. 125ra–127ra. *IMEV, NIMEV* 2078, *NIMEV* 1669 (see also 2817). *MWME* 9:2975 [43]. **Scribe:** B (Ludlow scribe). **Quire:** 14. **Meter:** Thirty-nine stanzas, mostly $aa_4b_3cc_4b_3$, with thirty-seven proverbs. Stanza 18 is four monorhyming tetrameter lines. A proverb and the phrase *Quoth Hendyng* are attached to stanzas 2–38. **Layout:** Double columns. Proverbs are written as prose. **Editions:** Wright and Halliwell, 1:109–16; Kemble, pp. 270–82; Morris and Skeat, pp. 35–42 (28 stanzas only); Böddeker, pp. 287–300. **Other MSS:** Cambridge, CUL MS Gg.1.1, fols. 476v–479v (ed. Varnhagen, pp. 182–91); Oxford, Bodl. MS Digby 86, fols. 140v–134r (Tschann and Parkes, p. xxvii [no. 52]; ed. Varnhagen, pp. 191–200). The three MSS are compared by Schleich, pp. 220–78. **Middle English Analogues:** See *MWME* 9:2972–79 [31–42, 44–56].]

1–6	This opening stanza, naming Hending as Marcolf's son, does not appear in the other two manuscripts. On the Marcolf and Solomon tradition in Latin and Middle English, see Ziolkowski 2008, Bradbury 2008; and Bradbury and Bradbury.
13–14	Compare Whiting, B 204.
22–23	Compare Whiting, W 417 (recorded only in *Hending*).
31–32	Compare Whiting, T 63.
40–41	Compare Whiting, C 216.
49–50	Compare Whiting, Y 27, Y 32, and C 210.
58–59	Compare Whiting, L 591.
67–68	Compare Whiting, E 206 (recorded only in *Hending*).
76–77	Compare Whiting, C 219.
85–86	Compare Whiting, F 141.
94–95	Compare Whiting, F 408.
103–04	Compare Whiting, F 366.
112–13	Compare Whiting, A 160.
121–22	Compare Whiting, B 505.
130–31	Compare Whiting, G 370 (recorded only in *Hending*).
139–40	Compare Whiting, C 633.
142–61	These two stanzas do not appear in the other two manuscripts.

148–53	Compare Whiting, M 194, and the saying attributed to Cato, in Chaucer's Miller's Tale, lines 3227–30, in reference to old John's ill-advised marriage to young Alisoun. For further background, see *The Riverside Chaucer*, p. 844.
156	*Bynd thine tonge with bonene wal.* Compare Chaucer's Manciple's Tale: "My sone, God of his endeless goodnesse / Walled a tonge with teeth and lippes eke" (lines 322–23).
159–60	Compare Whiting, T 384.
168–69	Compare Whiting, L 393: "He that gives me little is on (favorably disposed to) my life." The general sense of this proverb is "Something is better than nothing."
177–78	Compare Whiting, B 275.
186–87	Compare Whiting, B 609.
195–96	Compare Whiting, B 22.
199	*theyn.* The *MED* notes that this word may be an error for *tene.* See *thein* (n.), sense 3.
204–05	Compare Whiting, C 201.
213–14	Compare Whiting, L 415.
222–23	Compare Whiting, O 76. For the noun *edueth*, see *MED*, *edwit* (n.), sense b., "scorn, shame."
231–32	Compare Whiting, E 213.
240–41	Compare Whiting, T 217.
249–50	Compare Whiting, H 508 (recorded only in *Hending*).
258–59	Compare Whiting, C 166.
267–68	Compare Whiting, H 439.
276–77	Compare Whiting, W 264.
285–86	Compare Whiting, R 32.
288–96	This stanza does not appear in the other two manuscripts.
294–95	Compare Whiting, M 251 (recorded only in *Hending*).
303–04	Compare Whiting, W 571.
306–23	These two stanzas do not appear in the other two manuscripts.
312–13	Compare Whiting, M 191 (recorded only in *Hending*).
321–22	Compare Whiting, D 71.
330–31	Compare Whiting, D 402 (recorded only in *Hending*).
333–38	A version of these lines appears as a short lyric in London, BL, MS Royal 8.E.17, fol. 109r. See Brown 1916, 1:362.

339–40   Compare Whiting, H 468 (recorded only in *Hending*).

342–47   This closing stanza, which exploits the rhyme on *Hendyng* and *endyng*, does not appear in the other two manuscripts.

WHEN MAN AS MAD A KYNG OF A CAPPED MAN / THE PROPHECY . . . ERCELDOUNE [ART. 90]

The Prophecy of Thomas of Erceldoune delivers oracular pronouncements as incontrovertible truths. They are uttered in gnomic English, much like the proverbs of *Hending* (art. 89) that precede it, and like *Earth upon Earth* (art. 24b). In putting voice to Anglo-Scottish conflicts, it is comparable to *The Execution of Sir Simon Fraser* (art. 25). The prophetic signs for when the Scottish war will end form a cryptic list — amid real place-names — of inconclusive vagaries and impossible conditions. A French rubric heads the item, naming it as Thomas of Erceldoune's response to the Countess of Dunbar. Thomas was a thirteenth-century Scots poet and seer whose name attaches to several prophecies. This text is the earliest and one of the shortest. Its sympathies lie (maybe oddly for Thomas) with the English. The Countess of Dunbar has been identified as Black Agnes, sister of Robert the Stewart, who defended Dunbar Castle in 1337 or, alternatively, as Marjory, who surrendered the castle in 1296. The date of the poem therefore cannot be determined, though different dates between 1296 and 1337 have been proposed.

Metrically, the item is often classified as alliterative poetry, but it is more properly prose — in fact, the only English prose in the Ludlow scribe's share of the manuscript. (Elsewhere, there are the paint recipes [arts. 10–17] copied by Scribe C.) Some lines can be scanned as alliterative long lines, but most cannot, and many fail in full alliteration. Each item in the list begins with an incantatory "When," helping to build its impressive, authoritative tone. According to McSparran, *The Prophecy* is the "most linguistically eccentric and untypical text" among the book's English items (p. 396).

For commentary on the works of Thomas of Erceldoune and on this specific Harley item, see J. A. H. Murray (with a translation on p. lxxxvi); Robbins 1975, *MWME* 5:1524–28; Turville-Petre 1989, pp. 36–37, and 1996, pp. 195–97; J. M. Dean, pp. 4–5, 19–21; Scattergood 2000a, pp. 177–78; McSparran, pp. 396–99; and Flood.

[Fol. 127rb–va. *MWME* 5:1525 [288]. **Scribe:** B (Ludlow scribe). **Quire:** 14. **Layout:** Double columns. **Editions:** J. A. H. Murray, pp. xviii–xix; Brandl and Zippel, pp. 133–34; Robbins 1959, p. 29 (no. 8); Turville–Petre 1989, pp. 36–37; J. M. Dean, p. 11; Flood, pp. 11–27. **Other MS:** London, BL MS Arundel 57, fol. 8v (ed. Wright and Halliwell, 1:30.)]

5   *Londyon*. Turville-Petre 1989 reads *Loudyon*. As J. M. Dean notes, "This line may refer to Loudon Hill (Lothian) and its battle, 1307, when Robert Bruce defeated Aymer de Valence. Or it may refer to the city of London" (p. 20).

       felde. This word means either "field" or "felled, cut down."

9   *Rokesbourh*. Roxburgh, one of the four boroughs of Scotland.

       Forwyleye. This place-name has not been identified.

11   *Bambourne*. The battle of Bannockburn on June 24, 1314, was a stunning defeat for the English.

LA DESTINCCIOUN DE . . . / DISTINGUISHING FEATURES OF . . .   [ART. 91]

This prose work provides a portrait of Jesus Christ's physical features, with special attention given to his head and face. Its source is an apocryphal letter circulating in Latin, which purported to be addressed to the Roman Senate in the reign of Tiberius Caesar, from Publius Lentulus, governor of Judea before the time of Pontius Pilate. These stated circumstances do not fit historical fact. The letter reflects, instead, a conception of Jesus as imagined by pious Christians of the Middle Ages. The fake document seems to have been made and promulgated in the thirteenth century, perhaps originally in Greek and perhaps to promote the authenticity of a visual icon. This Harley text is the only version of the Lentulus Letter known in Anglo-Norman. Its placement opposite *The Way of Christ's Love* (art. 92) is probably a deliberate act of juxtaposition by the scribe. It has not been previously edited or translated.

[Fol. 127va–b. *ANL* 488. Vising §182. **Scribe:** B (Ludlow scribe). **Quire:** 14. **Layout:** Prose in double columns. The title is underlined in red. The *C* of *Cheveus* (line 4) and the *l* of *lé oyls* (line 10) are marked in red. **Editions:** None. **Other MSS:** None. **Latin Source:** Apocryphal Letter of Publius Lentulus: see *ANL* 488; *Catholic Encyclopedia*, s.v. Publius Lentulus; Kuczynski 2012, pp. 46–51. **Middle English Prose Analogue:** London, BL Addit. MS 10106, fol. 49v, ed. Kuczynski 2012, pp. 39–41. **Middle English Verse Analogue:** From *Cursor Mundi*; see *ANL* 488; Kuczynski 2012, pp. 51–57. **Translations:** None.]

6   *Grye né*. "Greek nose."

13   *reulé*. MS *resle* has been emended to *reulé*, "temperate, calm, ordered."

LUTEL WOT HIT ANY MON . . . / THE WAY OF CHRIST'S LOVE   [ART. 92]

The Way of Christ's Love is a religious lyric fashioned from what must have been a popular love song, *The Way of Woman's Love* (art. 93). The Ludlow scribe has copied the pair of contrastive poems as *contrafacta*, displaying them together on the same page. Two fragmentary analogues survive. These related lyrics suggest that there were formal competitions to remake secular songs into religious lyrics (Green 1989, pp. 304–12). It might even be that *The Way of Christ's Love*, which matches its predecessor in length, form, and emotive expression, was the winning entry in such a contest. This lyric represents Christ as supremely human, his flesh bleeding to make sinners whole. Christ's sacrificial blood dominates the imagery of stanzas 1, 2, 4, and 5 (compare *Song on Jesus' Precious Blood* [art. 56]). In stanza 3 (the middle one), Christ behaves as a filial child, "a suete Sone" (line 21), who, in seeing how angry his Father is with mankind, wants to placate him. He pleads to be the sole one to die in order to stave off the penalty all humans will face. In the last stanza the poet's final image is of a wan Savior, his cheeks thin and his body bled out: "His hert blod he yef for al monkunne" (line 38). Christ is cast here as the human lover of humanity, willingly sacrificing himself out of devotion. Thus the poem reforms a love lyric by imbuing it with religious strains drawn from the love-longings of the original. The borrowed refrain of *ever ant oo* (ever and always) suits the caring nature of an eternally loving God. For commentary on this poem, see the bibliography in *MWME* 11:4359–60; and Turville-Petre 1996, pp. 198–99, 211–12.

[Fol. 128r. *IMEV, NIMEV* 1922. *MWME* 11:4204 [31]. **Scribe:** B (Ludlow scribe). **Quire:** 14. Two verses per manuscript line. After stanza 1, the refrain is written to the right of the stanza. **Meter:** Five 8-line stanzas with refrain, $a_4b_3a_4b_3bb_5C_7C_5$. **Layout:** No columns. **Editions:** Wright 1842, pp. 111–12 (no. 40); Böddeker, pp. 231–32; Brown 1932, pp. 161–62 (no. 90); Brook, pp. 70–71 (no. 31); Silverstein, pp. 51–52 (no. 29); Millett (online edn.). **Other MSS:** None. **Middle English Analogues:** Cambridge, Gonville and Caius College MS 512, fol. 260v (ed. Brook, p. 88); London, BL MS Egerton 613, fol. 2v (ed. Brook, p. 88).]

7   *Ever ant oo.* Compare this phrasing to *The Sayings of Saint Bernard* (art. 74), line 143, where a similar expression describes the endless pains of hell.

LUTEL WOT HIT ANY MON . . . / THE WAY OF WOMAN'S LOVE   [ART. 93]

The Harley manuscript preserves the only copy of this love lyric, the book's last English item. It probably enjoyed a familiar currency, for it appears to have inspired three attempts to recast its content, manner, and refrain into a devotional poem. In itself, it may be derived from a French model beginning "Nus hom ne poroit savoir / Que c'est d'amer par amours" (Green 1989, p. 311). The scribe has copied it just below a successful imitation that recasts the lover as Christ (art. 92). He thus creates on a single page the manuscript's most dramatic instance of *contrefacta* (poems matched for likeness of form and for contrast of subject matter). Similar effects through juxtaposition occur with the side-by-side copying of the English lyrics *Spring* and *Advice to Women* (arts. 43, 44) and the consecutive copying of the Anglo-Norman poems on women, pro and con: *The Song on Women* and *The Blame of Women* (arts. 76, 77). Neither of these other examples, however, invert the secular to the religious in the same direct manner seen here. This type of reverse moral pairing occurs, in a more subtle manner, in the juxtaposed *Satire on the Consistory Courts* and *The Laborers in the Vineyard* (arts. 40, 41).

The speaker of *The Way of Woman's Love* complains about a certain woman's independence in a situation of *derne* (secret) love. He is faced with her perfidy: how she vowed her troth but then inexplicably withdrew her love. It seems that the speaker is less experienced than she is, and now he is suffering a painful lesson. Even so, he woos her with his song and continues to praise and love her. The refrain of *ever ant oo* (ever and always) utters the never-ending distraction suffered by the lover, his mind stuck in a state of confused hope and despair, remembered joy and anxious longing. For commentary on this poem, see the bibliography in *MWME* 11:4360–61; and Turville–Petre 1996, pp. 198–99, 211–12.

[Fol. 128r–v. *IMEV, NIMEV* 1921. *MWME* 11:4205 [32]. **Scribe:** B (Ludlow scribe). **Quire:** 14. Two verses per manuscript line. After stanza 1, the refrain is written to the right of the stanza. **Meter:** Five 8-line stanzas with refrain, $a_4b_3a_4b_3bb_5C_7C_5$. **Layout:** No columns. **Editions:** Wright 1842, pp. 113–14 (no. 41); Böddeker, pp. 178–79; Brown 1932, pp. 162–63 (no. 91); Brook, pp. 71–72 (no. 32); Silverstein, pp. 94–95 (no. 71); Stemmler 1970, pp. 28–29; Millett (online edn.). **Other MSS:** None. **Middle English Analogues:** Three religious lyrics (see art. 92).]

3   *fre*. The word means either "noble, generous" or "free, wanton."

12   *uch ende*. "All the members." See *MED*, *ende* (n.), sense 22b.

ENSEIGNEMENTS DE SAINT LEWIS . . . / THE TEACHINGS OF SAINT LOUIS . . .   [ART. 94]

The Teachings of Saint Louis to His Son Philip derives from an enormously popular Old French document, here provided in Anglo-Norman. Viewed as the true model of Christian kingship, Saint Louis IX (1214–1270) was the deeply pious monarch of France from 1226 until his death in Tunis while on crusade. He was canonized by Pope Boniface VIII in 1297. This letter formed part of the canonization effort. It was copied and recopied, and thus much promulgated, from the scriptorium at Saint-Denis, where lay the bodies of the kings of France. According to the incipit given here, Louis wrote the letter to his son Philip III of France (1245–1285) from his deathbed. The deathbed circumstance was a fiction spread widely to heighten the king's saintly repute. Despite that embellishment, the authenticity of Louis's authorship is not doubted.

The textual history of the epistle in Old French is complicated because copies are numerous and the letter frequently circulated inside other texts, such as Jean de Joinville's biography of Louis, a context that highlights its political cast. Louis's moral *gravitas* and royal status elevate *Teachings* above the genre of simple epistle from a noble father to his son, although it does share that element with *Urbain the Courteous* (art. 79). The letter is a mirror for a prince, that is, advice on sound governance. It is derived from a monarch of superior virtue and is to be bequeathed to his successor. *Teachings* stresses the necessity of good counsel to avoid bad decision-making, of seeking peace within the realm and outside it, and of exhibiting moral virtue. The ruler must maintain strong relations with the Church, award benefices wisely, reward all who exhibit virtue, and avoid oppression of the poor. He should administer finances with moderation. Pure intentions should guide all his actions.

Composed as a set of precepts and essential rules, the letter is aligned in MS Harley 2253 with *Urbain the Courteous* and *Hending* (arts. 79, 89), and, maybe more facetiously, with *The Jongleur of Ely and the King of England* (art. 75). As a reservoir of wisdom flowing from austere authority, it is like *The Sayings of Saint Bernard* and *The Prophecy of Thomas of Erceldoune* (arts. 74, 90). As a sanctified epistle that validates Christian belief, it is comparable to the Lentulus Letter extract and *Letter for Pilgrims on the Relics at Oviedo* (arts. 91, 97). Paragraphing in this edition follows the scribe's marks in the manuscript, except for lines 27 and 32, which are not marked. Oddly, R. Dean, *ANL*, does not include this text. Corrie speculates on possible links between the Harley compiler (that is, the Ludlow scribe) and the Joinville family (2003, pp. 78–79). This Harley item has not been previously edited or translated. For further commentary and background, see O'Connell, pp. 16–29; Corrie 2003, pp. 69–76; Krueger, pp. xviii, xxi, xxiii; and Ashley, pp. 3–6.

[Fols. 128v–129v. **Scribe:** B (Ludlow scribe). **Quire:** 14. **Layout:** Prose written with no columns. **Editions:** None. **Other MSS:** Numerous redactions in Old French; see Bossuat, pp. 345–46 (nos. 3688–97). For a critical edition, see O'Connell, pp. 55–63; for a translation, see Ashley, pp. 3–16. **Translations:** None.]

59   *seint Martyn.* Saint Martin (316–397), Bishop of Tours, was a soldier before he decided that his Christian faith prohibited him from fighting.

L'ENQUESTE QUE LE PATRIARCHE . . . / THE LAND OF THE SARACENS   [ART. 95]

This Anglo-Norman prose description of the Saracen rulers and their lands is found in three manuscripts. According to the incipit in MS Harley 2253, it is a report sent by the patriarch of Jerusalem to Pope Innocent III as a help to Christian crusaders. Cataloguers of the Harley manuscript have generally listed it as an extract from Jacques de Vitry's *Historia Orientalis,* but that work appears instead to be one of its various sources. Jacques de Vitry, Bishop of Acre and later of Tusculum (ca. 1160–1240), was a noted preacher and historian of the crusades.

As an informative guide on exotic sites that concern Christian pilgrims, this work is comparable to booklet 5's *Pilgrimages in the Holy Land* and *Pardons of Acre* (arts. 38, 39). In how it records distant geography and conveys diverse lore from faraway places, it seems to have been intentionally set beside the next two items: *Heraldic Arms of Kings* and *Letter for Pilgrims on the Relics at Oviedo* (arts. 96, 97). On the existence of a Latin source and several Old French analogues, see R. Dean (*ANL* 332). This work has not been previously printed. The paragraphing of this edition adheres in general to the markings of the Ludlow scribe, who also tended to mark in red the initials of its place-names.

[Fols. 129v–130v. *ANL* 332. **Scribe:** B (Ludlow scribe). **Quire:** 14. **Layout:** Prose written with no columns. **Editions:** None. **Other MSS:** Cambridge, CUL MS Gg.6.28, fols. 57r–61r; Oxford, Bodl. MS Bodley 761, fols. 195v–200v. **Translations:** None.]

29   *Mier.* Referring to Cyprus, this word seems a mistake for an original word meaning "island."

33   *le mount de Sardayné.* The Monastery Church of Sardenay in Saidnaiya, a pilgrimage destination because it was the site of a legendary icon of the Virgin Mary said to have been painted by Saint Luke. See Pringle 1998, 2:219–21 (no. 198). Reaching the monastery requires a steep climb. The site is mentioned briefly in *Pilgrimages in the Holy Land* (art. 38), line 174.

43   *le mount Lyban.* Mount Lebanon is the Lebanese mountain range that extends across the whole country, parallel to the Mediterranean coast. In the Douai Reims Bible, it is Mount Libanus; see Judges 3:3 and Ecclesiasticus 50:13.

45–46   For another mention of this icon, see the explanatory note to *Pilgrimages in the Holy Land* (art. 38), line 169.

47   *Abban e Phar*. Today these rivers are the Litani and the Orontes.

47–48   *ou Placidas perdi ces fitz*. By legend, Placidas was a Roman military commander under Titus (79–81) and Trajan (98–117) who converted to Christianity and became Saint Eustathius. As he attempted to flee with his young sons to escape a perilous situation, he was blocked by a raging river. Placidas carried one son over the river to safety, but the other was seized by a lion as he returned for him. Before he could go back to the first son, that one was seized and carried off by a wolf. See the romance *Sir Isumbras* for a similar situation.

49   *Jor e Dan*. The Dan River is the largest tributary of the Jordan river, located at the base of Mount Hermon. A tributary named the Jor is not known.

            le mont Sibboe. That is, Mount Gelboe or Gilboa, where Saul died in battle by falling on his own sword so that the Philistines would not be the ones to kill him (1 Samuel 3:1–6).

76   *Attanise*. Tennis or Tinnis, an ancient port city in Egypt, located southwest of present-day Port Said.

86   *le flum de Cobar*. The Khabar River, largest tributary to the Euphrates, which was the major river bordering the territory of the Chaldeans, associated with Nabuchodnosor.

LES ARMES DES ROYS / HERALDIC ARMS OF KINGS   [ART. 96]

This Anglo-Norman prose list of heraldic signs displayed on kings' arms demonstrates the interest by the scribe or patron in collecting information on diverse subjects. The manuscript contents evince someone's curiosity about, or pedagogical interest in, geography and distant places, a curiosity born perhaps of actual travel. It fits, therefore, with such items as *Pilgrimages in the Holy Land* and *Pardons of Acre* (arts. 38, 39) and the two texts that surround it: *The Land of the Saracens* and *Letter for Pilgrims on the Relics at Oviedo* (arts. 95, 97). For commentary on this text, see Corrie 2003, pp. 66–67.

[Fol. 131r. Compare *ANL* 390 (compare 391, 391.1). **Scribe:** B (Ludlow scribe). **Quire:** 14. **Layout:** No columns, written as a list in prose, items marked with paraphs. **Editions:** None. **Other MSS:** None. **Translations:** None.]

7   Corrie notes that "the English king is only the sixth in the list, two places after the king of France," indicating that "the compiler was not somebody who was interested only in England" (2003, p. 67).

17   It is unclear what the abbreviation *.s.* stands for.

26   *Mailogris*. Mallorca. In writing *gris* (*ri* abbreviated), the scribe seems to be reinterpreting letters he is unsure of in his copy: *Mailorqa*.

30   *Gryfonye*. The Pomeranian ducal house of Griffin (Livonia) in Poland.

31   *Hasteney*. Apparently Estonia.

SCRIPTUM QUOD PEREGRINI DEFERUNT / LETTER FOR PILGRIMS ... AT OVIEDO   [ART. 97]

This document replicates a letter provided to medieval pilgrims when they made pilgrimage to the Cathedral of San Salvador in Oviedo, a city located in the Asturias region of northern Spain. It lists a precise inventory of the holy relics housed inside the *Arca Santa*, a magnificent gilded silver casket that still draws pilgrims today. The *Arca* is claimed in this document to be authentically ancient, a priceless treasure transferred over time by God's plan from Jerusalem to Africa, then to Carthage, Seville, Toledo, and finally Oviedo and the Church of the Holy Savior, its ordained resting place. According to legend, the odyssey of the *Arca Santa* began around 614 and ended in Oviedo in 751 (Janice Bennett, pp. 28–44, plates 1–3).

This letter and the *Arca* itself are now both assigned to what historians call the *Corpus Pelagianum*, that is, a set of elaborate, historical fabrications designed by Pelagius [Pelayo], Bishop of Oviedo (1101–1130, 1142–1143; d. 1153), to promote and defend the privileges and prestige of the diocese (Barton and Fletcher, pp. 65–71). The *Arca Santa*, which is considerably less ancient than the letter claims, probably dates from the eleventh century (Harris, esp. pp. 82, 87 n. 18). In MS Harley 2253 the cross drawn by the scribe at the base of the letter appears to belong with this text and not the next one (Ker, p. xiv). This item has not been previously edited. The translation is by Jan Ziolkowski, prepared for this edition.

[Fols. 131v–132r. **Scribe:** B (Ludlow scribe). **Quire:** 14. **Layout:** Prose written with no columns. The incipit is underlined in red. **Editions:** None. **Other MSS:** None. **Translations:** None.]

14–18   The icon that bleeds, referred to here, is probably the famous one in Beirut, described in other Harley texts. See the explanatory notes to *Pilgrimages in the Holy Land* (art. 38), line 169, and to *The Land of the Saracens* (art. 95), lines 45–46.

25   *Yldefonti*. Saint Ildephonsus, Archbishop of Toledo (d. 667), author of *De virginitate perpetua sanctae Mariae*. A legend reports that the Virgin Mary appeared to him and presented him with artifacts of her son. Another legend associates him with the transport of the *Arca Santa* to Toledo (Janice Bennett, p. 31).

28–29   *Ananye, Azarie, et Mysaelis*. See Daniel 1:7.

30   *de oliva*. See John 12:12–13. The mention of the olive in addition to the palm may be the result of a confusion about Mount Olive.

32–33   *piscis assi et favum mellis*. On the biblical roast fish and honeycomb, see Luke 24:42.

37   Saints Eulogius, Lucretia, Eulalia, and Pelagius are all Spanish martyr saints: the priest Eulogius of Córdoba (d. 859); the two early female virgin martyrs Lucretia

of western Spain (d. 306) and Eulalia of Merida (d. 304); and the boy martyr Pelagius [Pelayo] of Córdoba (ca. 912–926). The church still claims the tombs of Saint Eulogius and Pelagius, but not the others.

38   *sancti Vincencii*. Saint Vincent of Saragossa, the patron saint of Lisbon, was martyred under the Emperor Diocletian around 304. His tomb is in Valencia.

      Alberis. Alvaro of Córdoba (d. 861), who wrote the life of Saint Eulogius.

38–39   *sancti Serani, episcopi, et sancti Iuliani, pontificis*. Seranus and Julian are named as holy men in the legend of the *Arca Santa*'s removal from Jerusalem (Janice Bennett, p. 36). Although they are not reputed to have moved it from Toledo to Oviedo, their presence in the legend may explain the names found here. Or it may be that *sancti Serani/Seraui* is an error for Saint Severus of Barcelona, a bishop reportedly martyred under Diocletian around 304, and *sancti Juliani* refers to Saint Julian of Toledo (642–690), a bishop.

40   *regis Costi*. "King Costus." This name is unexplained. The Church of the Holy Savior was founded by King Fruela I of Asturias in 761; he was assassinated in 768. He and his wife are interred there.

41   *sancte Florentine*. Saint Florentina (d. ca. 612) was the sister of three Iberian bishops (Leander, Isidore of Seville, and Fulgentius).

LEGENDA DE SANCTO ETFRIDO ... / THE LEGEND OF SAINT ETFRID ...   [ART. 98]

The legend of Saint Etfrid [Eadfrith] tells of the miraculous origin for the name of Leominster Abbey, founded in the year 660. God granted to the northern missionary Etfrid a peaceful encounter with a submissive lion (*leo*) as a token that he would successfully convert King Merewald to Christianity. Merewald (or Merewalh in most records) was the ruler of Magonsæte, a seventh-century sub-kingdom of Mercia. The happy effect of the king's conversion was the establishment of Leominster Abbey on the site of Etfrid's vision. Etfrid was then made priest of this new foundation and, later, its patron saint.

In the darkness of night Etfrid, traveling from Northumbria to Mercia, receives the omen: a terrifyingly huge lion approaches him. Unafraid, he offers it a share of his bread, and the lion, assuming the mild nature of a lamb, meekly accepts it. The author of the legend interprets this vision as a foreshadowing of how Merewald will accept from Etfrid the Word of God, the metaphoric Bread of Life. When Etfrid arrives as a stranger among the Magonsætes, it is revealed that the king has just suffered a nightmare about two frightful hounds that attacked him, with rescue offered by a venerable man with a golden key, which he wielded as a cudgel. Etfrid is called forth like Joseph before Pharoah (an allusion that the scribe may have added) to interpret the dream. The key-bearer is Saint Peter, and the hounds signify the jaws of hell, an "open maw" to which the mild-mannered lion seems to serve, figuratively, as a counterweight. Feeding on God's Bread, the king (as a lion) will avoid being fed to the frightful hell-mouth.

The legend is recounted in the *Life of Saint Mildburg*, whose authorship by Goscelin (ca. 1030–1107) has been proposed but rejected. Mildburg is one of Merewald's three sainted daughters; the others are Mildred and Mildgitha. She is the patron saint of Wenlock Priory, also founded by her father. The monastic church in Leominster was demolished during the Dissolution, but Etfrid continues to serve as patron saint of the Borough of Leominster, which still celebrates his legend. His feast day is October 26, and during the period of MS Harley 2253's copying it was observed with a four-day market and fair. Leominster is located south of Ludlow, midway between Ludlow and Hereford.

Like the other Latin legends in MS Harley 2253, this one celebrates an ancient Anglo-Saxon saint whose legend is tied to a neighboring locale. See *The Life of Saint Ethelbert* and *The Martyrdom of Saint Wistan* (arts. 18, 116). On the presence of these lives in the Harley manuscript, see Kuczynski 2000, pp. 138–40. For further commentary on the legend of Saint Etfrid, see Blair 2002a, p. 526; and Sims-Williams, pp. 55–58, 101, 118. For another Harley text with a possible tie to Leominster, see the explanatory notes to *A Song of Lewes* (art. 23). The Harley text has not been previously edited. The translation printed here is by Jan Ziolkowski, prepared for this edition.

[Fols. 132r–133r. Hardy, 1:257–58 (no. 673). **Scribe:** B (Ludlow scribe). **Quire:** 14. **Layout:** Prose written with no columns. The title is underlined in red. Division numbers are written in the margin, with large initials at the beginning of all sections, and red paraphs marking sections II–VIII. **Editions:** None. **Other MSS:** None. **Latin Analogue:** *De sancta Milburga virgine*, in London, BL Addit. MS 34633, fols. 207r–208r; and London, BL MS Lansdowne 436, fol. 72 (ed. Horstmann 1901, 2:189–90). **Translations:** None.]

5 *Reodesmouht*. This place-name, presumably in the vicinity of Leominster, is unknown there. There is a village in Northumbria called Redesmouth located near Bellingham on the River Rede, but Etfrid is said to be departing from Northumbria to be a missionary in Mercia, and he eventually comes to Magonsæte, a region in Mercia where Merewald is the ruler. In MS Lansdowne 436, the place-name is *Redewode*, another unknown place.

11 *clyno*. The word appears to mean "descending." Compare OF *cliner* and ME *clinen*.

24 Compare the story of Joseph as told in Genesis 41 and in *Old Testament Stories* (art. 71), lines 81–84, and the scribe's interest in dream interpretation, shown in his copying *A Book of Dreaming* (art. 85). This analogy may be the scribe's own addition. It does not appear in MS Lansdowne 436.

41 *soli ritu*. MS Lansdowne 436 reads *solicita*. The intended meaning seems to be: "Either way, put my mind at ease about this matter."

44 *violentium*. The MS reading *volentium* is emended. Horstmann 1901 reads the word in MS Lansdowne 436 as *molentium*.

60 *merearis*. Horstmann 1901 emends this word to *mereberis* in his edition of the text in MS Lansdowne 436.

65 *Viis*. The scribe writes *Hiis*, the same reading found in MS Lansdowne 436. A capital *V* may have been misread; the scribe's *H* is a capital.

75–77 MS Lansdowne 436 includes the following phrase: *hoc est anno gratie sexcentisimo sexagesimo*. The Ludlow scribe specifies the year in the margin.

QUY CHESCUN JOUR DE BON CUER CEST OREISOUN DIRRA / PRAYER FOR ...   [ART. 99]

A long Latin prayer with a lengthy French prose introduction, this item provides both the words to say and the occasions for their use. The writer explains that the prayer will provide protection in bad or risky situations, for example, during long trips by land, in bad weather at sea, before entering battle, and in the event of bewitchment. The prayer has prescribed parts: (1) an invocation of the Trinity, with "amen"; (2) recitation of three psalms (Psalms 66, 129, and 141); (3) a long petition, with "amen," for victory over enemies, in which the worshiper names himself; (4) another petition to God who has protected many, with heavy reference to events in the Book of Daniel; and (5) a reiteration of Psalm 141. The specificity of the instructions implies that the prayer will hold a binding effect if performed correctly. Another version of the Latin prayer appears in the fifteenth-century Thornton manuscript, where cross-signs are inserted to indicate gestures to be made as the prayer is recited.

In MS Harley 2253 this text closes both quire 14 and booklet 6. It anticipates the numerous prayers, hymns, and occasions for psalms and angels that comprise much of booklet 7. *Prayer for Protection* has not previously been printed. The translation of the Latin is by Jan Ziolkowski, prepared for this edition.

[Fol. 133v. *ANL* 949, 985. Compare *FDT* 3507. **Scribe:** B (Ludlow scribe). **Quire:** 14. **Layout:** Prose written with no columns. **Editions:** None. **Other MSS:** Similar items appear in Cambridge, Emmanuel College MS 106 (I.4.31), fol.27r–v; New York, Pierpont Morgan Library MS M 700, fol. 145r–v; Cambridge, Pembroke College MS 193, fol. 127v; Thornton MS (Lincoln, Lincoln Cathedral MS 91), fol. 177r (ed. Horstmann 1895, 1:376–77). **Translations:** None.]

17   Psalm 66. See also *Occasions for Psalms in French* (art. 101), line 16; and *Occasions for Psalms Ordained by Saint Hilary of Poitiers* (art. 111), line 26.

18   Psalm 129. See also *Three Prayers That Never Fail* (art. 109a), line 3.

22   *Set tu.* The Thornton version reads *Es tu*, which Horstmann 1895 emends to *Esto*.

24–25   In the Thornton version, there are crosses drawn between *Deus Habraham, Deus Ysaac, Deus Iacob,* and *Deus omnium* to indicate that the petitioner should make the sign of the cross as these words are said.

29   "*Christus in se confidentes salvat.*" Compare Daniel 13:60: "With that all the assembly cried out with a loud voice, and they blessed God, who saveth them that trust in him."

29–30   *Christus vincit, Christus regnat. Christus imperare.* A Gregorian chant begins "Christus vincit. Christus regnat. Christus imperat."

BOOKLET 7

QUANT VOUS LEVEZ LE MATYN / OCCASIONS FOR ANGELS   **[ART. 100]**

This Anglo-Norman prose item advises a Christian what angels to contemplate and invoke for aid in various situations. The eight-part list specifies ten guardians. Most names designate archangels, but a few, such as Rachel, seem to reference holy persons not commonly considered angels. Some names, such as *Abyel* and *Pantesseron*, cannot be identified with certainty. The source for this text is unknown. Variant versions exist in other English manuscripts.

[Fol. 134r. *ANL* 952 (2), 621. Rézeau 2:526. *FDT* 3499. **Scribe:** B (Ludlow scribe). **Quire:** 15. **Layout:** No columns, written as prose. Each item is marked with a red paraph and red-marked initial. **Edition:** Hunt and Bliss, pp. 240–41. **Other MSS:** Cambridge, Gonville and Caius College MS 451a, fol. 17r; London, BL MS Harley 1260, fol. 234; Oxford, Bodl. MS Rawlinson C.814, fol. 1v. **Translation:** Hunt and Bliss, pp. 240–41.]

1   *seint Michael*. The most widely invoked of the archangels, Michael (named in Daniel 10:3) is regarded the angelic leader of the heavenly host.

2   *seint Gabriel*. Like Michael and Raphael, Gabriel is recognized as an archangel in the Roman Catholic tradition, as well as by the Eastern Orthodox Church and Islam. As the angel used to convey spiritual mysteries to mankind, he was God's messenger at the Annunciation.

3   *seint Raphael*. Raphael is named in the apocryphal book of Tobit 3:17, 12:15. With Michael and Gabriel, he is among the three archangels recognized by name in the Roman Catholic tradition. Additionally, he is seen as an archangel in the Eastern Orthodox and Islamic traditions.

5   *seint Raguel*. Raguel is sometimes named as one of the seven archangels, although Michael, Gabriel, Raphael, and Uriel are the only ones named in the Bible. Raguel is also the name of Tobias's father-in-law in the apocryphal book of Tobit, which features other names on this list. See the explanatory notes to lines 3, 11.

6   *seint Rachel*. The Old Testament matriarch, wife of Jacob and mother of Joseph, and not an official saint.

8   *seint Pantesseron*. The identity of this figure is uncertain. The nearest angel name is "Phanuel," listed by Pope Gregory the Great as one of the seven archangels. More distant possibilities are Gabuthelon or Zebuleon, mentioned as angels in the Greek Apocalypse of Ezra. Given the scribe's spelling here, however, the most likely candidate seems to be the non-angel Saint Panteleon, honored widely in post-plague Europe as one of the fourteen guardian martyrs or "holy helpers." A remote possibility is Saint Pancras.

9   *seint Abyel*. This name is perhaps a mistake for Azrael, known, especially in Islamic tradition, as the angel who comes to comfort one during the passage to death.

seint Brachiel. Barachiel (named in the apocryphal Third Book of Enoch) is recognized as one of the seven archangels in the Eastern Orthodox tradition.

11 *seint Uryel.* Named in 2 Esdras, Uriel is one of the seven archangels in the Eastern Orthodox tradition, and Pope Gregory the Great also sets him in that category.

seint Tobye. The apocryphal book of Tobit relates the story of the father Tobias and his son Tobias, who are aided by the angel Raphael.

QUY VELT QUE DIEU SOVYEGNE DE LY / OCCASIONS FOR PSALMS IN FRENCH [ART. 101]

MS Harley 2253 holds three articles that advise one regarding what psalms are the most helpful to recite as prayers for particular needs. See also arts. 110 and 111. This anonymous work in Anglo-Norman prose is the first and most succinct of the psalm lists. It fills the lower portion of fol. 134r below *Occasions for Angels* (art. 100). Appearing as a matched pair, these articles open quire 15 and define it as a didactic booklet of practical religion, recording prayers and lists for their occasions. One may note that the Ludlow scribe's French psalter survives in MS Harley 273, fols. 8r–52v.

A cognate version exists in a Cambridge manuscript. The scribe marks off each listed item with a red paraph. In addition, each initial letter and psalm initial (except Psalm 53, in line 10) are marked in red. The sixteen psalms are in sequential order, generally speaking, with Psalm 30 listed twice. Psalms that recur in the later lists are noted in the explanatory notes. To match Latin titles to Douay-Rheims translations, I have expanded the scribe's Latin as needed, setting added words in brackets. For helpful commentary on the uses of the Book of Psalms in the Middle Ages, see Kuczynski 1995 and the essays edited by van Deusen.

[Fol. 134r. *ANL* 455(2), 986. Vising §320. **Scribe:** B (Ludlow scribe). **Quire:** 15. **Layout:** No columns, written as a vertical list. **Edition:** Hunt and Bliss, pp. 240–43. **Analogue:** Cambridge, Trinity College MS O.2.45, p. 4 (ed. Meyer 1903, p. 109). **Translation:** Hunt and Bliss, pp. 240–43.]

1–2 Psalm 12. See also *Occasions for Psalms Ordained by Saint Hilary of Poitiers* (art. 111), line 45.

3 Psalm 30. See also this item, line 6; *Occasions for Psalms in Latin* (art. 110), lines 5–6; and *Occasions for Psalms Ordained by Saint Hilary of Poitiers* (art. 111), lines 8–9.

5 Psalm 30. See also this item, line 3 (and explanatory note). On the psalm's power to deliver one from his enemy, see verse 16.

6–7 Psalm 34. See also *Occasions for Psalms Ordained by Saint Hilary of Poitiers* (art. 111), line 28.

8–9 Psalm 42. See also *Occasions for Psalms Ordained by Saint Hilary of Poitiers* (art. 111), lines 10–11.

10	Psalm 53. See also *Occasions for Psalms Ordained by Saint Hilary of Poitiers* (art. 111), line 22.
11–12	Psalm 63. See also *Occasions for Psalms in Latin* (art. 110), lines 1–2; and *Occasions for Psalms Ordained by Saint Hilary of Poitiers* (art. 111), lines 20–21.
13–14	Psalm 56. See also *Occasions for Psalms Ordained by Saint Hilary of Poitiers* (art. 111), lines 16–17.
15	Psalm 58. See also *Occasions for Psalms Ordained by Saint Hilary of Poitiers* (art. 111), lines 18–19.
16	Psalm 66. See also *Occasions for Psalms Ordained by Saint Hilary of Poitiers* (art. 111), line 26.
17	*Exurgat.* The word is *Exsurgat* in the Vulgate, *Exurgat* in the Douay-Rheims title of Psalm 67. For Psalm 67, see also *Occasions for Psalms Ordained by Saint Hilary of Poitiers* (art. 111), line 6.
18–19	Psalm 68. See also *Occasions for Psalms in Latin* (art. 110), lines 7–8; and *Occasions for Psalms Ordained by Saint Hilary of Poitiers* (art. 111), lines 47–48.
20–21	Psalm 69. See also *Occasions for Psalms Ordained by Saint Hilary of Poitiers* (art. 111), lines 37–38.
22	Psalm 78. See also *Occasions for Psalms in Latin* (art. 110), line 6.
23–24	Psalm 89. See also *Occasions for Psalms Ordained by Saint Hilary of Poitiers* (art. 111), lines 48, 49–50.
25	Psalm 138. See also *Occasions for Psalms Ordained by Saint Hilary of Poitiers* (art. 111), line 34.

GLORIA IN EXCELSIS DEO EN FRAUNCEIS / GLORY TO GOD . . . IN FRENCH　　　　**[ART. 102]**

Like the *Te Deum laudamus*, the ancient liturgical hymn *Gloria in excelsis Deo* became a "private psalm" for the devoted. It opens with the words sung by the angels to the shepherds at Christ's birth (Luke 2:14), and thus it was called the Angelic Hymn. As verses were added, it developed into a liturgical doxology. The prayer fits seamlessly in quire 15 with other religious memoranda that record and itemize efficacious prayers, rituals for commemorative masses, and the occasions for psalms. On its own, fol. 134v serves up three prayers in French and Latin. This vernacular item follows an Anglo-Norman prose listing of efficacious psalms, and it resides next to a confessional prayer in Latin. The *Gloria to God in the Highest in French* is notable for how the scribe references its language as something translated from Latin. The Ludlow scribe seldom flags a specific language in this way. Written as prose, the prayer is, in fact, a poem, and the scribe marks line breaks. For another reference to the *Gloria in excelsis Deo* in quire 15, see *Three Prayers That Never Fail* (art. 109a).

[Fol. 134v. *ANL* 869. *FDT* 3098. **Scribe:** B (Ludlow scribe). **Quire:** 15. **Meter:** Fourteen alexandrine lines on one rhyme, -é. **Layout:** No columns, written as prose, title underlined in red. **Edition:** Hunt and Bliss, pp. 242–45. **Other MSS:** None. **Translation:** Hunt and Bliss, pp. 242–45.]

title   *Gloria in excelsis Deo en frounceis.* As with a few other religious items (arts. 58, 72, 91, 97, 98, 113), the scribe supplies the title and underlines it in red. Here the title is noticeably multilingual, explaining to a reader that the sacred Latin hymn is rendered in French. This is a rare gesture on the part of the Ludlow scribe, though he does frequently display linguistic inquisitiveness regarding etymologies.

CONFITEOR TIBI, DEUS, OMNIA PECCATA MEA / PRAYER OF CONFESSION   [ART. 103]

This Latin prose prayer opens with the traditional word of confession, *Confiteor*. Not the prayer of general confession recited at the beginning of Mass, it is instead a prayer fashioned for another purpose, perhaps for private use, as a means to prepare oneself for attending mass. It forms part of quire 15's sequence of short prayers and occasions for psalms. Mention of the infernal angels allies it with *Occasions for Angels* (art. 100). Its psalmic cadences also befit its position here in the Harley manuscript. The translation is by Jan Ziolkowski.

[Fol. 134v. **Scribe:** B (Ludlow scribe). **Quire:** 15. **Layout:** No columns, written as prose. **Edition:** Hunt and Bliss, pp. 244–45. **Other MSS:** None. **Translation:** Hunt and Bliss, pp. 244–45.]

3   *per lignum salutiffere crucis tue.* "By the wood of your salvational cross." The prayer would have been said in front of or holding a crucifix.

10–11   *contra iacula Diabolica et contra angelos tartareos.* "Against the Devil's darts and against hell's angels." The phrase alludes to the war for souls fought by the good angels of *Occasions for Angels* (art. 100) against Satan and his minions, the infernal angels.

GLORIOUSE DAME / PRAYER ON THE FIVE JOYS OF OUR LADY   [ART. 104]

This frequently copied prayer has three parts: a long incipit that explains how it is an indulgence, a verse prayer on the Five Joys of Mary, and a prose prayer on the Five Joys. In other manuscripts, the first two parts appear together, alone, or in combination with different items. The third part is unique to MS Harley 2253 (*ANL* 742). With paraphs the scribe divides *Prayer on the Five Joys* into two sections (the incipit and the prayers), so that the article visually looks like two separate items. He copies it all as prose, punctuating the line endings of the verse prayer.

The incipit explains the item's authority as an indulgence, which rests on its imputed transmittal from the Virgin directly to Maurice de Sully, Bishop of Paris (1160–1196), who was Peter Lombard's successor in that post. The user is told to pray upon the Virgin's Five

Joys, a theme found elsewhere in MS Harley 2253 in an Anglo-Norman lyric (art. 49) and two English ones (arts. 63, 67). Appearing in at least six other manuscripts and a roll, the incipit in its various versions offers differing terms for the indulgence. Usually it is in prose, as here, but one is set in verse (*ANL* 751, 747). The subsequent verse invocation to Mary is found with the incipit or alone in twelve manuscripts (*ANL* 772). It appears in the Ludlow scribe's MS Harley 273, fol. 110, and both items are copied on fol. 27 of MS Digby 86 (Tschann and Parkes, p. xv [no. 9]).

A version of this prayer is printed by Meyer 1903 (pp. 118–19). Jeffrey and Levy print four different texts of the verse prayer and one of the incipit (pp. 64–67). They suggest that the *Salve Regina* inspires the verse prayer, but R. Dean believes the source to be *O gloriosa Dei genitrix* (*ANL* 772).

[Fols. 134v–135r. *ANL* 751, 747, 772, 742. *FDT* 2490, 2971, 3221. Vising §90, §94. **Scribe:** B (Ludlow scribe). **Quire:** 15. **Meter of Verse Portion:** Six alexandrine lines, aaaabb. **Layout:** No columns, written as prose, two red paraphs. **Editions:** Hunt and Bliss, pp. 244–47; partially transcribed in Parkes, Plate 1(ii). **Other MSS:** Many, as listed in *ANL*. **Translation:** Hunt and Bliss, pp. 244–47.]

7–8   These verses allude to the first two of Mary's Five Joys: Annunciation and Nativity.

12–18   This prose passage completes the enumeration of the Five Joys begun in the poem by adding references to the Resurrection of Christ, the Assumption of Mary, and the Virgin's Coronation in heaven.

REX SECULORUM ET DOMINE DOMINATOR / PRAYER FOR CONTRITION   [ART. 105]

This Latin prose prayer may be meant to be recited in the order given by the scribe, after the Latin prayer for confession and the French devotion to the Five Joys (arts. 103, 104). It has not been previously printed. The translation is by Jan Ziolkowski.

[Fol. 135r. **Scribe:** B (Ludlow scribe). **Quire:** 15. **Layout:** No columns, written as prose, with initial red paraph. **Edition:** Hunt and Bliss, pp. 246–47. **Other MSS:** None. **Translation:** Hunt and Bliss, pp. 246–47.]

UM DOIT PLUS VOLENTIERS JUNER LE VENDREDY / REASONS FOR FASTING . . .   [ART. 106]

This prose item in Anglo-Norman supplies another list for the devout, explaining why they ought to venerate Friday as a day of fasting. It records thirteen events believed to have occurred on Friday, starting with the Israelites coming to the Promised Land (recounted at length in the Ludlow scribe's *Old Testament Stories* [art. 71]). After this event come the death of Moses and the victory of David over Goliath. Next the list itemizes two events of importance to the author of *Pilgrimages in the Holy Land* (art. 38): the beheadings of Elijah and John the Baptist. In almost chronological order, more holy events are named: the Slaughter of the Innocents, cited oddly in advance of the Annunciation, then the Crucifixion and the Assumption of Mary. Tucked in are the martyrdoms of Saints Peter, Stephen, and Paul, with the earliest of these, the stoning of Stephen, set after the death of Peter. The reasons for Friday fasting conclude with the future battle of Enoch and Elijah against Antichrist.

A similar list in Anglo-Norman appears in Cambridge, Emmanuel College MS 106 (I.4.31), where a short preface attributes the text to Pope Clement. R. Dean describes a Continental version as well (*ANL* 699). The Fridays for Fasting motif derives from an ancient Christian tradition disseminated across many centuries and languages. A Middle English lyric in eleven eight-line stanzas with refrain, *Þe fryday þou fonde to fast and pray*, recounts the following holy Fridays: God's creation of Adam, the Fall, Moses receiving the law tablets, the Immaculate Conception of Mary, Mary's birth, Mary's presentation at the temple, the Annunciation, pregnant Elizabeth greeting pregnant Mary, Jesus' baptism, the Crucifixion, the Harrowing of Hell, Mary's Assumption, John the Baptist's beheading, the martyrdoms of Saints Peter, Paul, Andrew, Stephen, and Katherine, and, lastly, Saint Helena's discovery of the true Cross. Regarding the tradition of listing famous Fridays, one might also think of Chaucer's flamboyant catalogue of tragic Fridays in the Nun's Priest's Tale (*Canterbury Tales* VII 3338–52), even though it follows a different rationale. Its only overlap with these pious lists is the Friday of the Passion.

The paragraphing of the text and translation given here conforms to the scribe's rubrication.

[Fol. 135r. *ANL* 699. **Scribe:** B (Ludlow scribe). **Quire:** 15. **Layout:** No columns, written as prose. **Edition:** Hunt and Bliss, pp. 246–49. **Anglo-Norman Version:** Cambridge, Emmanuel College MS 106 (I.4.31), fol. 12 (ed. Suchier, pp. 580–81). **Middle English Version:** *Þe fryday þou fonde to fast and pray*, in London, BL MS Harley 3810, Part I, fol. 14r (*IMEV, NIMEV* 4275; ed. Jordan, pp. 262–65). **Versions in Other Languages:** See *ANL* 699. **Translation:** Hunt and Bliss, pp. 246–49.]

3   *mount de Alban*. Mount Nebo. See Deuteronomy 34:1–5. The scribe's word *Alban* probably comes from misreading a capital letter in his copy, with *Ne* being mistakenly read as *Al*.

5–6   The beheadings of Elijah and John the Baptist are implicitly connected. Taken up to heaven in a whirlwind (2 Kings 2:11–12), Elijah returned in the person of John the Baptist, according to prophecy (Malachi 4:5–6) and Gospel (Matthew 11:14, 17:9–13; Mark 9:11–13; and Luke 1:17). Compare the explanatory notes for *Pilgrimages in the Holy Land* (art. 38), where sites highlighted by the author are frequently places associated with the biblical stories of Elijah and John the Baptist. *The Life of Saint John the Baptist* (art. 5) appears in MS Harley 2253, fols. 43vb–45vb, in the hand of Scribe A.

QUY EST EN TRISTOUR / SEVEN MASSES TO BE SAID IN MISFORTUNE   [ART. 107]

This Anglo-Norman prose work offers another pious list intended to aid persons who find themselves in trouble, a condition defined as sadness or imprisonment, poverty or illness. By day of week, the appropriate masses and ritual actions are itemized. R. Dean identifies related texts in two other manuscripts, both unedited (*ANL* 948). In MS Harley 2253 this item joins with the next one, forming two lists of seven masses. The paragraphing of the text and translation given here conforms to the scribe's rubrication, except that the initial *F* (*Face*) of line 3 is not marked.

[Fol. 135r. *ANL* 948. **Scribe:** B (Ludlow scribe). **Quire:** 15. **Layout:** No columns, written as prose. **Edition:** Hunt and Bliss, pp. 248–49. **Other MSS:** London, BL MS Arundel 230, fol. 6v; London, BL MS Harley 209, fol. 120r. **Translation:** Hunt and Bliss, pp. 248–49.]

CELY QUE FRA CES MESSES CHAUNTER / SEVEN MASSES IN . . . SAINT GILES   [ART. 108]

A companion to the preceding article, this item lists seven masses, matching liturgical occasion to the sung introit. R. Dean (*ANL* 932) describes two other versions of this work (both unedited) that survive with an accompanying prayer (absent here). In the Boston manuscript, an incipit ties the singing of these masses to an indulgence obtained by Saint Giles from an angelic emissary. According to tradition, Saint Giles was celebrating a mass to gain pardon for Charlemagne (ca. 742–814), when an angel delivered on the altar a letter detailing one of the emperor's sins that he had never dared confess. Despite the impossibility of this story, for Charlemagne lived later than Giles's lifetime, the "Mass of Saint Giles" persisted as a legend, and it lends a divine aura to this list. Inscribing the item as prose, the scribe rubricates the initial of each itemized mass and the initial letter of each hymn title. That a church dedicated to Saint Giles stands in Ludford very near to Ludlow might be relevant to the scribe's interest in this piece.

[Fol. 135v. *ANL* 932. *FDT-1* 4050. **Scribe:** B (Ludlow scribe). **Quire:** 15. **Layout:** No columns, written as prose. **Edition:** Hunt and Bliss, pp. 248–49. **Other MSS:** Boston, Public Library MS 124, fol. 115v; Oxford, Bodl. MS Bodley 9, fols. 54v–55a. **Translation:** Hunt and Bliss, pp. 248–49.]

1	*seint Gyle.* Saint Giles (ca. 650–ca. 710). Born in Athens, this saint was a hermit whose legend is centered in Provence and southern France. He was a guardian saint, one of the fourteen "holy helpers" (compare explanatory note to *Occasions for Angels* [art. 100], line 9), invoked for protection against the Black Death.
3	*"Rorate cely."* Introit for the Advent Mass, taken from Isaiah 45:8.
4	*"Puer natus."* Either the plainsong chant *Puer natus est nobis*, Introit of the Third Mass in Christmas Day, or the Christmas chant *Puer natus in Bethlehem*.
5	*"Nos autem gloriari [oportet]."* Introit for the Holy Thursday Mass, drawn from Galatians 6:14 and Psalm 66:2.
6	*"Resurexi."* Introit for Easter Mass, drawn from Psalm 139:18, 5–6, 1–2.
7	*"Viri Galiley."* Introit for the Mass of Christ's Ascension, based on Acts of the Apostles 1:11 and Psalm 46:2.
8	*"Spiritus Domini."* Introit for the Mass of Whitsunday (Pentecost), based on Wisdom 1:7 and Psalm 67:2.

9   *"Gaudeamus" etc.* The Gregorian chant *Gaudeamus omnes in Domino* (Let us all
           rejoice in the Lord), based on Psalm 31:11.

JE VOUS REQUER . . . / PRAYER TO THE THREE KINGS   [ART. 108A]

MS Harley 2253 preserves the only known copy of this elegant Anglo-Norman prayer
to the Three Kings. It first addresses the Magi in honor of their desire to give to God and
how God so readily accepted their gifts. From there, the petitioner turns his address to God,
asking that God likewise accept this prayer as a gift and fill the petitioner with gifts of
gladness and joy.

[Fol. 135v. *ANL* 941. Rézeau 2:444. *FDT* 3037. **Scribe:** B (Ludlow scribe). **Quire:** 15.
Layout: No columns, written as prose and opening with a red paraph and an red-marked
initial. **Edition:** Hunt and Bliss, pp. 250–51. **Other MSS:** None. **Translation:** Hunt and
Bliss, pp. 250–51.]

1   *Jaspar, Melchior, e Baltazar.* The legendary names of the three Magi. See Jacobus
           de Voragine, *The Golden Legend*, trans. Ryan, 1:78–84. The Magi are unnamed
           in the Bible (Matthew 2:1–16).

           Jesum. On this Latin accusative form in French prose, compare *ABC of Women*
           (art. 8), line 313.

MUNDUS ISTE TOTUS QUODDAM SCACCARIUM EST / ALL THE . . . CHESS BOARD   [ART. 109]

This anonymous moralization likening the world to chess was tied in the Middle Ages
to two purported authors: Pope Innocent III (1198–1213) or John of Wales (a late
thirteenth-century Franciscan). Scholars now, however, ascribe it to neither. The title given
it here adopts the opening phrase and the Shakespearean title bestowed by Thorndike. An
alternate title applied to it in some manuscripts is *Quaedam moralitas de scaccario*, or *The
Morality of Chess*. H. J. R. Murray (p. 530) refers to it as *The Innocent Morality*. As a didactic
comment on society, it circulated frequently with John of Wales's *Communeloquium*, a popular
handbook for preachers crammed with extracts from a large variety of sources. When it is
preserved with John's treatise, which divides humanity's social strata into a host of
classifications, its interpolated position occurs in Part 1, distinction 10, chapter 7, a section
that discusses entertainments and games for the laboring classes. It appears often in early
printed editions of the *Communeloquium*, which received ten printings between 1472 and
1556. Little, pp. 232–34, prints it from the 1516 edition.
      Despite its anonymity, the presence of this moralization in MS Harley 2253 may suggest
that John should be counted among the Ludlow scribe's influences. Elsewhere in Part 1,
John critiques the legal system and also high taxation, and he expresses sympathy for the
poor. According to Swanson, John of Wales "gives every indication that he feels the present
system is too harsh, and . . . [he is] anxious that rulers should take proper advice before
making important decisions" (p. 100). Another of the scribe's selections in quire 15, *Against*

the King's Taxes (art 114), fiercely expounds similar sentiments. At the same time, the *Communeloquium* is a model of collecting, selecting, and arranging items from various writers, all the while expressing an authorial point of view, so it might have offered the Ludlow scribe a precedent of sorts for how he understood his own activity of creative compiling.

The author of *All the World's a Chess Board* muses on how chess pieces and their moves may be compared to different social stations and their habits or proclivities. The pieces represent the monarch (king), judges (rooks), women (queen), lords (knights), churchmen (bishops), and common folk and laborers (pawns). The only pieces that are just and straightforward are the king and the rooks. The others are devious and backhanded, as indicated by their crooked moves and greedy ambitions. While the author thus has an interest in social comment, he desires yet more, in the manner of a churchman, to deliver a soul-saving message: all who live will suffer a common fate, and the world should be recognized for what it is: the Devil's playground. To gain salvation, one must reject the game altogether and seek divine forgiveness.

For commentary, see H. J. R. Murray, pp. 530–34; Thorndike; and Adams, pp. 43–46. The paragraphing used here agrees with Thorndike's edition, which is based on a different manuscript. The Ludlow scribe marks in red the initial words of all the paragraphs except for those of the third and eighth ones. The translation printed here is by Jan Ziolkowski, prepared for this edition.

[Fols. 135v–136r. **Scribe:** B (Ludlow scribe). **Quire:** 15. **Layout:** No columns, written as prose. **Edition:** H. J. R. Murray, pp. 559–61. **Other MSS:** Numerous, as listed by H. J. R. Murray, pp. 559–60, e.g., Oxford, Balliol College MS 274, fols. 54v–56v (ed. Thorndike, pp. 461–65); London, BL MS Royal 12.E.21, art. 11 (cited by Ker, p. xv). **Translations:** None, but see English paraphrase by H. J. R. Murray, p. 530.]

10	*familia.* A collective term for the chess pieces, which, according to H. J. R. Murray, is "rare except in Latin works from the north of France and England," and lends an interesting element to allegories that compare chess to human life (pp. 532–34).
17	*ferce.* The term *fers* refers to the queen in medieval chess. In French love poetry and Chaucer, where the chess analogy is utilized in a different context, *fers* may refer to the poet's lady. See M. Taylor, pp. 303–05; and Peck 1970, p. 83.
22	*Pervertisti.* "You have perverted." The Vulgate word is *convertisti,* "you have turned."
26–27	*exactiones iniustas.* "Unjust taxations." The author shares a concern for the overtaxed poor with John of Wales, and also with interests recorded elsewhere by the Ludlow scribe. Compare *Song of the Husbandman* and *Against the King's Taxes* (arts. 31, 114).
39	*fierce.* The pawn becomes a queen (*fers*), perhaps with a French/English wordplay on "fierce."
43	*lyveret.* A technical chess term (variant *deliveret*), which H. J. R. Murray defines as "covered check," apparently meaning that a player in check is able to move out of check (pp. 532–34). Different versions agree that the word offered here

is spoken by the player as he makes an evasive move in response to his opponent's declaration of "check." The term is French. Its Middle English equivalent is (according to Murray) *neck*, a technical usage that does not appear in the *MED*.

QUY CHESCUN JOUR DENZ SEISSAUNTE JOURS / THREE . . . NEVER FAIL   [ART. 109A]

This item in Anglo-Norman prose offers a fail-safe formula for insuring that God hears one's prayers. Following it, though, would require extraordinary devotion, patience, and persistence. One is to recite daily three time-honored hymnal prayers — the *Veni Creator*, the *Gloria in excelsis Deo*, and Vulgate Psalm 129 (*De profundis*) — thirty times each, for four months. Tucked between two works in Latin, this article augments other texts of religious counsel occupying quire 15. As a work that references hymns, it can be compared to arts. 102 and 108, and it points, perhaps, to a musical component residing in the mind of one who would preserve lists of efficacious psalms (arts. 101, 110, 111).

[Fol. 136r. *ANL* 950, 985. **Scribe:** B (Ludlow scribe). **Quire:** 15. **Layout:** No columns, written as prose. **Editions:** None. **Other MSS:** None. **Translations:** None.]

1–2   *"Veni Creator Spiritus" etc. / "Qui [diceris] Paraclitus" etc*. A liturgical hymn, ascribed to Rabanus Maurus (ninth century), which was often sung in Gregorian chant. It is typically performed to celebrate the feast of Pentecost. The first line is "Veni Creator Spiritus"; the second phrase, "Qui [diceris] Paraclitus," opens the second stanza.

2   *"Gloria in excelsis [Deo]."* Another hymn or prayer of the mass. Elsewhere in quire 15, it appears in French (art. 102).

CONTRA INIMICOS SI QUOS HABES / OCCASIONS FOR PSALMS IN LATIN   [ART. 110]

This Latin item is the second of three in MS Harley 2253 that provide instructions on how to use psalms as aids on specific occasions. It may be compared, therefore, to arts. 101 and 111, both of which are in Anglo-Norman. This anonymous work is shorter than art. 101 in that it names only ten psalms (as compared to sixteen there), but it generally provides fuller instructions. Significantly, its author wants to convey the practical wisdom that when psalms are given material *written* form (not just recited), they hold charm-like potency. The instructor expects literacy and scribal competency to be skills embodied by the practitioner. In six instances, the user is told to write down the psalm on a scrap of paper and then, so as to obtain the desired result, tie that scrap to one's own arm, or tie it to a whining child's arm, or throw it into a fire, or use it with a censer. On the use of texts (and sometimes psalms) as amulets, see Skemer, esp. p. 86.

The latinity of these phylacteric instructions, along with their specific recipes for action, suggests practical use by someone who can read and write, probably, that is, by a person of formal religious training who prescribes them to others and conducts the rituals. A good deal of the material (recipes and prognostications) collected by the Ludlow scribe in London, BL MSS Harley 273 and Royal 12.C.12 exhibits comparable interests (see, for example, Skemer, pp. 14 n. 34, 83 n. 19). The scribe's French Psalter survives, as well, in MS Harley 273, fols. 8r–52v.

Visually, on fol. 136r, this item follows art. 109a — short, similar instructions in French — with a matched opening paraph. The scribe inserts paraphs to mark off each item on the list. Although there are two sequences (Psalms 68–70, 71–73), the psalms are not in consecutive order. The eleventh item is a hymn, *Te Deum laudamus*. Psalms recurring in the lists of arts. 101 and 111 are cited in the explanatory notes. The scribe's Latin titles for individual psalms are filled out as necessary (with words in brackets) to reflect their English translations. For helpful commentary on the uses of the Book of Psalms in the Middle Ages, see Kuczynski 1995 and the essays edited by van Deusen. The translation printed here is by Jan Ziolkowski, prepared for this edition.

[Fol. 136r–v. **Scribe:** B (Ludlow scribe). **Quire:** 15. **Layout:** No columns, written as prose. **Editions:** None. **Other MSS:** None. **Translations:** None.]

1–2	Psalm 63. See also *Occasions for Psalms in French* (art. 101), lines 11–12; and *Occasions for Psalms Ordained by Saint Hilary of Poitiers* (art. 111), lines 20–21. The scribe, writing *lxiiij*, misnumbers the psalm.
5–6	Psalm 30. See also *Occasions for Psalms in French* (art. 101), lines 3, 4–5; and *Occasions for Psalms Ordained by Saint Hilary of Poitiers* (art. 111), lines 8–9. This psalm is written in the bottom margin and inserted with a caret. It is identified as "the first" to distinguish it from Psalm 70 (as it is in art. 111).
6	Psalm 78. See also *Occasions for Psalms in French* (art. 101), line 22. Along with Psalm 30, this psalm is written in the bottom margin and inserted with a caret. The addition of a second psalm to this item may be an afterthought.
7–8	Psalm 68. See also *Occasions for Psalms in French* (art. 101), line 18–19; and *Occasions for Psalms Ordained by Saint Hilary of Poitiers* (art. 111), lines 47–48.
10–11	Psalm 69. See also *Occasions for Psalms in French* (art. 101), lines 20–21.
13	Psalm 70. See also *Occasions for Psalms Ordained by Saint Hilary of Poitiers* (art. 111), lines 39–40.
26	*"Te Deum laudamus."* An early Christian hymn of praise, also known as the Ambrosian hymn, which remains in regular use in the Catholic Church. By tradition, its authors are Saints Ambrose and Augustine, who composed it for the occasion of Augustine's baptism in 387. Another tradition ascribes it to Saint Hilary of Poitiers, to whom authorship of the next item in MS Harley 2253 is ascribed (see art. 111). The same hymn also closes art. 111.

SEINT HILLERE . . . / OCCASIONS FOR PSALMS ORDAINED BY SAINT HILARY . . . [ART. 111]

In this text ascribed to Saint Hilary, fourth-century Bishop of Poitiers and Church Doctor, the author lists the prayerful uses of twenty-three psalms and one hymn (the *Te*

Deum laudamus). The writer of many Latin patristic treatises, Saint Hilary composed *Tractatus super Psalmos*, which may bear an influence on this document or on its ascription. It represents the third of three articles in MS Harley 2253 that signal the best psalms to use in supplication to God on certain occasions. This list in French follows directly after its Latin counterpart (art. 110), also written as prose with paraphs to mark each item. As in the other French list (art. 101), one is told to *recite* these psalms, at times repetitively and with other prayers. The instructions never ask one to write out the psalms, as does the author of the preceding Latin list.

The psalms are not given in sequential order. Psalm 89 is listed twice. The several psalms repeated in the lists of arts. 101 and 110 are mentioned in the explanatory notes. The scribe's Latin titles for individual psalms are filled out as necessary (with words in brackets) to reflect their English translations. For helpful commentary on the uses of the Book of Psalms in the Middle Ages, see Kuczynski 1995 and the essays edited by van Deusen.

[Fols. 136v–137r. *ANL* 456, 986. **Scribe:** B (Ludlow scribe). **Quire:** 15. **Layout:** No columns, written as prose. **Edition:** Hunt and Bliss, pp. 250–55. **Other MSS:** None. **Translation:** Hunt and Bliss, pp. 250–55.]

6	*Exurgat.* The word is spelled this way in the Douay-Rheims title of Psalm 67; the Vulgate has *Exsurgat.*
	Psalm 67. See also *Occasions for Psalms in French* (art. 101), line 17.
8–9	Psalm 30. See also *Occasions for Psalms in French* (art. 101), lines 3, 4–5; and *Occasions for Psalms in Latin* (art. 110), lines 5–6. It is identified as "the first" to distinguish it from Psalm 70 (as it is in art. 110).
10–11	Psalm 42. See also *Occassions for Psalms in French* (art. 101), lines 8–9.
13–14	Psalm 54. Hunt and Bliss mistakenly identify the psalm as Psalm 63.
16–17	Psalm 56. See also *Occasions for Psalms in French* (art. 101), lines 13–14.
18–19	Psalm 58. See also *Occasions for Psalms in French* (art. 101), line 15.
20–21	Psalm 63. See also *Occasions for Psalms in French* (art. 101), lines 11–12; and *Occasions for Psalms in Latin* (art. 110), lines 1–2.
22	Psalm 53. See also *Occasions for Psalms in French* (art. 101), line 10.
23	Psalm 59. Hunt and Bliss identify this phrase as part of Psalm 53.
26	Psalm 66. See also *Occasions for Psalms in French* (art. 101), line 16.
28	Psalm 34. See also *Occasions for Psalms in French* (art. 101), line 6–7.
34	Psalm 138. See also *Occasions for Psalms in French* (art. 101), line 25.
37–38	Psalm 69. See also *Occasions for Psalms in French* (art. 101), lines 20–21.
39–40	Psalm 70. See also *Occasions for Psalms in Latin* (art. 110), line 13. It is identified as "the second" to distinguish it from Psalm 30 (compare lines 8–9).

45	Psalm 12. See also *Occasions for Psalms in French* (art. 101), lines 1–2.
47–48	Psalm 68. See also *Occasions for Psalms in French* (art. 101), lines 18–19; and *Occasions for Psalms in Latin* (art. 110), lines 7–8. Hunt and Bliss identify this psalm as Psalm 11.
48	Psalm 89. See also this item, lines 49–50; and *Occasions for Psalms in French* (art. 101), lines 23–24. Hunt and Bliss identify this psalm as Psalm 45.
49–50	Psalm 89. See also this item, line 48; and *Occasions for Psalms in French* (art. 101), lines 23–24. Hunt and Bliss identify this psalm as Psalm 45.
51–52	Psalm 21. Hunt and Bliss identify this psalm as Psalm 12.
52	*"Te Deum laudamus."* See explanatory note to *Occasions for Psalms in Latin* (art. 110), line 26.

EULOTROPIA ET CELIDONIA / HELIOTROPE AND CELANDINE   [ART. 112]

   This short prose item preserves two extracts from *The Book of Secrets of Albertus Magnus of the Virtues of Herbs, Stones and Certain Beasts*. The Ludlow scribe selects the first and fourth of sixteen herbs described in this work of natural lore, which circulated widely in Latin manuscripts from the late thirteenth century onwards. In the mid-sixteenth century the book was translated into English. The earliest printings of it came from the shops of William Copland (three editions) and William Seres (one edition), all undated; later it was printed by William Jaggard and then T. Coates in six editions dating from 1595 to 1637 (Best and Brightman, pp. xliii–xliv). The rationale for the scribe's two selections is not self-evident. Heliotrope is said to bring about calm speech. It also exposes the crimes of thieves and adulterous women. Celandine possesses ameliorative virtues, too, in its ability to quell enemies and end quarrels. It can give the prognosis for a man suffering a dire illness: if he is to live, he will weep; if not, he will sing. The virtues of both involve an additive from an animal (a wolf's tooth, a mole's heart) and the placement of the herb under a person's head. For further bibliography on medieval English herbals and their Latin sources, see *MWME* 10:3641–45, 3818–38. The translation printed here is by Jan Ziolkowski, prepared for this edition.

[Fol. 137r. **Scribe:** B (Ludlow scribe). **Quire:** 15. **Layout:** No columns, written as prose. **Editions:** None. **Other MSS:** See Best and Brightman, pp. lxiii–lxiv. **Translations:** None.]

| 1–8 | The corresponding early English translation reads: "The first herb is called with the men of Chaldea, *Elios*, with the Greeks, *Matuchiol*, with the Latins, *Heliotropium*, with the Englishmen, Marigold, whose interpretation is of *helios*, that is the Sun, and *tropos*, that is alteration, or change, because it is turned according to the Sun. The virtue of this herb is marvellous: for if it be gathered, the Sun being in the sign *Leo*, in August, and be wrapped in the leaf of a Laurel, or Bay tree, and a Wolf's tooth be added thereto, no man shall be able to have a word to speak against the bearer thereof, but words of peace. And if any thing be stolen, if the bearer of the things before named lay them under his head in |

the night, he shall see the thief, and all his conditions. And moreover, if the aforesaid herb be put in any church where women be which have broken matrimony on their part, they shall never be able to go forth of the church, except it be put away. And this last point hath been proved, and is very true" (ed. Best and Brightman, pp. 4–5; text produced by collation of the three Copland editions and the Seres edition).

2   *eulotropia*. "Heliotrope," an herbal name that figures in a rich rhetorical and metaphorical tradition, from Ovid to Machaut, Froissart, and Chaucer, where its reference point is the daisy (*marguerite*) rather than the marigold. See Travis, pp. 169–200.

           solsequium. The flower *solsecle* in Middle English, that is, marigold. It is used as a simile in two Harley lyrics to describe a woman's beauty and her health-bestowing sweetness. See *Annot and John* (art. 28), line 20, and *Blow, Northern Wind* (art. 46), line 67. Its open bloom is said to turn toward the sun as it makes its daily course across the sky.

4   *dens lupi*. Either the actual tooth of a wolf or the plant wolfsbane (Best and Brightman, p. 4). For comparison, the second herb, celandine, exhibits a virtue when combined with the heart of a mole.

9–12   The corresponding early English translation reads: "The fourth herb is named *Aquilaris*, of Chaldees, because it springeth in the time in which the Eagles build their nests. It is named of Greeks *Valis*, of Latins *Chelidonium*, and of Englishmen Celandine. This herb springeth in the time in which the Swallows, and also the Eagles, make their nests. If any man shall have this herb, with the heart of a Mole, he shall overcome all his enemies, and all matters in suit, and shall put away all debate. And if the before named herb be put upon the head of a sick man, if he should die, he shall sing anon with a loud voice, if not, he shall weep" (ed. Best and Brightman, pp. 6–7). See also Rohde, pp. 63–65, for quotations, including this one, from Copland's early printed text.

DE INTERROGANDI MORIBUNDIS BEATI ANSELMI / SAINT . . . THE DYING   [ART. 113]

This item attributed to Saint Anselm, Archbishop of Canterbury (1093–1109), lists the questions that a priest ought to ask of the dying to affirm belief and penance, as the proper means by which to ready the departing soul. The dying person is addressed *in habitu clericali* (as a cleric) and as "brother" or "sister," that is, as a person in religious vows. It may be that the Ludlow scribe has positioned this text in the manuscript as a conspicuous way to end it with thoughts of mortality and last things. The questions conjure the scene of a lonely soul's judgment before God, and the next article, *Against the King's Taxes*, will warn the rich that they may expect to ultimately face God's harsh penalties. This selection also adds to the pious lists and rituals recorded elsewhere in quire 15. This text of Anselm's questions has not been previously edited and translated. The paragraphing presented here conforms to the scribe's rubrication. The translation is by Jan Ziolkowski, prepared for this edition.

[Fol. 137r–v. **Scribe:** B (Ludlow scribe). **Quire:** 15. **Layout:** No columns, written as prose, title underlined. **Editions:** None. **Other Versions:** *PL* 158:685–88; Schmitt, pp. 5–6. **Translations:** None.]

DIEU, ROY DE MAGESTÉ / AGAINST THE KING'S TAXES   [ART. 114]

To judge by its clever macaronics and moral intensity, *Against the King's Taxes* was likely authored by a learned churchman. Its verses skillfully blend Latin and Anglo-Norman to produce a hybrid "variation of the goliardic stanza 'cum auctoritas,'" even as this "deliberate attempt to imitate a favourite medieval Latin stanza form . . . frequently does violence to the normal accentuations of French words" (Aspin, p. 108). Editors have printed the stanza as five lines — four of French and Latin, the last in Latin hexameter — but here it is presented as a ten-line stanza to display the poem's basic rhyme scheme (ababcbcbdd) and linguistic structure. Every stanza closes with a Latin couplet that makes an authoritative moral statement, much like the vernacular proverb sealing each stanza of the English poem *Hending* (art. 89).

In seventeen stanzas the poet of *Against the King's Taxes* voices precise objections to a grievous system of taxation and levies on wool, set in place to support royal adventures abroad. For these policies the poet blames not so much the king, whom he calls a *jeovene bachiler*, as he chastises the king's unnamed *maveis consiler* and the corrupt lesser officials who take more than they ought. Wright 1839 proposes that the complaint underlying the poem refers to events during the reign of Edward I (pp. 182–87), but modern scholarly consensus has settled on a later date of composition: the period of controversy and discontent, ca. 1337–1340, when King Edward III sought means to finance his war in France. In 1337 Edward III was twenty-five years old. The probable identity of the "evil counselor" is John Stratford, Archbishop of Canterbury and Edward's Chancellor. William Kilsby, Keeper of the Privy Seal, has also been proposed.

The circumstances for the poet's complaint seem thus to be contemporary with the scribe's making of the Harley manuscript. In dating the hand, Revard sets the copying of *Against the King's Taxes* at about 1339–1340 and no later than 1342 (2000b, pp. 62–64). Another item localized to the politics of 1340–1341 is *Trailbaston* (art. 80) (Revard 2000b, p. 75). Taxation of the wool trade, so vital to the Ludlow economy, was a burning local issue; another item that concerns the politics of wool is *The Flemish Insurrection* (art. 48) (Revard 2000b, pp. 28–29, 78–79). As for the subject of oppressive taxation viewed as a moral issue, one may compare this poem to another work in quire 15, *All the World's a Chess Board* (art. 109), and also to the English *Song of the Husbandman* (art. 31). By these selections, the scribe displays a persistent interest in how national policies and local corruption inflict hardship on the common people — and on clergy — who are forced to pay unfair taxes, levies, and what the poet of *Against the King's Taxes* even calls "tribute" (line 82).

For good commentary and historical background on this poem, see Aspin, pp. 105–15; Harriss, pp. 250–52; Coleman, pp. 79–81; Scattergood 2000a, pp. 163–67; and Scase 2007, pp. 29–33. Scase points out how the complaint, seemingly a plea for humble commoners, is really a grievance lodged on behalf of churchmen also affected and deeply offended. Opposition to abridgments of clerical privilege is an opinion implicitly espoused by the Ludlow scribe in the prose *Old Testament Stories* (art. 71) (Thompson 2000, pp. 284–87). A second copy of *Against the King's Taxes* supports the notion that the poem voices ecclesiastical protest. London, BL Addit. MS 10374 is a cartulary from Whalley Abbey that preserves the poem among the abbey's legal instruments, contracts, and documents. As a player in the wool trade, Whalley was subject to the levies addressed by the poet. The Whalley version is shorter, leaving out "those stanzas which contain criticism of the rich, and . . . those involved in military activities in France — perhaps because there was a desire not to upset the monastery's patrons" (Scattergood 2000a, pp. 166–67). The poet ultimately reminds readers that wicked tax-collectors and thievish policy-makers will get their due on Judgment Day (lines 101–20), and thus limns political complaint with the time-honored rhetoric of preaching.

[Fols. 137v–138v. *ANL* 95. Långfors, p. 96. **Scribe:** B (Ludlow scribe). **Quire:** 15. **Meter:** Seventeen 10-line stanzas in Latin and French (Ker, p. xvi; Aspin, p. 108). **Layout:** No columns; lines 1–8 of each stanza written on four MS lines, lines 9–10 written to the right. **Editions:** Wright 1839, pp. 182–87; Aspin, pp. 105–15 (no. 10). **Other MS:** London, BL Addit. MS 10374, fols. 145v–147r. **Translations:** Wright 1839, pp. 182–87; Aspin, pp. 111–14; Scattergood 2000a, pp. 163–66 (lines 21–60, 131–40 only); Scase 2007, pp. 30–32 (lines 11–50, 105–10 only).]

23   *Le quinzyme dener.* "The tax of the fifteenth." Scattergood summarizes how successive parliaments imposed taxes to raise funds for Edward's war with France: "In the autumn parliaments of 1333 and 1334, tenths and fifteenths were granted. In 1336 a grant of a tenth and a fifteenth was passed in the March parliament, and at the great council at Nottingham in the autumn a similar grant was made, as well as two-tenths from the clergy. A year later in September 1337, the great council of Westminster gave a tenth and a fifteenth for three years, and the convocation of Canterbury and York committed the clergy to a similar grant. Hence, the poet's complaint that the 'quinzyme' had been levied year after year" (2000a, p. 164).

25–26   Scase points to these lines as indicating that the injustices complained about extend to classes beyond the poorest: "those who used to sit in comfort are brought low" (2007, p. 31). Aspin cites Luke 1:52: "He hath put down the mighty from their seats" (p. 114).

42   *Collectio lanarum.* Scattergood defines this specific term: "in the summer of 1337, the king had come to an agreement with the principal wool contractors that, in return for a monopoly that would cut out foreign buyers, they would agree to buy and export 30,000 sacks of wool for the king's use — half the profits to go to the king. This is the 'collectio lanarum' . . . to which the poet objects" (2000a, p. 164–65). See also Wright 1839, p. 377; Aspin, p. 114; and Harriss, p. 251.

50   *mea lana.* "My wool." The first-person pronoun registers the poet's complaint as personally affecting him, while the third person *earum* (line 44) earlier in the stanza separates the speaker from the poor on whose behalf he also complains. See Scase 2007, p. 31.

73   *maveis consiler.* Probably John Stratford, Archbishop of Canterbury. There was a faction hostile to Stratford, Chancellor of England. Aspin proposes that *Against*

the King's Taxes was written as part of "a campaign of slander directed against him" (p. 115). Lines 7–8 seem also to allude to the evil counselor.

105   *le haut juggement*. "Last Judgment." In lines 105–10, the moral warning that God will punish the corrupt, greedy agents of unjust taxation, called thieves in the next stanza, exposes the moral core of a poem that voices a clerical point of view. The religious outlook of *Against the King's Taxes* pairs it with *All the World's a Chess Board* (art. 109). The scribe's placement of the poem near the end of quire 15 — and of MS Harley 2253 overall — may be because it reminds one to think of ultimate things.

150   *Pro victu solvere lignum*. "To pay for food with wood." *Lignum* refers to the wooden tallies or notched sticks given as receipts. As Scase comments, "The poet swipes at the practice of paying for prises with tally-sticks which often proved worthless, wittily pointing out that it is better to eat off wooden plates and pay with silver, than to eat off silver plates, and pay with wood" (2007, p. 31). Wright notes that people of the lower classes typically ate from wooden plates and vessels (1839, p. 377).

168   *Inter reges*. A specific reference, perhaps, to King Edward III of England and King Philip VI of France, and to the unsuccessful peace negotiations of 1337. See Scattergood 2000a, p. 166.

CONTEMPLACIOUN DE LA PASSIOUN JESU CRIST / SEVEN HOURS OF . . .   [ART. 115]

    This prose work in Anglo-Norman is unique to MS Harley 2253. It provides instructions for how a devout reader ought to meditate on the events of the Passion at each of the seven canonical hours. In pastoral fashion, the author supplies the penitential prayer to say at each hour, while successive scenes of Christ's torture are vividly recreated in word and mental image. Designed to stir fervent compassion and inward contrition, this exercise in devotion follows an ancient Christian trope that is standard in Latin Books of Hours and appears in many vernacular texts of the Middle Ages (Duffy 1992, pp. 225, 237–38). The Harley meditation begins at compline rather than matins because, according to the author, Judas betrayed Christ at compline. One must commence the meditation by thinking upon that betrayal, and thus tying it to one's own guilt and self-examination. For similar works in Anglo-Norman, see *ANL* 629, 959, 962, 966, 967. One of these, *Mirour de Seinte Eglyse*, appears in the Ludlow scribe's book London, BL MS Royal 12.C.12, fols. 17r–30v (ed. Wilshere 1982). On the tradition in Middle English, see Woolf 1968, pp. 234–37; and Brown 1952, pp. 39–44, 50–51, 69–70. Boulton 1996–97, pp. 54–55, offers a brief commentary on this work.

    In the context of MS Harley 2253, several other works invoke and visualize the Passion. In the early texts copied by Scribe A, there appear two Passion narratives in French: Herman de Valenciennes' *The Passion of Our Lord* and the prose *Gospel of Nicodemus* (arts. 2, 3). A sizeable number of lyrics also call for a commemoration of the Passion, that is, *A Spring Song on the Passion*; *Song on Jesus' Precious Blood*; *Jesus, Sweet Is the Love of You*; *Stand Well, Mother, under Rood*; *Jesus, by Your Great Might*; *I Sigh When I Sing*; *Maiden, Mother Mild* ; and *The Way of Christ's Love* (arts. 53, 56, 58, 60, 61, 62, 69, 92). This article is the next-to-last of the Ludlow scribe's items in MS Harley 2253. Analysis of the script indicates that it was inserted between 1338 and 1342 (Revard 2000b, pp. 62–64). Paragraphing in this edition follows the markings of the scribe, except that the paragraphs beginning at lines 62 and 96 are not marked.

[Fols. 138v–140r. *ANL* 958. *FDT* 2391–92, 2394–96, 2416, 3498. **Scribe:** B (Ludlow scribe). **Quire:** 15. **Layout:** No columns, written as prose. **Edition:** Hunt and Bliss, pp. 254–61. **Other MSS:** None. **Translation:** Hunt and Bliss, pp. 254–61.]

12–13   *"Requerez e vous receverez."* Compare Matthew 21:22, Mark 11:24, John 16:24.

17   *'Veilles e horez que vous ne entrez en temptacioun.'* Compare Matthew 26:41, Mark 14:38.

48   *'Crucifiez le! Crucifiez le!'* Compare Luke 23:21, John 19:6.

58–59   *'Dieu te salve, Roy des Gyus.'* Compare Matthew 27:29, Mark 15:18.

71–72   *'Iesu Nazarenus, Rex Iudeorum.'* Compare John 19:19. The author quotes the Vulgate Latin.

85–86   *'Dieux, Dieux, purquoi m'as tu guerpy?'* Compare Matthew 27:46, Mark 15:34.

93   *'Tout est acomply.'* Compare John 19:30.

94–95   *'In manus tuas, Domine, comendo spiritum meum.'* Compare Luke 23:46. The author quotes the Vulgate Latin.

99   *'Verroiement le Fitz Dieu estoit cesti.'* Compare Matthew 27:54, Mark 15:39, Luke 23:47.

106–07   *Josep de Arymathie e Nichodemus.* The prose *Gospel of Nicodemus* appears earlier in MS Harley 2253, in the hand of Scribe A (art. 3).

DE MARTIRIO SANCTI WISTANI / THE MARTYRDOM OF SAINT WISTAN   [ART. 116]

As in the two other Latin legends collected by the Ludlow scribe, the subject here is an Anglo-Saxon saint whose tale holds local resonance: Ethelbert of Hereford (art. 18), Etfrid of Leominster (art. 98), and now Wistan [Wigstan] of Wistanstow. Located ten miles northwest of Ludlow (the scribe's professional locale), Wistanstow was the site of Saint Wistan's martyrdom in the ninth century at the hands of his godfather Brithfard. Like Ethelbert, Wistan is a young prince murdered by an opponent with rival political ambitions. Ethelbert was an East Anglian ambushed in the Mercian court of King Offa. Here Wistan is caught in a web of rival family claims to the Mercian throne, the prize of which is his own mother, Queen Elfleda, daughter of the deceased King Ceolwulf.

When Ceolwulf died, he was succeeded by Wiglaf, whose son Wigmund married Elfleda. When Wiglaf died after a thirteen-year reign, he was succeeded by Wigmund. But Wigmund died soon thereafter, leaving the throne open for a new successor, Brithwulf, who wanted to have his own son (Brithfard) succeed him. To secure this end, Brithwulf arranged to have Brithfard marry Elfleda. In the Harley version, Brithwulf's role is left out, and Brithfard is an ambitious *consul* — both blood kinsman and godfather to Wistan — who demands the queen in marriage to secure his claim. Wistan opposes this plan not for his own ambition as the legitimate prince, but as a saint who seeks a better kingdom for himself and wants the same for his widowed mother. (His objections may also be based on grounds of consanguinity and the spiritual relationship of godparent to godson.) Wistan piously begs his mother to accept God as her "undying husband" (line 17), and she agrees. For this action, though, Wistan is treacherously called to meet with Brithfard, who feigns friendliness before he slices off the crown of Wistan's head.

According to legend, Wistan's martyred body was buried in the royal crypt that still exists under the chancel of Repton church (Yorke, p. 106, Fig. 10). The relics of Wistan were translated to Evesham Abbey in 1019. The oldest tale of the martyrdom, the *Vita sancti Wistani*, appears to have been written at this abbey. Its author may have been Dominic, Prior of Evesham, 1130–ca. 1144 (Jennings, pp. 298–304). The *Vita* is the source for the version in the Harley manuscript (ca. 1343–1349), which reduces it substantially. The *Vita* names Wistanstow, but the Harley text omits the place-name, perhaps because it was superfluous in its eponymous setting. The Harley adaptation may have been produced by the Ludlow scribe himself.

For commentary, see Blair 2002b, pp. 469, 483, and 2002a, pp. 558–59; Yorke, pp. 119–20; Walker, 38–39; and Sims-Williams, p. 167. The Harley text has not been previously edited. On its presence with the other Latin lives in MS Harley 2253, see Kuczynski 2000, pp. 138–40. It was apparently added to the manuscript later than other works, after an interval of several years (Revard 2000b, pp. 63–64), and, when it was inserted, at least one item was excised (Ker, p. xvi). The translation printed here is by Jan Ziolkowski, prepared for this edition.

[Fol. 140v. Hardy, 1:472 (no. 1023). **Scribe:** B (Ludlow scribe). **Quire:** 15. **Layout:** No columns, written as prose. **Editions:** None. **Other MSS:** None. **Latin Source:** *Vita sancti Wistani*, in Oxford, Bodl. MS Rawlinson A.287 (ed. Macray, pp. 326–32). **Later Latin Analogue:** John Capgrave's fifteenth-century *De sancto Wistano rege et martire* (ed. Horstmann 1901, 2:465–68). **Translations:** None.]

2   *Wiglafus rex Merciorum.* Wiglaf was King of Mercia, 827–840. His son Wigmund succeeded him, but died in the same year, leaving the throne to a kinsman Brithwulf [Berhtwulf], who ruled Mercia 840–52. The background of the tale involves three rival lineages of ninth-century Mercia: King Ceolwulf I (821–823) and his daughter Elfleda [Ælfflæd]; Ceolwulf's successor Wiglaf and his son Wigmund (who married Elfleda); and Wigmund's successor Brithwulf and his son Brithfard [Berhtfrith]. In his ambition to marry Elfleda and secure the Mercian kingdom — a plan opposed by Wistan — Brithfard becomes the villain of the legend.

26   By divine punishment, Brithfard is struck with insanity as soon as he commits the murders.

31   *die kalendas Iunii prima feria.* Wistan's feast day is June 1, the day of his martyrdom. Modern historians set the year of his death in 849, not 850.

✿ TEXTUAL NOTES

ABBREVIATIONS: As: Aspin; **Bö:** Böddeker; **Br:** Brook; **BS:** Bennett and Smithers; **BZ:** Brandl and Zippel; **B13:** Brown 1932; **Dea:** J. M. Dean; **Do:** Dove 1969; **Fl:** Flood; **Fö:** Förster; **Fu:** Furnivall; **HB:** Hunt and Bliss; **Kem:** Kemble; **Ken:** Kennedy; **Mi:** Millett; **Mo:** Morris and Skeat; **MS:** MS Harley 2253; **Mu¹:** H. J. R. Murray; **Mu²:** J. A. H. Murray; **NB:** Noomen and van den Boogaard; **Pa:** Patterson; **Rev:** Revard 2005a; **Ri:** Ritson 1877; **Ro:** Robbins 1959; **SP:** Short and Pearcy; **Si:** Silverstein; **St:** Stemmler 1970; **Tu:** Turville-Petre 1989; **Ul:** Ulrich; **W¹:** Wright 1839; **W²:** Wright 1841; **W³:** Wright 1842; **WH:** Wright and Halliwell.

BOOKLET 5

LUDLOW SCRIBE, ESTOYRES DE LA BIBLE   [art. 71]

15	*Rachel.* MS: *Lya.* See explanatory note.
46	*gonele.* MS: *gonenele.*
79	*come.* MS has mark over the *e.*
83	*come.* MS has a mark over the *e.*
149	*o.* MS: *e* (compare textual note to line 437).
172	*pez.* MS: *geȝ.* See explanatory note.
206	*velt.* MS: *verelt* (*er* abbreviated).
215	*bien.* MS: *bie.*
224	*quinte.* MS: *quite* (*ui* abbreviated).
227–29	Written at the base of the page with a mark for insertion.
267	*multeplia.* MS: *molteplia* (*o* abbreviated) in manner that indicates *mult* in Latin texts, *molt* in French texts, but compare *multiplierent,* line 271, which is not abbreviated.
276	*mie, ne.* MS: *ne ne.*
327	*primes estre.* MS: *primes primes estre* (the last word of fol. 96r is repeated on fol. 96v).
342	*fierement.* MS: *fieremont.*
372	*aungel.* MS: *anglel.*
410	*pur.* MS: *pu.*
437	*ov.* MS interlined above *e,* which is marked for deletion.
476	*desouz.* MS: *desouþ.* The scribe writes thorn instead of yogh.
506	*foyz.* MS: *foyht.* Instead of yogh, the scribe writes *ht,* which in his English texts often replaces *þ* (compare textual note to line 476).
547	*en autre.* MS: *e autre.* See Wilshere 1988, p. 86.

612	*Elysama*. MS: *Elysania* (*i* dotted).
616	*Ahiezel*. MS: *Abiezel*.
620	*Ahyrac*. MS: *Abyrac*.
629	*vintaunte*. MS: *vtaunte*.
630	*tabernacle*. MS: *taberacle* (second *a* abbreviated).
633	*encensers*. MS: *encersers*.
839	*Promissioun*. MS: *prousmissioun* (*ro* and *us* abbreviated).
870	*Arnon*. MS: *amon*.
905	*destourna*. MS: *bestourna*.
941	*Phasga*. MS: *Plasga*. See explanatory note.
980	*Cozby*. MS: *Corby*. The scribe writes *r* instead of yogh.

NOMINA LIBRORUM BIBLIOTECE [art. 72]

44	*Romanos*. MS: *Ronanos* (*an* abbreviated).

BOOKLET 6

GOD THAT AL THIS MYHTES MAY [art. 73]

16	*worst*. So Bö, Pa. MS, W³, B13, Br: *wrst*.
21	*Y stod*. So MS, W³, B13, Br. Bö, Pa: *ystod*.
30	*knowe*. So MS, W³, B13, Br. Bö, Pa: *knawe*.
32	*lowe*. So MS, W³, B13, Br. Bö, Pa: *lawe*.
53	*Unworth*. So Bö, Pa. MS, W³, B13, Br: *Unwrþ*.

LUSTNETH, ALLE, A LUTEL THROWE [art. 74]

4	*Y con*. So MS, W³, Fu. Bö: *ycon*.
7	*is*. So MS, Bö, Fu. W³: *his*.
11	*ys*. So MS, Bö, Fu. W³: *his*.
18	*wet*. So MS, W³. Bö, Fu: *whet*.
35	*fyht*. So MS, W³, Bö. Fu: *fyght*.
43	*swyketh*. So MS, W³, Bö. Fu: *swynkeþ*.
51	*conne*. So MS, W³, Bö. Fu: *wune*.
55	*thou*. So MS, W³. Bö, Fu: *þe*.
56	*wet*. So MS, W³. Bö, Fu: *whet*.
69	*ly*. So MS, W³, Bö. Fu: *by*.
71	*sit*. So MS, W³. Bö, Fu: *sihth*.
76	*worldes*. So MS, W³. Bö, Fu: *worst is*.
79	*feir*. So MS, W³, Bö. Fu: *feire*.
83	*bo*. So MS, Bö, Fu. W³: *so*.
95	*Arlebest*. So MS, W³. Bö, Fu: *alrebest*.
97	*notht*. So MS. W³, Bö, Fu: *noht*.
111	*hoke*. So MS (*e* abbreviated). W³, Bö, Fu: *hokes*.
114	*croke*. So MS (*e* abbreviated). W³, Bö, Fu: *crokes*.

116   *mist.* So MS, W³. Bö, Fu: *miht.*

120   *lye.* So MS, W³. Bö, Fu: *le3e.*

121   *hue.* So MS, W³. Bö, Fu: *hue þat.*

132   *buen.* So MS, W³. Bö, Fu: *weren.*

137   *weylaway.* So MS, Bö, Fu. W³: *weylawey.*

148   *champioun.* So W³, Bö, Fu. MS: *chaunpioun.*

Le jongleur d'Ely et le roi d'Angleterre   [art. 75]

13   *seignur.* So MS (*ur* abbreviated). Ul: *seignour.*

66   *fere.* So MS. Ul: *feyre.*

82   *yl ne fust.* So MS. Ul: *yl fust.*

110   *Qe.* So MS. Ul: *Que.*

162   *pus.* So MS (*us* abbreviated). Ul: *puis.*

169   *avre.* So MS. Ul: *aver.*

177   *Ore.* So MS. Ul: *Or.*

179   *pur.* So MS (*ur* abbreviated). Ul: *par.*

181   *ore.* So MS. Ul: *or.*

188   *Datheheit.* So MS (*Daþeheit*). Ul: *Dascheit.*

226   *bocerel.* So MS. Ul: *boterel.*

235   *fust.* So MS. Ul: *fist.*

251   *Yl.* So MS. Ul: *Il.*

254   *dirra.* So MS. Ul: *dira.*

308   *Pur.* So MS (*ur* abbreviated). Ul: *Par.*

316   *hountouse.* So MS. Ul: *hontouse.*

319   *descorreit.* So MS. Ul: *destorreit.*

321   *dirrount.* So MS. Ul: *dirront.*

324   *pecchiés.* So MS. Ul: *pechies.*

328   *Quar.* So MS. Ul: *Qar.*

337   *pecchiés.* So MS. Ul: *pechies.*

371   *Qe.* So MS. Ul: *Que.*

390   *simple.* So MS. Ul: *estre simple.*

Les trois dames qui troverent un vit   [art. 75a]

1   *que.* So MS, Ken, NB, SP. Rev: *qe.*

10   *Ja.* So MS, NB, SP, Rev. Ken: omitted.

13   *garda.* So MS, NB, SP, Rev. Ken: *garder.*

17   *meyntenaunt.* So MS, NB, SP, Rev. Ken: *mayntenaunt.*

25   *trovour.* So MS, Ken, NB, Rev. SP: *trover.*

       myen. So MS, NB, SP, Rev. Ken: *meyen.*

60   *il.* So MS, Ken, NB, Rev. SP: omitted.

78   *dreytures.* So MS. Ken, NB, SP, Rev: *droytures.*

83   *erroument.* So MS, Rev. Ken, NB: *erronment.* SP: *erraument.*

90   *Quei.* So MS, Ken, NB, Rev. SP: *Que celes.*

       il. So MS, Ken, NB, Rev. SP: omitted.

Le dit des femmes [art. 76]

11	*noun*. So MS, WH, Do. Ken: *nom*.
21	*espieces*. So MS, WH, Do. Ken: *espices*.
24	*espieces*. So MS, WH, Do. Ken: *espices*.
27	*beiser*. So MS, WH, Do. Ken: *besier*.
50	*nulle*. So MS, Ken, Do. WH: *nul*.
53	*blamer*. So MS, WH, Do. Ken: *flamer*.
66	*femmes*. So MS, WH, Do. Ken: *femme*.
78	*avauncé*. So MS, WH, Do. Ken: *auancé*.
89	*ay*. So MS, WH. Ken: *ayme*. Do: *aym*.
109	*dyre*. So MS, WH, Ken. Do: *dire*.

Le blasme des femmes [art. 77]

9	*pris*. MS interlined. So WH, Ken, Do.
10	*yl*. So MS, WH, Do. Ken: *il*.
37	*demostrer*. So MS, WH, Do. Ken: *demonstrer*.
41	*fotere*. So MS, WH, Ken. Do: *sotere*.
44	*houel*. MS (*b* written instead of *v*), WH, Ken, Do: *hobel*.
75	*forcyn*. So MS, WH. Ken, Do: *fortyn*.
77	*perdy*. So MS (*er* abbreviated), WH, Ken. Do: *pardy*.

Nicholas Bozon, Femmes a la Pye [art. 78]

3	*maners*. So MS (*er* abbreviated), W³, Do. Ken: *maneres*.
19	*pie*. So MS, W³, Ken. Do: *pye*.
29	*honme*. So MS, W³. Ken: *homme*. Do: *houme*.
31	*pye*. So MS, W³, Do. Ken: *pie*.
42	*desyre*. So MS, Ken, Do. W³: *de syre*.
66	*nous*. So MS, Ken. W³: *nus*. Do: *vus*.
73	*purveit*. So MS (*ur* abbreviated), W³, Ken. Do: *priveit*.
76	*Bien*. So W³, Do. MS, Ken: *bie*.

Un sage honme de grant valour [art. 79]

4	*molt*. So MS (*o* abbreviated). Ken: *mult*.
5	*molt*. So MS (*o* abbreviated). Ken: *mult*.
8	*sy*. So MS. Ken: *si*.
36	*Olyver*. So MS. Ken: *oliver*.
43	*autre*. So MS. Ken: *ange*.
50	*purpensez*. So MS (*ur* abbreviated). Ken: *porpensez*.
54	*penez*. So MS. Ken: *pensez*.
60	*amours*. So Ken. MS: *amurs* (*ur* abbreviated).
80	*pernez*. So MS (*er* abbreviated). Ken: *prenez*.
85	*pernez*. So MS (*er* abbreviated). Ken: *prenez*.
89	*pernez*. So MS (*er* abbreviated). Ken: *prenez*.

92	*apernez*. So MS. Ken: *aprenez*.
112	*Apernez*. So MS (*er* abbreviated). Ken: *aprenez*.
119	*sivilement*. So MS. Ken: *si vilement*.
124	*Apernez*. So MS (*er* abbreviated). Ken: *aprenez*.
137	*molt*. So MS (*o* abbreviated). Ken: *mult*.
144	*font*. So MS. Ken: *sount*.
161	*bosoynus*. So MS. Ken: *besoynus*.
163	*avenaunt*. So MS. Ken: *avenant*.
166	*molt*. So MS (*o* abbreviated). Ken: *mult*.
192	*molt*. So MS (*o* abbreviated). Ken: *mult*.
195	*vyleynye*. So MS. Ken: *vylenye*.
226	*seiez*. So MS. Ken: *serez*.
241	*Queiqu'il*. So MS. Ken: *quei qu'il*.
246	*apernez*. So MS (*er* abbreviated). Ken: *aprenez*.
249	*mesfet*. So MS. Ken: *meffet*.
265	*Pus*. So MS (*us* abbreviated). Ken: *pur*.
279	*deit*. So MS. Ken: *doit*.
284	*Meurement*. So MS. Ken: *menrement*.
285	*seignours*. So MS (*our* abbreviated). Ken: *seigners*.
308	*bien*. MS, Ken: *bie*.
322	*avower*. MS, Ken: *avowe*.
328	*Pernez*. So MS (*er* abbreviated). Ken: *prenez*.

TALENT ME PRENT DE RYMER E DE GESTE FERE [art. 80]

4	*que*. So MS, W[1], Ri. As: *qe*.
13	*pernent*. So MS, W[1], As. Ri: *paruent*.
21	*deseynes*. So MS, As. W[1], Ri: *doseynes*.
	n'eit. So MS, W[1], As. Ri: *neit*.
29	*maveis*. So MS, W[1], Ri. As: *mavois*.
36	*Si il*. So W[1], As. MS: *Sil il*. Ri: *S'il*.
37	*aprendroy*. So W[1], Ri, As. MS: *apredroy*.
38	*l'eschyne*. So MS, W[1], As. Ri: *leschyne*.
40	*tondroy*. So MS, W[1], Ri. As: *toudroy*.
45	*Ycel*. So MS. W[1], As: *Ytel*. Ri: *Y tel*.
54	*n'y*. So MS, W[1], As. Ri: *ny*.
56	*dotouse*. So MS, W[1], Ri. As: *doteuse*.
57	*coronee*. So MS, Ri, As. W[1]: *corouce*.
64	*n'averez*. So MS, W[1], As. Ri: *naverez*.
69	*savoy*. So MS, W[1], As. Ri: *sanoy*.
72	*escolage*. So MS, W[1], As. Ri: *estolage*.
74	*C'est*. So MS, W[1], As. Ri: *Cest*.
79	*volenters*. So MS, W[1], As. Ri: *volentiers*.
	ledenger. So MS, W[1], As. Ri: *legender*.
81	*pust*. So MS, W[1], As. Ri: *prist*.
82	*su*. So MS, Ri. W[1], As: *fu*.
88	*merra*. So MS, W[1], As. Ri: *menra*.

89   *sevent*. So MS, W¹, As. Ri: *sovent*.
90   *faus*. So MS, W¹, As. Ri: *fous*.
91   *ou deus*. So MS, Ri, As. W¹: *en d'eus*.
92   *seient*. So MS, W¹, As. Ri: *serent*.
98   *eyre l'esperver*. So MS, W¹, As. Ri: *cyre lesperver*.
99   *parchemyn*. So MS (*ar* abbreviated), W¹, Ri. As: *perchemyn*.

MON IN THE MONE STOND ANT STRIT   [art. 81]

1   *strit*. So MS, W³, Bö, B13, Br, BS, Tu. Ri: *streit*.
7   *wytht*. So MS (*wyþt*), W³, Ri, B13, BS, Tu. Bö, Br: *wyht*.
            wen. So MS, W³, Ri, B13, BS, Tu. Bö, Br: *when*.
11   *hithte*. So MS (*hiþte*), W³, Ri, B13, Br, BS, Tu. Bö: *hihþe*.
            sytht. So MS (*syþt*), W³, Ri, B13, BS, Tu. Bö, Br: *syht*.
20   *crokede*. So MS, W³, Ri, B13, Br, BS, Tu. Bö: *crockede*.
32   *schule*. So MS, Ri, Bö, B13, Br, BS. W³, Tu: *shule*.
35   *Ich*. So MS, W³, Bö, B13, Br, BS, Tu. Ri: *ic*.
            heth. So MS (*heþ*), W³, Ri, BS, Tu. Bö, B13, Br: *heh*.
37   *hosede*. So MS, W³, Ri, B13, Br, BS, Tu. Bö: *osede*.
38   *amarscled*. So MS, W³, B13, BS, Tu. Ri, Bö, Br: *amarstled*.
39   *teh*. So MS, W³, Ri, B13, BS, Tu. Bö, Br: *teþ*.
40   *cherld*. So MS, W³, Ri, B13, BS, Tu. Bö, Br: *cherl*.

LE CHEVALER E LA CORBAYLLE   [art. 82]

2   *chevaler*. So MS, Ken, Rev. NB: *chevaller*.
23   *l'ageyte*. So MS, NB, Rev. Ken: *la geyte*.
25   *l'aust*. So MS, NB, Rev. Ken: *la vst*.
28   *tro*. So MS, Ken, NB. Rev: *trop*.
38   *remuer*. So MS, Ken, NB. Rev: *remut*.
42   *E il*. So MS, Ken, Rev. NB: *Cil*.
54   *a le*. So MS, NB, Rev. Ken: *al*.
61   *molt*. So MS (*o* abbreviated), NB, Rev. Ken: *moult*.
73   *clope*. So NB, Rev. MS, Ken: *clepe*.
77   *jamés*. So MS, Ken. NB, Rev: *ja mes*.
            ces. So MS, Ken, Rev. NB: *ses*.
86   *tro*. So MS, Ken, NB. Rev: *trop*.
95   *pieté*. So MS. Ken, NB, Rev: *piece*.
103   *Lumbardye*. So MS, Ken, Rev. NB: *Lumbardie*.
105   *pust*. So MS, NB, Rev. Ken: omitted.
109   *quidroi*. So NB, Rev. MS, Ken: *quidoi*.
129   *ad*. So MS, Ken. NB, Rev: *od*.
130   *assise a pentis*. So MS. Ken: *assis e apentis*. NB, Rev: *assise e apentis*.
135   *ces*. So MS, Ken, Rev. NB: *ses*.
144   *Pus*. So MS, Ken, NB. Rev: *puis*.
183   *endormie*. So MS, Ken, Rev. NB: *endormye*.
203   *vaillaunt*. So MS, Ken, Rev. NB: *vaillant*.

207	*trycherye.* So MS, NB, Rev. Ken: *trycherie.*
221	*ele.* So MS, Ken, Rev. NB: *cele.*
233	*autre.* So MS (*re* abbreviated), NB, Rev. Ken: *autro.*
238	*Qaunt.* So MS, NB. Ken, Rev: *Quant.*
248	*ad.* So MS, Ken. NB, Rev: *ont.*
249	*dames.* So MS, Ken. NB, Rev: *damos.*
254	*Unque.* So MS, NB, Rev. Ken: *vnqe.*
257	*issyr.* So MS, Ken, Rev. NB: *isser.*
260	*bosoigne.* So MS, Ken, NB. Rev: *besoigne.*

DE MAL MARIAGE [art. 83]

2	*d'enconbrement.* So MS, W², Ken. Do: *d'encombrement.*
5	*provee.* So W², Ken, Do. MS: *prorree* (*ro* abbreviated). See explanatory note.
8	*d'enconbraunce.* So MS, W², Do. Ken: *d'encombraunce.*
11	*prendre.* So W², Do. MS, Ken: *predre.*
19	*cele.* So MS, W², Ken. Do: *vele.*
22	*Quaunt.* So MS (*ua* abbreviated), Do. W², Ken: *Quant.*
64	*bon.* So MS, W², Ken. Do: *bone.*
76	*Un.* So MS, W², Ken. Do: *vu.*
84	*saulee.* So MS, Ken, Do. W²: *saulce.*
100	*que.* So MS, W², Ken. Do: *qe.*
111	*tierz.* So MS, W², Do. Ken: *tirez.*
124	*purchassaunt.* So MS, W², Do. Ken: *perchassaunt.*
130	*hounie.* So MS. W², Ken: *honnie.* Do: *houme.*
131	*l'orra.* So MS, W², Ken. Do: *lerra.*
133	*unqe.* So MS, W², Do. Ken: *unque.*
134	*unque.* So MS, W², Do. Ken: *unqe.*
139	*allas.* So MS, W², Do. Ken: *alas.*
140	*Yl.* So MS, Ken, Do. W²: *Il.*
144	*seigneur.* So MS, W², Ken. Do: *seignur.*
149	*prodhonme.* So MS (*ro* abbreviated), W². Ken: *prudhonme.* Do: *prudhoume.*
158	*pluz.* So MS (*plu3*), W². Ken, Do: *plus.*
162	*col.* So MS, W², Ken. Do: *doel.*
167	*trois.* So MS (*ro* abbreviated), Ken, Do. W²: *treis.*
170	*seigneurs.* So MS, W², Ken. Do: *seignurs.*
172	*merci.* So MS, W², Do. Ken: *merdi.*
173	*Fis.* So MS, W², Do. Ken: *fils.*
175	*gloire.* So MS, W², Ken. Do: *glorie.*

LA GAGURE, OU L'ESQUIER E LA CHAUNBRERE [art. 84]

14	*Qe.* So MS, Ken, NB. Rev: *Que.*
23	*ma dame.* So MS, Ken, NB. Rev: *Madame.*
32	*que.* So MS, Ken, NB. Rev: *qe.*
37	*oblié.* So MS, Ken, NB. Rev: *oublie.*
38	*repeyré.* So MS, Ken, Rev. NB: *reperye.*

43	*Pur*. So MS (*ur* abbreviated), Ken. NB, Rev: *Por*.
44	*S'il*. So MS, Ken. NB, Rev: *Si*.
74	*Si*. So MS, Ken, NB. Rev: *Ci*.
83	*la*. So MS, Ken, Rev. NB: *sa*.
88	*J'ay*. So MS, NB, Rev. Ken: *J'ai*.
89	*en riaunt*. So MS, Ken. NB: *en riant*. Rev: *enriant*.
96	*Ay*. So MS, Ken, Rev. NB: *Sy*.

A BOK OF SWEVENYNG [art. 85]

4	*gret*. So MS, Fö. WH: *grete*.
6	*gret*. So MS, Fö. WH: *grete*.
27	*bestes*. So MS, Fö. WH: *beste*.
58	*is*. So MS (interlined), WH. Fö: omitted.
72	The scribe has written the word *ydel* in the right margin.
116	*of*. So MS, Fö. WH: *to*.
128	*worth*. MS, WH, Fö: *wroth*.
183	*Drynke*. So Fö, WH. MS: *Dynke*.
253	*syth*. MS, WH, Fö: *syht*.

ORDRE DE BEL AYSE [art. 86]

15	*sonme*. So MS, W[1]. As: *soume*.
16	*prodhonme*. So MS (*ro* abbreviated), W[1]. As: *prodoume*.
29	*lerroi*. So MS, W[1]. As: *lerrei*.
59	*fount*. So MS, As. W[1]: *font*.
65	*collacioun*. So MS, W[1]. As: *collatioun*.
69	*chandeille*. So MS, W[1]. As: *chandelle*.
115	*chanoynes*. So MS, As. W[1]: *chanoygnes*.
122	*sueres*. So MS, As. W[1]: *freres*.
144	*execucioun*. So MS. W[1], As: *executioun*.
150	*nos*. So MS, As. W[1]: *no*.
155	*Charthous*. So MS, As. W[1]: *Chaichons*.
163	*De l'herber*. MS, W[1], As: *Del herber*.
167	*entreoblier*. So MS, As. W[1]: *entreoublier*.
169	*fuer*. So MS, As. W[1]: *suer*.
182	*a eese*. So MS. W[1]: *acese*. As: *a oese*.
188	*en*. So MS, As. W[1]: *ne*.
213	*aukes*. So MS, As. W[1]: *ankes*.
232	*mesfet*. So MS. W[1], As: *meffet*.
246	*bonz*. So MS, W[1]. As: *bons*.

LE CHEVALER QUI FIST LES CONS PARLER [art. 87]

14	*grant*. So MS (*ra* abbreviated), Ken, NB, SP. Rev: *graunt*.
36	*ly*. So MS, NB, SP. Ken, Rev: *le*.
37	*consail*. So MS, Ken, NB, SP. Rev: *consaile*.

79	*E il.* So MS, Ken, NB. SP, Rev: *Eles.*
80	*savereit.* So MS (*er* abbreviated), Ken, SP, Rev. NB: *saueit.*
97	*Donc.* So MS, Rev. Ken, NB, SP: *Dont.*
100	*cortois.* So MS, Ken, NB, SP. Rev: *corteis.*
102	*enmerviller.* So MS, Ken, NB, SP. Rev: *enmervuiller.*
115	*chevalchant.* So MS, NB, SP. Rev. Ken: *cheualachant.*
116	*va.* So MS, Ken, NB. SP, Rev: *le va.*
126	*a mesoun.* So MS, NB, Rev. Ken: *a mesoune.* SP: omitted.
129	*marcz.* So Ken, NB, SP, Rev. MS: *mrarcz* (*ar* abbreviated).
135	*mars.* So Ken, NB, SP, Rev. MS: *mrars* (*ar* abbreviated).
140	*grant.* So MS (*ra* abbreviated), Ken, NB, SP. Rev: *graunt.*
141	*demesure.* So MS, NB, SP, Rev. Ken: *demensure.*
142	*merveillouse.* So MS, Ken, NB, SP. Rev: *merveilleuse.*
148	*grant.* So MS (*ra* abbreviated), Ken, NB, SP. Rev: *graunt.*
151	*Yleque.* So MS, NB, SP, Rev. Ken: *yleqe.*
153	*chastiel.* So MS, NB, SP, Rev. Ken: *chastier.*
159	*serjauntz.* So MS, NB, SP, Rev. Ken: *seriaunts.*
168	*velsist.* So MS, NB. Ken, SP, Rev: *volsist.*
175	*come.* So MS, Ken, NB, Rev. SP: *quant.*
179	*mi.* So MS, Ken, SP, Rev. NB: *me.*
185	*Coillouns.* So MS, Ken, NB, SP. Rev: *Coillons.*
187	*abay.* So MS, Ken, NB, Rev. SP: *abaye.*
203	*grauntay.* So MS (*ra* abbreviated), Ken, NB, SP. Rev: *grantay.*
216	*ele.* So MS, Ken, NB, SP. Rev: *el.*
219	*saunz.* So MS, Ken, NB, SP. Rev: *sauntz.*
220	*grant.* So MS (*ra* abbreviated), Ken, NB, SP. Rev: *graunt.*
232	*chevaler.* So MS, Ken, NB, SP. Rev: *Chevalere.*
234	*mon.* So MS, Ken, NB, SP. Rev: *moun.*
	sy. So MS, Ken, NB, SP. Rev: *si.*
235	*Que.* So MS, Ken, NB, Rev. SP: *Qe.*
241	*suzryst.* So Ken, NB, SP, Rev. MS: *suȝryst.*
242	*chaunbre.* So MS, Ken, NB, SP. Rev: *chambre.*
255	*quaunt.* So MS, NB, SP. Ken, Rev: *quant.*
258	*Syre.* So MS, NB, SP, Rev. Ken: *Sire.*
260	*respoundra.* So MS, NB, SP, Rev. Ken: *respondra.*
270	*Fyrent.* So MS, NB, SP, Rev. Ken: *ferent.*
272	*respounce.* So Ken, NB, SP, Rev. MS: *rospounce.*
285	*quaunt.* So MS (*ua* abbreviated), NB, SP, Rev. Ken: *quant.*
289	*son.* So MS, NB, Rev. Ken: *soun.* SP: *a son.*
290	*Le.* So MS, Ken, NB, Rev. SP: *Mistrent le.*

OF RYBAUDS Y RYME ANT RED O MY ROLLE   [art. 88]

1	*my.* So MS, Bö, Tu. W[1], Ro: *mi.*
3	*by.* So MS, W[1], Bö, Tu. Ro: *bi.*
4	*tolyvre.* So MS, W[1], Ro. Bö: *to lyure.* Tu: *tolyuer.*
7	*weren.* So MS, W[1], Bö, Tu. Ro: *were.*

18	*momeleth.* So MS, W[1], Bö, Tu. Ro: *momeleþe.*
20	*hyre.* So MS, W[1], Ro. Bö, Tu: *hym.*
38	*fleis.* So MS, W[1], Ro, Tu. Bö: *fleish.*

MON THAT WOL OF WYSDAM HEREN   [art. 89]

2	*leren.* So Bö. MS, WH, Kem, Mo: *lernen.*
10	*Lene.* So MS, WH, Kem. Mo, Bö: *Leue.*
13	*biginning.* So MS, WH, Kem. Mo, Bö: *beginning.*
17	*non.* So MS, Kem, Mo, Bö. WH: *none.*
20	*where feh.* So MS, WH, Kem. Mo, Bö: *were foh.*
29	*ysotht.* So MS, WH, Kem. Mo, Bö: *ysoht.*
31	*thede.* So MS (*þede*), WH, Kem, Mo. Bö: *þedes.*
35	*lere.* So Bö. MS, WH, Kem, Mo: *lerne.*
39	*fule.* So MS, WH, Kem, Mo. Bö: *file.*
43	*lerest.* So Bö. MS, WH, Kem, Mo: *lernest.*
49	*lerneth.* So MS, WH, Mo, Kem. Bö: *lereth.*
52	*biste.* So MS, WH. Kem, Bö: *luste.* Mo: stanza omitted.
62	*unmytht.* So MS, Kem. WH: *un-might.* Bö: *unmyht.* Mo: stanza omitted.
66	*ne.* So MS, WH, Kem. Bö: *neuer.* Mo: stanza omitted.
74	*Thenne.* So MS, WH, Bo, Mo. Kem: *Þen.*
80	*fiht.* So Mo, Bö. MS, WH, Kem: *fist.*
83	*Thath.* So MS (*þaþ*), WH, Kem, Mo, Bö: *þah.*
85	*fytht.* So MS, WH, Kem, Mo, Bö: *fyht.*
119	*stoke.* So MS (*e* abbreviated), Mo. WH: *stokes.* Kem, Bö: *stok.*
122	*Oune.* So MS, Kem, Mo, Bö. WH: *onne.*
124	*clotht.* So MS, WH, Kem. Mo, Bö: *cloþ.*
125	*wrotht.* So MS, WH, Kem. Mo, Bö: *wroþ.*
126	*Thath.* So MS, WH, Kem, Mo, Bö: *þah.*
	ant. So MSS CUL Gg.I.1 and Digby 86. MS, WH, Kem, Mo, Bö: omitted.
127	*ploth.* So MS, WH, Kem, Mo, Bö: *ploh.*
134	*notht.* So MS, WH, Kem, Mo, Bö: *noht.*
151	*wot.* So MS, WH. Kem: *wat.* Bö: *whet.* Mo: stanza omitted.
	brohte. So MS, WH, Kem. Bö: *broȝte.* Mo: stanza omitted.
153	*Er syth his lyf.* MS, WH, Kem, Bö: *Er his lyf syth.* Mo: stanza omitted.
155–60	Written as prose in the MS.
158	*mytht.* So MS, WH, Kem. Mo, Bö: *myht.*
160	*nad.* So MS, WH, Kem, Mo. Bö: *naþ.*
163	*him.* So MS, Mo, Bö, Kem. WH: *hym.*
164	*unsatht.* So MS, WH, Kem. Mo: *un-saht.* Bö: *vn saht.*
183	*wone.* So MS, Kem, Mo, Bö. WH: *woue.*
184	*mone.* So Mo, Bö. MS, WH, Kem: *mowe.*
198	*Drath.* So MS, WH, Kem. Mo, Bö: *Drah.*
199	*theyn.* So MS, WH, Mo, Bö. Kem: *þayn.*
200	*ys.* So MS, Kem, Mo, Bö. WH: *is.*
207	*land.* So MS, Kem, Mo, Bö. WH: *lend.*
	cloth. So MS, WH, Mo, Bö. Kem: *claþ.*

208	*fol.* So MS, Kem, Bö. WH, Mo: *ful.*
221	*wythoute.* So MS, WH, Kem, Mo. Bö: *wiþ oute.*
223	*edueth.* So MS, Kem. WH, Mo: *edneth.* Bö: *eduiteþ.*
239	*bord.* So MS, Kem, Bö. WH: *boord.* Mo: stanza omitted.
254	*bette.* MS, WH, Kem: *bettre.* Bö: *betere.* Mo: stanza omitted.
255	*fere.* So WH, Kem, Bö. MS: *fore.* Mo: stanza omitted.
256	*yef.* So Kem, Bö. MS, WH: *ye.* Mo: stanza omitted.
	were. So WH, Kem, Bö. MS: *wore.* Mo: stanza omitted.
258	*Lyht.* So MS, WH, Kem. Bö: *Lyht.* Mo: stanza omitted.
264	*botht.* So MS, WH, Kem. Bö: *boht.* Mo: stanza omitted.
278	*Quoth Hendyng.* So WH, Kem, Mo, Bö. MS: line omitted.
302	*wythynne.* So MS, WH, Kem. Bö: *wiþ ynne.* Mo: stanza omitted.
306	*riche.* So MS, Kem, Bö. WH: *ryche.* Mo: stanza omitted.
308	*Thath.* So MS (*þaþ*), WH, Kem. Bö: *þah.* Mo: stanza omitted.
327	*rytht.* So MS, WH, Kem. Bö: *ryht.* Mo: stanza omitted.
328	*nytht.* So MS, WH, Kem. Bö: *nyht.* Mo: stanza omitted.
343	*hevene.* So MS, WH, Kem. Mo, Bö: *heuenne.*

WHEN MAN AS MAD A KYNG OF A CAPPED MAN [art. 90]

2	*d'Escoce.* So BZ. MS, Mu², Ro, Dea, Fl: *descoce.* Tu: *de scoce.*
	prendreit. So MS, Mu², BZ, Ro, Dea, Fl. Tu: *predreit.*
5	*Londyon.* So MS (*y* interlined), Mu², BZ, Ro, Dea, Fl. Tu: *Loudyon.*
9	*Forwyleye.* So MS, Mu², BZ, Tu. Ro: *Fforweleye.* Dea, Fl: *Forweleye.*
10	*don.* So MS, Mu², Ro, Tu, Dea, Fl. BZ: *dou.*
13	*markes.* So MS (*es* abbreviated), Mu², BZ, Ro, Dea, Fl. Tu: *marke.*
15	*forme.* So MS, Mu², Ro, Tu, Dea, Fl. BZ: *forwe.*
	shal. So MS, Ro, Tu, Dea, Fl. Mu², BZ: *sal.*
18	*levedis.* So MS. Mu², BZ, Ro, Tu, Dea, Fl: *louedis.*
19	*drouneth.* So MS, Ro, Tu, Dea, Fl. Mu², BZ: *drowneþ.*

LA DESTINCCIOUN DE LA ESTATURE JESU CRIST NOSTRE SEIGNEUR [art. 91]

13	*reulé.* MS: *resle.*

LUTEL WOT HIT ANY MON HOU LOVE HYM HAVETH YBOUNDE [art. 92]

13	*ydon, Y rede.* So MS, W³, B13, Br, Si, Mi. Bö: *y don, yrede.*
15–16	MS, W³, Bö, B13, Br, Si, Mi: *Ever ant oo nith ant day &c.*
20	*Whe.* So MS, W³, B13, Si. Bö, Br, Mi: *We.*
23–24	MS, W³, Bö, B13, Br, Si, Mi: *Ever ant oo &c.*
31–32	MS, W³, Bö, B13, Br, Si, Mi: *Ever ant oo &c.*
39–40	MS, W³, Bö, B13, Br, Si, Mi: *Ever ant oo &c.*

LUTEL WOT HIT ANY MON HOU DERNE LOVE MAY STONDE   [art. 93]

6	*wyth.* So MS, W³, B13, Br, St, Si, Mi. Bö: *myþ.*
8	*on.* So MS, W³, Bö, B13, Br, St, Mi. Si: *of.*
14	*Who.* So MS, W³, B13, Si. Bö, Br, St, Mi: *Wo.*
	ywynne. So MS, W³, Bö, B13, Br, St, Mi. Si: *ywyne.*
15–16	MS, W³, Bö, B13, Br, St, Si, Mi: *Ever ant oo &c.*
23–24	MS, W³, Bö, B13, Br, St, Si, Mi: *Ever ant oo &c.*
31–32	MS, W³, Bö, B13, Br, St, Si, Mi: *Ever ant oo &c.*
39–40	MS, W³, Bö, B13, Br, St, Si, Mi: *Ever ant oo &c.*

L'ENQUESTE QUE LE PATRIARCHE DE JERUSALEM FIST   [art. 95]

15	*Nota.* MS: *ta.* In the left margin the scribe inserts a mark of notation (abbreviation for *ta*), apparently planning to add *No* later in red ink. Compare art. 83, lines 83, 153 (fols. 117v–118r).
	Sarce. MS: *Sarco.*
40	*veniment.* MS: *venimez.*

SCRIPTUM QUOD PEREGRINI DEFERUNT   [art. 97]

49	*iniuncte.* MS: *inuncte.*

LEGENDA DE SANCTO ETFRIDO, PRESBITERO DE LEOMINISTRIA   [art. 98]

7	*sacerdos.* MS: *sacrier* (*ri* abbreviated).
33	*tenebat.* MS: *teneros.*
44	*violentium.* MS: *volentium* (*m* abbreviated).
65	*Viis.* MS: *Hiis.*
75	The roman numerals *lx* and *vi^c* are interlined.
83	*faleratur.* MS: *soleratur.*

BOOKLET 7

QUANT VOUS LEVEZ LE MATYN   [art. 100]

2	*Qaunt.* So MS. HB: *Quaunt.*
6	*pensez.* So HB. MS: *pensez pensez.*

QUY VELT QUE DIEU SOVYEGNE DE LY   [art. 101]

7	*expungna [expungnantes me].* MS: *expungna.* HB: *expugna.*
8	*vostre.* So MS (*ost* abbreviated). HB: *votre.*
13	*vostre.* So MS (*ost* abbreviated). HB: *votre.*
13–14	*Miserere mei Deus [miserere mei] quoniam in te confidit [anima mea].* MS, HB: *Miserere mei Deus quoniam in te confidit.*

17   *Exurgat.* So MS. HB: *Exsurgat.*
18   *tribulacioun.* So MS. HB: *tribulatioun.*
23–24   *refugium [tu factus es nobis].* MS, HB: *refugium.*

GLORIA IN EXCELSIS DEO EN FRAUNCEIS [art. 102]

4   *vostre.* So MS (*ost* abbreviated). HB: *votre.*
9   *Les preeyeres.* So MS (first *re* abbreviated). HB: *Le preyeres.*
         nostre. So MS (*ost* abbreviated). HB: *notre.*
12   *trehauncé.* So MS. HB: *trehauucé.*

CONFITEOR TIBI, DEUS, OMNIA PECCATA MEA [art. 103]

3   *mihi.* So MS (*ihi* abbreviated). HB: *in.*
5   *indulgencie.* So MS. HB: *indulgentie.*

GLORIOUSE DAME [art. 104]

2   *ov.* So MS. HB: *en.*
18   *tresdouce.* So MS. HB: *tredouce.*

REX SECULORUM ET DOMINE DOMINATOR [art. 105]

1   *mihi.* So MS (*ihi* abbreviated). HB: *michi.*
3   *mihi.* So MS (*ihi* abbreviated). HB: *michi.*
5   *misericordiam.* So MS (*isericord* abbreviated). HB: *manum.*
         mihi. So MS (*ihi* abbreviated). HB: *michi.*

UM DOIT PLUS VOLENTIERS JUNER LE VENDREDY [art. 106]

6   *Baptiste.* So MS (*iste* abbreviated). HB: *Baptistre.*
10   *A.* So MS. HB: omitted.

QUY EST EN TRISTOUR [art. 107]

9   *Baptiste.* So MS (*iste* abbreviated). HB: *Baptistre.*
10   *offrer.* So MS (*er* abbreviated). HB: *offrir.*

CELY QUE FRA CES MESSES CHAUNTER [art. 108]

2   *ov.* So MS. HB: *en.*
3   *premere.* So MS (*re* abbreviated). HB: *primere.*
         Annunciacion. So MS. HB: *Anunciation.*
5   *gloriari [oportet].* MS, HB: *gloriari.*

MUNDUS ISTE TOTUS QUODDAM SCACCARIUM EST   [art. 109]

7	*condicio*. So MS. Mu[1]: *conditio*.
10	*contingit*. So Mu[1]. MS: *contigit*.
20	*in linia*. MS: *cum linia* (*m* abbreviated). Mu[1]: *in linea*.
21	*obliquari*. So Mu[1]. MS *oliquari*.
26	*exigenciam*. So MS (*m* abbreviated). Mu[1]: *exigentia*.
	tertium. So MS. Mu[1]: *tercium*.
	obliquant. So MS (*n* abbreviated). Mu[1]: *obliquat*.
31	*latrant*. So MS (*ra* abbreviated). Mu[1]: *latrent*.
32	*tradant*. So MS (*ra* abbreviated). Mu[1]: *tradunt*.
43	*lyveret*. So MS. Mu[1]: *liqueret*.

QUY CHESCUN JOUR DENZ SEISSAUNTE JOURS   [art. 109a]

1	*foiz*. MS word interlined.

CONTRA INIMICOS SI QUOS HABES   [art. 110]

1	*lxiii*. MS: *lxiiij*.
5–6	*In te Domine speravi, i^m Deus venerunt*. MS: written in lower margin and inserted with a caret.
14	*Deus laudem [meam ne tacueris]*. MS: *Deus laudem*.
16	*martiris*. MS: *mris* (an abbreviation for either *martiris* or *matris*).
19	*Quam bonus Israel [Deus]*. MS: *Quam bonus Israel*.
21	*Ut quid Deus rep[p]ulisti*. MS: *Vt quid Deus repulisti*.
25	*Nonne Deo subiecta [erit anima mea]*. MS: *Nonne Deo subiecta*.
26	*dic*. MS: *dice* (*e* abbreviated).

SEINT HILLERE ARCHEVESQUE DE PEYTERS ORDINA CES SALMES   [art. 111]

1	*archevesque*. So MS. HB: *archeveque*.
6	*meam [ne tacueris]*. MS, HB: *meam*.
8	*Dites*. So MS. HB: *e dites*.
9	*premer*. So MS (*re* abbreviated). HB: *primer*.
10	*Iudica*. So HB. MS: *Iudicer* (*er* abbreviated).
14	*Deus*. So MS (*eu* abbreviated). HB: *Dominus*.
	conculcavit [me homo]. MS, HB: *conculcavit*.
16	*Deus*. So MS (*eu* abbreviated). HB: *Dominus*.
19	*Deus*$_1$. MS, HB: *Deus meus*.
	insurgentibus [in me libera me]. MS, HB: *insurgentibus*.
23	*repulisti [nos]*. MS, HB: *repulisti*.
29–31	Written in the bottom margin, with the place of insertion indicated by scribal mark.
30	*tribularer [clamavi]*. MS, HB: *tribularer*.
32	*conffesse*. So MS. HB: *confesse*.
34	*les*. So MS. HB: *le*.

35	*iniquo [eripe me]*. MS, HB: *iniquo*.
37	*adiutorium [meum intende]*. MS, HB: *adiutorium*.
43	*preeyere*. So MS (*re* abbreviated). HB: *preyere*.
44–45	The titles of Psalms 27 and 12 appear to be later additions by the scribe.
46	*ou tribulacion*. MS words interlined. HB: *ou tribulation*.
47	*Deus*. So MS (*eu* abbreviated). HB: *Dominus*.
47–48	The titles of Psalms 68 and 89 are added in the right margin, inserted with a caret.
48	*refugium [tu factus es nobis]*. MS, HB: *refugium*.
49	*refugium [tu factus es nobis]*. MS, HB: *refugium*.
52	*respice [me]*. MS, HB: *respice*.

EULOTROPIA ET CELIDONIA [art. 112]

10	*habuerit*. MS: *huerit* (*er* abbreviated).

DE INTERROGANDI MORIBUNDIS BEATI ANSELMI [art. 113]

26	*premissa*. MS: *permissa* (*er* abbreviated).

DIEU, ROY DE MAGESTÉ [art. 114]

19	*est*. So As. MS, W[1]: *eat*.
26	*scannum*. So MS (*m* abbreviated), As. W[1]: *scamnum*.
44	*Divicias*. So MS, As. W[1]: *divitias*.
87	*rien*. MS, W[1], As: *ren*.
93	*deit*. So MS. W[1], As: *doit*.
114	*Gratia*. So MS (abbreviated *gra*), W[1]. As: *gracia*.
145	*manger*. So W[1], As. MS: *mager*.
149	*vicii*. So MS, As. W[1]: *vitii*.

CONTEMPLACIOUN DE LA PASSIOUN JESU CRIST [art. 115]

4	*ciel*. So MS. HB: *tiel*.
6	*qe*. So MS. HB: *que*.
17	*temptacioun*. So MS. HB: *temptatioun*.
18	*porreit*. So MS. HB: *porroit*.
22	*pointe*. So MS (*e* abbreviated). HB: *point*.
34	*court*. So HB. MS: *comt*.
	jugié. So MS. HB: *jugé*.
	ciel. So MS. HB: *tiel*.
37	*ycel*. So MS. HB: *ytel*.
39	*subjeccioun*. So MS. HB: *subjectioun*.
42	*icel*. So MS. HB: *icil*.
50	*A icele*. So HB. MS: *A icele A icele* (words are repeated at the top of a new folio).
	houre. So MS. HB: omitted.

51	*Diable*. So MS. HB: *Deable*.
	nostre. So MS (*ost* abbreviated). HB: *notre*.
56	*sanglante*. So MS. HB: *sanglant*.
60	*mauntel*. So HB. MS: *maunterel* (*er* abbreviated).
	de. So HB. MS: *te*.
69	*quar*. So MS (*ua* abbreviated). HB: *qar*.
74	*nostre*. So MS (*ost* abbreviated). HB: *notre*.
86	*quar*. So MS. HB: *qar*.
89	*peynes*. So MS. HB: *poynes*.
	quar. So MS. HB: *qar*.
90	*vostre*. So MS (*ost* abbreviated). HB: *votre*.
94	*Adonqe*. So MS. HB: *Adonque*.
99	*Verroiement*. So MS. HB: *Verreiement*.
100	*Gews*. So MS. HB: *Guws*.

DE MARTIRIO SANCTI WISTANI   [art. 116]

4	*Repedone*. So MS (*ne* written on stub; see Ker, p. xvi).
15	*mortuus*. So MS (*s* written on stub; see Ker, p. xvi).
16	*sustinuisti*. MS: *sustinusti*.
20	*notificavit*. So MS (first *i* written on stub; see Ker, p. xvi).

APPENDIX: FULL CONTENTS OF MS HARLEY 2253

BOOKLET 1 (quires 1–2, Scribe A)

1.	fols. 1ra–21vb	French verse	The Lives of the Fathers
1a.	fols. 21vb–22ra	French verse	The Story of Thais

BOOKLET 2 (quires 3–4, Scribe A)

2.	fols. 23ra–33rb	French verse	Herman de Valenciennes, The Passion of Our Lord
3.	fols. 33va–39rb	French prose	The Gospel of Nicodemus
3a.	fol. 39rb	French prose	The Letter of Pilate to Tiberias
3b.	fols. 39va–41va	French prose	The Letter of Pilate to Emperor Claudius
4.	fols. 41va–43vb	French prose	The Life of Saint John the Evangelist
5.	fols. 43vb–45vb	French prose	The Life of Saint John the Baptist
6.	fols. 45vb–47vb	French prose	The Life of Saint Bartholomew
7.	fols. 47vb–48vb	French prose	The Passion of Saint Peter

BOOKLET 3 (quire 5, Scribes B and C)

8.	fols. 49r–50v	French verse	ABC of Women
9.	fols. 51ra–52va	French verse	Debate between Winter and Summer
10.	fol. 52va	English prose	How To Make Red Vermilion
11.	fol. 52va	English prose	How To Temper Azure
12.	fol. 52vb	English prose	How To Make Grass-Green
13.	fol. 52vb	English prose	How To Make Another Kind of Green
14.	fol. 52vb	English prose	Another for Yellow-Green
15.	fol. 52vb	English prose	How To Apply Silverfoil
16.	fol. 52vb	English prose	How To Make Iron as Hard as Steel
17.	fol. 52vb	English prose	How To Make White Lead

BOOKLET 4 (quire 6, Scribe B)

18.	fols. 53ra–54vb	Latin prose	The Life of Saint Ethelbert
19.	fol. 54vb	Latin verse	Soul of Christ, Sanctify Me
20.	fol. 55ra–b	French verse	A Goliard's Feast
21.	fols. 55va–56vb	English verse	Harrowing of Hell
22.	fols. 57r–58v	English verse	Debate between Body and Soul
23.	fols. 58v–59r	English verse	A Song of Lewes
24.	fol. 59r–v	French verse	Lament for Simon de Montfort

24a.	fol. 59v	French verse	Carnal Love Is Folly
24a*.	fol. 59v	Latin verse	What Allures Is Momentary
24b.	fol. 59v	English verse	Earth upon Earth
25.	fols. 59v–61v	English verse	The Execution of Sir Simon Fraser
25a.	fol. 61v	English verse	On the Follies of Fashion
26.	fols. 61v–62v	French verse	Lesson for True Lovers
27.	fol. 62v	English verse	The Three Foes of Man

BOOKLET 5 (quires 7–11, Scribe B)

28.	fol. 63r–v	English verse	Annot and John
29.	fol. 63v	English verse	Alysoun
30.	fol. 63v	English verse	The Lover's Complaint
31.	fol. 64r	English verse	Song of the Husbandman
32.	fols. 64va–65vb	English verse	The Life of Saint Marina
33.	fol. 66r	English verse	The Poet's Repentance
34.	fol. 66v	English verse	The Fair Maid of Ribblesdale
35.	fols. 66v–67r	English verse	The Meeting in the Wood
36.	fol. 67r	English verse	A Beauty White as Whale's Bone
37.	fols. 67va–68va	French verse	Gilote and Johane
38.	fols. 68va–70rb	French prose	Pilgrimages in the Holy Land
39.	fol. 70rb–v	French prose	The Pardons of Acre
40.	fols. 70va/71ra/71va	English verse	Satire on the Consistory Courts
41.	fols. 70vb/71rb	English verse	The Laborers in the Vineyard
43.	fol. 71va	English verse	Spring
44.	fols. 71vb–72ra	English verse	Advice to Women
45.	fol. 72ra–va	English verse	An Old Man's Prayer
46.	fols. 72va–73rb	English verse	Blow, Northern Wind
47.	fol. 73r–v	English verse	The Death of Edward I
48.	fols. 73v–74v	English verse	The Flemish Insurrection
49.	fol. 75ra–b	French verse	The Joys of Our Lady
50.	fols. 75rb–va	English verse	Sweet Jesus, King of Bliss
51.	fol. 75va–b	English verse	Jesus Christ, Heaven's King
52.	fol. 75vb	English verse	A Winter Song
53.	fol. 76r	English verse	A Spring Song on the Passion
54.	fol. 76r	French verse	I Pray to God and Saint Thomas
55.	fol. 76r	Trilingual verse	While You Play in Flowers
56.	fols. 76v–77r	French verse	Song on Jesus' Precious Blood
57.	fol. 77va	French verse	Mary, Mother of the Savior
58.	fols. 77vb–78va	English verse	Jesus, Sweet Is the Love of You
59.	fols. 78vb–79rb	French verse	Sermon on God's Sacrifice and Judgment
60.	fol. 79rb–vb	English verse	Stand Well, Mother, under Rood
61.	fol. 79vb	English verse	Jesus, by Your Great Might
62.	fol. 80ra	English verse	I Sigh When I Sing
63.	fol. 80rb	English verse	An Autumn Song
64.	fol. 80v	English verse	The Clerk and the Girl
65.	fols. 80v–81r	English verse	When the Nightingale Sings
66.	fol. 81r–v	English verse	Blessed Are You, Lady
67.	fol. 81va–b	English verse	The Five Joys of the Virgin
68.	fols. 82ra–83r	English verse	Maximian
69.	fol. 83r	French & English verse	Maiden, Mother Mild

70.	fols. 83r–92v	English verse	King Horn
71.	fols. 92v–105r	French prose	Ludlow Scribe, Old Testament Stories
72.	fol. 105va–b	Latin prose	Names of the Books of the Bible

BOOKLET 6 (quires 12–14, Scribe B)

73.	fol. 106r	English verse	God Who Wields All This Might
74.	fols. 106ra–107rb	English verse	The Sayings of Saint Bernard
75.	fols. 107va–109vb	French verse	The Jongleur of Ely and the King of England
75a.	fol. 110ra–va	French verse	The Three Ladies Who Found a Prick
76.	fols. 110vb–111rb	French verse	The Song on Women
77.	fol. 111rb–vb	French verse	The Blame of Women
78.	fol. 112ra–b	French verse	Nicholas Bozon, Women and Magpies
79.	fols. 112rc–113vc	French verse	Urbain the Courteous
80.	fols. 113vb–114v	French verse	Trailbaston
81.	fols. 114v–115r	English verse	The Man in the Moon
82.	fols. 115va–117ra	French verse	The Knight and the Basket
83.	fols. 117ra–118rb	French verse	Against Marriage
84.	fol. 118rb–vb	French verse	The Wager, or The Squire and the Chambermaid
85.	fols. 119ra–121ra	English verse	A Book of Dreaming
86.	fols. 121ra–122va	French verse	The Order of Fair Ease
87.	fols. 122vb–124va	French verse	The Knight Who Made Vaginas Talk
88.	fols. 124va–125r	English verse	Satire on the Retinues of the Great
89.	fols. 125ra–127ra	English verse	Hending
90.	fol. 127rb–va	English prose	The Prophecy of Thomas of Erceldoune
91.	fol. 127va–b	French prose	Distinguishing Features of the Bodily Form of Jesus Christ Our Lord
92.	fol. 128r	English verse	The Way of Christ's Love
93.	fol. 128r–v	English verse	The Way of Woman's Love
94.	fols. 128v–129v	French prose	The Teachings of Saint Louis to His Son Philip
95.	fols. 129v–130v	French prose	The Land of the Saracens
96.	fol. 131r	French prose	Heraldic Arms of Kings
97.	fols. 131v–132r	Latin prose	Letter for Pilgrims on the Relics at Oviedo
98.	fols. 132r–133r	Latin prose	The Legend of Saint Etfrid, Priest of Leominster
99.	fol. 133v	French & Latin prose	Prayer for Protection

BOOKLET 7 (quire 15, Scribe B)

100.	fol. 134r	French prose	Occasions for Angels
101.	fol. 134r	French prose	Occasions for Psalms in French
102.	fol. 134v	French verse	Glory to God in the Highest in French
103.	fol. 134v	Latin prose	Prayer of Confession
104.	fol. 134v–135r	French verse & prose	Prayer on the Five Joys of Our Lady
105.	fol. 135r	Latin prose	Prayer for Contrition
106.	fol. 135r	French prose	Reasons for Fasting on Friday
107.	fol. 135r	French prose	Seven Masses To Be Said in Misfortune

☙ VOLUME 3: INDEX OF FIRST LINES

This index lists first lines, titles, and incipits. Titles that differ from the first line or incipit are in italics.

❦ VOLUME 3: INDEX OF MANUSCRIPTS CITED

This index lists proper names found in the articles of MS Harley 2253. Each entry is listed by variant spellings (if any), article numbers, and line. Translated forms are indicated by italic font. Excluded from this list are terms for God ("Creatour," "Crist," "Dieu," "Jesu," "Salveour," etc.), terms for Mary ("Marie," "Nostre Dame," etc.), and titles ("Child," "cuens," "Bisshop," "E(o)rl," "Kyng," "Seint(e)," etc.).

Aaram (Haran): art. 71.17

Aaron (Aaron): art. 71 passim

Abab (*Hobab*): art. 71.641, 644, 647

Abacuc (*Habakkuk*): art. 72.34

Abban (*Abban*): art. 95.47

Abdyas (*Obadiah*): art. 72.30

Abel (*Abel*): art. 95.14

Abidon (*Abidan*): art. 71.614

Abiram. See Abyron

Abraham. See Habraham

Absolon (*Absolon*): art. 79.38

Abyel (*Abiel*): art. 100.9

Abyron (*Abiram*): art. 71.738, 745, 747, 751, 756, 757, 762, 777

Acres (*Acre*): art. 95.30, 42, 52, 53

Actus Apostolorum (*Acts of the Apostles*): art. 72.55

Adam (*Adam*): art. 71.2

Affrica (*Africa*): art. 97.7

Aggeus (*Haggai*): art. 72.36

Ahiezel (*Ahiezer*): art. 71.616

Ahyrac (*Ahira*): art. 71.620

Alban (*Nebo*): art. 106.3

Alemaigne (*Germany*): art. 96.6

Aleppo. See Halape

Alexandre (*Alexander*): art. 109.41

Alisaundre, Alysaundre (*Alexandria*): art. 95.7, 90, 91

Amalech (*Amalek*): art. 71.643, 695, 722

Ammiel. See Amyel

Amminadab. See Amynada

Amon (*Ammon*): art. 71.884

Amorey, Amorei, Amoreye, Amorienz, Amoreum (*Amorite, Amorites*): art. 71 passim

Amorite. See Amorey

Amos (*Amos*): art. 72.29

Amyel (*Ammiel*): art. 71.688

Amynada (*Amminadab*): art. 71.606

Anak. See Enach

Ananye (*Ananias*): art. 97.29

Anathema (*Anathema*): art. 71.847

Andre (*Andrew*): art. 97.43

Annunciation: art. 108.3

Anselm (*Anselm*): art. 113.1

Antecrist (*Antichrist*): art. 106.14

Antichrist. See Antecrist

Antioche (*Antioch*): art. 95.35, 48, 52

Apocalipsis (*Apocalypse*): art. 72.60

apostles, apostoille, apostolus (*Apostles*): art. 94.65; art. 95.2; art. 97.6; art. 107.11. *See also* Actus Apostolorum

apostoille de Rome (*Apostle of Rome*): art. 95.19. *See also* Piere

Arabye, Arabie (*Arabia*): art. 95.27, 65

Arad (*Arad*): art. 71.845

Aragoun (*Aragon*): art. 96.17

Domesday (*Doomsday*): art. 73.38

Dominicans. See prechours

Donbar. *See* countesse de Donbar

Doomsday. See Domesday

Dotaym (*Dothan*): art. 71.32

Dunbar. See countesse de Donbar

Durham. See Laurence

Dyna (*Dinah*): art. 71.12

Ealfleda (*Elfleda*): art. 116.5

Easter. See Pasche

Eawe de Contrediccion (*Waters of Contradiction*): art. 71. 840

Ecclesiam Sancti Salvatoris [Oviedo] (*Church of the Holy Savior*): art. 97.1, 8–9, 41, 49

Ecclesiastes (*Ecclesiastes*): art. 72.17

Ecclesiasticus (*Ecclesiasticus*): art. 72.20

Edom (*Edom*): art. 71.832, 834, 836, 848

Effraym, Effrem, Effrahym (*Ephraim*): art. 71.115, 238, 241, 244, 611

Egal (*Igal*): art. 71.687

Egipciene, Egipcienz, Egipcien(e)s (*Egyptian, Egyptians*): art. 71 passim

Egipciene Complegnement (*Mourning of Egypt*): art. 71.253

Egipte (*Egypt*): art. 71 passim; art. 95 passim

eglise (*Church*): art. 71.731. *See also* seinte Eglise

Egypt. See Egipte

Egyptian. See Egipciene

Eleazar. See Eleazar; Eliezel

Eleazar (*Eleazar*): art. 71.772, 813, 837, 838, 974

elevatione, elevacion (*Levation*): art. 110.27; art. 111.52

Eleyne (*Helen*): art. 76.96, 100

Elfleda. See Ealfleda

Eliab. See Elyab

Eliasaph. See Elysab

Eliezel, Eleazar (*Eliezer*): art. 71.334, 642

Elijah. See Elye

Elim. See Elym

Elishama. See Elysama

Elizur. See Elyzur

Elon (*Helon*): art. 71.609

Ely (*Ely*): art. 75.28, 29

Elyab (*Eliab*): art. 71. 609

Elye, Elyas, Helyas (*Elijah*): art. 87.50, 52; art. 97.26; art. 106.5, 14

Elym (*Elim*): art. 71.448, 450

Elysab (*Eliasaph*): art. 71.604

Elysama (*Elishama*): art. 71.612

Elyzur (*Elizur*): art. 71.599

Enach (*Anak*): art. 71.695

England. See Engleterre

Engleter(r)e (*England*): art. 96.7; art. 114.21

Englysshe (*English*): art. 90.15

Enoc (*Enoch*): art. 106.14

Enymy (*Enemy*): art. 104.3. *See also* Deable; Devel; Feond; Feond; Gost; Lucifer

Ephesios (*Ephesians*): art. 72.47

Ephraim. See Effrahym

Epistola Jacobi (*Epistle of James*): art. 72.56

Epistola Johannis (*Epistle of John*): art. 72.58

Epistola Jude (*Epistle of Jude*): art. 72.59

Epistola Petri (*Epistle of Peter*): art. 72.57

Erceldoune. See Thomas de Essedoune

Ermenye (*Armenia*): art. 96.11

Erminak (*Armagnac*): art. 96.14

Esau (*Esau*): art. 71.4

Escoce (*Scotland*): art. 80.26; art. 90.2; art. 96.15

Escripture. See seinte Escripture

Esdras (*Ezra*): art. 72.11

Espaigne, Espaygne (*Spain*): art. 82.103; art. 96.3

Espernement (*Burning*): art. 71.654

Essebon (*Heshbon*): art. 71.871

Essedoune. See Thomas de Essedoune

Ester (*Esther*): art. 72.14

grey frere (gray friar, i.e., Franciscan): art. 81.19. *See also* frere menours
Griffony. *See* Gryfonye
gris moignes (*Gray Monks*): art. 86.133
grye. *See* grece
Gryfonye (*Griffony*): art. 96.30
Gryu (*Greek [language]*): art. 115.70. *See also* grece
Guerin. *See* Gwaryn
Guhel (*Geuel*): art. 71.688
Gwaryn (*Guerin*): art. 87.4
Gyle (*Giles*): art. 107.1
Gyus, Gyw, Giw, Jedeux, Iudei (*Jews*): art. 71.727; art. 73.29; art. 95.45; art. 97.16; art. 115 passim

Habakkuk. *See* Abacuc
Habraham, Habrahe (*Abraham*): art. 71.2, 254; art. 99.25; art. 109.12
Haggai. *See* Aggeus
Haifa. *See* mont Cayphas
Halape (*Aleppo*): art. 94.5
Hasteney (*Estonia*): art. 96.31
Hazeroth. *See* Asserot
Hebreu, Hebrewe (*Hebrew*): art. 71 passim; art. 115.70, 84
Hebreus, Hebrus, Hebreos (*Hebrews*): art. 71 passim; art. 72.54, 62; art. 95.64
Helen. *See* Eleyne
Heliopolis. *See* Helyopoleos
Helon. *See* Elon
Helyas. *See* Elye
Helyopoleos (*Heliopolis*): art. 71.107
Hendyng (*Hending*): art. 89 passim
Herodes (*Herod*): art. 106.7; art. 115.41
Heshbon. *See* Essebon
Hillere (*Hilary*): art. 111.1
Hippomedes. *See* Ypomedes
Hittite. *See* Ethey
Hivite. *See* Evey
Hobab. *See* Abab
Holy Church. *See* seinte eglise
Holy Land. *See* terre seinte

Holy Scripture. *See* seinte Escripture
Holy Wryt (*Holy Writ*): art. 74.5
Hor (*Hor*): art. 71.836
Horeb. *See* Oreb
Horma (*Hormah*): art. 71.846
Hosea. *See* Ozeas
Hospitlers (*Hospitallers*): art. 86.71
Hubert (*Hubert*): art. 81.37
Huet (*Huet*): art. 87.22, 73, 289, 291
Hungrie (*Hungary*): art. 96.20
Hur. *See* Ur

Iacob. *See* Jacob
Idumea. *See* Ydumee
Iebarym (*Iye-abarim*): art. 71.859
Ierosolimatana. See Jerusalem
Igal. *See* Egal
Ildephonus. *See* Yldefontus
India. *See* Ynde
Innocens (*Innocents*): art. 97.28; art. 115.7
Iohannis baptiste. *See* Johan le baptiste
Iosep. *See* Josep
Isaac. *See* Ysaac
Isaiah. *See* Ysayas
Iscariot. *See* Judas
Isle of Man. *See* Man
Israel (*Israel*): art. 71 passim; art. 97.22, 33; art. 106.2
Issachar. *See* Yzacar
Iudei. *See* Gyus
Iudeorum (*of the Jews*): art. 115.71
Iulianus (*Julian*): art. 97.40
Iunius. *See* joyn
Iye-abarim. *See* Iebarym

Jabbok. *See* Jeboc
Jacob, Iacop (*Jacob*): art. 71 passim; art. 99.26. *See also* Epistola Jacobi
Jaffa. *See* Japhet
Jahaz. *See* Jasa
James. *See* Epistola Jacobi
Japhet (*Jaffa*): art. 95.55
Jasa (*Jahaz*): art. 71.869
Jaspar (*Jaspar*): art. 108a.1
Jazer (*Jazer*): art. 71.874

lundy (*Monday*): art. 107.5
Lya (*Leah*): art. 71.11
Lyban. See mount Lyban
Lyons-sur-Rhone. See Leons-sur-Rone

Maccabees. See Machabeus
Machabeus (*Maccabees*): art. 72.39
Machy (*Machi*): art. 71.688
Madianyte, Madyanytes (Midianite, Midianites): art. 71.972, 980, 981
Madyan, Madian (*Midian*): art. 71.322, 643, 645, 881
Magdalen. See Maria Magdalena
Magdalom (*Migdol*): art. 71.426
Mahomet (*Mahomet*): art. 95.18, 26
Mailogris (*Mallorca*): art. 96.26
Makemet (*Makemet*): art. 95.16
Malachias (*Malachi*): art. 72.38
Mallorca. See Mailogris
Man (*[Isle of] Man*): art. 96.28
Man (*Man*): art. 116.12
Manassen, Manasses, Manasse (*Manasseh*): art. 71.115, 238, 241, 243, 611
Marache (*Marah*): art. 71.445
March. See mars
Marcolf. See Marcolve
Marcolve (*Marcolf*): art. 89.3
Marcus (*Mark*): art. 72.40
mardy (*Tuesday*): art. 107.7
Mare Rubrum. *See* Rouge Mer
Maria Magdalena (*Mary Magdalen*): art. 97.30
Marie (*Mary [sister of Moses]*): art. 71 passim
Mark. See Marcus
mars (*March*): art. 95–70
Martyn (*Judge Martin*): art. 80.33
Martyn (*Martin [of Tours]*): art. 84.67; art. 94.60
Mary Magdalen. See Maria Magdalena
Mass. *See* messe
Mathana (*Mattanah*): art. 71.865
Matheus, Matheu (*Matthew*): art. 72.41; art. 95.93
Mattanah. See Mathana
Matthew. See Matheus

Maurice. See Moris
Mediterranean. See Mier Gregeis
Melalyn (*Melalin*): art. 95.7
Melamadaim (*Melamadaim*): art. 95.12
Melchifas (*Melchifas*): art. 95.10
Melchifitan (*Melchifitan*): art. 95.14
Melchior (*Melchior*): art. 108a.1
menours. See frere menours
Merciorum, Mercio (*Mercians*): art. 98.2, 5, 76, 85; art. 116.3, 5, 13
Merwaldus (*Merewald*): art. 98.2, 76
mesgredy (*Wednesday*): art. 107.9
messe (*mass, Mass*): art. 76.54; art. 94.19; art. 107 passim; art. 111.33
Micah. See Mycheas
Michael (*Michael*): art. 71.688
Michel (*Michael*): art. 75.364; art. 100.1. *See also* Mount-Seint-Michel
Michel (*Michael*): art. 107.5
Midian. See Madyan
Mier Gregeis (*Greek Sea [Mediterranean]*): art. 95.28
Migdol. See Magdalom
Misael. See Mysaelis
Moab (*Moab*): art. 71 passim
Moabites, Moabytes (*Moabites*): art. 71.862, 930
Monastery of the Lion. See Leonis monasterium
Monday. See lundy
mont Cayphas (*Mount Haifa*): art. 95.54
mont Sibboe (*Mount Gelboe*): art. 95.49
mont Tabor (*Mount Tabor*): art. 95.54
montis Oliveti (*Mount Olive*): art. 97.22
montis Synay, mount Synay (*Mount Sinai*): art. 71.538; art. 97.32
Mont-Saint-Michel. See Mount-Seint-Michel
Moris (*Maurice*): art. 104.1
Moses. See Moyses
mount de Calvarye (*Mount Calvary*): art. 115.60

Salu (*Salu*): art. 71.980

samadi, samady (*Saturday*): art. 86.88, 90; art. 107.14

Sampson (**Samson**): art. 77.75; art. 95.60

Samson. *See* Sampson

Samuad (*Shammua*): art. 71.687

Saphadin. *See* Saphadyn

Saphadyn (*Saphadin*): art. 95.3, 6

Saphat (*Shaphat*): art. 71.687

Sapiencia (*Wisdom*): art. 72.14

Saracens. *See* sarazyns

Saraphas (*Saraphas*): art. 95.20

sarazyn, sarazyns (*Saracen, Saracens*): art. 95.16, 18, 85, 89

Sarce, Surie (*Syria*): art. 95.14, 29, 48

Sardayné (*Sardenay*): art. 95.33

Sardenay. *See* Sardayné

Sarepta. *See* Sarepte

Sarepte (*Sarepte*): art. 95.42

Saturday. *See* samadi

Saul (*Saul*): art. 95.50

Scot (*Scotsman*): art, 90.15

Scotland. *See* Escoce

Scotsman. *See* Scot

Scotsmen. *See* Scottes

Scottes (*Scotsmen*): art. 90.19

Scripture. *See* seinte Escripture

Sea of Cyprus. *See* Meir de Cypre

Sedeur (*Shedeur*): art. 71.599

seinte Eglise (*Holy Church*): art. 79.63; art. 94.15, 43, 48–49, 50, 54, 58. *See also* eglise

seinte Escripture (*Holy Scripture*): art. 83.47

Sempringham. *See* Sympringham

Seon (*Sihon*): art. 71.867, 871, 872, 877

Sephor (*Zippor*): art. 71.881, 897

Sephora(n) (*Zipporah*): art. 71.333, 370, 371, 373

septembre (*September*): art. 95.69

Sepulchre Nostre Seignor Jesu Crist (*Sepulcher of Our Lord Jesus Christ*): art. 95.21

Sepulcres de Covetyse (*Graves of Covetousness*): art. 71.655

Seranus (*Seranus*): art. 97.39

Seth (*Seth*): art. 71.2

Sethur. *See* Stur

Seville. *See* Yspali

Shammua. *See* Samuad

Shaphat. *See* Saphat

Shedeur. *See* Sedeur

Shelumeiel. *See* Salamyel

Shiphrah. *See* Suphia

Shittim. *See* Sythem

Sibboe. *See* mont Sibboe

Sicily. *See* Cicile

Sidon. *See* Sydoygne

Sihon. *See* Seon

Simeon. *See* Symeon

Simon. *See* Symoun

Sin. *See* Syn

Sinai. *See* Synay

Sodi. *See* Zoty

Solomon. *See* Salamoun

Sophonias (*Zephaniah*): art. 72.35

Soudan (*Sultan*): art. 95.89, 92

Spain. *See* Espaigne

Spigurnel (*Spigurnel*): art. 80.35

Stephanus, Estevene (*Stephen*): art. 97.26; art. 106.13

Stur (*Sethur*): art. 71.688

Suhar (*Zuar*): art. 71.608

Sultan. *See* Soudan

Sunday. *See* digmange

Suphia (*Shiphrah*): art. 71.272

Sur (*Zur*): art. 71.981

Surie. *See* Sarce

Surs (*Tyre*): art. 95.42, 44

Susanna (*Susanna*): art. 99.34

Sydoygne (*Sidon*): art. 95.43

Symeon (*Simeon*): art. 71.11, 139, 142, 601

Symoun (*Simon*): art. 75.271

Sympringham (*Sempringham*): art. 86.34, 36, 40

Syn (*Sin*): art. 71.450, 464, 820

synagoge (*Synagoge*): art. 71.731

Synay (*Sinai*): art. 71 passim; art. 95.62, 75. *See also* montis Synay

Syria. *See* Sarce

Sythem (*Shittim*): art. 71.966

Tabor. *See* mont Tabor

Tars. *See* Tharse

Tartarus (*Tartarus, hell*): art. 98.50; art. 103.11; art. 109.44

Temese (*Thames*): art. 85.103

Tennis. *See* Attanise

Terre de Promissio(u)n (*Promised Land*): art. 71.840; art. 95.9; art. 106.2

Terre Seinte (*Holy Land*): art. 95.3

Thames. *See* Temese

Tharse (*Tars*): art. 96.18

Thesalonicenses (*Thessalonians*): art. 72.50

Thimotheum (*Timothy*): art. 72.51

Thobias (*Tobit*): art. 72.12

Tholeto (*Toledo*): art. 97.8, 26, 40

Thomas (*Thomas [of ?Canterbury, ?Cantilupe]*): art. 84.93

Thomas de Essedoune (*Thomas of Erceldoune*): art. 90.1

Thursday. *See* jeovedy

Timothy. *See* Thimotheum

Titum (*Titus*): art. 72.52

Tobias. *See* Tobye

Tobit. *See* Thobias

Tobye (*Tobias*): art. 100.13

Toledo. *See* Tholeto

Trayl(l)ebastoun, Traillebastoun (*Trailbaston*): art. 80.5, 37, 50

Trene (*Lamentations*): art. 72.23

Triple (*Tripoli*): art. 95.43

Tuesday. *See* mardy

Tunes (*Tunis*): art. 94.2

Tyre. *See* Sur

Uolyab (*Oholiab*): art. 71.491

Ur (*Hur*): art. 71.511, 512

Urban (*Urbain*): art. 79.3

Ury (*Uri*): art. 71.491

Uryel (*Uriel*): art. 100.13

vendredi, vendredy (*Friday*): art, 86.87; art. 106 passim; art. 107.13. *See also* bon vendredy

Vincencius (*Vincent*): art. 97.39

Virgo (*Virgo*): art. 112.3

Waters of Contradiction. *See* Eawe de Contrediccion

Wednesday. *See* mesgredy

Wibaldus (*Wibald*): art. 116.12

Wiglafus (*Wiglaf*): art. 116.2, 28

Wigmundus (*Wigmund*): art. 116.3, 4, 15

Wille (*Will*): art. 90.7

Wisdom. *See* Sapiencia

Wistanus (*Wistan*): art. 116 passim

Wit. *See* Wyt

World (*World*): art. 74.92

Wrong (*Wrong*): art. 90.17

Wyt (*Wit*): art. 90.7

Ydumee (*Idumea*): art. 95.51

Yibna. *See* Gibelete

Yldefontus (*Ildephonus*): art. 97.25

Ynde (*India*): art. 95.8

Ypomedes (*Hippomedes*): art. 79.39

Ysaac (*Isaac*): art. 71.2, 254; art. 99.26

Ysacar. *See* Yzacar

Ysayas (*Isaiah*): art. 72.21

Yspali (*Seville*): art. 97.8

Yzacar, Ysacar (*Issachar*): art. 71.11, 607

Zabulon, Zabulun (*Zabulon*): art. 71.11, 609

Zacharias (*Zechariah*): art. 72.37

Zambry (*Zimri*): art. 980

Zareht (*Zered*): art. 71.860

Zechariah. *See* Zacharias

Zelpha (*Zilpah*): art. 71.14

Zephaniah. *See* Sophonias

Zephone. *See* Jephunneh

Zered. *See* Zareht

Zilpah. *See* Zelpha

Zimri. *See* Zambry

Zippor. *See* Sephor

Zipporah. *See* Sephoran

Zoty (*Sodi*): art. 71.687

Zuar. *See* Suhar

Zur. *See* Sur

BIBLIOGRAPHY

Adams, Jenny. *Power Play: The Literature and Politics of Chess in the Late Middle Ages*. Philadelphia, PA: University of Pennsylvania Press, 2006.

Allen, Rosamund, ed. *King Horn: An Edition Based on Cambridge University Library MS Gg. 4.27 (2)*. New York: Garland, 1984.

Andrew, Malcolm, and Ronald Waldron, eds. *The Poems of the Pearl Manuscript: Pearl, Cleanness, Patience and Gawain and the Green Knight*. Fifth edition. Exeter: University of Exeter Press, 2007.

Anglo-Norman Dictionary (AND). Online at http://www.anglo-norman.net.

Anselm of Canterbury. *"Admonitio morienti et de peccatus suis nimium formidanti."* In *Patrilogia cursos completus . . . series latina*. Ed. J.-P. Migne. Paris, 1844–64. 158.685–88.

Archibald, Elizabeth. "Macaronic Poetry." In *Companion to Medieval Poetry*. Ed. Corinne Saunders. Oxford: Blackwell Publishing, 2010. Pp. 277–88.

Ashley, Kathleen, trans. "The French *Enseignemenz a Phelippe* and *Enseignement a Ysabel* of Saint Louis." In *Medieval Conduct Literature: An Anthology of Vernacular Guides to Behaviour for Youth, with English Translations*. Ed. Mark D. Johnston. Toronto: University of Toronto Press, 2009. Pp. 3–16.

Aspin, Isabel S. T., ed. *Anglo-Norman Political Songs*. Anglo-Norman Texts 11. Oxford: Basil Blackwell, 1953.

Baker, Benedict, trans. *Vitae Patrum: Lives of the Desert Fathers*. 2004. Online at http://www.vitae-patrum.org/uk.

Barton, Simon, and Richard Fletcher, trans. *The World of El Cid: Chronicles of the Spanish Reconquest*. Manchester: Manchester University Press, 2000.

Bede. *A History of the English Church and People*. Trans. Leo Sherley-Price. Second edition. Rev. R. E. Latham. Harmondsworth: Penguin, 1968.

Beer, Jeanette, trans. *Master Richard's Bestiary of Love and Response*. Berkeley: University of California Press, 1986.

Bell, Kimberly K. "'holi mannes liues': England and Its Saints in Oxford, Bodleian Library, MS Laud Misc. 108's *King Horn* and *South English Legendary*." In *The Texts and Contexts of Oxford, Bodleian Library, MS Laud Misc. 108: The Shaping of English Vernacular Narrative*. Ed. Kimberly K. Bell and Julie Nelson Couch. Leiden: Brill, 2011. Pp. 251–74.

Bell, Kimberly K., and Julie Nelson Couch, eds. *The Texts and Contexts of Oxford, Bodleian Library, MS Laud Misc. 108: The Shaping of English Vernacular Narrative*. Leiden: Brill, 2011.

Bennett, J. A. W., and G. V. Smithers. *Middle English Verse and Prose*. Oxford: Clarendon, 1966.

Bennett, Janice. *Sacred Blood, Sacred Image. The Sudarium of Oviedo: New Evidence for the Authenticity of the Shroud of Turin*. Littleton, CO: Libri de Hispania, 2001.

Best, Michael R., and Frank H. Brightman, eds. *The Book of Secrets of Albertus Magnus of the Virtues of Certain Herbs, Stones, and Beasts, also A Book of the Marvels of the World*. Oxford: Clarendon, 1973.

Bevington, David, ed. *Medieval Drama*. Boston: Houghton Miffllin, 1975.

Biggs, Frederick M. "A Bared Bottom and a Basket: A New Analogue and a New Source for the *Miller's Tale*." *Notes and Queries* 254 (2009), 340–41.

Birkholz, Daniel. "Harley Lyrics and Hereford Clerics: The Implications of Mobility, c. 1300–1351." *Studies in the Age of Chaucer* 31 (2009), 175–230.

405

Blair, John (2002a). "A Handlist of Anglo-Saxon Saints." In *Local Saints and Local Churches in the Early Medieval West*. Ed. Alan Thacker and Richard Sharpe. Oxford: Oxford University Press, 2002. Pp. 495–565.

———— (2002b). "A Saint for Every Minster? Local Cults in Anglo-Saxon England." In *Local Saints and Local Churches in the Early Medieval West*. Ed. Alan Thacker and Richard Sharpe. Oxford: Oxford University Press, 2002. Pp. 454–94.

Blamires, Alcuin, ed. *Woman Defamed and Woman Defended: An Anthology of Medieval Texts*. Oxford: Clarendon Press, 1992.

Bloch, R. Howard. *The Scandal of the Fabliaux*. Chicago: University of Chicago Press, 1986.

Boas, Adrian J. *Jerusalem in the Time of the Crusades: Society, Landscape and Art in the Holy City under Frankish Rule*. London: Routledge, 2001.

Böddeker, Karl, ed. *Altenglische Dichtungen des MS. Harl. 2253*. Berlin: Weidmannsche, 1878.

Boffey, Julia. "Middle English Lyrics and Manuscripts." In *A Companion to the Middle English Lyric*. Ed. Thomas G. Duncan. Cambridge: D. S. Brewer, 2005. Pp. 1–18.

Boffey, Julia, and A. S. G. Edwards. *A New Index of Middle English Verse*. London: British Library, 2005.

Boklund-Lagopoulou, Karin. *'I have a yong suster': Popular Song and the Middle English Lyric*. Dublin: Four Courts Press, 2002.

Bonnard, Jean. *Les Traductions de la bible en vers français au moyen âge*. Geneva: Slatkine Reprints, 1884.

Borland, Lois. "Herman's *Bible* and the *Cursor Mundi*." *Studies in Philology* 30 (1933), 427–44.

Bossuat, Robert. *Manuel bibliographique de la littérature française du moyen âge*. Melun: Librairie d'Argences, 1951.

Bossy, Michel-André, ed and trans. *Medieval Debate Poetry: Vernacular Works*. New York: Garland, 1987.

Boulton, Maureen (1996–97). "Le langage de la dévotion affective en moyen français." *Le moyen français* 39–41 (1996–97), 53–63.

———— (2009). "The Lives of the Virgin by Wace and Herman de Valenciennes: Conventions of Romance and Chanson de Geste in Religious Narratives." In *Church and Vernacular Literature in Medieval France*. Ed. Dorothy Kullmann. Toronto: Pontifical Institute of Mediaeval Studies, 2009. Pp. 109–23.

Bradbury, Nancy Mason (2008). "Rival Wisdom in the *Latin Dialogue of Solomon and Marcolf*." *Speculum* 83 (2008), 331–65.

———— (2010). "Popular Romance." In *A Companion to Medieval Poetry*. Ed. Corinne Saunders. Oxford: Blackwell Publishing, 2010. Pp. 289–307.

Bradbury, Nancy Mason, and Scott Bradbury, eds. *The Dialogue of Solomon and Marcolf: A Dual-Language Edition from Latin and Middle English Printed Editions*. Kalamazoo, MI: Medieval Institute Publications, 2012.

Brandl, A., and O. Zippel, eds. *Middle English Literature*. Second edition. New York: Chelsea, 1949. Rpt. 1965.

Breeze, Andrew (1992). "The Instantaneous Harvest and the Harley Lyric *Mayden Moder Milde*." *Notes and Queries* 237 (1992), 150–52.

———— (2004). "Jonas, Jason, and the Harley Lyric *Annot and John*." *Notes and Queries* 249 (2004), 237–38.

Brereton, G. E. "*La riote du monde*: A New Fragment." *Medium Ævum* 4 (1935), 95–99.

Brook, G. L., ed. *The Harley Lyrics: The Middle English Lyrics of Ms. Harley 2253*. Fourth edition. Manchester: Manchester University Press, 1968.

Brown, Carleton (1916, 1920). *Register of Middle English Religious and Didactic Verse*. 2 vols. Oxford: Bibliographical Society, 1916, 1920.

———— (1932), ed. *English Lyrics of the XIIIth Century*. Oxford: Clarendon, 1932.

———— (1952), ed. *Religious Lyrics of the XIVth Century*. Oxford: Clarendon, 1924. Second edition. Rev. G. V. Smithers. Oxford: Clarendon, 1952.

Brown, Carleton, and Rossell Hope Robbins. *The Index of Middle English Verse*. New York: Columbia University Press, 1943.

Burnley, David, and Alison Wiggins, eds. *Auchinleck Manuscript*. Edinburgh: National Library of Scotland, 2003. Online at http://auchinleck.nls.uk/editorial/project.html.

Butterfield, Ardis. "English, French and Anglo-French: Language and Nation in the Fabliau." In *Mittelalterliche Novellistik im europäischen Kontext: Kulturwissenschaftliche Perspektiven*. Ed. Mark Chinca, Timo Reuvekamp-Felber, and Christopher Young. Berlin: Erich Schmidt, 2006. Pp. 238–59.

Cable, Thomas. "Foreign Influence, Native Continuation, and Metrical Typology in Alliterative Lyrics." In *Approaches to the Metres of Alliterative Verse*. Ed. Judith Jefferson and Ad Putter. Leeds Texts and Monographs, New Series 17. Leeds: University of Leeds, 2009. Pp. 219–34.

Cannon, Christopher. *Middle English Literature: A Cultural History*. Cambridge: Polity Press, 2008.

Cartlidge, David R., and J. Keith Elliott. *Art and the Christian Apocrypha*. London: Routledge, 2001.

Cartlidge, Neil. "Medieval Debate-Poetry and *The Owl and the Nightingale*." In *A Companion to Medieval Poetry*. Ed. Corinne Saunders. Oxford: Blackwell Publishing, 2010. Pp. 237–57.

Catholic Encyclopedia. http://www.catholic.org/encyclopedia.

Cazelles, Brigitte, trans. *The Lady as Saint: A Collection of French Hagiographic Romances of the Thirteenth Century*. Philadephia: University of Pennsylvania Press, 1991.

Chaucer, Geoffrey. *The Riverside Chaucer*. Ed. Larry D. Benson et al. Third edition. Boston: Houghton Mifflin, 1987.

Chevalier, Ulysse. *Repertorium hymnologicum: Catalogue des chants, hymnes, proses, séquences, tropes en usage dans l'église latine Depuis les origines jusqu'a nos jours*. Tome 1. Louvain: Lefever, 1892.

Child, Francis James. *The English and Scottish Popular Ballads*. 5 vols. 1882–98. Rpt. New York: Dover, 1965.

Choong, Kevin Teo Kia. "Bodies of Knowledge: Embodying Riotous Performance in the Harley Lyrics." In *"And Never Know the Joy": Sex and the Erotic in English Poetry*. Ed. C. C. Barfoot. Amsterdam: Rodopi, 2006. Pp. 13–32.

Christine de Pizan. *The Book of the City of Ladies*. Trans. Earl Jeffrey Richards. New York: Persea Books, 1982.

Clanchy, M. T. *England and Its Rulers: 1066–1307*. Third edition. Oxford: Blackwell, 2006.

Clough, William Overton, ed. *Gesta Pilati: or, The reports, letters and acts of Pontius Pilate, procurator of Judea, with an account of his life and death: being a translation and compilation of all the writings ascribed to him, as made to Tiberius Cæsar, emperor of Rome, concerning the life of Jesus, His trial and crucifixion*. Indianapolis: R. Douglass, 1880.

Clugnet, Léon, ed. "Vie de sainte Marine." *Revue de l'Orient Chrétien* 8 (1903), 288–311.

Coleman, Janet. *Medieval Readers and Writers 1350–1400*. New York: Columbia University Press, 1981.

Conlee, John W., ed. *Middle English Debate Poetry: A Critical Anthology*. East Lansing, MI: Colleagues Press, 1991.

Connolly, Margaret. "Compiling the Book." In *The Production of Books in England 1350–1500*. Ed. Alexandra Gillespie and Daniel Wakelin. Cambridge: Cambridge University Press, 2011. Pp. 129–49.

Cooke, Thomas D. "Pornography, the Comic Spirit, and the Fabliaux." In *The Humor of the Fabliaux: A Collection of Critical Essays*. Ed. Thomas D. Cooke and Benjamin L. Honeycutt. Columbia, MO: University of Missouri Press, 1974. Pp. 137–62.

Cooper, Helen. *The English Romance in Time: Transforming Motifs from Geoffrey of Monmouth to the Death of Shakespeare*. Oxford: Oxford University Press, 2004.

Corrie, Marilyn (2000). "Harley 2253, Digby 86, and the Circulation of Literature in Pre-Chaucerian England." In *Studies in the Harley Manuscript: The Scribes, Contents, and Social Contexts of British Library MS Harley 2253*. Ed. Susanna Fein. Kalamazoo, MI: Medieval Institute Publications, 2000. Pp. 427–43.

———— (2003). "Kings and Kingship in British Library MS Harley 2253." *Yearbook of English Studies* 33 (2003), 64–79.

Crane, Susan. *Insular Romance: Politics, Faith, and Culture in Anglo-Norman and Middle English Literature*. Berkeley: University of California Press, 1986.

Cross, J. E. "The Sayings of St. Bernard and *Ubi Sount Qui Nos Fuerount.*" *Review of English Studies*, n.s. 9 (1958), 1–7.

Da Rold, Orietta, Takako Kato, Mary Swan, and Elaine Treharne, eds. *The Production and Use of English Manuscripts 1060 to 1220.* Leicester: University of Leicester 2010. Online at http://www.le.ac.uk/ee/em1060to1220.

Dane, Joseph A. "Page Layout and Textual Autonomy in Harley MS 2253: 'Lenten Ys Come wiþ Loue to Toune.'" *Medium Ævum* 68 (1999), 32–41.

Daniel, Hermann Adalbert. *Thesaurus Hymnologicus sive Hymnorum Canticorum Sequentiarum Circa Annum MD Usitatarum Collectio Amplissima.* 5 vols. Leipzig: J. T. Loeschke, 1855–56.

Dante Alighieri. *La Divina Commedia.* Ed. G. H. Grandgent. Rev. Charles S. Singleton. Cambridge, MA: Harvard University Press, 1972.

D'Arcy, Anne Marie. "The Middle English Lyrics." In *Readings in Medieval Texts: Interpreting Old and Middle English Literature.* Ed. David F. Johnson and Elaine Treharne. Oxford: Oxford University Press, 2005. Pp. 306–22.

D'Arcy, Anne Marie, and Alan J. Fletcher, eds. *Studies in Late Medieval and Early Renaissance Texts in Honour of John Scattergood: The Key of All Good Remembrance.* Portland, OR: Four Courts Press, 2005.

Davies, R. T., ed. *Medieval English Lyrics: A Critical Anthology.* London: Faber and Faber, 1963.

De Wilde, Geert. "The Stanza Form of the Middle English *Lament for the Death of Edward I*: A Reconstruction." *Anglia* 123 (2005), 230–45.

Dean, James M., ed. *Medieval English Political Writings.* Kalamazoo, MI: Medieval Institute Publications, 1996.

Dean, Ruth J., with Maureen B. M. Boulton. *Anglo-Norman Literature: A Guide to Texts and Manuscripts.* London: Anglo-Norman Text Society, 1999.

Degginger, Stuart H. L. "'A Wayle Whyt Ase Whalles Bon': Reconstructed." *Journal of English and Germanic Philology* 53 (1954), 84–90.

Dobson, E. J., and F. Ll. Harrison, eds. *Medieval English Songs.* New York: Cambridge University Press, 1979.

Dobson, R. B., and J. Taylor. *Rymes of Robin Hood: An Introduction to the English Outlaw.* Pittsburgh, PA: University of Pittsburgh Press, 1976.

Donaldson, E. Talbot. *Speaking of Chaucer.* Durham, NC: Labyrinth, 1983.

Douay-Rheims Bible + Challoner Notes + Vulgate Bible (Clementine). http://drbo.org.

Dove, Mary (1969). *A Study of Some of the Lesser-Known Poems of British Museum Ms. Harley 2253.* D.Phil. dissertation. Cambridge: Girton College, 1969.

——— (2000). "Evading Textual Intimacy: The French Secular Verse." In *Studies in the Harley Manuscript: The Scribes, Contents, and Social Contexts of British Library MS Harley 2253.* Ed. Susanna Fein. Kalamazoo, MI: Medieval Institute Publications, 2000. Pp. 329–49.

Dubin, Nathaniel E., trans. *The Fabliaux.* New York: Liveright, 2013.

Duffy, Eamon (1992). *The Stripping of the Altars: Traditional Religion in England c.1400–c.1580.* New Haven, CT: Yale University Press, 1992.

——— (2006). *Marking the Hours: English People and Their Prayers 1240–1570.* New Haven, CT: Yale University Press, 2006.

Dunbar, William. *The Complete Works.* Ed. John Conlee. Kalamazoo, MI: Medieval Institute Publications, 2004.

Duncan, Thomas G., ed. *Medieval English Lyrics: 1200–1400.* Harmondsworth: Penguin, 1995.

Dunn, Charles W. "I. 1. Romances Derived from English Legends." In Severs et al. Pp. 17–37, 206–24.

Dunn, Charles W., and Edward T. Byrnes, eds. *Middle English Literature.* New York: Harcourt, 1973.

Durling, Nancy Vine. "British Library MS Harley 2253: A New Reading of the Passion Lyrics in Their Manuscript Context." *Viator* 40 (2009), 271–307.

Edgar, Swift, ed. *The Vulgate Bible, Volume I: The Pentateuch; Douay-Rheims Translation.* Cambridge, MA: Harvard University Press, 2010.

Elliott, J. K., trans. *The Apocryphal New Testament: A Collection of Apocryphal Christian Literature in an English Translation*. Oxford: Clarendon, 1993.

Fein, Susanna (1998), ed. *Moral Love Songs and Laments*. Kalamazoo, MI: Medieval Institute Publications, 1998.

——— (2000a), ed. *Studies in the Harley Manuscript: The Scribes, Contents, and Social Contexts of British Library MS Harley 2253*. Kalamazoo, MI: Medieval Institute Publications, 2000.

——— (2000b). "British Library MS Harley 2253: The Lyrics, the Facsimile, and the Book." In *Studies in the Harley Manuscript: The Scribes, Contents, and Social Contexts of British Library MS Harley 2253*. Ed. Susanna Fein. Kalamazoo, MI: Medieval Institute Publications, 2000. Pp. 1–20.

——— (2000c). "A Saint 'Geynest under Gore': Marina and the Love Lyrics of the Seventh Quire." In *Studies in the Harley Manuscript: The Scribes, Contents, and Social Contexts of British Library MS Harley 2253*. Ed. Susanna Fein. Kalamazoo, MI: Medieval Institute Publications, 2000. Pp. 351–76.

——— (2005). "XXVII. The Lyrics of MS Harley 2253." In Severs et al. Pp. 4168–4206, 4311–4361.

——— (2006). "Harley Lyrics." In *The Oxford Encyclopedia of British Literature*. Ed. David Scott Kastan and Gail McMurray Gibson. 5 vols. Oxford: Oxford University Press, 2006. 2:519–22.

——— (2007). "Compilation and Purpose in MS Harley 2253." In *Essays in Manuscript Geography: Vernacular Manuscripts of the English West Midlands from the Conquest to the Sixteenth Century*. Ed. Wendy Scase. Turnhout: Brepols, 2007. Pp. 67–94.

——— (2009), ed., *John the Blind Audelay, Poems and Carols (Oxford, Bodleian Library MS Douce 302)*. Kalamazoo, MI: Medieval Institute Publications, 2009.

——— (2013). "The Four Scribes of MS Harley 2253." *Journal of the Early Book Society* 16 (2013), 27–49.

——— (2014). "Of Judges and Jewelers: *Pearl* and the Life of Saint John." *Studies in the Age of Chaucer* 36 (2014), forthcoming.

——— (2015). "Literary Scribes: The Harley Scribe and Robert Thornton as Case Studies." In *Insular Books: Vernacular Miscellanies in Late Medieval Britain*. Ed. Margaret Connolly and Raluca Radulescu. Proceedings of the British Academy. London: The British Academy, 2015 (forthcoming).

Fiero, Gloria K., Wendy Pfeffer, and Mathé Allain, eds. and trans. *Three Medieval Views of Women: "La Contenance des Fames," "Les Bien des Fames," "Les Blasme des Fames."* New Haven, CT: Yale University Press, 1989.

Finberg, H. P. R. *The Early Charters of the West Midlands*. Leicester: Leicester University Press, 1961.

Fisher, Matthew. *Scribal Authorship and the Writing of History in Medieval England*. Columbus, OH: The Ohio State University Press, 2012.

Flood, Victoria. "Imperfect Apocalypse: Thomas of Erceldoune's Reply to the Countess of Dunbar in MS Harley 2253." *Marginalia* (October 2010), 11–27. Online at http://www.marginalia.co.uk/journal/10apocalypse.

Ford, Alvin E., ed. *L'Evangile de Nicodème. Les versions courtes en ancien françaises et en prose*. Publications romanes et françaises 125. Geneva: Librairie Droz, 1973.

Förster, M. "Beiträge zur mittelalterliche Volkskunde." *Archiv für das studium der neueren Sprachen und Literaturen* 127 (1911), 31–84.

Foster, Frances A. "V. Saints' Legends. 6. Legends of Jesus and Mary." In Severs et al. Pp. 447–51, 639–44.

Fowler, David C. "XV. Ballads." In Severs et al. Pp. 1753–1808, 2019–70.

Frankis, John. "The Social Context of Vernacular Writing in Thirteenth Century England: The Evidence of the Manuscripts." In *Thirteenth Century England: Proceedings of the Newcastle upon Tyne Conference 1985*. Ed. P. R. Coss and S. D. Lloyd. Woodbridge: Boydell, 1986. Pp. 175–84.

French, Walter Hoyt, and Charles Brockway Hale, eds. *Middle English Metrical Romances*. 2 vols. New York: Russell & Russell, 1964.

Fulk, R. D., ed. and trans. *The Beowulf Manuscript*. Cambridge, MA: Harvard University Press, 2010.

Fuller, David. "Lyrics, Sacred and Secular." In *A Companion to Medieval Poetry*. Ed. Corinne Saunders. Oxford: Blackwell Publishing, 2010. Pp. 258–76.

Furnivall, F. J., ed. *The Minor Poems of the Vernon MS. Part II*. EETS o.s. 117. London: Kegan Paul, Trench, Trübner, 1901.

Garbáty, Thomas J., ed. *Medieval English Literature*. Lexington, MA: D. C. Heath and Co., 1984.

Gerald of Wales. *The Jewel of the Church. A Translation of Gemma Ecclesiastica by Giraldus Cambrensis*. Trans. John J. Hagen. Leiden: Brill, 1979.

Gibbs, A. C., ed. *Middle English Romances*. London: Edward Arnold, 1966.

Goering, Joseph, ed. *William de Montibus (c. 1140–1213): The Schools and the Literature of Pastoral Care*. Toronto: Pontifical Institute of Mediaeval Studies, 1992.

Gordon, E. V., ed. *Pearl*. Oxford: Clarendon, 1953.

Gower, John. *Confessio Amantis*. Ed. Russell A. Peck, with Latin translations by Andrew Galloway. 3 vols. Kalamazoo, MI: Medieval Institute Publications, 2000–06.

Gray, Douglas. *Themes and Images in the Medieval English Religious Lyric*. London: Routledge and Kegan Paul, 1972.

Green, Richard Firth (1989). "The Two 'Litel Wot Hit Any Mon' Lyrics in Harley 2253." *Mediaeval Studies* 51 (1989), 304–12.

——— (1999). *A Crisis of Truth: Literature and Law in Ricardian England*. Philadelphia: University of Pennsylvania Press, 1999.

Greene, Richard Leighton (1962), ed. *A Selection of English Carols*. Oxford: Clarendon, 1962.

——— (1977), ed. *The Early English Carols*. Second edition. Oxford: Clarendon, 1977.

——— (1980). "XIV. Carols." In Severs et al. Pp.1743–52, 1940–2018.

Hall, Joseph, ed. *King Horn: A Middle-English Romance Edited from the Manuscripts*. Oxford: Clarendon, 1901.

Halliwell, James Orchard, ed. and trans. *The Harrowing of Hell, A Miracle Play Written in the Reign of Edward the Second*. London: John Russell Smith, 1840.

Hanna, Ralph. "The Matter of Fulk: Romance and the History of the Marches." *Journal of English and Germanic Philology* 110 (2011), 337–58.

Hardy, T. D. *Descriptive Catalogue of Materials Relating to the History of Great Britain and Ireland to the End of the Reign of Henry VII*. 3 vols. London: Longman, Green, Longman, and Roberts, 1862–71; repr. New York: Kraus, 1966.

Harris, Julie A. "Redating the Arca Santa of Oviedo." *Art Bulletin* 77 (1995), 82–93.

Harriss, G. L. *King, Parliament, and Public Finance in Medieval England to 1369*. Oxford: Clarendon, 1975.

Hathaway, E. J., P. T. Ricketts, C. A. Robson, and A. D. Wilshere, eds. *Fouke le Fitz Waryn*. Anglo-Norman Texts 26–28. Oxford: Basil Blackwell, 1975.

Hellman, Robert, and Richard O'Gorman, trans. *Fabliaux: Ribald Tales from the Old French*. London: Arthur Barker, 1965.

Herrtage, Sidney J.H., ed. *The early English versions of the Gesta Romanorum*. EETS e.s. 33. London: Oxford University Press, 1879. Rpt. 1962.

Herzman, Ronald B., Graham Drake, and Eve Salisbury, eds. *Four Romances of England: King Horn, Havelok the Dane, Bevis of Hampton, Athelston*. Kalamazoo, MI: Medieval Institute Publications, 1999.

Hindley, Alan, Frederick W. Langley, and Brian J. Levy, eds. *Old French Dictionary*. Cambridge: Cambridge University Press, 2000.

Hines, John. *Voices in the Past: English Literature and Archaeology*. Cambridge: D. S. Brewer, 2004.

Holbrook, Richard. "The Printed Text of Four Fabliaux in the *Recueil général et complet des fabliaux* Compared with the Readings in the Harleian ms., 2253." *Modern Language Notes* 20 (1905), 193–97.

Holthausen, F., ed. "Die Quelle des mittelenglischen Gedichtes 'Lob der Frauen.'" *Archiv für das Studium der neueren Sprachen und Literaturen* 108 (1902), 288–301.

Honeycutt, Benjamin L. "The Knight and His World as Instruments of Humor in the Fabliaux." In *The Humor of the Fabliaux: A Collection of Critical Essays*. Ed. Thomas D. Cooke and Benjamin L. Honeycutt. Columbia, MO: University of Missouri Press, 1974. Pp. 75–92.

Horobin, Simon. "Manuscripts and Scribes." In *Chaucer: Contemporary Approaches*. Ed. Susanna Fein and David Raybin. University Park, PA: Pennsylvania State University Press, 2010. Pp. 67–82.

Horstmann, Carl (1876), ed. "Die Evangelien-Geschichten der Homiliensammlung des Ms. Vernon." *Archiv für das Studium der neueren Sprachen und Literaturen* 57 (1876), 241–316.

——— (1878), ed. *Sammlung Altenglischer Legenden*. Heilbronn: Von Gebr. Henninger, 1878; rpt. Hildeshein: Georg Olms, 1969.

——— (1895, 1896), ed. *Yorkshire Writers: Richard Rolle of Hampole and His Followers*. 2 vols. London: Swan Sonnenschein, 1895, 1896.

——— (1901), ed. *Nova Legenda Anglie: As Collected by John of Tynemouth, John Capgrave, and Others, and First Printed, with New Lives, by Wynkyn de Worde a.d. mdxui*. 2 vols. Oxford: Clarendon, 1901.

Hough, Carole. "A Note on Harley Lyric No. 3 Line 21." *Review of English Studies* 214 (2003), 173–77.

Hrothsvitha. *Paphnutius*. Trans. Mary Marguerite Butler, R.S.M. In *Medieval and Tudor Drama*. Ed. John Gassner. 1963; rpt. New York: Applause, 1987.

Hulme, William Henry, ed. *The Middle-English Harrowing of Hell and Gospel of Nicodemus*. EETS e.s. 100. London: Oxford University Press, 1907.

Hunt, Tony. "Anglo-Norman Rules of Friendship." *French Studies Bulletin* 30 (1989), 9–11.

Hunt, Tony, ed., and Jane Bliss, trans. *"Cher alme": Texts of Anglo-Norman Piety*. Tempe, AR: Arizona Center for Medieval and Renaissance Studies, 2010.

Izydorczyk, Zbigniew. *Manuscript of the Evangelium Nicodemi: A Census*. Subsidia Mediaevalia 21. Toronto: Pontifical Institute of Mediaeval Studies, 1993.

Jacobus de Voragine. *The Golden Legend: Readings on the Saints*. Trans. William Granger Ryan. 2 vols. Princeton: Princeton University Press, 1993.

James, M. R. (1917). "Two Lives of St. Ethelbert, King and Martyr." *English Historical Review* 32 (1917), 214–44.

——— (1924), trans. *The Apocryphal New Testament, Being the Apocryphal Gospels, Acts, Epistles, and Apocalypses with Other Narratives and Fragments*. Oxford: Clarendon, 1924.

Jeffrey, David L. (1975). *The Early English Lyric and Franciscan Spirituality*. Lincoln, NE: University of Nebraska Press, 1975.

——— (2000). "Authors, Anthologists, and Franciscan Spirituality." In *Studies in the Harley Manuscript: The Scribes, Contents, and Social Contexts of British Library MS Harley 2253*. Ed. Susanna Fein. Kalamazoo, MI: Medieval Institute Publications, 2000. Pp. 261–70.

Jeffrey, David L., and Brian J. Levy, eds. *The Anglo-Norman Lyric: An Anthology*. Toronto: Pontifical Institute of Mediaeval Studies, 1990.

Jennings, J. C. "The Writings of Prior Dominic of Evesham." *English Historical Review* 77 (1962), 298–304.

Jones, Trefor. *The English Saints: East Anglia*. Norwich: The Canterbury Press, 1999.

Jordan, Richard, ed. "Kleinere Dichtungen der Handschrift Harley 3810." *Englische Studien* 41 (1910), 253–66.

Jubinal, Achille, ed. *Nouveau Recueil de contes, dits, fabliaux et autres pièces inedites des xiiie, xive et xve siècles*. Paris: Eduoard Pannier, 1839, 1842.

Keiser, George R. "XXV. Works of Science and Information." In Severs et al. Pp. 3593–3967.

Keller, Von Henning. "Die me. Rezepte des Ms. Harley 2253." *Archiv für das studium der neueren Sprachen und Literaturen* 207 (1971), 94–100.

Kemble, John M., ed. *The Dialogue of Salomon and Saturn, with an Historical Introduction*. London: Ælfric Society, 1848.

Kennedy, Thomas Corbin. *Anglo-Norman Poems about Love, Women, and Sex from British Museum MS. Harley 2253*. Ph.D. dissertation. New York: Columbia University, 1973.

Ker, N. R., intro. *Facsimile of British Museum MS. Harley 2253*. EETS o.s. 255. London: Oxford University Press, 1965.

Kerby-Fulton, Kathryn, Maidie Hilmo, and Linda Olson. *Opening Up Middle English Manuscripts: Literary and Visual Approaches*. Ithaca, NY: Cornell University Press, 2012.

Kinch, Ashby. "Dying for Love: Dialogic Response in the Lyrics of BL MS Harley 2253." In *Courtly Literature and Clerical Culture*. Ed. Christoph Huber and Henrike Lähnemann. Tübingen: Attempto, 2002. Pp. 137–47.

Kingsford, C. L., ed. *The Song of Lewes*. Oxford: Clarendon, 1890.

Kölbing, E., ed. "Klein Publicationen aus der Auchinleck-Hs. I. Lob der frauen." *Englische Studien* 7 (1884), 101–25.

Kremer, Eugen, ed. *La Bible von Hermann de Valenciennes*. Teil IV (Von der Speisung der fünftausend bis zum einzug in Jerusalem). Greifswald: H. Adler, 1914.

Krueger, Roberta L. "Introduction: Teach Your Children Well: Medieval Conduct Guides for Youths." In *Medieval Conduct Literature: An Anthology of Vernacular Guides to Behaviour for Youth, with English Translations*. Ed. Mark D. Johnston. Toronto: University of Toronto Press, 2009. Pp. ix–xxxiii.

Kuczynski, Michael P. (1995). *Prophetic Song: The Psalms as Moral Discourse in Late Medieval England*. Philadelphia, PA: University of Philadelphia Press, 1995.

———— (2000). "An 'Electric Stream': The Religious Contents." In *Studies in the Harley Manuscript: The Scribes, Contents, and Social Contexts of British Library MS Harley 2253*. Ed. Susanna Fein. Kalamazoo, MI: Mediaeval Institute Publications, 2000. Pp. 123–61.

———— (2012). "An Unpublished Middle English Version of the *Epistola Lentuli*: Text and Contexts." *The Mediaeval Journal* 2 (2012): 35–57.

Kuehne, Oswald Robert. *A Study of the Thaïs Legend with Special Reference to Hrothsvitha's "Paphnutius."* Philadelpha: University of Pennsylvania, 1922.

Kuryluk, Ewa. *Veronica and Her Cloth: History, Symbolism, and Structure of a "True" Image*. Oxford: Basil Blackwell, 1991.

Labarge, Margaret Wade. *Simon de Montfort*. London: Eyre and Spottiswoode, 1961.

Lacy, Norris. *Reading Fabliaux*. New York: Garland, 1993.

Lagorio, Valerie M., and Michael G. Sargent, with Ritamary Bradley. "XXIII. English Mystical Writings." In Severs et al. Pp. 3049–3137, 3405–71.

Lambdin, Laura Cooner, and Robert Thomas Lambdin. "Debate Poetry." In *A Companion to Old and Middle English Literature*. Ed. Laura Cooner Lambdin and Robert Thomas Lambdin. Westport, CT: Greenwood Press, 2002. Pp. 118–53.

Långfors, Arthur. *Les Incipit des poèmes français antéreurs au XVIᵉ siècle: Répertoire bibliographique*. 1917; rpt. New York: Burt Franklin, 1970.

Lerer, Seth (2003). "Medieval English Literature and the Idea of the Anthology." *PMLA* 118 (2003), 1251–67.

———— (2008). "'Dum ludis floribus': Language and Text in the Medieval English Lyric." *Philological Quarterly* 87 (2008), 237–55.

Liszka, Thomas R. "Talk in the Camps: On the Dating of the *South English Legendary*, *Havelok the Dane*, and *King Horn* in Oxford, Bodleian Library, MS Laud Misc. 108." In *The Texts and Contexts of Oxford, Bodleian Library, MS Laud Misc. 108: The Shaping of English Vernacular Narrative*. Ed. Kimberly K. Bell and Julie Nelson Couch. Leiden: Brill, 2011. Pp. 31–50.

Little, A. G. *Studies in English Franciscan History*. Manchester: Manchester University Press, 1917.

Louis, Cameron. "XXII. Proverbs, Precepts, and Monitory Pieces." In Severs et al. Pp. 2957–3048, 3349–3404.

Lucas, Angela M., ed. and trans. *Anglo-Irish Poems of the Middle Ages*. Dublin: The Columba Press, 1995.

Lynch, Andrew. "Genre, Bodies, and Power in Oxford, Bodleian Library, MS Laud Misc. 108: *King Horn*, *Havelok*, and the *South English Legendary*." In *The Texts and Contexts of Oxford, Bodleian Library, MS Laud Misc. 108: The Shaping of English Vernacular Narrative*. Ed. Kimberly K. Bell and Julie Nelson Couch. Leiden: Brill, 2011. Pp. 177–96.

Lyons, W. H. "Doctrinal Logic and Poetic Justice in the Twelfth Century: The Case of Herman de Valeniennes, Solomon and Henry II." In *Currents of Thought in French Literature: Essays in Memory of G. T. Clapton*. Ed. J. C. Ireson. Oxford: Basil Blackwell, 1965. Pp. 21–32.

MacCulloch, J. A. *The Harrowing of Hell: A Comparative Study of an Early Christian Doctrine*. Edinburgh: T. & T. Clark, 1930.

Macray, William Dunn, ed. *Chronicon abbatiae de Evesham ad annum 1418*. London: Longman, Green, Longman, Roberts, and Green, 1863.

Maddicott, J. R. *Simon de Montfort*. Cambridge: Cambridge University Press, 1994.

Margherita, Gayle. *The Romance of Origins: Language and Sexual Difference in Middle English Literature*. Philadelphia: University of Pennsylvania Press, 1994.

Martin, Ernst, ed. *La Bible von Hermann de Valenciennes*. Teil V (Von Christi einzug in Jerusalem bis zur himmelfahrt). Greifswald: H. Adler, 1914.

Martin, Lawrence T., ed. *Somniale Danielis: An Edition of a Medieval Latin Dream Interpretation Handbook*. Frankfurt am Main: Peter D. Lang, 1981.

Marx. C. W[illiam] (1995). *The Devil's Rights and the Redemption in the Literature of Medieval England*. Cambridge: D. S. Brewer, 1995.

——— (1997). "The *Gospel of Nicodemus* in Old English and Middle English." In *The Medieval Gospel of Nicodemus: Texts, Intertexts, and Contexts in Western Europe*. Ed. Zbigniew Izydorczyk. Tempe, AR: Medieval and Renaissance Texts and Studies, 1997. Pp. 207–59.

——— (2013), ed. *The Middle English Liber Aureus and Gospel of Nicodemus Edited from London British Library, MS Egerton 2658*. Heidelberg: Winter, 2013.

Marx. C. William, and Jeanne F. Drennan, eds. *The Middle English Prose Complaint of Our Lady and Gospel of Nicodemus ed. from Cambridge, Magdalene College, MS Pepys 2498*. Heidelberg: Carl Winter, 1987.

Matthews, John. "The Games of Robin Hood." In *Robin Hood: Anthology of Scholarship and Criticism*. Ed. Stephen Knight. Cambridge: D. S. Brewer, 1999. Pp. 393–410.

Maulsby, Stephen C. *The Harley Lyrics Revisited: A Multilingual Textual Community*. Ph.D. dissertation. Washington, DC: Catholic University of America, 2008.

McCarthy, Conor, ed. *Love, Sex and Marriage in the Middle Ages: A Sourcebook*. London: Routledge, 2004.

McKitterick, David, ed. *The Trinity Apocalypse (Trinity College Cambridge, MS R.16.2)*. London: The British Library, 2005.

McKnight, George H., ed. *King Horn, Floriʒ and Blauncheflur, The Assumption of our Lady*. EETS o.s. 14. London: Oxford University Press, 1901; rpt. 1962.

McSparran, Frances. "The Language of the English Poems: The Harley Scribe and His Exemplars." In *Studies in the Harley Manuscript: The Scribes, Contents, and Social Contexts of British Library MS Harley 2253*. Ed. Susanna Fein. Kalamazoo, MI: Medieval Institute Publications, 2000. Pp. 391–426.

Menner, Robert J. "The Man in the Moon and Hedging." *Journal of English and Germanic Philology* 48 (1949), 1–14.

Meyer, Paul (1895). "Notice sur le manuscrit fr. 24862 de la Bibliothèque nationale contenant divers ouvrages composés ou éscrits en Angleterre." *Notices et extraits* 35 (1895), 131–68.

——— (1889). "Notice du ms. Egerton 2710 de Musée britannique." *Bulletin de la Société des anciens textes français* 15 (1889), 72–95.

——— (1903). "Les manuscripts français de Cambridge." *Romania* 32 (1903), 18–120.

Michelant, Henri, and Gaston Raynaud, eds. *Itinéraires à Jérusalem et descriptions de la Terre Sainte rédigés en français aux XI*^e, *XII*^e *& XIII*^e *siecles*. Preface by Comte Riant. Publications de la Société de l'Orient latin, Série Géographique 3: Itinéraires français. Geneva: Jules-Guillaume Fick, 1882.

Middle English Dictionary (*MED*). Online at http://quod.lib.umich.edu/m/med.

Migne, J.-P., ed. *Patrologiae cursus completus . . . series latina*. Paris: J. P. Migne, 1844–64.

Mill, Anna J. "XII. Dramatic Pieces. 1. The Miracle Plays and Mysteries." In Severs et al. Pp. 1315–56, 1557–98.

Millett, Bella. *Wessex Parallel WebTexts*. 2003. Online at http://www.soton.ac.uk/~wpwt/.

Monda, Joseph B. "'The Sayings of Saint Bernard' from MS Bodleian Additional E 6." *Mediaeval Studies* 32 (1970), 299–307.

Montaiglon, Anatole de, and Gaston Raynaud, eds. *Recueil général et complet des fabliaux des XIIIᵉ et XIVᵉ siècles*. 6 vols. Paris: Librairie des bibliophiles, 1872–90. Repr. New York, 1964.

Mooney, Linne, Simon Horobin, and Estelle Stubbs. *Late Medieval English Scribes*. York: University of York, 2011. Online at http://www.medievalscribes.com.

Mooney, Linne, and Estelle Stubbs. *Scribes and the City: London Guildhall Clerks and the Dissemination of Middle English Literature 1375–1425*. York: York Medieval Press, 2013.

Morris, Richard, and Walter W. Skeat, eds. *Specimens of Early English. Part II: From Robert of Gloucester to Gower, A.D. 1298–A.D. 1393*. Second edition. Oxford: Clarendon, 1873.

Muir, Lawrence. "IV. Translations and Paraphrases of the Bible, and Commentaries." In Severs et al. Pp. 1385–1536, 1631–1725.

Murray, H. J. R. *A History of Chess*. Oxford: Oxford University Press, 1913.

Murray, Hilda M. R., ed. *The Middle English Poem, Erthe upon Erthe, Printed from Twenty-Four Manuscripts*. EETS o.s. 141. 1911; Oxford: Oxford University Press, 1964.

Murray, James A. H., ed. *The Romance and Prophecies of Thomas of Erceldoune*. EETS 61. London: N. Trüber, 1875; rpt. Felinbach: Llanerch, 1991.

Muscatine, Charles. *The Old French Fabliaux*. New Haven, CT: Yale University Press, 1986.

Nelson, Ingrid Lynn (2010). *The Lyric in England, 1200–1400*. Ph.D. dissertation. Cambridge, MA: Harvard University, 2010.

—— (2013). "The Performance of Power in Medieval English Households: The Case of the *Harrowing of Hell*." *Journal of English and Germanic Philology* 112 (2013), 48–69.

Newhauser, Richard. "Historicity and Complaint in *Song of the Husbandman*." In *Studies in the Harley Manuscript: The Scribes, Contents, and Social Contexts of British Library MS Harley 2253*. Ed. Susanna Fein. Kalamazoo, MI: Medieval Institute Publications, 2000. Pp. 203–217.

Nicholls, Jonathan. *The Matter of Courtesy: Medieval Courtesy Books and the Gawain-Poet*. Woodbridge: D. S. Brewer, 1985.

Nichols, Stephen G., and Siegfried Wenzel, eds. *The Whole Book: Cultural Perspective on the Medieval Miscellany*. Ann Arbor, MI: University of Michigan Press, 1996.

Nolan, Barbara. "Anthologizing Ribaldry: Five Anglo-Norman Fabliaux." In *Studies in the Harley Manuscript: The Scribes, Contents, and Social Contexts of British Library MS Harley 2253*. Ed. Susanna Fein. Kalamazoo, MI: Medieval Institute Publications, 2000. Pp. 289–327.

Noomen, Willem, and Nico van den Boogaard, eds. *Nouveau recueil complet des fabliaux*. 10 vols. Assen: Van Gorcum, 1983–98.

Nykrog, Per. *Les Fabliaux: Nouvelle édition*. Geneva: Librairie Droz, 1973.

O'Connell, David, ed. *The Teachings of Saint Louis: A Critical Text*. Chapel Hill, NC: University of North Carolina Press, 1972.

O'Connor, Br. Basilides Andrew, ed. *Henri D'Arci's* Vitas Patrum: *A Thirteenth-Century Anglo-Norman Rimed Translation of the* Verba Seniorum. Washington, DC: The Catholic University of America, 1949.

O'Farrell-Tate, Una, ed. *The Abridged English Metrical Brut Edited from London, British Library MS Royal 12.C.XII*. Heidelberg: C. Winter, 2002.

Ogilvie-Thomson, S. J., ed. *Richard Rolle: Prose and Verse, Edited from MS Longleat 29 and Related Manuscripts*. EETS o.s. 293. Oxford: Oxford University Press, 1988.

O'Gorman, Richard. "The *Gospel of Nicodemus* in the Vernacular Literature of Medieval France." In *The Medieval Gospel of Nicodemus: Texts, Intertexts, and Contexts in Western Europe*. Ed. Zbigniew Izydorczyk. Tempe, AR: Medieval and Renaissance Texts and Studies, 1997. Pp. 103–31.

O'Rourke, Jason (2000). "British Library MS Royal 12 C. xii and the Problems of Patronage." *Journal of the Early Book Society* 3 (2000), 216–25.

———— (2005). "Imagining Book Production in Fourteenth-Century Herefordshire: The Scribe of British Library, Harley 2253 and his 'Organizing Principles.'" In *Imagining the Book*. Ed. Stephen Kelly and John J. Thompson. Turnhout: Brepols, 2005. Pp. 45–60.

Ovid. *Metamorphoses*. Trans. David Raeburn. London: Penguin, 2004.

Parkes, M. B. *English Cursive Book Hands 1250–1500*. Oxford: Clarendon Press, 1969.

Parsons, H. Rosamond. "Anglo-Norman Books of Courtesy and Nurture." *PMLA* 44 (1929), 383–455.

Patterson, Frank Allen, ed. *The Middle English Penitential Lyric: A Study and Collection of Early Religious Verse*. New York: Columbia University Press, 1911.

Pearcy, Roy J. (1978). "Chansons de Geste and Fabliaux: 'La Gageure' and 'Berenger au long cul.'" *Neuphilologische Mitteilungen* 79 (1978), 76–83.

———— (2007). *Logic and Humour in the Fabliaux: An Essay in Applied Narratology*. Cambridge: D. S. Brewer, 2007.

Pearsall, Derek. *Old English and Middle English Poetry*. London: Routledge and Kegan Paul, 1977.

Peck, Russell A. (1970). "Theme and Number in Chaucer's *Book of the Duchess*." In *Silent Poetry: Essays in Numerological Analysis*. Ed. Alastair Fowler. London: Routledge, 1970. Pp. 73–115.

———— (1975). "Public Dreams and Private Myths: Perspective in Middle English Literature." *PMLA* 90 (1975), 461–68.

———— (1991), ed. *Heroic Women from the Old Testament in Middle English Verse*. Kalamazoo, MI: Medieval Institute Publications, 1991.

Perman, R. C. D., ed. "Henri d'Arci: The Shorter Works." In *Studies in Medieval French Presented to Alfred Ewert in Honour of His Seventieth Birthday*. Ed. E. A. Francis. Oxford: Clarendon, 1961. Pp. 279–321.

Pfaff, R. W. *New Liturgical Feasts in Later Medieval England*. Oxford: Clarendon, 1970.

Phillips, Helen. "Dreams and Dream Lore." In *Studies in the Harley Manuscript: The Scribes, Contents, and Social Contexts of British Library MS Harley 2253*. Ed. Susanna Fein. Kalamazoo, MI: Medieval Institute Publications, 2000. Pp. 241–59.

Pickering, Oliver. "Stanzaic Verse in the Auchinleck Manuscript: *The Alphabetical Praise of Women*." In *Studies in Late Medieval and Early Renaissance Texts in Honour of John Scattergood*. Ed. Anne Marie D'Arcy and Alan J. Fletcher. Dublin: Four Courts Press, 2005. Pp. 287–304.

Pringle, Denys (1993, 1998, 2007, 2009). *The Churches of the Crusader Kingdom of Jerusalem: A Corpus*. 4 vols. Cambridge: Cambridge University Press, 1993, 1998, 2007, 2009.

———— (2012). *Pilgrimage to Jerusalem and the Holy Land, 1187–1291*. Crusade Texts in Translation, 23. Burlington, VT: Ashgate, 2012.

Ransom, Daniel J. *Poets at Play: Irony and Parody in the Harley Lyrics*. Norman, OK: Pilgrim Books, 1985.

Raskolnikov, Masha. *Body Against Soul: Gender and Sowlehele in Middle English Allegory*. Columbus, OH: Ohio State University Press, 2009.

Raymo, Robert R. "XX. Works of Religious and Philosophical Instruction." In Severs et al. Pp. 2255–2378, 2467–2582.

Reichl, Karl (1973), ed. *Religiöse Dichtung im Englischen Hochmittelalter*. Munich: Wilhelm Fink, 1973.

———— (2000). "Debate Verse." In *Studies in the Harley Manuscript: The Scribes, Contents, and Social Contexts of British Library MS Harley 2253*. Ed. Susanna Fein. Kalamazoo, MI: Medieval Institute Publications, 2000. Pp. 219–39.

Reimer, Stephen R., ed. *The Works of William Herebert, OFM*. Toronto: Pontifical Institute of Mediaeval Studies, 1987.

Revard, Carter (1982). "*Gilote et Johane*: An Interlude in B. L. MS. Harley 2253." *Studies in Philology* 79 (1982), 122–46.

———— (2000a). "From French 'Fabliau Manuscripts' and MS Harley 2253 to the *Decameron* and the *Canterbury Tales*." *Medium Ævum* 69 (2000), 261–78.

———— (2000b). "Scribe and Provenance." In *Studies in the Harley Manuscript: The Scribes, Contents, and Social Contexts of British Library MS Harley 2253*. Ed. Susanna Fein. Kalamazoo, MI: Medieval Institute Publications, 2000. Pp. 21–109.

————— (2004). "*The Wife of Bath's Grandmother*: or How Gilote Showed Her Friend Johane that the Wages of Sin Is Worldly Pleasure, and How Both Then Preached This Gospel throughout England and Ireland." *Chaucer Review* 39 (2004), 117–36.

————— (2005a). "Four Fabliaux from London, British Library MS Harley 2253, Translated into English Verse." *Chaucer Review* 40 (2005), 111–40.

————— (2005b). "*A Goliard's Feast* and the Metanarrative of Harley 2253." *Revue Belge de Philologie et d'Histoire* 83 (2005), 841–67.

————— (2005c). "The Outlaw's Song of Trailbaston." In *Medieval Outlaws: Twelve Tales in Modern English Translation*. Ed. Thomas H. Ohlgren. Second edition. West Lafayette, IN: Parlor Press, 2005. Pp. 151–64.

————— (2007). "Oppositional Thematics and Metanarrative in MS Harley 2253, Quires 1–6." In *Essays in Manuscript Geography: Vernacular Manuscripts of the English West Midlands from the Conquest to the Sixteenth Century*. Ed. Wendy Scase. Turnhout: Brepols, 2007. Pp. 95–112.

Rézeau, Pierre. *Les Prières aux saints en française à la fin du moyen âge*. 2 vols. Geneva: Droz, 1982–83.

Rigg, A. G. (1986), ed. *Gawain on Marriage: The Textual Tradition of the De coniuge non ducenda with Critical Edition and Translation*. Toronto: Pontifical Institute of Mediaeval Studies, 1986.

————— (1992). *A History of Anglo-Latin Literature 1066–1422*. Cambridge: Cambridge University Press, 1992.

Ritson, Joseph (1877), ed. *Ancient Songs and Ballads from the Reign of King Henry the Second to the Revolution*. Third edition. Rev. W. Carew Hazlitt. London: Reeves and Turner, 1877.

————— (1884, 1885), ed. *Ancient English Metrical Romances*. Second edition. Rev. Edmund Goldsmid. 2 vols. Edinburgh: E & G Goldsmid, 1884, 1885.

Robbins, Rossell Hope (1959), ed. *Historical Poems of the XIVth and XVth Centuries*. New York: Columbia University Press, 1959.

————— (1975). "XIII. Poems Dealing with Contemporary Conditions." In Severs et al. Pp. 1385–1536, 1631–1725.

Robbins, Rossell Hope, and John L. Cutler. *Supplement to the Index of Middle English Verse*. Lexington, KY: University of Kentucky Press, 1955.

Rock, Catherine A. *Romances Copied by the Ludlow Scribe*: Purgatoire Saint Patrice, Short Metrical Chronicle, Fouke le Fitz Waryn, *and* King Horn. Ph.D. dissertation. Kent, OH: Kent State University, 2008.

Rohde, Eleanour Sinclair. *The Old English Herbals*. London: Longmans, Green, 1922.

Rosenthal, Constance. *The Vitae Patrum in Old and Middle English Literature*. Philadelphia: University of Pennsylvania, 1936. rpt. Folcroft, PA: Folcroft Library Editions, 1974.

Russell, Delbert W., ed. (1976). *La Vie de Saint Laurent: An Anglo-Norman Poem of the Twelfth Century*. Anglo-Norman Texts 34. London: Anglo-Norman Text Society, 1976.

————— (1989). *Légendier apostolique anglo-normand: édition, critique, introduction et notes*. Montréal: Les Presses del'Université de Montréal, 1989.

Russell, Norman, trans. *The Lives of the Desert Fathers*. Kalamazoo, MI: Cistercian Publications, 1981.

Salisbury, Eve, ed. *The Trials and Joys of Marriage*. Kalamazoo, MI: Medieval Institute Publications, 2002.

Salter, Elizabeth. *Fourteenth-Century English Poetry: Contexts and Readings*. Oxford: Clarendon, 1983.

Samuels, M. L. "The Dialect of the Scribe of the Harley Lyrics." *In Middle English Dialectology: Essays on Some Principles and Problems*. Ed. Angus McIntosh, M. L. Samuels, and Margaret Laing. Aberdeen: Aberdeen University Press, 1989. Pp. 256–63.

Sands, Donald B., ed. *Middle English Verse Romances*. New York: Holt, Rinehart and Winston, 1966.

Saupe, Karen, ed. *Middle English Marian Lyrics*. Kalamazoo, MI: Medieval Institute Publications, 1998.

Sayings of the Desert Fathers. Online at www.orthodoxwiki.org/Sayings_of_the_Desert_Fathers.

Scahill, John. "Trilingualism in Early Middle English Miscellanies: Languages and Literature." *Yearbook of English Studies* 33 (2003), 18–52.

Scase, Wendy (2005). "*Satire on the Retinues of the Great* (MS Harley 2253): Unpaid Bills and the Politics of Purveyance." In *Studies in Late Medieval and Early Renaissance Texts in Honour of John*

Scattergood. Ed. Anne Marie D'Arcy and Alan J. Fletcher. Dublin: Four Courts Press, 2005. Pp. 305–20.

——— (2007). *Literature and Complaint in England 1272–1553*. Oxford: Oxford University Press, 2007.

Scase, Wendy, ed., and Nick Kennedy, software. *A Facsimile Edition of the Vernon Manuscript, Oxford, Bodleian Library MS. Eng. poet. a. 1*. Bodleian Digital Texts 3. DVD-ROM. Oxford: Bodleian Library, University of Oxford, 2012.

Scattergood, John (2000a). "Authority and Resistance: The Political Verse." In *Studies in the Harley Manuscript: The Scribes, Contents, and Social Contexts of British Library MS Harley 2253*. Ed. Susanna Fein. Kalamazoo, MI: Medieval Institute Publications, 2000. Pp. 163–201.

——— (2000b). *The Lost Tradition: Essays on Middle English Alliterative Poetry*. Dublin: Four Courts Press, 2000.

——— (2005). "The Love Lyric before Chaucer." In *A Companion to the Middle English Lyric*. Ed. Thomas G. Duncan. Cambridge: D. S. Brewer, 2005. Pp. 39–67.

——— (2010). "Alliterative Poetry and Politics." In *A Companion to Medieval Poetry*. Ed. Corinne Saunders. Oxford: Blackwell Publishing, 2010. Pp. 349–66.

Schleich, G. "Die Sprichwörter Hendings und die Prouerbis of Wysdom." *Anglia* 51 (1927), 220–78.

Schmitt, P. Franciscus Salesius, ed. *Ein Neues Unvollendetes Werk des HL. Anselm von Canterbury*. Münster: Aschendorffschen, 1936.

Severs, J. Burke, Albert E. Hartung, and Peter G. Beidler, eds. *A Manual of the Writings in Middle English, 1050–1500*. 11 vols. New Haven, CT: Connecticut Academy of Arts and Sciences, 1967–2005. [For specific chapters cited in the explanatory notes, see: Dunn (vol. 1), Fein 2005 (vol. 11), Foster (vol. 2), Fowler (vol. 6), Greene 1980 (vol. 6), Keiser (vol. 10), Lagorio and Sargent (vol. 9), Louis (vol. 9), Mill (vol. 5), Raymo (vol. 7), Robbins 1975 (vol. 5), and Utley (vol. 3).]

Seymour, M. C. (1963), ed. *The Bodley Version of Mandeville's Travels*. EETS o.s. 253. London: Oxford University Press, 1963.

——— (1973), ed. *The Metrical Version of Mandeville's Travels*. EETS o.s. 269. London: Oxford University Press, 1973.

——— (1993). *Sir John Mandeville*. Authors of the Middle Ages 1. Aldershot: Variorum, 1993.

——— (2002), ed. *The Defective Version of Mandeville's Travels*. EETS o.s. 319. Oxford: Oxford University Press, 2002.

——— (2010), ed. *The Egerton Version of Mandeville's Travels*. EETS o.s. 336. Oxford: Oxford University Press, 2010.

Shields, Hugh. "*The Lament for Simon de Montfort*: An Unnoticed Text of the French Poem," *Medium Ævum* 41 (1972), 202–07.

Short, Ian, trans. "Translation of the Life of St John and the Apocalypse." In *The Trinity Apocalypse (Trinity College Cambridge MS R.16.2)*. Ed. David McKitterick, Nigel Morgan, Ian Short, and Teresa Webber. CD-ROM. London: The British Library, 2005. CD81–CD94.

Short, Ian, and Roy Pearcy, eds. *Eighteen Anglo-Norman Fabliaux*. ANTS Plain Texts Series 14. London: Anglo-Norman Text Society, 2000.

Shuffelton, George, ed. *Codex Ashmole 61: A Compilation of Popular Middle English Verse*. Kalamazoo, MI: Medieval Institute Publications, 2008.

Silverstein, Theodore, ed. *Medieval English Lyrics*. London: Edward Arnold, 1971.

Sims-Williams, Patrick. *Religion and Literature in Western England 600–800*. Cambridge: Cambridge University Press, 1990.

Sinclair, Keith V. (1979). *French Devotional Texts of the Middle Ages: A Bibliographic Manuscript Guide*. Westport, CT: Greenwood Press, 1979.

——— (1982). *French Devotional Texts of the Middle Ages: A Bibliographic Manuscript Guide, First Supplement*. Westport, CT: Greenwood Press, 1982.

——— (1988). *French Devotional Texts of the Middle Ages: A Bibliographic Manuscript Guide. Second Supplement*. New York: Greenwood Press, 1988.

——— (1997). "The Translations of the *Vitas patrum, Thaïs*, Antichrist, and *Vision de saint Paul*. Made for Anglo-Norman Templars: Some Neglected Literary Considerations." *Speculum* 72 (1997), 741–62.

Skeat, W. W., ed. "'Elegy on the Death of King Edward I' from a New MS." *Modern Language Review* 7 (1912), 149–50.

Skemer, Don C. *Binding Words: Textual Amulets in the Middle Ages*. University Park, PA: Pennsylvania State University Press, 2006.

Solopova, Elizabeth. "Layout, Punctuation, and Stanza Patterns in the English Verse." In *Studies in the Harley Manuscript: The Scribes, Contents, and Social Contexts of British Library MS Harley 2253*. Ed. Susanna Fein. Kalamazoo, MI: Medieval Institute Publications, 2000. Pp. 377–89.

Spiele, Ina, ed. *Li Romanz de Dieu et sa mere d'Herman de Valenciennes chanoine et prêtre (XIIe siècle)*. Leyde: Presse Universitaire de Leyde, 1975.

Stemmler, Theo (1970), ed. *Medieval English Love-Lyrics*. Tübingen: Max Niemeyer, 1970.

——— (2000). "Miscellany or Anthology? The Structure of Medieval Manuscripts: MS Harley 2253, for Example." In *Studies in the Harley Manuscript: The Scribes, Contents, and Social Contexts of British Library MS Harley 2253*. Ed. Susanna Fein. Kalamazoo, MI: Medieval Institute Publications, 2000. Pp. 111–21.

Suchier, Walther. *L'Enfant Sage (Das Gespräch des Kaisers Hadrian mit dem klugen Kinde Epitus)*. Dresden: Max Niemeyer, 1910.

Sugano, Douglas, ed. *The N-Town Plays*. Kalamazoo, MI: Medieval Institute Publications, 2007.

Swanson, Jenny. *John of Wales: A Study of the Works and Ideas of a Thirteenth-Century Friar*. Cambridge: Cambridge University Press, 1989.

Tamburr, Karl. *The Harrowing of Hell in Medieval England*. Cambridge: D. S. Brewer, 2007.

Taylor, Andrew (2002). *Textual Situations: Three Medieval Manuscripts and Their Readers*. Philadelphia, PA: University of Pennsylvania Press, 2002.

——— (2011). "'Her Y Spelle': The Evocation of Minstrel Performance in a Hagiographical Context." In *The Texts and Contexts of Oxford, Bodleian Library, MS Laud Misc. 108: The Shaping of English Vernacular Narrative*. Ed. Kimberly K. Bell and Julie Nelson Couch. Leiden: Brill, 2011. Pp. 71–86.

Taylor, Mark N. "Chaucer's Knowledge of Chess." *Chaucer Review* 38 (2004), 299–313.

Thompson, John J. (1997). "The Governance of the English Tongue: The *Cursor Mundi* and Its French Tradition." In *Individuality and Achievement in Middle English Poetry*. Ed. O. S. Pickering. Cambridge: D. S. Brewer, 1997. Pp. 19–37.

——— (2000). "'Frankis rimes here I redd, / Communlik in ilk[a] sted . . .': The French Bible Stories in Harley 2253." In *Studies in the Harley Manuscript: The Scribes, Contents, and Social Contexts of British Library MS Harley 2253*. Ed. Susanna Fein. Kalamazoo, MI: Medieval Institute Publications, 2000. Pp. 271–88.

——— (2007). "Mapping Points West of West Midlands Manuscripts and Texts: Irishness(es) and Middle English Literary Culture," In *Essays in Manuscript Geography: Vernacular Manuscripts of the English West Midlands from the Conquest to the Sixteenth Century*. Ed. Wendy Scase. Turnhout: Brepols, 2007. Pp. 113–28.

Thorndike, Lynn. "All the World's a Chess-Board." *Speculum* 6 (1931), 461–65.

Travis, Peter W. *Disseminal Chaucer: Rereading the Nun's Priest's Tale*. Notre Dame, IN: University of Notre Dame Press, 2010.

Treharne, Elaine, ed. *Old and Middle English c.890–c.1450*. Third edition. Chichester: Wiley-Blackwell, 2010.

Tristram, Philippa. *Figures of Life and Death in Medieval English Literature*. New York: New York University Press, 1976.

Tschann, Judith, and M. B. Parkes, intro. *Facsimile of Oxford, Bodleian Library, MS Digby 86*. EETS s.s. 16. Oxford: Oxford University Press, 1996.

Tucker, Samuel Marion. *Verse Satire in England before the Renaissance*. New York: Columbia University Press, 1908; rpt. AMS, 1966.

Turville-Petre, Thorlac (1989), ed. *Alliterative Poetry of the Later Middle Ages: An Anthology*. Washington, DC: The Catholic University of America Press, 1989.

——— (1996). *England the Nation: Language, Literature, and National Identity, 1290–1340*. Oxford: Clarendon, 1996.

——— (1997). "English Quaint and Strange in 'Ne mai no lewed lued.'" In *Individuality and Achievement in Middle English Poetry*. Ed. O. S. Pickering. Cambridge: D. S. Brewer, 1997. Pp. 73–83.

Tyson, Diana B. "'Against the King's Taxes': The Second Manuscript." *Nottingham Medieval Studies* 54 (2010), 73–92.

Ulrich, J. "La riote du monde." *Zeitschrift für Romanische Philologie* 8 (1884), 275–89.

Utley, Francis Lee. "VII. Dialogues, Debates, and Catechisms." In Severs et al. Pp. 669–756, 829–902.

Valois, Noël. "Jacques Duèse, pape sous le nom de Jean XXII." *Histoire littéraire de la France* 34 (1914), 391–630.

van Deusen, Nancy, ed. *The Place of the Psalms in the Intellectual Culture of the Middle Ages*. Albany, NY: State University of New York Press, 1999.

Varnhagen, Hermann. "Zu mittelenglischen Gedichten. XI. Zu den sprichwörtern Hending's." *Anglia* 4 (1881), 180–210.

Vincent, Nicholas. *The Holy Blood: King Henry III and the Westminster Blood Relic*. Cambridge: Cambridge University Press, 2001.

Vising, Johan. *Anglo-Norman Language and Literature*. London: Oxford University Press, 1923.

Voragine. See Jacobus de Voragine.

Walker, Ian W. *Mercia and the Making of England*. Stroud, Gloucestershire: Sutton, 2000.

Walpole, Ronald N., ed. *The Old French Johannes Translation of the Pseudo-Turpin Chronicle: Supplement*. Berkeley: University of California Press, 1976.

Wanley, Humfrey, D. Casley, et al. *A Catalogue of the Harleian Manuscripts in the British Museum*. London: Dryden Leach, 1759; rev. and repr. in 4 vols., London, 1808–12.

Ward, Benedicta, trans. *The Sayings of the Desert Fathers: The Alphabetical Collection*. Kalamazoo, MI: Cistercian Publications, 1975.

Waters, Claire M., ed. and trans. *Virgins and Scholars: A Fifteenth-Century Compilation of the Lives of John the Baptist, John the Evangelist, Jerome, and Katherine of Alexandria*. Turnhout: Brepolis, 2008.

Whatley, E. Gordon, ed., with Anne B. Thompson and Robert K. Upchurch. *Saints' Lives in Middle English Collections*. Kalamazoo, MI: Medieval Institute Publications, 2004.

Whiting, Bartlett Jere, with Helen Wescott Whiting. *Proverbs, Sentences, ands Proverbial Phrases from English Writings Mainly before 1500*. Cambridge, MA: Belknap Press of Harvard University Press, 1968.

Wiggins, Alison. "Middle English Romance and the West Midlands." In *Essays in Manuscript Geography: Vernacular Manuscripts of the English West Midlands from the Conquest to the Sixteenth Century*. Ed. Wendy Scase. Turnhout: Brepols, 2007. Pp. 239–55.

Wilmart, André. *Auteurs spirituels et textes dévots du moyen âge latin*. 1932; repr. Paris: Études augustiennes, 1971.

Wilshere, A. D. (1982), ed. *Miroir de Seinte Eglise (St. Edmund of Abingdon's Speculum Ecclesiae)*. Anglo-Norman Texts 40. London: Anglo-Norman Text Society, 1982.

——— (1988). "The Anglo-Norman Bible Stories in MS Harley 2253." *Forum for Modern Language Studies* 24 (1988), 78–89.

Wogan-Browne, Jocelyn, Carolyn Collette, Maryanne Kowaleski, Linne Mooney, Ad Putter, and David Trotter, eds. *Language and Culture in Medieval Britain: The French of England, c.1100–c.1500*. Woodbridge: York Medieval Press, 2009.

Woolf, Rosemary (1968). *The English Religious Lyric in the Middle Ages*. Oxford: Clarendon, 1968.

——— (1970). "Later Poetry: The Popular Tradition." In *The Middle Ages*. Ed. W. F. Bolton. London: Barrie & Jenkins, 1970. Pp. 263–311.

Woolgar, C. M., ed. *Household Accounts from Medieval England, Part 1: Introduction, Glossary, Diet Accounts (I)*. Records of Social and Economic History n.s. 17. Oxford: Oxford University Press for The British Academy, 1992.

Wright, Thomas (1839), ed. *Political Songs of England, from the Reign of John to That of Edward II*. 1839; repr. with an Intro. by Peter Coss. Cambridge: Cambridge University Press, 1996.

——— (1841), ed. *The Latin Poems Commonly Attributed to Walter Mapes*. London: John Bowyer Nichols and Son (for the Camden Society), 1841; rpt. New York: AMS Press, 1968.

——— (1842), ed. *Specimens of Lyric Poetry, Composed in England in the Reign of Edward the First*. London: Percy Society, 1842; repr. New York: Johnson Reprint Corporation, 1965.

——— (1844), ed. "Early English Receipts for Painting, Gilding, &c." *Archaeological Journal* 1 (1844), 64–66.

Wright, Thomas, and James Orchard Halliwell, eds., *Reliqiuae Antiquae*. 2 vols. London: John Russell Smith, 1845.

Yorke, Barbara. *Kings and Kingdoms of Early Anglo-Saxon England*. London: Seaby, 1990.

Ziolkowski, Jan M. (1998), ed. and trans. *The Cambridge Songs (Carmina Cantabrigiensia)*. Tempe, AR: Medieval & Renaissance Texts and Studies, 1998.

——— (2008). *Solomon and Marcolf*. Cambridge, MA: Harvard University Press, 2008.

🖉 COMMENTARY SERIES

🖋 DOCUMENTS OF PRACTICE SERIES

Love and Marriage in Late Medieval London, selected, translated, and introduced by Shannon McSheffrey (1995)

Sources for the History of Medicine in Late Medieval England, selected, introduced, and translated by Carole Rawcliffe (1995)

A Slice of Life: Selected Documents of Medieval English Peasant Experience, edited, translated, and with an introduction by Edwin Brezette DeWindt (1996)

Regular Life: Monastic, Canonical, and Mendicant "Rules," selected and introduced by Douglas J. McMillan and Kathryn Smith Fladenmuller (1997); second edition, selected and introduced by Daniel Marcel La Corte and Douglas J. McMillan (2004)

Women and Monasticism in Medieval Europe: Sisters and Patrons of the Cistercian Reform, selected, translated, and with an introduction by Constance H. Berman (2002)

Medieval Notaries and Their Acts: The 1327–1328 Register of Jean Holanie, introduced, edited, and translated by Kathryn L. Reyerson and Debra A. Salata (2004)

John Stone's Chronicle: Christ Church Priory, Canterbury, 1417–1472, selected, translated, and introduced by Meriel Connor (2010)

🖋 MEDIEVAL GERMAN TEXTS IN BILINGUAL EDITIONS SERIES

Sovereignty and Salvation in the Vernacular, 1050–1150, introduction, translations, and notes by James A. Schultz (2000)

Ava's New Testament Narratives: "When the Old Law Passed Away," introduction, translation, and notes by James A. Rushing, Jr. (2003)

History as Literature: German World Chronicles of the Thirteenth Century in Verse, introduction, translation, and notes by R. Graeme Dunphy (2003)

Thomasin von Zirclaria, *Der Welsche Gast (The Italian Guest)*, translated by Marion Gibbs and Winder McConnell (2009)

Ladies, Whores, and Holy Women: A Sourcebook in Courtly, Religious, and Urban Cultures of Late Medieval Germany, introductions, translations, and notes by Ann Marie Rasmussen and Sarah Westphal-Wihl (2010)

🖋 VARIA

The Study of Chivalry: Resources and Approaches, edited by Howell Chickering and Thomas H. Seiler (1988)

Studies in the Harley Manuscript: The Scribes, Contents, and Social Contexts of British Library MS Harley 2253, edited by Susanna Fein (2000)

The Liturgy of the Medieval Church, edited by Thomas J. Heffernan and E. Ann Matter (2001; second edition 2005)

Johannes de Grocheio, *Ars musice*, edited and translated by Constant J. Mews, John N. Crossley, Catherine Jeffreys, Leigh McKinnon, and Carol J. Williams (2011)

🖋 TO ORDER PLEASE CONTACT:

Medieval Institute Publications
Western Michigan University
Kalamazoo, MI 49008-5432
Phone (269) 387-8755
FAX (269) 387-8750
http://www.wmich.edu/medieval/mip/index.html

Typeset in 10/13 New Baskerville
and Golden Cockerel Ornaments display
Manufactured by Sheridan Books, Inc.

Medieval Institute Publications
College of Arts and Sciences
Western Michigan University
1903 W. Michigan Avenue
Kalamazoo, MI 49008-5432
http://www.wmich.edu/medieval/mip

 WESTERN MICHIGAN UNIVERSITY